AN
ILLUMINATED
LIFE

ALSO BY HEIDI ARDIZZONE

Love on Trial:
An American Scandal in Black and White
(with Earl Lewis)

AN
ILLUMINATED
LIFE

Belle da Costa Greene's
Journey from Prejudice to Privilege

HEIDI ARDIZZONE

W. W. Norton & Company
New York London

"The Young Dead Soldiers" from *Collected Poems, 1917–1982* by Archibald MacLeish.
Copyright © 1985 by The Estate of Archibald MacLeish. Reprinted by permission of
Houghton Mifflin Company. All rights reserved.

For information about permission to reproduce selections from this book,
write to permissions, W. W. Norton & Company, Inc.,
500 Fifth Avenue, New York, NY 10110

Manufacturing by RR Donnelley, Harrisonburg, VA
Book design by Anna Oler

Library of Congress Cataloging-in-Publication Data

Ardizzone, Heidi.
An illuminated life : Belle da Costa Greene's journey
from prejudice to privilege / Heidi Ardizzone. — 1st ed.
p. cm.
Includes bibliographical references and index.
ISBN 978-0-393-05104-9
1. Greene, Belle da Costa. 2. African American librarians—New York
(State)—New York—Biography. 3. Women library administrators—New York
(State)—New York—Biography. 4. Pierpont Morgan Library—History.
5. Manuscripts—Collectors and collecting—New York (State)—New
York—History. 6. Art—Collectors and collecting—New York (State)—New
York—History. 7. Berenson, Bernard, 1865–1959—Friends and associates.
8. Passing (Identity)—United States—Case studies. 9. New York
(N.Y.)—Intellectual life—20th century. I. Title.
Z720.G83A89 2007
020.92—dc22
[B]
2007004967

W. W. Norton & Company. Inc., 500 Fifth Avenue, New York, N.Y. 10110
www.wwnorton.com

W. W. Norton & Company Ltd., Castle House, 75/76 Wells Street, London W1T

1 2 3 4 5 6 7 8 9 0

For the librarians, archivists, and curators who protect and give access to humanity's intellectual and cultural treasures . . .

. . . and for my own beloved, stereotype-defying librarian: Conrad Rader

Contents

AN
ILLUMINATED
LIFE

Introduction

PRESENTING
BELLE DA COSTA GREENE

Seated massively at his desk that day in 1905, John Pierpont Morgan seemed lost in thought. He hardly even bothered to look up when his nephew Junius appeared before him with a slim, grey eyed girl in tow. . . . Scarcely out of her teens, "quaking with fear and shaking like an aspen," Belle da Costa Greene began her career as head of the Pierpont Morgan Library.

—Time, 1949[1]

I really must be grudgingly admitted the most interesting person in New York, for it's all they seem to talk about.

—Belle da Costa Greene, 1911[2]

IT BEGAN, OF COURSE, at the Library. A small elegant white marble building, it sat tucked around the corner from Madison Avenue on a quiet block of East Thirty-sixth Street. Nearly complete at the end of 1905, it would soon house J. Pierpont Morgan's private office and his growing collection of European art, rare books, and manuscripts. For Morgan, it was a quiet, private retreat a few blocks from his Manhattan residence, away from the demands of his Wall Street office. The businessman was aging. The aggressive—some would say rapacious—growth of his financial capital was no longer the center of his energies. "Mr. Morgan's Library" would become his retreat from the frantic world of finance, and an outlet for his new interest in acquisitions of a different sort. As quickly as tariff laws could be reformed, Morgan was bringing European art and Western culture to New York. Not many there had yet seen his treasures.

When she arrived at Morgan's Library for her first appointment with the great man that winter, Belle da Costa Greene was a complete unknown in the New York worlds of society and art. Her family had lived in Manhattan for a decade, but she was currently residing in Princeton, New Jersey, working at Princeton University's library. Her father was gone; her mother and the eldest children had struggled to support the family. With a brother in graduate school, two younger sisters to help support, and an appetite for intellectual challenge, Belle was ambitious for professional development and money. At Princeton she had begun her informal studies of rare books and illuminated manuscripts, and she caught the attention of Assistant Librarian Junius Morgan, a Princeton graduate with an avid interest in early books. Junius had been helping his more famous uncle with his developing library, which was now overflowing his home study and the attic storage room of the Lenox Library. He wanted to be sure the priceless and often unique manuscripts would be in good hands. Surely the elder Morgan would not object to hiring a young unknown woman, if she had ability. J. Pierpont appreciated talent wherever he found it, and everyone knew he had an eye for beautiful women.

So Belle found herself approaching the new building on Thirty-sixth Street one winter day in late 1905. It is a wonderful moment to imagine, this meeting. Of course, she was nervous, perhaps even terrified, but her face would not have betrayed it. Passing through the solid metal doors, feeling the mosaic stone floors of the vaulted foyer ring beneath her heels, she stepped into a building that sought to re-create the architecture and artistry of ancient Greece and Renaissance Italy. Today tall lapis lazuli pillars pull a visitor's gaze upward to high arching ceilings painted in the style of the Italian Renaissance masters. These paintings were among the last touches added to the Library and were probably not there for her first visit. Three interior doors flanked the entryway. To the left was the West Room, Morgan's office; to the right was the East Room, which became the reading room for visitors. The North Room was straight ahead, directly opposite the imposing entrance. This office would soon be hers. These doors, these high frescoed ceilings, damask and tapestried and art-laden walls, the heavy wood shelves soon to house the collected treasures—these would become her home and her legacy.

We do not know what words were exchanged, what first impressions were made, yet we can imagine the two sizing each other up: Mr. Morgan trying to judge her ability and her character; Miss Greene anxious to impress and trying not to try too hard, making her own judgments of the notorious man now quizzing her. They certainly made a very odd couple. Morgan was a formidable figure, gruff, blunt, and used to getting his way. A large man with a bulbously scarred nose and small dark eyes, he glared ferociously out at the world. This was the man who had the power to sway—and save—the national economy, and who was single-handedly bringing more artwork, including the manuscripts that were already Belle's passion, to Manhattan. In turn-of-the-century New York, no one was more famously and infamously powerful than J. Pierpont Morgan. He had grown up in modest wealth but had made his own enormous fortunes speculating in the Civil War and leading the movement of capital into new technologies (railroads, steel, oil, electricity) and the development of corporate monopolies. At the age of sixty-eight, Morgan was also more than forty years Belle's senior.

By contrast, Belle da Costa Greene was small and slender, her dainty figure squeezed even thinner into the wasp-waisted corsets of the period's fashion. Her delicate silhouette only accentuated his bullishness. By all accounts she was as beautiful as she was brilliant, although her beauty was usually qualified as exotic or unusual. With a cloud of dark hair and huge eyes, olive skin, and a proud carriage, she dressed elegantly and conducted herself with poise and dignity beyond her apparently youthful age. Later reports estimated that she was only eighteen, nineteen, at most twenty-one, when she first came to Mr. Morgan's Library.

Belle knew that her chosen work as a librarian hardly fit the image and attitude that her flamboyant, mischievous soul demanded. "Just because I *am* a librarian . . . doesn't mean I have to *dress* like one," she reportedly boasted.[3] And she didn't. Often described as wearing fashionable gowns with brilliant jewels and a large silk handkerchief that she used with dramatic effect, Belle da Costa Greene was no typecast librarian. Nor did she perform her tasks quietly and demurely. Still, for most of her adult life, Belle oversaw Morgan's growing collection of rare books and art housed at his new building. Oddly kindred spirits, the two became partners in the acquisition of manuscripts and art and were suspected of being lovers—a rumor both denied. (Belle reputedly quipped, "We tried," when asked whether she had been his mistress.)[4] Morgan, secure in his tremendous wealth and his even more intimidating reputation, could occasionally turn off the bluster and turn on the charm. Belle, confident beyond her age and experience, could turn off the charm and turn on the bluster.

Rumor and speculation swirled around the young Belle Greene; she was notorious in her time. Her uncertain background did not prevent her from gaining access to the dinner tables and salons of the rich and the famous. She became a local celebrity in New York. Protected by her position as Morgan's librarian and confidante, she shocked, impressed, disgusted, and delighted those who knew her with her alternately dignified and coarse manner, her acerbic and sometimes stinging tongue, and her indomitable vitality and presence. People still tell tales that highlight her outrageous behavior, her haughty power, and her legendary and unusual beauty. Some even write ghost stories in which she haunts the Morgan Library, protecting her treasures and her reputation from would-be thieves and disrespectful biographers.[5]

Most of those who remember her today are scholars, librarians, and museum curators—those whose work keeps them in constant touch with her strongest legacy. She had, as one admirer put it, "transformed a rich man's casually built collection into one which ranks with the greatest in the world."[6] And she was lauded as a leading scholar, although she had never worked in academia or published scholarly books or articles. During her lifetime it was these fellow lovers and protectors of books and art who filled her professional and social calendar. But she also cut a much broader social swath through New York and in Europe. Opera stars, actresses, artists from the avant-garde to traditional portraitists, poets, political activists and politicians from socialists to presidents, newspaper editors, writers, millionaires, Wall Street traders, and European royalty and aristocracy—all invited her to their tables and called her a friend. The grand elite and bohemian bevies of New York City in the first half of the twentieth century felt her touch, as did their counterparts in London, Paris, Rome, and Florence. She was a beloved "daughter" of priests and bishops, including Cardinal Ratti, who would become Pope Pius XI. But her favorite "Petit Saint Pere" (Dear Sainted Father) was Father Henri Hyvernat, who worked with her on one of Morgan's most famous purchases, a collection of Coptic Christian manuscripts discovered in Egypt in 1911. The task of repairing, copying, and publishing a catalogue describing this fantastic find took over three decades and was typical (although on a larger scale than most) of the work Belle oversaw every day in her position as the Morgan librarian.

In her twenties and thirties Belle lived in a seemingly endless whirl of work and fun, toiling over her priceless art treasures and ancient manuscripts by day, and enjoying wild nights of opera and theater, cigarettes and champagne by night. Her daytime work and her nightlife often stood in stark contrast to one another, but there was never any doubt which took priority. Her friends knew that she loved the party life of a socialite. One described her as a woman "who arrests even the casual if astute observer with her overflowing joie de vivre and impresses him as having the best of times in this best of all possible worlds." But if any male admirer attempted to follow up on an evening flirtation by visiting her at the Library the next morning, he would quickly find himself back out in the street, "moved to a higher admiration or cursing the well-known caprice of woman, according to his own equipment."[7] Eventually, she reached a level of professional stature that few women of her generation were able to attain. An independent and impatient soul, Belle never married. Nevertheless, she did become "hipped," as she put it in her customary slang, to a new man once or twice a year and took several lovers. New York was on the cusp between Victorian ideals and modernity. Belle was far from alone in flouting the traditions of monogamy and marriage, but she was in an unexpectedly vulnerable and exposed position.

Slightly exotic compared with the "old-stock" Americans of western and northern European ancestry who worked and socialized with Morgan and his peers, Belle's physical appearance prompted much comment. Belle herself attributed her beige complexion to a Portuguese grandmother, like the hundreds of thousands of New Yorkers who were adding their southern and eastern European faces to the mixture of American ethnicities. But one of Belle's secrets that she did not keep very successfully was that her darker features came not from one Portuguese grandparent but from two African American parents of mixed ancestry.

Belle could not have achieved the social and professional prominence she did at the turn of the twentieth century had she been completely open about her background. She certainly could not have reached such heights without her quick wit, fearless persona, and extraordinary ability to handle millionaires, art dealers, scholars, and the occasional obsessed would-be or ex-suitor. Scholars estimate that thousands of people of mixed ancestry left communities of color to live as white every year in the early twentieth century.[8] Had Belle followed her mother and siblings into historical obscurity, she and they would have been simply a few more anonymous members of this quiet response to segregation and racism. But when Belle met J. P. Morgan on that fateful day in 1905, she stepped out of obscurity and into history.

It is not exactly a rags-to-riches story; Belle's childhood was not one of poverty. But she and her family did live with prejudice, even as a relatively comfortable family of color, or light-skinned "Negroes"—the polite term of the time roughly equivalent to today's "African American." Her family's history includes enslavement and active struggle at first against slavery, then against segregation, and always against discrimination and racism. And she did not end up marrying riches, or even becoming independently wealthy—at least not by the standards of the Morgans and their ilk. But she certainly did achieve privilege. And she did so despite constant rumors about her ancestry and her identity.

Belle's emergence from nowhere into such an intoxicating existence evokes Americans' love of the self-made man—or woman, in this case. This heroic figure re-creates herself in the open opportunities of America's society and economy, making her fortune through hard work, character, and ability. In this myth there are no insurmountable obstacles to wealth, no uncrossable lines dividing the democratic society. That there are so few examples of actual self-made men, and fewer still of women, illuminates the real power of social class to restrict opportunity. But it was a story many believed in, and Belle was one of them. In some sense she absolutely was a self-made woman, a success story of the promise of the American dream. But the patronage and protection of J. Pierpont Morgan and his son were crucial to her rise.

When Belle stepped out into the cold winter air of Manhattan after her interview with Morgan, her life had changed. She could not yet have realized how much. She knew she had a job, a good job, working for an important man to whose rare-book collection she would now have access. With a starting salary of $75 a month, almost twice what she was making at Princeton, she must have returned to her family exultant. Her mother, now well into her sixties, could stop working; her sisters could continue their schooling. And she had found a mentor and defender of unprecedented power in Morgan.

Belle's story is a compelling one for many reasons. The force of her personality alone explains her strong presence in the memories and imaginations of many who knew her and knew of her. I confess I have, like many of her contemporaries and peers, succumbed to the vitality of her presence as it lingers in the stream-of-consciousness scrawl of her letters. The energy and personality that so many of her contemporaries marveled at leap off the page and reveal a woman who was con-

stantly thinking and learning and seeking inspiration and new ideas.
Belle was capable of laughing sarcasm and gentle empathy. She could
be brutally succinct in her dismissal even of people whom she
respected and loved. ("If a person is a worm, you step on him," she
apparently said.)[9] She habitually numbed herself with work, with play,
perhaps with alcohol as well, certainly with parties and socializing. But
she also was capable of deep introspection, taking spiritual retreats—
more and more as she reached middle age. Throughout her life she
spent long hours reading, losing herself in her thoughts, staring into a
favorite piece of art, or leafing through a beloved manuscript. It was in
the art and the manuscripts that she purchased and cared for that she
left her mark on the world.

I have learned a fair amount about the art and book worlds that
Belle Greene worked in and about the rare illuminated manuscripts
she treasured and often purchased. Wherever I went to read her
archived correspondence, researchers around me were looking at
ancient yellowing manuscripts, brightly colored pages of medieval biblical texts, or photographs of pre-restoration Italian Renaissance frescoes. And I have found myself haunting the Internet stores for the relatively rare, relatively expensive original editions of printed books in
my own field of history, infected perhaps by this "gentle madness" of
bibliomania that Belle and many of her cronies manifested.[10] It is my
hope that something of this world will come through in this book. But
I approached this project with the gaze, experience, and tools not of an
art scholar or a paleographer but of a social historian and a biographer.

The result is a study that focuses on Belle de Costa Greene's background and experiences, on the social worlds and times she inhabited.
Belle grew up in the struggling elite community of people of color in
Washington, D.C., and eventually lived as a nominally white upper-
middle-class New Yorker. In the earliest chapters, when we have very
little direct evidence of Belle the child, Belle the schoolgirl, Belle in
her first library experiences, the social and cultural history serves to
reconstruct the period and places in which she lived. Even in the central chapters, when Belle's voice and the voices of her contemporaries
offer rich descriptions of her experiences in the 1910s and 1920s, the
cultural context plays an important role. Belle lived through two world

wars and suffered losses in each of them. She saw social norms open up—for women, for sexual expression, for eccentricity—and close again. She rode financial booms up the economic ladder to privilege, and watched the stock market crash and fail to recover for a decade. She lived in New York as it transformed itself from an island city into a multiborough modern metropolis of skyscrapers and motor cars, connected by bridges and tunnels, first competing with and then surpassing European cities in size and power.

That one woman lived in so many different worlds offers the opportunity to examine this history through the eyes of an individual and watch a single person navigate her way through the cultural shifts of communities and time. Belle lived in a series of social realities, moved in and out of different circles (sometimes permanently), and embraced complicated public identities. Of course, we all live in multiple worlds, bringing different parts of ourselves to those we encounter in each world. We all have multiple identities and parts of ourselves that we keep separate from others. In Belle's time this was even more true than it is today. At the turn of the twenty-first century, hardly a public figure emerges without a written or televised biography explaining his or her personal and family background and its impact on his or her career or public activities. But in her generation Belle was not alone in scorning personal history as irrelevant, in destroying personal papers, and in maintaining very different public and private personas.

Her attitude on this issue throws some obstacles into the path of those who have tried to tell her story, including myself. Belle was remarkably successful in limiting and controlling publicity about her private life both during and after her lifetime. No published study of Belle exists. A number of essays and a few public lectures focus on her, and she appears in biographies of Morgan and the other great men in her life, most notably Bernard Berenson. The absence of more published information is due in no small part to her decision to burn all of her personal papers shortly before her death, in 1950. And, as her own protégée and friend Dorothy Miner wrote in her posthumous tribute collection, *Studies in Art and Literature for Belle da Costa Greene*, few of her intimates felt they really knew her well.[11]

Had Belle not destroyed her own papers, someone else would surely have tried to write her story much sooner. Despite the lack of information, Belle has been an object of curiosity and interest to many people during her lifetime and since her death, particularly within the fields of art and book history and among librarians. Did she have any formal training in librarianship or rare books? Did she know that one of her lovers, the famous art critic Bernard Berenson, was a secret business partner of the Duveens, art dealers with whom she worked for decades? Did she know more about the deals and deceptions, forgeries and unknown treasures, that haunted the world of art collecting? Was her relationship with Morgan or his son more than friendship? Did her relationships with men hide, as a few observers suspected, intimate affairs with women? Did she retain any connections to members of her family—especially her father—who, unlike her, openly identified with their black ancestry? How did she identify herself racially?

This book cannot answer all of these questions. Belle took some secrets, especially about her early life and career, to her grave. And the friends and colleagues who knew her best have passed away. So too have her siblings, who might have been greatly affected had her story been told during their lifetimes. Belle was not completely successful, however, in destroying her papers. She left shelves full of her professional, and occasionally not so professional, correspondence in her records at the Morgan Library. A few key folders have disappeared in recent years, but the files are still a rich source. Moreover, since written correspondence was the main way people did business in the early twentieth century, she left thousands of letters in the files of dealers, curators, and scholars, many of which have since been archived. The bulk of these papers document Belle's daily work in acquiring, assessing, and making accessible the artistic and scholarly treasures of the Morgan Library, but some—in handwritten postscripts or letters that stood in for both professional and personal updating—contain clues to Belle's social life and experiences that are the focus of this book.

Most significantly Bernard Berenson kept a trunk of her letters—over six hundred of them—dating from the period 1910–44. The bulk were written during the initial years of their friendship, 1909–16, when the two maintained a passionate although mainly long-distance love affair. These letters are a gold mine of information about her social life, about her work, about the people and events around her, about her own life and thoughts. Belle wrote so prolifically and engagingly about New York and the world in the early twentieth century that her letters to Berenson beg to be published in full. No doubt his letters to her were much the same, and he was devastated when he heard they were gone. "She has burned my autobiography," he lamented, an action for which he never forgave her.[12] After his death his longtime companion and literary heir Nicky Mariano came across the trunk that stored Belle's letters at Berenson's home in Florence, Italy. Mariano was no great fan of Greene's. She knew that Belle had wanted the letters to be destroyed, but also that Bernard had chosen not to do so. So she carefully tucked the letters into folders. And there the collection remains archived at Berenson's library, now Harvard University's Center for Italian Renaissance Studies, available to researchers fortunate enough to travel to Florence.[13] I was one of these, and the months I spent in Italy allowed me to visit firsthand many of the towns, churches, and sites that Belle returned to again and again and wrote about so glowingly. These letters, which Belle called her diary, contain a record of her life. Not a complete record, not an unbiased one, but almost no biographer has that to work with.

Through a combination of these letters, the professional papers kept at the Pierpont Morgan Library, and her correspondence scattered through dozens of archives, as well as public records, memoirs of her contemporaries, and stories told by those who knew her, I have tried to derive the events and patterns not just of Belle Greene's life but of the many social circles and worlds she inhabited. Over the course of her life, she moved between and across lines of color, class, culture, nation, and world views. Perhaps most astonishingly, she also illuminated her inner world, where she lived "behind the curtain of my mind."[14]

1

RAISED EXPECTATIONS

Even those who knew Belle Greene best never knew all the facets of her personality or of her career. She herself refused to cooperate with efforts to record her life, scorning such personal history as unimportant.

—Dorothy Miner, employee and friend, 1954[1]

In 1880, elite blacks based their social status on ties with prominent whites, their skin color, and their family backgrounds. . . . The generation of black leaders that rose to prominence during Reconstruction and the 1880s had faith that the race would ultimately be assimilated into white society. As educated men and women and, in many cases, with ancestral ties to the white community, elite blacks fully expected that they would be the first to be accepted as equals. . . . The dramatic rise of racism in the 1890s came as a great shock to the black elite.

—Jacqueline Moore, 1999[2]

IF J. PIERPONT MORGAN asked about Miss Greene's background when he hired her as his librarian, she mostly likely gave him the same information she gave others, more or less. She was born in Alexandria, Virginia, or Richmond, or somewhere in the South. If he asked what her ancestry was, as some apparently did, curious as to the source of her smoky, Mediterranean coloring, she would have explained that "da Costa" was a Portuguese name. She might have described her mother as a Southern lady, "cultivated but impoverished." Reduced by circumstances and widowed, the beautiful Mrs. Greene made a modest living teaching music, sacrificing a great deal to educate her son and four daughters.[3] This story was a blend of fact and fiction.

Belle was born in Washington, D.C., not in Virginia; D.C. was below the Mason-Dixon line, yet the extent of its southern identity is still debated. In the context of the northeastern world of her adulthood, Belle's identity and repeated references to her southern upbringing and cultural inheritances made sense. When caught in an act of superstition, for example, she blamed her "Southern birth and blood"; when an English maid disparaged her family, she silently reposted with her mother's "grand Southern blood" and swore to replace the annoying employee as soon as possible.[4]

Belle was also several years older than she claimed, a masquerade she shared with many American women in a society in which youth was highly valued and single women past a certain age were disdained.

Most dramatically, however, Belle's name at birth was Belle Marian Greener, not Belle da Costa Greene. For the first nine years of her life, she grew up in an elite family in D.C.'s large and well-established colored community. Her mother's family had been free from slavery since the turn of the eighteenth century; her father was a rising star in African American political circles, a self-described black man whose complexion was "near-white" but whose career was dedicated to promoting black civil rights.[5]

If Morgan had known that Belle was actually twenty-six when they met in 1905, and that her father was a Harvard graduate, a former university librarian, professor, and dean, her confidence and abilities might have been less startling. But these details about her father might have revealed his identity: Richard T. Greener, a prominent Negro professional. Greener was the first black graduate of Harvard College, the first colored librarian and professor at the University of South Carolina during its brief post-Emancipation program of racial integration, former dean of historically black Howard University, and former secretary for the Ulysses S. Grant Monument, for which J. Pierpont Morgan himself served as treasurer. It was a résumé of high accomplishments and "firsts" marking the career of a man who had always represented the Negro race. Greener was a reflection of the professional elite, the "Talented Tenth" of the Negro race, whose accomplishments the leader W. E. B. Du Bois believed would both persuade white America to endorse social and political equality and actively help other members of the race to improve their educational, cultural, economic, and political standing. This could be said of many middle-class Americans of African ancestry (both mixed and unmixed) of Greener's generation. But Du Bois had specifically identified Greener as a member of this special group, recognizing not only his accomplishments but also his hard work on behalf of the race.[6]

Knowledge of her father's identity and biography might have significantly altered how his daughter was received as she began her career. Still, for someone trying to obscure questions about her past, Belle did not stray too far from the truth in her stories about her family background and childhood. Not everything Belle said about her family and background was a lie; most of it was just far enough away from the truth to prevent complete exposure. Belle has been described as passing for white, but her family background and her performance of race offer a much more complicated tableau than a simple shift from black to white.

Belle's parents reflect the experiences of many freeborn African Americans in the late nineteenth century. Regardless of how Belle identified herself racially, or how she lived that identity publicly, she was their daughter. Their story gives us a deeper understanding of her story: how she was raised, what values, messages, and lessons they would have tried to pass on, and who her earliest role models were for womanhood and for scholarship. Their history also reveals the impact of race on families of mixed ancestry, and how Belle's understanding of her identity and her connection to blackness came to diverge from that of her father.

The bits we can piece together of their families' histories form a mosaic of American experience in the eastern seaboard, a story that included interaction and intermixing with many of the ethnicities and races that made up the new nation in the late eighteenth and early nineteenth centuries. Belle's family was African, including African Americans who were enslaved in the eighteenth and early nineteenth centuries, Spanish (by way of Puerto Rico), and almost certainly several other white European nationalities as well. A friend later said that she was the "product of a singular moment in the history of civilization of the American continent."[7]

Belle's father, Richard Theodore Greener, was born free in Philadelphia in 1844, but not to an elite family. His father, Richard Wesley Greener, was the son of a former slave, Jacob C. Greener. Jacob, thought by his descendants to have been born in Africa, was enslaved in Virginia until the first decade of the nineteenth century, when he left, either freed or fleeing enslavement. He settled in Baltimore, where he worked as a whitewasher, helped organize the Colored Episcopal Church, and was active in antislavery and anticolonization circles. He also married a local woman, whose identity is now unknown but who was probably of mixed ancestry. They had two sons: Richard Wesley and a similarly named Jacob C. Both men followed their father into the abolitionist movement, working with the white radical antislavery leader William Lloyd Garrison in the 1830s.[8]

Richard Wesley, Belle's paternal grandfather, worked as a laborer and bootblack in Baltimore. Around 1840 he married Mary Ann La Brune, or Brun, and the couple moved to Philadelphia. Richard T. Greener thought that La Brune's father was Spanish, born in Puerto Rico; he described La Brune's mother only as "a Negress." Greener's very light skin suggests that he must have had more than one white or mixed grandparent. The lack of information about the white ancestors in Greener's history suggests that they were not closely aligned to the darker members of their family. Although some white women had children by African American men, the majority of children of interracial parentage in the nineteenth century were the offspring of enslaved African American women and the white men who owned them or were otherwise in positions of power over them. In some instances these men acknowledged their offspring and took responsibility for them, granting them freedom and support. In most cases, however, white fathers treated their mixed-race children as the slaves they legally were. This was more likely the case in Greener's family, because there is no evidence of financial support or of the presence or acknowledgment of white ancestors except for the Spanish grandfather.[9]

After Richard T., Belle's father, was born, Richard Wesley continued to work for several years as an agent for Garrison's antislavery newspaper *The Liberator*. Soon he took work as a seaman and was often away on voyages for months at a time. At the age of seven Richard T. had the chance to accompany his father on a trip to Liverpool. This transatlantic trip must have expanded the young boy's vision, and it offered a rare chance to spend time with his seafaring father.[10]

Young Richard's maternal uncle, Josiah C. Wears, was the more stable adult male presence in Belle's father's life. Wears was a barber, very successful, and highly active in black politics, particularly in the campaign for black suffrage. Both Josiah and his son Isaiah were prominent members of Philadelphia's black abolitionist community. Isaiah was also a strong influence on his younger cousin Richard T. and provided emotional and occasionally financial support until Isaiah's death.[11]

In 1853 the Greeners moved to Boston. This was an educational disaster for nine-year-old Richard: Boston public schools did not admit Negro children. Richard's light complexion, "a shade darker than a Caucasian's," might bring some social advantages, but he was still black in the official classification system, and the public schools were white-only. Eventually his mother found a private school that would accept him, one that offered a comprehensive education in Latin, English, mathematics, literature, and the physical sciences to students from "four different races . . . the Anglo Saxon, Teutonic, Celtic, and African." Within a few years, however, his father had taken one last trip: to California to join the gold rush. For a while Richard Wesley stayed in touch with his family and, most likely, sent money. But Richard T. never saw his father again. And when the letters and the money stopped arriving, Richard left school and began working a series of jobs to help support himself and his mother.[12]

It was in his jobs as an office boy or clerk in stores, hotels, and other businesses that young Richard Greener began to attract the attention of white patrons who opened up their libraries and their tutoring skills to the young teenager. While he learned French and read voraciously, the boy dreamed of studying art in Europe. But this ambition was far beyond his means, and he soon turned to the more attainable goal of resuming his formal education. This was difficult enough to achieve. Indeed, Greener's immense talents and intellect might easily have been lost to the system of discrimination that kept so many African Americans, like his father and grandfather before him, in menial jobs. But his patrons and supporters helped him realize his dream.

Throughout his teenage years in Boston, Greener attended political meetings and abolitionist lectures by leading politicians, writers, and activists, including Senator Charles Sumner, the philosopher Ralph Waldo Emerson, and the national African American leader Frederick Douglass. He also befriended several prominent Bostonians, most notably Oliver Wendell Holmes Sr., writer and dean of Harvard's Medical School, and the Harvard anthropology professor Louis Agassiz.

It was a much more modest patron, however, his white employer, businessman August Batchelder, who encouraged him to apply to Oberlin College and offered to fund his education. As the Civil War broke out, Greener left the vibrant city of Boston for the small midwestern town of Oberlin, Ohio. Having given up formal schooling at the age of eleven, he struggled to catch up with students whose education had been far superior to his own. He was not alone. With a long history of admitting women and African Americans, many of whom had been denied a rigorous education, Oberlin offered a preparatory school to help students with less schooling bridge that gap. While the war raged on, Greener studied for two years at Oberlin, then returned to Boston, where he enrolled in Phillips Academy, another preparatory school, where he was the only African American student. There was some conflict and bitterness in his leaving Oberlin; this would become a troubling pattern in his career. In this case he charged that racism had prevented him from receiving honors he believed he had deserved.[13]

In 1865 Greener entered Harvard College, part of an experiment in Negro education launched in the immediate post–Civil War era. He lived alone in the dorm and struggled through his freshman year, which he had to repeat. His academic difficulties were shared by other Phillips Academy graduates, but Greener also bore the social burden of being the only African American at Harvard College, and the first to graduate. Although he did not report hostilities, he found his class-mates continually curious and confused by him. Rumors spread that he was an escaped slave, that he had no prior education, or that he had served in the Civil War. The next year Harvard admitted a second black student, whom Greener had known at Phillips.[14]

To some extent Greener was just another Harvard student. The 1870 census taker recorded him living in a student dorm in 1870 with a dozen other male students: all were listed as white. Perhaps the enu-merator never saw Greener, did not notice his slightly darker skin, or simply assumed that he must be white to attend Harvard and to live among other white students. In any case, it does seem to reflect Greener's insistence that he never experienced direct prejudice or overt hostility at Harvard. Not one to overlook mistreatment, he reported that he was generally accepted by and found friendships within the Harvard student body, joining social and literary clubs as well as a secret society. He wrote articles for the student paper and—as he had at Oberlin and Phillips—earned a reputation as an orator.[15]

But Greener was certainly not accepted as white, no matter how light his skin. The persistent stories that connected him directly to slavery, the Civil War, and the South all point that out. And all records and accounts of his time at Harvard identify him as a Negro or colored student. Nor did Greener seek to disassociate himself from the black community. Although his years at Harvard made him feel "isolated from the race," he maintained social connections to African Americans in Boston. For example, he was one of Frances Rollin's many "gentleman callers." Rollin, who had been born free in Charleston, South Carolina, and had also attended Oberlin, was now living in Boston, writing a biography of Martin R. Delany. She described Greener (after he critiqued a draft of her writing perhaps a bit too harshly) as living "in a grand intellectual sphere and accustomed to only perfection."[16]

Much as Greener continued to work and socialize with African Americans, he recognized that both personal and racial success meant working with white Americans to promote social change. Many middle-class African Americans, whether of mixed ancestry or not, shared this attitude in the post–Civil War period. Greener was as brilliant and ambitious as his daughter Belle would become, hoping to take advantage of the slowly increasing opportunities for African Americans in the post-Emancipation generation. However, Greener specifically sought to use his talents to advance the cause of equality, for African Americans and, later, other ethnic minorities in the United States.[17] Raised in an extended family in Baltimore and Philadelphia whose members were active in antislavery and anticolonization movements and in promoting educational opportunities for African Americans, Greener naturally gravitated to those around him who were advocating on behalf of the newly emancipated freedmen and women and "the race" in general.

Greener's activities now caught the attention of two men whose careers he had followed for years: Frederick Douglass and Senator Charles Sumner. Douglass was arguably the most famous African American man in the North. He had escaped from slavery and risen to prominence as a commanding orator and as a leader in the abolitionist, civil rights, and women's rights movements. He also edited a series of abolitionist newspapers and had published several autobiographies, which recounted his experiences under slavery and in freedom. Douglass's story in many ways mirrored that of Greener's grandfather Jacob: growing up enslaved and moving North to make a new life. And Greener's father and uncle, like Frederick Douglass, had worked closely with white abolitionist leaders like Garrison to raise white Northerners' opposition to slavery, lobbying Congress as they considered a series of proslavery and antislavery bills and compromises through the 1840s and 1850s.[18]

Charles Sumner was one of the strongest allies the abolitionist movement had in the Senate. He was a white Republican from Massachusetts and a leading member of the Radical branch of the party that most consistently supported abolition, women's rights, and civil rights. Also known as a powerful orator, Sumner had promoted African American opportunities (the enlistment of black soldiers in the Union Army), protection (the establishment of a Freedmen's Bureau to assist former slaves), and political equality (suffrage for African American men). He was such a notorious political figure that he was lampooned in Thomas Dixon's highly popular novels, which lionized the Ku Klux Klan and portrayed Reconstruction from a white Southern slaveholder's perspective. These novels were adapted for the stage and then became the basis of D. W. Griffith's 1915 blockbuster film *The Birth of a Nation.* In the film Sumner was portrayed as a clubfooted carpetbagger, blind to the dangers racial equality posed to his young daughter and the excesses of his mulatto protégé Silas Lynch. (The senator's white daughter is kidnapped and threatened by Lynch with "forced marriage" and is saved by a heroic Southern white suitor in his newly designed white-hooded Klan robes.)[19]

By the time Greener graduated from Harvard, in 1870, he had established working relationships with both Sumner and Douglass. The United States was still grappling with the political fallout of the Civil War and the social and economic realities of a suddenly nominally free black population. Congress had just passed the highly contested Fifteenth Amendment to the Constitution, giving black men the right to vote. Even some supporters of black suffrage had challenged the amendment, wanting to hold out for universal suffrage, which would include black and white women, as well as black men. Former slaves, male and female, quickly organized to protect the men's new right and to strategize on how best to use their voting power on behalf of the entire community. But those families and communities that had already achieved freedom were in a particularly crucial position to lead and organize such efforts, having already formed political alliances as well as great social and financial stability.[20] Greener did not have economic stability, but his Harvard education and his years of activism gave him the networks and the credentials to join these efforts.

His first priority, however, was finding work, and Greener took a series of teaching and administrative jobs at various schools for African American students. He first returned to his hometown, Philadelphia, to teach English at the Quaker-run Institute for Colored Youth. But he was soon pulled into the local political fray, which was being repeated in cities and towns throughout the nation. The dangers of the time were highlighted for him with the 1871 murder of Octavius Catto, principal of the institute's male section. Catto had been a leader in organizing African American men to vote in Philadelphia for the first time since the passage of the Fifteenth Amendment. On the day of the first election open to black men, gangs of armed white men roamed the streets threatening and attacking black men trying to vote. Most victims survived the assaults: the intent was to terrorize and prevent election participation. Catto was shot and killed; his friend Richard T. Greener was the first to reach his body. Despite the presence of witnesses, the killers were never brought to trial. In response, Greener became a leader in African American organizing, working with local activists like his cousin Isaiah Wears, Robert Purvis, and William Forten.[21]

In 1872 Greener was hired as principal of the Preparatory School in Washington, D.C., a move that fit well with his political aspirations and activism. It was clear that the federal government would continue to be the focus of civil rights legislation and protections for the near future, so Washington was the place to be. By this time Richard had already gained a reputation among Republicans for his speeches and petitions in support of the Fifteenth Amendment and for Senator Sumner's proposed civil rights bill. He also began working for Frederick Douglass's newspaper, the *New National Era*. Now he was in the thick of the political struggle at its highest level, but problems with his job began to overshadow his political and journalistic activities.

The D.C. public schools were segregated, and the Preparatory School was the pinnacle of the colored public school system. By 1869 over half of the teachers working in D.C.'s black schools were African American, a relatively well-paid position for nonwhites at that time. So Richard Greener occupied a very visible and important place in the community. His hire, however, had been controversial, largely because his promised salary of $1,500 was much higher than the $900 his predecessor (an African American woman) had earned.[22] From this uncertain start, Greener struggled with the board over hires, curriculum issues, operational costs, and student discipline. By the end of the year he had begun to write articles in the New National Era criticizing the trustees for mismanaging the schools. Despite outside reports of his success as a principal and the parents' support, he was removed from his position by the end of the school year.

Caught up in a community controversy over his firing, and the broader issue of integration of the D.C. school system, Greener scrambled for work, drawing on his relationships with Senator Sumner and, increasingly, with elite African American political and social organizations in D.C. In the color-conscious world of the D.C. elite, some of these groups were traditionally restricted to light-skinned people of mixed ancestry. Greener's complexion would have qualified him for membership under these informal rules. However, he and a new generation of African Americans in Washington were more concerned with uniting to break down barriers that affected all people of African ancestry than with maintaining color boundaries between them. Greener continued to champion the integration of the D.C. school system and began working closely with Sumner on both national and local race politics. He also continued his work at the New National Era, clerked for the district attorney, and started to prepare for law school. And he was courting one of the D.C. elite's eligible daughters: the beautiful Genevieve Ida Fleet.

Genevieve, or Genie, as she was known to her family, was an accomplished pianist and well-respected music teacher, born in the late 1840s to James H. and Hermione (Peters) Fleet. Genevieve's family history had much in common with her husband's: origins in slavery, racial mixing, most likely between enslaved women and white men, and a few generations of freedom before 1865. The Fleets, and to some extent the Peterses, had a long history in Georgetown as free families of color. And although some were menial laborers, many were teachers, musicians, skilled workers, and independent business owners like barbers, and one was even a physician. In fact, in part because of their prominence, we can trace more of the Fleets' history in the late eighteenth and early nineteenth centuries than that of any other branch of Belle's family.

Between 1797 and 1812 Belle's great-great-grandfather Henry Fleet, himself a free man of color living in Georgetown, purchased his wife, "Negro Nan," and at least five children who were described as his, as well as several other young "yellow" or "mulatto" slaves who may or may not have been related to him. Henry may have been born free and married an enslaved woman, or he may have first purchased his own freedom from his owner. It is even possible that he was himself the son of a white slaveowner who granted his freedom and assisted Henry in developing a trade that allowed him to purchase his own off-spring. Among the children he freed in 1797, along with his wife, were Genevieve's grandfather James Fleet and her great-aunt Patience. In all cases where an owner was recorded, the Fleet family members were purchased from George Beall or his estate and heirs.[23]

Henry legally owned his wife and several of his children for over twenty years, freeing them either in childhood or as they came of age. For example, he freed his son, Henry Jr., in 1818, stating that the young man was a shoemaker and had "made me full compensation for the money I expended on him to this date."[24] Henry Fleet was not the only member of his family to own family members. His mother, Patience Turner, freed a Milly Turner and her three children in her will, while leaving property to her children Robert Hicks, Henry Fleet, and Sally Turner.[25]

Owning family members because one had purchased them out of slavery and had not yet freed them was quite different from the system of chattel slavery, in which enslaved people and their children were legal property to be bought, sold, and exploited for their labor. In D.C. it was quite common for free people of color to assist others, especially relatives, out of enslavement. The Fleets were not the only family to come to freedom slowly over time in this way, nor were they the only ones to own family members in the process.

Of course, many white slaveowners also owned family members, particularly when white men fathered children with enslaved women, whose children were legally slaves as well. This was the case for some people in Genevieve and Richard Greener's circles: Frederick Douglass's father was a white man. Francis Grimké and his brother Archibald were also born into slavery, the sons of a white plantation owner and a black enslaved woman. After the war, they began their education and were aided in going to college by white patrons in Pennsylvania. There they became involved with the antislavery movement, where they met their white aunts, Sarah and Angelina Grimké, who financed Archibald's tuition at Harvard Law School. Archibald Grimké was an influential activist who, like Greener, was working with Republicans to expand opportunities for African Americans. Francis became a minister and was a pastor at the Fifteenth Street Presbyterian Church, of which Genevieve and her family had been members for decades. In addition to his ministerial relationship, Francis and his wife, Charlotte Forten Grimké, were good friends of Richard and Genevieve Greener.[26]

Still, Henry Fleet was a man of color, probably a former slave himself, who legally owned most of his family. In some places nonwhites (usually people of mixed black and white ancestry, or Native Americans) owned African American slaves and exploited their labor as chattel. But there is little evidence that the Fleets were part of this pattern. African American ownership of family was more commonly an economic step toward freedom. In fact, in some states or cities it was easier, and sometimes legally necessary, not to free family members who had been purchased out of slavery. Sometimes freed slaves had to leave the area within a not period of time after manumission. If other family members were still enslaved, or simply had economic and social ties to that community, it was more expedient to keep the legal status of enslavement. In D.C., residence was allowed after manumission, and the process was a simple one. Once laws were passed requiring free people of color to register and establish their freedom, it became more advisable to do so.[27] It is also important to remember that all free husbands and fathers had a legal right to the assets and earnings of their wives and children. Henry Fleet's belief that his children should work to pay him back for the money he spent purchasing them made both economic and social sense in this context.[28]

Once freed, Henry's children did well. Daughter Airy inherited a house in Georgetown; Patience married a prominent man of color, William V. Grant, a master bricklayer.[29] James was a gifted musician, as was his son James H., Genevieve's father. But James H. Fleet was also a trained physician. He and two other African American men received a medical education paid for by the American Colonization Society. The ACS was a white-led organization whose members sought to end slavery, but assumed that blacks were naturally inferior and could not live freely in the United States. Instead, the ACS proposed to send people of African descent "back" to the American colony of Liberia, in northern Africa. Some African Americans agreed with the general idea of removing blacks to Africa, although their reasoning was that white racism would never allow blacks to live freely in the United States. Still, the three new physicians refused to go after completing their education. In fact, Fleet was apparently the only one who worked as a doctor. He also became active in the 1830s convention movement, as African Americans began organizing regional and national meetings to discuss and debate political issues and strategies.[30]

Genevieve's mother, Hermione Constantia Peters, was also born in the District of Columbia. She was one of six children of John Peters and Louisa Gaines, both listed as mulatto or colored.[31] The Peterses have also been described as an elite family of free people of color in D.C., but there is much less information available about them. Hermione Peters married James Fleet on 21 April 1845.[32] Genevieve was the firstborn, followed by four brothers and several infants who did not survive. It was a very musical household. Hermione was a pianist and her husband a violinist; both performed publicly as well as teaching.[33] Although their first son was named James, after his father and grandfather, the next three boys were Mozart, Bellini, and Mendelssohn. The youngest girl was Minerva. Hermione kept house while the children were growing up, a mark of the family's relative comfort.

The Fleets lived in an extended family household for all of Genevieve's childhood. Besides her grandfather James, Genevieve's great-aunt Patience, her husband, William, and their youngest son, Henry T. Grant, lived with them. For a while another older woman, H. Ray, perhaps another of James's married sisters, lived there as well. The elder

James Fleet and William Grant both died in the 1850s, but Patience continued to live with the growing Fleet family. All members of the household were consistently labeled mulatto throughout the decades. Hermione and her family were also founding members of the Fifteenth Street Presbyterian Church, established in 1841 as white churches began to push black members to leave. Grants, Peterses, and Fleets all appear in their membership records, including Hermione, James H., Genevieve, Mozart, and Bellini.[34]

Genevieve's family was clearly more established, more elite than Richard's. Both families were racially mixed; both Genevieve and Richard were very light-skinned, by all accounts. But the Peterses and Fleets had been part of a stable community of free people of color in Georgetown and then Washington, D.C., for most of the nineteenth century. Besides their Georgetown address, the Fleets had worked in higher-status professions as engineers, barbers, music teachers, and printers. When Genevieve's mother began to work for the first time in 1880, it was as a dressmaker. A few years later she took a job as a clerk in a government office.[35]

However, income and occupation were not the defining factors for membership in the elite class. In contrast to that of the white middle class, the economics of racial prejudice simply did not allow for the development of a money-based elite until after World War One. And there was absolutely no African American counterpart for the white aristocracy of the Morgans, Vanderbilts, and Astors. Many members of the "black Four Hundred," as the black papers dubbed the D.C. elite, worked in service occupations.[36] From this perspective, then, the Fleets were doing very well indeed.

What we know of Genevieve's childhood and young adult years suggests that she was in many ways a quite typical young middle-class woman of color. She taught school for several years before marrying Richard, no doubt helping support her younger brothers after the loss of their father.[37] And she was, like her mother and father, an accomplished musician. In fact, when Richard arrived at his new position in Washington, Genie had been working as a music teacher in the colored public school district for several years. She had received praise and recognition for her teaching, her discipline, and her activities with her students. She had organized a literary society with other teachers and students. In 1872, shortly before Richard's arrival, she temporarily served as principal of one of the smaller schools in the district.[38] Genevieve may have met Richard through their work in the school system, or at one of the social or community functions that defined Georgetown's free community of color.

When Richard and Genevieve married, in 1874, their union brought together two patterns of free African American experience: the generations of freedom and relative status the Fleets had achieved, and the rise in opportunities in the postbellum era that Greener's education represented. Both paths wound through struggle, discrimination, and limitations. As they launched their life together in the post-Emancipation period, Richard and Genevieve would have been aware of the divide between them and the whites with whom their families associated and worked. They would have been equally aware of the gulf between themselves and the hundreds of thousands of recently freed slaves.

The young couple, however, began their married life in a social setting very different from the ones in which either had been raised. Eight months before their marriage, Richard Greener accepted a professorship at the University of South Carolina. It was here that he brought his new bride to live within two weeks of their September 24, 1874, wedding. Columbia, South Carolina, was at the time an extraordinarily turbulent place to begin a life together.

South Carolina in the 1870s was in the throes of a heated and sometimes violent political battle over the future role and status of African Americans in a post-Emancipation state. With a new state constitution in 1868, the political world had been "turned upside down," as representatives of the state's African American population had a voice in framing the new constitution, and Republicans, including many African Americans, were now in power in the former slaveholding state.[39] Richard's very appointment was a significant step in the Republican attempt to promote a model of racial equality. The 1872 elections had allowed Republicans to take over the university by electing an all-Republican, black-majority board of trustees, transforming the formerly all-white school into a racially integrated one overnight. Whether they had the power to support and enforce those changes was far less certain. Furious white parents withdrew their sons, and white community members made their outrage clear in verbal and physical attacks. For the Republicans hiring a "colored Professor," especially such a "cultivated and refined . . . honored graduate of grand old Harvard," was a great boon to the experiment in Reconstruction.[40] And, just as he had at Phillips Academy and Harvard College, Richard T. Greener again represented the potential of the Negro race to enter fully into American political and economic life. But now the stakes were much more explicit and the prejudice much more violent.

Greener threw himself into his new job, again gaining a reputation as a hard worker and eloquent orator. In addition to teaching, he organized the university library and attended classes in the law school, eventually earning his long-desired law degree. Fully aware that the university had only four years (until the next election) to prove itself, he also traveled to publicize and recruit black students for the struggling school. The "integrated" school had lost all of its white students, as well as most of the faculty. Locally, the school became the focus of statewide debates over the education and enfranchisement of African Americans, and Greener placed himself center stage in the turmoil. By 1875 he was working the equivalent of three jobs—teaching, running the library, and recruiting students—in addition to pursuing his law degree, campaigning for the Republican party, and fighting the university for repairs to the poorly heated house provided for his residence.[41]

The Deep South must have been a shock for Genevieve and Richard. It is likely that neither of them was prepared for the open hostility of Southern racism. Genevieve in particular, although a young woman of color, had been protected from the harshest facets of racism, living in a community of free people of color in the safety of her parents' home. When Genevieve left D.C., segregation had not yet solidified and African Americans had not yet been disenfranchised, although they had never had all the rights and privileges of white citizens. South Carolina, on the other hand, had been one of the largest slaveholding states of the Deep South and was now a battleground over "the Negro question." Larger cities like Charleston had had a "Brown Fellows Society" from 1790, admitting only light-skinned, mixed-race people of color. But South Carolina was one of the first states to legalize the one-drop rule, defining as black anyone of any black ancestry. Social distinctions between brown and black remained, but there was no longer room in the state's racial categories or policies for such divisions.[42]

For a while the birth of their first child, born on September 11, 1875, may have distracted Genevieve from the world outside. But when Horace Kempton Greener died on the very day he turned eight months old, there were no friends or family for Genie to turn to.[43] It must have been a painfully lonely time; even her husband was not fully there.

Richard had begun to travel frequently, which would become a tiresome pattern in their marriage. At this point his trips were primarily to recruit more students of color to fill the newly integrated university, whose white student body had vacated. But soon the preelection debates heated up, and Greener's was a crucial voice in support of continued Republican reform. Rallies and meetings throughout the state, however, were constantly threatened by the presence of armed young white Democrats called Red Shirts who screamed Republican speakers down, disrupted meetings, and threatened violence. Often the only African American speaker, Greener was the target of many verbal and physical attacks, vilified in Democratic papers, heckled with calls of "God-damned nigger" while trying to orate, and threatened with guns when leaving and arriving at meetings. On voting day he served as an election official and was assaulted twice during his twenty-hour shift.[44]

In 1876 the Republicans lost the election, signaling the end of Reconstruction attempts to support African Americans' emergence into full citizenship. It was a reversal that was asserted throughout the South and eventually within the federal government. During the interim between the election and the actual change of power, Greener traveled back and forth between Columbia and Washington, giving testimony on the violence of the Democratic Red Shirts and trying to assure payment of back salary owed to him. Much of it was never paid. Once the university was again established as a white institution, Richard Greener resigned.[45]

In 1877 the Greeners left South Carolina, leaving a small grave behind in the state Richard had hoped to help transform. But they were not alone. Their first daughter, Mary Louise, was born on January 27, 1877, just months before their retreat. She survived, a tiny testament to the hope all parents have for a good life for their children, and a better world for them to know.

Back in Washington the Greeners settled into life as members of the extended Fleet-Peters family. They found a home near Genevieve's mother, who was now working as a dressmaker. Mary Louise was baptized a bit belatedly at the Fifteenth Street Presbyterian Church, where the Greeners' friend Francis Grimké had just become an assistant pastor. (Grimké would become senior pastor in 1889.) Russell Lowell was born on February 1, 1878, the first surviving son. A year later Genie was pregnant again, this time with Belle.[46]

Two small children and a pregnancy would have kept Genevieve very busy. Richard threw himself back into work and political projects. Money was tight, and several times he had to borrow from his cousin Isaiah Wears to make ends meet. Greener entered a law partnership with a prominent African American attorney, John H. Cook, who died a few months later. And he continued to practice law and served as acting dean of the Law School in Cook's place at the newly formed school for African American students, Howard University. Greener later cofounded the National Benefit & Relief Association, an insurance company that served people of color, which white-owned insurance companies refused to do. Six months before Belle was born, her father helped organize and spoke at a memorial service for William Lloyd Garrison, held at the Fifteenth Street Presbyterian Church.[47] He worked closely with Frederick Douglass on this and several other projects during this period.

The 1870s were a remarkable time for African Americans in Washington, D.C. Men and women of color were entering professions and positions (like Cook's and Greener's positions at Howard University, and the election of African American representatives in Congress) that would have been closed to them a decade earlier.[48] Leaders like Richard Greener had every reason to hope and even expect that political and social equality was a reachable goal, attainable if not by them then by their children.

In the midst of this optimistic time, Belle Marion Greener entered the world on November 26, 1879. Her birth certificate listed her as colored (the only options were "White" or "Colored"). It was now possible to trust that this label would not keep her from reaching her goals, as it had so many in her parents' and grandparents' generations. Her father was on another lecture tour—this time through the Midwest—when she was born. Still, there were plenty of family members around to help Genevieve recover and care for three children under the age of three. The extended family lived on a quiet street of recently built two-story row houses in the 1400 block of T Street, about ten minutes west of Howard University on foot. The 1880 census captured them there: Genevieve and Richard with their three children: Louise (Mary) Russell, and Belle, and an older servant named Mary A. Askins.[49] Hermione lived next door with her sons James, a schoolteacher, and Bellini, a printer. Mendelsohn had died in 1878 at the age of twenty-one. Genie's fourth brother, Mozart, was now married and living on the other side of the Greeners with his wife, Adalaide, and their infant son, Clafton L. Fleet, born just a few months before his cousin Belle. Mozart was working as an engineer. Genevieve's cousin Henry Grant was married as well, working as a schoolteacher, and living in D.C. with his wife, Julia, and four children, including one by Julia's previous relationship. Henry's mother, Patience, was now living with her son.[50] Genevieve was already pregnant again, and gave birth on December 20, 1880, to a third girl, Ethel Alice.

And oddly, just at this moment that Genevieve was back home on familiar ground, the family's racial identity came under new scrutiny. Having been classified as "colored," "mulatto," and even "black" for generations, the Greeners and their children were all listed as "white" in 1880. Only the servant, Mary Askins, was denoted as "black." (Their cousins, the Grants, living in another neighborhood, were listed as "black.") There had been no change in the census. In 1880 "white," "black," and "mulatto" were all options, as were "Chinese" and "Indian." The instructions to census takers specified that "mulatto" should include "quadroons, octoroons, and all persons having any perceptible trace of African blood," cautioning that "[i]mportant scientific results" would rely on accurate determination of the mulatto category.[51]

However important color distinctions may have continued to be within some communities, they were disappearing from institutional systems of racial categorization. As the country began to develop segregation as a legal system in the South and as a social one in the North, the category of "mulatto" became less and less visible. States literally rewrote their definitions of "black" and "white," expanding definitions of "black" or "Negro" to include people of mixed ancestry. The one-drop rule was gaining dominance over American racial ideologies throughout the country. One-drop racialism held that African ancestry was so powerful and significant that any amount of "black blood," even one drop, should designate a person as black. This was not a universal belief, by any means. Like many states, the District of Columbia did not have a legal definition of race, leaving cultural assumptions to determine who was colored and who was white.

The Greeners had not shifted their racial identity. Richard was still a prominent activist, campaigning for civil rights and working with black and white leaders. However, it is likely that they occasionally took advantage of their ambiguous appearance. As segregation and discrimination imposed more and more limits on African Americans' access to jobs, cultural activities, education, and hotels, there were more and more occasions on which simply not proclaiming black ancestry could get one a job, a meal, a place to stay. Richard reported that he sometimes did just this when he traveled. Still, the most likely explanation for this census anomaly is that the enumerator recorded what he thought he saw—a white family with a black maid. Census takers were notoriously imperfect at identifying people of mixed ancestry. Enumerators often made their own judgments about an individual or family, and often saw or spoke only to whoever was in when they called at the door, not the entire family (or dormitory). Unless they were in a black neighborhood, it was considered rude to ask an apparently white person what his or her race was.[52] The presence of a dark-skinned maid may also have further whitened the Fleets' and Greeners' appearance to enumerators.

Nevertheless, the Greeners were popular members of Washington's community of color, whose activities revolved around social events, from lavish weddings and parties to small dinners, outings, and entertainments. While rarely at the center of their social world, Richard and Genevieve attended many major events. Newspapers noted their presence at local birthday celebrations, dinner parties, literary club meetings. And they seemed to have developed the friendships that brought them to more informal socializing as well. Richard also gave local talks, which were often mentioned in the newspapers.[53]

Washington was a political and cultural center for African Americans in the 1870s and 1880s, attracting talented and ambitious people of color from across the states, much as Harlem in New York City would half a century later. In the late nineteenth century the African American elites in D.C. tried to distinguish themselves from the lower classes and prove their respectability to middle-class whites through their behavior and their self-representation. They emphasized decorum, dignity, gentility, and good taste, scorning gaudiness in dress or décor. Refined behavior, they believed, would bring respect, and the first chance to demonstrate respectability was in one's personal appearance and comportment.[54] Archibald Grimké passed on advice to his own daughter when she went off to school: "[T]he treatment which will be accorded her by all will be at once felt favorably if she be well dressed." A young woman should therefore be respected if she "appears at once to be a young girl of refined manners and tastes and used to the best Society."[55]

Yet, cultural assimilation did not mean racial assimilation for D.C.'s elites. They were certainly color conscious and even snobbish: dark skin could exclude an otherwise exemplary individual from their social circles.[56] But they also stressed racial pride and survival, declaring a bond of identity, history, and shared position in white America with their darker-skinned and lower-class fellow citizens. Interracial marriage was not encouraged, and the black-published *Washington Bee* preached against passing and denounced practices like skin bleaching. Ironically, at the same time that the newspaper editorialized that "the color of one's skin should be a source of pride rather than humiliation," it published ads for "beauty" products that touted lighter skin and straighter hair.[57] Still, the elite believed they had a responsibility to use their higher economic, educational, and cultural attainments for the betterment of the entire race. This call to maintain loyalty and connection to the "black masses" was strengthened and solidified between 1880 and 1920, but was already present in the writings and actions of Washington's black elite in the 1860s and 1870s.

Genevieve's community also had certain expectations for marriage and family life. Marriage was supposed to be based not only on affection but also on partnership and mutual support as well as a shared background. Moreover, families like the Greeners and the Fleets were expected to take pride in their racial ancestry and have a sense of responsibility to the race. They were expected to be leaders and role models and, in exchange, to receive respect and status within the community, as well as support if they should need it.[58] Richard Greener did not have the same privileged background of his wife and her family, and his ability to support his family had already been inconsistent. Although his education and accomplishments made him an acceptable suitor and husband, Richard and Genevieve may have found that they had fundamental differences in their expectations and their values. One of these differences was surely in their understanding of their racial identity and loyalties. Both were racially mixed; both had very light complexions. But Richard had experienced racial prejudice from a working-class vantage point and had never lived in a community in which class divisions were so clearly divided along color lines as they had been in D.C. during Genevieve's childhood and early adulthood. Richard's white ancestry made him even more aware of and outraged at the illogic of racism and prejudice; Genevieve's had offered a cushion against the harsher aspects of that illogical put powerful system.

In fact, the category "mulatto" was undergoing intense scrutiny and change as the system of segregation divided everyone into black and white, and increasingly defined people of mixed ancestry as black. This was a familiar identity for Richard—he used the term "black" often to refer to himself and others—but almost certainly not for Genevieve. Nationwide, the social position and racial identity of people of mixed ancestry was varied and in flux. Some were from families or regions where that ancestry denoted a community distinct from both black and white. Others came from communities in which color might be a source of difference or tension, but where shared ties of experience, history, and family defined "Negro" as containing a spectrum of skin color and facial features.

In the late nineteenth and early twentieth centuries though, it was black ancestry that most Americans, including the majority of those of mixed ancestry, deemed most important. What connected most people of color was a shared set of values and goals and a pride in being identified with "the race." There may have been a wide social gulf between this largely mixed-race middle class and the working-class "negro," but the elites were nevertheless proud "race men" and women.[59] The only alternative was to break off ties to the community of color and live as white.

This, then, was the world in which Belle lived for the first eight years of her life. Clearly she grew up in a home and environment where education and culture were valued and family bonds were strong. Belle spent her childhood surrounded by an extended family that could nurture all of her abilities and curiosity. She was not the baby for long, with the birth a year later of Ethel, who would quickly become her favorite sister. Still, what Belle loved best, she later often said, was to be "petted and spoiled" as she had been as a child.[60] And it was here in Washington's community of color, surrounded by siblings and cousins and aunts and uncles, that she must have learned to crave attention, to expect love and praise, to know herself to be worthy of "high" culture, education, and accomplishment.

It was here that Belle would also have learned how to dress, stand, sit, and speak "like a lady," to control anger or resentment in the face of rudeness or even outright abuse from a white person. Middle-class African American parents raised their children to understand appropriate behavior, embrace hard work, and value a community consciousness—all necessary strategies to encourage success for the first post-slavery generation of race men and women. Parents sought to imbue their children with the same armor of respectability and trained them in the proper behavior they employed to avoid negative attention and contradict whites' stereotyped beliefs about the Negro race.[61] Belle would have been encouraged in her skills and tutored in those not offered by the school system. Her mother may have taught her to play the piano; her father could have given her lessons in French or Latin. She was surrounded by music, lectures and lessons, references to classical literature, and the constant knowledge that her family had status and respect in a community that valued respectability, thrift, hard work, self-respect, and genteel dress and comportment. In these ways the D.C. elite prepared their children "not simply for life, but for life as African Americans."[62]

Belle was also raised in a family with an often absent father, whose work was focused on defending African American civil rights. Richard traveled almost constantly during her young life: to talks, meetings, conferences, and trials. A week after Ethel Alice was born, for example, Greener left again: this time to meet with Johnson C. Whittaker, a West Point cadet who had been found tied to his bed with his ears mutilated. White cadets had beaten him to make it clear that they did not want a black student in their class. White officers seem to have felt the same way: Whittaker was facing a court of inquiry, charged with mutilating himself. Despite Greener's attempts to help this former South Carolina student of his, the young cadet eventually faced a court-martial, by then accused not only of self-mutilation and forging a threatening letter to himself but also of falsely swearing at the court of inquiry. Greener served as a witness and assisted Whittaker's counsel before a military court-martial board overseen by Judge Advocate Asa Bird Gardiner. Whittaker was found guilty, but, after several months of awaiting sentencing, the finding was overturned on a technicality.[63] This would become one of the most memorable cases of

Greener's long and varied career.[64] It was the sort of surreal and outrageous transgression of justice that embittered and inspired race men like Richard T. Greener.

When Belle was almost four, the anti–civil rights backlash culminated in a U.S. Supreme Court decision, *Civil Rights Cases,* overturning the Civil Rights Act of 1875, which her father and many others had fought for. Greener considered the decision despicable and immediately began to give interviews and lectures protesting the shift. He went on the road again, along with Frederick Douglass, the lawyer and diplomat John Mercer Langston, and many other black leaders. During these travels Greener experienced firsthand the segregation that relegated him and other African Americans out of first-class accommodations and into colored-only sections and train cars. On one trip in 1884 he refused orders five times to move to the second-class coach (there were no first-class train cars for colored people). He wrote appeals defending his right to travel across the country "without fear of being put off a car or denied food and shelter solely because I had a trace of negro blood in my veins."[65] As the progressive momentum of the Reconstruction era was pulled under by a backlash of white supremacy, Greener and hundreds of thousands of others were experiencing a new kind of racism and disenfranchisement. It would be another century before America again passed civil rights legislation and resumed the long, slow process of addressing discrimination and segregation.

At the same time, ironically, he was also beginning to experience hostility from a few African Americans because of his light skin and his perceived desire to associate only with whites. When Greener and Robert H. Terrell had been refused membership in the Harvard Club of Washington, D.C., the *Washington Bee* editorialized that the club had the right to limit membership. Greener and Terrell, the *Bee* charged, were simply "fair-complexioned, well-educated blacks" who wanted to abandon their race to associate with whites.[66] Greener's attempts at integration, he complained bitterly, were being misunderstood.

Richard's own frustration with the increasing solidification of segregation was due mostly to its inherent inequity. But his position as a very

light-skinned man, and his ability to operate as white when his identity was unknown, made him particularly aware of the illogic and injus-
tice of racism. As William Henry Crogman pointed out when speaking
to a white audience in 1884, Greener had a Harvard degree and was
"nearer your color than mine," being only a "very little tinged" with
black ancestry. But Greener's friend and supporter asked, "What does
society care about a Harvard graduate, if his complexion is tinged with
the hated color?"[67]

Greener publicly addressed the issue of racial ancestry, color, and
ability in an 1886 publication. It was a topic he felt should be raised
only when absolutely necessary. He noted that, among "the colored
people," those of mixed ancestry seemed to be doing better socially and
economically than those who were "pure black." But that was merely
because they had come from "superior stock on both sides . . . inherit-
ing the several strains of the very best blood of the South," and because
they benefited from greater opportunities and preferential treatment
by whites. They shared the experience of discrimination, and Greener
called for continued unity among all colored people to fight prejudice.
He expected more opportunities for his "blacker brethren" to open up,
and in the meantime thought that "mixed-bloods" like himself should
use the access they had to speak and write publicly to appeal to whites
and inspire African Americans.[68]

However, like many other African American leaders, Greener was
becoming disillusioned with politics and with campaigns for civil
rights. When he was offered the opportunity to leave such work, to
leave Washington, D.C., even to leave his family temporarily, he
jumped at it. By 1885, as the family moved into its next stage and
Richard and Genevieve's marriage began to deteriorate, Belle and her
siblings found themselves, as many children do, caught between
increasingly hostile parents. New York would bring new opportunities,
new temptations, and new decisions to Belle and her mother and siblings. Richard Greener would eventually give up his expectations for
his family, just as they gave up any expectations for living full, unfet-
tered lives as people of color.

GILDED DREAMS IN NEW YORK

Those who know me will not accuse me of building up a race wall in politics or otherwise. All my efforts have tended to destroy the one which now exists . . . My solution of all the political and social problems is the union and co-operation of blacks and whites on the basis of manhood and fitness. All that I am I owe to privileges and advantages enjoyed from free association with the better class of white people.

—Richard Greener, 1881[1]

I wonder if any living being has greater imaginative powers than I. Since my childhood I have lived in them.

—Belle Greene, 1909[2]

IN 1885 RICHARD T. GREENER moved to New York. Belle was six years old. Once again Richard left his family behind for a job, this time for a very high-profile one: secretary of the Grant Monument

Association. When Ulysses S. Grant, former president and Union general, died on July 23, 1885, his family and New York politicians began to make plans for a memorial tomb in New York City. Because of Grant's association with the Civil War and Emancipation, organizers wanted a black representative on the committee coordinating the monument. As one of the most prominent African American intellectuals and Republican Party activists of his generation, Greener was an obvious choice. Within a week of Grant's death, he was in New York meeting with political leaders and the officers they appointed to oversee the Grant Monument Association (GMA). Former President Chester A. Arthur was chair; New York City's mayor, William Russell Grace, and Hamilton Fish, former secretary of state under Grant, were vice chairmen; J. Pierpont Morgan, the powerful financier who would hire Belle twenty years later, was treasurer.[3]

Frustrated with the direction racial politics were taking, and beset by mounting debts after the collapse of the National Benefit & Relief Association, Richard accepted the appointment as secretary of the GMA. It was a key position in the work of raising the $1,000,000 to build a fitting monument to Grant. With his salary of $200 a month, Greener hoped to recover from his debt and pull himself out of the financial tailspin he had been in since he was denied his back pay from the University of South Carolina. By the fall of 1885 he had moved to Long Island and was operating the GMA office in Manhattan on the second floor of the Mutual Life Insurance Building, at 146 Broadway, just a two blocks north of Wall Street.[4] By 1886 he had relocated to Manhattan. Genevieve and the children stayed in Washington, where they consolidated households and lived with Hermione.[5]

Manhattan was a rising metropolis in the 1880s, growing in almost every possible direction and meaning. The island city was a study in contrasts. The most visible disparity was that of class: fabulous wealth emerged amid indescribable poverty. Diamonds glittered on women's arms, ears, necks, and dresses in the gaslit ballrooms of spacious brownstone mansions and exclusive clubs. Blocks away, tenements packed impoverished adults and families into small dark rooms, which often lacked running water; children worked beside their parents in

factories six days a week, ten to twelve hours a day, in dangerous conditions for meager wages. Although part of the growing middle class,
Greener quickly became a familiar figure in the upper echelons of
Gilded Age New York. His work was no longer focused on racial
reform, but he continued to challenge the informal system of racial
segregation, joining previously white-only clubs, parades, and organizations.[6] His job brought him into daily contact with New York's elite
and gave him the opportunity to use his formal and informal artistic
training. Although he had long ago given up his dream of studying art
in Europe, Greener had scoured the libraries at Oberlin, Harvard, the
University of South Carolina, and Howard, soaking up everything their
holdings had to say and show about decorative, artistic, and monumen-
tal art. He played a large role in the selection of the Grant Monument
design.[7]

Richard enjoyed New York. Its culture, he found, was "much more
to [his] taste than the fetid and vitiated political and social atmosphere
of Washington which we have breathed so long."[8] The city was undergoing a cultural renaissance. In the decade and a half before Greener's
arrival, the Museum of Natural History (established in 1869) had been
joined by the Metropolitan Museum of Art (1872), Madison Square
Garden (1879), and the Metropolitan Opera (1883). All were funded
by the donations or bequests of New York's millionaires. In the
post–Civil War era, Manhattan (still a separate city) had emerged as a
center of industry and the center of finance in the nation. Technological advances in the postwar economy and the development of corporate capitalism concentrated unprecedented riches in the hands of a
few businessmen. Telegraph cable and railroads, steel and oil, made
Cornelius Vanderbilt, John Pierpont Morgan, Andrew Carnegie, and
dozens of others into the equivalents of multibillionaires today. Now
many of these men were investing their assets into cultural institutions, and New Yorkers like Greener could take advantage of some of
these newly opened institutions.[9]

Richard visited his family for Thanksgiving and Christmas. Genie
was pregnant again, and it was a difficult pregnancy this time. Put on
bed rest in early February 1886, she gave birth on the twenty-second

to Theodora Genevieve. Richard was away for most of her pregnancy, even for the birth. In fact, the night before Theodora was born, Richard was dining at the exclusive Delmonico's restaurant with two hundred of his fellow Harvard alumni. The New York Harvard Club had accepted this prominent African American as a member. A few weeks later Greener marched in the Saint Patrick's Day parade with T. Thomas Fortune, a well-known African American organizer and newspaper editor in New York. Greener's presence at the parade with Fortune indicates that he was connected with black leadership in New York, even as his new job brought him into increased contact with exclusively or predominantly white circles.[10]

Greener also took a second job, on the Municipal Civil Service Examining Board. He was now supporting two households, and hoped finally to make enough money to bring himself financial stability. Unfortunately, he made some bad investments; the solution to his money problems remained elusive. The extra work left Greener little time for visiting D.C., but he was there for the holidays again in 1886. They had, he said, spent every Christmas Day at home together as a family since their marriage. In August of 1887 Genevieve gave birth again, this time to a boy. Richard must have been thrilled—after four girls and the death of his first son, it was clear from his letters that Russell was his favorite. If he showed that favoritism at home, it must have baffled Belle and her sisters, until they were old enough to understand the limitations on women's opportunities. But little Charles Woodman Greener lived only for three months. Belle would surely have remembered his short life and his death, so impossible to explain or understand. She turned eight years old that November, the same month her baby brother died.[11]

Richard went home for Christmas as usual. This time when he returned to New York, his family went with him. Once again, Genevieve followed her husband to an unfamiliar place, probably with no little trepidation. In New York, Richard was busy with work, so Genevieve must have stayed mainly at home. She now had five children between the ages of two and twelve, and the loss of her infant son was still a fresh grief. Eventually, other members of her extended Fleet family migrated to New York, including Belle's uncle Bellini and her cousin's son Henry L. Grant.[12] But Richard's letters make no mention of contact with these family members. Still, New York in the late 1880s was a much more comfortable place to adjust to than South Carolina in the 1870s had been: the weather was colder, the Northern customs different. But here they were far from the only newcomers.

As the Greeners arrived in New York, they were part of a much larger migration of Americans to the city that was quickly becoming the national economic and cultural capital. Although many American migrants were white, the most visible new arrivals were African Americans coming from the South for the jobs in the urban North's new industrial expansion, and with the hope of freedom from southern racism and segregation. Most African American migrants were working-class, but all, like Richard, were seeking work and better lives, hoping to find the North less racist than the increasingly limited and violent forms of white supremacy that the South was developing to replace slavery. The Greeners' relationship to African Americans in New York reflected a shift in their racial experience and identity.

African American migration in the late nineteenth and early twentieth centuries altered the racial demographics of most northern and midwestern urban centers, including New York. Manhattan had actually lost a sizable portion of its black population during the Civil War, in part because of its notorious draft riots, in which white working-class men attacked black people and institutions, lynching and killing over 100 and burning the Colored Orphans Asylum to the ground. But by 1900 there were 60,000 blacks in New York, 36,000 in Manhattan. (The five cities and towns united into a single, multiborough city in 1898.) Most blacks in Manhattan lived in small neighborhoods in the southern area (Five Points, Greenwich Village), in the West Side area between Twenty-fourth and Fortieth Streets known as the Tenderloin, or in the area north of Central Park that would later be known as Black Harlem. In 1901 the sociologist W. E. B. Du Bois estimated that one-half of New York's African American population was employed in domestic service or menial work. One-quarter was working in higher vocations, and one-quarter consisted of the poor, struggling and failing or turning to crime. Du Bois also advised that "no respectable negro family should linger a week in the Tenderloin of New York," and it is unlikely any member of the Greener family ever did.[13]

The Greeners were, again, both part of this history and distinct from it. Their first home together, for example, was not in one of the black districts described by Du Bois. Their apartment at 29 West Ninety-ninth Street was in a largely white area just west of Central Park, far north of the Tenderloin district and south of Harlem. Native-born New Yorkers, Germans, Scandinavians, Irish, Canadians, and white migrant Americans lived in multifamily dwellings; twelve families lived in number 29. It was a solidly working-class, lower-middle-class neighborhood. Men worked as salesmen, butchers, bookkeepers, carpenters, policemen; women earned wages as dressmakers, stenographers, or store clerks or worked at home caring for children. Most school-aged children went to school. Some washerwomen and janitors lived there, as well as some nurses and teachers. Rarely, a black family appeared in one of the surrounding blocks. More rarely still, a black servant lived with a white family. But right around the corner on Central Park West, fortunes went up. Stockbrokers, physicians, and engineers now outnumbered clerks and salesmen. Many families there had live-in servants, either African American or foreign-born.[14]

And then there was the park, literally a block away from the Greener residence. The largest public space in metropolitan America, Central Park provided a haven of walking paths, open squares, fountains, gardens, and lush greenery for New Yorkers of all backgrounds. Later in her life, Belle often retreated to country estates and wilderness sanctuaries when the stress and pace of her life overwhelmed her. Perhaps she and her siblings already did the same when they wanted to escape their homework and the stuffy confines of the apartment. On the other side of the park was the Metropolitan Museum of Art, which offered free admission several days each week. One of Manhattan's two public libraries—or, rather, privately funded libraries open to the public— was also across the park. (The Lenox Library, at Fifth Avenue and East Seventieth Street, was also the storage site for J. Pierpont Morgan's overflow of rare books and manuscripts.)[15] Genevieve and her children must have taken advantage of these opportunities. Russell was taking drawing lessons and seemed to have an artistic gift. And he was not the only one interested in art. Several years later an "Aunt Julia" (possibly her great aunt Julia Grant) gave Belle a copy of Bernard Berenson's *The Venetian Painters of the Renaissance*. A young up-and-coming art critic, Berenson, in soon-to-be signature commentary, pointed out patterns in the artists' works, offering new ways to determine attributions, as well as meditating on the transcendence and significance of the individual pieces.[16]

While the opportunities that New York offered were exciting, in the short term it was probably just enough that the Greener family was together again after over two years apart. Richard was once more present in his children's daily lives, he was no longer on the lecture or activism circuits, and for a while they lived a quiet yet busy life. The four older children were in school and doing well. The "baby," two-year-old Theodora, was plump and healthy. At the end of 1888, however, Richard's mother died, and he brought her body to New York for burial. His mother had never met his wife and children. And when Genevieve asked his cousin Isaiah for help with the burial expenses, Richard was furious. He needed the money, he admitted, but he could not forgive Genie for going behind his back to ask for it.[17]

Meanwhile, the criticism from the *Washington Bee* continued, and rumors began to spread that the Greeners were now avoiding former friends—at least those who were not white. Richard was at first annoyed at the rumors, then embarrassed and angry. When Francis and Charlotte Grimké came to New York but did not call on their old friends, Richard wrote to them. He feared that the Grimkés had believed the reports and thought their presence would be unwelcome, and he wanted to assure them otherwise. Passing was an uncomfortable reality to many families of mixed ancestry. As a minister, Francis had sermonized on the subject the summer before Richard moved to New York. Grimké called passing a sin, warning his congregants to avoid the temptation to "sail under false colors, to masquerade," although he acknowledged there were many good reasons for people who could to do so.[18] As a friend, though, he seemed to be following the usual practice of leaving alone individuals who were thought to be living as white, avoiding anything that might "unmask" them.

Richard continually denied that there was anything to the rumors. The Greeners did live in a predominantly white neighborhood, and Richard worked in an entirely white workplace, although he tried to bring other African Americans into the GMA office and activities. In part the problem was that Richard was no longer doing work that was actively focused on black civil rights and racial politics. He believed that the work he was doing for the Grant Monument did serve that greater cause, but he was working primarily with white New Yorkers— and prominent ones at that. The black-published *New York Age* noted that since his arrival in New York, Richard had focused on his job. "He has not mingled much with his race, but he has kept close watch of race affairs." The *Age* speculated that Greener may have been frustrated by political failures, or believed that "the race had failed to sustain him as it should have done." Whatever the problem, the editor defended Professor Greener as "one of the best critical scholars the race has produced" and "one of the most eloquent Afro-Americans in the country." At least part of the New York African American community still claimed Richard T. Greener and believed—as he did—that he was still identified with them.[19]

In 1892 Richard Greener resigned from the Grant Monument project, along with the other paid officers, when wealthy board members voted to eliminate their salaries.[20] His job at the Civil Service Board kept the family afloat, but new expenses were arising. The children were growing. By 1894 "Weezie" (Louise) and Russell had both started college already: she at the Girls' Normal School, he at the College of the City of New York. Belle was finishing school and would begin to attend the new Teachers' College the next year, at the age of sixteen. Baby Theodora had started grammar school.[21]

As Greener began looking for work in his previous fields—Republican Party organizing and civil rights activism—the rumors of his racial identity became an obstacle. When a friend approached Booker T. Washington about a possible job for Richard, mentioning twice in one letter that the Greeners looked "almost white," Washington made some inquiries. These seemed to focus as much on Genevieve as on Richard, and the results suggested that it was Genie's behavior, not Richard's, that was behind the confusion. One correspondent wrote in 1894 that although Genevieve "is colored and never passed for anything else while here [in D.C.]," it was generally known that "she associates only with whites in New York."[22] Washington did not hire Greener, but did begin a correspondence with him.

In 1896 Richard attended the Republican National Convention with a delegation from the National Federation of Colored Men. Afterward he was hired by the Afro-American News Syndicate and hired to head the Republican Party's Western Colored Bureau in Chicago to campaign for William McKinley, the Republican presidential candidate, as well as several important local elections. Greener planned to stay in Chicago with his cousin Ida Platt, who had just become the first black woman to graduate from an Illinois law school and was now practicing law. But other black Republicans in New York intervened. They reported that both Greener and his wife had been passing for white, charging that Richard had rented from white landlords even before his family joined him in New York, and that he had deserted his race, refusing to involve himself in African American organizations or socialize with colored people in New York. It was only because of his financial straits that he was now returning to race politics. Greener defended himself, pointing out that he had appointed other African Americans to the Grant committees and invited them to public affairs connected with the building. Despite the charges, Greener went to Chicago and campaigned hard for the Republican candidates. When McKinley won the presidency, Greener returned to New York, where reports that he and his family had been passing in the late 1880s and early 1890s persisted. Alexander Crummell, an African American minister and leader who had once been Greener's friend, blocked his membership to the American Negro Academy, charging, "For years he has been a white man in New York and turned his back upon all colored acquaintances."[23]

Although Richard, as a public figure, bore the brunt of the controversy over his racial identity, Genevieve was the one who wanted to identify and live as white. Perhaps it began when she realized her fellow New Yorkers were not recognizing her as colored, assuming instead perhaps that she was southern European. Although there was no official segregation in New York, this presumtion would have greatly improved the way Genevieve and (probably more important) her children were received and treated. Teachers and schoolmates would likely have assumed that the Greener children were white. Did Genevieve instruct them not to explain otherwise? Did she instill in them a white identity? Perhaps she explained to them that they were more white than black, or perhaps the older children had already learned that being labeled black could lead to very different treatment.

One odd piece of evidence suggests that Genevieve and her children had already begun using the name Greene by 1894. The inscription in the *Venetian Painters* book that Belle apparently received as a gift that year reads, "Belle Greene with love from 'Aunt Julia.' March 5, '94." This is a puzzling note. In 1894 Richard was still with the family and Genevieve and her children were still using the name Greener, in all official records anyway. But it is possible that Belle, and perhaps her siblings, were already playing with both a name change and an identity change. Finding records of the children during the 1890s has been particularly frustrating. Most schools do not have surviving student records going back that far, and children were listed individually only in census data. Was Belle already using the name Greene in 1894? Or did she, or someone else, write the inscription later and backdate it?

It seems pretty clear that Genevieve, and probably her children as well, were already working, going to school, and socializing in contexts where they were presumed to be white. Doing this while still living with Richard T. Greener, the man whom any newspaper reader could identify as the Negro former secretary of the Grant Monument Association, was unusual, to say the least. Of course, it would be assumed by outsiders that Richard was also trying to shift to living as white. How could a husband and wife present such different images of themselves to friends and neighbors? Perhaps Richard agreed not to mention his race around the building (although other African Americans lived on their block). This issue was very likely either at the core of their marital conflict or at least the topic through which they struggled over other concerns: whether he was faithful, whether adult children should work their way through college and beyond or be supported by parents, how much influence extended family should have, how much a husband and father was expected to earn to support his family.

Little, if any, evidence of these issues filtered into letters and other public records. But the question of racial identity was apparent. Richard was painfully aware that he was generally believed to have betrayed his loyalties to the colored community. He wrote to John E. Bruce, one of the few African American journalists, he said, who had defended him. Greener recalled that Bruce had also been one of the few black men who "dared to come and see" him in his office on Broadway when "other Negroes passed by," not giving him the chance to prove he had not changed. Greener was grateful that at least some fellow race men knew that his heart and loyalties were still with them.[24]

But Richard gave up on returning to race politics and headed to Washington to consult with Republican leaders who had been offering him a position in the McKinley administration. He had hardly been home for the past year or two, and the marriage did not survive either the distance of his travels or the equally expansive gap between Genie's and Richard's ideas about where to live in the racial and ethnic spectrum of New York. By the end of 1897 the Greeners had separated. The 1898 city directory lists only a "Genevieve I. Greener" at the West Ninety-ninth Street address.[25] Married women rarely merited a separate entry unless they had a residence separate from their husband's; dependent children were never named unless they had a professional position to publicize. Richard moved around a great deal, but when he was in New York over the next months he stayed in temporary lodgings or his office.

Now alone and estranged from his family, Richard yearned to get away from New York and his family. He began to pursue a foreign service job and was offered an appointment in Bombay, which would pay $2,000 a year. Was he restless enough to go that far to a place with which he had no experience or connection? In the spring of 1898 he stood in front of the Fifth Avenue Hotel, at Madison Square, and watched the news bulletins flash reports of the Spanish-American War in electric lights while new recruits marched and drilled in the square. "I feel a slight touch of the fever myself," he wrote his cousin, and considered enlisting in "some naval capacity." But he was too old for war. And Genie, with the help of her uncle Charles Peters, was able to block the Bombay appointment. In a confrontational meeting between husband and wife, mediated by Genie's aunt, and in a threatening letter to Peters, Richard warned his wife and her powerful family not to block his aspirations.[26]

Exactly what Genie's motives were is not clear. Perhaps she had heard the rumors in D.C. that her husband had a mistress there and wanted revenge, or she may have been trying to keep her children's main source of support closer to home. Whatever the reason, she gave up her efforts after this meeting. In late 1898, with no further interference from his estranged wife, Richard T. Greener was appointed to a consular post in Vladivostok, Russia, a port city close to Japan. Russia would not recognize a consul, so Greener's title was adjusted to "Commercial Agent." There he would later be joined or rejoined by a Japanese woman with whom he eventually had a common-law marriage and several children.[27]

By the time he left, his marriage to Genevieve was over, although there is no record of an official divorce in New York or Washington, D.C. In a final meeting the couple negotiated terms of support. Richard's letters do not mention meeting with his children during the year or two that he was not living with them, or before his departure. Most seem to have broken off all ties. Richard wrote bitterly to his cousin about his family situation soon after he arrived in Vladivostok:

> I have had two letters from Louise; but none from Mrs. G or any of the other children. Louise seems to be ambitious and is taking a course for a degree, besides her daily teaching. I am willing to do my part, when I get on my feet; but I want it settled on a legal basis: for I am firmly resolved, never to live in the Fleet family any more, I have had my

dose of them, and Mrs. G. has shown she cannot live with me and for me alone. She has ample grounds now, on which to secure a divorce and I should interpose no objections. All they want of me, is my money, and I don't see, why she does not see what is her only course. If they attempt to bother or harass me, I shall simply remain abroad until death relieves one or the other of us. There are only two children, I am bound to support, in fact only one, for Ethel was 18 in Dec. Lowell and Louise are self-supporting, and Belle and Ethel will be soon in the same position. Mrs. G. has shown herself a good enough business woman, when her own individual interests are concerned, and she has made friends in New York, at my expense, and by disparagement of me, to an extent I can never forgive, and she knows my determination full well; for I told her so, in plain terms at our last interview.[28]

If anyone other than Louise wrote to Richard in Siberia, he left no record of it.

Clearly, multiple issues were involved in the dissolution of the Greeners' marriage. That he felt taken over by the Fleet family is not surprising, given their long history and deep ties in the Washington, D.C., elite. That dominance had apparently followed him even to New York. His complaint about Genie's making friends in New York in a way that threatened or belittled him probably refers to her socializing only with whites.

Richard's refusal to support his children after they turned eighteen was a blow to Genevieve, who aspired to higher education for all her children.[29] To help them pay for tuition, she began to work again as a music teacher.

In 1899 Hermione Fleet, née Peters, passed away. She was buried in Harmony Cemetery, a graveyard organized by free Negroes in 1825 as part of a mutual aid society whose membership (any free adult Negro man was eligible) paid dues in exchange for financial assistance in medical and burial expenses.[30] It was far from Genevieve's last link

to her family; the presence of her aunt and uncle in mediating her separation from Richard attests to that. But it may have helped her make
the decision or confirm the path she was on.

By 1900 the official transformation was complete. Still living at 29
Ninety-ninth Street, Genevieve reported herself as "Ida Green,"
widow. "Mary L" was a teacher, "De Costa" (Russell) was a clerk, "Marian" (Belle) was a "libaryberian," and Alice Ethel and Theodora were
both in school. The entire family was listed as white. This was not the
first time enumerators had seen them as white, but it was the first
appearance of "Green" or "Greene" rather than "Greener." (City directories soon established the correct spelling as "Greene," but the final *e*
would often be omitted in private and public records alike.) This was
also the first use of "De Costa" or "Da Costa" in either Russell or Belle's
name.[31] What discussions went into these name changes? What did
the children think about their father's departure? How much impact
could he be said to have had on them if they changed their name to
disassociate from him and never wrote while he was in Vladivostok?

The children of famous men and women are usually influenced
more by their parents' private lives than by the public stances and
accomplishments for which they are known. Greener's frequent
absences may have prevented him from having a stronger effect on his
children. They seem not to have adopted his perception that mixed-
race ancestry was a subdivision of the colored race and that unity was
the path to the common goal of ending prejudice. But surely Belle, a
keen observer of human behavior, a woman known for soaking up
information like a sponge, would have learned from and even picked
up some of her father's attitudes.

What would she have remembered about Richard Greener while he
was gone, and what lessons would she have consciously or unconsciously internalized? Belle's father supported women's activism and
suffrage, publishing his belief that women needed the vote to escape
their present position of servitude and fulfill their potential abilities in
civil society.[32] Although his letters about his children tended to focus
on his one son, his daughters were all encouraged in their schoolwork
and were expected to enter an appropriate profession. It was common

among middle-class African American families to place equal emphasis on educating their daughters and on women's work as part of their
role as wives and mothers, and the Greeners were no exceptions to
this rule.[33] Greener would have encouraged, even pressured, his children to work hard, to excel at their studies, and to aim high in their
ambitions.

Belle's father also admired the struggles and character of other ethnic minorities in the United States, especially Jews, whom he held up
as a group that African Americans should use as a model for their own
development. And he knew how to interact with people from different
backgrounds, including elite white society—his fellow students at
Phillips Academy and Harvard were the sons, now the leaders, of that
society. Richard looked forward to a time when the colored schools he
taught at would be integrated; when the migration to the Midwest he
helped support would no longer be necessary; when the informal bans
among African Americans against interracial marriage, passing, and living outside of one's racial community no longer made sense; and when
a man of color could simply be a man. (For example, he was one of the
few African American leaders to defend Frederick Douglass when he
married a white woman.)[34]

Belle probably developed her love of art and her fascination with
rare books from her father as well. While Greener was still the librarian at the University of South Carolina, he submitted a paper on the
"Rare and Curious Books" of that institution to the American Philolog-
ical Association meeting in 1876. He had also had a personal collection of rare books and documents related to African American history,
including a 1792 edition of Benjamin Banneker's *Almanac* and a facsimile of a letter written by Banneker to Thomas Jefferson. His continued interest in classical European art was evident in a small scrap-
book of reproductions from European museums that he presented to
Francis and Charlotte Grimké in 1913.[35] There was definitely something of Richard T. Greener in his daughter Belle da Costa Greene.

Still, in changing their names, Belle and her family cut this connection with Richard Greener. This official name change from Greener to
Greene is an intriguing one. The elimination of the *r* was a conscious

indication that the family members had altered their public identity. We cannot say for sure what their personal identity was (mixed? colored? white with some black ancestry?), but we do know that they were signaling a change from their previous public identity as colored, and an intention to hide a part of their past and their ancestry. It was not a complete change, however: Greene is very close to Greener. Perhaps it was necessary to be able to use some old records and papers? If Belle and her siblings were already distancing themselves from their well-known father by using a different name, they may have needed one that he would think was a mistake if he caught someone using it. Before computer databases and Social Security numbers, changing one's name was a relatively simple matter. But there were other permutations as well: Genevieve added "Van Vliet" to her name, most likely a Europeanized version of her own maiden name, Fleet. She continued to shift her name around for decades, appearing variously as Van Vliet Greene, Genevieve V. V. Greene, and Ida Green, later as Victoria Greene—sometimes listing herself as a widow of DeAcosta, sometimes as a widow of Van Vliet. Most often, however, she seems to have been using Van Vliet as her maiden name. (When her youngest daughter married, for example, she listed her mother's maiden name as Genevieve Van Vliet and her father as Russell Da Costa.)[36] Using both her maiden name and her husband's name may also have been an attempt to suggest a higher-class background. It was common practice among New York's social elite for women to incorporate their family names into their married names, either formally or informally. Children were also sometimes given their mother's family name as a middle name. In both cases the practice indicated the prominence of the woman's family. Genevieve may already have been creating the image Belle would propagate of her mother as a genteel woman fallen on hard times. That much was certainly true.

But whatever names Genevieve cycled through over the next forty years, she never went back to Greener, either the name or the man, and neither did her children.

Genevieve did not make this decision alone. Her four eldest children were old enough to understand fully the significance of what they were doing, and to leave the family if they disagreed strongly with it. By 1900 Louise was twenty-four, Russell twenty-three, Belle Marian twenty-one, and Ethel Alice twenty. (The "baby," Theodora, was fourteen.) There is no question that the older four knew that both their parents were of white and black ancestry. They had seen their father struggling to make a political career, championing and representing "his race," even as he wished to unify the races and break down the walls between blacks and whites. And they had seen the toll that white America's unrelenting racism had taken on him.

Furthermore, the Greener children had grown up in a racial world different from that of Genevieve's childhood. Black and white communities were becoming even more segregated and distinct. The social ties (sometimes family ties) that families like the Fleets had once had to the white community were growing weaker and even breaking. Genevieve had grown up in a time when associating with whites was a part of being in the elite colored class. In her world, there were privileges that could be enjoyed if one were willing to live within certain restrictions and conduct oneself carefully. Her children had experienced a different racial context; the social advantages that light skin had given their parents may have been far less forthcoming for this new generation. Since they were all physically light enough to be perceived as white, they had probably also experienced the very different ways some whites treated them when they were perceived as white and when they were perceived as colored. Did they identify themselves as colored? Did they see their black ancestry as only an obstacle to their goals and dreams? Or were they willing to give up an identity and a community that had nurtured them for the sake of freeing themselves of the burden of racism?

In New York there was also the very pressing question of money. Despite Richard's assurances that his family did not need the money they demanded from him, they were actually struggling without their father. If Richard, a colored man who graduated from Harvard and was a lawyer, had had such difficulties supporting five children, how would Genevieve as a colored woman with much less education and work experience ever manage?

And so Genevieve Ida Fleet/Greener/Van Vliet/D'Acosta/Greene crossed the color line and began to live as white, bringing her five children with her. It was probably just the last step in a decadelong process. In the lingo of the day, they were said to be passing. But this term is ineffective in conveying the meaning, motivation, and performance of what Belle Marion Greener was doing as she became Belle da Costa Greene. And who Belle da Costa Greene became.

Passing had always been a reality in American society, and a curiosity to many white Americans. It was a growing phenomenon at the turn of the twentieth century. But the term "passing" itself reflects nineteenth-century racial definitions, suggesting that people who were really black were now pretending to be white. In nineteenth-century white literature, people who passed were usually found out, and their black "blood"—or at least its discovery—almost inevitably led to their tragic downfall. Historically, however, passing has been experienced and understood in many ways: as a rejection of the fiction of race, as a betrayal of the African American community, as an acceptance of the dominant racial ancestry of a mostly white person, as a form of assimilation, as a cultural adaptation comparable to the Anglicization of European ethnic names, as resistance to the illogic of the one-drop rule. Belle's experience was certainly less dramatic than stories of passing found in literature, pulp fiction, and film. She had, for instance, brought one parent and all of her siblings along with her. This kind of continuity belies the image of someone giving up all of her family ties and past connections to enter an entirely new social world.[37]

More important, the term "passing" suggests a masquerade and deception. What if Belle had never considered herself colored? She was eight years old when she moved to New York. It is hardly possible that she was unaware she had black ancestry, but she may not have believed that that made her black or even colored in any significant way. What if she understood her father's strong social connections with that part of his ancestry, but—once out of D.C.—had no such connections herself? What if her name change was a conscious or unconscious rejection not only of her father's name but of his racial identity as well? Because we cannot really know her self-identity, I prefer the term "living as white" because it allows for the possibility that Belle was a woman of color who believed her predominantly white ancestry made her just as white as her Italian, Jewish, and other white ethnic neighbors and schoolmates.

Throughout her life Belle made a variety of comments about her identity, references to race, color, and ethnicity that help further illuminate her self-perception. I will discuss these as they come up in her life either in her own writings or (more often) as others' observations or surrounding events raised them for her. These movements further illuminate Belle's understanding and public performance of her racial and ethnic identity. The first clue lies in her new name. When Belle Marion Greener became Belle da Costa Greene, she also added a fictitious Portuguese ancestry.[38] Only Belle and her brother used the "da Costa"; none of her sisters seems to have done so. Why?

Casual observers and intimates alike took note of Belle's appearance. She had what her own brother called a "peculiar style of beauty,"[39] one that journalists and biographers struggled to describe: "the young Belle da Costa Greene with the alluring pug-dog face and lidded green eyes and tiny waist."[40] Even in biographies and monographs in which she merits only brief mention, her physical attributes are carefully noted. She is described as "strangely beautiful," and her ethnic background was a constant source of speculation during her lifetime as well as afterward. Her skin is called "dark," "olive," "Mediterranean," "yellowish." Her appearance was "exotic." Her origins were "obscure"—"the dusky oval of her face suggested an exotic origin."[41]

In other words, her appearance—and that of her brother—may have been different enough that they could not pass for Anglo. Even in New York's mix of ethnicities and races, Belle's identity and ancestry drew attention and questions. With the in-pouring of immigrants of "new" ethnic European backgrounds to New York, any non-Anglo features of the Greene family could blend more easily into this melting pot of faces and skin tones and accents and cultures. Of course, in such a context, their cultured upbringing, mildly southern but very American accents, and fine comportment and values could render them far less threatening and suspicious than these newcomers.

Claiming Portuguese ancestry was a carefully chosen tactic. Belle and her family may not have anticipated the extent to which anti-immigrationists would argue that southern Europeans were as dangerous to the racial integrity of white America as people of mixed ancestry were. Even then, the focus was mostly on southern Italians, who had long been suspected—probably quite rightly—of having some North African ancestry.

But perhaps the most consistent characteristic of American racialism has been its inconsistency. The one-drop rule was increasingly becoming the law of the land and the dominant way of thinking about race in terms of African Americans of mixed ancestry. In fact, had Belle really been from Virginia, as she claimed, she might have run into more serious difficulty in adopting a white identity after being born colored. By the early twentieth century Virginia officials were vigilantly guarding against attempts by people of mixed ancestry to live as anything but black. As the state revised its definition of blackness in 1904 (anyone with one-quarter or more black ancestry), and again in 1924 (anyone with any amount of black ancestry), individuals and families found themselves literally reassigned from white to mulatto, from mulatto to black, and even from white to black.[42] But Italians were legally white, and Portuguese immigration never reached the same numbers or levels of national concern.

Many self-identified Negroes, mixed-race and otherwise, were quick to point out the illogic of the one-drop rule and of the racialism that underlay it. The Harlem Renaissance writer Jessie Fauset, for example, compared the treatment a young women would receive in the United States as colored with her treatment as an Italian American. She described a young girl living in New York: "[W]avy brown hair, rosy cheeks, and gray eyes make my Fabiola like one of those rare Italian girls born on the East Side from roots firmly planted about sunny Naples. You may call that Italian Fabiola a jewel or a flower; but my Fabiola is a Negro. What must I call her?" She might have called her Belle da Costa Greene.[43] But what did Belle da Costa Greene call herself?

One thing we know she called herself was "librarian." By 1900 Belle was listing that as her occupation. A friend later reported that she had worked as an apprentice in the New York Public Library system (which means at either the Lenox or the Astor Library) and that she took a bibliography course at Amherst College's Fletcher Summer Library School. The former cannot be confirmed; but "Belle M. Greene" does appear in a July 1901 listing of former students of Amherst's Library Class of 1900. By then she was working at the University of Princeton Library.[44] She may have had previous jobs, but this is the earliest position where Belle's early life and career begin to come into focus.

3

PRINCETON: EARLY INFLUENCES

[W]hile there is nothing in the law of the University to prevent a Negro's entering, the whole temper and tradition of the place are such that no Negro has ever applied for admission and it seems extremely unlikely that the question will ever assume a practical form.

—Woodrow Wilson, 1904[1]

I am having an awfully good time—being "rushed" to my vanity's content and renewing my youth in this my beloved Princeton—I have a peculiar fondness for the place as I have spent so many happy days here.

—Belle Greene, 1910[2]

HOW DID BELLE make the transition from being a high school graduate with a few extra library courses to becoming arguably the most powerful woman in the New York art and book world? Belle's early career is difficult to trace. Even during her lifetime, her pre–Morgan Library work and training remained obscure. In part this was because her rise to fame under Morgan's name overshadowed anything that came before it. But largely it was Belle's own covering of her tracks. Her formal schooling, for example, is a mystery. At Teachers' College she would have learned the latest in educational methods and psychology, but that hardly explains her emergence as an expert on pre-fifteenth-century books. She herself never mentioned the Amherst summer program where she seems to have taken a summer course in 1900, and no records tell us what classes she took there. The brochure for the five-week session in 1901 promises daily morning lectures introducing students to the basics of library work and cataloguing—using several systems—and afternoon practical work suited to students' needs. Admission required only a high school diploma and a fee of fifteen dollars.[3]

Still, much of the answer to her professional and social transition lies in the three years she spent in her early twenties working at the Princeton University Library. It may not have been her first library job, but it is the first one whose influence on her future career is traceable. How she got the job, and exactly when she started, is unclear. According to Amherst's records she was already there by the summer of 1901; the first mention of her in the Princeton archives is 1902.[4] And there are few details on the specifics of her job or social life during this period. The local and student papers make no mention of Belle during this time, and the library records mention her only briefly. But her few years at Princeton gave Belle practice in the basic librarian skills that she would have learned at Amherst. She also gained a grounding in rare books and manuscripts, as well as experience in conducting herself as a working woman, as a girl surrounded by male students, and as a white person in a highly segregated town. What Belle's life was like during her years in Princeton can only be speculatively reconstructed through accounts of news and community events and her own later reminiscences, but that context tells us a great deal.

Belle and her family were already living as white by the time she began working at the Princeton Library.[5] She had used the name

Greene at Amherst (but kept the middle initial M). Still, Belle was leading a double life of sorts, maintaining residence in New York and New Jersey. The Pennsylvania Railroad ran a line between Princeton and New York—a trip of less than two hours. The trains ran twelve times a day Monday through Saturday, and three times on Sunday evenings.[6] This would have made visits between Belle and her family relatively easy, and she could have readily spent weekends with them. In fact, when New York and New Jersey conducted state censuses in 1905, both listed her. In Manhattan, Belle was Marian Greene, twenty-two-year-old librarian, daughter of Van Vliet Greene. Her sisters Louise and Ethel were working as teachers. Russell and her sister Theodora were both students. Russell was now in the Engineering School at Columbia University, where he eventually received his master's degree in mining, electrical engineering, and steam engineering. It was probably to support him that the family moved in 1903. Their new apartment was at 507 West 112th Street, between Broadway and Amsterdam, just a few blocks south of Columbia's campus, northwest of Central Park, around the corner from Morningside Park. On the far side of Columbia University stood the marble tomb of the Grant Monument that Richard Greener had worked to raise funds for. Dedicated in 1897, it was still a popular New York attraction in Riverside Park.

In Princeton she appeared as Belle Green, twenty-one-year-old library worker, a single woman boarding with an extended family.[7] Belle's apartment in Princeton was on University Drive, right next to the campus, just a brief walk from the library. She could have made her daily way across campus with two of her apartment mates. Charlotte Martins was a librarian, in charge of the purchasing department in 1902; her salary was $100 per month.[8] Belle later referred to herself as "one of Miss Martins' pupils" and recalled the "excellent training" Charlotte gave her.[9] In her midfifties in 1905, Martins had worked at the library for over twenty years when Belle arrived. She lived with her father, John Martins, and her widowed sister, Anna Hyde, whose daughter Gertrude also worked at the library. Anna and her other daughter, Clara, do not seem to have worked for wages.[10] The Martinses and the Hydes had rented their portion of the house since at least 1900 and often took in a boarder. But Belle was more than a boarder.

Working with Gertrude at the library, probably under Charlotte's direct supervision, Belle adopted Gertrude's aunt as her own as well. Letters between Charlotte and Belle a few years later demonstrate their fondness for each other, with Belle writing to Charlotte as "Aunt Lottie" and Charlotte to Belle as "darling Bella." The same train that allowed dual residency for Belle before her move to the Morgan Library also allowed her to return repeatedly to Princeton for weekends and visits for the rest of her life, often including a stay or visit with the Martins-Hydes, even after Belle became a "high-flyer."[11]

The little information we have about Belle's fellow librarians and housemates in Princeton is tantalizing. Although all the Hydes and Martinses are listed as white in the records, their reported ancestries suggest a complex history, perhaps even mirroring that of Belle's family. John Martins, Anna and Charlotte's father, was born in the West Indies in the 1810s. John Martins had worked as a bookkeeper in Roxbury, Massachusetts. He and his wife, Anna, raised five children with the help of an Irish domestic servant. John listed his father's birthplace as Spain.[12]

Did the Martins-Hydes' West Indian and Spanish background reflect their own racial ambiguity? Certainly Anglo-Americans associated the West Indies with racial mixing. In an interesting departure from her New York records, Belle told the 1905 New Jersey census taker that her birthplace was D.C. and that her father was born in England and her mother in Spain. Oddly, it was her father's grandfather who was thought actually to be Spanish, and in 1900 the Greene children told New York enumerators that their father was born in Philadelphia, their mother in Maryland. Was it the Martinses and Hydes' Spanish ancestor who inspired Belle to begin embellishing her southern European ancestry? She never claimed Spanish ancestry again. Had she found a white family whose national and ethnic history she could model as her own? Or were these three librarians and their families further united by a shared black or mixed ancestry that they had to hide to in order keep their jobs?[13] Certainly being born in the West

Indies did not mean that Charlotte's grandfather was black or colored. However, in 1910, with John Martins gone (probably dead), Charlotte and her sister told federal census enumerators that their ancestry was English on both sides.

Princeton University was a particularly interesting place for Belle to first be on her own and living as white. Like New York, New Jersey had never offered a legal definition of black or white. But Princeton was culturally very southern despite its northern location, and the university was largely responsible for this. Throughout the nineteenth century Princeton had drawn its upper-class male student body, as well as much of its faculty and administration, primarily from the slaveholding South. In the first half of the 1800s, students even brought slaves with them as personal servants during their school residency.[14] Moreover, Princeton was the only Ivy League school that had not begun to admit any African American students by the turn of the twentieth century. Under Woodrow Wilson's presidency (1902–10), the university maintained its white-only student body, although a few Japanese students appear to have been in residence. On African American admission, however, Wilson held firm.[15] In fact, the first black students did not attend Princeton University until the late 1940s, a handful of servicemen and veterans participating in a special wartime program. It was enough to prompt a small, though unsuccessful, campaign to open admissions, but Princeton did not knowingly admit or actively recruit black students until the mid-1960s.[16]

Still, African Americans were a visible part of the borough and surrounding township of Princeton, New Jersey. With a total population of 7,173 in 1905 (including students), more than 90 percent of the 1,123 "colored" residents lived in the center borough near the university. With the exception of live-in domestic servants, virtually all residents labeled "colored" by the 1905 state census resided in all-black neighborhoods, sometimes with a few recent immigrant families sprinkled among them. (Immigrant neighborhoods, most notably Italian, were also highly segregated in Princeton.)[17] There had been a free black community in Princeton since the late seventeenth century, but most blacks living in Mercer County in the eighteenth and nineteenth

centuries were slaves or former slaves. Gradual emancipation in New
Jersey began in 1804, continuing until 1830 as those born to slavery
"aged out" to freedom. By the late nineteenth and early twentieth centuries, a strong community had developed in the area south of campus,
just a few blocks from Belle's apartment. Centered on black churches,
black-owned businesses, and the university's employment of African
Americans as laborers and service workers, this community thrived
until the expansion of the university and the downtown business district forced its removal.

Although not legislated in Princeton, segregation was institutionalized in practices of discrimination and exclusion. Churches had been
segregated since the early nineteenth century. Hotels and restaurants
barred African Americans, except for the exclusively black establish-
ments. African American children could attend only a black grammar
school; there was no black high school they could attend. In other
words, Princeton operated with exactly the kind of two-tiered racial
segregation that made it virtually impossible to maintain a mixed-race
identity in public.

Separated from her family in a new city, Belle would have found it
both easier and harder to live as white. She was unknown, less likely
to run into anyone who knew her family background or her father's
identity. But she was now surrounded by evidence of the discrimination and prejudice that people defined as black lived with in Princeton. Not only was she living physically closer to a black community
than she had been since moving to New York, or perhaps ever, but the
town was small enough that local papers took notice of African American events and accomplishments. Segregation in small towns did not
prevent daily contact and mutual knowledge between those defined as
black and those defined as white.

For example, in 1899 the first African American Princeton resident
graduated from high school in nearby Trenton. Lauded by the black
community and the local paper, William D. Robeson Jr.'s accomplishment would soon be eclipsed by that of his then infant brother Paul.[18]
The actor, singer, and activist became Princeton's most famous African
American resident. Paul Robeson lived in Princeton from 1898 to

1910. Belle would probably not have known him, but she might have known of his father, who was the former minister of the oldest black church and a community leader. And in 1904 she would have known about the horrifying death of Paul's mother, Maria (or Marie) Louisa Bustill Robeson. Maria suffered terrible burns after her dress caught fire when hot coals spilled out of her stove; she died hours later. If Belle missed the newspaper story, she would certainly have heard the talk about such a gruesome event. But did Belle know that the woman who died was a distant relative? Maria was a first cousin of Jacob C. White, who was Belle's second cousin on her father's side.[19] Like Genevieve Fleet, Maria was a very light-skinned, mixed-race woman from an elite family of color. The Bustills were one of the most prominent colored families in Philadelphia. But Maria married a darker-skinned, lower-class, well-educated man. Like Richard Greener, William Robeson was descended more closely from slavery and was the first in his family to attain a college education. The Robeson children were as talented and ambitious as the Greener/Greenes, and they were unambiguously black.[20]

Belle's treatment and experience in Princeton would have been entirely different from that of the Robesons simply because white Princetonians accepted her as one of them. Nevertheless, the small town that she would later call "the most adorable spot in the world" had a reputation among African Americans in New Jersey as being virulently racist. And the university that was the site of her fondly remembered "many happy days" would continue to work hard to maintain its southern identity and white supremacy throughout her lifetime.[21]

In fact, in the 1930s when a Missouri newspaper erroneously mentioned that the then famous Paul Robeson had attended Princeton University, a local alumnus Roger Slaughter wrote to Princeton's president, John Hibben, enclosing the article and asking that he publicly correct the statement: "As you know one of the reasons that Princeton is popular here and through the south is because it is the one eastern school which does not enroll negroes. Under the circumstances I am afraid that the parents of prospective Princeton students may get the wrong impression."[22] Apparently President Hibben agreed with those concerns, for he had the university secretary write the newspaper's editor that Paul Robeson had never attended Princeton, but was a graduate of Rutgers University.[23]

We can only speculate on Belle's reactions to Princeton's system of segregation and discrimination during her few years there. Did she feel any connection with the African Americans that she would have constantly encountered as servants, waiters, and janitors on and off campus? Did she feel the guilt that other mixed race individuals reported when they used their light skin and white features to gain access to good restaurants, interesting lectures, or a better job? Or did she feel removed from the mostly working-class black population of Princeton, coming from her middle-class background? Elitism was not something with which Belle was later identified. Quite the contrary. She became renowned for her practice of befriending workers, servants, and cab drivers.[24] Had she yet learned how to maintain the racial difference between herself and those whose darker skin and social status was already at a remove? Perhaps she already knew how to mimic, maybe even internalize, the racial language and attitude of her white peers. She definitely adopted these habits during her Morgan years. But would she, like the white students and faculty with whom she worked and socialized, have been blind to and unaffected by the accomplishments of Princeton's black community? The ministers, the teachers, the small-business owners, and the craftsmen and women who had made up her parents' social world in Washington—their counterparts were present in Princeton as well.

But Belle fell in love with the university and the social life she enjoyed there. Even after she was the famous Belle da Costa Greene, J. P. Morgan's librarian, Belle remained closely tied to Princeton University.[25] She continued to return to Princeton for social weekends and graduation celebrations into the 1940s. Being a part of this culture also meant accepting the explicit racism of its hierarchies and traditions: the annual weeklong graduation celebrations featured, among the bands and parties and games, the regular appearance of black-faced minstrel musicians.[26]

It is possible that the strong division between blacks and whites and

the full exclusion of blacks from the academic and intellectual activities of the university made Belle more determined than ever to claim
her white identity. Living in Princeton would have tested any continued connection she may have felt with the black community. Perhaps
the reality that she thrived in this environment suggests that she never
had any such connection. As a white woman, she could work in the
library among the books that she loved, she could attend lectures by
the constant stream of local and visiting speakers on subjects ranging
from philosophy to archaeology to politics, and she could participate in
the elaborate campus social life. And, of course, as a slender, attractive, white young woman on a heavily male campus, she had opportunities for socializing. And she did plenty of that, as her later reflections
make clear. She often went to Princeton dances and greatly resented
some of the chaperones there who spoiled her fun.[27] Much later in her
life she reflected that if she had not gotten the job with Morgan, she
probably would have ended up marrying a Princeton man.[28]

Had they known her family history, what would white Princetonians
have called Belle da Costa Greene? Most likely "Negro" or "black."
"Mulatto" was a term that was disappearing in social usage, even
though the presence of people of mixed ancestry was acknowledged.
When reporting a 1905 interracial marriage in Massachusetts, for
example, the *Princeton Press* noted that the woman was "light complex-
ioned and of fine figure, but unmistakably a negress."[29] And the majority southern student body had largely grown up in states where, by the
turn of the century, the lines between black and white were being
heavily policed by local and state governments through antimiscegena-
tion laws, blood-quantum definitions of race, and the increasing categorization of people of little or remote black ancestry as black.[30] State
legislatures were beginning to police the presumed biological boundaries between the races by adding or hardening their definitions of
racial categories and outlawing marriage between the nonwhites and
the whites.

For news outside their little world, most Princetonians no doubt followed the daily papers of New York, Trenton, or Philadelphia. The
local paper, the *Princeton Press*, came out only once a week during the

years Belle lived there. It did pick up news from around the country and the world, reprinting matter-of-fact stories about lynchings (usually the only references to black Americans in national news), politics, and the activities of alumni and faculty in other places. While the campus had its own student-run newspaper, the *Princetonian*, the centrality of the university to the town is apparent in the consistent focus on academic activities. The community, or at least the white community, was welcome at campus events. We can easily imagine Belle at some of the many lectures, concerts, and social events advertised in the town and campus papers during those years.

There was also some international news that might have caught her attention. From 1904 to 1905 the *Press* ran a series of stories following the Japanese-Russian war. It was the biggest foreign news story of the period.[31] Many Americans became familiar with the name Richard T. Greener, unofficial U.S. Consul, often mentioned in news coverage of the war. But only Belle among her fellow Princetonians would have known that it was her father who was the most important American official on the ground in Siberia during these years. (Unless Maria Bustill Robeson or someone else had known of the connection and passed it on.) In May 1904 the *Press* ran a story about "Siberia in Winter" focusing on the very city where Richard Greener lived— Vladivostok. The article described a four-month period of "Black and Deadly Frost," the dangerous cold of nights, the abuse of alcohol, women's skirts lined with fur, and a harbor frozen into a dull gray ice block.[32] It must have been uncomfortable for the Greenes when Richard Greener once again rose to public prominence, even from Siberia.

But what Belle gained most from her few years at Princeton was her training for what would become her lifework. This opportunity alone was surely a reason for Belle to put aside whatever discomforts the southern racial atmosphere may have brought. Rare books—whether the handwritten pre–printing press volumes or the early editions produced by presses—were hardly the kind of riches most children dreamed of. But Belle claimed to be uniquely predisposed to love them. She later explained,

I knew definitely by the time I was twelve years old that I
wanted to work with rare books. I loved them even then, the
sight of them, the wonderful feel of them, the romance and
thrill of them. Before I was sixteen I had begun my studies,
omitting the regular college courses that many girls take
before they have found out what they want to do.[33]

Belle may have been referring to her summer course at Amherst or
Princeton when she mentioned specialized studies, cutting four to ten
years off her age, as would be her practice for her entire life.

Her interest in books was also an artistic one. Decades later Belle
explained that manuscripts were generally better preserved than paintings and therefore contained the "fullest, most authentic, and most
convenient source for the comparative study of painting and the allied
arts during the Middle Ages."[34] Her fascination with illuminated manuscripts, especially, was not a popular or easy interest to pursue at the
turn of the twentieth century. Illuminated manuscripts were hand-
printed books named for their colorful, artistic illustrations. Most were
produced before the development of the printing press allowed multiple copies of the same text to be reproduced exactly. Illuminated manuscripts were unique, even when they were carefully copied versions
of common texts like the Old Testament, the Gospels, or the Koran.[35]
Few examples of such manuscripts were available in the United States,
and fewer experts able to analyze their historical, artistic, and scholarly
value. Greene may have dated her interest in rare books to her childhood, but it is quite likely she had never seen any rare pre-fifteenth-
century illuminated manuscripts, which were to become the basis of
her work for Morgan and her lifelong passion, until she began working
at Princeton University Library.

Belle later told people that she had apprenticed with "the best bib-
liographer in America," going to Princeton for the express purpose of
working with Ernest Cushing Richardson. Richardson held the position of Librarian of Princeton University from 1890 to 1925.[36] There
is no archival record at Princeton to link Greene directly with Richardson as an apprentice or protégée. Library reports did not detail the daily

activities and interactions of the librarians and their assistants and clerks. Belle probably began her work as a general clerk or cataloguer. But by the time she left, she had begun to work with the rare books and manuscripts, whether informally or formally.[37] And even if she had no structured work relationship with Richardson, she would have used the resources of the library, attended any talks he gave, and learned as much as she could from Richardson, from Charlotte Martins, and from others working in the library whom Richardson had taught.

In fact, Richardson trained many younger librarians while working at Princeton, both through his classes and through his work at the library. Belle considered herself one of his students, and it is not a far stretch to presume that she had already developed her skill at gaining information and informal training in fields that interested her from experts firsthand. These were the years of hard work that she later credited with preparing her for her success as curator of Morgan's Library.[38] At Princeton she learned many crucial skills and gained invaluable experience in precisely the fields that Morgan would need. And Ernest Richardson was just the person to orient her to these fields.

Professionally, Richardson is probably best remembered for devising a cataloguing system and constructing the National Union Catalog of the Library of Congress. However, as a teacher as well as a librarian at Princeton, Richardson focused on teaching bibliography and paleography (the study of ancient manuscripts) in his classes. And this emphasis in his teaching and his own scholarship offers the strongest indication of his influence on the young Belle Greene. (That Belle also learned the importance of a good catalogue at Princeton is evident from her 1914 letter to the *New York Times* in which she corrected an error in a previous interview and noted that she had begun to study the British Museum's printed library catalogue ten years previously at the Princeton University Library.)[39]

With a semester release from residency each year, Richardson took near-annual trips to Europe, where he frequented libraries and book dealers, bringing back originals when he could afford them and facsimiles when he could not. He also used the time to study rare and sometimes unique manuscripts held in European museums, libraries, and churches.[40] Greene followed Richardson's example of making regular pilgrimages to Europe's museums and libraries and dealers as soon as she was financially able. He made his European trips in 1902, 1903, and 1904, so Belle would have heard about these trips and seen whatever books he brought back to the library. Richardson had not been able to purchase the rare and expensive illuminated manuscripts for Princeton, but by 1898 Princeton's library boasted a large number of facsimiles: exact copies of ancient texts for students (and aspiring young librarians) to study. Princeton was also developing a collection of early editions of printed books, which Belle would also come to admire and study.[41]

Richardson's emphasis on paleography reflected his loyalty to European traditions and materials. He believed that the study of handwritten, especially ancient and medieval, texts was erroneously absent in American scholarship; Europe was still the center of these fields of study. Belle would later share Richardson's goal of teaching American librarians and scholars the basics of paleography and raising American scholarship to be on par with that of Europe. Under Richardson, Belle could have learned to distinguish and decipher ancient scripts and languages as well as the history and development of writing itself. At a more advanced level, scholars would be able to determine the region or origin, approximate date of production, and sometimes even the individual writer of a manuscript. Belle would eventually reach this level of expertise as well. She had already begun to learn European languages, a requisite ability for students of many fields.

Richardson sought to elevate America's intellectual standing by immersing Americans in the art and culture of European and ancient Western civilization. But he looked beyond the popular paintings and sculpture of the Italian Renaissance, which were creating a stir in America, to recognize the artistic and scholarly significance of early books and manuscripts. In this interest, Richardson was supported by Junius S. Morgan, J.P.'s nephew and Associate Librarian at Princeton during Belle's time there.[42]

Junius Morgan must indeed also be counted as a major influence in

Belle's book training at Princeton. A class of 1888 Princeton graduate, Junius was an avid bibliophile and member (along with his uncle) of New York's Grolier Club. Dedicated to the study and production of books, the Grolier Club had been founded in 1884 and named for a French Renaissance bookmaker, collector, and art patron, Jean Grolier. By 1890 it had a home at 29 East Thirty-second Street, right in the Murray Hill district near the homes of "everyone worth mentioning" to the society men who made up its exclusive membership. Junius had initiated most of Pierpont Morgan's first purchases of his pre–printing press books, and dropped by often to examine his uncle's collection and advise on new or potential buys.[43]

Junius also presented the Princeton University Library with several fifteenth- and sixteenth-century rare editions of printed books. These early printed books, or incunabula, represented the first century of publications after the development of the printing press around 1450. He began purchasing editions of Virgil as a student and, beginning in 1894, donated dozens, even hundreds of books to the library. The Junius S. Morgan Virgil Collection now boasts over nine hundred volumes. The local newspaper often noted the library's acquisitions, which usually took the form of gifts, and Junius Morgan's name appeared regularly as a donor. In 1905 alone, Morgan gave fifty volumes, mostly bibliographical works. And in 1904 the library received a fifteenth-century manuscript from another alumnus, purchased through Bernard Quaritch of London.[44]

Belle and Junius Morgan became fast friends while she was at Princeton. Belle later confessed that she had started loving him "simultaneously with putting up my hair from pig tails." As a "kid," she recalled, she had a huge crush on Junius—"which I secretly gloated over as the tragedy of my young life." (Junius was married.) And he apparently took great pride in her, if not open credit for her subsequent rise in fortune and reputation. He told her once of listening with amusement when someone highly praised her to him, since that speaker "evidently did not know or realize that I had brought you up."[45]

In recommending Belle to his uncle, Junius brought another passionate bibliophile, one he had influenced and trained, into his project of developing Morgan's book collection. At the same time he brought Belle to the opportunity of her life, affording her unlimited access to rare and invaluable treasures. No wonder she was so devoted to her benefactor, later calling him her "mad, bad, Beloved Junius."[46] She also put aside her crush and became good friends with his wife. Through-out the decades she spent weekends in Princeton with Junius and his family, declared herself "dreadfully fond of him," and told a friend, "[We] have always been perfectly frank and openly confidential—he evidently has told me more of his troubles than anyone else."[47] After Pierpont Morgan's death, she drew even closer to Junius, declaring, "I am very much devoted to him and would choose him as my own from all the Morgan family if I had to choose."[48]

The summer at Amherst, these few years at Princeton, and Junius's recommendation were probably all the credentials Belle brought with her to her interview with Morgan. But her lack of institutionalized library education was far from uncommon for her time and field. After all, Richardson himself had no formal library training. Neither had her father, for that matter, when he became Librarian of the University of South Carolina. On the other hand, while he participated in the apprentice-mentor method of training the next generation, Richardson strongly championed the formation of a formal, specialized education for librarians and advocated the development of library schools at major universities even before the profession and educational institu-tions adopted this path. Belle's was probably the last generation in the United States in which an individual with no formal training or degrees in library science could become a director of a major archive or library.

And Belle had not been Junius's first choice for his uncle's position. He had already tried to hire Henry Watson Kent, a fellow member of the Grolier Club. While Belle was at Princeton, Kent had been a librarian for the Grolier Club, earning $2,400 per year. In 1905 he was offered the Morgan position for $3,000 a year, but he turned it down for a position at the Metropolitan Museum of Art. By the time Belle found out that Kent's proposed salary was more than three times what she was given, she was no longer in a position to object, because she herself was making $10,000 at that point. She could afford to dismiss "him as was offered my job" now that she had proven her own worth—and thoroughly convinced J.P. that Kent was completely unworthy. She speculated that Kent might be making only $5,000 at most at the museum, "so the Joke is on him—at least for the present. Of course he may be a Museum director some day."[49] It would have been taken for granted by all parties that a woman would earn markedly less than a man for the same job. Belle herself later recommended individual women as bibliographers or research assistants, reminding prospective employers that women were cheaper to hire. And the difference in starting offers was further justified by Kent's college education. He was in the first class of the Columbia Library School, where he studied with Melvil Dewey, creator of the Dewey Decimal System.[50]

Compared with Henry Kent, Belle was a gamble of a hire. She had no degree, no formal library training, no experience managing or overseeing a library collection. But Junius, a "latent creator" of Morgan's collection, could not have regretted the outcome of his search.[51] Junius hoped not only to help his uncle but also to further his own interest in Morgan's continued appreciation and acquisition of such items. Who better to place in a position to guide and assist his uncle than a brilliant but unknown woman who shared Junius's passion and owed her leap in fortune to him?

And so, sometime toward the end of 1905, Junius Morgan brought Belle to meet his financial mogul uncle, J. Pierpont Morgan. By the time Belle came to work for him, probably in January 1906, Morgan had established his collection of incunabula and illuminated manuscripts.[52] The printed portion of his collection was kept largely in his home in New York, in a room literally overflowing with papers and books, or was on loan or otherwise scattered. The newly constructed Library would meet his need for a place to keep them all. Initially Belle's job was simply to take charge of the organization and care of the books. It quickly became much, much more.

In 1906 Richardson's annual report on the Princeton University Library mentioned the loss of several unnamed key librarians and two more in lesser positions,[53] but Belle's departure was not noted in local newspapers. Nor did her arrival at Morgan's Library merit any particular recognition outside of her family and close circles of friends. It was only later that curious reporters, friends, and fans would try to trace the path of Belle da Costa Greene's rise in fortunes.

BELLE GREENE, GIRL LIBRARIAN

People who meet for the first time the young tutelary genius of Mr. Morgan's Library, take for granted that any girl so fond of society, so fashionable in dress and appointments, and with such a comet's tail of admirers, must owe her position with its large salary to "pull," and that it is probably a sinecure anyway. Little they know.

—Gertrude Atherton, 1917[1]

She wears her hair long and does not use glasses, runs to Europe on secret missions, and is the terror of continental collectors' agents. Her name is Belle Green.

—*Chicago Daily Tribune*, 1921[2]

IN EARLY 1906 Belle da Costa Greene returned to full-time residence in New York and began her work at the Morgan Library. She resumed living with her family: brother Russell was taking graduate courses at Columbia; sisters Louise and Ethel were, like their mother, working as teachers. Young Theodora was in school. The family members were doing better than they had since their father's departure. But in the 1905 New York State census, only Ethel and Belle (listed as Marian) reported regular wage income. Mary was probably a tutor or music teacher, like her mother, working out of the home with private students. All were listed as white and would be white in official documents for the rest of their lives.[3] Belle's new job, and its $75-a-month salary, was a relief to the whole family.

The salary was only the icing on the cake. This was Belle's dream job. The Princeton University Library may have introduced Belle to the colorful artistry and careful calligraphy of pre–printing press books, but now she was surrounded by treasures of art and literature from all corners of the world. A few years later she wrote Henry Guppy, her counterpart at the John Rylands Library, in Manchester, England, which boasted the 40,000-volume Althorp Collection as well as numerous other rare books and manuscripts. Belle told Mr. Guppy that she would envy him his association with such riches, which she had only seen in the printed catalogue, "if my work lay anywhere else but here."[4]

As the finishing touches were put on the Library building in 1906, Belle began that work. Crates of books from Morgan's overflowing personal library soon filled the largely empty rooms, each volume needing to be identified, catalogued, and housed in the two stories of built-in glass-doored bookshelves in the East Room, or in the vault where the unique and very expensive manuscripts were stored. A later visitor described this vault as a "magic cavern . . . that amazing room [where] one touched hands with the immortals and caught from their strangely eloquent pages the very sound of their voices."[5] There was absolutely no collection like it in the United States. She dealt with all of Morgan's eclectic treasures, but it was the books that always were her priority and her pride. In 1909, in a rare surviving letter between the two, she wrote Morgan that her goal was to make his Library *pre-eminent, especially for incunabula, manuscripts, bindings and the classsics.* She thought their only rivals were the British Museum and the Bibliothèque Nationale, but hoped someday to claim "that there is neither *rival* nor *equal*."[6] By the 1920s she considered that they had succeeded.[7] But that was a far-off dream when she first entered the still incomplete Library and set about to make sense of Morgan's files and purchases.

John Pierpont Morgan was a looming figure in American finance and a powerful presence in turn-of-the-century New York. He was born to an old-stock New England family. His father, Junius Spencer Morgan (for whom J.P.'s nephew was named), moved to New York and apprenticed as a banker, but settled in Hartford after his marriage to Juliet Pierpont. Their firstborn arrived in 1837, John Pierpont Morgan. Nicknamed J.P. as a child, the young Morgan preferred to be called Pierpont, but the J.P. stuck. Even Belle privately referred to him by his initials, sometimes dubbing him "Big Chief," "Boss," or even "Mr. Stick," when she was peeved at him. Of course, she would have called him "Mr. Morgan" to his face.[8] As Junius's business and wealth grew, he trained his son to follow in his footsteps, supervising his education and helping him during J.P.'s own early business career.

Morgan's first marriage, in 1861 to Amelia Sturges, was tragically short. Amelia had tuberculosis, and J.P. brought her to Algiers for their honeymoon in hopes that the warm climate would heal her. She died a few months later. Grief stricken, Morgan threw himself into a new business. He paid the standard $300 fee to be excused from military service during the Civil War, and launched into loans and market speculation, to his great profit (and his father's growing consternation), during the war.

After the war he married Frances Louisa Tracy and became a partner in the banking firm that would become J. P. Morgan & Co. Morgan's businesses and partnerships continued to grow and evolve over the years, collectively coming to be known as the House of Morgan. J.P.'s family grew as well. He and Fanny had four children: Louisa Pierpont was the eldest, born nine months after the wedding. A year later John Pierpont Jr., always called Jack, joined them. Juliet followed a few years later, and finally Anne Tracy in 1873. While growing up, Jack was always closer to his mother than to his father. He married first, in 1890, a year after he graduated from Harvard. Of his wife-to-be, Jessie Grew, Jack wrote that he had been drawn to her illustrious Boston "family line" before "any other feeling" entered in. Still, love did come and the couple had a close relationship. Jack followed his father into banking, as was expected of the only son. By the time Belle joined J.P. at the Library, Jack was conducting much of the company business.[9]

Juliet, considered the prettiest of the three Morgan daughters, also helped the family business continue by marrying a banker in 1893 and becoming Mrs. William Pierson Hamilton. Her father gave her a $10,000 annuity and a house, and Hamilton joined his business, eventually becoming a partner. Louisa, the eldest, was the last to marry. She was her father's favorite and his frequent travel companion. She married lawyer Herbert Livingston Satterlee in 1900 at the age of thirty-three and also received a $10,000 annuity and a house. Only Anne, the youngest, never married. She was twenty-nine by the time Belle came to work for her father, only a few years older than Belle. Anne Morgan and Belle Greene would move in many of the same circles but would never become friends.

By 1880 Morgan was earning between $700,000 and $900,000 a year. The family bought a brownstone mansion at 219 Madison Avenue, very near the plot that would later be the site of his marble Library. By the 1890s he was earning over $1,000,000 a year. Beyond his personal wealth, he commanded hundreds of millions of dollars through his own companies and through his influential connections with other financial and industry leaders. The powerful Morgan represented, and often led, the consolidation of capital into corporations. He seemed to have a finger in almost every financial and cultural project in Manhattan.

It was not until late in his life that Morgan began focusing his attention on the literary, artistic, and material collections that would be the basis of Belle's work for him. By 1902, when work began on his new Library, Morgan had already begun to retreat somewhat from the business world. Rare-book collecting was only one new arena for his energy. Long before he began purchasing in earnest, Morgan had inherited and amassed a significant collection of autographs and letters by famous men: signers of the Declaration of Independence, Robert Burns, George Washington. He began his habit by soliciting the autograph of President Millard Fillmore in 1851. He also had a few original manuscripts, including one of Walter Scott's *Guy Mannering*, which his father had given him.

It was not until the 1890s, however, that Morgan, with the encouragement of his nephew Junius, began making the kind of major purchases that would come to define his Library. Before construction even started on the new building, he owned a Gutenberg Bible—the first printed Bible—on vellum; a ninth-century manuscript of the Gospels that was handwritten, illustrated, and bound with jewels; four Shakespeare folios; the original autograph manuscript of Dickens's *A Christmas Carol*; and the list goes on.[10] Most such transactions were private, their details known only to those involved or—if the item was significant or the transaction major—others in the business of selling, collecting, or studying. Larger purchases did attract media attention, however. Morgan's purchase of a block of thirty-two Caxtons along with other rare books from the late William Morris's estate, for example, caught the attention of New York and London papers. William Caxton was one of the earliest English printers of incunabula in the fifteenth century, and his books were (and are) highly prized by collectors. The London papers bemoaned the loss of English national treasures to an American. The *New York Times* noted smugly, "Mr. Morgan's library is rapidly becoming the most valuable private book collection in the world. Its owner does not seem to be collecting books, however, but to be absorbing collections formed by others." This most recent acquisition included editions of Chaucer's *Canterbury Tales,* a fragment of Cicero's essay "On Old Age," as well as numerous histories, philosophical writings, and a *Book of Divers Ghostly Matters.*[11]

Just as his interest in business began to stray to books and art, Morgan's romantic attentions had become diffused as well. By the 1890s he was involved in an endless series of extramarital affairs, collecting wealthy widows and married women, whom he often took with him on his European journeys. After Louisa's marriage, Anne became her father's preferred traveling companion, often serving as an unwilling chaperone when his mistresses joined them. Marriage, for J.P., meant "discretion, not fidelity."[12] Morgan also visited museums and dealers' shops, bringing home pieces of Old World culture and artifacts to distribute between his various homes and offices and the cultural institutions he supported.

Morgan was also a major fixture in the New York cultural world. He had been a trustee of the American Museum of Natural History since it was founded in 1869, elected a trustee of the Metropolitan Museum of Art in 1888, and served as senior warden of St. George's Episcopal Church. Through his work as treasurer of the Grant Memorial Association, he had surely known Belle's father. How closely the two men worked together is unclear. Morgan may have forgotten Richard Greener—it had been more than fifteen years since Greener resigned from the project. If so, the newspapers could have reminded Morgan of the former GMA secretary in Belle's first few months at the library. In the spring of 1906 Greener returned from his posting in Siberia, arriving in San Francisco just in time to lose most of his papers and belongings in the April 18 earthquake.

Greener was probably recalled largely because of the region's growing political importance, but he was accused of mishandling both his personal and governmental business, drinking, gambling, and living with a mistress. His replacement was a white man who was immediately named consul and given double Greener's salary. Once back in the States, Greener faced newspaper stories about his reported behavior in Vladivostok. He defended himself passionately against the charges, but gained little ground. Although he had friends supporting his quest for another foreign service appointment, no further government appointments were forthcoming. Greener cast around for a while trying to reintegrate himself into black politics, working for Booker T. Washington and taking a tour of the South with Francis Grimké. He even visited the University of South Carolina, now an all-white campus. Only an African American library worker recognized him. Eventually, Greener settled in Chicago with his cousins the Platts. He had left the pinnacle posting of his career, just as his daughter was beginning what would undoubtedly be hers.

But if Morgan had suspicions about Belle's connection with Greener, or even about her ancestry in general, he left no sign. He is remembered as a man who might have been able to overcome prejudice for the sake of talent and beauty. A probably apocryphal story still circulates that when St. George's Church hired a black choir director, many of its white patrons objected, threatening to withdraw their financial support. After hearing the choir perform gloriously under their new conductor, Morgan promised to replace the withdrawn donations if the man stayed.[13]

But there is no evidence that Morgan extended such opportunities in his companies. Nor is there any mention of Morgan's reactions when his nephew George Morgan married a Japanese woman, Yuki Kato. The family initially closed ranks in support of George's choice. He had been living in Japan, collected Japanese art, and was expected to remain there. But when the couple arrived in New York for their honeymoon, the Morgan family refused to accept her and the couple retreated to Europe.[14]

Morgan's world was one in which nonwhites could fill prescribed roles: servants, entertainers, laborers. Racial slurs and slang terms were commonplace in his business and social circles.[15] Jews, Asians, and African Americans were all outsiders, at best. Belle's dusky skin and even her invented Portuguese ancestry already marked her as exotic and different. But she also had insider status in many ways. Although her family was far from wealthy, she had been raised with the values, the aesthetics, and the attitude of a daughter of the elite classes.

It is possible, however, that even if Morgan had known she had some African ancestry, he might have been one of an unknown number of northern white Americans who believed that while "black blood" carried inferior traits, a small amount could be overcome in a predominantly white person. Belle's youth and beauty may have further helped white New Yorkers like Morgan overlook the question of her ancestry.

And Morgan's social world was also an international one. If Belle had not yet encountered these circles, in which race and ethnicity often had meanings very different from the ones in the American domestic scene, she quickly entered them. In 1907 she was listed in the *New York Times* as a guest at an "Oriental barbeque" celebrating the Fourth of July. The party featured Middle Eastern cuisine, and the attendants included Armenian and Turkish dignitaries and Americans.[16] In addition to introducing Belle to new tastes and cultures, such events reflected the complicated palette of ethnic identities that a global perspective presented. Where did Armenians fit in the system of American racial categories in 1907?

Meanwhile, Belle's job was stretching her horizons in other directions. Soon after she began, Morgan hired another assistant, Ada Thurston, to help her. Unlike Belle, Ada had a college degree and years of formal librarianship training and experience. She graduated from Vassar in 1880 and taught at several colleges before taking a year of classes at Pratt Institute's program in library studies. At Pratt her courses included cataloguing and classification. Nearly twenty years older than Belle, Thurston was either hired as or quickly became Belle's assistant.[17] Belle seemed up to the challenge of supervising an older woman with more education and quickly dubbed her assistant Thursty. Belle admired her co-worker, her intelligence and character more than her appearance. "Thursty may be plain," she warned a friend in a letter of introduction, "but she is very keen." Belle confided in Ada, and the two women often socialized together with visiting scholars, or with Ada's Vassar friends.

It may have been uncomfortable at first, given that the two women worked so closely together and had such an apparent discrepancy in their experience and positions. But in addition to her great familiarity with incunabula and illustrated manuscripts, Belle had the advantage of being comfortable around Morgan. Even after five years of working together, Belle reported that Ada was still "dreadfully afraid of J.P. and hates to be here alone with him."[18] Belle, by contrast, had quickly grown to respect and even revere her employer, and was notorious for her ability to stand up to his temper.

By the summer of 1906 Belle and her small staff were dealing not only with the items from Morgan's home study but also with many of his pieces that had been in other institutions. Morgan's son-in-law Herbert Satterlee described the scene:

> The books and engravings in the Lenox Library were moved
> down and also other collections that were out on loan; and
> many, many volumes that had been bought and paid for but
> were still in the hands of the dealers were called in. The
> new building was a busy hive. Every day there was unpack-
> ing, dusting, arranging on shelves and the entering of items
> on cards that were to be the basis of the catalogue.

Morgan brought family and friends in to see progress, but kept
other visitors out while the librarian and her assistants were busy
organizing.[19]

Belle's responsibilities increased, and she was under mounting pressure to develop a familiarity and even expertise with the wide range of
treasures her boss had assembled. But, especially in these early years,
it was her connection with Morgan himself that mattered most. His
estimation of her outweighed all others, and it was clear to anyone
observing her that his estimation was high. Within a few years she was
making purchases on her own and had replaced Junius as Pierpont's
primary adviser on manuscript matters. It was a mutual respect, but
given her humble beginnings, it was his trust of her that amazed
onlookers.[20]

Belle earned that trust. Over the next five years she studied Italian
and German and continued French with private tutors, attended lectures, grilled visiting scholars, and read voraciously: scholarship on art
and manuscripts, collection catalogues, and trade magazines. She also
read a dizzying array of classic texts and modern fiction and nonfiction,
from Dante to Gertrude Stein to Keats. (She much preferred Dante
and Keats.) But in her work it was other librarians, curators, and even
dealers who helped her learn the ropes. In fact, she was often entering
ongoing relationships between these individuals and J. P. Morgan, the
nuances of which were not always clear to her. In some cases it was
part of her job to pick up where Morgan had left off, and dealers in particular were not always sure whether this new assistant was anyone of
account, an improvement on or an obstacle to dealing directly with the
man himself.[21]

Once the collection was united, catalogued, and shelved, Belle eased into this more exciting process of adding to the collection. Toward the end of her first year there, Belle wrote to the London booksellers Pearson & Co., who had sold Morgan Keats's *Endymion* manuscript in 1897, asking for information on former sales. Pearson & Co. had been one of Morgan's main sources for books for the past fifteen years, and, in their correspondence, Pearson and his agents began to explain to Miss Greene how their transactions were generally conducted.[22] From the end of 1906 through 1907, sometimes with a definite tone of restrained impatience, Pearson employee F. W. Wheeler guided her through the process of purchases that had previously been negotiated directly with Morgan. At one point Belle half playfully warned him not to be "too kind with your offers of aid as I shall probably impose upon you most heartlessly."[23]

It was very much in the interest of those in the book world, particularly dealers, to offer assistance to even a young, unknown woman in Belle's position. Without direct access to Morgan himself, dealers must have anticipated that they could butter up his inexperienced assistant instead. Perhaps they expected her youth and her sex would even make her more vulnerable to their influence or manipulations. Aware of the potential exploitation of her position, Belle eagerly accepted advice and information, but she often double-checked it. Furthermore, she routinely refused books and other, more material offerings. When Wheeler sent her some books as a personal gift a year later, she returned them, apologizing for her "seeming rudeness," but explaining that while she was sure he had good intentions, she had to avoid the appearance of partiality. Later she was more willing to personally accept offerings from long-standing business associates, but in this case she added the volumes to the Library's growing collection of reference works. Decades later a co-worker recalled hearing Belle "inveigh from time to time against Directors and Librarians who put all the books they received into their private libraries, to hear her talk, it was nearly as bad as absconding with library property." Belle always remained suspicious when valuable gifts were offered.[24]

During these early years Belle's written interactions with dealers show her gradually taking on a larger role and greater independence in making decisions and running the day-to-day business of the Library.

By 1907 she was screening books and works offered by dealers for Morgan's consideration and starting to develop her own relationships with these men. She also handled correspondence with the many scholars whose work Morgan privately supported, usually paying the costs of publication of a manuscript. In one case, Morgan had committed $75,000 over five years to Edward Curtis for a twenty-volume set of photographs and information entitled *The North American Indian*. At first, Morgan's business secretary, Charles King, handled the correspondence. But once Belle was established in the Library and the early rush of the cataloging and setting up was completed, she took over. The project continued for over twenty years and cost much more than the original $75,000.[25]

Despite her increasing responsibilities for the collection, she still checked with Morgan and cited him as the authority of her decisions. An observer described the process: Miss Greene would give Mr. Morgan letters and take instructions either in writing or orally. She would then reply to the correspondence. Once he had his able amanuensis, Morgan rarely wrote business letters himself. He hated to answer mail. When Belle chided him that his pile of letters that could wait was getting too high, he informed her that his experience had taught him that "if you leave letters alone long enough, they 'Die out.'"[26] Belle may have learned this lesson too. When her own correspondence became too tedious or (in her mind) unnecessary, she tended to just ignore it.

Not all of her duties were work related. Belle later described long talks with Mr. Morgan in his West Room office, as well as extended periods of just sitting in silence. Even before they developed their full camaraderie and confidence in each other, she would sit in his office and read to him, often from the Bible. Once, J.P. requested the story of Jonah, who survived being swallowed by a whale. After complying, Belle asked whether he believed it. A staunch biblical literalist, Morgan answered that he did. Belle left her own position unrecorded, although her question itself implies skepticism. But she, too, loved the Bible and often mentioned reading it alone and with friends, interspersed with poetry and literature.[27]

There is no doubt that Morgan had a profound impact on Belle both professionally and personally. At the same time, however, she began to show her independence of character. In fact, it did not take long for her soon to be famous temper to emerge. For example, she deeply offended the Florence-based dealer Leo Olschki when she refused his offer of a particular manuscript with a decided lack of tact: "In regard to the Cicero 1468, Mr. Morgan agrees with me that the price asked is absurd. . . . It annoys me exceedingly to have Mr. Morgan offered a book such as this, the rarity of which is doubtful, at so very exorbitant a price." It was far from the last time Greene would wrangle with a dealer over pricing. She complained bitterly and incessantly that dealers regularly overpriced items offered to Morgan because of his wealth. And Morgan regularly overpaid because he did not know, or care.[28] But while Olschki took umbrage at Greene's outrage, objecting that the item was appropriately priced, he soon discovered that annoying Belle da Costa Greene was a bad idea, and not a difficult achievement. Olschki was persistent, writing repeatedly to Greene, trying to convince her that her information regarding the manuscript's value was inaccurate. She ignored a number of his letters and finally, after telling him, "I am most astonished and annoy[ed] that you should trifle with me in [this] manner," she countered a complicated offer he had made.[29] Their purchase agreement didn't end this particular problem, however. The following spring Olschki appealed directly to Morgan because, he claimed, Greene was ignoring his letters regarding the shipping and processing of the items in question. This led to another argument over whether the items had actually arrived at the Library.

Once received, the manuscripts disappointed Greene greatly, and she renewed her complaints over the price. Olschki finally gave up and agreed to take the manuscript back "with the greatest pleasure of the world in spite of having printed in the catalogue that it has already been sold and in spite of the delay of eight months past since you received it until you wrote a word of reception with remarks which are not justified at all." Complaining that Belle had to have a reason to "show animosity" against him, he threatened to tell Mr. Morgan he would rather not correspond with her anymore. Her reply expressed regret at their difficulties but still attributed the problem to the "exorbitant" price Olschki had initially set.[30]

Many such squabbles emerged in Belle's business transactions. In this case Olschki did go to Morgan with his complaints, with mixed results. No doubt he was hoping that the young upstart assistant would be upbraided by her notoriously gruff employer and that future business could be conducted directly with the great man himself. Instead, as Olschki reported to Belle, J.P. was "very much surprised to hear of your irritated correspondence with me," but blamed her silences on her busy schedule. Most importantly he had emphasized that Olschki should continue to notify Miss Greene, not Mr. Morgan, when he had books to sell. But Morgan also undermined Belle's attempts to control his spending by purchasing books directly from Olschki.[31]

Belle's ability to project confidence and assume authority was off-putting to many, but invaluable to her employer. Morgan needed someone who would stand up to dealers, even be willing to offend them, far more than he needed to keep dealers' good will. Belle proved up to the task, and her approach saved him money and avoided many purchases of forgeries and misattributions. Before her arrival Morgan had been less vigilant and had caught many such items in his nets. In short, Belle had begun to act as Morgan's agent, much to many dealers' dismay.

"Librarian," then, included purchasing agent, personal reader, companion, and more. By the end of 1906 Morgan was conducting financial business at the Library as well. Belle was privy to the private meetings and musings of the powerful man. She also sometimes assisted him at his work. Never was this more apparent than during the panic of 1907 when Belle was present at a historic meeting in which Morgan brokered a deal that stopped a threat to the stock market, New York's economy, and the banking and trust networks of the nation.

The 1907 panic followed an economic plunge that threatened to be one of the worst in a period of volatile swings in the stock market. This was a long-feared, even long-expected crash. Bouts of fearful selling in the spring led to short-term recovery but long-term uncertainties owing to a series of factors: overinvesting in trust funds, a market characterized by much speculation in railroad, mining, and copper stocks. Trusts were a relatively new and less well-regulated alternative to banks. As of 1906 they were required to keep only 15 percent of their worth in cash reserves, and only 5 percent on their premises. (Banks in New York were required to hold a 25 percent reserve.) This made trusts particularly vulnerable to a "run"—if too many depositors demanded their money at once, the institution would quickly run out of cash. As it turned out, it was an attempt to corner the copper market in late October that started the trouble, leading to a general market decline and a widespread run on a few trust companies. Once people began pulling out of the market, and trying to withdraw funds from trust companies and banks, the whole system was in danger.[32] The Knickerbocker Trust Company, which had links to the failed copper takeover, was the first to fall. But Morgan had taken control, organizing the bank presidents (who already shared many social and business ties) and trying to organize the trust presidents (who did not). A few days later, when the stock market was on the verge of closing, Morgan helped raise $25 million to keep the market open and save the endangered brokerage houses. The next week it was New York City that needed $30 million to meet its bills. Morgan and several other financiers obliged.[33]

Finally, on November 2, Morgan hosted a meeting of New York bankers at his Library. Ensconcing the bankers in the East Room and the trust men in his West Room office, Mr. Morgan sat late into the night with Miss Greene in her office in between and played solitaire, as was his habit when he needed to clear his thoughts. The big bronze doors to the street were locked. Did the bankers wonder at the presence of this young woman who floated in and out of the rooms and held silent counsel with Morgan in the North Room? (Belle later told the story that Morgan left one of these crucial meetings to inspect a collection of Abraham Lincoln's correspondence, which he purchased.) Sometimes she ran messages back and forth; sometimes individual men entered his domain to offer an idea. "Why not just tell them what to do?" an exhausted Belle Greene finally asked him. "I don't know what to do," he told her, "but I'll know it when I hear it."[34]

By dawn there was a solution, one that saved the weaker trusts (and therefore the entire economic domino array of the financial market) and profited Morgan's U.S. Steel by allowing it to buy Tennessee

Coal. This last piece violated the antitrust laws, but President Theodore Roosevelt, usually staunchly opposed to big business monopolies
and interference with government, gave his approval and the stock
market immediately rallied. Local papers noted that with the 1907
panic the "financial hospital" that was Morgan's office had now moved
to the Library. Much more important were the whole transaction's
implications for the extent of Morgan's power. Controversy over the
U.S. Steel deal followed quickly.[35]

Belle continued to play a role in Morgan's financial business but
never left a record of what she did. Her work at the Library was where
she would make a public mark. By 1908 newspapers and magazines
were beginning to pay more attention to the regular purpose of the
Library itself. The first stories focused on Morgan. The *Nation*, for
example, noted that the Library had made public the surprising bibliophile aspect of the man better known to the world as a financier. More
than in the building, the *Nation* was interested in the story of Morgan's
entrance and developing connoisseurship in the world of book collecting, in which the collector must become in part a scholar.[36] The same
month the *New York Times* offered a front-page story devoted to "Mr.
Morgan's Great Library" as "One of the Chief Treasure Houses of the
World." His fellow collectors Henry Clay Frick and Peter Widener had
taste, the New York writer noted, but only Morgan had genius. The
remainder of the article was actually an advance copy of a *Times* of
London story written by an unnamed English writer who was clearly
familiar with the world of books. He lauded the Library as a "Bookman's Paradise," calling it "the most carefully, jealously guarded
treasure-house in the world" and comparing J. Pierpont Morgan to
Lorenzo de Medici in his catholic taste and intimate knowledge. Only
a few friends and highly placed individuals had been allowed inside his
marble palace. Every room and many items were described in loving
and admiring detail. The only sour note sounded when the writer
reached the English manuscripts, which he asserted should never have
been taken from England. Morgan was not to blame—he had purchased the Byron manuscripts, for example, from Greece. But the
nationalism of an Englishman lamented that these "heirlooms of Eng-

land" were forever lost. The displacement of Chaldean, Assyrian, and Babylonian tablets did not elicit similar censure. England, of course, had long been gathering the cultural and intellectual treasures of the world. The "courteous librarian" who showed the writer those ancient artifacts merited only brief mention.[37]

By then, that polite person was signing herself "Belle Greene, Librarian." The slender, well-coiffed young woman who arrived every morning and stayed all day, sometimes into the night, provoked much interest and speculation in New York. Who was she exactly? Another mistress? Morgan was rumored (correctly) to have several, and the Library did become a place for them to meet him. But none had ever stayed so long, let alone taken a paying position. Could she be an illegitimate daughter? Morgan had never been proven to have a child from any of his extramarital affairs, but the rumors of such a possibility persisted even after his death.

Part of the reason for such speculation was simply that the person chosen for such an important position was a young, unknown woman. As more schools offered degrees in library science, the profession was becoming more formalized. Like teaching and nursing, librarianship was a field that was open to women—indeed, dominated by women at its lower and middle levels. Despite the Victorian ideal that white middle-class women's proper position was in the home, many women, especially single women, worked for wages outside the home. Working-class white women and African American women often continued to work after marriage. Their definition of being a wife and mother included contributing to the family income, when needed. But in the professions that white middle-class women dominated, it was expected that a woman worked only until she married. In many cases, as with J. P. Morgan's companies, women were let go once they married. This partly explains why Belle so consistently passed as a younger woman.

Belle's appearance may have brought her ethnic background into constant question, but not her age. Photos from the 1910s show her looking every bit as young as she claimed to be. And with a strong cultural premium on women's youth, women commonly lied about their age. At twenty-six, Belle would have been considered to be nearing spinsterhood: almost too old for marriage and destined to live alone or with her parents, and to support herself or be supported by family her entire life. This was certainly not the image she wanted to project. As a younger woman, she would be considered eligible for immediate employment and could comfortably put marriage off another five or ten years.

But in a high-profile, influential post such as Belle's, many clearly expected to find a man. Even a man named Belle! In the summer of 1908 George C. Williamson's letters addressed her several times as "My dear sir" and "Dear Mr. Greene" before he realized his error. Williamson was an art historian and a book dealer, who both advised Morgan and sold to him. He had just completed work on the first of three catalogues he compiled for Morgan's Library. Published between 1906 and 1908, it presented Morgan's portrait miniature collection.[38] Belle did not correct his error, signing herself as usual "Belle Greene, Librarian." Finally, after being "a little puzzled" by her signature, Williamson asked Morgan directly.

Like many of New York's upper class, Morgan and his family spent four to six months each year abroad. For Morgan this offered the opportunity to see and evaluate possible purchases. This year his trip had allowed the London-based dealer Williamson to consult on the matter of her sex, and Olschki to complain about her behavior and do business behind her back.

Williamson's next letter was full of apologies, explaining, "I was not aware that I was addressing a lady." By the end of the year Williamson had met Belle in person, a meeting that could have left no doubt as to her sex. But others continued to expect a man, calling her "Mr. Blle da Costa Greene" or, like Williamson, convincing themselves that a Belle could be a "Sir."[39]

Nor did Belle try to "bury [her] sex," as many women in her field did, or to fit the stereotype of either career woman or librarian. When the British photographer Ernest Walter Histed complained about her extravagant hats, she retorted with one of her most oft-quoted, perhaps apocryphal Belle-isms: "Just because I am a librarian doesn't mean I have to dress like one!" Whether accurate or not, the statement reflects her image. At her retirement Lawrence C. Wroth, head of the John Carter Brown Library at Brown University and consultant to the Pierpont Morgan Library, remarked that there had never been "a librarian so little like the conventional librarian of fiction, gliding, rubber-heeled, with finger to lips, among tables and files and shelves. Miss Greene's work was carried on heartily, noisily, in a whirl of books and papers."[40]

In fact, Belle very much used her femininity and her allure in both her personal and her professional life. She attracted a series of admirers and loved a good flirtation, preferably with someone creative, knowledgeable, or otherwise "<u>interesting!</u>" She felt no inhibition in interspersing witticism, slang, and other personal comments in her professional correspondence, and after the first few years such inclusions were characteristic. In an early example, a New York rare-book collector, J. O. Wright, mixed a running banter into his correspondence. (J.O. was probably James Osborne Wright, who published a number of catalogues of book collections and early print books.)[41] As Miss Greene and Mr. Wright discussed business, they began to slip in comments about seeing each other more often, even "twice a day" visits. When she apparently relayed a compliment she received from someone else, his repartee promised, "The M. compliment is not so much. I could do better without stretching my imagination." It was a literary flirtation as well, Belle's favorite kind. At one point, alluding to how he felt about her presence, Wright referred her to an illustration in one of Morgan's rare editions of *Oliver Twist*. The referenced page portrays the hungry orphan's plea "More!"[42]

This exchange represents the first evidence of one of Belle's many flirtations. That Wright shared her love of books and was able to exchange such intellectual bons mots was no doubt part of the attraction. That he was married (to writer Mabel Osgood Wright) only made such interactions safer and more dismissable when Belle was ready to move on.

Frustratingly few details are available about Belle's social life during this time. The men and women who filled her world did not leave archival or other evidence of their presence in this period of her life.

Some clues drift out from her much more documented later life. In addition to the book collectors, dealers, and other book and art world associates who occupied her professional correspondence, Belle was drawn to the company of writers, actors, singers, musicians—to talented creative people of all types. Her social life revolved around dinner parties, theater, music, and the opera. She was probably in Morgan's seats at the opera more often than he was, and she loved to attend dress rehearsals, when she could, for the "electric atmosphere" that made the performance "pulsate." *La Bohème* was one of her favorites— "an opera which I hate because I love it so," she sighed. "[B]y the end of the evening I am invariably desperately enamoured of the man who sits next me, be he old or young, black or white, lame, halt or blind."[43]

The year 1908 also brought losses for Belle. Arthur Upson, a poet and good friend, drowned while boating that summer, at the age of thirty-two. Upson was a promising young poet who had begun to receive critical acclaim. Belle called him a "genius" who she knew would be appreciated one day. "[H]e knew the harmonies of words and tone and made them one," she later recalled. She particularly loved Upson's "Octaves in an Oxford Garden." How Belle knew the poet and in what capacity is unknown. Upson grew up in upstate New York until 1894, when he moved with his family to St. Paul, where he attended the University of Minnesota. But Belle apparently knew him quite well. They had, she said, a "soul-attachment." She described him as being so "vital" that "he simply took me up and carried me over the hard places—and taught me to revel in this 'divine adventure called life.' " But his vitality was offset by periods of depression. In 1906 Upson had attempted suicide. He spent a lot of time overseas during his final few years trying to recover from his health and emotional problems. He must have passed through New York City on those voyages; he also corresponded with the New York papers, which regularly reviewed his publications after 1902.[44]

Arthur was attracted to Belle because she "issued a sense of light and radiance," a claim almost everyone who knew her would agree with. After his death she mused that this phrase described him better than her, that he had carried in him "the joy—the intensity of life—

which I believe is creation."[45] Their friendship indicates that Belle had a rich social life in her early years at the Morgan Library and that she already radiated the energy and vitality that many would later record in their impressions of her. Upson's death affected her so deeply she swore never to "allow another human soul to become necessary to my happiness." The losses in her life were already beginning, and taking their toll.

Once Belle began working for Morgan, a whole new world of New York society opened up to her. By 1909, it is clear, she had begun to socialize with Morgan's friends and was on invitation lists everywhere, from the luxurious mansions of the Long Island Gold Coast, blue-blood resorts like Newport and Hot Springs, Virginia, as well as city celebrations of music, dance, drinking, and leisure activities. Exactly when this began is not certain, but Belle did not enter Morgan's Library entirely without social connections. Some of her friends from Princeton and even her school days were part of her new life as well, for example, the wife of Judge Peter Hendricks, whom Belle identified as an "old school mate," presumably from Teachers' College or Amherst. Peter Hendricks was a New York Supreme Court justice and a friend of J.P.'s whom Belle considered a "restful and lovable creature."[46]

As for Mr. Wright and his Dickensian pleas for more, Belle claimed not to take such encounters seriously, particularly when they over-lapped with her professional life. Although she later became renowned for what a friend called her "indiscriminate man switching,"[47] Belle seems to have kept her romantic life separate from the Library. At the same time, however, her professional world *was* also a social world. Friendships and personal animosities could, and did, sway deals, determine information sharing, and helped maintain the elaborate net-work of favors, alliances, and gossip that connected dealers, curators, buyers, and art experts.

William Laffan, for example, was widely rumored to be having an affair with Belle. Laffan was the editor of the *New York Sun*. He was also a close friend of Morgan's and often advised him on his art pur-chases, especially the Asian pottery that Laffan himself loved and col-lected. Laffan contributed to the *Catalogue of the Morgan Collection of*

Chinese Porcelains, as well as to a similar catalogue of Henry Walters's *Oriental Ceramic Art.* He also persuaded Morgan to set up an Egyptian section at the Metropolitan Museum of Art and to fund a series of archaeological digs to fill it.[48]

Work on the Morgan catalogue had begun before Belle's arrival. The collection was housed at the Metropolitan Museum of Art, but there is no doubt that Laffan was often in the Library (and Miss Greene in the museum) during Belle's first few years there. In fact, many of the men who knew him, including Walters, believed Laffan to be in love with her, and rumors continued for years after Laffan's sudden death, in 1909.[49]

Belle herself later attested that William had "made love" to her almost daily and that she found him more amusing than tempting. (The phrase "make love" then referred to romance, especially verbal protestations of devotion; it was not yet a synonym for sex.) William Laffan was also married, as were many of the men Belle flirted with. An intrigue with a married man was relatively safe for a single woman who was not looking to be married herself. The presence of a wife could prevent a playful romance from becoming a real entanglement, and it allowed Belle not to take professions of love very seriously. It is also worth noting that in the aftermath of his death, Laffan's widow suddenly began leaning on Belle, wanting to talk, first about anything but her husband, then all about him. Belle continually expressed impatience with the woman, writing to a friend that she was tempted to rid herself of the social burden by telling her "how funny William was when he made love to me."[50] This attitude was unsympathetic and appalling indeed. But it is important to distinguish here between Belle's harsh words and her actual behavior. Although she was famous for shocking people by saying irreverent things, Belle was far more likely merely to threaten or fantasize about being so outspoken. In this case she almost certainly never told Georgiana Laffan off. Instead, Belle continued to spend time with the grieving widow, whose company she did not particularly enjoy, listening to her mourn her dead husband as a saint without contradicting her. Her written threats to do so must be understood as a form of venting, an insight into the complexity of her own emotional response to the death of a man whose attentions may not have been entirely welcome but whose knowledge of Oriental and Near Eastern art and cultures must have opened intellectual doors for the young librarian.

And Laffan was hardly the only powerful man Belle was meeting in these early years as Morgan's assistant. Two and a half years after her first meeting with J. P. Morgan, Belle received a reward for her hard work: a business trip to Europe. Accompanied by her mother, she spent time in London on business for Morgan and was able to meet curators, scholars, and dealers. Her mother's presence provided Belle with the necessary chaperone for a single woman traveling abroad alone. Neither had been outside of the United States before.[51] Belle's primary purpose on her trip to Europe was to collect purchases that Morgan had made during his own annual trip earlier in the year or through other agents. And she performed at least one very big transaction on his behalf herself. The full story was not revealed for several years, but Belle was actually behind Morgan's purchase of sixteen more Caxtons from Lord Amherst, acquired privately just before his collection went up for auction. One was the earliest-known printed book in English, *The History of Troy*.

In a 1912 interview for the *New York Times*, Belle described her approach. She had arrived a week before the sale and met immediately with Lord Amherst.

> "You see, I just had to have them," Miss Green said, getting flushed with excitement as a soldier does whenever he recounts a hard-earned victory, "so I said to my lord, 'Mr. Morgan offers you this,' naming a goodly sum. Oh it was a hard and trying moment. I felt that there were members of the family who eyed me suspiciously. Possibly they didn't like the way I dressed, they were so staid and so prim."[52]

Belle's concern about her dress at this crucial professional moment is telling. Perhaps it was simply something less consequential to worry about as she tried to persuade Lord Amherst to sell some of the plums of his collection before the bidding of the auction began. Or perhaps she had already learned that her appearance and her dress were likely to cause as much comment as her intellectual brilliance. But whatever concerns she had about her appearance, she continued to negotiate. She promised immediate payment and warned that Mr. Morgan would not bid at the auction if he did not get the Caxtons in private sale— and his withdrawal would have the effect of keeping auction prices lower.

Belle left Lord Amherst and waited nervously for his answer. She had brokered other purchases before, had negotiated with men who had decades of experience over her own few years. But this was her first attempt at a major purchase, and with "staid" British aristocracy no less. Days went by. Belle spent time in London with her correspondents and new friends at the British Museum and took day trips to other museums and collections as well. The night before the sale she was dining with several of her friends—all "bookmen" who would be attending the auction to bid for themselves or for their institutions. The men were questioning her on her bidding plans and trying to find out which items she was aiming for:

> "One of them turned to me during the evening. 'Miss Green,' he said, 'will you promise me that in the morning you'll not bid against me for such and such a Caxton?' I was on the qui vive, waiting for my telegram which would tell me whether or not I had swept the collection from under the hammer. And as luck would have it, just before I replied the missive was placed in my hands. I read the gladdening news. Our offer had been accepted. 'Yes,' I said, 'I'll promise not to bid against you at the sale to-morrow.' I believe that was my greatest coup."[53]

It certainly was. When the news broke the next day that the Caxton volumes had been sold already, the London curators and dealers knew who had trumped them. And Morgan knew that he had an agent capable of dealing with private owners, who were often wealthy and titled, as well as she dealt with professional dealers. Belle was probably also the agent who purchased a King Charles I copy of the Cambridge Bible for Morgan at the Amherst auction for $5,000.[54]

During her brief trip to London, Greene met with dealers like George Williamson face-to-face for the first time and saw private and public art collections the likes of which even Morgan could not yet hope to match. The journey certainly made her role much more visible to her European correspondents. Not only did they see Miss Greene; some also met Mrs. Greene, often sending regards to Belle's mother for decades afterward. Following Belle's return, letters to English contacts tended to be even more chatty. Socializing was part and parcel of the art business world, and Belle excelled at it. Williamson discussed plans he and his wife had for coming to New York, and offered Belle congratulations "on the delightful position you have in that wonderful library, and on the success with which you have been able to add great treasures to it."[55]

George Durlacher of the Durlacher Brothers art dealership in London, whose 1908 correspondence consisted primarily of bills and receipts, began writing much more informally in 1909. In January he asked for a "few lines" indicating Belle's "safe return." By the summer he was commenting on her "usual happy spirits" and writing notes in the margins: "Fitz has just left and sends his love, so do I and so would my wife if she knew."[56] In addition to expertise and experience, Greene was learning—often quite imperfectly—how to connect and separate her social and her professional lives.

"Fitz" was probably scholar and dealer Joseph H. Fitzhenry, who had helped Morgan in his collections, particularly French porcelains, many of which were on loan at the Victoria and Albert Museum, in South Kensington. Belle had spent a memorable day there, alone in the company of the museum men and other scholars (all over the age of sixty, she made a point of noting). Fitzhenry quickly became a confidant and adviser, addressing her in letters over the next year as "my dear charmer" and "dear and charming lady" and sending her his insights into the motives and attitudes of powerful New York dealers Joe and Henry Duveen and Jacques Seligmann.[57]

And Williamson made a sizable sale to Morgan through Greene. Included in his correspondence file is a copy of a notarized statement signed by Belle, presented to customs upon her return, with an assortment of books she and Morgan had purchased. In the statement she deposes that as "the librarian of J. Pierpont Morgan" she is "in personal charge of the private collection of books and manuscripts of the said J. Pierpont Morgan . . . that she is personally familiar with the details of the purchases of books and manuscripts by the said J. Pierpont Morgan." In other words, the books were for Morgan's private collection and not for sale, an important distinction for customs that allowed Belle to import valuable and rare books for Morgan without having to pay a duty on them. In 1897 the U.S. government had passed a law that levied a 20 percent import tax on works of art coming into the United States, with an exemption for books and manuscripts that were used for research, educational, or cultural purposes.[58]

Customs continued to pose a problem for American art collectors. Although, with Morgan's powerful influences, tariff laws were lightening, import taxes limited the number of items that could practically be brought into the United States. Many of Morgan's more valuable pieces were still in museums and in his own home in England, waiting for the laws to change. When asked why he did not just pay the tariffs, Morgan pointed out that the cost would be several million dollars. This meant that much of his collection was out of Belle's reach for the first years of her work at the Library. Some pieces she waited anxiously to see, like a Petrarch bust about which she had heard great things from everyone who had seen it. As she told another dealer, "Mr. Morgan very rightly does not wish to bring it over (as well as the other objets d'art) until our stupid tariff is settled. We hope this will happen very shortly now and I will write you immediately [when] it is safe to ship things."[59]

In England (whether she visited Paris, too, is not clear), Belle also met some of the professionals who would become close friends and allies in the decades to come. Charles Hercules Read, keeper of the British Museum Department of British and Medieval Antiquities, was one, although Belle did not make it to the museum itself. (She was accused by another British Museum employee of "cruelly" boycotting their collection on that trip.)[60] Read had recently established a relationship with Morgan on a visit to Egypt.[61] Prior to her trip they had corresponded about a Shakespeare autograph that Morgan was considering purchasing. Belle doubted its authenticity, and Read confirmed that it was a forgery. Again, the character of their letters changed markedly after her trip, from a formal tone to one much friendlier and more personal. A month after her return, he wrote,

> I should like to know the result of your matured reflections on yr. visit. It was such a rush that your impressions must have succeeded each other very rapidly. I can only trust the completed effect was not unsatisfactory. Another point equally important—or perhaps more so, is whether Mr. Morgan was content with your results.—I trust he was satisfied with your trip.[62]

Read certainly would have known of Belle's accomplishment and may have been one of the men at her dinner of quiet triumph before the auction. If he was hoping to win one of the Caxtons, he did not hold it against her. Charles Read and Belle Greene would become allies and friends in future years.

If the overseas tour had tested Belle's ability to navigate an international visit and conduct business for Morgan outside of the Library, she passed with flying colors. The trip highlighted her transition from cataloguer to influential representative of Morgan and the Library. From that point on she began to make more and more decisions about purchasing, and soon was a powerful figure in the world of collecting. Even those who did not respect her personally had to acknowledge the unique power of her position.

This shift in her standing was also noted upon her return by Vladimir Simkhovitch, a scholar at Columbia University. Simkhovitch wrote jokingly that he felt guilty for not visiting her since her return: "I understood that you have seen such famous people in London that you would not even look at plain common mortals like myself."[63] He need not have worried. However high her social status rose, Belle never lost her love for those scholars and bibliophiles who shared her passions and provided her with greater knowledge and understanding. Columbia was only one of the many New York and East Coast universities where she established close relations with faculty and administration. And it still had the distinction of sharing her neighborhood. In 1908 the Greene family moved to 403 West 115th Street, just a few blocks north of their previous home. Their new building overlooked Morningside Park, east of the university campus. It was an all-white, mostly native-born, solidly middle-class neighborhood.

Not everyone rejoiced in Belle's step into public and social recognition. Olschki, who heard that she had been in Paris when he was, felt snubbed that he did not merit a meeting. They continued to do business, but when a billing problem emerged the next year, she sent it on to Morgan's business secretary, Charles King, with a note, "The gentleman is—as usual—full of glib explanations."[64] Belle had a long memory—and she could carry a grudge. This sort of favoritism and merging of personal and professional dealings lingered on in some people's unfavorable image of her. But it was the way of the art world. Belle often complained about the intricate web of secrets and gossip and deals, the personal likes and dislikes that characterized her work, even as she participated actively herself.

With her trip to Europe in December of 1908, Belle had entered a transatlantic world of high society, culture, and art. Her trip, quick and incomplete as it was, had introduced her not only to new vistas but also to a wider community of people whose interests and expertise could only further feed her insatiable appetite for knowledge.

A TURN IN THE ROAD

So began the one romance in Berenson's life that would stand apart from all others in depth and intensity. None would cause him longer seasons of lovesick anguish.

—Ernest Samuels, Berenson biographer[1]

Let me tell you a secret—beloved—if you continue to like me you will find that it is in spite of the things I do and say and think and not because of them. Has your love strength sufficient for that?

—Belle Greene, 1909[2]

IN THE SAME SEASON that Belle made her first triumphant trip to Europe, she also met the love of her life. Meeting Bernard Berenson was as consequential for her emotional life as her meeting two years earlier with J.P. had been for her professional one. It would begin as a flirtation but this time Belle's relationship with Bernard would develop into a decadelong affair, an even longer friendship, and the lingering combination of longing, frustration, and passion that only thwarted love can bring.

Bernard Berenson had arrived in New York in late October 1908. His wife, Mary, had actually come to the United States a month before him, with her two daughters Rachel (Ray) and Karin Costelloe. Bernard had remained in Europe another month, meeting with dealers, museum curators, and art scholars in preparation for this trip. Upon landing he immediately joined Mary in Boston, his childhood home from the age of eleven.

Bernard was the prodigal son, returning to the United States after achieving greater success than even his proud family could have dreamed of, although perhaps not in any field they had ever imagined. At forty-two years old, Berenson was an established art critic and scholar who had helped transform Western understanding of art, especially of the Italian Renaissance period. His books on Italian art were now in multiple printings. His reputation made him valuable to dealers and collectors alike. And his commissions from dealers and profits from his own sales had allowed him to purchase a villa in Tuscany and travel annually throughout Europe. This American trip came at a crucial financial point, however, since the villa required extensive renovations. The Berensons needed new contacts to wealthy collectors and to the dealers who sold to them.

It began as a routine visit—for a couple to whom "routine" meant a fast-paced schedule of meetings and dinners, outings and exhibitions. Married eight years, together for almost eighteen, the Berensons habitually traveled on extended trips several times a year, both together and separately. During their regular individual trips—she to visit her mother, sister, and daughters in England; he to socialize with the Anne Morgans, Edith Whartons, and Henry Adamses of the transatlantic world in Paris and Versailles—they kept in constant contact through almost daily letters. It was an expensive lifestyle, which they supported by using their knowledge of art to appraise, advise, and sometimes purchase works on behalf of dealers or wealthy patrons and customers. Bernard's best-known patron was the socialite Isabella Gardner, who, largely with Bernard's and Mary's help, had amassed the collection now institutionalized as the Gardner Museum in Boston.

Like Belle, Bernard had other lives and even other names in his past. His journeys had brought and would bring him through several identities: Bernhard Valvrojensik to Bernhard Berenson to Bernard Berenson; Lithuanian to American to transatlantic expatriate; Orthodox Judiasm to secular Judaism to Episcopalian Christianity to Roman Catholicism to a secular humanism of sorts. These transformations, however, were well known, accepted as part of the successful white immigrant experience. Tens of thousands had changed their names, Anglicized and shortened them, assumed some outward appearance of assimilation. The same year (1908) the Berensons arrived back in the United States, Israel Zangwill's hit play *The Melting Pot* popularized the term that described the merging of races and ethnicities in the Northeast. The late nineteenth and early twentieth centuries saw a rise of immigration from southern and eastern Europe, and New York was one of the centers of immigrant settlement on the East Coast. Zangwill's fictional hero, David Quixano, a musician and composer born—like Berenson—in the Russian pale, celebrated his vision of America as "God's Crucible, the great Melting-Pot where all the races of Europe are melting and re-forming" to make the American.[3]

Bernard Berenson was one of those hundreds of thousands of real European immigrants. He was born Bernhard Valvrojenski in 1865, the eldest son in an Orthodox Jewish family in Butrimonys, a small village in the Vilna province of Lithuania near the German border. Bernard's intelligence was quickly evident and nurtured. He read German at the age of three and began informal and formal education in religious texts and secular political and philosophical works.[4] His father, with little education but great intellectual eagerness, had embraced the Haskalah movement of anticlerical skepticism. The status of Jews in the region was steadily worsening, and a series of violent pogroms in neighboring Odessa prompted Bernard's father to emigrate to Boston in 1874, bringing his wife and three children in 1875.[5] Once in the United States, the newly renamed Berensons ceased attending synagogue but tried to assimilate into the German-Jewish community that had established itself in Boston. Bernard focused on his education, and the Berenson family poured all of its resources into their blue-eyed, fair-haired eldest son and brother. With their help, Ber-

nard's high ambitions and thirst for learning brought him to Harvard
College in 1884, after a year at Boston University. Exactly who paid his
expenses and tuition is not clear. Tuition alone was $155 a year by the
time Berenson graduated. By then he had been taken up by white
Christian patrons, including Thomas Sergeant Perry, a lecturer at the
new Radcliffe Society for the Collegiate Instruction of Women, later
Radcliffe College of Harvard University. Perry was at the center of
Boston literary circles, a close friend of the writers Henry James and
William Dean Howells and the socialite and artistic patroness Isabella
Stewart Gardner. Known as a "millionaire Bohemienne," she and her
husband, Jack, an international businessman, had begun a small collection of English contemporary paintings. When she and Berenson
met in 1885, the Gardners had just returned from a world tour of the
Orient and the Middle East. Her father's death in 1891 left her the
funds to begin serious collecting over the next two decades, even after
her husband's death.[6]

Berenson was very much an outsider in these Protestant circles that
surrounded Harvard. He was an immigrant who had to learn English
at the age of eleven while adjusting to a new culture and life. His Judaism further marginalized him. Although his father had turned away
from Orthodoxy or, indeed, any religious practice, in the United States
the family had maintained a Jewish identity. One of Bernard's cousins
was training to be a rabbi, and his mother kept her faith. Once he
entered college, however, Bernard began attending Christian services,
which was compulsory at both Boston University and Harvard. Anti-
Semitism was quite common in such circles far beyond the requirement to attend Christian rites. Indeed, in a few decades Harvard
would institute restrictive admission quotas on Jewish students. But
Bernard was about to undergo another transformation that further distanced him from his Jewish immigrant identity. Within a year of entering Harvard, Bernard began attending Trinity Church of his own
accord. He was soon baptized under Episcopalian minister Phillip
Brooks's guidance. His new Christianity brought him further into the
circles of patrons who began to support him, especially among the
largely female attendants of Perry's gatherings and Gardner's salons.[7]

Bernard graduated from Harvard in 1887, seventeen years after Richard T. Greener had received his degree there. The contrast between their experiences is evocative. As a Jew, even a highly intelligent, very handsome, and fair-haired Jew, Bernard would always be on the margins of the American culture he now embraced. As a Christian he could, and did, have full entrée into the highest echelons of that society, although some prejudice against his origins, which he never hid, may have lingered. All he lacked now was money, and Bernard set about to rectify that situation. Greener, on the other hand, could not have made an analogous "conversion" to whiteness to better fit into Harvard's intellectual and cultural circles. Those who patronized his education did so in large part because he was not white, wanting to provide the opportunity of higher education to a brilliant young man whose race would otherwise deny him access.

And what a contrast between Richard's and Bernard's post-Harvard careers. Both wanted to go to Europe to study art, but only Bernard realized that dream. After graduating from Harvard, several of Bernard's supporters contributed to a $700 fund for him to spend a year in Europe, where he sat in on university courses, collected photographs of his favorite paintings in museums for later study, and sought out experts in the developing fields of art history and art criticism in order to learn from them. Jean Paul Richter took him on as an informal apprentice in Florence and eventually introduced Berenson to his own teacher, Giovanni Morelli. A well-published leader in the new scientific approaches to art connoisseurship, Morelli brought methodological approaches from his medical training to previously highly subjective task of dating and attributing Italian art. When Bernard's money ran out, his sister Senda sent more, and Bernard began to advise wealthy friends in the purchase of art, gaining further financial support in the process.[8]

In 1890 Bernard met Mary Costelloe at her parents' country home outside of London at the invitation of a mutual friend. His reputation had proceeded him, and Mary was excited to meet the brilliant young intellectual and art student. She later recalled that Bernard "exhaled an enticing if frightening atmosphere of foreign culture."[9] His years of travels and dazzling opinions on every topic pulled her mind to the path not taken. She made a strong impression on him as well: she was tall and fair with reddish-brown hair and blue-green eyes, handsome and quick-witted. She was also married and raising two young daughters. But not for long.

Mary was born Mary Smith in 1864 to Philadelphia Quakers.[10] Her mother, Hannah Whitall Smith, was an early advocate for women's rights who, with her husband, Robert, focused her life on evangelical Christianity. For much of Mary's childhood, the Smiths moved back and forth between Philadelphia and England as Robert preached. In 1875 Hannah published *The Christian's Secret of a Happy Life*, which quickly became a beloved evangelical classic and is still in print. Although she had two brothers and one sister, Mary was her mother's favorite, indulged and encouraged in her intellectual development as a child and sent to Smith College and then the Harvard Annex (later Radcliffe College), overlapping Bernard's student days by several years. The two had heard of and caught glimpses of each other there but never met, although Bernard was a friend of Mary's brother Logan. At Harvard, Mary had been exposed to cultural expressions not encouraged in her family's circles, falling in love with art and poetry. She befriended Walt Whitman (although she promised her mother she avoided the "bad parts" of his writing) and brought him and other literary and artistic acquaintances into her family's home.[11] She did retain from her Quaker upbringing, however, the archaic-sounding second-person informal, using "thee" and "thine" with loved ones throughout her life.

Independent of spirit and unconventional in behavior, Mary surprised everyone who knew her in her marriage to a Catholic English barrister, Frank Costelloe. After giving birth to two daughters, she struggled with the contradictions between her socially prescribed role and her own desires and interests. Mary was not alone in this dilemma, in a period when a married woman was expected to focus her energy on the domestic sphere and subsume her identity in her husband's. Middle-class women in the United States and England found ways to pursue their own activities without transgressing these roles, usually by immersing themselves in volunteer work, church-related activities, or reform movements. Women who desired an independent identity and career either remained single or waited to find a similarly reformist and supportive husband. But Mary found her husband unsympathetic and the demands of motherhood overwhelming. It was, as her family had feared, an unhappy match.

Nevertheless, when Mary met Bernard through a mutual friend, she had immersed herself in her domestic duties and was actively supporting and assisting Frank's political aspirations and work. Berenson initially became friends with both Costelloes: with Frank he talked about Catholicism; with Mary he roamed London's museums studying paintings. When Bernard left for a tour of Italy in 1891, he converted to the Roman Catholic Church, regretting that Frank was not a priest and thus could not be the one to usher him into his new faith. Back in London he began giving lecture tours, under Mary's management. Bernard was finally earning something of a living on his growing expertise and interpretation of art. And as he continued to travel, Mary began to follow him, first to Paris, then moving to Florence for a year to study Italian art under his tutelage. Frank may have hoped that a period of freedom would satisfy her restlessness. But Mary was already moving into the position she would hold throughout Bernard's career: working partner, friend, and lover.

It was a slow process, but eventually Mary and Frank separated. He refused to grant her a divorce. Legal or informal separations were far more common at the time in England and the United States, anyway, but Frank followed Catholic teachings on the matter of marriage and divorce. A separation maintained the economic and legal structure of a marriage, but allowed a couple to live apart and conduct separate lives. Mary originally hoped to keep her daughters, especially her elder and favorite, Ray. But Bernard had no patience for children, and Frank refused to give up the girls, as was his right as a husband and father under English law. Costelloe hired a governess and wrote a will forbidding Mary to get custody in case of his death. Mary, whose own conversion to Catholicism when she married Frank had never been wholehearted, was particularly upset that the girls would be raised Catholic. She tried to visit them regularly and wrote often.

For several years Mary Costelloe and Bernard Berenson traveled and worked together, always maintaining separate living quarters as a thin veil of propriety. Neither one's family was happy with the situation, which threatened the reputation of their wayward daughter and son. By 1893 Mary and Bernard had finished their first book, based on an essay Mary had written and both had expanded on and edited. But Mary asked the publisher to omit her name; her mother wished to avoid further scandal and feared that a coauthored book could bring disastrous attention to her married daughter's illicit relationship. Thus 1894 saw the publication of *The Venetian Painters of the Renaissance*, by Bernard Berenson, and the much more modest *Guide to the Italian Pictures at Hampton Court*, by Mary Logan, a pen name she had used before.[12] It was *The Venetian Painters* that Belle's "Aunt Julia" gave her in 1894. Belle was then fourteen; Bernard and Mary were just turning thirty—she a year older than he. The Berensons' joint career was launched, and each would earn income over the next decade both individually and collectively, giving lectures, buying and selling pictures, and offering appraisals. And both would continue to write and publish on art, although Bernard's name alone would appear on the books to keep their brand consistent.

In 1899 Frank Costelloe was diagnosed with terminal cancer after several months of illness. Mary returned to his side during the last weeks of his life, but whatever reconciliation may have been made did not extend to Costelloe's relenting to give Mary custody of or even visitation rights with her daughters. After Frank's death Mary and her family challenged his will, and Mary's mother won custody of the girls, allowing Mary to be a part of her daughters' lives. After waiting the traditional year of mourning, Mary and Bernard married.

Now in New York in 1908, the Berensons were well established and looking forward to several months of visiting friends and family, and strengthening their professional and social connections among art scholars and collectors. Leaving Italy had been especially tumultuous that year. They had just purchased their beloved Villa I Tatti, a centuries-old stone house tucked into the country hills overlooking the red roofs of Florence. It had been their rental home for years, and now they determined to make it their permanent residence. Before leaving, they had launched an ambitious renovation and landscaping project that they hoped (somewhat overconfidently) would be completed before their return. The expense of the purchase and reconstruction heightened their need to enhance Bernard's developing reputation as an expert and assessor of art. The Berensons were on the road to a life of luxury that they could not yet afford.

New York City was still relatively new terrain for the Berensons, but it was slowly becoming familiar as Bernard's reputation grew. Both were more at home in the Boston area: Bernard's family still lived in Boston, as did his patron and friend Isabella Stewart Gardner. Gardner's collection of paintings held in her Boston home at Fenway Court was attracting notice, and Berenson earned great credit for selecting its most important pieces. He began to seek out, and be sought out by, a new pool of museums curators and private collectors, and New York was the next logical place to expand his business. The Morgan Library was only one of the Berensons' scheduled stops. And its fascinating, sharp-tongued librarian provided an unplanned diversion in the itinerary.

The Berensons had been in New York since late November, and they were not exactly enjoying their taste of the social and cultural scene. During her preparations for the trip—twenty-four trunks for her daughters on top of her own and Bernard's—Mary had expressed increasing reluctance to make the journey to America altogether. She wrote her mother from the ship that this would be her last trip to the States. "With so much in Europe, and <u>this</u> between, I cannot imagine being tempted to cross again." But Mary's contribution to the work in Bernard's name was not unrecognized at the time. She was also developing a reputation in the field to which they both devoted their lives, and her presence was expected on his American trips. In fact, she had planned a series of lectures of her own in New York and Boston.

Their business required socializing, but they found the social elite extravagant and pompous. Mary described the dinners they attended as generally "banal, somewhat vulgar, extremely pointless," and noted that Bernard was "so overcome with the pointlessness of all those people being asked to meet us that he could scarcely speak at dinner."[13] At

the age of forty-four, Mary much preferred the company of her husband, her family, and a few close friends. But her worries about
Bernard's career and their expenses forced her to endure the frivolities
of those whose wealth could buy classical paintings just as easily as
diamonds.[14]

One of New York's rich art collectors was, of course, J. Pierpont
Morgan. His daughter Anne arranged for the Berensons to visit her
father's Library. Anne had attended several of these social events,
which Mary disparaged in such detail. Miss Morgan, along with her
two friends Elsie de Wolfe, an interior designer, and Elisabeth (Bessie)
Marbury, an actress turned theater producer and agent, were longtime
friends of Bernard's, often summering, as he did, in Paris.[15] Elsie and
Bessie lived together and were assumed to be lovers, especially by the
younger transatlantic set, who flaunted their own sexuality and affairs,
whether homosexual or heterosexual, monogamous or promiscuous.
Bessie was particularly notorious as a lover of women. Anne Morgan's
close association with them brought her sexuality into question even
more than did her failure to marry.

Of the three, Anne was the most socially connected, one of the top
Four Hundred of New York society. She lived off an income provided
by her father and had tremendous independence as a single wealthy
woman. Each of these three women hosted the Berensons for a meal
or social event during their trip, but Anne was the one who arranged
for Mary to lecture in New York.[16] The location for this lecture was the
new Colony Club, an exclusive women's club, which Anne had
cofounded and Elsie de Wolfe had famously decorated. The Colony
Club was a female version of elite men's clubs of the time, a place for
society women, but with a large membership of authors, actresses, and
professional women as well. The first of its kind, its six stories boasted
sleeping rooms, restaurants, halls, a swimming pool, and a gymnasium,
including a squash court. Wolfe's stylistic innovations eschewed the
heavy drapes and gilded Victorian standards in favor of glazed cotton
chintz, light colors, and floral motifs that soon became the model for
interior decorating. Anne was arranging for "all society" to come to
Mary's lecture, including her mother, Mrs. J. P. Morgan. Arranging for

a visit with her father at his Library was another way for Miss Morgan to help her friends and show her family that she was still cultured and knew important people.[17]

From the Berensons' perspective, the invitation to Mr. Morgan's Library was a chance not only to see an exclusive collection but also to make a connection with a wealthy collector. Dealers sometimes went through convoluted schemes to engineer such meetings. A. S. Drey, a dealer in Munich, once heard that Morgan had bought a Ghirlandaio in Florence. Desperate to meet, and sell expensive art to, an eager buyer of such means, Drey immediately traveled to Florence and stalked a church, confident that Morgan would not leave Florence without seeing its famous Ghirlandaio fresco *The Last Supper*. Sure enough, after a few weeks Morgan showed up, and Drey was able to "accidentally" meet him and eventually make a very lucrative sale.[18] Bernard, though not openly a dealer, had similar motives for potential gains. He was familiar with this kind of tactic but hated all the wasted time necessary to try to approach people like Morgan. Thus, Mary noted with particular relish that they had not even had to ask for the appointment but had been invited by Morgan to see "his famous Library. . . . It is he, his daughter says, who wants to show us his things."[19] If Morgan had invited them himself, all the better their chance to make a favorable impression.

Most of Berenson's biographers have understandably assumed that Bernard and Belle met during the Berensons' highly documented visit to Mr. Morgan's Library on December 3, 1908. It would indeed have been oddly fitting had Mary been present when her husband met Belle da Costa Greene. Mary's proximity had never prevented Bernard from seeking the company of other women, or even conducting extramarital affairs. They had an open marriage long before the term was popularized. In fact, Mary had been the first to stray, falling in love with German sculptor Hermann Obrist even before she and Bernard were able to marry. She believed then that pure monogamy was contrary to human nature, and wanted Bernard to understand that she could still have primary loyalty to him. Bernard was keenly jealous and could not accept Mary's reasoning, until he began to pursue liaisons with other women. By the time of their New York trip, Mary had come to regret her own participation in and agreement to the arrangement. At the beginning of 1908 she wrote in her diary that she was finding her marriage difficult and the romance gone. It was particularly bitter to watch her husband "indulge in the most romantic feelings" about another.[20] Still, she had become resigned to their situation, and sought more to improve their own relations than to discourage his affairs. So it came as no great surprise that, on this trip, she would once again watch her husband fall in love.

But on December 3, if Belle's own recounting of buying the sixteen Caxtons directly from Lord Amherst is to be believed, she could not have been at the Library or anywhere in New York. The *New York Times* reported the private sale on December 3, from a news cable sent from London on December 2, and not even J. P. Morgan had money enough to bring his librarian back across the Atlantic so quickly. And, in fact, the only documented suggestion that Bernard met Belle at the Library is in a letter he wrote months later to Isabella Gardner, and he does not specify when the meeting took place.[21]

Even without Belle's presence, the stop at the Morgan Library would have been noteworthy to those trying to follow the intrigues of the world of art dealers, sellers, and buyers. And the circumstances and back story of their visit laid the foundation for an odd triangle that would form between Belle, Bernard, and J.P. over the next few years. Probably unbeknownst to Belle, the two men who would become the most important people in her life had some history, and she would long have to contend with events and charges that had occurred before her arrival at the Library.

Although his collection was growing in scope and significance, Morgan had completely ignored Berenson's advisory services. In fact, there was a significant chill between the two men. In 1903 Morgan had helped keep Berenson from being offered the position of director of New York's Metropolitan Museum of Art. Berenson had been courted for the job by then board president, Frederick Rhinelander. However, Morgan, who had been a board member for fifteen years, and New York art dealer Henry Duveen suspected Berenson of being connected with a con man they knew to be dealing forgeries. Known as Uncle Henry to many of his business associates, Henry Duveen and his brother Joe were the heads of the powerful Duveen Bros. business, which had offices in New York, London, and Paris. (One of Belle's most often-repeated bons mots was supposedly made when viewing a collection the Duveen Bros. had helped created. She pronounced, "How utterly Duveen!")[22] The Duveens had worked with Morgan on several purchases that would amount to multimillion-dollar deals in today's currency, sometimes bankrolled entirely by Morgan. And Duveen brought his reservations to the powerful Morgan.[23]

The evidence of Berenson's involvement with this particular con man was tenuous, and Duveen's case against him melted away. But Morgan's doubts about his character lingered. When Morgan succeeded Rhinelander as president of the museum's board of trustees, Berenson's candidacy was completely off the table. He probably would not have accepted the position, preferring to remain in Europe with the art he loved and the business he needed, but losing the offer no doubt rankled.

Ironically Henry and Joe Duveen had recently approached Berenson themselves and suggested that he go on their payroll. They were one of the business contacts Bernard and Mary hoped to nurture during this trip. If Bernard could receive regular pay for appraisals or attributions, many of their financial pressures would be eased. Given that such appraisals were more valuable if Berenson's opinion was seen as impartial, neither the dealers nor the art critics publicized their developing relationship, of which Morgan was probably unaware.

For his part, Berenson had been critical of Morgan's approach to collecting, mocking his lack of experience in pricing and choosing pieces. In 1901, for example, Morgan purchased a Raphael painting, *Madonna and Child Enthroned with Saints,* that Berenson had previously advised his patroness not to purchase. At the time he told Gardner that he could not ascertain that the piece, a central panel from a Colonna altarpiece, was actually a Raphael, as attributed. After Morgan obtained it (for a stunning $400,000, a then record price for a painting), Berenson further dismissed the *Madonna,* claiming,

"Raphael barely looked at [it]." With a rising market for Italian Renaissance art making his career, Berenson profited from skyrocketing
prices. Yet he also blamed the escalation on "people like Pierpont
Morgan . . . who buy anything at prices to make your hair stand on
end."[24] When Morgan died, the *Madonna* was considered one of the
most important paintings in his collection, and went to the Metropolitan Museum of Art, where it is now established as early Raphael.[25]

In 1906 Berenson had visited Morgan's London home at Princes
Gate. Morgan's residence for almost half of the year, the mansion
housed a good part of his collection and was open to select visitors in
his absence. Berenson derided the art there as a random assortment of
pieces. It looked, he famously wrote his patroness, "like a pawnbroker's
shop for Croesuses," although he admired some of the pieces.[26] Gardner and Morgan were sometimes competing for the same items, and
Bernard kept his buyer updated on Morgan's purchases, appealing to
Gardner's sense of superiority and competitive spirit. Now there was a
new "shop" of treasures in New York, guarded and defended by Belle
da Costa Greene.

If Belle had been aware of this history, it would surely have prejudiced her against Berenson. Though barely three years into her tenure
with the financier, Belle already considered herself Morgan's protector.
If Berenson became an enemy of Morgan, he would be an enemy of
Belle Greene. As Mary would later warn her husband, that could harm
him professionally as much as her friendship could help him.

Regardless of what she knew of previous friction between Berenson
and her boss, or of Bernard's character, Belle definitely knew of his
scholarship and importance in the new and developing field of art criticism, specializing in one of the many fields in which Morgan collected. She still had her copy of that first *Venetian Painters,* and she
must have read, if not owned, his later publications on central Italian
art and on the drawings of Florentine painters, if not on her own, then
certainly in her work for Morgan.[27]

The visit itself was not life changing. Mary described the Library as
"a fine building, although hideously decorated with modern ceiling
paintings." But it was the treasures within that drew her interest.

He has the most wonderful collection of books, and a great
many fine objets d'art. Although these are mixed with forgeries, some quite blatant, others more successful. There is
in particular one picture for wh[ich] Roger [Fry] is responsible, which we are dreadfully afraid is a forgery. . . . However, probably we shan't have to speak of it at all. And do not
mention it. . . . We may be wrong after all.[28]

A new market was opening up in art, especially Italian Renaissance
painting, and new pieces were being discovered or sold from collections and churches throughout Europe. With most pieces in private
collections, without the technology or even the records to identify and
date them, forgeries were everywhere. No dealer or collector was
immune from the occasional misattributed or carefully prepared forgery, but it was, of course, a great embarrassment for the purchaser and
scandal for the dealer when one was discovered after a sale.

For his own part, Berenson was "duly impressed" with the illuminated
manuscripts. And even Belle would have been forced to agree with his
assessment of the rest of the collection as being a mix of good and bad—
"punk!" she called the latter.[29] Since Berenson was known as an expert
in art criticism, and made his living and reputation on his ability to provide accurate attributions, he often faced a forged or misattributed
piece. With scholarship in the field of art in its infancy and a high-priced
market subject to intentional or unintentional misrepresentations, the
danger that a collector or even a museum would make a false step was
high. It was not unusual for the Berensons to hold their tongues in such
a situation, especially if the owner seemed to suspect nothing. In this
case, the involvement of Roger Fry, with whom they had done business,
posed an added awkwardness.

The collector merited a better review than the collection. Mary
described Morgan as "very genial and pleasant" and was surprised to
find "the plain Yankee just under the surface, in fact, peeping out every
now and then, in some homely expression or thought." Morgan offered
"all his wonderful catalogues." This was a rich gift indeed: limited editions that provided descriptions, provenances, and reproductions of

parts of the Morgan collection. Such limited publications were in high demand, and usually offered only to major museums and research collections. For Berenson, who had begun a collection of photographs of artwork that even now attracts scholars of Italian Renaissance art, these were valuable additions to his private research collection. For Morgan it increased the possibility that his holdings would find their way into future articles and books by the important scholar.

Morgan also offered to bring the Berensons to see another collection of pictures at "Benny" Altman's.[30] Benjamin Altman was a New York philanthropist, art collector, and self-made businessman and senior partner of B. Altman & Co. His home on Fifth Avenue housed a remarkable collection of paintings, tapestries, sculpture, and—his specialty—Chinese porcelains and enamels. Such private collections were accessible by invitation only. A stranger could not call or request a visit without an introduction through a mutual friend.

But Altman would have to wait until 1909. Within a few days of their visit to Mr. Morgan's Library, the Berensons headed south, Mary to Bryn Mawr to check on her daughters, Bernard to Washington, D.C. (where Mary later joined him), to renew his passport and meet more important people, including President Theodore Roosevelt, who addressed him as "Berrington."

The larger jobs the Berensons were in the States to perform included cataloguing the collections of John Graver Johnson and Peter Widener. Peter Widener was, like Morgan, an investment financier with powerful control in many dominant fields, including steel, oil, tobacco, and railroads. The Berensons had been invited to stay at Widener's palatial residence, Lynnewood Hall, outside of Philadelphia, while they consulted about his collections to sort out the fake from the authentic pieces and to reappraise some of the questionable attributions. During their stay at the Wideners', Mary was overwhelmed by the size of her rooms, half marbled, half carpeted, with a dozen different perfumes in cut-glass bottles, "acres" of fresh flowers daily, and French maids jumping up to serve her. They were, she said, "the richest millionaires I ever struck . . . so rich that it seemed to me really awful."[31]

John Graver Johnson was a lawyer whose collection focused on European paintings: Dutch, French, Flemish, English, and Italian. At the Johnsons', as at the Morgan Library, the Berensons were presented with possible forgeries or misattributions. This time it was four pictures just purchased as Botticellis. In fact, both Roger Fry and Herbert Horne had guaranteed the attribution. But whereas in New York they were only visitors quietly questioning some of Morgan's pieces, here they had been hired to ascertain and add Bernard's name to such determinations. With his relationship to the British art critics already strained to the breaking point, the Berensons agonized over what to do. Eventually he decided to leave the attributions as given.

By early January, Mary and Bernard were back in New York; Belle had returned in late December and was ensconced once more at the Library, receiving congratulations and resuming her usual routine. Like most first-time visitors to Europe, she hoped to go back again soon. For now, though, there were letters to reply to and business to catch up on.

The Berensons most likely met her on a follow-up visit to the Library in January. Morgan did not make good on his promise to bring them to Altman's, and arranged to have Belle do the honors instead. Belle missed that appointment because of illness, so Bernard made the visit alone. The next time Altman saw Belle, he grilled her on what Berenson had thought of his things, and what Morgan thought of Berenson.[32] Or she may have been dispatched by J.P. to entertain the Berensons, bringing them to dinner or the opera on his behalf. Indeed, they could have met repeatedly in the few weeks after their return to New York. Belle frequented many of the places they did and could have attended any of the events planned to introduce the art critic and lecturer to the New York cultural lights. Despite their many misgivings, the Berensons were successful in socializing with the "squillionaires" in New York. Mary reported triumphantly that she and "B.B." were "the fad . . . of the moment. . . . [A]ll those palatial doors on Fifth Avenue are open to us." It was, she reminded herself, the only way to approach collectors.[33]

Belle might have gone, for example, to Mary's lecture at the exclusive Colony Club, where she often lunched with friends. The talk went just as Anne Morgan had planned, including her mother's attendance—a substantial social coup for Mary. This lecture was the highlight of the trip for Mary, who excitedly reported every compliment and accolade to her own mother. The society women, she reported, had decided that Mary was "the brains of the 'Berenson outfit' . . . the 'only begetter' of all that goes under BB's name!"[34] Belle's presence at this conquest would explain her enthusiasm for Mary, almost equal to her interest in Mary's husband.

Elsie de Wolfe also hosted a large dinner, followed by a trip to the theater. The dinner had been bearable, the play—a farce in which a man uses his wife's charms on his employer to work his way up in the company—was not. Mary and Bernard were disgusted, and they avoided theater for the rest of the trip. Elsie was very helpful, however, in helping Mary select clothing and purchase new corsets for her thickening waist. Never a small woman, Mary was finding her weight becoming more of a problem as she aged.[35]

Another event, which Mary described to her mother in weary bemusement, featured a red dinner, at which everything was colored red, including food, décor, and favors. And the guests were all bejeweled to the point of ridiculousness with "about two million worth of diamonds and no lady except myself had on a dress that cost less than £75."[36] At least they made one valuable connection there: Archer Huntington, who was already a multimillionaire and would inherit even more when his widowed mother, Arabella, passed away. Mary did not mention that the hosts of this dinner were Joseph Duveen and his wife. The negotiations had gone well, and Bernard had assisted the dealers in several transactions, to their mutual financial benefit. By the end of their visit, Duveen and Berenson had a verbal agreement that he would act as their exclusive adviser for all Italian purchases and sales.[37]

But however they met, Belle and Bernard did not record their first impressions of each other. If Bernard immediately felt the depth of attraction he later proclaimed for Belle, he left no sign. He required beauty, intellectual challenge, strong character, and a quick wit; Belle had them all. With an air of arrogance much more refined than that of Morgan, Bernard could also be both intimidating and charming. According to Mary, "B.B. betrays his sense of misfit by fiendish brilliancy which leaves people uncomfortable and gasping and I betray mine by extreme and heavy amiability."[38] Of course, Bernard's gruff manner and superior attitude would scarcely have cowed the young librarian: her legendary ability to stand up to Morgan's rages was ample proof of that. Belle was used to attitude, not afraid of the formidable. Usually in control of her public persona, she did not betray her feelings easily, but could appear to be open and even oblivious to social propriety and constraints. Slender and dignified, with rather patrician features and a well-groomed beard, Berenson was quite a handsome man.

In between his fancy dinners and lucrative deals, Mr. Berenson found time to get better acquainted with Miss Greene. At first their meetings were public, and perfectly understandable to anyone who cared to question them. For example, Belle accompanied Bernard to tour the Metropolitan Museum. Later she recalled that they admired a recent acquisition: a Greek marble statue of a young boy's torso.[39]

By mid-February, Belle had begun to pursue Bernard, and his extended family, fairly aggressively, and the first documented evidence of their relationship appears. Upon hearing that one of Mary's daughters, Rachel (Ray) Costelloe, would be traveling to New York with a friend, Belle offered to entertain them. Mary excitedly relayed her invitation to Ray: "Mr. Pierpont Morgan's secretary, Belle Greene, a most wild and woolly and EXTRAORDINARY young person, wants thee and Ellie to go to the opera with her, in her box, on Thursday March 4th."[40] The word "extraordinary" is uncharacteristically capitalized and spread across the page of Mary's usually cramped, consistent writing. (In fact, it is a style of expressive writing more characteristic of Belle's own hand.) And Mary repeated the depiction as she reported to her mother of the "gaieties" arranged for Ray and her friend Ellie Renfel. "Americans *are* so kind!! Mr. Pierpont Morgan's extraordinary young librarian, Miss Belle Greene, is going to take them to the opera."[41]

A third-generation proponent of women's rights, Ray was touring the Northeast, giving lectures and holding meetings on women's suffrage. Mary had set up several introductions for the girls in Boston and New York and guided her daughter through her first independent experience of American society. She consoled her when a meeting with the formidable Isabella Gardner went awry—Gardner was infamous for the delight she took in humor at others' expense. And when a play Ray wrote was politely declined for production by Bessie Marbury, Mary broke the news gently.[42]

As the New York trip neared, Mary coached the English-raised Ray on American "social laws":

> This venturing upon an unknown society on the frail back
> of one or two introductions is immense fun, especially as
> one feels so detached. There is one thing you must be care-
> ful about—Leave cards on everybody who has called and on
> all the people who do you a politeness or ask you to a meal.
> This is the chiefest of the American social laws.[43]

She sent Rachel to call on Rita Lydig in New York, instructing her to write, "Sent by my mother, Mrs. Berenson," on the back of her card.

Rita De Acosta Lydig was a New York society woman renowned for her beauty. Her parents were Spanish, although she was born in New York, and descended from Albas. Rita was also known for her extravagant lifestyle, and for having divorced her first husband before marrying Philip Lydig, a banker and Wall Street broker. Rita, like Belle, was considered an exotic beauty. Her Spanish ancestry set her apart from her cohorts and made her character suspect. Mary assured Ray that Mrs. Lydig was "nicer than she seems," and warned her daughter that the socialite was "very Creole and Spanish, and one uses a different standard." Belle knew the Lydigs as well, although she was not intimate with them. She considered Rita a "fascinating lady" but deliberately kept her distance, perhaps uncomfortable with a woman whose name and ancestry where a bit too close to that which she had adopted.[44]

Of all of Ray's visits in New York, it was the evening spent with Miss Greene that she described most enthusiastically. It was, Ray reported to her family, "the most wild experience of all." After a successful strategizing session on suffrage at the Bryn Mawr Club in New York and a series of lunches and social engagements, Ray and Ellie got ready for their first trip to the opera. Belle picked them up, accompanied by several "curious people" who departed after the show. Then the fun began. Belle and two unnamed men, "both repulsive, in different ways," took Ray and Ellie for supper and commenced "the queerest conversation!" After some "amusing frivolous" conversation, the topic turned to suffrage, an issue near and dear to Ray's own heart. "Miss Greene and I got one of them between us and fairly slaughtered him. He was a southerner, and said that the Divine order of things was that no woman should be allowed to earn money or to think for herself." The other man, a German, was less "prehistoric," and Ray felt she and Belle had gotten the best of the southerner. It was a late night for Ray, but "a most entertaining evening. We liked Miss Greene tremendously, and I hope I shall meet her again"[45]

Entertaining the family of a prospective art associate may have been part of Belle's duties, and pleasures, in her work for Morgan. "Her box" was actually Morgan's box at the Metropolitan Opera. But Belle was pursuing her own interests in "taking up" Mary's daughter socially. She was very interested in the Berensons and used every method in her grasp to ingratiate herself with them.

And the interest was mutual. A few days after receiving Ray's glowing report, Mary invited Belle to Boston to keep her daughter company. Mary had developed a painful case of shingles, and Ray had left her own tour to assist her, even giving one of Mary's scheduled lectures for her. Mary thought the "two girls" would have fun together.[46] Although there were only fifteen years between Mary and Belle, the distance was exaggerated by Belle's continued habit of claiming to be five or six years younger than she actually was, and by Mary's habit of dealing with prospective competitors by adopting and mothering them. Ray was then a college student, still at Bryn Mawr, ten years younger than Belle. But to a wife and mother reaching middle age with a series of health problems, the "wild and woolly" Belle no doubt seemed to belong to her daughter's younger and more spirited generation.

By the time Mary issued her invitation, however, a parallel correspondence of a very different nature had commenced between Belle
and Bernard. "Dear Mr. Berenson," begins Belle's first existing letter to
Mary's husband, written on February 23, 1909. They had had a lunch
date; he had canceled. Eager to ensure she would have another occasion to see him alone, Belle wrote to express her disappointment. This
first note was simple and short, a far cry from what would become her
characteristic rambling effusions, sometimes running to eight or ten
pages. By comparison, it was a model of restraint:

> I am so glad that you are going to be a <u>real</u> friend (than
> which there is no rarer thing in god's world) that I can
> <u>almost</u> forgive you for not lunching with me. For I must
> confess that I am really dreadfully disappointed about that
> for I did hope to have a quiet chat with you there. I should
> like to feel that before you went away we were at least
> <u>started</u> on the road of friendship. This is a <u>very</u> frank letter
> but I think you understand. It's [more European?] to
> understand it. Why don't you come and have tea with me
> some day.[47]

His first note to her was equally formal in its address, beginning, "Dear
Miss Greene."[48] However, Berenson was experienced enough to
understand she was expressing an interest beyond friendship.

In barely veiled language Belle's first letter suggests that Bernard
and Belle had already begun a serious "friendship" and flirtation,
which she hoped would become much more. It was not exactly proper
for a single woman to invite any man to her home unaccompanied. But
since Belle lived with her mother and sisters, she often entertained at
home, which was within the bounds of social acceptability. Here she
made no mention of familial chaperones. Her family was very willing
to grant her privacy with a visitor if she requested, but the implication
of their presence provided a cover of respectability to Belle's invitation.
Still, it was undeniably a forward letter by the day's standards, as she
proposed to advance their intimacy to another, perhaps uninvited level.
Her awareness that he had only another month in the States may have

prompted her to take the risky step of putting her interest and her invitation in writing.

Yet Belle still had commitments that kept her from seeing Bernard. Although she tried at least once to visit him in Boston—it is not clear whether this was in response to Mary's invitation—she had to cancel. "I know you will share my disgust on not being able to come to Boston and play with you all," she wrote Bernard in early March, "I am truly distressed because it has made my dear Alice Ditson unhappy." Alice Ditson, with whom Belle often stayed on her frequent trips to Boston, was the wife of the music publisher Charles Ditson, who had taken over his father's business in 1907.[49] Alice informally supported many singers and musicians and opened up a world of musical artists to Belle, both in Boston and during her visits to New York. Belle hoped Bernard would meet Alice in her absence and "show her the golden side of you," suggesting Belle had already by then come to know his various sides quite well. But Mrs. Ditson was not really her concern. Belle would see her Boston friends again before long; Bernard and Mary were returning to Italy in less than two weeks. She pressed her desire to see him. Giving Bernard her home telephone number, and asking him to wire her his itinerary, she tried to arrange a visit for the following week, when he would be back in New York.[50]

Meanwhile, she wrote to Mary expressing her "real pleasure" in spending time with Ray. "I think you and she have great reason to be mutually very proud of each other and the greatest good I can wish her is that she may grow to be as much like you as possible." Knowing that Mary would be returning to New York to catch her ship home, Belle begged her to make time for a visit and invited her to lunch: "I shall be so proud if you will."[51]

To Bernard, however, Belle sent a clipping of a poem entitled "The Turn in the Road." ". . . Far have I fared alone . . . / And then, by the alder thicket / A turn in the road—and you!"[52] And the next day she wrote, "Dear Man of my Heart,"

> I have been with you in thought every moment since you
> left me—have wished for you at dinners—at the theater
> and opera, in the morning afternoon and night. My

thoughts have been wrapped around you as I should have
wished to be and my absorbing occupation has been to chop
off, day by day, the long many hours that lie between us,
Love—. . . How I wish that you might gather me up and
take me to the Wood beyond the world where we two might
learn to know Life and each other.[53]

This letter went far beyond Belle's flirtatious notes in professional
correspondence. She was falling in love, and she was now confident
enough in his feelings to no longer hide her own.

They did eventually dine alone in his rooms at the Hotel Webster, a
few blocks from the Library. Three years later the memory of her first
private time together with Bernard was still vivid:

> I remember every little bit of that evening so well, even to
> the clothes I had on and how you liked my hair and how you
> went back of my chair and kissed it—and I did not move or
> let you know (actively) that I knew you had done so.[54]

By official societal standards, it was beyond inappropriate. But Belle
was in love, and she was far from alone in stretching the boundaries of
women's comportment. Many people around her, beginning with J.P.
himself, were conducting affairs, protecting reputations and marriages
by hiding liaisons and meetings. Of course, Morgan was a wealthy
man, whose class and gender granted him the privilege of having extramarital sex with little danger to his reputation or marriage; he could
bring his mistresses to his yacht or to Europe, and could pay servants
and workers to keep his secrets. Belle was a single woman with far
fewer resources, and had only her family and the Morgan name to protect her. Although she had had friendships and romances with men,
and was willing to flirt openly and even flaunt her relationships with
men, she had not yet (she repeatedly claimed) become sexually active.

Whatever reasons or promises she may have made to herself about
not crossing that line, she found herself quite tempted to put them
aside with this man, who had caught her heart and her mind more than

anyone she had ever known. Belle and Bernard met alone at least once
more before he left. The Berensons had a dinner at the Astors' that
night and he had a luncheon, but they carved out one more private
meeting. And of that last encounter, what she remembered most was
what they had not done. Although they "wanted to give ourselves completely unto each other's keeping" before he left, they did not dare.[55]
Convention, her own sense of propriety, or an unwillingness to invest
herself sexually and emotionally just before his departure prevented
her from yielding to her own desires.

The ache of that denial haunted them both for months to come. But
those last hours were not all sweet talk and forbidden fruit. Before
their final goodbyes, Berenson told her in a "brutal speech" that in
making her love him he was "only making things easier for someone
else." And then their time was up. Belle dropped him off at the Beaux
Arts for his luncheon. A year later she cold still recall her emotional
state at that moment, "I felt as if I had left all the sun and warmth
behind me."[56]

She could not bear to see him off at the docks the next day. Instead,
she wrote him a letter, dated only "The night of the day that you
left me."

> Desire of my heart—To settle for what is before me—the
> hours, the days the weeks and years without you—is to set-
> tle for a dull gray despair or else certain madness. For I can
> never cease imagining and I doubt [sic] that will be my
> undoing! I make vows <u>not</u> to dream of you—<u>and break
> them!</u> And then "all the doubts that assail thinking men"
> come over me and I lie awake dreading annihilation. I help
> myself out of my depression by remembering that you and
> one or two other "worthy people" care a bit for me. I use my
> friends to reflect any virtues I may have.

Oddly, she closed with a few lines of a poem given to her "by a young
man I have been trying to help." It reminded her, she said, of something Bernard had once said.[57] No doubt it also served to remind

Bernard that he was leaving her behind, alone and unattached in a world of interesting men.

As Belle tried to maintain her old life, feeling in her heart that everything had now changed, the Berensons made their way back to Europe. Much had changed for them as well, although neither could yet know how much. In the short term, the American trip had been a financial success. They had solidified their relationship with Duveen, sold several paintings brought with them for that purpose, and received at least $3,000 (enough to buy a car in Italy) as commissions for other sales. They took a parlor suite on the *Mauretania* for their return trip and, having now entered the circles of the New York, Boston, and Philadelphia elites, dined on board in the "Millionaires' Corner."[58]

But before leaving New York, Bernard had ordered a gift for Belle: the sixteen-volume French edition of *A Thousand and One Nights*. Perhaps he was wondering how many nights there would be before he and Belle were together again, and whether they would ever spend a night together.

"THE WHIRL IN WHICH I LIVE"

*My fate is bound round my neck in bonds of iron, rather gold,
glittering gold and locked with the Eternal $.*

—Belle Greene, 1910[1]

*When the world began to change, the restlessness of women was
the main cause of the development called Greenwich Village,
which existed not only in New York but all over the country.*

—Hutchins Hapgood[2]

THROUGHOUT THE SUMMER of 1909 Belle's and Bernard's letters flew fast and furious. Settling into an affair of letters did not
always suit Belle's schedule or nature, and she was not the kind of
woman whom even such an experienced collector of mistresses as
Bernard had ever encountered. Belle had a job, and not simply a job
but a career. And not just any career but one of the most unusual positions in the world, perfectly suited for her. Her work at the Library

totally engrossed her days, and she had a city of people, events, and culture at her fingertips by night. For a long time Bernard remained the only man in her heart, but he had a great deal of competition and would soon discover that even he did not come before her life's true passion.

Belle relied on the memories of her "brief but happy hours" spent with Bernard to sustain her.[3] But her inconsistent writing did not suit Bernard's expectations. He and Mary wrote each other daily during their regular separations, and both corresponded regularly with dozens of friends and, in Mary's case, with family as well. Both loved to write letters and devoted hours a day to reading and responding to the copious correspondence each received daily. Berenson's assistant later recalled that both Bernard and Mary were "intensely letter-conscious," always impatient for the mail to arrive.[4] For Belle writing was a necessary evil of her work, and the imperative to respond to every letter she received, professional and personal, dismayed and overwhelmed her.

There was much to keep her from writing. The letters she did write reveal a life of controlled chaos and show her own struggle to embrace contradictory activities, people, and paths. In addition to tracing the development of her relationship with Bernard, she discussed her equally intense, if somewhat more contentious, relationship with J.P. And as the two men maintained their mutual skepticism, she tried to balance her loyalty to each. Her passion for her work was sometimes lost in the daily grind of annoying visitors and constant debates over attribution, provenance, and value of her books. Above all, her growing resentment of Morgan's control over her life emerged, countered largely by her even greater devotion to him. The privileges and luxuries she began to acquire made her even more aware of what she did not have. She resented the wealthy who provided much of her entertainment, and she longed for the access to art, culture, and especially travel that they had, but could not join their ranks because of her job. Of course, it was her job that gave her entrée into that world to begin with. At the same time, she was beginning to grapple with modernity in several forms. The art of Matisse and Rodin, so unlike that of any of the periods or styles she was surrounded by at the Library and the museums she haunted, baffled and intrigued her. New ideas about sexuality and women's behavior, pushed to new limits by the bohemian movement, seemed to embrace both her own position as a career woman and her growing desire to step off the pedestal of Victorian womanhood and become sexually active. And throughout it all, Belle's long-distance relationship with her beloved Bernard evolved, tempered by her own emotional ups and downs.

For the first few months after his departure, Belle's letters were full of passion and exhortations for their quick reunion. In April she wrote tantalizingly that she trusted the day would come "when sans fear et sans reproach I can be all that you wish to you." In May she demanded, "Egoist—listen—I doubt if I shall be able to love you much longer without seeing you so you had better plan to come back to these shores soon." And in June she mused that although she had never known "the mystery of the completion of love between a man and a woman" and although she and Bernard had "not yet known the fulfillment," she took comfort in the belief that, despite their "unrealized joys," their love was "safe from spoiling" precisely because it was "incomplete."[5]

Her longing to be with him was multifaceted. She missed the intellectual opportunities as much as the romantic ones. She told him she wished she could be with him in London "to see those wonderful things with your eyes—I am sure that I could amount to something with you to help me—but who is there here to teach me?" Yet their lost opportunity to become sexually intimate weighed heavily on her mind. Was it unwise to have "let the moment slip"? Her instincts said not: "I think of all that I want to be to you and I know I am right to wait."[6]

Belle left Bernard no doubt that she intended them to have a fully sexual relationship when next they met. Although middle-class ideologies of proper womanhood stressed premarital chastity (not to mention marital fidelity), many women and men transgressed these official proscriptions but maintained a façade of respectability. Whatever fears may have kept Belle from joining their numbers before Bernard departed did not prevent her from planning to be sexual with him when they reunited—at least as long as that reunion remained in the misty, undetermined future.

Moreover, social mores regarding sex were changing in the first decades of the twentieth century. The spreading influence of Freudian theories of human psychology and development opened a discussion of sexual desires and behaviors. Sigmund Freud himself gave a series of lectures at Clark University in Worcester, Massachusetts, in the summer and fall of 1909 that further popularized psychoanalytic ideas in the United States. In Freud's world view, sex was a natural and universal human need. Socially inappropriate expressions of sexuality were traced to developmental problems in an individual's early life. This was a provocatively positive image of sex in the context of Victorian European and American attitudes in the late nineteenth century. At the same time progressive reformers' interest in issues like prostitution and sexually transmitted diseases, as well as eugenic interest in controlling reproduction, led to a carefully expanded public discussion of sexual behavior. Reformists sought to control, not understand, sexual behavior that was considered inappropriate or illicit. But both Freudian and reformist discourses revealed that for all of the attempts to cover up and deny sexuality, Americans—including white middle-class and elites—were having a lot of sex, and by no means was it limited to married couples. Still, women in Belle's position (single, dependent on her job) had to protect their reputation, not to mention worry about an unwanted pregnancy. That she had no idea exactly when and where she would see Bernard again made it all the more titillating, and safe, for Belle to write to Bernard about her plans to "be all she could be" to him when that far-off day arrived.[7]

In addition to the usual desire to read reassurances of continued love, Bernard also wanted Belle to write about what she did every day—a request Belle found "absurd." She deemed her daily activities

of no consequence whatever! I go to luncheon party and a dinner party every day. I automobile almost every afternoon. I flirt and I study . . . I meet some people whom I love and lots who I detest—I scratch and am scratched and all this is of no consequence to me like you who is touring the Earth. When—if ever—I do anything worthwhile I will let you know—until then I will write to you of what is behind the curtain of my mind—your commands to me not withstanding.[8]

In fact, she did both. Her letters, often written over days, provide both a periodic calendar of her work and social appointments and a reflection of her thoughts and emotions on pretty much everything: her work at the library, the people around her, current events, books she was reading, plays and operas she attended, artists and writers she spent time with, parties and weekends she went to, political movements and events, spirituality, marriage, motherhood, her family. She certainly did not tell him everything, and some of her reflections on marriage and men may have been carefully filtered for a lover's eyes. But in their detail and length the letters are incredible.[9]

One of her favorite subjects was, as she promised, herself and her emotions. By the end of April she was already trying to explain why she didn't write as much as he wanted: "if you knew the mad (and useless!) whirl in which I live you would forgive me and love me still." She was finally writing that day because she was lonely for him, "for all the blue devils in the cosmos are sticking their poisonous tongues into me tonight."

A chance conversation at a dinner party that night had reminded her of the loss of Arthur Upson, her poet friend who had drowned in 1908. That loss had made her reluctant to love again. Until she met Bernard. And now she confessed one of her emotional scars to him: she was afraid "almost physically" of deep emotional attachments. The few she had known had all ended in loss "because of some outer unreachable inalterable and unfightable force."[10] Granted, we know almost nothing of the close attachments formed in her early career, but surely those of her youth must count among them. Her father had left the family and gone to Siberia. No matter what the circumstances between husband and wife, for a child, even a teenager, the parent who leaves has abandoned them. Then her grandmother, who helped raise her from infancy through adolescence, had died. What other connections with aunts, uncles, and cousins had been strained or lost with the advent of living as white?

And now the combination of reliving this loss and Bernard's departure had overwhelmed her. For the first time since he left, she let her loneliness and despair spill into a letter, feeling the distance between them in a way she had not felt before. "I can't even send my spirit 'singing through the spheres' to find you—I feel hemmed in—isolated and altogether blue—," she moaned. So far was she from the vitality and energy that he had seen that she feared she was "not the Belle that you think you love." But the sun rose on another day, and her blues receded into the shadows. She wrote again, but enclosed the "horrid tearsome letter" of the night before without rereading it for fear she might not send it at all. This became something of a rule for her: no matter how crabby, ill-advised, or disconcerting her words, she generally let him "see" her in all her moods. Nevertheless, with the next day's metamorphosis, she focused on reassuring him about her love for him and her faith in their future, although her unhappiness crept back as she wrote.

> Dear if you were only here I could make you know what I want you to be to me but somehow I can't write it all—I think I could stand a long absence—not feeling your touch or hearing your dear unAmerican voice—. . . I wish—but then one can't wish away mountains and of course one has no moral right—but I wish I could feel that I was all in all to you and that no-one else could claim you. You see dear I am only a very jealous very unhappy very lonely girl and I am by no means sure that I am all to you that I can [and] would be.[11]

In other words, she wished he were not married. Imagining Mary, even in a cliché, as a mountain suggests both that she saw her lover's wife as a formidable force and that she felt Mary's presence to be natural and unchangeable. Belle understood that his marriage took priority even over what she believed to be the love of her life, reflecting not only the morals of the time but the laws as well. A woman (or man) in Belle's position, involving herself in an emotional or sexual affair with a married person could find herself sued for "alienation of affection" by an abandoned spouse. In fact, anyone who interfered in a marriage, especially sexually, was vulnerable to such a suit.

She seemed certain they would not see each other for a while. What, she wondered, would they feel for each other after perhaps one or even two years of separation?[12] The distance between them, both spatial and temporal, hit her hard occasionally, and she often turned to him for solace in her letters. It was because she was so seldom "blue," she said during a similar spell later that fall, that it seemed during those times that "all the devils real and imaginary in the universe were bent on my destruction."[13]

For the rest of the year, she wrote less often, but still regularly, rarely letting more than a week or two pass without a letter. Some letters lost their way or were delayed, and Bernard often complained that she was not writing enough. He had high expectations and was an avid letter writer. She was not, although she realized full well that letters were necessary to maintain a connection, at least for him. She wrote in stolen moments at work or on weekend trips, on trains, in bed before or after her day. Her letters went on for pages, sometimes for days. Sometimes they got lost or forgotten as work or an illness or family problem took over her life.[14] She wrote eight letters in April 1909, but only three each in May and June.

In May the letters had stopped for a while, and each thought the other was ignoring him/her. She sat down to write him about her "surprise anger dismay and despair" at not hearing from him for three weeks, and her growing fear that he was ill. Before she could even send the note, she had received a letter from him, but she enclosed her anxious note in her reply anyway. And his letter, it turned out, also complained about not hearing from her for a few weeks. She had a good excuse: she broke her wrist when thrown from a horse. (She later returned and successfully "broke" the horse in question.) In this second letter she also confessed that she had feared that he had met some "femme blonde—such devils as they are!" She was particularly worried Bernard would lose interest in her upon meeting a blond woman because she felt particularly jealous of and inferior to any "beautiful blonde."[15]

When they are in the field I make as graceful a bow as a raging heart permits and retire to sulk in the arms of some
blind foolish and altogether undesirable creature who
assures you he "prefers brunettes." You see how I was tormented last month. Don't you feel the slightest pangs?—
heartless wretch.

Blond women were "the joy and bane" of Belle's life. "I adore them and
hate them," she admitted. Blond hair and white skin were the ideals of
American feminine beauty, and women of all ethnicities had long used
homemade and commercial skin lighteners to achieve this ideal.[16]

Belle's constant open envy of blond women was only one way in
which she drew defiant attention to her own beige skin. By her own
accounts, Belle probably had the darkest complexion not only of the
social crowds she moved with but in her family. Yet, the first image of
herself that she sent to Bernard that spring was a printed card, not of
her, but of a small, peach-skinned child with light brown hair. Belle
explained that her nurse, who had known her since infancy, had purchased it because it looked just like Belle at five.[17] All photographs and
most paintings and drawings of Belle show her with very dark brown or
black hair, so if she did have light brown hair as a child, it darkened
considerably as she matured.

Bernard indeed fed Belle's insecurities by flirting with blond women,
and lots of other women as well. As he wrote to his patroness that
spring, "When I am not hard at work I must have women I might, and
I would be in love with." (This was written on a trip to Portugal as
Bernard was sizing up the women in the place he was staying in for
their potential as objects of love.) But, perhaps in part because of his
own emotional promiscuity, he also feared Belle would be distratcted
from his attentions. Very few of his letters to her, probably some of the
least personal ones, have survived in archives. His hundreds, perhaps
thousands, of letters written during the 1910s can never be recovered,
but some glimpses of their content and even brief quotations appear in
her replies and references. When he complained about the burden of
his work, perhaps openly envying J. P. Morgan his librarian, Belle

responded she would love to be free to work with Bernard, if she were not in the position that she was. When he worried why she should love a "bald and middle-aged" man, she assured him that she hadn't noticed either state—only that he had "a most enchanting fashion of wrinkling [his] nose."[18]

Her letters might not have been consistent or regular, but they were heartfelt. "Why are you not here beloved to kiss me and pet me and correct my English?" she complained on that first "glorious" Easter Sunday after he left. Then, she was euphoric, a "pagan pure and simple," celebrating the return of spring as "the reincarnation of the virginal bacchante." She wrote glowingly of the radiance of the sun, the call of nature, "the world—like myself is bubbling over with joy."[19]

Other days she was fatalistic and saw no future for their relationship. If he stayed away long enough, she warned, they would forget about each other and go their separate ways: Bernard toward "fame and glory," Belle "the path of all 'sordid victims.' " Sometimes she felt that the distance between them was part of the attraction. "I have," she warned him prophetically, "a nasty trick of loving some people more in their absence."[20] And she was very realistic as to the unrealistic nature of her attachment to him. They had known each other such a short time that she had to rely on her imagination to build her image of him; "not to know all, to see miles of untrodden way stretching ahead leaves me queerly ecstatic possibilities with a limitless playground for one's imagination." She claimed to have tremendous "imaginative powers," which she had lived in since childhood, "and now with their aid my love for you runs absolute riot." And she warned him that if he continued to like her it would come to be despite her behavior, not because of it. "Has your love strength sufficient for that?" she challenged. If all this seemed a bit too honest, Bernard had only himself to blame. He had asked to hear her " 'naughty' feelings," by which he apparently meant not only her hunger for him but her jealousies and fears as well.[21]

But these personal musings and emotions seldom made up the bulk of her multipage letters. As Bernard demanded, and despite her own protests, she regularly filled pages recounting the parties, weekends, lunches, dinners, theater, opera, and, most of all, the people in her life.

Belle often wrote to Bernard from some "gay and giddy house party" she was attending. She was generally kept very busy at these social events, dining, drinking, dancing, driving, horseback riding, and always talking, talking, talking, but she usually had more leisure time to write than she did during the work week.[22] Throughout the summer of 1909, but especially in the fall and winter seasons of 1909 and 1910, Belle's letters to Bernard offered the first surviving description of her incredible life. In some sense these glimpses were random, giving great detail about the events taking place just before she happened to find time to write. Since time was not something she had in abundance, her letters were often interrupted. She routinely repeated herself, forgetting that she had already described an event or person or conversation. And she certainly withheld information from him, especially about her personal life.

There were few details about her family, although she reported on them occasionally. In the summer of 1909 the Greenes were staying in the Adirondacks while she stayed in the city with her brother, Russell, communicating with her sisters and mother by letter. When she fell off the horse and broke her wrist, she also cut her face, which resulted in a "most alluring" scar on her cheek that she believed only enhanced "what my brother calls my 'peculiar style of beauty.'" As she recuperated from the fall, she was "most beautifully spoiled and petted." By the end of the summer she reported that she was finally going up to pay her "respects" to her family, as the tone of their letters had become "quite disgusted" with her. She was not looking forward to the visit, she told Bernard, since they refused to spoil her as she liked to be and instead always put her in her place within a day. Russell confirmed that she was spoiled, but he would not be there to help deflate her head. By then he had left New York for a job in Florida.[23]

Once in a while a remnant of her pre-Morgan social life appeared. That summer, for example, she spent a weekend with a group of female "college chums," presumably from Teachers' College or Amherst, who rented a houseboat in New Jersey. They all lived in their bathing suits and acted like "tomboys," swimming and canoeing. If the suits were old-fashioned, they covered all but calves and forearms. If they were the newer modes, they revealed shoulders and knees as well. Either way, modesty was preserved. Men were not allowed except for dinner parties, by which time the young ladies had resumed full and proper dress. Nevertheless, it was a prolonged sleepover-picnic with fourteen "girls" sharing six beds and having a wonderful time.[24]

Other references to older friends were much more oblique. In April she had mentioned lunching with someone who had been traveling the world for seven years. They were each taking stock of the changes those years had wrought on the other, and he found her "much changed" and was "unreasonably angry with me for 'growing up' and especially for not wearing a pig-tail."[25] If it had literally been seven years, she would have been in Princeton working at the library. But reporting the passage of time accurately was never Belle's strong suit.

Such anonymous references to Belle's Princeton or even pre-Princeton life were not on her usual social calendar and certainly not the core of her current life as a New York figure and Morgan's protégée. By 1909 her social circles were so varied and colorful as to encompass names from New York's high society, theater, writers, artists, publishers, millionaires, and scholars. Nevertheless, she claimed she refused to be adopted by the "Smart Set," only spending social time with people who interested her or who could connect her with interesting people. "I would rather spend a whole evening with my Italian teacher a most enchanting and learned albeit cross cantankerous and rough creature—than dine with Mrs. Reggie Vanderbilt," she claimed.[26]

But, like it or not, Belle was connected with the "set" she loved to hate. She had in fact dined with Mrs. Reginald Vanderbilt, along with sixty other guests, over the Fourth of July weekend. She loved the Vanderbilts' home, a 280-acre estate in Newport, Rhode Island, and she enjoyed the yachting.[27] And although she vowed never to do it again, she did. "The horrid part of being a 'poverina' and visiting the 'predatory rich,'" she explained to Bernard, was that she was always expected to be at their disposal and to be social and entertaining.[28] The Berensons had some experience with such visits, of course, but for Belle there was no direct professional reason to attend weekends and dinners of this sort. Much as she complained and disdained the social elite, she chose to continue to associate with them.

It is not difficult to see why. What she loved most about the wealthy, besides their access to luxury, was their access to culture, entertainment, talent, and extraordinary people. When the New Theatre (later called the Century) opened in the fall of 1909 at Central Park West and Eighty-second Street, it brought a new uptown venue for the lavish theatrical and operatic productions that Belle adored. In one week alone that fall she attended a dress rehearsal at the new New Theatre, went to the opening (*Anthony and Cleopatra*) Monday night, ran up to Boston Tuesday for the opening of its new opera house, attended the Philharmonic back in New York on Wednesday, and was at the New Theatre again on Thursday for a production of a new play. She worked at the Library that week as well.[29]

Opera and theater were part of the upper-class social scene in New York. J. P. Morgan had a box and season tickets at the Metropolitan Opera and at the New Theatre as well. Other box holders at the New Theatre included Philip Lydig, John Jacob Astor, William K. Vanderbilt, Clarence MacKay, Otto Kahn, Archer Huntington, Edward H. Harriman, Peter A. B. Widener, and Daniel Guggenheim. Belle was often there in her boss's box, or as a guest of some of these other big names in New York business and cultural circles. She considered the New Theatre itself beautiful, but complained that the acoustics in the cavernous hall were "exceedingly bad."[30] But she absolutely loved the opera and would shut out idle chatter, poor sound, and any distraction to lose herself in the story and the music.

Not all of the "predatory rich" bored her. She still loved her "great chum" Junius Morgan and spent a weekend in Princeton with his wife that summer as well. And she ran into John D. Rockefeller while staying one weekend at Hot Springs, Virginia, a wealthy resort that dated back to the late eighteenth century. The self-made millionaire and Morgan's librarian had met before. This time, however, they talked for hours, grilling each other on their stories. He wanted to know her life history, especially her age; she wanted to know about his origins as well. Although Rockefeller later seemed to feel he had told her too much about his business machinations, including things she was sure Morgan did not know, their friendship continued, at least through the week.[31] Much to the delight of the other vacationers and the horror of her friends, the unlikely pair took to each other, despite the forty years' difference in their ages, "like two penny postage stamps on a hot day." They spent the week golfing, talking, and riding in his car. He even taught her how to drive. (Cars were one of the few things Belle would admit she envied the rich for. When she had an opportunity to be driven in a car at over seventy miles per hour, she called it "the most exciting thing I have ever experienced.")[32] Belle teased Bernard that she and J.D. might soon be "united in the bonds of Holy Standard Oil." And when Rockefeller wrote to her a month later, she refused to tell Bernard the contents of the letter from her "latest mash." But when the gossip caught up with her, she was unrepentant: "Headlong was I born and headlong I continue precipitously rushing forward through all manner of nettles and briars instead of keeping to the path," she bragged blithely.[33]

Belle's confessed impetuousness and her disdain for the wealthy could sometimes combine with lethal effect. She once called William K. Vanderbilt a "rotten branch of a rotten tree" and his wife "an underbred, underborn, impossible creature."[34] These Vanderbilts were members of the Four Hundred, having entered the New York/Newport society reigned over by Mrs. John Jacob Astor. This insult never circulated, but others did.

Isabella Stewart Gardner invited Belle to visit her private collection in November on one of her many trips to Boston. As Belle described the visit to Bernard, she found the "ensemble" very fine and particularly admired a Raphael, a Velasquez, and a terra-cotta Madonna and Child. Belle had far less praise for her hostess. While she did note that Mrs. Gardner had been very kind, she still found her a "rude, boresome, underbred, unlovable person," and said she had declined Mrs. Gardner's offer to return for a play later in the evening. Bernard would probably not have been surprised or particularly offended by Belle's depiction of Isabella. His wealthy patroness had a reputation for taking advantage of her position at the expense of others, but Belle had probably picked up on her own employer's rivalry with the Boston art collector.

Belle was more interested, however, in describing the effect of seeing a portrait of Bernard himself at the Gardner Museum. It had been painted by Denman Ross in the spring of 1909 before Bernard left Boston. Ross, a collector and a Boston Museum of Fine Arts trustee, was part of the literary and artistic circles Bernard had frequented as a Harvard student. Belle had asked Bernard for a photograph of it, but now that she saw it she was quite disappointed. She called it "hopelessly bad," because it did not fit her mind's portrait of him: "alert, vital, entreating and glowing, enthusiastically inspiring and so entirely lovable."[35]

This time, however, Belle did not limit her criticism of the wealthy woman to her private letters to Bernard. Back in New York a few days later, she apparently spoke disparagingly of Mrs. Gardner and her collection at a dinner in the presence (unbeknownst to Belle) of a friend of Gardner's who reported the conversation back to Boston. It was the sort of gossipy talk that often took place at such dinners. Alcohol flowed freely at these gatherings, and the opportunities for social faux pas were many. But it was not the first time Belle had bad-mouthed Isabella to her friends. Over the summer she told Chris Barnes, who claimed to be good friends with Mrs. Gardner, that she was "impossible socially."[36] And when Mrs. Gardner came to the Morgan Library, Belle complained that she tried her patience and called her "the most unattractive woman in every way that I have ever met and the monotone colour of her skin hair and eyes gets on my nerves—(Meeow!!)." Belle would later dub her "Grisabella."[37]

But after hearing about Belle's comments at that dinner, Isabella wrote to Bernard with the "nasty" tale. All of Belle's dinner account of the trip, she told Bernard, had been a lie. Furthermore, Belle had reportedly claimed that there were several forgeries in her collection and had mentioned the Berensons quite intimately as well. Did Bernard know her? What did he think of her and of this story? "It turns out she is a half-breed, and I suppose can't help lying," Isabella concluded. "But let me know what you think."[38]

Mrs. Gardner also wrote to Miss Greene directly, a "rather bitterly plaintive letter." A harried Belle urged Bernard to tell his patroness that Belle had thought the collection was lovely. "[S]ome villain" had told Gardner that Belle had disparaged it.[39] Bernard defended Belle, calling the story "incredible" and questioning the accuracy of "the reported utterances of Miss Greene." He quoted Belle's paragraph that listed the paintings she enjoyed; the only critique he mentioned was that she had disliked the Denman Ross portrait of himself.[40] On Isabella's opinion that Belle was a "half-breed," Bernard made no comment. He had his own ideas on that subject. And of course he did not reveal the extent of his intimacy with Belle.

Belle's other Boston visits that winter were more successful, both socially and professionally. And the two often overlapped. The home of Annie Fields, for example, was a regular stop in Belle's Boston rounds. Belle enthusiastically described the "enchanting hours" she spent with the "dear old Mrs. James Fields, who I love passionately." They talked about Browning, Thackeray, Tennyson, Emerson, Thoreau—Great Men of literature and philosophy whom Mrs. Fields had known. Annie Fields was a Boston native, whose marriage to James Fields, editor of the *Atlantic Monthly* had brought her into literary circles, as well as Boston's cultural and social circles in the late nineteenth century. In addition to the men Belle listed, Fields also supported women writers, including Harriet Beecher Stowe, Rebecca Harding Davis, Willa Cather, and Sarah Orne Jewett. She was also a poet in her own right. At the time Belle befriended her, Annie had lost her second life companion. After her husband died in 1881, Annie and Sarah Orne Jewett had lived together in a "Boston marriage" for almost two decades. Although the term at the time was used to describe two women living together, it could be used as a synonym for "lesbian" as well. However, this is a controversial label. Biographers of Fields and Jewett are careful to note both the obvious intimacy and primacy of the women's relationship and the difficulty in defining the nature and meaning of that bond to them. This was an association that was defined less by sexual orientation than by an intimate domestic arrangement between two unmarried women. Respectability was possible simply because no one publicly questioned, or cared, what went on behind closed doors.[41]

Belle may have been unaware of the nature of the relationship between Fields and Jewett, but she certainly knew about Jewett. A few years later Belle reported that she and Annie had had a "tiny falling out" over Jewett, whom Belle called Annie's protégée, but she hoped the older woman had forgiven her for that. And she warmly recalled her visits with Annie Fields as "the most delightful hours I have ever spent in Boston."[42] But this was not the only Boston marriage Belle would encounter, and she would encounter women who were far more open in their romantic and sexual relationships with other women.

Amy Lowell, whose home was another frequent social stop in Boston that winter, would soon be in a similar partnership. Primarily known as a socialite, Lowell was just about to emerge as a poet with the publication in 1910 of her first poem. But she had not yet met Ada Dwyer Russell, a widow with whom she would live in her own Boston marriage from 1914 until Lowell's death in 1925. Belle already knew Ada Dwyer when she was a stage actress. And Lowell's contact with Belle extended into the 1920s, so Belle would eventually experience Lowell's transformation while in a relationship with Russell: large dogs running loose in the house, masculine clothing, and cigar smoking.[43] Greene, Dwyer, and Lowell were contemporaries, born within five years of one another. And although there is less of a paper trail between Belle and Amy Lowell than between Belle and Annie Fields, it is likely that their primary connection was their shared love of books. Lowell was also a book collector, who purchased through a Philadelphia dealer Belle loved to fence with: A. S. W. Rosenbach. Moreover, she was a scholar: in 1925 Lowell sent the Morgan Library a copy of her book on Keats and gave a lecture there.[44]

In Mrs. Fields's case Belle had clear professional motives for her social attentions, much as she enjoyed the older woman's company. As a result of her close connection with so many writers, Mrs. Fields had amassed a valuable collection of manuscripts. At the beginning of 1909 an agent, Gardner Lane, had been trying to get a complete list of her manuscripts for Mr. Morgan with the help of Sarah Jewett.[45] After Jewett's stroke that spring and her death in the summer, the behind-the-scenes maneuvering was over. Once she had waited an appropriate period Belle ventured a personal visit. And somewhere in the hours of conversation about the literary lights of New England, Belle raised the subject of Mrs. Fields's manuscripts and the Morgan Library's interest in them. In the correspondence that followed, Mrs. Fields sent the Morgan Library one "Pierpont letter" written by J.P.'s father and promised to look for others that she had. She also mentioned a number of manuscripts and autograph letters in her possession that she had forgotten to show Belle. Perhaps Belle would come again, and Mr. Morgan might accompany her. Mrs. Fields also promised to leave her book of manuscript poems to the Library, where "it will be cared for by him and by you in his exquisite building."[46] Belle enthusiastically followed up with more correspondence and visits. Fields called her "dear Librarian and my young friend," and J. P. Morgan sent the Boston widow extravagant flowers. Mr. Lane soon found himself cut out of the loop of these genteel negotiations; Miss Greene and Mrs. Fields amicably settled on the price of $1,000 for her first edition of Washington Irving's *The Life of George Washington.*[47]

It was another Morgan-Greene success.

Belle's letters leave no doubt of the centrality of J. P. Morgan in her life, whether he was in residence in New York or in England, or touring other countries. When Morgan was in town, he was a looming presence. One of her friends would later tell her that she was never quite herself when Mr. Morgan was out of town.[48] Although her relationship with Morgan was not specifically romantic or sexual, it was far more than professional, and her loyalty to and love for him was probably more threatening to her relationship with Berenson than any of the crushes she recounted, or even those she conveniently never mentioned. J. P. Morgan was, she told Bernard, "the most exhausting person I know. He often tells me he 'likes my personality' and yet when I leave him I feel utterly divested of it—as if a glove one draws off and gives to a friend because he admires it." Her work with him, as we have seen, had extended beyond the manuscripts and business of the library. She had become a personal assistant of sorts and was involved in some of his financial and other business doings as well. "The Big Chief has succeeded in acquiring all of the world here now, and most of the world without," she groaned, "and it keeps us very busy every minute."[49]

It quickly became evident that their bond would be an obstacle in her relationship with Bernard. That summer, for example, Belle had mentioned that she might be able to spend five months of 1910 in England, France, Italy, and Egypt with her friends the Truesdales, but only if J.P. would let her. Actually, she confessed, the question was more if she could bring herself to leave Morgan for so long. "I almost wish I did not like him so much or that I liked him a great deal more— it would simplify things so."[50]

Throughout 1909 and into 1910 Belle tried to negotiate her position between the two men. When Bernard sneered at Morgan and his taste in art, Belle, used to hearing all manner of negative things about her boss from people whose opinion she disdained, could not stand to hear them from one whom she loved and respected. For pages she tried to explain the man she knew behind the power that was J. P. Morgan. She saw in him the "ultimate symbol of humanity" and a "Christ-like genius of suffering," and described a close and emotionally intimate relation- ship in which they sat together for hours, sometimes silently, some- times confessing to each other: J.P. telling her his unfulfilled hopes, his failures, and his visions. "He is the hero of my soul and the child of my heart," she explained, "and when you say belittling things of Him, although you can injure him not at all, you can hurt me." Bernard later referred to such praise as Belle's "hagiology" of the man B.B. believed was "cyclopic, demoniac."[51]

The tension between Bernard and J.P. continued. Morgan refused to let Belle send some photographs (presumably of pieces of his col- lection) to Berenson, which Belle chalked up to his inexplicable prej- udice against her beloved "B.B.," as he was almost universally known to friends and family. J.P. even objected to her writing to Bernard, but as that was her private business she felt free to ignore him. Bernard was quite aware of Morgan's priority in her life. Even Mary com- mented on it. She judged Belle a "true friend" who would stand by Bernard "through thick and thin—at least provided the thick weren't J.P.M."[52]

Throughout 1909 Belle angled to bring J.P. and Bernard into a mutually profitable working relationship. She wanted desperately to use some of her ties and inside knowledge to help Bernard expand his work. Belle also claimed increased influence over Morgan, bragging about "queering a deal" when her "Big Chief" was asked to influence a sale to the Metropolitan Museum. The crossed dealer, Belle expected, would call her "all sorts of things which I am not (at least yet)," but she protected herself by getting a friend of Morgan to support her. Still, Belle sought always to protect Morgan's name and money. At one point Belle and Bernard debated the attribution of a supposed Pinturicchio that Morgan had purchased. Bernard supported the attribution, but Belle was not convinced. More importantly she did not want Morgan dragged into the controversy and so decided to keep the painting out of the public eye until things had calmed down. She warned Bernard not to air his views too loudly. "I do not think it kind or fair to the Big Chief to make him a buffer for your various factions, and I think you know that my first thought is for him."[53]

And however much Belle wanted to help Bernard, she would not do so at the cost of her own professional standing. For example, she drew a line in providing Bernard with copies of the various catalogues published for the Morgan Library. She sent him one on painting and manuscripts without checking with Morgan, but did not send him the "Miniature Catalogue." When Bernard complained, she explained that while the one was obviously in line with his work, the other was not, and that with a limited edition she had to place those that were in her disposal very carefully. Bernard was also using his new connection, if somewhat tentatively. He wrote her about a "friend" who had some Rembrandt prints to sell; she asked for a list, but there is no record of the matter going any further.[54]

Although Belle and Bernard often wrote about art matters, both practical and aesthetic, her letters always began and ended, and often middled, with descriptions of her longing for him and the various ways it impacted her life. Throughout her work and play, she said, she constantly carried on a relationship with him in her head. He was so much a part of her emotional life that she thought about him and imagined him everywhere: a big roomy sofa in a guest suite on a weekend visit prompted her to imagine him there with her and describe in detail the Viennese negligee she was wearing "like a shower of falling rose leaves

. . . all covered with filigree lace." Writing to Bernard while waiting for a car to pick her up and take her to her next engagement made her fantasize about finding him hidden in a dark corner of the car so that she could cancel everything and bring him back home. "I shall shut you in my heart and lock the door and throw all the bolts—I kiss you until my breath leaves and my body melts into you."[55]

The would-be lovers exchanged gifts for Christmas: books for both. She gave him her copy of Dante's *Vita Nuova,* which they both loved and referred to, comparing their love for each other with Dante's for Beatrice. Bernard sent her one of his *Painters* series. Two of his books had been revised and reprinted in 1909: *The Florentine Painters of the Renaissance* and *The Central Italian Painters of the Renaissance.* Both eventually joined her 1894 copy of *Venetian Painters of the Renaissance* in her personal library.[56]

Her interest in Bernard started to affect her social interests as well. If any one mentioned knowing Mr. Berenson, she would inevitably "attack" them to talk about her new favorite subject: Bernard. In one case she allowed a near-stranger to come home with her after a dinner, just to hear him talk about his visit to I Tatti.[57]

But on a day-to-day basis it was still Morgan who shaped her emotional and professional life. At the end of the year Belle explained she was unhappy because a disagreement with J.P. had stretched into a weeklong coolness and silence. "[A]lthough I know I am in the right and Mr. Stick is not—still it makes me wretched." It helped little to know that J.P. was even more miserable and was taking it out on everyone else. "It amuses even while it depresses me. He is such an *enfant.*" Belle did not mention the subject of this disagreement. Now she was just counting the days until she could ship him off to Europe, such was her exhaustion: "although I really adore him, he absorbs my strength and vitality to an alarming degree."[58]

By January they had mended their quarrel, and J.P. began making demands on Belle's after-hours time again. She was regularly invited to join him and some of his family for quiet dinners and larger outings. She usually complained, but went to make him happy. Of a dinner with the Jack Morgans she said she was "bored to extinction" and joked

that the topic of conversation had been "the theology of sleep." Belle
loved Jack, she said, but his wife was "too much Boston" for her taste:
"her icy aura chills my very soul."[59]

Another command invitation from J.P. delayed Belle from meeting
Bernard's sister Senda, who was in New York for a visit. Instead, Belle
accompanied the Morgan family ("Ye Gods! How I hate them!") to dedicate a memorial building in Hartford for J.P.'s deceased father, Junius
Spencer Morgan. Even the most luxuriously commoded private rail car
in the country did not make her happy, but at least she was left alone
to write to Bernard. Morgan slept on the trip, probably "resolving some
new merger" even in that state, she surmised. Or he may have been
contemplating his mortality. For the next day she found herself clos-
eted with him for hours going over his new will. She was, he told her,
the only person except his lawyer who had read it, and she did not
divulge any tidbits, even to Bernard. Although this was not the final
version, she apparently knew that he was planning to leave her a sizable sum of money.[60] Soon it would be clear that some very constrain-
ing strings were attached.

Eventually Belle was able to see Senda, although not as much as she
had hoped. Senda was now a physical education instructor at Smith
College. Belle declared she loved her simply for reminding her of
Bernard, but also for her own personality and intelligence. In turn, Bernard's sister had only good things to say about Belle, who had arranged
opera parties, a lunch, and a dinner, showed her around the Library,
and extended other invitations, which Senda could not fit into her
schedule. Senda reported to her brother that she was quite charmed
by this "distinctly American" woman, "a most vivid and alert [and] at
the same time human person." Senda herself was charmed by Belle's
friendly spirit and thought she was "a stunning looking creature."[61]

Belle lost whatever attempt she made to finagle the five-month
travel vacation in the summer of 1910. But her social calendar was
extremely full that spring. Belle attended one of the social events of the
season: the marriage of Marjorie Gwynne Gould to Anthony J. Drexel
Jr. Crowds of curious onlookers, mostly women, crowded the streets
outside St. Bartholomew's Church despite the pouring rain. Police had

to contain the throngs of people, many of whom waited for hours to catch a glimpse of the bride as she arrived. Belle was one of the six hundred invited guests present at the ceremony. The *New York Times* took three paragraphs to describe Miss Gould's dress of white satin charmeuse and Dutch lace, with a veil of Brussels netting setting off her bouquet of orange blossoms and white roses. Belle reported only that the bride looked "pretty and happy."[62]

Newspaper accounts also recorded the most elite and noteworthy guests. Belle herself was never mentioned in these published accounts, but many among her and J.P.'s professional and social acquaintances were prominently listed. Clarence Mackay's daughter was a flower girl; Mackay had inherited the Postal Telegraph & Cable Corporation from his father and served with Morgan on a number of fine arts boards. One of the bridesmaids was Helen Morgan Hamilton, daughter of William Pierson and Juliet Morgan Hamilton and granddaughter of J. Pierpont Morgan. One of the ushers was William Rhinelander Stewart Jr., a cousin to the groom. William Rhinelander Stewart Sr. had been president of the Rhinelander Real Estate Company, which controlled large tracts of prime real estate in Manhattan. Stewart had also been a key figure in fund-raising for the Ulysses S. Grant Monument. Juliet Morgan Hamilton was also related to the Rhinelanders by marriage: her husband's sister Helen Maria Hamilton had married Philip Mercer Rhinelander, a cousin of William Rhinelander Stewart. The Philip M. Rhinelanders were also in attendance. This link between the Morgans, Rhinelanders, Hamiltons (who themselves were descendants of Alexander Hamilton), and Stewarts exemplifies the complicated threads of marriage, business, and philanthropic work that held the social elite together as a community and an economic and cultural power. Belle could never claim that kind of connection, and she certainly would never have mentioned her connection to many of these families through her father's work with the Grant Monument. By now she was at home with the people, places, and activities of this world.

The reception was catered by the Delmonicos, whose restaurant was a favorite stop for Belle's pre-opera dinners and post-opera suppers (which consisted largely of cigarettes and drinks). Other guests

included Mr. and Mrs. John D. Rockefeller Jr., Mrs. Reginald Vanderbilt, Mrs. Thomas Ryan, Mr. and Mrs. Philip Rhinelander, Charles
Lanier, Mr. and Mrs. Henry Clay Frick, Mr. and Mrs. Andrew Carnegie, and Francis W. Crowninshield. Any New Yorker who read the
papers would have recognized these names. Belle knew many of the
people behind the names, and obviously knew the Goulds well enough
to merit an invitation. The Fricks, Vanderbilts, Rockefellers, Laniers,
and Carnegies were famous for their money and business power. Belle
spent time regularly with Henry Clay Frick's art and particularly loved
his Rembrandt *Self Portrait*, which reminded her of Morgan. She considered Charles Lanier, a banker who was friends with Morgan, one of
her "octogenarian lovers" and called him her "darling old Mr. Lanier."[63]
Belle counted Thomas Ryan as a friend despite his "villainous 'business' standing" and admired his Italian art collection. Ryan was a
financier who gambled, mostly successfully, on a series of business
ventures with questionable tactics.[64] Frank Crowninshield was a magazine editor and Manhattan socialite who helped create the practice of
mingling of artists, musicians, and writers with the social elite. (Belle
seemed to tag along with the artists-musicians-writers at these events,
although she was not one of them either.) His interest in the blue
bloods of New York mirrored Belle's. Crowninshield appreciated the
"immense number of things which society, money, and position bring
in their train: painting, tapestries, rare books, smart dresses, dances,
gardens, country houses, correct cuisine, and pretty women." He was
known to stop by the Library for a chat with Belle.[65]

Belle dismissed this august gathering as "not especially good."[66]

Certainly the spectacle of riches that the Gould-Drexel wedding
represented no longer served, as it had a generation ago, simply to represent the promise of America. Observers noted that the crowds that
stood outside watching the guests and wedding party arrive like
celebrities walking the red carpet were not as big as they would have
been twenty years before.[67] Belle's dismissal of the guests may have
reflected this new social dissatisfaction with such ostentatious dis-
plays of wealth. But it was also yet another example of Belle's determination to disparage her social superiors and judge them below her in

moral character and taste. In her habitual dismissal of the rich as
"underbred," Belle's resentment of the "idle rich" revealed the limits of
her own rise in fortunes. No matter how far she reached in attaining
her own ambitions (and those of her mother for all of her children), she
would never have the leisure and luxuries their wealth could afford.
So, too, she may well have internalized her mother's community's
sense of superiority and even snobbery, reserving the right to make her
own standards of social superiority and good breeding.

Belle's presence at such events also stood in odd contrast to her
interest and growing immersion in bohemian and modernist circles in
New York. Nor were her tastes limited to the Renaissance styles and
medieval and classical arts that the Morgans, Fricks, Ryans, and their
crowd were collecting. She was a regular, for example, at the Photo-
Secessionists gallery. Under the combined energies of Edward Steichen and Alfred Stieglitz, the gallery, better known as "291" after its
address on Fifth Avenue, presented New Yorkers with exhibitions of
modern art. Both Steichen and Stieglitz were photographers committed to promoting photography as an art, but they introduced New Yorkers to many new painters and sculptors as well. It was here that Belle,
steeped in the classic arts, ancient cultures, European, Renaissance,
and medieval writings, encountered modern art and photography. The
gallery also became a gathering place of the political and cultural
avant-garde. Norman Hapgood, Max Eastman, Margaret Sanger,
Mabel Dodge, and Leo Stein all frequented it, as did Belle.[68]

Belle's two artistic worlds were not entirely separate. For example,
Steichen had done some portrait photographs of the Morgans when he
came to town that January. He wrote to "Miss Greene" to make
arrangements but noted he was "tempted to make it out in full, Belle
da Costa Greene, for it sounds great. I knew it had to be something
else besides just plain Miss Greene."[69] However, Belle's involvement
with 291 and the avant-garde artists who frequented it was usually outside of her work as a librarian and curator for medieval and Renaissance books and art.

In March 1910 Belle went to see an exhibit of Henri Matisse's work.
The artist's "most extraordinary" style confounded her, and she stayed

at the exhibit for two hours trying to comprehend it. But the "extravagant contortions" of Matisse's figures were completely new to her (and to most Americans). She left that first exposure to his work with only a "slight glimmer of understanding." Belle found the Rodin sketches and drawings more accessible but less fascinating. Nevertheless, she left with a photograph of Rodin's sculpture *Balzac*, a gift from the photographer, Stieglitz.[70]

In contrast, Bernard admired Matisse's work and had met the artist in the fall of 1908 during one of his solitary sojourns in Paris. He purchased *Trees near Melun,* and further shocked and antagonized many art critics when he began to support Matisse's artistry.[71] Eventually Belle would grapple more with the modern art scene, both through friendship with this circle of artists and aesthetically.

In fact, the socializing that Belle seemed to enjoy most during this period was with the musicians, artists, writers, publishers, actors, actresses, and singers who buzzed around the New York cultural and literary scene, whether they were avant-garde or more classically oriented. Many of the individuals Belle listed as in attendance at the various parties and dinners on her calendar were currently performing, working, writing, or exhibiting in one of the many concert halls, orchestras, operas, theaters, magazines, newspapers, or art galleries of New York and its environs. For example, Belle was a guest at several of the Long Island Gold Coast mansions, including the Roland Conklins' Rosemary Farm, with its outdoor amphitheater. Her description of one such visit shows how her connections to the wealthy class supported her interest in art, music, and writing—and vice versa. The crowd at the Conklins' that weekend included the English actor Johnston Forbes-Robertson, Olive Fremstad, a well-known Wagnerian soprano, Gertrude Atherton, a writer, and Nance O'Neill, a stage actress who was currently performing in *The Lily*, a play written and produced by impresario David Belasco. Creative performers were expected to provide a bit more structured entertainment than guests like Belle. That evening's performances included a bit of *Macbeth* and a "very bad young poet" reading his "very bad young poetry."[72]

Belle was meeting most of these people for the first time. A few would become friends. Gertrude Atherton, whom Belle described in this first encounter as "very amusing—very good looking and very risqué," was one. Atherton was a widow who defied the Victorian feminine ideal in her life and her novels. Belle continued to socialize with Gertrude for years, and at least one of Atherton's books, the 1922 *Sleeping Fires,* remained in Belle's possession until her death.[73]

Similarly, in the spring of 1910 Belle's Boston friend Alice Ditson was in New York preparing to depart for a summer abroad. Before leaving, Ditson arranged a lunch with Belle, French tenor Edmond Clément, Russian basso Reinhold von Wahrlich, and Madame Nazarian, an actress whom Belle had adored in *Elektra.*[74] At this lunch Belle listened transfixed as Nazarian described living in a lunatic asylum to prepare for a role. Belle had already admitted to falling in love briefly with Clément. Twelve years her senior, Clément was a handsome dark-haired man, the leading tenor at the Paris Opéra-Comique. Clément joined the Metropolitan Opera Company for the 1909–10 season, making his New York debut at the New Theater performing the lead in *Fra Diavolo.* But he left after one year, complaining about the predominance of Italian operas under Gatti-Casazza.[75]

Clément was only one of many men Belle admitted falling in love with. She also professed a "frenzied case" on Johnston Forbes-Robertson, the English actor whom she reported as unfortunately devoted to his wife, Gertrude. Forbes-Robertson gave her a photograph of a bust of his head, which she promised Bernard she would only adore for one day and one night, then quickly amended that to one day only, as the nights were reserved for Bernard.[76] Other men were memorable only for their physical beauty and charm. On a weekend at Newport and Bar Harbor, Belle met two enchanting men. One was coming to the Library, and she could not recall his "most unpronounceable name," only that he was an Austrian count. She did remember that the count was gorgeous, "a living incarnation of the sun god," and wondered whether she would like him as much without the "glittering background of Newport." Another young boy, who was "cut out by nature as a heart breaker," tried to explain his "rabid" interest in Christian Science to her. Belle was not at all interested, but was quite happy to sit, smoke a cigarette, and look at his handsome face while the youth talked on and on.[77]

Obviously, Belle did not hide the fact of her crushes and associations with other men from Bernard, but she did shift her message on how he figured in her local pantheon of intrigues. Most often, she told him that these trifles did not diminish her love for him. "When anyone seeks to assure me of his or her affection for me I am so astonished that they do not know that I belong to you—and I laugh and play and flirt with them to while away the dull hours till your return."[78] Later she mused that her love for him made loving someone else the same way impossible. She had become almost cruel to those who tried. And in a rare moment of looking into the future of this passion for a married man, she considered that even her own marriage would not change her love for Bernard, if, that is, she was ever "so foolish or blind as to marry." Just then her freedom was her priority. Still, being an "old maid" at the age of thirty or forty did not appeal.[79] Belle was then only three months shy of thirty.

On the other hand, Belle was not always above throwing the specter of other men in Bernard's face, especially when she was upset with him. For example, when he announced that he would not be returning to the United States in 1910, she suddenly began to wonder what it would be like to spend a night with him. At first she simply tried to imagine "how it would really feel to go to sleep in your arms and wake in your arms!" If she could be with him in Italy, they would go through Rome, Venice, and Siena hand in hand, seeing the sights by day and making love all night. Then she moved on to wonder how she had kept herself from succumbing to him while he was there: "was I wise or foolish I wonder." She was still sure that he would be the man "to teach me all and I am glad glad glad that no other man has shown me the way." But, and this must have thrown Bernard into despair, she said she was "so infernally human" that she often doubted she could avoid falling into a sexual relationship with another man, especially if it would be years before she was with Bernard again.[80]

By April she had given up on going to Europe at all in 1910. Never was her so-called poverty, relative to the wealthy and the just well off, more painfully apparent to her than in the spring. With each boat departure another group of her friends left New York shores for the summer season in Europe. (Morgan had also departed on his annual trip, but that was an event that offered Belle some relief from his constant demands.) Belle, who had spent only a scant few weeks across the Atlantic, yearned to get away for a year or two of study and travel. But she had become so indispensable to Morgan by this time that she could not leave and had to stay behind every year and wish her friends farewell. When he was there, he demanded her presence and attention; when he was on his own annual sojourn, she was needed to attend to the Library. Of course, Belle would probably not have had the opportunity for European travel without her job at the Morgan Library. But how different the ability to travel seemed now that she had tasted Europe, and now that she was surrounded by Europeans and Americans who routinely crossed the Atlantic every year. "I am so envious of the masses that 'run over' to Europe every season," she raged, furious that they were indifferent or ignorant to its sights and culture, while she, who burned to see everything, could not.[81]

Instead, she said goodbye to Morgan and her friends, as usual, and leased a "shanty-bungalow" in Tuckahoe, New York, twenty miles north of Manhattan in Westchester County. She installed her family in this summer home in a wooded area by Tuckahoe Lake to escape the summer heat of the city. Most New Yorkers could never have afforded such a luxury, but it was common for middle-class men to send their wives and children away for the summer, remaining behind to work and spending some weekends with their family on the shore or in the country. And Belle's "hole in the ground" could not have been too small: it would sleep herself, her mother, three sisters, and two guests.[82] Throughout the summer Belle commuted by train back into the city, often bringing a few men back with her in the evening for dinner with the family. This provided entertainment for her sisters and gave her the opportunity to get to know the men better in the quieter environs of a family meal.

At the Library without her boss, Belle managed to squeeze socializing into her busy workdays. In fact, socializing was expected as part of her job. She usually lunched one on one or with a small group. And her lunch hour might extend into the afternoon if she squeezed in a visit to a dealer or gallery to see the latest exhibits, new arrivals from Europe, or pieces held aside for her private perusal. Her lunch or dinner partners were often men, especially in the summers, when professional men seemed to be the only other people left in Manhattan.

Quite often Belle's companions were publishers of books, magazines, and newspapers. Mitchell Kennerly, who had owned his own publishing house, was a regular lunch partner. Richard Watson Gilder had been one as well. Editor in chief of the *Century Monthly Magazine*, Gilder was known for hosting the gatherings of artists, writers, and musicians with whom Belle loved to socialize. When he died in late 1909 Belle mourned the loss of a very good friend.[83] Belle also often dined alone with Jack Cosgrove, editor of *Everybody's Magazine*, "simply because it is the only chance we have to really talk and get to know each other." He was her complete opposite "in almost every way— quiet, sane, socialist, working living and giving all that he has to the peepul (who do not interest me in the slightest) determined to right the peepul's wrongs and most determined of all to convert me to his way of thinking." He was her "Rock of Gibraltar." And he, like Gilder, had another quality Belle adored: the ability to find interesting people to come to his parties.[84]

Belle also hosted dinners and teas, inviting the same eclectic mixture of artists, movers and shakers, political ideologues, and interesting socialites who attended many of the events she attended. Few such invitations survive, but one invites Mary Fanton Roberts, a writer, critic, and fellow lover of art and artists, to a tea at Belle's home with Frances Alda Gatti-Casazza, the wife of Metropolitan Opera director Giulio Gatti-Casazza, and several other operatic lights. Fanton and Belle were also both friends of the famous dancer Isadora Duncan. Duncan was a self-defined feminist who defied social conventions in her life as she defied dance conventions on stage. She believed that women had the right to have children whether married or not, without shame or social censure. Duncan took pride in her children, but could not avoid the cultural stigma of being an unwed mother, especially when she toured in the United States.[85]

In cultivating a friendship with Duncan, Belle put her passion for

the arts and interesting people over any concerns for propriety. Similarly, Belle regularly stepped over social norms in her friendships with
men by seeing them without other company. She was as likely to dine
alone with them as with a larger party, and—following the custom of
the time—she allowed and expected them to pay for her meals and
perhaps purchase small gifts as well.

At times Belle seemed to prefer the company of men: she confessed
a "weariness" of women's luncheons and to generally not being "'long'
on wives," a rather stupid trait, she admitted. But she did have several
good female friends and flirted with and enjoyed female artists, writers, and other interesting women. In fact, a few rumors later circulated
that Belle used her open flirtations with men to mask her affairs with
women.[86] Little archival evidence survives from this period to support
this suggestion, but it should be noted that most of the archival evidence takes the form of letters to her decidedly heterosexual would-
be lover.

Bernard was never happy to hear about Belle's flirtations, whatever
the gender of her interest, and it is uncertain what his response would
have been had he discovered that Belle was bisexual. He had had
ample social experience with homosexual men. He once wrote a friend
that while he could not understand why a man would "leave women,"
he did not object to homosexuality per say. He did, however, have some
uncomfortable memories of gay men pursuing him when he was
young, "first erotically and then for many years vindictively."[87] What he
thought of gay women was not yet clear, and his response to any hints
or evidence of Belle's flirtations or even relationships with women is
even harder to gauge. In addition, the language and social conventions
of the time allowed both men and women to express friendship and
platonic love in terms that sound romantic and even sexual to modern ears.

Still, women seemed as fascinated by Belle as men were, even if the
feeling was not mutual. Lillie Lawlor, a tall, blond female singer,
wanted Belle to "keep house with her" in Paris. Belle was tempted, at
least in her fantasies. She never said much about Lawlor, except that
she was a companion to Arabella Huntington (widow of the railroad

tycoon Collis Potter Huntington) and that she had "the most extraordinary faculty of attracting weird men and isms to her." Lawlor later broke with Huntington and went into art dealing.[88]

Despite her stated preference for socializing with men, Belle had many close female friends. In the early 1910s Ethel Grant was a particular favorite. Under the name Ethel Watts Mumford, Grant was a noted playwright, poet, novelist, and wit. Belle pronounced her "a terror" whom she loved, part of a "wicked crowd" with whom Belle spent many happy hours.[89] Born Ethel Watts, Ethel was divorced from her first husband, George Dana Mumford, with whom she had had a son. Ethel's second husband, Peter Geddes Grant, was also part of their group. Better known as P.G., he was a partner in the investment brokerage firm Leavitt & Grant. The Grants had a large home in the fashionable Sands Point neighborhood on Long Island. Some among their society neighbors may have shunned them for her dissolved marriage, but divorce was losing its aura of scandal, perhaps especially in this upper crust of society.[90]

In the late spring of 1910 Belle realized it had been a year since Bernard had left New York. It seemed, she said, perfectly incredible. "How have I managed to live through it, I wonder? It makes me despise the human frame which persists in going on and on and on when one's real life has stopped—is dead." Ignoring his previous decision not to travel across the Atlantic that year, she began begging him to visit. If he really loved her, she pleaded, he would come.[91]

But already there was some friction between them. Bernard often voiced objections to Belle's choice of friends. For example, the Truesdales (who had now left for Egypt without Belle) stood low in his esteem, especially the wife: he seemed to think her unintelligent and without purpose. Belle was not moved by Bernard's negative opinion of her friend: "She is restful and lovable and I don't ask more of her." Mindless amusement was not below her. When there was no opera or party to divert them, Belle and her friends could find amusement at a circus, followed by a late supper at Delmonico's.[92]

In this context, in these crowds, Belle could relax and be herself. This part of the cultural movement derisively called the bohemians, cultivated values and beliefs about sexuality and relationships that set them apart from the American elite. While the elites hid their improprieties behind a façade of respectability when at all possible, bohemians wanted to change cultural restrictions and flaunted their affairs, sexual explorations, and experiments in dress, living, writing, and art.[93] Belle was not of the elite, but worked in a position where she had to conform to their code of respectable demeanor, if not always respectable behavior. Still, she delighted in spending time in Greenwich Village and other communities where people were transgressing social boundaries much more egregiously and openly than she did, or could. There was a danger in doing so because association implied influence, and clearly there was some influence, but Belle maintained her own standards of propriety, although she was willing to relax them at times for shock value.

At other times, however, she was reminded again of the necessity of maintaining more control over her words and behavior. When she went to a dance with a bishop's wife, for example, she had really had to be careful to "mind my p's and q's—which is difficult for me."[94] When she found herself staying at the College Club of Boston, a women's club and residence founded in 1890, she was confronted with a very traditional and, in her eyes, laughable set of values and expectations. She first somehow shocked the desk clerk by asking for a room with an attached bath and sitting room, then drew the outraged attention of the "managress" by requesting her breakfast in bed. Such luxuries were apparently inappropriate at this club. Then, in the evening, Belle entertained two male friends in the club's parlor under the disapproving eyes of the other female guests. Once those women retired "to their Virgin Couches," Belle and her friends began to relax and really talk, only to be frostily informed that gentlemen had to leave by ten. The men complied, one walking on his hands to the door. Belle, now considered beyond the pale, was treated for the rest of her stay like a "Chinese or Abyssinian Princess" traveling incognito.[95] With this description she meant to emphasize the cultural gap between her crowd and these Bostonian women. Yet it was no accident that she chose two nonwhite ethnicities to describe her own outsider status.

In fact, Belle often referred to herself racially, ethnically, and spiritually as other than white. When her friends the Truesdales came back after their two months in Egypt, Belle was completely overcome with envy. Although she yearned to travel almost anywhere, Egypt had captured her imagination in a particularly personal way: "I know that I was an Egyptian princess . . . in one of my former incarnations. I am simply soaked with the love of it [Egypt], the joy and despair of it and the ever increasing mystery of it. Someday I am going there to live and I doubt if I shall ever come back."[96] A belief in past lives was not uncommon in the early twentieth century. And certainly former lives as exotic princesses were popular among white women. However, Belle's imagined and actual connection with Egypt would continue. And in the context of her family history and her continued attempts to play with, cover, reveal, and question her own racial identity, these comments are quite poignant.

Egypt was not considered to be culturally or ethnically a part of Africa, although it certainly was geographically. At the time, however, the accomplishments of ancient Egyptian culture and its high civilization contradicted European and white American perceptions of Africa as a continent of primitive savages. Wherever evidence of African civilizations, architecture, technological development, or culture was found, Europeans trying to maintain colonial control found ways to deny that those achievements had anything to do with *black* Africans. At the same time, African Americans identified Egypt as African, and as an example of the ability of Africans to build a civilization to rival those of Europe and the United States.

Belle's interest in Egyptian culture and identity may have been complicated by the fact that she was either unable or unwilling to embrace a totally white identity. Belle actively participated in circulating the rumors that led Isabella Gardner to dismiss her as a "half-breed." There are several accounts of Belle's making explicit references to having black ancestry. One Berenson biographer, who was able to speak to dozens of people in the 1960s who had known Belle well, recounted one such story. On her way to dinner with a friend, Belle noticed that her lace sleeve was torn, revealing her arm. "Belle Greene grinned and said, 'The nigger blood shows through, doesn't it?'" Without knowing the origin, source, or date of this supposed comment, it is dangerous to read too much into it.[97] For example, did Belle use that exact wording? She certainly was willing to use other racial and ethnic slurs— "chink," "coolie," "Jap," and "dago" are all sprinkled through her personal correspondence—although if she really didn't like an individual she was likely to find a much more creative and specific insult. If the incident described above did happen, Belle's wording may have been altered by memory or retelling. She may have said something like "The black blood really shows."

Or not. She was known for using language to shock and outrage, and she did use "nigger" a few times in her letters. Once she was recommending a popular novel by one of her favorite authors, Ronald Firbank, titled *Prancing Nigger*. The other times it was a synonym for "African" and used to describe art, as when she mentioned reading "a new book on 'Nigger' art." (Berenson occasionally used the same phrase to describe African art.)[98]

Using a term whose history is so heavy with violence and pain that it is now referred to in polite circles as "the 'n' word" may have been part of the process of distancing herself from other or real African Americans (or, in the latter case, Africans). People who consciously hid their black ancestry sometimes used racist language to further distance themselves from the part of their ancestry that they were denying.[99] Although the term was a common one in casual usage among whites, even in 1910 it was understood that it should not be used in certain circles. Adopting the language of racism was one way for Belle to assimilate into American whiteness, by assimilating into white American racism.

The "blood shows through" quotation was also a challenge. What was her companion expected to reply? Certainly not "Yes." If Belle's question, then, required a negative answer, its apparent confession of black ancestry also served to contradict such rumors. *If she really was black, she wouldn't use such language, she wouldn't draw attention to herself,* we can imagine her unnamed companion thinking. Both in her identification with Egypt and her reported reference to her own skin

as showing her black ancestry, Belle both claimed and denied a connection to that part of her background. The racial ambiguity of Egyp-
tians may have appealed to Belle as well.

It is also significant that Belle (like many other American women)
visualized herself not just as an Egyptian or an Oriental woman but as
a princess or other royalty. This elevation represented a much more
universal desire to be relieved of the burdens of work and her constant
awareness of the large economic gap between her and many of the
people with whom she socialized. Belle may have been able to talk,
dress, and socialize like them, but she was clearly differentiated from
them in her work. Her job had to come first, and her boss's desires or
the demands of the Library often overrode her own plans and priorities.

For example, that spring Belle had been looking forward to a vacation in Hot Springs, Virginia. But the day before she was supposed
to leave, an English scholar appeared with his new wife. Dr. Johns,
an Anglican minister and master of Queen's College, Cambridge,
required her assistance in his work cataloguing the Morgan collection
of Babylonian and Assyrian tablets, and the Johnses needed entertaining. In both attempts Belle was struggling. She knew little about the
tablets and less about how to entertain a sixty-year-old Cambridge
provost and his new wife, an Egyptologist. Clearly Belle's own "giddy
and frivolous crowd" would not do, so she began calling on "some
learned and scientific people" for meals.

Harder still was finding common ground with the new Mrs. Johns,
despite their shared interest in Egypt. The Englishwoman's appearance and dress appalled Belle as much as Belle's shocked her. By this
time Belle had definitely acquired her reputation for dressing stylishly
and extravagantly, more in the manner of an upper-class lady than the
stereotype of a bookish, spinster librarian. Early biographers describe
her wearing Renaissance gowns, draped with jewels and waving silk
handkerchiefs around as she talked.[100] This is likely an exaggeration,
at least in her work clothing. Belle herself complained the next year
when a temporary maid began insisting she wear her "ball-dresses" to
the Library. And the narrow stairs and high walkways required more
practical attire. Belle also suspected that this unsatisfactory maid bor-

rowed her underclothes and silk stockings but sighed, "[A]s I never know how many things I have there is no way of telling."[101]

Underclothes were much more substantial at this time (1920s dresses were sometimes perceived as underwear by shocked elders), and Belle's maid was apparently not the only woman interested in her slips, chemises, corsets, stockings, and garters. When the Johnses dined at the Greene home, Mrs. Johns inspected Belle's wardrobe and seemed particularly interested in her undergarments. "I could see doubts of my respectability creeping over her countenance so plainly that I grew reckless and showed her some really 'loose' ones. Our relations have been a bit strained ever since much to my relief." Belle described the situation as a standoff of racial temperaments. She wished that English people could be "more flexible and understandable" since they also were "so innately worthy and interesting." But she feared that her own nature would make her do something to put her "forever beyond the pale," and chafed under the strain to overcome her "all too-Latin soul."[102]

It was quite common at the turn of the century to ascribe, as Belle did, innate cultural, intellectual, and temperamental differences to one's racial ancestry. And "race" at this time included distinctions between European groups that we now call national or ethnic. Of course, the difference between Negro and Caucasian was, under this ideology, seen as the widest of all. But Belle was not alone in considering "Latin" and "mulatto" to be analogous if not overlapping categories of identity.

Relations with Dr. Johns had been deteriorating anyway. He apparently wanted more money for his work on the catalogue and ultimately resigned as editor. It is unlikely that Mrs. Johns's inspection of Belle's wardrobe played any role in this Library drama, but it could not have helped matters much.[103]

Not all scholarly visits were so fraught with cultural tensions. Since she couldn't leave New York, Belle's best opportunity to learn was through her work at the Library. Scholars and experts came to her there, mostly welcomed, and she soaked up everything they could tell her. Alfred Pollard of the British Museum had visited the preceding

summer, much to her joy. He was one of the top experts on incunabula, the early printed books that Belle loved. They worked together
while he was in New York, and she wanted to study with him in London, if she could. She loved scholars mostly for the knowledge that
they represented. "Beloved," she wrote to Bernard, "it frightens me
when I stop long enough and think of how much I have to learn."[104] To
fill the gap, she continued her own education, taking a course in Italian and one in bookbinding. Her French lessons had progressed to the
point where she was not only reading Anatole France's *Jeanne d'Arc* in
French but also writing essays and criticism on it. In typical schoolgirl
slang she complained that her professor was "hard as nails."[105]

But she was learning, and her hard work was paying off. More and
more, her professional correspondence included evidence of her rising
authority in her field. She continued to make purchases and was
increasingly independent in selecting items and negotiating prices.
"This morning," she boasted, "I spent some of my bosses' hard earned
money in buying part of the original manuscript of Poe's *Raven* and a
beautiful Francis I in bindery." She claimed partial responsibility for
George Blumenthal's appointment as a trustee of the Metropolitan
Museum and was working to have Archer Huntington made one as
well.[106] George Blumenthal and his wife, Florence (Florrie), would
become good friends: both were interested in art and collecting. When
she had received a program for the Exhibition of Historical Writing
held at Columbia University, she was outraged at the quality of the list
and wrote to Professor Simkovitch to complain about "this bibliographical outrage," which she protested "as a friend of Columbia and
fellow worker of yours."[107] Asserting her right to speak to a leading
scholar as a peer marked a clear change from the tone of her professional correspondence in the first years of her work. (This was the
same man who had jokingly worried that she would have no time for
the likes of him after her triumphant return from London.)

Similarly, she began to join, and be invited to join, professional
organizations like the Bibliographical Society of London, whereas
before she had relied on Mr. Morgan's membership, through which
she had access to newsletters and publications.[108] And scholars began

to turn to her for advice. Albert T. Clay was a leading Assyriologist whose chaired position, the Laffan Professorship in Assyriology at Yale University, had been created for him and endowed by Morgan. When Professor Clay had a problem with Dr. Johns, he first sent a draft of his letter of complaint to the colleague to Belle, asking her to "add, change or cut out as you see fit. . . . Frankly advise me in the matter." Since Clay had essentially replaced Dr. Johns in assisting Morgan, it was reasonable for him to involve the Morgan Library. But he turned only to Belle, not to Mr. Morgan, for advice and approval on his intervention.[109] And a new Ph.D. who wished to work as a librarian of rare books wrote to the un-degreed Miss Greene to ask whether she knew of any library positions or wealthy collectors who might hire him.[110]

Belle had also worked out her relationship with all the major dealers who regularly approached her in seeking to sell to Mr. Morgan. She was particularly fond of Bernard Quaritch, whom she trusted (with good reason) not to inflate his prices for her. That year Quaritch noticed that a fifteenth-century Venetian early print Bible had sold at auction for almost £99.15. He immediately wrote Belle, warning that whoever had purchased it would probably offer it to Morgan and that he had another copy of the same book, which he offered her for £18. She bought it immediately for the £18. Both felt angered at the "fictitious prices" such books sometimes reached.[111]

Belle was also particularly loyal to the Seligmanns, and asked Bernard to be friendly when he saw Jacques Seligmann, because he and his partner Emile Rey were "very useful to me." But, still unaware of B.B.'s connection with the Duveens, she told him she disliked and distrusted Joseph Duveen "intensely and thoroughly." She knew that Duveen controlled Benjamin Altman, another collector with whom she wanted Bernard to work.

Belle had no high regard for Altman either; he had earned her scorn by always trying to bring her gifts, which she in turn always refused. She also scoffed at "how much snubbing he will smile under—the burden of his race I suppose." Altman was Jewish. Belle was consistent in referring to individuals' characteristics as ingrained in their ethnic heritage. While she did not share the strong anti-Semitic views that many

Gentile Americans held at that time, she did accept that there were Jewish characteristics—and German ones, English, etc.[112] Despite her feelings about Altman, and her distaste for dealing in general, Belle was eager to provide business opportunities for her new love.

With all of her activities, Belle's writing pace slowed until a month gap in May 1910 prompted an unexpected and extremely jolting letter from Mary Berenson, telling her that "B.B.," as both women and most of his friends fondly referred to him, was sick and unhappy. That was putting it mildly. Belle seems to have had absolutely no idea of the turmoil and torment her year of passionate love letters and a busy life had brought to Bernard. The year had been a lucrative one for the Berensons, but extremely trying as well. Their relationship was buckling. The depth of Bernard's attachment to Belle was probably the most obvious factor, but there were many others as well: Mary's friendships with other men, Bernard's moral quandary over the Duveen deal, the inevitable complications with the seemingly endless renovations. B.B.'s chronic dyspepsia had become worse, confining him to his bed for much of the fall and early winter of 1909. In early 1910 he recovered enough to travel to London briefly for business. But by spring, his hysterical (sometimes violent) rages had begun to result in fainting spells. Finally, his doctor recommended psychiatric counseling.[113]

Mary blamed Bell's latest monthlong "silence" for her husband's downward spiral. Despite her very well-founded fear that this woman might be the inadvertent cause of the destruction of her marriage and her husband's health, she hoped that Belle's attention in the short term would help him rally. Belle wrote to Bernard immediately to assure him that her love had not changed or lessened "one iota." She was silent for a month only because her usual whirl of activity had become a "maelstrom of business, society and emotion." But Mary's letter had stopped her cold, and she immediately found the time to write to Bernard, pouring out her love, her frustration at their distance, her desire for him, her feeling that the people she was with were only seeing her physical self. The real one was "far far away in a little town of Italy."[114]

And here she was brought up short again, this time literally interrupted in her writing by a cable from Bernard, saying he was ill but "progressing satisfactorily." Belle demanded details and swore that had she known, she would have come to him, ignoring everything that kept her there—"my duty, my pleasure, and my poverty"—to care for him.

> We can't go on this way much longer—the thought of you is an obsession with me—and I am so afraid of its becoming in some way unnatural, abnormal and so, unlasting— whereas if we could be with each other for even a little while it would be enough to tide us over another few years—[115]

And so Belle determined to find a way to get to Europe sometime that year. She would start to work on Morgan as soon as he returned from Europe, she promised. In the meanwhile, as she had before, she sent B.B. a photograph of a portrait of her.

In fact, over that year, Belle sat for several artists for portraits and sketches. In February 1910 she described an unnamed man painting her portrait in an old Spanish shawl that Morgan had given her. By July, Belle was also sitting for a portrait with Carlos Baca-Flor, an artist who had painted J.P. and Jack Morgan, and Harry Walters. This may have been the portrait she referred to earlier in the year, but she describes her dress very differently: an arrangement of "Egyptian blue gauze" that Baca-Flor had designed himself.[116] What Belle sent Bernard to console him was a photograph of a miniature portrait that the Boston artist Laura Coombs Hills had begun that April. Although Hills initially wanted Belle to pose sitting on a leopard skin, which Belle thought was a horrible idea, the final pose was standing wrapped in a "wonderful glowing Saffron" veil. The vivid sunset colors of pink-salmon and orange were the "whole value" of the portrait, Belle thought. She regretted that she could send Bernard only a black-and-white photograph of it. She wanted him to see it because it portrayed a Belle he did not yet know, but would some day: "the Belle of one of my former incarnations 'Egyptienne.'" "I think you will like her," she noted, but if he didn't, he should tear it up. Bernard kept it whole.[117]

Belle's mother reportedly had a very different view of what "incarnation" the portrait evoked. The story is told that she said it made Belle look like a hussy. Two years later, when the artist asked to borrow the miniature for an exhibition of her work, Belle refused. "It seems to occasion so much comment, being a bit unusual, and I fear is not always appreciated."[118]

The Egyptian self that Belle saw in this portrait may reside in the nature of the dress, which is very sheer, even translucent, and brightly colored. It is draped over one shoulder and around the other, something like a sari. The line of a pale undergarment is visible across her chest, and her right hand is clearly visible under a layer of the pink-orange wrap. Or the "Egyptienne" may be in her face, painted with the full features that she was often described as having, but which did not always appear in her portraits and photographs. Her eyebrows are thick and dark, her eyes look black, her nose is delicately rounded, and her lips closed in a slight pout. Her hair is piled up in a mass on top of her head, with a colorful scarf holding it back from her face. If her skin were darker, she would indeed look the part. But her face is a creamy ivory with pink overtones reflecting the colors of her dress.

Belle continued to send Bernard images of herself. A month after the Hills portrait, it was a photo in which she said she looked sad because she was thinking about B.B. when it was taken.[119] In fact, Belle sat for more than half a dozen photographers and artists over the next two years. She sent copies of almost all of them to Bernard in an attempt to bring her physical presence to him, and find a pose that captured his idealized memory of her. But getting there in person was a far greater challenge.

In June, J. P. Morgan returned to New York renewed in health and spirit. Belle was so happy to see him that she allowed him to kiss her in greeting, which crossed "all my principles and established an unfortunate precedent." But Morgan apologized and pointed out he was old enough to be her grandfather—age adjustment or not, this was true, although Belle was not much younger than his youngest daughter. But Belle forgave him. She was, after all, "very fond" of her boss. And he had brought more treasures. Three illuminated manuscripts were articularly wonderful: a Greek *Aesop's Fables* from the early tenth century, a Bible from the same period with three hundred miniature illustrations, and a sixteenth-century manuscript that she had to wait to see.[120]

Now that the Big Chief was back, Belle's life shifted again to focus on his demands. Instead of going to Newport, as she had planned, for the Fourth of July, perhaps to the Vanderbilts' as she had the year before, she was called into the library to keep J.P. company, and there they sat alone together until he invited himself to dinner at her summer house in Tuckahoe. He was not the only guest, but he seemed bored in the company of her sisters and mother. Belle was not concerned.[121]

More annoying was the return of "the harem" in J.P.'s wake. Much as Belle loved her Boss, she did not understand all the "damned fools" who lost their heads and their dignity in their efforts to become yet another one of his mistresses. "They flock to him all day long in rapid and sickening succession, each one pluming her feathers and thinking she is the hen pheasant. . . . All fat—all pouty—all neurotic—Bah!"[122] The one exception was Lady Johnstone, whom Belle found "extremely attractive." When Bernard pressed her for details, she promised to provide them in person, but wrote only that Johnston was "neither fat (which I loathe) nor a fossil." Belle herself was quite smug that she had lost over twenty pounds since Bernard's departure, and now weighed in at a most satisfying 105 pounds.[123]

Still, Belle had a hard time respecting any woman who would willingly be a part of a harem. So disgusted was she by this "discouraging aspect" of Morgan that at times

> all the wonderful points seem to drop away and this one festering sore seems to fill one's vision—then one swears to pack one's trunk and be up and off—which of course one never does. Instead you give him your brain, blood, heart and soul and life, all that one has to give to such an extent that the minute he leaves one collapses like a house built of cards. Isn't it amusing and isn't it ridiculous![124]

She, too, was caught by some combination of Morgan's power and magnetism, her feeling that she had a special connection to the great man, and, of course, the tremendous value of her position and his protection.

Nevertheless, Belle was able to convince Morgan that she needed to go to Europe again that year. She had some important business in London that she did not want people to know she was pursuing "until it is quite finished and I have won the battle." She would be there in August but then would be free to spend several weeks in Italy—alone. She knew Bernard had made plans already for August and September, but she hoped he could change them. The thought of seeing him again was "almost too much." She had to see whether their love could "stand the test of flesh and blood contact."[125]

Bernard could change his plans, and he did, with Mary's encouragement. "People one cares for are worth upsetting one's plans for," she encouraged, adding less supportively, "Thee is growing old and probably this is the last. Make the most of it, if thee can without doing her harm."[126]

Make the most of it, they would. After almost a year and a half, Belle would see Bernard again. And, after nearly two years, she would finally return to Europe and make her first trip to Italy, having time to travel for her own pleasure this time. How could it be anything but wonderful?

BELLA ITALIA

I feel so near you tonight darling—the miles and miles and the horrid ocean seem to be utterly eliminated and I am with you— . . . sitting beside you on the sofa at Claridges while you read me the book of French verse—walking about the narrow streets of Urbino, holding your hand and my breath as I sit beside you in the Choir stalls at Arrezzo.

—Belle Greene, 1911[1]

I am trying, tonight, to "analyze" my antagonism—I know that its roots lie in the remembering of the really innocent (that sounds funny, but its true) utter, and world-excluding worship I once gave you. Certainly I can never give anything approaching it to anyone else—for the simple reason that it is no longer existent. In fact, I think it really ceased to exist when I left you to go to London— Only I did not know it then—or for a long time afterwards.

—Belle Greene, 1921[2]

IN AUGUST 1910 Belle finally went to Europe again. This time she
had two months to spend overseas; this time her mother stayed home.
And, although she had work to do in London for the Library, this time
she had another agenda. She wanted to reunite with Bernard, but she
was also dying for the chance to explore Europe. Armed with a stack
of introductions and calling cards identifying her as Morgan's librarian,
Belle candidly looked forward to open doors, private tours, and personal tutelage. But she also secretly planned to have Bernard at her
side providing many of those services, while commencing the love
affair she had been dreaming about for over a year.

Bernard's role in Belle's plans, however, had to be hidden from Morgan and from prying eyes in order to protect her position and her reputation. Morgan was under the impression that she would be traveling
alone. He would have known, from his own annual stays in London
and Italy, the art education that could be attained only by visiting European museums and collections. Belle was taking a social risk traveling
without her mother, indeed without any chaperone, save her maid,
Marie, who would leave her for much of the trip to visit her own family in Switzerland. Sex brought its own hazards. Did Belle worry about
pregnancy? Did she know how to protect herself against sexually transmitted diseases? Nothing in her prior communications suggests that
she did, but these were precisely the kinds of subjects that a
respectable woman never discussed. Of course, respectability was no
longer Belle's primary goal. She was determined to lose that part of her
innocence.

Belle was not the only American taking advantage of a foreign context to transgress the social rules of her home. Traveling without a
chaperone was acceptable in some circumstances. Having business to
attend to would help. While in London, Belle would be surrounded by
enough familiar business and social acquaintances not to fall under
suspicion. As a businesswoman with a good reputation and Morgan's
name to protect her, she could now afford to bend a few rules. Her
plans to have an affair with Bernard, however, went much further
beyond the limits of appropriate behavior. Nor could she completely

escape the networks and ties that maintained American social standards. New York society, at least the portion of it that was transatlantic,
replicated itself to a great extent in London and Paris during the summer months. Belle was bringing some of home along with her.

This was apparent even on the weeklong sea journey. In that moving hotel and seaside resort, Belle had time to relax and socialize, no
doubt basking in the microcosm of society that was onboard with her.
Some of her fellow travelers in first class suffered from seasickness and
disembarked in Europe miserable and exhausted. Not Belle. She
arrived in a bustle of excitement and was so overwhelmed by her surroundings that she could not even focus on Bernard, who met her in
London—eventually. But not even their miscommunication about
which train she would take and where they would meet could dampen
her exhilaration at finally returning to Europe. On the way to the hotel
together, she was a flurry of chatter and excitement, craning her neck
to look at all the sights. Bernard declared her "the most incredible combination of sheer childishness, heydenishness, gayety girl, with sincer-
ity, cynicism and sentiment." Those first few hours were a blur, during
which they managed to check Belle and her maid, Marie, into her suite
at Claridges and find dinner.[3]

London was bustling, and both Miss Greene and Mr. Berenson
had business to take care of. The next day Mary arrived, on her way to
Oxford. Belle had a dinner engagement, and the Berensons dined
together while Bernard poured out his impressions of Belle. They had
had such little time together in New York, and more than a year had
passed since then. It was as if he were meeting her for the first time.
He was ecstatic and appalled. She seemed to live a wild life in New
York, he told Mary; she drank, she smoked, she caroused. He disapproved of most of her friends, of her language ("chorus girl and bowery"), of her manner. He could not figure her out. Her vitality and talent, her youth and uncouthness, both enticed him and disturbed him.[4]

At some point Mary joined the couple. Belle had met Mary before,
of course, but this was the first time the women were meeting now that
Belle and Bernard's romance was in the open. For Mary it provided
another opportunity to size up the woman who had caused so much

havoc in her husband's and her emotional life. Mary was probably the only one remembering how bad things had gotten over the past year, how sick Bernard had become in his obsession with Belle's memory. She recorded two points about this meeting: that Bernard had talked a great deal about himself and that Belle had disliked it. When Bernard got on the subject of himself, his work and his emotional state, Belle's astonished reply was, "You do think a lot about your precious happiness!"[5] Mary reminded her husband several times about the exchange and warned him not to boast of his talents, but to let Belle and others discover his assets for themselves. Of Belle herself Mary expressed only optimism and praise, filtered for her husband's eyes:

> I was really quite charmed by Miss Greene, and wish this
> all might be the beginning of a permanent relation, such as
> our middle-aged, bourgeois, romantic souls sigh for. Men
> are supposed to like Episodes, but I do not think thee is that
> kind, and I hope thee will make this into something lasting
> and agreeable. I shall certainly help thee . . . , for I love her
> youth, her élan, her intelligence. I find her remarkably
> attractive too.[6]

The feeling, if it was sincere on Mary's part, was mutual.

Belle had long worried that Mary thought her a silly and inconsequential person.[7] She had already confided to Bernard that the only reason she had not yet thrown herself at Mary was that she suspected "if I have the chance to learn to know her at all I should like her much better and longer than you."[8] Now she seemed desperately to want Mary's approval but did not know how to proceed. In fact, much to Bernard's and Mary's amusement, Belle was so disinclined to speak about Mary for the next few weeks that the Berensons dubbed it her "Taboo." Her later remarks about Mary, however, demonstrate a strong magnetism, genuine admiration, and a desire on Belle's part for a friendship. Mary was, in many ways, living the life Belle yearned for in her moments of dissatisfaction. Of course, she was married to the man Belle loved. In addition, Mary lived in Europe and focused her life on art, just as Belle aspired to do. And then there was Mary's emotional maturity and calm. Belle later said that Mary made her "pray to be big and simple."[9]

After Mary's departure for Oxford, in between work meetings and social commitments, Bernard began to show Belle the architectural sites and artistic collections that made London one of the centers of the art world. He also accompanied her to dealers' galleries and auctions. When he showed her a manuscript that was for sale, Bernard got his first insight into her buying power and independence. When Belle cabled J.P. about the manuscript, Morgan's only reply was to use her judgment. "I must say she uses it well," commented the great art critic and quiet dealer, equally surprised and impressed.[10]

Before they left London for Paris, Bernard also got his first taste of Belle's more eclectic social connections. Belle gave a dinner party (out of obligation, she told him) for her friends Ethel and P. G. Grant, and an unnamed Persian prince and his wife. Bernard considered Ethel a "spoiled American woman, but with an overpowering temperament and deliberate purpose to give it will."[11] After suffering through the dinner (Bernard was even less impressed with the Persian royalty than with the Grants), they went to an even worse play. The only saving grace of the evening for Bernard was that Belle also seemed to have had a terrible time, calling it the worst evening she had ever spent.[12]

It was in Paris that the art seeing and hunting and buying began in earnest. The two went to a manuscript sale, where Belle purchased several thirteenth- and fourteenth-century books. Bernard then took her to Notre Dame, which was a revelation to her. His great delight on their journey was to introduce her to great art, both famous and unknown, to "talk art" to her about the pieces, the artists, the techniques, the periods. He was, at first, surprised at her mastery of this world.[13] She already had a formidable expertise and instinct of her own. And as they journeyed together from Paris to Munich and then through Italy, he was astonished that despite such a narrowness of expertise (manuscripts), she had a quick aptitude for appreciating the broader world of "Art." "B.G. scarcely ever failed to appreciate the real things—just how and why beats me, the Titian Crowning with Thorns for instance wh[ich] is a marvel." He described her as going into ecstasies over several of his favorite pieces (the series of the Master of the Life of Mary and Fra Filippo's *Annunciation*).[14] Her taste was astonishing, given her lack of experience. Bernard questioned Belle closely about her training, and she told her story about apprenticing herself to Richardson at Princeton.[15]

Both were trying hard to make a good impression. In the evenings Bernard read French and English poetry to her, an "old trick" from his early romance with Mary. Always willing to try to fake it a bit, Belle at first assured Bernard that she "doted" on Shelley, but further conversation revealed she had read very little of him. He added more Shelley to his arsenal. But she could hold her own in a conversation about Keats. Bernard was alternately amused and impressed. "She likes my reading," he told Mary, a bit too honestly, "probably because she likes to look at my eyes while I read." Belle ever after associated Baudelaire with those nights at Claridges.[16]

Both Mary and Bernard saw Belle as talented, but young and relatively ignorant. "What she may grow into, who shall tell? Perhaps I shall count for something in that," Bernard mused in one of his daily letters to Mary.[17] Mary encouraged him to think of Belle as a potential protégée, whose life path could be permanently altered by her time with Bernard. "Thee can perhaps give her a great deal, and she needs—at least from our point of view—a more refined ideal of life and human intercourse. She is perhaps sufficiently assimilative to get a lot in a couple of months, and it may make a lot of difference to the kind of life she leads."[18] Mary certainly preferred this image of her husband's relationship with Belle to the more emotional path he seemed to be on.

Yet, despite Belle's presence, Bernard's depression began to overtake him again in Paris. He tried to hide his suffering from Belle, perhaps mindful of her scorn for his preoccupation with his emotional state. But he poured out his misery in his daily letters to his wife, grieving that even the incredible and unexpected gift of love could be transformed by his "melancholy."[19]

Bernard's openness with Mary was not complete, but it was remarkable by most standards. His letters were scattered with references not only to his emotional responses to Belle and their detailed itinerary but also to his love for and appreciation of Mary. "Even tho' polygamous," he ended one letter, "I am not the less yours."[20] When he left London for Paris and Munich, he told her he was mourning to be away from her for several weeks and would not feel whole until he was with her again. "I feel so grateful to what you are for the way you are taking this new situation—so simple, so natural, and yet fr. any conventional point of view so extraordinary."[21]

Always mindful that it was her own affair that had opened their relationship, Mary tried to stay philosophical about her husband's finally realized affair. Love between humans, she wrote her husband, was so fundamental and even mystical. Mary also noticed that Bernard had become more tender toward her in his letters since Belle's arrival. His love for Belle seemed to have opened him back up to his love for Mary.[22]

In truth, though, Mary was not exactly enjoying herself while Belle and Bernard saw the sights of Paris. She was at a "cure" in Oxford, England. Along with other upper-class women, she was staying at a health resort and trying to "reduce" by fasting. Mary had never been fashionably slender, and in her middle age was finding the pounds mounting. To add insult to injury, she was failing to lose weight even with these drastic measures. Happily, or unhappily, the doctors put her on a grape juice diet after a few days. "How different from one Miss G. and Bernard!!" she commented wryly, probably imagining the rich French cuisine they were enjoying.[23]

After a few days in Paris, Bernard and Belle took the Orient Express to Munich, which had been on Bernard and Mary's itinerary before Belle's surprise announcement of her trip. Bernard and Belle took rooms in separate hotels but spent most of their days together. And the separate hotels did not keep them apart after day was done: they spent at least one wonderful night together in Belle's room under an awkwardly thick down comforter.[24] By day they spent hours at an exhibition of Islamic art, which Bernard recommended that Mary come see in September. The Berensons and Mary were constantly trying to expand their own areas of expertise in art; they had been in Munich together over a decade previously, but the Persian show was new. He wanted her well versed.

And in Munich began the "terrible business of dodging acquaintances." After the relative quiet of Paris, it turned out now that several
other New York society and art people were around, including Rita
Lydig and Arabella Huntington. Both Belle and Bernard knew the
Lydigs and Huntingtons. Despite the need to evade others, Bernard
wanted to stay and spend more time at the exhibition. He thought they
had avoided detection. But after several run-ins with hotel staff not
used to American expectations for service, Belle had had it. She
declared she hated Munich and "everything German," and the two prepared to move on to Italy. Belle's aversion to things German would not
soon fade.

As Bernard began to make plans for their trip to Italy, the question
of propriety arose. With Belle's maid gone, Belle and Bernard were on
their own. (He never traveled with a servant.) They had been counting
on avoiding people who knew them as their only protection from discovery. But Italy was Bernard's home and one of Morgan's regular
stops. He was well known there, practically an honorary citizen.
Bernard later remarked drily that he could barely look at an Italian
church's treasure without being told that "Birbo Morgo had offered
cento mila lire for it."[25] They might be safe enough on the first planned
leg: a tour of several small towns off the usual tourist routes in northern Italy and Tuscany. But when they reached Rome, they would certainly run into dealers who had long-standing loyalties to Morgan.
Belle feared that her boss might have enlisted them as spies or, at the
very least, that they would send word of her doings back to her
demanding and territorial boss and patron. Accordingly, she tried to
arrange for her Boston friend Alice Ditson to meet her in Rome and act
as chaperone. But when Alice proved unreachable, Belle appealed to
Bernard, who appealed to Mary to join them, first raising it as a remote
possibility and then as a compelling necessity. Mary did not see the
urgency; she believed Munich and Venice were more dangerous than
Rome at that time of year. "No one will be in Rome then," she assured
her husband. The third leg of the trip was a two-week stay in Venice.
Both Belle and Bernard expected Mary to meet them there, and she
had agreed.[26]

Meanwhile, Bernard was beginning to have doubts about his affair

with Belle. Despite her written promises that this time she would
become all that she could be to him, he reported that he found her
"much more cérebrale than sensual. Of the erotic there is little in her."
This judgment would certainly change. Decades later Berenson
remembered her as a wonderful lover. It may have taken Belle a while
to become comfortable with her sexuality. Bernard was also grappling
with his expectations and the overwhelming reality of her presence.
On the eve of his journey to meet her, he had questioned whether he
was too old for a true affair, scolding himself to stick to "ideated sen-
sations, to dreams," instead of real and physical emotional love.[27]

But still, their shared passion for art and their emotional connection
were enough to confirm his hopes for her. He implored Mary to look
beyond the surface of Belle's behavior: "[U]nder the mask and manner,
and giggle there is something so genuine, so loyal, so vital too, so full of
heart." And he increasingly believed that her instinct for art was true,
that she could make a real contribution to the art world, under his guidance. He described the time they spent looking at art as "unalloyed joy.
Either I am enchanted or she is the most responsive person—excepting
possibly your beloved self—I have come across."[28]

As he prepared to return to his adopted homeland, Bernard dreaded
the trip. Usually he escaped to northern Europe to avoid the heat of
late summer in Italy, and now there were reports of another cholera
outbreak in the south. Then, too, Italy represented the pressures of his
business and the problems with I Tatti, still undergoing renovations
under Mary's distant supervision. But Belle was determined to see
Italy. And Bernard's depression was lifting, allowing him to bask in her
attentions and let go of his uneasiness about their differences in age,
experience, and temperament.

He wrote his wife that he could not imagine anyone loving him more
than Belle did: a "sheer miracle" to bask in and then look back on later
as a glory. Mary replied, rejoicing that he had finally gained the perspective she wanted him to and "glad thee has something that makes
thee happy. . . . I hope it will make us understand each other better."[29]
But it must have been painful to hear her husband suggest that Belle
loved him more than Mary herself did. Mary may have been able to

brush it off as a lover's exaggeration at the time. She was preoccupied with her weight-loss efforts, a developing illness, and the impending possibility of having to travel to Rome instead of returning home as she planned.

With future plans still up in the air, the happy couple arrived by train in Verona. Once in Italy, Belle was in heaven, and Bernard, however reluctantly, was in his element. He was one of the experts, perhaps *the* expert, in Italian art, especially the Renaissance paintings, frescoes, architecture, and sculptures that adorned churches and museums throughout northern Italy. They drove from town to town through the endless postcard-perfect vistas of northern Italy and Tuscany's gold-and-green countryside. He gloried when she reacted as he had his first time seeing Verona, Ravenna, Siena, and Orvieto.

In these smaller towns they were largely safe from running into acquaintances, but not completely. They had a close call in Verona when dealer Jacques Seligmann ran into Bernard at his hotel while Belle was waiting in the cab. She escaped notice, he thought. Then in Ravenna, Belle was caught by friends of the Morgans and had to abandon Bernard to dine with them.[30] This time Bernard lay low. And so they avoided detection, mostly, and spent the next week taking in the sights "hard": all day, every day.

Free to meet during the day in Ravenna, they visited the library's collection of early manuscripts, which Bernard deemed "fine early things throwing floods of light on the evolution of art." Belle was in her strength here, and she further impressed Bernard when they found a collection of Rembrandt etchings. Belle knew them intimately and astounded her companion with her ability to identify not only the masterpiece each sketch was the basis of but which stage each represented. Berenson had apparently missed the several hundred Rembrandt etchings in his tour of the Library; Morgan had purchased them in 1900. Belle added to Morgan's collection, purchasing more Rembrandt etchings at the end of her trip.[31]

One evening they sat together writing letters. Belle wrote to J.P., telling him about conversations she had had with dealers and pieces she had seen for purchase or delivery to the Library. Bernard was probably writing his usual one- to two-page letters to Mary and half a dozen other people. But he noticed that as he wrote letter after letter, Belle was still working on that one to Morgan. With a bitter sigh, perhaps suddenly recalling all the times he had waited for a letter from her, he complained that she had never written him so long a letter.[32] It was a dissonant moment in their idyll as the memory returned of their difficulties communicating by letter, and their very different habits of writing—he obsessively and daily, she in fits and starts when she found the time and was in the mood. They would soon be apart again, she pulled back into her life as J.P.'s librarian, and reliant on this unsatisfactory medium to maintain a relationship. Would B.B. fall again into a depression upon her departure?

But despite the ever-present knowledge that their time together was finite, each tried to bask in the other's presence, and in the perfect Mediterranean sun. In Ravenna they had gloried in the museums, the churches, and especially the mosaics. In Siena they were almost the only tourists. The sepia-toned town of small churches nestled into small plazas was celebrating a holy day. Public museums were closed; the narrow curving roads were quiet. Belle loved every bit of it. One evening they sat on the ancient walls that surround the medieval city center and watched the sun set. Years later she vividly recalled looking back up the hill at the decidedly unmodern skyline of Siena silhouetted against a pink sky. Bernard pronounced the temperature and atmosphere ideal. They had missed the oppressive heat of summer and enjoyed the more temperate warmth and cool evenings of September.[33]

It was a blissful time. Bernard was happy. Belle was happy. In these little towns tucked into the Italian countryside or perched up on hills, they had more freedom to be alone together than they had in the larger cities. For years to come Belle would remember their romantic and sexual intimacies in Siena, Ravenna, and Perugia and "live in the memory of our all too brief honeymoon." Her weeks in Italy with Bernard transformed her internal life.[34]

But the external world still intruded. While in Siena, Belle wrote her own appeal to Mary to join them in Rome. Citing "certain complications at home," she explained that even such a "careless and hopeless unconventional person" as herself had to appear respectable in

Rome. But she assured Mary that she also wanted to spend time together simply to get to know her. Adopting some of the Berensons' private language, Belle struggled to explain why. She wanted, she said, to feel some of Mary's " 'life-enhancing' . . . presence near me and about me and within me. It is impossible for me to tell you here all that I feel about you—and your uncalled for and rather unexpected bigness to me."[35]

"Bigness" was perhaps an unfortunate choice of words, given Mary's failed weight-loss treatment and Belle's diminutive figure. But generosity of spirit aside, Mary was not eager to make the trip to Rome. As the lovers were exploring Tuscany, Mary arrived in Venice. Still feeling poorly, she hoped to conduct her art business quickly and move on to Florence and her bed. But rumors about her husband and his companion had preceded her. An Italian friend of theirs from Florence, Carlos Placci, reported with a raised eyebrow that he had heard that Bernard was traveling with a "young lady." Mary hastened to convince him that nothing scandalous was happening and begged him not to feed the gossip. She told Placci that her husband had formed a platonic art-based friendship with Belle and that she and Bernard did not care about conventions. Mary explained that she knew the young woman and approved of her husband's behavior. Placci knew Bernard well enough that he was unlikely to be convinced by this story. Nevertheless, he promised to protect the Berensons, laughing that when he met Bernard with this mystery woman he would "tell everyone she is a man."[36]

Faced with this evidence of potential scandal and barraged with letters from Bernard and Belle, Mary gave in and began to make plans to join them in Rome. She had hoped to postpone it, but Belle and Bernard were running out of places they could visit without meeting acquaintances. Even quiet Siena was not completely empty. George Perkins (one of J.P.'s partners) and his wife were there, getting ready to accompany the Blumenthals and the Lydigs on a tour.[37] The Blumenthals were in Perugia until September 15. Thomas Ryan kept popping up, as did the Huntingtons. (Any one of these could have been the friends of Morgan with whom Belle had to dine in Ravenna.) Too many connections, too much risk: Belle and Bernard modified their itinerary.

The couple had left Siena with mixed feelings, reluctant to head to

Rome. In the hilltop town of Orvieto, they examined the familiar high façade of the ornamental duomo with its mosaic of golds, blues, and rosy pinks. Belle still remembered it in detail two years later. Orvieto was beautiful and dirty, "picturesque and smelly." The two did not stay long; scaffolding hid the Signorelli frescoes in the San Brizio Chapel. But the discovery of art and each other went on. Throughout, Berenson focused more on Belle's reactions than on the familiar sights themselves. She was, he marveled, "incredibly, miraculously responsive, and most of all to the things I really care most about." And yet she was still devoted to her work on rare books and manuscripts. Her project of the moment was to catalogue the first century of printed books. Bernard was mystified. He saw the appeal of preprint books, especially the illuminated manuscripts that contained gorgeous, well-preserved pieces of art within their bindings. But he saw no artistic value in printed books, even the earliest examples.[38]

From Orvieto the lovers drove through pouring rain to Toscanella and Viterbo on their way to Rome. When they finally arrived, the sun came out, Alice Ditson turned up, and there didn't seem to be anyone else around who would recognize Belle.

Mary thankfully retreated to I Tatti to recover from her own travels. Artist René Piot was still in residence in a nearby villa, working on his commission to fresco some inner walls. Workers were tearing up the main floor. Too ill to care about the renovations, Mary took to her room and waited for her husband and Belle to finish their stay in Rome and head back to Florence.[39] She remained in bed for the entire week.

Alice Ditson's arrival had let Mary off the hook temporarily, but her presence brought a disquieting reminder of the gulf in social taste and expectations between the lovers. Alice was another friend of Belle's of whom Bernard almost instantly disapproved. He pronounced her "a poor specimen of a poor type of striving, silly, moneyed American female. And Belle remembers how already in New York I begged her to shake that type of acquaintance." Their idyll was, he proclaimed, over. Belle, too, was appalled by Alice Ditson, after three weeks under Bernard's influence, he surmised. She fell into "one of the worst fits of the blues I have beheld." Coming from a man who suffered himself from severe depression for much of his life, that was saying something.[40]

With the suddenly unwanted Mrs. Ditson in tow, Bernard took Belle to the Sistine Chapel. Alice chattered intolerably; Belle snapped waspishly; Bernard was miserable. And to make matters worse, they encountered that grievous bane of all travelers: other tourists. The Sistine Chapel was a particularly awful place to meet a crowd. Even whispers echo off the frescoed walls and bounce down from the high ceilings painted with Michaelangelo's timeless biblical scenes and figures.[41] The unhappy threesome went through the rest of the vast Vatican Museum, and into the nearby St. Peter's Basilica, where popes had held mass for centuries.

The mounting unease was suddenly broken when Bernard received news that his sister Bessie had fallen ill. Fearing tuberculosis, he rushed to Paris, at Belle's insistence. He also had some work to attend to in France, but she did not seem to be aware of that. Bernard left her with a list of places and pieces to see, which she followed carefully, spurning anyone else's attempts to "tell her things" about the sights. Belle reported faithfully to Bernard in letters on her impressions of particular statues or paintings she claimed as hers in spirit. A Sano di Pietro painting of a gold-robed Virgin tempted her to thievery; a Francesco Sponza of Dei Conti made it clear to her that Morgan's was a forgery; a Virgin and Child by Francescuccio Ghissi reminded her of some of the Persian paintings from the Munich exhibition.[42] Throughout their journeys Bernard had been tutoring Belle in his methods of determining authenticity and attributions. But his approach combined a sharing of the artistic impact of each piece on the individual. Belle's quick comments about these three pieces show that she was responding in kind: Did she love (and therefore covet) a painting? Could she see how to distinguish a forgery from the real thing? Could she discern an artistic continuity, perhaps even influence, between works from two cultures or two time periods? Bernard's reply might have given his answer to these questions.

One moonlit evening Belle and Alice went with a friend of Alice's to the ruins of the Colosseum and persuaded a guard to show them the

lowest levels of the ancient stadium. Belle soaked up the sight and
feeling, standing in the silhouette of the half-crumbled open stone
walls filtering the moon's light. These sights—the ruins, landscapes,
medieval walls, pagan temples, and hilltop vistas—affected Belle as
deeply as the fine art and classical masters she highlighted in her letters to Bernard. The natural and human-made beauty of Italy and
everything he showed her was now "stamped into my memory and a
part of my very flesh and blood." Italy was an exotic locale in the Anglo
imagination: its warmth and art pulled them southward every season.
But Italians' darker skin and cultural differences made them a convenient "other" for their neighbors to the north. Belle's appearance, so
mysterious and suspect in New York, would have seemed perfectly
normal in Italy. Her self-image as Latin and southern European would
have been supported in this context, even as the strangeness of food,
language, and customs would have emphasized her (white?) American
identity. And then, of course, there was the art, the ruins, the ancient
world overlaid with contemporary life and architecture—it would forever be her beloved Italy.[43]

Belle was less impressed, however, with a return visit to Vatican City,
this time featuring a meeting with a cardinal whose name she could
not recall. Much to her surprise and dismay, this forgettable man had
arranged a meeting with Pope Pius X a few days later, after her planned
departure for Florence. Although the dismayed cardinal promised to
try to find an earlier time, the appointment was not rescheduled, much
to Belle's relief. Belle then suffered through a tour of the Vatican
Museum, which she had already seen with Bernard, and a private
viewing of silver and gold pieces used in special celebrations of the
Mass at St. Peter's Basilica. Finally she was rewarded for her patience
with a personal visit the next day at the Vatican Library with Prefect
Franz Ehrle.[44] For centuries the Catholic Church had been collecting
manuscripts, ancient and modern, of not only Roman Catholic texts
but also those of world religions and cultures. It was a library that had
no peer, and under Ehrle's direction it was undergoing a recataloguing
and reorganization to make it more accessible to scholars. Belle could
have seen only a smattering of the tens of thousands of manuscripts

collected there, but it was enough to make an indelible impression and make up for her boredom with the cardinal. She would return to the Vatican Library many times over her lifetime, and would develop a much deeper interest in the Catholic Church itself as she matured.

That afternoon Belle and her maid, Marie, who had rejoined her in Rome, set out for Florence with a few stops along the way back in Orvieto and Siena. Mary promised her husband she would make Belle feel welcome in his absence, as much as her health allowed. But Bernard had bigger plans. He hinted broadly that Mary should invite her to stay at I Tatti while in Florence, although Belle planned to stay at a hotel in the city and had some business to do. And he instructed Mary to show Belle around in his absence, writing out an itinerary that must have sent her under the covers in despair: the Piazze, the Giottos at Santa Croce, the Medici tombs, the Opera del Duomo, and a run through the best art in the four biggest museums—the Bargello, the Academy, the Palazzo Pitti, and the Uffizi Gallery.[45] Florence was, and is, a center of Renaissance art—the best of the artists having already been collected there by wealthy Italian Renaissance patrons. Mary and Bernard, of course, had been in every nook and cranny of the famous city, which their country villa overlooked. Every time visitors came (and the stream was fairly constant when renovations were not in progress), one or both descended into the red-roofed city to act as tour guides.

Upon hearing that Mary was not feeling well, however, Belle quickly declined her invitation to stay at I Tatti. Instead, Belle and Marie took rooms at the Grand Hotel, and Belle made the rounds of churches, museums, and plazas by herself. She did journey up to I Tatti for an afternoon to visit Mary and finally see her lover's home, somewhat against her will, and certainly not under her desired circumstances. Much as she may have been seeking Mary's acquaintance, she probably had not planned on a one-on-one meeting quite so soon. Nevertheless, Bernard also extracted a promise from Belle to "meet [Mary's] kindness frankly," and she pledged to try to behave as he asked, although she said it was difficult for her to go to I Tatti without him there. It was only Bernard's own advice and lecture on controlling her behavior during one of their last jaunts together in Rome that allowed her to bring herself even to try to meet with Mary alone. "I do hope I shall be able to control myself and behave decently. If not, perhaps your wife will forgive me."[46]

Mary picked Belle up by car in Florence and drove her up into the hills for an excursion before bringing her back to Villa I Tatti. They drove along now familiar winding Tuscan roads, rising up out of the outskirts of Florence through green farmland dotted with the narrow, high pine trees and bright-colored villas of the Tuscan countryside. The drive would have enchanted Belle, had she not been so nervous about being alone with Mary.[47]

Crossing the Ponte di Mensola, a small bridge over a creeklike river just below I Tatti, Mary could have pointed out the tiny local church of San Martino above on the hill as they rounded the corner toward the stone walls and metal gates around the estate. I Tatti boasted acres of farmland but did not yet have the Renaissance-style gardens it is now known for. It was not the only, or even the largest, villa in the neighborhood. But to Belle's eyes it was pure enchantment. Inside, the house was still in disarray: Mary had returned to find things much improved— a new hallway, some landscaping, Piot's fresco in progress—but not complete. She lamented the unfinished floor that required Belle to use the back staircase. Despite the mess, I Tatti was Bernard's home, representing a life that Belle yearned for. Belle was largely unaware of the depth of Bernard's emotional illnesses, of the rages and frustrations of his marriage, of the extent of his business dealings and financial pressures. Bernard had attained what her father could not even strive for, and what she had not yet achieved. To her his life seemed to be one of comfort and privacy, money to travel, the freedom to study and work.

It was clear, though, that things were not quite settled in the Berenson home. Belle looked with some consternation at the vivid colors René Piot had begun to apply to the fresco. The artist repeated his assurances that the colors would fade upon drying and had to be applied brightly. He also may have taken a break to sketch the young visitor. A charcoal portrait in the Berenson archives contains on the back a note in Bernard's handwriting: "extraordinarily like Belle Greene when I first knew her in 1908." Mary also showed Belle their own collection of paintings, furniture, and statues, which Mary was still gathering for the new look.[48] The resident architects and hangers-on Geoffrey Scott and Cecil Pinsent joined them for dinner. Scott and Pinsent were supposed to have overseen the completion of the renovations during the Berensons' trip to America, but were not performing as expected. Still, they remained at I Tatti, much to their friends' amusement and Bernard's annoyance.

Geoffrey Scott was Mary's emotional answer to her husband's affairs. Although the younger man had made it clear he was not interested in her sexually (he was more attracted to men than to women), he and Mary were quite emotionally intimate. At the same time that Bernard had been falling in love with Belle, Mary had been increasingly preoccupied with Geoffrey and had still hoped that he might reciprocate her interest. She assured her husband that there was no "spark of romance" on Geoffrey's part, but continued to rely on him for male attention and a deep friendship. Of course, part of her denial to Bernard was based on Mary's own realization that her own romantic affairs would not be received nearly as sympathetically, either by her husband or by her culture in general. "Literature," she observed in her diary, "has nothing but contempt for an old woman growing fond of boys."[49]

The men thought Belle "rather awful," so apparently she was not as successful in repressing her behavior as she had hoped. Mary attributed their objections to Belle's "manner rather than herself," and told her mother that she "really liked her. . . . I find her plucky and sensible and energetic and capable and very sincere."[50] But this must be taken as a surface description only; Mary did not confide to her mother the nature of Belle and Bernard's relationship. Most details of her and Bernard's interactions with the visiting New York woman from the Morgan Library were left out of such correspondence.

Once she left Mary, Belle returned to her hotel room and her business in Florence. There was too much to do and too many people to see. Her failure to visit rankled some. Leo Olschki, the Florence bookseller who had early felt her scathing pen, was miffed that she did not grace him with her presence or her business while she was there.[51]

Meanwhile, in Paris, Bernard had ascertained that Bessie did not have tuberculosis and that her condition was already improving. He made plans to return to I Tatti, but, Belle warned him, Florence was full of New Yorkers that mid-September. Not only were there more people around who knew Belle, but several of them had already run into her with Bernard or had otherwise caught wind of their travels together during their previous trips. The Blumenthals had arrived, as had the Van Vechtens, and the Lydigs were expected on Monday. Carl Van Vechten, a New York–based journalist and writer whose connections to Harlem artists and writers shaped his career, was traveling with his wife. There were also some art people in from London. Belle related the list of acquaintances "brutally, stating as you see mere facts which will enable you to plan accordingly."[52]

Bernard returned to Florence on September 19, throwing I Tatti "topsy-turvy" as everyone scurried around tidying and adjusting to arrange things perfectly. "Strange little man!" Mary wrote her family. "Why are we all so terrified of him?" Despite their preparations the master of the house arrived in a rage, and, hoping to hide some of the renovation's less successful projects from him, Mary persuaded her husband to spend the night in town. Bernard was doubtless more than happy to be closer to Belle.[53]

The next day the reunited couple left Florence for Perugia. With the visit from Belle over, and everyone scheduled to meet in Venice, Mary returned to her ruminations on the effect this affair might have on her marriage. She wrote to her husband about the "radical change" she hoped might result from this experience with Belle. She had fallen into the habit, she confessed, of not telling him things to avoid his rages. This behavior began even before her affair with the sculptor Obrist and was a result of Bernard's belief at the time that Mary's outside interests were a threat to their relationship. Now that Bernard was experiencing his own affairs, he realized as she had that such side interests "need not alter a really devoted already existing relation." She even suggested that Belle might stay at I Tatti on a future visit, consoling him that "this time thee has given her Italy!"[54]

Meanwhile, Bernard and Belle had reached the northern city of

Bologna and found the inescapable Blumenthals already there. Belle spent an evening with them to allay suspicion and learn their travel plans. Bernard thought his presence was unknown and again tried to reconfigure their own itinerary to avoid future chance meetings. He also appealed once more to Mary to cut short her own plans to meet them and save them from having to dodge acquaintances.

After a few more days in Florence, Mary went up to Venice, much to her mother's dismay, to prepare for Bernard's and Belle's arrival. Mary's mission was to secure a "really splendid suite," which she did in the Hotel de l'Europe: four bedrooms, two baths, a room for the maid, and a large living room and balcony. Mary carefully explained to her mother that she and Belle had the adjoining rooms overlooking the Grand Canal, while Bernard and Geoffrey's room had a shared bath and a street view. Hannah may not have been fooled.[55] The actual arrangement of the bedrooms was a matter of some speculation.

Mary's mother and daughters showed an avid interest in Mary's relationship with Bernard. They were half amused, half outraged, but well acquainted with his rages and her attempts at placating, avoiding confrontation, and working hard to soothe him. Their relationship seemed like something out of a novel to Ray and Karin, and a constant source of concern for Hannah.[56] They were somewhat dismayed by the extravagance of Mary's life with Bernard, so different from their own: the stream of important visitors, the frequent travel, their exotic life in Italy, the huge villa always filled with servants and workers and guests. Part of their disapproval was certainly based on Bernard himself and the circumstances of his marriage to Mary. Although Bernard seldom failed to grant any request Mary made for financial support for her family, he spent little time with them, having no real relationship with his stepdaughters and mother-in-law. And he was, after all, the reason Mary had abandoned her daughters' father, and her daughters themselves. Hannah also constantly warned Mary against "bowing down to materialism" and hoped she and Bernard might make good their frequent vows to start following a simpler life.[57]

The Venice trip thus seemed absolutely incomprehensible to them. Ray wrote with "commiseration" because Venice seemed "too gay and

too expensive and we don't see what there is in it." Many visitors would
have disagreed with Ray's assessment of Venice. Crowded and gaudy
and charmingly Old World, the city of seaports and water canals, ornate
buildings, and tiny, hidden residential squares has a magical beauty
that still entrances crowds of tourists every summer. Its popularity as a
resort was what required Mary's presence there from the start.

For those four tourists in September of 1910, the Venice trip did not
start well. Belle, Bernard, and Marie arrived in pouring rain, which did
not let up for several days, threatening to flood the famous square in
front of San Marco, one of the city's most popular public sites. Then
Belle became ill and grew worse, even after taking a liver pill, a common medicine. Leaving her behind in her maid's care, the others set
out despite the rain and waded into the highly gilded San Marco
Church, where Bernard declared he hated pictures and now liked only
"the art of unselfconscious savages." Mary blamed it on the Persian
exhibition in Munich and worried that her own fatigue was a sign of
returning illness.[58]

But Venice and the foursome improved. The sun came out. Mary
discovered her health was perfectly fine for once. Bernard met with
dealers, with profitable results. And Belle recovered enough to venture
out, take care of some business, see some Venetian sights, and bury
herself in one of several libraries that held manuscript collections.
Belle and Bernard took a boat to Murano Island, where artisans created sculptures of color and light caught in blown glass. Belle later
remembered entering the small Santi Maria e Donato church with
B.B. "I . . . felt—before I saw" a Byzantine mosaic of the Virgin Mary
there.[59]

With the weather increasingly warm and brilliantly sunny, the foursome spent much time sitting out on their balcony talking and teasing.
Mary even proclaimed herself sorry that she and Belle would be going
their separate ways in a week, portraying her as very "jolly," able to take
teasing and still see "what things are."[60] True, Belle was a "rather insol-
uble element" at several social events the Berensons had arranged with
friends, but by all accounts (at least all surviving written accounts),
Mary was well pleased with the Venice trip and with Belle. She even

hoped that her own protégé, Geoffrey Scott, might benefit from Belle's influence if he moved to New York.[61] Best of all, Belle had intervened to support Mary in one of her ongoing arguments with Bernard, much to Mary's pleasure.

Still immersed in her desire to improve her relationship with Bernard, Mary promised him not to manage and deceive him anymore in order to avoid his rages. So when some news came that Mary knew would, for several reasons, enrage Bernard, she told him immediately, with Belle and Geoffrey there. B.B's predicted fury emerged "black as thunder," and Mary took the opportunity to prove her point that his behavior was unreasonable and the source of many of their problems. After Bernard left when dealers came to meet with him, Belle promised to "give it to him hot" when they went out that day, so shocked was she at his behavior. Mary was quite satisfied that she had gotten through to her husband, with the help of his other woman, no less.[62]

Belle and Bernard's last day trip together in Venice was to the island of Torcello. Once the center residence and trading place in the Venetian Lagoon, Torcello was by then relatively deserted, with few residents but a steady stream of tourists. Its main attraction was the Byzantine Basilica of Santa Maria Assunta. They spent the afternoon wandering hand in hand, rarely speaking, but, Belle later recalled, "we were one that day thank God. We were one!" But as their boat neared their hotel, she knew the end had come.[63]

Belle prepared to leave for London, Bernard for Paris, and Mary and Scott for I Tatti again. Belle had business in London to attend to. But her departure marked a mysterious turning point in her relationship with Bernard, one that Mary struggled to understand. A few nights before spending that quiet afternoon in Torcello, Belle clung to Bernard all night, despairing that "the world seemed slipping away." They slept peacefully their last night together, holding each other close, breathing in each other's breath. As Belle had written longingly the year before, "Who could be aught but a lover in Venice?"[64] But by the time they went their separate ways, that ideal had been shattered. The probable cause was one Mary would never discover.

Something happened to Belle. She had recovered from her illness in Venice, but in London she was suddenly taken ill and on strict bed rest by the time she was heard from again. At least that's what she told Mary and how it seemed to observers.[65] Under the care of a London doctor, her good friend Ethel Grant, and Ethel Harrison, a friend of Bernard's, Belle struggled to meet her business obligations and recover from—what exactly?

The first hints came from Bernard. No sooner had he left Venice than he immediately fell apart. He wrote Mary that he was ashamed of himself, full of self-recriminations for never-specified reasons, unable to bear it, unable to sleep. He understood now, he said, the temptation of Saint Anthony. (Famously depicted in a Hieronymus Bosch triptych, Saint Anthony was tempted by sins of lust and pleasure and tormented physically by demons.) Bernard said little about Belle's condition, except that she was somehow at the root of it.

Despite his desperation, Bernard could not join Belle in London, because she was too sick and too busy. A visit to the Louvre, an attempt at socializing, nothing helped. A three-hour conversation with the writer Henry Adams only led him to contrast Adams's world with Belle Greene's. Bernard was relieved to be in the former; in hers he now saw no future. He was, he finally concluded, in hell itself.[66] Hell at the Ritz in Paris, socializing with literary lights, but hell nevertheless. And to make matters worse, the Blumenthals had shown up again, looking "sly and knowing." Apparently Bernard and Belle had not been as inconspicuous as they had thought. He was forced to meet with them, hoping to secure their silence.

Inured as she was to her husband's depressions and fits, Mary was completely baffled by this latest turn. At first she thought he was mourning the end of his time with Belle. Then she surmised that Belle was not behaving as Bernard wanted, not putting aside her duties and friends in London to try to spend more time with him. Mary reminded her husband that it was Belle's vitality, her "thousand irons in the fire" life that had attracted him to her in the first place, and probably her youth that made her unable to realize how rare their love was.[67]

From Belle there was a strange gap in correspondence, or rather there is a telling gap in the surviving correspondence. Although Belle left Venice on September 30 (and Bernard departed for Paris the next day), her first surviving letter to him is dated October 9. Yet Bernard was clearly hearing from her or about her during that week, because he wrote to Mary during the first week of October with news of Belle. Whether the communication was by telegram or through third parties, or whether these letters were not saved or were even destroyed, is not clear. The two Ethels were with Belle in London, helping to take care of her along with Marie and a doctor. Ethel Harrison lived in Naples and had known Bernard for a while. She met up with Belle and the Berensons in Venice and may have traveled with Belle to London. Whatever the specifics, Bernard had clearly charged her with Belle's care. Ethel Grant was Belle's friend from New York who had dined with Belle and Bernard in Munich. Either Ethel could have been writing to him that week if Belle had been unable to do so. Still, her own letters pick up as if she had been writing to him all along. And the gap is suspiciously timed.

It appears that Belle was not merely ill but pregnant when she left Venice, and that she went to London seeking to end the pregnancy. She could have been no more than a month or two along, and several medical options were available for bringing on a miscarriage in England at that time. It is also possible that the "liver pill" she took in Venice was an abortifacient, intended to "bring on" a late period, but had not done its job. In fact, there is some evidence that two years later Mary Berenson also journeyed to England to have an abortion, taking pills under a doctor's care and staying with her daughters as she waited for the miscarriage to happen. She was a bit regretful, but she had long since resigned herself to Bernard's utter lack of interest in having children.[68] Had Bernard likewise insisted that Belle end her pregnancy? Did Belle also want an abortion? Both must have seen the impossibility of the situation. She could not hope to hide a pregnancy in New York. As a single unwed mother in 1911, she could never have maintained her professional status, nor could she disappear for seven or eight months and quietly carry to term and give up the child. And there was no question that Bernard would leave Mary, would leave Italy, would want to be a father. It was an awful end to Belle's great romantic tour of Italy, and to her first sexual affair.

On the other hand, London was a better place for her to be than

New York. While abortions were readily available in New York for those who had the money and knew where to look, they were illegal and dangerous. And there was also the danger of blackmail or exposure. In London, laws were rarely enforced. Belle was fortunate to find, probably with the help of Bernard's friend Ethel Harrison, a safe and sympathetic doctor who apparently also took it upon himself to educate her in preventing another unwanted pregnancy. Toward the end of her recovery Belle and her doctor had talked for four hours about "forbidden topics." By the time she wrote her first surviving letter to Bernard from London, she assured him she was now well informed on these unmentionable subjects.[69]

One such subject must surely have been birth control. It was a common practice for modern women of means at the turn of the century to procure in Europe methods of barrier contraceptives that were still illegal in the United States. American women did not have to leave the country, or even leave their homes, to obtain "hygienic" devices like douches, which were also commonly used for contraceptive purposes. Despite the illegality of contraception, stores and mail-order catalogues marketed many such devices in coded terms. Marketers routinely claimed that their products were for other purposes but hinted or promised they would also prevent conception or end an early pregnancy. But the more reliable barrier methods had to be purchased from Europe, and untold numbers of upper-class American women brought home more than fine clothes and perfume from their trips abroad. Belle may well have joined their ranks, and received a much needed education on preventing further pregnancies.[70]

How Belle felt about ending her pregnancy was not immediately clear, even to her. She was still thinking about it a decade later. In 1919 Belle herself referred to this experience when she, for the only time in written record, wondered whether she had made a mistake in not having children. Writing to Bernard that he was one of two men she had known with whom she would have considered having a child, she asked rhetorically, "Why did we ship me off to London?" In 1921 she remembered the "really innocent . . . utter and world-excluding worship I once gave you." She commented that her ability to have that kind of feeling for anyone ceased to exist "when I left you to go to London," although she did not realize it at the time.[71]

But in the fall of 1910 there were no such regrets or recriminations, unless they came during the weeklong gap in the archive. By mid-October, though still under medical scrutiny, Belle was well enough to resume the meetings and art seeing that were her work. She did not discuss her condition very much in her letters, but instead listed her activities and meetings for Bernard. She met with the Duveens to arrange the shipment of some of Morgan's paintings. Her friends Charles Read and Alfred Pollard took her through their departments at the British Museum. Read also brought her to South Kensington to see the new wing of the Victoria and Albert Museum featuring more of Morgan's collection, some of which she adored and some of which she hated. She found herself surrounded by men at the museums and at the dinners and teas that several of them threw for her. She found it at first "queer" to be the only woman, noting that she had no chance to eat in such an environment, because she was so busy talking. But one of the things that struck her about the English men with whom she worked and socialized with was that they treated her "just like a man here" and never seemed to consider that they should provide a chaperone or at least another female to accompany them. Belle said she rather liked it.[72]

In London many men were falling over themselves to show her around. But not all men were swayed by her charms. Bernard himself lunched with a man who had met Belle, probably in New York, but at first didn't remember her when Bernard mentioned her name. Finally, however, he recalled the "young lady who expected a great deal of attention."[73]

Despite all the male attention, Belle was socializing with several women, including Ethel Harrison, who was still in London and whom she brought to see J. P. Morgan's estate at Princes Gate. Ethel Grant had left England to drive to France (where she got stranded, needing money from Belle to get back to London). But Bernard must have noticed that she was spending most of her time with men, especially museum men, scholars, and collectors. Sidney Colvin showed her around his prints department at the British Museum, and the "enchanting" Arthur Hind, also of the museum, taught her "all sorts of things in a few moments." This was what Belle lived for: to see new things and learn about them from other scholars and experts.[74]

After a lunch with Sydney Cockerell, director of the Fitzwilliam Museum in Cambridge, she was so enchanted that she canceled two afternoon appointments in order to spend more time with him. It is not clear whether Belle had met Cockerell on her first visit. In 1908 Cockerell had just been appointed to his position, even though he, like Belle, had no university degree. He had worked for a printing press that used woodblock methods, and as an adviser to Henry Yates Thompson, a wealthy book collector who specialized in medieval manuscripts and became a good friend to Belle. Cockerell took Belle to see some manuscripts at the Society of Antiquaries and revisit the cavernous British Museum. Roger Fry, an art historian and art critic who had just left his post as director of the Metropolitan Museum and returned to his native England, was also showing her around. He presented her with two paintings as gifts that she decreed "punk!" She later recalled dumping the paintings overboard as soon as she boarded her ship.[75]

With all this activity, she was already ignoring her doctor's advice to stay quiet for several more days. "Piffle, says I," she wrote with cheerful determination not to be overly upset by events. Belle was, it seemed, returning to her riotous life. Ethel Grant arrived in Paris, where she reported to Bernard that Belle had always been like that, throwing herself into things, activities, and people with great intensity and then suddenly losing her passion.[76]

Nor had Belle told her doctor she was planning to follow Ethel to Paris, and to Bernard, in a few days. Belle planned to stay there with her friend Mrs. Hyde and had social arrangements for several dinners and lunches. She also seemed hesitant to throw herself back into an affair with Bernard, and he would have received the distinct impression from her letters that he was not at the center of her plans. She did not want him to meet her at the train; she would be tired, and they wouldn't have time to talk.

And talk they must. In the meantime her letters to him were light and airy, calling him a "silly infant" for thinking she might not want to see him, warning him that she would have much shopping to do in Paris, for herself and for her family. And his letters to Mary were morose and tortured as he began to dread Belle's return and mourn that he was fundamentally unable to love and enjoy love. Mary was understandably baffled. Wasn't he in love with Belle? Was this just the pain of separating? Indeed, Mary was appalled at the extent of her husband's agony and his sudden certainty that all had ended. Bernard never wrote anything to Mary about the cause of Belle's "illness." He explained his misery as feeling rejected by Belle, depressed that the affair was over, unable to recover from it emotionally. Perhaps he really believed that was the fundamental problem. But Mary was not convinced. After two weeks of such letters she complained she still had no idea what had happened to change Bernard's mind and emotional state so quickly. At first she wrote back soothingly, sure that Belle's impending arrival would transform everything, including her husband.[77]

But unfortunately for the lovers and their endangered romance, a train workers' strike in Paris threatened Belle's travel plans. Day after day she postponed her trip, expecting that the strike would end and travel conditions would improve the next morning. But day after day the situation grew worse and she grew more and more frantic, wishing she had left when she first had planned, when at least some trains were getting through. The departure date for the return voyage to New York began to close in. While she continually assured Bernard that she did not want him to interrupt his plans and business to come to her, she yearned for him to do just that. And her tendency to cover her own pains and losses in a social whirl only made matters worse. Belle was still being dined and guided around the British Museum and the many other sights and collections, and she wrote about it in such glowing terms that Bernard was convinced that she did not come to him only because she was having too much fun in London. He feared that if she were in Paris, he would just get "mere, hasty glimpses of her," which would be worse than not seeing her at all. His friend Ralph Curtis, an artist who resided in Venice, reported gossip that Belle had used Bernard as a "valet du place" (local servant) in Italy. Bernard feigned unconcern to Curtis, but worried to Mary that it might be true.[78]

So Bernard pulled back from the romance and approached Belle, in writing, as a "platonic angel," which she claimed to find quaint and amusing but then confessed, "[Y]our letter moves me to either laughter or tears. I think I shall laugh—at least until I see you." And when Belle, amid reports of strikers' violence and derailed trains, finally gave up on reaching Paris before her sea journey, Bernard tried to be philosophical. Forwarding her cable to Mary, he told her that he believed that Belle had been "genuine" to him all along, but that she had a "divine freedom from sentimentality."[79]

But Belle's letter, sent the same day as the missing cable, betrayed a much more complicated emotional response. "I feel quite wretched about not seeing you," she wrote, "—more so than I would have, if our relations of August had never changed. I feel very much to blame and torment myself a great deal about it all." But she did try to rationalize their situation, suggesting that it might be for the better of their future relationship that they not see each other for a while. The closest she came to telling him what she really wanted was mentioning that Ethel H. had suggested she ask Bernard to join her. Then she got to her real concern: Where should they go from here? Did Bernard even want to hear from her again? Should they keep writing? Or wait and see whether fate ever brought them together again? Until she knew what he wanted, she didn't have the heart to write about anything: not her visit to the National Gallery to see "his" pictures, not the daily accounting of her "giddiness" that he had demanded. These things had lost all interest to her now that she knew they wouldn't see each other again on this trip. "Fate is doing queer things with me these days. I feel so forlorn and hopeless—but perhaps in the end I will find it to have been the better way for us all."[80]

Bernard wrote back immediately. Of course he wanted to see her. She could still come to Paris, even if only for a day or two. And of course he could make the trip to London. Belle was delighted. She dashed off a note with all of her schedule and location details and left London to spend one night and a day with the Yates Thompsons in the English countryside.[81] But Bernard was not waiting for her when she returned, although he promised to send her some Fortuny nightgowns and other things he had purchased for her in Paris. Nor did he show up in the few days remaining before she left to meet her ship. To Mary, Bernard claimed he stayed away from London and Belle because he wanted to make their parting as easy on her as possible. "I am not talking any more of being in love." He was also completely overwhelmed by his emotional pain and depression, even longing for death, as he walked through the hours he could have been spending with Belle and knowing she would think that his failure to come meant he did not care. Even an attempted lunch with Bessie Marbury and Anne Morgan went awry when they decided the way to cure his obvious melancholy was to bring him along on the *Oceanic* for their voyage to New York—the same boat that would be picking Belle up on its way from Europe to New York.[82] Taking a transatlantic boat just for the journey would have been an impulsive move, but not entirely unknown in circles that could afford it.

As Bernard had feared, Belle was furious to find that he could have come but chose not to. She wrote a cross and pointed letter, telling him that while his decision might be wise, it revealed "a weakness in us both which is not much to our credit and rather annoys me." Furthermore, she told him that the beauty of the robes and nightgowns he had bought for her "will not offset the remorseful and unhappy moments I should have in wearing them."[83]

By the end of the day she had calmed down and wrote again, apologizing for her earlier anger. She had realized that he, like she before him, had been listening more to other people than to his own mind and heart. If only they could have talked together and tried to mend things between them, without the interference of well-meaning friends who did not understand the situation. In person they could have understood each other's feelings. Slipping from her high road a bit when she told him he couldn't expect her to believe he still loved her when he wouldn't come to see her, she recovered enough to leave him with these final thoughts:

> No matter what the future brings forth—two months out of each of our lives has gone to the other and nothing can alter the fact that I loved you as absolutely completely and utterly

as one human being can love another and that I am glad of
it all—glad that it was so spontaneous—so sincere and so
deep. You know I never attempted to "flirt" with you—to
deny one bit of it or to withhold one bit of it—that I am sure
you will acknowledge.

Weighty words indeed. But literally in her next breath, Belle began to
recount a surprise visit from an infamous kept woman, Emilie Grigsby.

Grigsby's reputation was so scandalous, Belle said, that "all the men
in the world" knew her, but no women would acknowledge her. Nevertheless, Belle let her in. "I just lay back and studied her, such an exquisite angelic looking creature. Of course many gentlemen's fortunes
have gone into her tiny hands, but the one that made us all give her a
wide berth was Yerkes—that was really too much." Grigsby had indeed
been the mistress of several prominent men, most notably Chicago
railroad magnate Charles Yerkes. She had met Belle at a dinner back
in New York and sought her out when she heard Belle was in London.
"Her affection for me seemed so intense tonight that I decided she had
wearied of men and was turning her attentions to 'Topic no 2.' But not
for little Belle!" "Topic no. 2," or just "No. 2," was Belle's slang for
homosexuality. Oddly, Grigsby also wanted to give Belle a wrap of the
same design as the ones Bernard was trying to persuade her to accept
from him. Mariano Fortuny was a dress designer whose free-flowing
pleated-silk fashions represented a total departure from the corseted
dresses Belle had worn throughout her adulthood.[84] She was curious
enough to look at the Fortuny gown Grigsby offered, but did not accept
it. How typical of Belle, Bernard must have thought. Even as she was
mourning their missed opportunity to talk and trying to rescue their
relationship before she left for America, she was distracted by an
unknown and probably quite undesirable social acquaintance.

Belle promised to write Mary from the boat, but asked Bernard not
to tell her everything that had happened between them. "[I]t really is
not necessary and after all it belongs to us to you and to me alone." No
more should they take their friends or even family into their full confidence about their relationship. There is no evidence that Mary ever

found out about the pregnancy. She might have been more sympathetic than Belle would have expected. She would aid other women
who fled to Italy to give birth to illegitimate children.[85] But this particular pregnancy would have been rather more personal.

Mary had already given up her summer-long stance of support and
approval of Belle. In the midst of the strikes, Mary finally voiced her
own long-held suspicion that Belle had only wanted to have Bernard
Berenson, the famous Italian art critic, escort her through Italy. It was
this vanity that motivated her, Mary suggested, not love or interest in
Bernard as a person outside of his reputation and knowledge. Although
Bernard's own doubts were growing, he refused to acknowledge them
to Mary. He knew "the child was perfectly sincere, disinterested,
utterly abandoned in her love for me," at least while it lasted. Now, he
mused, Belle seemed so strange to him, "perhaps an incomprehensible
being, almost as if she belonged to another species." Yet, while wondering whether he had made "the greatest mistake" of his life in avoiding London, Bernard still spent time with a new friend, the writer
Edith Wharton, and started planning a trip to Spain with Mary.[86]

8

HIDING IN THE LIGHT

*I am . . . trying to assemble all the beautiful blonds in New York
for him [Charles Read]. I shall probably look like a huckleberry
in a bowl of milk!*

—Belle Greene, 1910[1]

*What does it matter if someone at some time, any time should see
my letters to you or yours to me. The whole world may know how
I feel about you as far as I am concerned.*

—Belle Greene, 1911[2]

ON THE TRAIN FROM LONDON to meet her ship, Belle began to
think about her return to New York. Her secrets had now multiplied,
and she had much more than ever to hide. The tactic she would take,
whether regarding her ancestry or her affair with Bernard, would be
one of misleading openness. Consciously or not, Belle dealt with suspicions about first her ethnicity and now her sexual behavior by

acknowledging, even drawing attention to, the rumors and the questions. But she stopped short of complete revelation, except to a small, intimate group. This tactic of hiding in the light flirted with true exposure, but it also allowed her the appearance of frankness, which veiled her growing collection of secrets. It was a complicated dance, and one in which she missed more than a few steps.

As she started on the journey home, Belle felt like a very different person from the one who had left the States three months before. This sense was confirmed when she met a slight acquaintance from New York on the train to the boat. The unnamed man could not put his finger on what exactly had altered, but told Belle that she seemed "much older and distressingly cynical and . . . much better looking." Perhaps to divert him from speculation on what caused such sudden maturity and cynicism, Belle responded that her "beauty" was a sore subject. Then she found herself telling him of a "certain" man (Bernard) who was sure she was her "mammy-nurse's" daughter! The New Yorker was appalled at such slander and warned Belle to stay away from men who would say such awful things about her.[3]

This story speaks volumes about Belle and her multiple performances of race and ancestry. Bernard had confided to other friends, and obviously to her as well, his speculations about her ethnic ancestry. He suggested to one that she might be Malaysian. At the time, "Malay" was a common stand-in for the "brown" or "Other" category of the popular five-group system taught in schools throughout the United States. His own patroness had called her a "half-breed."[4] Obviously, in Italy, Bernard had shared another theory with her: he thought Belle had black ancestry.

Although this version of her family Belle produced on the train identified her as mixed-race (never offered as fact, of course), it was as far from her real story as the Portuguese grandmother story. Her mother was not a maid or a "mammy"; she was a teacher and a musician. Her father was not a white seducer, using his racial and class status to force or seduce a young black domestic worker into a sexual relationship. He was a Harvard graduate and a lawyer who had married her mother and raised five children with her for almost two decades before their marriage dissolved. By comparison, in fact, the Portuguese grandmother story was actually pretty close to the truth: Belle at least had a Spanish great-grandfather. (Although for Rita Lydig even having just Spanish ancestry was enough to make her "Creole" and "exotic" to Mary Berenson and many others in her circles.) Conversely, Bernard's "mammy-nurse" theory, which Belle herself was now propagating as rumor, reduced her ancestry, her legitimacy, and her therefore status. Why would she present this new story of her origins, even as a joke?

Perhaps Belle was still so shaken by her experience in London and her failed attempts to reunite with Bernard that she just blurted it out without considering the consequences. She may even have been unsettled enough to be playing, consciously or unconsciously, with the potential dangers of disclosure: a self-destructive impulse, a moment of lowered defenses. It is also interesting that this episode took place just as Belle began her return trip back to the color-conscious world of New York. Many African Americans who journeyed to Europe felt far freer there, less confined by the limitations and weight of American racialism. In Europe a person with some rumored or known black ancestry might be accepted as white, even if a particularly exotic form of whiteness. Many Europeans who made the transatlantic trip in steerage to become Americans also found their ethnic and racial identities shifting in the New World.

Once Belle was on board the *Oceanic,* she was surrounded again by friends and acquaintances from home, some welcome, some not, another microcosm of her New York world. Here, too, people noted a change in her, which Belle blithely chalked up to the miscarriage. So many people were telling her that she had never looked better, so, she joked to Bernard, she had decided "that if I have one of those XXXXXXXXXXXXX yearly I stand a chance of being a blond at forty— which is the height of my earthly ambition!" Ethel Grant and her husband, having returned from Paris in time to catch the boat, were on board. So were Anne Morgan and Bessie Marbury. Miss Morgan was perhaps not so innocent when she suggested that Bernard join her on the return trip. For she grabbed Belle and immediately started grilling her about Italy. Where had she gone? What had she seen? How had

Belle found out about "all those little towns"? Belle wanted to know how much Annie knew and replied suggestively that she had had an exceptional guide. To which the Morgan daughter laughed and rejoined, "I suspect you did, and I suspect I know who it was." Having made their points and gotten their information, Miss Morgan and Miss Greene largely ignored each other for the remainder of the trip, except for a few times when Anne tried to persuade Belle to intercede on her behalf with her father.[5]

But Belle had Ethel and P. G. Grant to dally with. The crossing was particularly "curlycuetous," and this time Belle succumbed to the seasickness that the boat's tossing movements often brought. Ethel dubbed her "Billious Breene" and laughed at Belle's "vociferous objections to the Lord of Tempests."[6] When Belle recovered, Ellen Terry, the legendary English actress, kept Belle and Ethel entranced with her stories of her early theatrical career and her friendship with George Bernard Shaw. Belle pronounced herself "madly in love" with Terry and eagerly abandoned any handsome man she was flirting with to rush to Terry's rooms when summoned. They also talked about Terry's love affair with Henry Irving, who had died in 1905 after they had been separated for several years. Terry had taken several lovers very openly, beginning with architect Edward William Godwin, with whom she had two children.

And Ellen Terry guessed Belle's secret: that she had recently been "dreadfully in love." Belle worried that she would be so transparent to everyone. At least her secret was safe with this older woman, who would not judge her, having discovered for herself that becoming a fallen woman could be wonderfully freeing. Terry would probably even still consider Belle an innocent, so young and inexperienced in matters of love and sex. For her part, Belle found Ellen, and her morals, absolutely enchanting, and she reported that the feeling was mutual. Ellen called her "Childie" and decided that Belle should marry her son. ("'But, I said, he doesn't approve of marriage—he only wants children.' She sighed and said 'Yes.'")[7]

Alice Ditson was on board, too, but annoyingly distracting, now seen through the filter of Bernard's eyes. Belle tried to spurn her, but

Alice was oblivious and went around announcing that Belle was "her soul-mate and she could never love a man as she loves me etc. ad disgustum." Belle worried that people would take it for "a case of Topic No. 2," as they apparently had in London.[8] The George Williamsons, whom Belle now disliked personally for reasons never explained, were also on board. They wanted to be more friendly than Belle desired. She solved two of her problems by introducing them to Anne Morgan and leaving them all to talk.

When they were alone, Ethel and Belle compared notes about Bernard's behavior, beginning the long process of dissecting the last month of the affair. But Ethel and P.G. were also starting to annoy Belle—only Ellen Terry seemed incapable of annoying Belle on that trip. One morning the Grants cornered her and implored her to give up her avowed plan of marrying for money. Belle had inadvertently raised this concern when she assured them she had no interest in breaking up the Berensons' marriage. P.G. and Ethel had taken her seriously and obviously discussed it with each other. Belle assured them it would be several years before she would consider it. But she was getting quite tired of such interference in her affairs, real or imagined.[9]

Still, Belle greatly enjoyed her trip. She hosted a tea in her stateroom for Ellen Terry (who recited) and Marguerite Sylva (whom Belle had admired as Carmen at the Metropolitan Opera and who sang some bits from *Carmen* and *Thaïs*, another of Belle's favorites). Other guests included Admiral Brownson, who told stories about his experiences in the English navy and a writer who read some of his short stories. "As usual," Belle admitted, "I was the stupid one who just sat and enjoyed the others," making no contribution to the formal entertainment.[10]

Throughout the week Belle dreaded the day when the journey would end and she would be back in New York. J. P. Morgan, the person she missed the most, would not be in town for a few more days. Another man, identified only as "my future lord and master," would meet her boat, although Belle was hardly looking forward to seeing him. He had no chance with her, unless Bernard wrote that he no longer loved her.[11]

Ethel had her own theory about why Belle had such trepidation about her homecoming: her family. Belle was, she reported, "looking forward with shrinking to the society of her precious family." Now that Belle had enjoyed "freedom and good company," Ethel imagined, "the file edge of daily family is going to be very irritating. I only hope it would make her too prone to kick it all out." Ethel may have been biased here. She is credited with coining the witticism "God gave us our relatives; thank God we can choose our friends."[12]

Belle disembarked on October 26. The weather was a perfect autumn combination of dazzling sunshine and cool air. Most traveling Americans were back or due back soon. J.P. was waiting for her reports; correspondence had piled up in her absence. Her family and friends were there to welcome her home and fill up her evenings and weekends. And there was all the gossip to catch up on and control. Back in New York, Belle began to plan for her future with Bernard in their resumed correspondence. But her return to her New York life also brought a new sense of imbalance and loss. To distract herself, she returned to her "whirl" of work by day and play in the evenings and on weekends.

It all began nearly from the moment Belle stepped off the *Oceania*. Newspaper reporters recorded her arrival, estimating that she brought $30,000 worth of items back for the Morgan Library. The customs agent, ever on the lookout for Americans smuggling luxury items and artworks in without paying the proper taxes, confiscated two pieces Bernard had given her: a sixteenth-century Italian painting and an antique box. To get those back, she had to ask Bernard to fill out paperwork and obtain an affidavit from the American consulate in Paris attesting to the age and value of the items.[13]

But the inconvenience caused by this supposed discovery masked a greater coup, another example of Belle's hiding a deeper truth by seeming to confess to it. Belle knew that "their" man at the customshouse would pass her personal luggage through without examining it. Despite this arrangement, she took extra precautions to prevent detection of some decidedly nonpersonal art. Tucked between her clothes in her own trunks—even inside her boots—she hid a number of smaller items, including three bronze statues, a small painting, and some jew elry for the Library. Then she showed elaborate hesitancy when declaring three manuscripts, and the two gifts from Berenson, knowing that the manuscripts would be accepted and the gifts only confiscated until she got an affidavit from Berenson attesting to their value. Her feigned indignation when they were taken, however, did the trick. The inspector accepted her claim that the sixteenth-century Spanish illuminated manuscript and an incunabula from the same period were hers. "They don't belong to Mr. Morgan," a local journalist overheard her saying. "This is a private affair and concerns no one but myself." Satisfied that they had caught her out, the agents let the other trunks go. When she and J.P., back from his own travels, were finally alone at the Library, she showed off the smuggled items, and she and J.P. "did a war dance and laughed in great glee."[14]

It was a dangerous but relatively common trick employed by private collectors and professional dealers to avoid steep tariffs on imported art. In fact, just a week before Belle's arrival in New York, Joe and Henry Duveen as well as Ben and Louis Duveen had been arrested by customs and fined a total of $50,000 for differences between their shipments' declared and actual values, which they claimed was the result of clerical error.[15] Still, Belle bragged about her "little trap" not only to Berenson but also around New York. Her story pointed out the ignorance of the customs agents in determining the age, authenticity, and value of items, and their inconsistency in enforcing the new import laws. And Belle soon got her confiscated items back. The antique box sat on her desk at the Library until Morgan noticed it one day and commented, that "You had better not let 'your' friend Mr. Berenson see it, he'll say it's no good." Belle replied, "Oh! he has seen it and thinks it fine—otherwise I would not keep it." She may have reconsidered the wisdom of having a gift from Berenson at work, for she brought it home soon after that.[16]

The smuggling, undervaluing, and misrepresentations that the Duveens stood accused of were common practices among art collectors and dealers. A few years earlier Isabella Gardner had been caught shipping art in boxes labeled "household items." Gardner's suspect story was that she had lent some furniture and art to a friend who was

Richard T. Greener,
Belle da Costa Greene's
father, circa 1870.

Richard T. Greener,
circa 1890.

Fifteenth Street Presbyterian Church, the Fleets', Peters', and Greeners' church during Belle's childhood, circa 1899.

Howard University, where Richard T. Greener taught and served as dean during Belle's childhood, circa 1900.

T Street N.W. Greener and Fleet residences during
Belle's childhood. Photo 2006.

Princeton University Library, 1900–1906.

J. Pierpont Morgan, circa 1902.

Puck magazine cartoon depicting Morgan's collection of art
and treasures coming to New York, 1911.

The Morgan Library, exterior.

Morgan Library, North Room (Belle da Costa Greene's office).

Morgan Library,
West Room
(J. P. Morgan's office).

Morgan Library,
East Room
(reading room).

Belle da Costa Greene, photograph by Clarence White, 1911.

Belle da Costa Greene, photograph by Clarence White, 1911.

Belle da Costa Greene, photograph by Theodore Marceau, 1911.

Belle da Costa Greene, photograph by Theodore Marceau, 1911.

Belle da Costa Greene, photograph by Walter Histed, 1910.

Bernard Berenson at home in his Villa I Tatti, outside of Florence, Italy.

Gardens and landscaping behind the Villa I Tatti.

Mary Berenson at I Tatti.

"The Cleverest Girl I Know," Says J. Pierpont Morgan

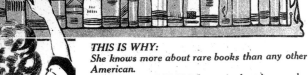

THIS IS WHY:

She knows more about rare books than any other American.

She has spent $42,000 for a single volume and outwitted a rich duke at an auction.

Her opinion on Caxton editions is sought by the greatest scholars.

She is chic, vivacious, and interesting, in fact, a "dandy, wholesome American girl," says

Mr. Morgan. She wears her hair long and does not use glasses, runs to Europe on secret missions, and is the terror of continental collectors' agents. Her name is Belle Green.

All day Miss Green works among books most of which were printed before America was discovered.

MISS BELLE GREEN

Chicago Tribune, August 11, 1912, page G2.

in a hostile separation dispute with her husband. Gardner had asked her to keep everything until the tax laws changed, but the woman decided to return to the United States and took it upon herself to bring Gardner's belongings as a surprise. The friend's angry husband alerted customs, and Gardner was threatened with fines of over $150,000 and prison.[17]

Not everyone knew how to play the game, however. When the George Williamsons debarked from the same ship, their luggage was opened and examined piece by piece. The customs' art expert declared that a seventeenth-century miniature painting Williamson wanted to bring in to sell was only a colored photograph and could be brought in for forty cents in tax. Williamson, an English expert on miniature portraits, was so outraged at the claim that his valuable antique was neither valuable nor antique, that he refused to pay the small tax, letting the customs agent confiscate it instead. (His catalogue of Morgan's miniature collection had just been completed and published that year.) The Williamsons dropped by the Library to tell Belle their mournful story, and she brought it straight to her boss, who laughed as hard as she did. So prevalent was the issue that at least one newspaper asked her to write an article about customs and art imports. But, as usual, Belle declined, opting to leave well enough alone and stay out of the limelight, given the widening dragnet of the Duveen investigation. Some lights were too bright, even for the fearless Belle.[18]

Belle was so busy already in the first hours and days of her return that she did not even cable Bernard to assure him that she had landed safely until two days after the fact. As she explained to him, when she finally found time to write, she had been surrounded by people for twenty-four hours straight—literally holding her hand and not letting her out of their sight. But, of course, she wrote, she had thought of him every minute.[19]

Not likely. There was too much to distract her, for one thing. Belle was suddenly involved in local and national politics, attempting to keep Theodore Roosevelt out of running for the presidency. She said that all the Wall Street men (including Morgan) were voting Democratic in the primary for the first time in their lives, just to try to block

Roosevelt. Roosevelt's antitrust stand threatened their business expansion, and he had targeted Morgan (as did much popular opinion) as the symbol of voracious capitalist greed. Belle was vocal, if not active, in these campaigns, saying the whole time that "no woman really cares a damn about any politics."[20] Such obvious contradiction between her words and her actions was one of Belle's hallmarks, and her friends loved to point them out to each other, if not to her face.

Several Europeans were also in town now, demanding attention with varying success. She gave her dear friend Charles Hercules Read, of the British Museum, a dinner party at the Colony Club, and invited a party of "beautiful blonds" for him to flirt with. In such fair company, she feared, she would "probably look like a huckleberry in a bowl of milk!" She also brought him to visit several other collections in galleries and private homes, including those of Benjamin Altman, Henry Clay Frick, and the late Henry O. Havemeyer, a sugar mogul and avid art collector. She owned up to Bernard that Miss Greene and Mr. Read were actually on a first-name basis, but promised that she had not fallen in love with Charles. When he left in November, after they had seen each other almost daily for a month, she described her "peculiarly tender feeling for him" as motherly. Read was twenty-two years her senior and had been married almost as long as she had been alive.[21]

Nevertheless, Belle and Charles continued to carry on a "mock" flirtation. Mock in Belle's eyes, at any rate, though it may have been more serious on her part than she let Bernard know. Six months later she sent Bernard an "addendum" Read had sent after writing an "adorably indiscreet" twelve-page letter. In general, she said she found Read (and most other English men) far too uptight and repressed to be much fun to flirt with. The only surviving note from Read from that period tells her she is one of the few people he is frank with, and it signs off, "Keep nice and limpid and frivolous. Your pal."[22]

Not all visitors were so welcome. Belle refused to give a party at her own expense for the Williamsons. Morgan also didn't want to bother with them. They remained ignored.

And Ethel Harrison was also planning to come to New York, posing an interesting dilemma for her supposed friend Belle da Costa Greene.

Ethel, of course, knew the one secret Belle never hinted about or made joking references to (except to Bernard): her pregnancy and subsequent abortion. Since Belle had not had the opportunity to talk to Bernard as she had wished about Ethel H., she finally disclosed the full situation to him, as she saw it. She recognized that Ethel H. had been "a perfect brick to me and stuck to me like a sister," arranging social events as well as helping to take care of her in the "all-important matter," along with Ethel G. But gradually Belle had come to realize in London that Ethel H. was not her friend. So sure was she of this that she and Ethel G. dubbed Harrison "Black Ethel," while Grant began referring to herself as "Ethel Bianca."[23]

It turned out Ethel Harrison had a grudge against Bernard. In hindsight (and after much discussion with Ethel G.), Belle realized that during her illness she had allowed herself to be swayed by the decidedly negative picture Harrison was painting of Bernard. For example, Harrison talked as if Bernard had pushed himself on Belle, even though Belle repeatedly protested that she had come to Europe with the intention of giving herself to him, "alive to the possible consequences." Then Harrison began to tell her she was a fool, that Bernard did not love her. Furthermore (perhaps most painfully), Harrison claimed that Bernard had begged *her* to go off with him *and have a child with him* but that she had refused. In fact, Harrison said she planned to insist that Bernard leave her alone in return for her help with Belle's situation. In her state in London, it took Belle a while to determine that Harrison's intention throughout this drama was to turn her against Bernard and to break them up. Belle now feared that Harrison, still in Europe with access to Bernard, would turn her strategy on Bernard, since Belle had stopped listening.

Perhaps a bit naïvely, Belle began to tell her lover some unflattering things about his friend: Ethel H. had begun an affair with a doctor in London (it is not clear whether it was with the same doctor who attended Belle); Ethel wanted only the physical contact of sex, not the emotional experience; she was not acknowledged socially by "decent" women. The distinctions Belle implied between Harrison's behavior and Belle's own illicit affair with Bernard were twofold. First, Ethel was motivated by physical lust, while Belle's affair was based on love, of which sex was only one expression. Second, Ethel's behavior was so well known that she was ostracized from society as an indecent woman, while Belle was taking great pains to cover her one affair and maintain the all-important façade of respectability. Still, there was something a bit ironic in her indictment of Harrison. Belle was facing similar claims of unromantic motives and therefore indecent behavior. In fact, Ethel Grant's husband, P.G., had just announced plans to enlighten Bernard as to "what a cold, hard proposition" Belle was, incapable of loving a man for longer than a week. P.G. had been a secondary witness to the affair between Belle and Bernard, through his wife's involvement.[24]

Of course, Belle also was in the position to compare numbers of affairs—Bernard was her first and only lover, whereas Ethel apparently had numerous liaisons. She did not mention this, perhaps because Bernard himself was so promiscuous. Even so, Belle might well have harbored the common double standard that multiple sexual conquests were acceptable, even admirable, in a man but indecent in a woman. She certainly held many other double standards. In other words, a woman might have an affair if motivated by true love and affection, and she might retain social respectability, but only if she did not flaunt her behavior.

Restraining the rumors was therefore a priority for Belle, to protect her reputation and her own definition of respectability. Within a few weeks of Belle's departure, for example, Bernard had lunch with Rita Lydig, one of the New Yorkers they had been dodging in Italy. Mrs. Lydig let him know she knew everything and suggested that Bernard, who was ill again, go to New York and let Belle take care of him. Bernard told her that Belle did not return his feelings: a lie. Meanwhile, Belle wrote to Philip Lydig to find out where he stood and invite him to the Library. But Mr. Morgan inadvertently blocked her plan to further sweeten the Lydigs by allowing them access to his private collection. For the next few months Morgan repeatedly refused their continued requests to visit the Library and him, once even literally running away an hour before an appointment Belle had scheduled.[25]

Other people were trusted confidants. Throughout the fall she declared Ethel Grant the only "outsider" she would entrust with the emotional truth of her affair with Bernard.[26] But she was also forced to rely on the good will and friendship of others in the know. When Eugene Glaenzer came into the Library in early November, they quickly established an amicable understanding without ever elaborating on the nature of her relationship with Bernard. Glaenzer was a New York art gallery owner and manager of the New York office of Jacques Seligmann & Co., art dealers with whom Belle was very sympathetic. He had also been in Europe that summer and had apparently heard the rumors; he knew why she had been too busy to see him in Paris and Italy. But he also knew that she knew he was "quite as busy" himself. They laughed over this mutual acknowledgment of their European departure from American standards of proper behavior. Fearing that the Blumenthals had been spreading the story, Belle enlisted Glaenzer's help. Later Belle would embrace Florrie Blumenthal as a friend and come to respect and admire her taste and knowledge in art and design.[27] But in the months following her Italy trip, Belle considered her a threat and the most likely source of gossip. So she sent a distinct warning to Florrie through Glaenzer to "mind her own business or I would have to see her personally."[28]

But it was too late. If not the Blumenthals, then someone else was talking, at least in Paris, where Bernard still lingered. Belle later blamed her boss's former partner George W. Perkins for spreading the story. Ironically, Bernard was more upset about other rumors that she had spurned him or, worse, had used him only as a guide than about whether or not people had figured out that they were lovers. He repeatedly told Belle of rumors that her interest was only in his expertise and panache as an art expert, and continued to ask her for months whether they were true.[29]

Later, at Florrie Blumenthal's insistence, she and Belle did meet and agreed to be "friends." Belle was by then as much concerned about Bernard's fears as about her own reputation. So she made it clear to Florrie that Bernard had taken her through Italy not as a tour conductor but as a "good friend."

> I told her that nothing incensed me so much as for any one
> to think that I cared more for your knowledge (much as I
> appreciated it) than I did for you personally and that I
> was greatly disappointed that I could not get back to Paris,
> as my chief reason in going there was to see you again
> before I sailed.[30]

Again, without actually discussing the nature of her relationship with
Bernard, Belle emphasized the great respect and admiration she had
for Mr. Berenson. This would become her primary response to any
mention of Bernard. She was always loyal to him intellectually, defending, for example, any opinion he had given on any artistic subject. And
she never feigned indifference to him, but always proclaimed her great
fondness and even love for him, sometimes waxing eloquent with jealous thoughts when his other women were mentioned.

Sometimes this meant expressing jealousy of herself. For instance,
when she met a Mrs. Ripley and realized they both were friends of
B.B., they immediately began talking about him and recent reports of
his illness. Their conversation was a great example of social gossip
gone awry. Mrs. Ripley divulged to Miss Greene that she had heard
from another friend that Bernard's illness was due to his being in love
with a mystery woman who was also in love with him. Mrs. Ripley was
determined to find out who it was. No one seemed to know, and she
was writing to the sister of a friend to find out. Miss Greene laughed
and joked, "[H]e promised to be true to me but of course I fear I'm too
far away to keep him to his word." Mrs. Ripley swore to let her know if
she found out the woman's name. Belle was momentarily paralyzed.
Would the woman actually write to her if she found out that Miss
Greene *was* the mystery woman?[31]

But there were dozens of projects and people and things demanding
her attention to keep her from dwelling too long on Bernard and what
had happened in Europe. The Duveen affair was threatening to go to
trial. An independent valuation of the items involved and an examina-
tion of business records had made it clear that there was no simple
error behind the matter. The Duveens were now charged with evading

five million dollars in tariffs over 1909 alone. Joe had hired a lawyer, and the question now was how many other dealers and collectors would get pulled into the legal mess. Belle's opinion on the topic swung back and forth as various figures, including Joe Duveen himself, discussed the matter with her. First she and J.P. hashed the matter out. Neither liked the dealer, but both felt he was being treated unfairly. Belle told J.P. that the art world in London sympathized with Duveen and she had heard that the same held in Paris. Even Jacques Seligmann, the dealer's main rival who had been burned himself, said he would stand by him. Seligmann seemed to be safe; he was no less guilty than the Duveens of doctoring customs papers, but he had destroyed the evidence of his misdeeds. Morgan seemed safe but did not want Duveen seen at the Library, just in case. Instead, he dispatched Belle to dine with the accused and to report back.[32]

And then the parade began. Thomas Ryan, George Blumenthal, and Emile Rey all came to the Library to talk to Belle about the customs business and Arnold Seligmann's potential involvement.[33] When the collectors Peter Widener and Benny Altman became entangled in the mess, Belle began to focus her anger more on the Duveens, hoping that rumors that they would settle with huge fines were true. "It's what I always felt about them—they rob the people they buy from—they rob the people they sell to and they rob the government," she sniffed self-righteously to Bernard.[34]

At some point during the crisis Bernard revealed to Belle some details of his financial involvement with the Duveens. This did not seem to affect her attitude toward the Duveens or their situation, but it did put a damper on her desire to have Bernard come visit her. Although she yearned to see him and knew she could not make the trip for a while, she always stopped herself from begging him to come. If he had a contract with the Duveens, he might be dragged into the trial as a witness or even find himself under threat of arrest if he came to the United States.[35]

Besides the unusually dramatic events in the art and book world that fall, there was the opening of the opera and theater season to occupy Belle's attentions. In addition to her usual near-nightly atten-

dance of all the plays and operas she could fit into a week, Belle
became involved in the management of the New Theatre. Only a year
after it opened, it was already in financial trouble. According to Belle,
J. P. Morgan and Otto Kahn asked her to help them try to salvage it.
Belle considered Kahn a great friend whom she judged sincere in his
interest in art. Kahn was also the primary supporter of the Metropolitan Opera Company and had been responsible for bringing Giulio
Gatti-Casazza as director and Arturo Toscanini as conductor. Moreover, he had been one of the primary planners for the New Theatre, in
which the Metropolitan Opera Company regularly performed.[36]

Over the fall and early winter Belle called a series of meetings and
began trying to find a new manager. When the New Theatre was
reconstituted as the Century Theatre, Belle was one of sixteen incor-
porators in the new "Century Opera Company," along with Otto Kahn,
Philip Lydig, Clarence Mackay, and Harry Payne Whitney. But when
it came time to appoint the board, she opted—as usual—to remain
behind the scenes.[37]

Not surprisingly, theater and opera productions, and theater and
opera people, were the center of Belle's social life in the fall of 1910
and early winter of 1911. Promising Bernard she would "sober down"
in February after "my divine Sara" left, Belle reveled in her tumult of
dinners, rehearsals, and shows.[38] Belle's divine Sara was *the* divine
Sarah Bernhardt, a French actress born in 1844. (Bernhardt, like Belle
and countless other women of the time, routinely subtracted years
from her biological age. In 1909 the sixty-five-year-old great grandmother proudly played the nineteen-year-old Joan of Arc to wildly
enthusiastic audiences.) The impetuous and ambitious Bernhardt had
long since established her star status on stage and was moving into cinema as well. But in New York that season she was revisiting some of
her most famous stage roles: the title roles in *Phèdre* and *La Femme X*.
Like Ellen Terry, whose friendship had sustained Belle on the long
ocean voyage home, Bernhardt left a trail lovers—and a few husbands—in her wake, earning her a reputation as a femme fatale for the
romantic and as a promiscuous woman for the righteous. In 1910 she

was on her second farewell tour of the United States, accompanied by her twenty-seven-year-old lover.[39]

It is impossible to tell how far back Belle's acquaintance with these women went. Scattered pieces of evidence suggest that she hung around theatrical circles long before she began writing Bernard and therefore leaving detailed evidence of her movements. It is clear, however, that by the 1910–11 season Belle was very friendly with these most famous and most fascinating older women.[40]

Bernhardt attended a small party at Belle's apartment in early December. At the end of December, Belle went to see the Divine Sarah in *La Femme X*, a play by Alexandre Bisson. Later revamped as *Madame X*, the plot depicts a woman who sinks into depravity after her husband casts her out. She is redeemed by sacrificing herself for her child years later, although he (in later versions sometimes she) does not recognize his lost mother. In the intermissions between the histrionic acts, Bernhardt sent for Belle to come backstage, an unusual privilege. She also invited Belle to come to Philadelphia with her for several days in February, but that trip was later canceled.[41]

Belle's interest in Terry was also primarily social. She and Ellen went together to the new Engelbert Humperdinck opera *Die Königskinder (The King's Children)* and the Russian Ballet, where Anna Pavlova performed her signature piece, "The Dying Swan," which Belle pronounced "too wonderful." (Isadora Duncan would have scoffed at that.) After a supper at the Metropolitan Club with friends, hosted by Frank Sturgis, a close crony of J. P. Morgan's, the two women returned to Belle's apartment and stayed up until five in the morning talking. Belle described Terry in much the same way others described Belle— "so overflowing with vitality and the joy of living." Later she described Terry's behavior at a party in her apartment as "like a kitten" dancing around with many men. She was, Belle said approvingly, a mischievous woman.[42]

Bernard would have been disappointed with Belle's reversion to socializing with actresses, dancers, and the like, even ones at such heights as Bernhardt and Terry. When she confessed in February that, far from sobering up as promised, she was now hanging out with Mary Garden, she knew he would be annoyed. She defended her decision, saying that Garden interested her greatly and that she didn't believe that half the gossip about her was true. And Mary was performing that season as well, in *Thaïs* and in *Pelléas et Mélisande*. Mélisande was her signature role, which she had premiered for Claude Debussy in 1902 amid scandal involving another soprano and the librettist, and controversy over its artistic merit—which soon gave way to adoration. Garden came to New York in 1907, joining Oscar Hammerstein's Manhattan Center Opera Company—the Metropolitan Opera's biggest competition. Her first performance as Thaïs was most memorable for the pale pink skintight dress she wore that made her appear to be nude. But her most scandalous role was as Salome and its still famous "Dance of the Seven Veils," which she first performed in 1909. Garden became a media celebrity and fell in with theater crowds and the transatlantic aristocracy (rumors persisted for years that she was engaged to a Russian prince).[43]

Gossip abounded about her love affairs, and Mary loved to tease the press, announcing alternately that she would never marry and that she was on the verge of giving up her career for love; that she had no use for voting and that she was a suffragist.[44] Although Garden played out her supposed ambiguities with full media coverage, her competing declarations sound similar to Belle's willful failure to notice her own apparent contradictions. So far only Belle's friends and colleagues noticed when she threw herself into politics while claiming women had no place there or denounced the idle rich as underbred while staying at their mansion parties and eating at their tables. Soon, however, Belle's audience would broaden considerably. She may have been learning some lessons in media manipulation from one of the best.

Indeed, Belle seemed more interested in Mary Garden socially than artistically. When she saw her in *Thaïs* in 1911, Belle admired her costume and acting but dismissed her singing as "punk," and when she went to see her in *Carmen* in 1912, she anticipated that it would be "pretty bad." But Mary the person interested Belle tremendously, and she loved to keep the star company when she was studying a part, but promised to drop her if Bernard insisted. He did.[45]

Belle said she stopped seeing Mary Garden, but she probably did not stay away from her or other female performers very long. These women's independence, frank enjoyment of their sexuality, and willingness to reject marriage, or treat it as a temporary arrangement, clearly enthralled Belle. She watched all of them—Garden, Duncan, Bernhardt, Terry, and others—with fascination, frankly admiring the lives they had led. "Do you suppose," she asked Bernard breathlessly, "I will ever have all those exciting experiences?"[46] There may have been some recognition in her envy and ambition. Descriptions of the performers and the librarian sound familiar: they were full of vitality, impulsive, dramatic, loving to tease, to feed and create some scandal while taking great offense at other rumors. Belle's particular enthrallment with actresses is significant. She studied them as they studied their roles, attended their shows even when she did not expect an outstanding performance, made herself part of their social circles. There is a sense in which we all have that fascination, because we all understand the connection between acting a role on stage or before cameras, and the performance we each carry out in our everyday lives. This may have been of special interest to a woman with such secrets as Belle's.

Still, Belle did not only gravitate toward artistic celebrities. One of J.P.'s mistresses, Lady Alan Johnstone, also captivated her.[47] Johnstone initiated their friendship after hearing about Belle's travels, and probably about her affair with Bernard. Johnstone was the one member of the "harem" for whom Belle had any respect, although she amused herself trying to keep Johnstone and three of J.P.'s other "pets" apart from one another when they were all in the Library at the same time. But she liked Johnstone better than the rest and agreed to have lunch with her at the Colony Club. Her description of her interactions with J.P. and his mistress reveal that, while she may not have been one of the great man's mistresses, Belle occupied a somewhat analogous position in his life. For example, when Johnstone told her that J.P. had said Belle was the "most important person in his life," Belle responded that it was "all rot" and that she was thrilled to see that Johnstone was in New York so she could take J.P. off her hands for a while and give her some breathing space. Even so, J.P. did break a date with Johnstone to talk with Belle for several hours that very evening.[48]

As Belle threw herself back into her tumultuous life, Bernard tried to settle back into his significantly quieter one. By mid-November, Bernard finally left Paris for I Tatti, although Mary was suddenly ill again and dreading his return. She alternately promised to soothe his troubled emotions and tried to postpone his arrival.[49] She was beside herself about the Piot fresco, still shockingly vivid in color and showing no signs of fading, as the artist continued to promise. (They still have not.) She was sure Bernard would agree with her that they should be removed but wanted him to make the decision. On the other hand, she joked, if Piot turned out to be the next Michelangelo, they would be famous just for having him in their home.[50]

But Bernard arrived mostly peaceful and loving almost everything that had been renovated and added to the villa—except the frescoes, which he pretended not to see after one brief, horrified look. They were later covered up. Despite Bernard's failure to become enraged, it was clear he was not in good shape. He was so nervous that he quivered at the slightest noise. A doctor was called in the next morning and eventually diagnosed him with an "unspeakable neuralgia" (neural or nerve pain) and suggested daily massages.[51]

His illness was both physical and emotional. Mary ultimately concluded that it was all emotional. Certainly Bernard's digestive troubles, his increasingly violent rages, his refusal to leave his bedroom for days on end, all seemed connected to his emotional stability—or instability. In either state, the immediate cause was clear: Belle. Within days of Bernard's return, Mary wrote to the other woman about his health, hoping perhaps that Belle would be able to write something to alleviate his suffering. Belle agreed that she was the cause, but perhaps not in the same way Mary or even Bernard understood it. For Belle the problem was that she was not with him, but the solution—to join him again—was just not possible.[52]

Nor was she able to provide the continuous stream of letters Bernard's fragile state seemed to require to keep him stable. When her maid Annie became ill later that month, Belle stopped writing for a few weeks, sending only a brief note explaining that she was giving all of her attention to the "mammy-maid" who had raised her since infancy. A chronic pain in Annie's leg had worsened, and a botched cauterization led to an operation. Belle hired a nurse but spent all her non-working time caring for her caregiver herself until her hospital stay. After a month of silence, during which Bernard broke down completely, sure that she no longer loved him, Belle wrote again. Annie was gone. After two operations, the second of which seemed to be a complete success, she had caught an infection and died.

In her grief, and realizing belatedly the effect her silence had had on Bernard, Belle tried to explain why she felt this loss so keenly. Annie had been, she wrote, her "faithful and adoring slave" who had been by her side all of her life, who had loved and spoiled her like no other. She was "more dear than a mother" to Belle, and the first time they had been separated for a significant period was during Belle's trip to Europe the preceding year. Belle felt lost without her, alone and uncared for.[53]

The intimacy Belle described between herself and Annie sits awkwardly with the language of race she uses to portray her. Despite Belle's grief, she presented Annie as a painfully stereotyped figure. Annie, as translated by Belle for Bernard, was a "poor little black thing," a "faithful and adoring slave" who spoke in humorous dialect and loved Belle "in a slave's way or a dog's way. Something quite outside of human love she gave me."[54] Who was this woman, and why did Belle describe her in such terms?

A hired black woman did indeed take care of Belle early in her childhood. Mary A. Askins worked as a live-in domestic servant in the Greener household in Washington, D.C., when Belle was an infant. She was listed as seventy years old in 1880. She could not read or write and very likely had been born a slave. It is possible that Mary's middle initial A stood for "Ann" or some form of that name, or that the Greeners had given her the name Annie. (It was not uncommon for employers to assign names to servants, sometimes even using the same name for a series of individuals working in the same role.) But there is no record of her living with the Greenes in New York or of any Mary or Ann (or Anne) Askins matching her age and birth information in Manhattan between 1890 and 1910. If by chance this woman moved with Genevieve and the children to New York, this might fit the story Belle told Bernard in 1910 when Annie became ill and died. Certainly she could have played the role of helping to raise Belle, providing the apparently unconditional love and loyalty that defined the mammy figure for whites. But if Askins was really seventy years old in 1880, she would have been a hundred in 1910. Not impossible, but very improbable. If the Annie who died in 1910 was Mary A. Askins, it is far more likely that her age was overestimated in the 1880 census.[55] Likelier still is that this was not the same woman whom Belle mourned in 1910.

Indeed, in 1910 an Annie Ferguson was living with the Greenes as a servant. This Annie was listed as mulatto and a widow. This Annie was forty years old, which would have made her only nine years older than Belle. Nor does she seem to have been working there long. Impossible, then, that this was the Annie whom Belle remembered from her childhood, unless census takers in 1880 and 1910 mistook her age by several decades. It may be that Belle was combining her memories of an earlier domestic servant who helped raise her and this woman.[56]

There are a few other references to a nursemaid living with Belle and Genevieve in New York. In 1909 Belle mentioned that her "dear old nurse maid" had shown her the postcard she declared looked exactly like Belle as a child. And then again there was Bernard's suggestion, repeated by Belle to an acquaintance on a train, that Belle was her "mammy-nurse's" child. This may well have been a reference to a specific woman. If Bernard ever did have tea at Belle's home, he might have met Annie.[57]

The incident also raises another layer in the question of Belle's identity. Did she describe Annie as slavelike and doglike to emphasize for Bernard the difference between herself and Annie? Her explicit purpose was to explain her monthlong silence and emphasize the difference between Annie's love for her and hers for Bernard. But Bernard's suggestion that Annie, not Genevieve, was Belle's biological mother may have made Belle nervous. Again, as she did when using the "n" word, Belle may have been using racist language to further affirm her identity as white, or at least as not-black. Annie's stereotypical blackness would then operate to cast Belle and her family more firmly as white. Or perhaps Belle had internalized her position as superior to her dark-skinned "mammy" either by virtue of being white, having white ancestry, or simply being comfortable enough to hire a maid rather than work as one.

Whoever she was, Annie clearly represented blackness for Belle. Her complicated emotional response to Annie's death pulled on feelings she had about her, about other black women who had nurtured her, about the link with blackness she had lost when she made the decision over ten years before to change her name.[58]

In the months following Annie's death, Belle seemed to cling to Bernard even more. She had purchased a new apartment, or two adjoining apartments, for herself and her family on East Fortieth Street.[59] Their building was across the street from the blocklong Murray Hill Hotel on Park Avenue, and just four blocks north of the Morgan Library. It was also conveniently close to Grand Central Station, still under construction, due to be completed in early 1913, and the New York Public Library on Fifth Avenue, which opened in May 1911.

Throughout the fall of 1910 and into 1911 as she selected furnishings and décor for her rooms, Belle imagined Bernard living with her there: "[E]very time I put in a chair or place a book or hang a picture or lay a bedspread I say some day—'Daarrling' will sit there—some day 'Daarrling' will read that, some day 'Daarrling' will look at that and say 'no—its not Joshua Reynolds—its an Amico of Tossetta.'" Dubbing her bedroom her "Berenson room," she created a bookshelf with art books he had sent her and portfolios of photographs of his collection. She asked for three cabinet-sized photos of him for her dressing table. She considered his tastes when ordering her bathroom mirror, and bought a sofa made with him in mind: large and cushiony for him to sleep on. And she purchased slippers and a robe for him, which hung in her closet awaiting his arrival.[60]

For Christmas, Belle sent Bernard her "only decent possession": an ancient Greek coin. He sent her a series of increasingly expensive gifts, including a set of books about the Tuscan towns they had visited together, a "little San Timiniceso legend," and a Piero della Francesco.[61]

Belle was also adding to her modest collection and arranging her new rooms to showcase them. When she received a $2,000 raise, she immediately purchased two Han period pottery jars. And she had her eye on more pieces, speculating that she could sell her collection of six eighteenth-century English mezzotints for $10,000. The copper intaglio prints had "said all they ever can to me." She also installed silk rugs, several Chinese porcelains, and an Italian "primitive" of unspecified origins.[62] On a limited scale, Belle had become a collector herself.

Bernard encouraged this and began giving her ever more significant art pieces as gifts. Later that year he presented her with a Spinello Aretino painting, *The Angel of the Annunciation*. Mary bitterly complained that B.B. had given "some of his loveliest pictures" to the undeserving Belle, at great cost to Mary's pride and her pocketbook.[63]

But not all of his gifts were artistic in nature. Even before she moved into her "Berenson room," Belle had the Fortuny gowns he had sent, which she finally consented to keep. Belle seemed to wear hers at home only (except for an opera cape) and thought she looked "very queer in them—like a Hindoo." But she loved the feel of them against her skin without all the layers of undergarments normally required by her dresses. "I feel very oriental and dreamy and lazy and as if I had no bones."[64]

Caught up in the fantasy of her inner life with Bernard, exhausted by the demands of her social life in New York, and unaware of the extent of his illness, Belle continued to write. But her letters became less frequent and less consistent. Some of her lapses in writing were easily explainable, as with Annie's death; others were not. Throughout the year following their idyll in Italy, gaps in her correspondence, whether caused by her neglect or the vagaries of the international mails, kept letters from reaching Bernard time and again. And each time her apparent silence threw him into paroxysms of doubt and anxiety.[65]

Mary and Bernard both thought she should prove her love to Bernard with a visit, but Belle was, as she put it, not a free agent. Morgan's ever-increasing dependence on her made it impossible for her to leave until at least the summer of 1911. She assured Bernard over and over of her love, calling him "daaarling" and "fiamma mia" (my flame). Ethel Grant also wrote to Bernard confirming from a third party that Belle was still smitten with him, if anything, even more now than while in London. Belle herself repeatedly said that their difficulties during and after their stay in Venice had made their love stronger. "Sometimes I think it was just as well that we had that Hellish time in September," she even mused, so much had their love grown and deepened in the thorny aftermath.[66]

Although both Mary and Bernard repeatedly begged and pressured Belle to visit, she repeatedly refused. She simply was not in a position to drop everything—her job, her ties to J.P., her duty to her family— and leave again. And she continued to caution Bernard not to come to the United States. There was not only the customs problem but also the problem of avoiding further scandal. Where could they go, other than Canada, where they could be together?[67]

Once she was in her new apartment, at the end of January 1911, however, she immediately began to plan for him to come visit and stay there safely with her.[68] She had arranged the perfect combination of absolute privacy and the appearance of family presence. She had taken two adjacent apartments and had a doorway cut between the drawing rooms. The door had a lock, but technically Belle still lived with her mother, which made her "eminently respectable," she concluded smugly.[69] Belle's short-term plan was for Bernard to come to New York and stay with her in her new apartment, once the Duveen case was settled. But she had bigger plans for them as well. She was never quite clear about her long-range vision, but Morgan seemed to play a key role.

Morgan was about to leave again for his annual season in Europe. And this time he was planning to meet with Bernard one-on-one. In fact, Belle orchestrated the meeting. Still trying to figure out why J.P. was "unaccountably prejudiced" against Bernard, Belle tried to show her boss that Bernard had become an ally and friend to her professionally and, by extension, to Morgan as well. One Sunday afternoon she and J.P. were alone in the Library and talked, as was their habit, for hours. Among other things, she told her boss she had spent time with the famous Mr. Berenson in Italy. Of course she mentioned only the educational aspect of their visits, omitting any detail on how often and in what capacity the couple had traveled together. Morgan thereafter referred to Bernard as "Miss Greene's friend Mr. Berenson," which Belle found very amusing.[70]

But much as she wanted the two most important men in her life to meet in Europe, she worried about the dangers, warning her lover to be "very careful" when talking to Morgan about her, to be sure to show only "a scholar's interest in a student." J.P., after all, could hardly object to this renowned scholar tutoring his protégée—it would only make Belle "fitter" for her work. Months before the anticipated meeting, she also began imploring Bernard to be tactful about discussing Morgan's art things, to avoid criticism and not tell Morgan that his things were "punk," even when they were. Above all, she lectured, remember that Morgan loved flattery. Buttering him up would be for their own good as a couple in the long run.[71] Most importantly, Morgan must not guess that Belle and Bernard were lovers.

> There must be nothing of what really has happened for he is terribly jealous and considers me his property and would never speak to you if he learned otherwise and daarrling you must be friends for my sake if for no other—the two people that I love best in the world must love each other.

And she was sure, having stressed the presence of Mary Berenson and Alice Ditson at their meetings, that J.P. suspected nothing untoward. "So be wise angel—our time will come and we might as well all three be friends while he lives. Don't think I'm deceitful, for I'm really planning more for you than for myself although you may be inclined not to believe it."[72]

The meeting itself was anticlimactic. No deals came out of it, no decisions were made, no relationships forged. However, the great men were friendly to each other, and Belle breathed a sigh of relief when J.P. left Florence and wrote her a positive report. "[H]e still loves us," she reported gleefully back to Bernard. And apparently he still hadn't heard any "nasty gossip." Even so, Belle continued to worry that J.P. had caught wind of the affair.[73] Certainly several people in their overlapping social circles knew, including his daughter and one of his mistresses.

At the same time Morgan's emotional demands on her were growing. Throughout the next two years Belle constantly complained about his erratic expectations of her. He demanded her complete fidelity, not as a lover, but as an employee and a paid confidante. But J.P. also wanted (and received) an emotional loyalty and friendship from her. And there was sometimes an edge of sexual tension in the mix:

> He asked me tonight if I would like him better if he were
> thirty years younger and I said no, I'd leave the library—he
> would be too dangerous—which seemed to please him and
> then he said he never wanted to be younger except when he
> was with me and thought of me. I don't doubt he has said
> that to every woman he knows but I love him just the same.[74]

This kind of teasing fit both Belle's and J.P.'s personalities, and their relationship combined many shared interests. The two spent long hours together talking about almost everything: books, people, politics, finance, the Library, Morgan's family.

A while later Bernard's name came up again in one of Miss Greene and Mr. Morgan's chats. Belle mentioned that Mr. Berenson had written to her about a book he was going to send to Morgan. Apparently Belle had mentioned a few too many letters. (If Bernard was writing at the same rate as Belle, she would have received nine or ten in the preceding month alone; he later claimed to have written almost daily during this period, not at all improbable, given his penchant for letters and his obsession with Belle.)

[J.P.] said "It seems to me you hear very often from Berenson" and I lied brave[ly] and said "not so very often but he
is so good to me and writes me of all the interesting things
he sees and does in the art and literary world and I am so
anxious for you both to be friends for he admires you so
much" (at which J.P. visibly brightened).

Belle and J.P. then had it out about who had said what about whom—
both J.P. and Bernard had been told about "horrid things" the other
had said about him. J.P. denied having said anything negative; Belle
assured him that Berenson admired him. Finally, Belle was thrilled to
report, Morgan concluded that the two men had simply disagreed
about an attribution.[75]

This outcome perfectly fit Belle's plan to have the two men be great
friends. And there was little she loved better than sitting down to talk
with an influential person and untangling an apparent mix-up to her
own benefit, or twisting and cajoling and convincing him until her
desired outcome was reached. In a world dependent on social ties,
trust, and loyalty, and riddled with scandal, deceit, and greed, such
talks were not treated as merely feminine gossip but were the stuff that
dealers and collectors alike depended on to chart their business
courses.

But Belle could also use these skills for her own purposes. One of
the more extreme examples of this came when Ethel Harrison arrived
in New York in late January. Belle now hated "Black Ethel," but she had
to be careful, even kind to her adversary. Ethel H. knew at least two
secrets that could destroy Belle. How to punish her without losing her
good will and thereby risking retaliation?

Belle and Ethel Grant hatched a plan. Upon their victim's return,
several of Belle's male friends were enlisted, two to pretend to be completely in love (or lust) with the visiting Ethel, and several more to rush
her with invitations to dinners, drives, and theater parties during her
visit. One of the false crushes was Frank Pollock, a handsome tenor
whom Belle persuaded to play the role by pointing out that Harrison
was in a position to get him an engagement in opera houses in and

around her home in Naples. Ethel fell for it, and the whole party, all in the know, had much amusement at her expense. The game went on all week in an endless string of dinners and performances and parties. Belle was elated at her plan's success. Ethel H. could never say that Belle hadn't repaid her kindnesses in London, but Belle could feel she had repaid her for her deviousness. "I am used to the game of staying out all night," Belle smirked, but Ethel was not. She dragged around "looking like a sick cat." It was likely this kind of behavior that made Mary Berenson later comment that while she wanted to think well of Belle, "she often makes it hard."[76]

Of course Belle knew that Ethel H. would soon be returning to her home in Italy and would eventually meet up with Bernard. This posed a dilemma, since "the viper" had now been introduced to several of Belle's beaus, and one in particular. Frank McComas was an Australian-born landscape painter who had fallen in love with Belle. In order to distract Ethel H. from the subject of Bernard, Belle played up her interest in the unknowing "fine boy of 35," during the week of rushing and false romance and hidden laughter. But Frank was apparently unaware that Belle's sudden deeper interest in him was all part of her plan for dealing with Ethel. Even Belle felt a bit guilty, for this time she could not hope that Frank's feelings for her were superficial or ephemeral. She promised herself that she would let him down easy after Ethel was gone. "Poor child."[77]

In fact, she felt she was now attracting even more men than usual. She told Bernard it was because she was in love with him that "half the world" seemed to be in love with her. Trying to explain the impossibility of anyone's taking Bernard's place in her heart, she told him about another unnamed "young man" who had proposed to her four times. In her final refusal she confessed she was in love with someone else. The man later saw Bernard's picture and realized this was his rival. After staring at the portrait for a while, the unsuccessful wooer admitted, "I could never hope to take you from a man like that and yet I shall hope until I die."[78]

When Ethel Harrison finally returned to Europe, Belle breathed a sigh of relief. Apparently she was not as immune to the physical toll of late nights and heavy partying as she claimed. She spent the next two evenings home alone, even postponing a dinner with her beloved Ellen Terry to stay in her bed rereading two years of Bernard's correspondence.[79]

Eventually Bernard's letters began to contain some pointed questions about the "beaus" Belle kept mentioning. He asked for more information about Frank McComas, and Belle tried to explain that she saw him as "exterior to us." She was glad he would be in California again for a few months; she felt quite bad about the situation and genuinely liked him, but could not love him. He was, she said, more in love with her than Bernard was "because it came over him so suddenly that it rather swept him off his feet." She was hoping Frank would recover so they could be friends. And, oh yes, he was already married "like almost all the men who love me."[80]

Once back in Italy, "Black Ethel" did indeed tell Bernard all about McComas's interests in Belle. Belle had to remind Bernard that she had told him about Frank and that all of their socializing had been a farce, created to mock Ethel. But the intended victim had caught on to at least some of the underlying truth. She had noticed, for example, that the handsome tenor who was supposed to be flirting with her actually seemed to be far more interested in Belle. Under Bernard's barbed questioning Belle finally admitted that Frank Pollock had also proposed to her twice—unsuccessfully.[81]

That Belle flirted with other men was no secret. Bernard also had many other women in his life besides Mary and Belle. But Belle still used a strange combination of open disclosure and denial when dealing with the subject. How, for example, was Bernard to take her sudden interruption of a letter-writing session because she had to meet her "future husband" for lunch? Belle promised not to consider him unless Bernard dumped her, and she never mentioned him again, unless one of the above Franks was the "nice great big polar bear" in question.[82]

Bernard had often accused her of being a flirt, and Belle had always tried to explain the nature and purpose of her relationships with men:

You call me a flirt—I'm not really—I can't flirt very well because if I am really interested it very soon passes beyond the flirting stage and difficulties of all sorts present themselves, and invariably the time arrives when you wonder how you are going to gently insinuate that the dream is over and that you find you are not really his soulmate. The whole trouble with me is my insatiable curiosity—a perfectly mad irresistible desire to know every thing and every body every situation and every emotion, every human, divine and hellish relation and the result is that I come away with little scraps of knowledge but generally bruised and with a determined resolve "never again" but of course one is caught again and so the game goes on. It is probably going to be the ruination of me but I don't seem to be able to help it.

And, as always, Belle sought to distinguish her relationship with Bernard, assuring him that her interest in him was not driven by curiosity but by a sense of "at-homeness" and that the stimulation she felt for him was "a champagne to my soul, mind and body."[83]

In addition to the danger such flirtations held for her position and her status as a woman in the public eye, Belle was marginally aware that her approach to relationships might be hurtful. But she did not believe she had ever caused a man pain. "I never heard yet of a man, who very soon did not find solace in some other (fair) dame."[84] Again, the specter of the blond beauty.

Meanwhile, Belle was also bracing for another visitor. Senda Berenson, Bernard's sister, had been in touch arranging a visit. At first Belle was thrilled, thinking it was just another social tour of New York, although she idly wondered whether Senda knew anything about the affair.[85] Senda and Belle had last met in 1909, soon after Bernard and Mary left New York. On this second visit, however, Senda was looking for answers, not a night on the town. She did know about the affair, and probably much more than Belle did about Bernard's declining physical and emotional state over the five months since he had last seen Belle. Mary and Bernard had been keeping Senda apprised of the situation, and, as their desperation peaked, Mary dispatched her sister-in-law to appeal directly to Belle and find out what her intentions were.[86]

When Belle realized that Senda was actually coming to talk to her about Bernard, she asked him for permission to discuss the situation if Senda asked about it. Belle had her position statement ready: "that I love you very much and that I don't believe we either of us can ever be really happy apart."[87] But this blithe line did not suffice for the gentle but pointed grilling Senda employed. In fact, the actual meeting completely unnerved Belle. Senda, "with the awful eye of a third person," had immediately exposed the truth of the situation by asking her what the result of the affair was going to be. "It was a sickening moment— only the second time I had ever looked the question in the face." Belle didn't say when the first time had been. Now Senda's quiet challenge made her face the reality that she and Bernard would always live apart, at most able to be together a month or two each year. "It makes me feel that life is but a long grey stretch—the endless desert with here and there an oasis formed by our meeting."[88]

Senda also asked Belle whether she would marry Bernard, if he were available. Belle said no. Relieved that her brother's marriage was not in external danger, Senda came away from the meeting quite convinced of Belle's sincere fondness for and loyalty to Mary. But Bernard seemed to be wavering. He would later admit that the affair with Belle was the one affair that had tempted him to end his marriage. He had had many mistresses, and would have many more, but only Belle seemed worth giving up Mary for. Senda, in the meantime, tried to convince him that marriage to Belle would never work. "You would be separated in two months," she counseled her elder brother. "She could never for one moment wait upon you—care for you (in the homely sense) make paths smooth and easy for you." This affair, Senda feared, was blinding Bernard to all Mary did and was for him.

Furthermore, Belle revealed that she was not interested in marriage at all. She told Senda she preferred not to marry and, if she did, it would be for money—"lots of money." Apparently this was her standard line. Belle explained to Bernard that she never planned to marry, didn't feel she was cut out for marriage, and did not see how marrying would add anything to her relationship with him. She did mention the role money might play in changing her mind, promising that even if she were "forced into an 'alliance financially,'" she would still be his emotionally.[89] When Senda and Rachel Costelloe (Mary's daughter) each married later that spring, Belle hoped the men were worthy and commented that it made her happy to hear of "some nice girl" marrying because it made her feel that she could still more "afford single blessedness."[90]

Belle's pronouncements on marriage were confusing, to say the least. It is difficult to know how seriously to take her continued threats to marry only for money. That attitude was certainly belied by both her other pronouncements on marriage and her own failure to take her own supposed advice and marry money. At a time when marriage was expected to be every young woman's goal, and a single woman past a certain age was an object of pity and scorn, Belle's options—both in practice and in attitude—were limited.

Belle had been engaged herself, however, at least once. The man was a Princeton graduate, and the engagement took place either while she was working in Princeton or in the first couple of years when she began working for Morgan. And by her own account, she was routinely presented with proposals from men well able to support her in comfort, if not style. Belle reassured Bernard that she would always love him, "even if I am ever so foolish or so blind as to marry." Marriage might come, especially since she did not relish the thought of being an old maid at thirty or forty (Belle was then a few months shy of thirty), but at that point she prized her freedom above all else.[91]

Senda also spoke to the triad Greek chorus to the Belle-Bernard drama: Anne Morgan, Elsie de Wolfe, and Bessie Marbury. All three were baffled by the situation. Anne said she could not believe that Bernard was so affected by Belle. "B.B. with his exquisite refinement—his delicate almost squeamish attitude toward loudness and vulgarity—it is impossible." Senda actually defended Belle to the trio, calling her "wonderfully clever and interesting." But despite this avowed affection for Belle, Senda warned that Belle's life and position were so extraordinary that "her very virtues may be her undoing—and her keen love of luxury and amusement will make her undoing more easy." She considered the situation with Belle completely hopeless. "I can see her fascination for you—she has a splendid intellect and she is so wonderfully alive, so ready to greet all expressions of life." But there were also many reasons for caution. Belle's friends were vulgar and cheap—P. G. Grant had appalled Senda by making a pass at her. Bernard, of course, already shared this opinion of some of Belle's social circles. In fact, Belle's life and surroundings were so distasteful to Senda that she was sure a few weeks in New York would cure Bernard of his passion, if only the Duveen problem did not threaten.[92]

Senda predicted that Belle's life would be a series of flirtations, few real attachments, but "no man's love for life." Perhaps coming to a similar conclusion, Belle grew so overwhelmed trying to explain the encounter to Bernard that she gave up writing and spent a fitful night thinking and crying over the situation. Oblivious to Belle's inner turmoil, Senda left New York liking her more than ever, but even more concerned about the affair and its effect on her brother.[93]

After facing her realization that she and Bernard would never be completely together, Belle recovered enough to write her own detailed account of the meeting. She assured Bernard that Senda had only his happiness in mind, but added "[S]he thinks your happiness cannot come through me." Still not sure how much Senda actually knew, Belle decided she had "divined all" but misunderstood Belle's motives. Although Senda made no accusations, Belle believed Senda considered her a " 'body-snatcher' and professional flirt." Belle agreed that Bernard could not live without Mary and should not leave her. She also added her own obligations to her "beastly family and dear J.P." that kept her from being with Bernard. However, after an emotional night she had concluded they could be "a great deal to each other if we are not every thing." Finally, she asked Bernard whether she should withdraw from his life, since she did not seem to bring him happiness or peace. "Daarrling it makes me rage and weep and sick to think I may become—or am now a drag upon you. I can't bear it. . . . I feel like a cork adrift on the ocean." And she wrote Senda the next day, repeating that she was willing to give up Bernard if it was better for him.[94]

Belle had to wait almost two weeks for Bernard's response. In the meantime, she threw herself into her overscheduled social life to avoid thinking about her emotional one. She wrote Bernard again at the end of the week, explaining that it was once again all her social engagements that kept her from writing. She was also getting ready to throw a costume party for several hundred of New York's "clever" people, planning some plays, tableaux, and musical performances. But it was also a particularly eventful two weeks in her home life. She finally moved herself and her family into the new apartments she had spent so long arranging. Almost immediately they had to move out again because of a house fire in the top floor of the building. The damage to her floor was minimal, mostly water damage, but she and her family had been forced into the streets in their nightgowns and were now staying at a nearby hotel until repairs were complete. A week later she was back in her "Berenson" bedroom and enjoying her "chaste solitude." She loved being able to close and lock the door between her rooms and those of her family. With the silk wall covering ruined, she hung sixteenth-century tapestries on the living room walls and put one on the floor.[95]

Finally, Bernard cabled: much to Belle's relief, he was not ready to give her up. "I am yours forever," she rejoiced, "and shall not worry again." A week later she wrote of the "blessed peace" and joy she felt loving him, "as if I were walking on air," she added unoriginally. She promised she would do nothing to threaten their love. "Many people may tell you I am a flirt—or worse—but it is not true."[96]

Mary meanwhile wrote Belle a carefully sweet letter inviting her to join them in Turkey or Greece that fall. Mary did tell Belle that Bernard was still sick and depressed, but did not blame her. The timing was odd because Mary had just had final confirmation that Bernard's situation with Belle was as bad as, or worse than, she had imagined. She had come across part of one of his lengthy letters to Belle (accidentally, she told him) and read it. It was not the first time she had "accidentally" read one of her husband's love letters. But what she read this time was devastating. The "death of love" she had felt in her marriage was painfully confirmed, and now she also realized he had not been honest with her about the depth of his feelings for Belle.[97] To her husband she put a brave face on it, listing the comforts she had: her daughters, her mother, Geoffrey Scott's friendship. She expected that eventually he would settle into a "better proportion" of emotion and learn to be a more balanced "homme à deux femmes." Bernard assured her that he still loved her but threatened that if "keeping you obliges me to let go of Belle, it will be so hard that it may not be worth while." Her own mother gently suggested that some distance might be healthy, and Mary eventually left I Tatti to spend some time with her family in Oxford. But she was determined to stick with the marriage. Bernard promised Mary that all he wanted was to live with Mary and to dream of Belle, and be with Belle once in a while.[98] As the couple tried to work out the biggest crisis in their twenty-year relationship, they also tried to plan for Belle's promised visit in September.

Belle, for her part, had not stopped her carousing. Her costume party had been a huge success. Frank Pollock, Mary Garden, Edmond Clément, and Geraldine Farrar all sang. There was a performance by two of the Russian dancers, a "wonderful clog dance by a darkey," and a "fine Apache dance" by Ben Ali Haggin (James Ben Haggin), a portrait painter and theater designer. There were also some tableaux, which Belle said would have shocked Bernard. If Haggin had a hand in the tableaux, they perhaps involved his famous nude or near-nude "Living Pictures."[99] These entertainments allowed Belle's guests to both witness and participate in the culture and dress of non-Europeans, a popular pastime among white Americans. The dancing lasted until 5:30 A.M., and Belle didn't get to bed until 6:30, sleeping only a few hours before getting up to drive Ada Thurston to the docks for her boat to Europe.[100]

Finally, in early March, Belle began trying to slow down, even considering early bedtimes (before midnight) and vowing to give up "the demon drink, and the Goddess Nicotine," at Bernard's request. But it took a fainting spell and doctor's orders to do the trick. In mid-March she was diagnosed with nervous exhaustion and anemia and lectured sternly on her late-night habits. She was so tired that she did not even mind for once. Besides it was time for all her friends to head for Europe again. Not two days later Belle snuck out to hear Mary Garden sing in *Thaïs*, an opera she adored so much she said she never missed a performance. But she came straight home and canceled all of her engagements for the rest of March.[101]

A new man entered her life, whom she identified only as Baird. This may have been Edward Kellogg Baird, a lawyer and fellow opera lover who came to her home regularly to talk and read to her. Belle found him restful, which meant that she would soon find him boring. He compensated for her lack of a social life, occupying her time when she could not do anything really interesting.[102]

Ethel Grant confirmed that Belle was following orders, mostly, but that she had the collapse coming, staying up until all hours and still working in the day, not to mention smoking heavily. Now she had a new man to match her new quiet lifestyle, and Ethel heartily approved of him as "good for her." Unfortunately, however, Ethel expected that Belle would recover quickly and was worried about her long-term prospects. Since she would not suffer much, she probably would not learn the lesson of moderation and would soon stop paying attention to her health. Ethel ranted to Belle about all the "pug-uglys, vampires, hangers on, mutts, liars, scandal mongers, looselivers, loosetalkers, loosethinkers" she had in her life. Ethel had warned her before to prune her calling list, and now she had evidence of the poor outcome of Belle's lifestyle. The problem was, Ethel thought, that Belle could not discern human character and opened herself to people far too quickly.[103]

Many of her friends, in fact, took the opportunity to say, "I told you so." They offered various explanations for Belle's collapse: smoking, partying, bad company, bad habits—even her nail chewing was blamed for her poor health! But Ethel was right: within a few days Belle was feeling so much better that she was able to brush off any concern or advice her friends offered. She even started to worry that she would get fat.

And within a week Belle was hosting a "tiny little tea" for Isadora Duncan and ten of the most handsome men she knew. Belle joked that

Duncan, who famously had two children with two different men, was looking for another man to have a child with. Isadora apparently hit it off with one of the men she met at the party, a man who (much to Belle's delight) returned at the end of his weekend tryst to give Belle all the details. Then she was dragged to a luncheon at the Colony Club that she had forgotten about. The hostess, Kate Douglas Wiggin Riggs, best known as the author of *Rebecca of Sunnybrook Farm* (1903), insisted. Belle and Geraldine Farrar, the soprano, were the guests of honor. One thing led to another, and Belle didn't get home until eleven-thirty, pretty tired out, after dinner with Baird. He was still her "steady" in Bernard's absence.[104]

Belle's letters to Bernard dwindled throughout April. She wrote every four to seven days, but after the first week her letters became brief notes. Part of the problem may have been that Bernard wrote her some "vituperative" letters scolding her (quite belatedly from Belle's point of view) for bad behavior she had given up weeks ago. The one- to two-week lag in their correspondence led to many such problems. When he complained that her letters were too short and too far between, Belle snapped back that he should recall how much she hated writing letters altogether. She would just as soon not write again for a month, except that he would think she had abandoned him. Belle even complained to Mary, appealing to her, "Please beat B.B. for me. He writes me such scolding letters. . . . And the way he talks about my 'set' is trying."[105]

Mary was not likely to be sympathetic. Bernard's emotional tumult over Belle, which he later described as near-suicidal, was coming close to destroying the Berensons' marriage. It was no longer Belle and her interests that were the biggest threat; Bernard's depression was wearing away the last intimate bonds between husband and wife. Accustomed to being the center of attention and care, Bernard was simply unable to maintain the civility and calm that Mary needed, and unwilling to consider the effects of his physical and emotional demands on her. His moods so clearly hung on Belle's level of attention and affection that Mary soon came to resent more than he did Belle's every slight and pout.

Still largely oblivious to the fragility of her lover's stability, Belle continued to respond to events as she understood them. Nonetheless, her anger melted when she heard that yet another gift had arrived in customs: a pre-Duccio Madonna. But Bernard did not even receive her affectionate letter thanking him for several more weeks. Before it arrived, he cabled to find out what was wrong. She cabled back immediately, baffled, "don't understand have written all love."[106] That was April 24. On April 25 the long-anticipated Hoe sale began.

One of the problems, surely, was that Bernard had never before fallen in love with a woman who had a job, let alone a career. No matter how many times Belle told him how busy her work kept her, he never seemed to believe that her schedule might at times truly leave no space for the hours-long letter-writing sessions he desired of her. And April 1911 was one of those times. The Hoe sale was actually one of a series of New York auctions dispersing the book collection of Robert Hoe. Everyone in the book world was in town, and those who weren't kept writing and calling. Belle was extremely busy.

Many important books were on the block, and Mr. Morgan and Miss Greene were not the only ones who wanted a share. The British Museum, for one, had hoped to purchase a rare early William Caxton edition of Thomas Malory's *Le Morte d'Arthur* and appealed to Belle to help reserve it for them. Alfred Pollard, who headed the print and rare books department, asked Charles Read to use his friendship with Belle to request the "mere trifle" of not bidding on that piece. Belle and Morgan had certainly done this in the past, refraining from purchasing a piece and pressuring other dealers to do likewise in order to allow a public or national institution to acquire it. Both believed strongly that some pieces of cultural history properly belonged in national archives. But in this case other private collectors were after the prize, and Belle explained to Pollard and Read that she did not think the British Museum could compete with the prices that the Hoe books would bring.[107]

In fact, this Caxton print was no "trifle." It was Belle's biggest target at the Hoe auction. From overseas Morgan had empowered her to pay up to $100,000 for it—more than she had paid for all sixteen Caxtons collectively purchased from Lord Amherst in 1908. But, never one to spend her boss's money unnecessarily, Belle had done her own ground-work, persuading several potential competitors not to bid against her. As the sale began, however, her plan was threatened by the surprise appearance of a new collector from California, Henry Huntington. His agent, George Smith, began buying up item after item at previously unheard-of prices. On the first day a Gutenberg Bible sold for $50,000 and made front-page news.[108] Huntington's wealth and determination to procure the bulk of the Hoe collection drove prices far beyond what had previously been considered reasonable and justifiable.

Belle was appalled. After a few days of this she gave a rare, lengthy interview to the *New York Times* decrying the high prices as "more than ridiculous," even harmful. The reporter took time to note that "Miss Green bore no earthly resemblance to the traditional bookworm, so far as appearance went." Unusually succinct in describing her only as an "alert young lady, wearing a few orchids," the writer emphasized that although she might not look like a rare-book expert, she certainly was one. Then he gave Belle her soapbox from which to make her com-plaints public.

It was already clear that one collector was walking away with nearly all of the collection, his agent spending over $150,000 in the first two days alone. The danger, Belle said, was that libraries could no longer keep up with the prices and that therefore these rare books would be in the hands only of wealthy collectors, inaccessible to the public and to scholars. Mindful that she herself represented a wealthy collector, she admitted that her own interests were not threatened. "Everybody knows if I wanted a book, all I would have to do would be to buy it, but I care too much for the art of collecting to put rare books out of the reach of ordinary people." The reporter also noted that many of the big London and Paris dealers were dropping out of the race as prices soared. This seemed to support Miss Greene's assertion that the prices were beyond the items' value. It appeared, he concluded, that a "book collector's trust" had formed.[109]

In this interview Belle gave her first public hint that she had a much broader agenda in building a collection of incunabula and preprint illuminated and text manuscripts for the Morgan Library. She wanted the rare books she prized so highly to be available to the public, not locked in the vaults of private collectors. J.P. already made his books available to scholars and highly selected visitors, but Belle's early vision of the Library competing with the national libraries of Europe suggested a much bigger, more public institution. That would be a long time coming, but meanwhile her commitment to the development of public libraries and museums won her the respect and gratitude of curators and librarians around the world.

The very next week Belle took on George Smith/Henry Huntington herself. And she walked away with her prize, at far less than her boss's top price: the Caxton edition of Malory's *Le Morte d'Arthur* for $42,800. This purchase bought tremendous publicity for the Morgan Library and for Miss Belle da Costa Greene. It was by no means the highest price, or the most important sale. But it was one of the few major items to go to a local collector. For the New York papers, then, Belle's purchase was a home-team triumph. It was also a purchase with which the public could identify. Thomas Malory's *Le Morte d'Arthur* was a version of the perennially popular King Arthur legend. If readers did not know or care about the significance of Caxton as one of the earliest and finest book printers, they would at least recognize the name of King Arthur. That it was a beautiful young woman who carried the day only added to the drama of the news story.

"Fifty Thousand Dollars for That Book!" screamed the headline on the cover of the New York *World Magazine*. With a full page, including both sketches and photos of Belle, the "Bachelor Girl, Still in Her Twenties," the story promised to explain "How She Engages with Bibliophiles and Museum Curators in Battles of Thousands." The article described the final moments of the bidding war for the Caxton book between Belle Greene and George Smith, Huntington's representative, emphasizing the disparity of an "alert young woman" taking on the buyers and collectors of the world. "She knew what she wanted and with J. Pierpont Morgan's money she was able to get what she wanted—in almost every instance." The *World* pronounced her the leading authority on rare books, at least "among the fair sex."

Unlike the staid *Times* interview, the stories in most papers paid as much attention to the details of Belle's appearance and lifestyle as to the auction itself. She looked more like a society girl than a librarian. She was dark with an olive complexion and flashing black eyes. She was strikingly vivacious with a "slight girlish figure," and her fashionable dress was completed with a corsage of violets. Her sex and her appearance set her apart from the gallery filled with "bibliophiles, college professors, curators of museums and collectors." Even her living quarters and social life merited note: her "attractive studio apartment" on East Fortieth Street, where she lived with her mother (the ruse worked!), her close ties to J. P. Morgan (true) and his daughter Anne (not entirely true) as well as his wife (definitely not true). It was Belle, as much as the "time-worn tome" she had obtained, who was the focus of attention at the auction and afterward. She was indeed, at the auction and in the press coverage that followed, the "cynosure of all eyes."[110]

Belle was triumphant in her purchase and appalled at the publicity. After the sale, she fled New York for the weekend. Her mother woke her in the morning, showing her the "horrible vision" of herself in the *World*. Thrown into a fit of rage and despair that left her with a violent headache, Belle bemoaned the portrayal of herself as "half actress and half college girl." It was hardly the image of quiet dignity and self-containment that she sought in her professional conduct. And having her photographed and sketched image so prominently displayed must have made her nervous. After more than ten years as Belle da Costa Greene, she was now comfortable in her adopted name, as any woman who changed her name upon marriage would become. But might it now have seemed that the shift was not far enough? The name Belle da Costa Greene with a photo would have been recognizable, or at least suspiciously familiar, to anyone who had known the young Belle Marian Greener. Her father was now in Chicago, but there were many still in New York who had known him and his family. Hiding in full view was a clever disguise. But it was also risky, and Belle tried to contain publication of her name as much as possible. A journalist later suggested she had "learned the Morgan rule" to avoid the public gaze, and her name rarely appeared in print.[111]

If that was Belle's goal, she was not altogether successful that year. A week later the *New York Daily Tribune*'s "In the Public Eye" highlighted Belle in its regular society page, with a photo. The brief article identified her as "one of the most active and most interested bidders at the great Hoe sale of rare books" who won *Le Morte d'Arthur* "with all the enthusiasm of a true bibliophile added to the spirit engendered by rivalry."[112]

Belle was suddenly the toast of the town, and she complained that every newspaper and magazine seemed to be running a story about her. She was now refusing all interviews, and not all local papers published a story on her, as she complained to B.B. She may have exaggerated the interest in her, either because of her very real fear of too much publicity or because of vanity, or she may have been successful in stopping some of the stories. She did have ties to reporters, publishers, editors, and owners in the newspaper and magazine world by that time.

The publicity of the Hoe sale and her purchase may have brought unwanted publicity, but it also cemented her status within the art world as a powerful and highly effective figure, even if diminutive and corseted and of the "fairer sex." Congratulations poured in from curators and collectors, some with a slightly bitter aftertaste. Pollard and Read both sent theirs. After the fact, the museum men had to agree that the British Museum could not have competed, as they bemoaned the outrageous amounts that threatened to keep public institutions out of future acquisitions and speed up the drain of European books and artworks to the newly enriched and interested American collector. Belle defended her own participation in this auction to her European friends, noting that she had bid on other pieces only to force Smith, "the most villainous man in the trade," to pay more and that the Malory book seemed likely to go for $60,000—$70,000 just hours before it actually went on the block.[113]

In the short term, however, despite the triumph of the purchase, the Hoe sale itself shifted the expectations of dealers and sellers on the prices they might place on rare books. Dealers immediately raised their prices, much to Belle's disgust and annoyance, and she had to storm at many of them, threatening to remove Morgan's business if they didn't return to pre–Hoe sale figures. Even book dealers who specified that the Hoe prices would not affect their own used the occasion to make a new bid for Greene's attention. F. Wheeler wrote that having noted the rates gained for vellum printed books at the Hoe sale, he wanted to send over all of his vellum stock for her to inspect and select from. Even this mention of the Hoe prices was enough to set Greene off. In a marked contrast from the tone of her early correspondence with this dealer, she flew into a fury and made clear her ability to influence Wheeler's business with Morgan.[114]

But in this case Belle may have made some behind-the-scenes deals on her own behalf with the private collectors who could afford the shockingly high prices emerging from the Hoe sale. For example, Belle had apparently made some arrangement with her friend Luther Livingston, of Dodd & Livingston, a local book dealer and friend whom Belle had long respected and helped in the past.[115] She even promised him part of the commission she expected to earn as Morgan's representative. Livingston was a dear friend who tutored her in bibliography. But exactly what he did to merit a piece of any commission is unclear. He had bid against her for the Caxton until the price reached $30,000. Whatever role this played in her triumph, Belle subsequently discovered that Morgan had no intention of paying her the commission usually given to an agent transacting a major art sale, whether from private sale or public auction. Because she was a salaried employee, Morgan felt she did not merit a bonus payment, nor did he want her to use other agents to procure books.[116]

This must have been a huge disappointment to the ambitious Miss Greene, although none of her correspondence to Livingston betrays it. Her salary, by now $10,000 a year, was more than enough to keep herself and her mother and three sisters living in comfort, with a maid and a cook. But in the circles she traveled in, this was not wealth, and Belle's tastes in fashion, entertaining, and, most important, art were expensive. The standard commission rate could have earned her anywhere from $2,000 to $5,000 for this purchase alone. A lost opportunity, indeed, for a woman with very high aspirations and no resources other than her own skills and name. A few such sales a year could have doubled her income.

Even though she was living far more comfortably than the Greeners ever had, Belle was now surrounded by riches in a world in which money was earned largely on the backs of other people's labor. Against this standard, she constantly felt herself a hopelessly poor "working girl."[117] Summer after summer she stayed behind in the hot, dirty city to work while all her friends and social hosts left for months abroad. On a good year she could get away for a month or two herself. Only twice in the six years she had worked for Morgan had she been able to travel to Europe. Most years she just endured the New York heat and planned for a future when she could live a modestly wealthy life of leisure. In her case, of course, leisure meant a residence in Europe and the time and money to devote herself to learning and soaking up art.

Although it brought her no closer to this monetary goal, the *Morte d'Arthur* purchase was one of the most important—certainly the most publicized—of Greene's early career. Some even went out of their way to make sure Morgan (who had been in Europe when Greene won her prize) realized just how well Belle had performed. The scholar Albert Clay wrote to Morgan praising Greene's performance, particularly in contrast to Huntington's behavior, which "generally disgusted" people in the know. "She seems to have made a profound impression upon those who attended the sale by her dignified demeanor, and for refusing to pay unreasonable prices for what she desired to purchase for the Library, every person, of course, recognizing that she had unlimited means back of her." Her refusal to try to match the "ridiculously high prices" had earned Belle the strong approval of all who were outraged by Huntington's coup. She had represented herself and Morgan well.[118] For the rest of her life, and even after her death, this purchase would consistently be listed as an, or even *the*, example of the power she held over Morgan's acquisitions. Later histories and biographies of American art collecting recall her as a "notable also-ran" at the Hoe sale, a glamorous, near-celebrity in the art world.[119]

It was here, then, that Belle began to gain the public reputation, already growing among her colleagues, for being "fearless in the auction room and determined in the bookshops." Stories of her purchasing coups abound, some apocryphal, some based in truth. As her fellow librarian Margaret Stillwell later recalled, "When Mr. Morgan commissioned her to secure some treasure for his collection, she did. That was a foregone conclusion. She expected to get it. Mr. Morgan expected her to get it. And so did everyone else—except perhaps, for a time, her poor opponents."[120] It was after the Hoe sale that Belle's triumphant first auction in London became public fare and her clout in and out of the auction room the stuff of legend. That was the point, at least in the opinion of one *Times* reporter, at which she came into her power in Pierpont Morgan's eyes.[121] Morgan had recognized her ability then and subsequently allowed her a fair amount of latitude in spending his money on rare books. Belle was continually described as small, dainty, graceful—a girl librarian in a man's world. Her diminutive figure, ebullient nature, and magnetic energy made her appear youthful long after the calendar would agree. Still, over the next few years Belle would mature and develop new interests while deepening her intellectual expertise. And she would do so during a decade in which the world around her was changing even faster.

9

A MODERN WOMAN

I'm terribly afraid of becoming an haranguer and being called a suffragette. In these days of wild crazy emotional erotic and neurasthenic women I would rather be called a masculinist than a feminist. They are a sickening sight these women—most of them.

—Belle Greene[1]

I think I would have been a much nicer person if I had not taken or "gotten" my present job—but I would have been married—perhaps to Princeton man—more likely to a (very) moderately rich Jew—as my ideas of millionaires was different in them days—But I would at least have been a more natural female and with some ideals left, and—a dozen children. Query—was it the Kindness or the Revenge of the Gods?

—Belle Greene, 1914[2]

AFTER THE FLURRY of publicity over the Hoe sale died down, Belle's life did not immediately seem to be skyrocketing to fame and glory. Quite the opposite. Yielding again to the demands of her body and her doctors, Belle gave up alcohol entirely and kept to quiet evenings and reduced socializing. As a result, the summer of 1911 was not a very exciting one. Belle's letters described oppressive heat in the city and a life of reform. She redecorated her apartment for the warm season, draping the library in green-gray chintz with a thick green rug, lots of plants in the windows, and cool green window shades. The bedroom she hoped to share someday with Bernard was now pale blue English glossy chintz with pale lavender roses and white floor matting.[3]

She sent her family away for the summer again, this time to Tokeneke, in the Pennsylvania Poconos, too far away for her to join them nights and weekends. (The summer home she described as a "shack" actually had four master bedrooms with three servants' rooms and a water view.)[4] Her letters to Bernard groaned and whined about her boredom, even as she tried to plan for a trip abroad to see him at the end of summer or sometime in the fall. But there was another secret she was keeping that year. This time Bernard was decidedly out of the loop. Even so, true to her character, her letters were sprinkled with hints, red herrings, and near-admissions. Surely Bernard read and reread and analyzed her words as carefully as any biographer. But he also had mutual friends, the very ones who left Belle behind to escape the summer heat, to clue him in.

Despite her attempts to reform, Belle fell ill again in June. Her diagnosis was more complicated, and her illness lasted several weeks. She had, she said, a typhoid fever, which seemed to be developing into malaria. A dubious transition, but it was clear she was sick. Her doctor prescribed quinine, abstention from alcohol, and rest.[5] As Belle was already "firmly seated" on the "Water Wagon," she promised to stay there until the end of the year. A temperance movement term, "being on the water wagon" meant that a person had pledged to avoid alcohol, in Belle's case temporarily. Belle had also been ordered to limit her cigarettes to ten a day. "Life seems hardly worth living," she sighed.[6]

By early July she had recovered enough to return to work, lower her quinine doses, and hope to be able to make the trip to Europe, if not during the summer then certainly in October for another book auction, the Huth sale. She and Bernard began corresponding about travel options to accommodate her fragile health: she could stay at I Tatti (Mary was not enthusiastic), or she could join him on one of his rest cures. Europe was dotted with elite resorts, often clustered around some natural location, whose waters, vapors, mud pools, or airs were believed to have healing powers. Bernard needed something; he was still not well. Mary started thinking about leaving him again, exhausted at having to deal with his "dreadful blackness," the "bitterness of spirit that hangs around him" that was increasingly aimed in her direction.[7] To make matters worse, he had begun to accuse her of not caring about him and not loving him. Mary once again took refuge with her daughters. Rachel had just married Oliver Strachey, which brought her and Karin even deeper into the Bloomsbury circle that surrounded Virginia Woolf and Vanessa Bell. From there Mary wrote to her husband about his attitude. "It simply dries me up. There is apparently nothing I can say or do that will convince thee." She bitterly added that "one 'daarling' from Belle," even after weeks of silence, was apparently more convincing to Bernard than her own months and years of faithful companionship.[8]

But Belle's ability to convince so easily was waning. Or perhaps it was Bernard's desire to believe that lapsed. In either case, by July, Bernard's letters slowed to a trickle. A few too many reports had reached him about Belle's philandering, and Belle's explanations and alibis were indeed starting to show cracks. When Bernard called on Charles Read at the British Museum that summer, he was startled to discover that Read was "very much taken with 'Little Belle.'"[9] Read apparently gave Bernard an earful about his own budding romance with Belle (unaware of Bernard's relationship with her). Read even mentioned that he and Belle were carrrying on a frequent correspondence—this would have made Bernard doubly jealous, both for the passionate nature Read implied the letters had and for their daily arrival from she who claimed to be too hot and exhausted to write to Bernard. Belle tried to brush it off, denying she had written to Read daily, and reminding Bernard she

had already told him about the "correspondence flirtation." But she
finally admitted that on Read's part, at least, the fascination was real,
and the letters passionate, at least for an Englishman she qualified
dryly. Read was scheduled to return to New York soon thereafter and
Belle was a bit nervous, "realizing that he had good reason to think her
hopelessly in love with him."[10]

Read's arrival also gave Belle ample opportunity to punish him for
teasing Bernard. When Read arrived "as good looking as ever," Belle
made sure Bernard knew how coolly she treated him. However, Read
was too interesting and knowledgeable for her to find him really boring; besides he brought her several "adorable Egyptian things" to add
to her personal collection. And after he returned to England he sent
her another Chinese statue.[11] Belle's attitude toward Read was probably not as cool as she led Bernard to believe.

And the reports continued. By midsummer of 1911 stories about
Belle and other men began to eclipse any remaining talk linking her to
Bernard. Belle tried in vain to brush it all off. Bessie Marbury (perhaps
dispatched by Bernard) began pumping Belle's friends for information
and resurrected some stale rumors about Belle and Jack Cosgrove.
Belle advised Bernard to consider the source, sniffing, "All the scandal
about them [Bessie and her women friends] has never interested me
so why can't they leave me alone?" Ultimately Belle refused to care
about her reputation, joking that she would "paralyze them by marrying J.P. some fine day—wouldn't it be a beautiful scandal?"[12]

Still more ships were sailing east across the Atlantic, bringing
Bernard more news and gossip. But which was which? Belle tried to
preempt both by starting to mention to Bernard other men with
whom his friends would likely say she was connected. William Gibbs
McAdoo, president of the Hudson and Manhattan Railroad Company,
who oversaw the building of the first tunnels under the Hudson River
was one. McAdoo had his charms, she granted, but she noted that she
always took a chaperone except when they lunched in his private
office.[13] And then there was the faithful fellow opera-lover Mr. Baird,
whom she had already "bounced," much to Ethel G.'s outrage.

Belle's assistant at the Library, Ada Thurston, had also visited Bernard and Mary at I Tatti, and Belle's lifestyle had been a topic of conversation. Belle could not pull all of the details out of Thursty when she returned, but gathered that everyone had agreed that Belle should stop smoking cigarettes. She had to laugh. For one thing, she had been smoking the entire time she and Ada talked about her trip. For another, she did not see the point of her friends' trying to impose further modifications on her. No one could change her but herself. "I am doing it, but by degrees." The cigarettes would likely be the last to go, Belle grimaced.[14]

Not all of the news carried from New York was bad. Bernard had lunch with Arnold Brunner and his wife; he was a prominent architect and she a close friend of Belle's. The Brunners encouraged his hope that Belle would prevail in her current campaign to cast off "all her drinking and gigging and stupid Bohemianism." Interestingly, the Brunners blamed Belle's family as the source of the trouble, claiming that it was they who enabled and even encouraged her "very worst conduct." The Brunners hoped for a "complete break" between Belle and her family. It seemed Miss Thurston thought so too.[15] These glimmers of disdain or discomfort with Belle's family on the part of her co-workers and friends form a faint but evocative pattern. There are no sources from the family to counter or explain this tendency of Belle's friends to look down on them. Belle herself constantly complained about her family in a general way, but she did that about almost everyone. She never gave any clues, directly or indirectly, that suggested her family might be having an ill effect on her. And her actions speak volumes. She continued to live with and support her mother and remained close to her siblings even after they finished their schooling and started to work.

Ada was not the only self-appointed transatlantic messenger that summer. Ethel G., whose own friendship with Belle was starting to wear a bit thin, arrived in Europe to give B.B. her two cents. Perhaps because he relied on her to tell him what was happening with his New York lover, Bernard exempted Grant from his indictment of Belle's pals. But Belle herself was growing tired of this particular friend. When Ethel bent his ear about Belle's "seven devils," Belle tried to explain that Ethel was just angry because she thought Belle had treated Baird shamefully. "He bores me horribly at times," Belle explained, "and I can't help showing it."[16] Then there was the young banker Harold Mestre, whom Ethel G. detested. When Belle not only liked him but began to play with him, Ethel grew exasperated. Belle tried again to explain. Mestre was not important, she insisted. They had had a "fevered flirtation," but the problem was really only that Harold and Ethel Grant did not like each other. He thought Ethel very "coarse and vulgar" (she was drunk when they met) and advised Belle to drop her socially. Ethel found out and was offended. And, yes, Belle and Harold had been engaged "for a brief space" when Belle was "horribly bored," but that was all "an experience of the past." She chided Bernard that he really should not approve of Ethel so much, since she was the "chief" hoodlum. Nor would the traitorous Grant go unpunished. Belle promised to beat her to a pulp upon her return and ignore her letters in the meanwhile.[17]

Engaged? Belle was in no mood to explain. In fact, she was becoming very tired of defending herself against every rumored flirtation B.B. heard about. She railed at him: He knew it was part of her nature to "do crazy things" and to be a "beastly correspondent." She would probably play with other men until she was "too old to move or speak or hear or see." But he must know that he was not just the object of another one of her flirtations—if he did not believe that by now, why did he continue to write to her at all? Furthermore, Bernard was hardly in a position to berate her for her philandering. "In fact no island was ever more completely surrounded by water than you are by dames. . . . [I]sn't [it] a bit the case of the pot calling names?"[18] It certainly was; Bernard consoled himself with plenty of other women when Belle was not around. But he could not grant Belle the same latitude. Not only was the familiar gendered double standard in play, but Belle's likely marriage could threaten their affair far more than his taking yet another mistress. What man, he may have wondered, would put up with the unfaithfulness in a wife that Mary tolerated in Bernard. Belle did not agree; marriage for her was an economic arrangement, not a life partnership or chastity vow.

Still, Belle's goal that summer was to try to get to Europe for a trip to Spain with the Berensons in September and a visit to Italy in October. While her doctor wanted her to take a vacation sooner than that because she was still not well, it was impossible. Belle insisted on Mary's presence in Spain, however, still very concerned about maintaining a proper appearance and aware that people seemed to be watching them.[19] So the Berensons began to make arrangements. Mary reluctantly agreed to go and enlisted Geoffrey Scott as a fourth— he immediately started planning for a month in Spain with "the Enchantress" (Belle).[20]

But the flurry of Berensonian preparations was interrupted by a cable from Belle. She would not be able to come in September after all. It turned out that getting J.P.'s approval for her trip was not the simple matter Belle had hoped it would be. He "flared up into the air" with many objections and was not even interested in sending her to the Huth sale in October. Apparently he had heard about Belle's brief engagement to Harold Mestre as well, and the news "made him rave and foam at the mouth." Belle swore she had never been engaged, but still got mad right back because it wasn't his business anyway. After a few days of strained interactions, he approached her "with tears and crocodile heart breakings beseeching me not to leave him, not to marry any one and not to look at any man." Belle was not impressed, but decided to pick her battles and let the matter rest.[21]

When the Huth sale was postponed to November, Belle's hopes of reaching Europe by October dwindled. She was still optimistic that J.P. would come around and let her attend the auction, but it is difficult to see why. He rarely let her out of his sight now and continued to add to her duties. She generally stayed at work with him until seven or eight at night (the one night she left at five to go to bed early he referred to as her "desertion"). She was so exhausted, she said, that she had no social life at all. She was still being good, keeping to her daily exercises, baths, and massages. The diagnosis now was that she was "nervous," and she told Bernard that if it were not for him she would not even want to face the ocean voyage at all that year.[22]

By late September rumor had it that Belle was engaged again. This

time Mary heard it from the ever interested Bessie Marbury, who gleefully wrote that "BB's inamorata is engaged to be married." "Is it true?"
Mary asked B.B. doubtfully. "I wonder how it will affect thee. . . . I am
so sorry."[23]

It was true. The engagement had been off, but was back on again.
This time Belle was not able to brush it off as lightly has she had in
August. This time she had announced her engagement to friends and
introduced him socially as her fiancé. Harold Mestre was obviously a
significant man in her life. Who was this man, and why had he been
successful where so many others had reportedly failed?

Harold Mestre was Harold de Villa Urrutia Mestre, who would later
establish a career as a biologist and academic. But in 1911 he was
working as a stockbroker with his father at Alfred Mestre & Co.
Mestre's parents were both born in Cuba, where his grandfather had
been a professor of law at the University of Havana.[24] Belle repeatedly
referred to Harold as a youth and a boy, although he was only five years
younger than her true age, or about the same age she claimed to be.
This did not fit her pattern of being drawn to older, usually married
men. But Mestre was one of a number of Wall Street brokers Belle
tried unsuccessfully to fit into her life. By October the engagement
was off again. Later in the fall, friends suspected it might be back on
yet once more, but by December even the overly suspicious Ethel
Grant dismissed it all as "absurd fancy."[25]

In all official records, Mestre is listed as white. Could his Cuban
background have made him less concerned about the implications of
marrying an ethnically ambiguous woman? Outside of the United
States it was quite common for light-skinned mixed-race people to
become white, socially and legally. Race may have played a role in
Belle's feelings about marriage. At the time a commonly believed myth
held that a person of mixed ancestry, no matter how white, could produce a "coal-black" baby. This theme often appeared in popular fiction
(where it usually dramatically revealed the black identity of an apparently white person) and was given scientific credence by leading scholars of what we now call scientific racism. By the 1920s studies of racial
mixing would emerge to debunk the idea that two phenotypically white

people could give birth to a phenotypically black child. But the fear prevented many people who wished to keep their black ancestry private from having children.[26] Perhaps Belle simply could not take the risk of marrying and having children (she often said she saw no reason to marry except to have children).

Unable to get a straight answer from Belle about her off and on engagements to Harold, Bernard turned to Ethel for information and insight. Ethel obliged with relish. She confided that Belle was "forever tickling her fancy with the marriage idea—and then haranguing with the particular object." As evidence that the engagement had not been genuine, Ethel cited other instances when Belle had insincerely declared her intention to marry. Belle, it turned out, had wanted Frank McComas, the landscape painter roped into rushing Ethel Harrison, to divorce his wife. Belle had gone so far as to tell her mother that she was going to marry him after the divorce. But at the same time she told Ethel that she never intended to marry Frank. She simply believed that it was absurd for a man to remain married to a woman he did not love. (Belle's definition of marriage for others was not consistent with her own plans.) Frank had not yet "gone to Reno" (divorce capital of the county), Ethel reported. But the main point was that Bernard should not take Belle's engagement too seriously. "Belle may marry," Ethel predicted, "but she won't stay married. She is too utterly unconventional." Still, the whole episode had severely damaged Belle's reputation. In fact, it had made her some bitter enemies.[27]

Unfortunately for Bernard, this letter, written in late October, did not arrive until the end of November. By then Ethel's standing as an intimate observer of Belle's affairs had been lost, another outcome of the Harold Mestre episode. He had apparently become such a sore spot between the two women that Belle finally made good on her earlier threats to cut Ethel off. After avoiding her for several months, Belle confronted her. She had heard from several people that Ethel was gossiping about her and at first did not believe it, but when Harold came to her with the same story, she was finally convinced that Ethel had spoken the "unspeakable," at least to him. Whatever this gossip was, it had not done any harm, and Belle admitted that Ethel might be justified in evening a score for something that had happened concerning Ethel's husband, P.G., but she had had enough: "so now we're quits."[28]

Ethel could hardly take her seriously, resorting to her voyage nickname: "Billious," she retorted, "You are a dear old Jackass!" Ethel denied ever saying anything bad about Belle, except possibly to her face. Someone (one Harold Mestre), she suggested, was trying to drive them apart by spreading lies about Ethel; the only person she had ever discussed Belle with so frankly was Bernard, and she "considered that circumstances gave [her] that right." She did not blame Belle for the incident with P.G. and offered to try to work things out. (Since P.G. was the man who had offended Senda by making a pass at her, it might be surmised that one of Belle and P.G.'s teasing exchanges had gone a bit too far.) But Belle wasn't having any of it. She thought it was quite possible that Ethel did not mean what she had said or remember saying it, because she was often drunk. Having given up alcohol, Belle now had precious little patience for those who continued to imbibe, and no tolerance whatsoever for the loss of inhibitions and control that too much alcohol evoked. This, more than anything else, was the likely underlying cause of the break. Belle was still determined to reform her life, and that meant no longer spending time with people who were continuing the lifestyle she was now avoiding. And she was more loyal to Harold's friendship than to Ethel.[29]

Belle's renewed engagement with Harold also led to a second confrontation with J.P.[30] This time he issued an ultimatum: "[T]he day you get married will be the last day I shall set eyes on you and you won't get anything from me if you do." Belle responded with fury. She had no intention of marrying anyone anytime, she claimed. But if she did, Morgan's threats to remove her from his will would not be a deterrent: "he could buy a great deal with his gold but not me or my affections." Furthermore, she told J.P., she lost all respect for him when he treated her as if she were was something he "had bought and paid for." Even after he apologized, she was not appeased. She would rather leave him and lose her high salary than let him talk to her as he would to his mistress or a servant. Pity the three dealers who were waiting in the lobby to see her after this encounter.[31]

Clearly Belle's resentment of Morgan had only risen since their last recorded scuffle. Through these accounts of Belle's personal and even intimate interactions with Morgan and Berenson and Mestre, we begin to see what it meant for her at this point in her life to be working and to some extent living her life at Morgan's pleasure. In order to maintain her career and her financial security—far above that of most single working women—Belle was willing to sacrifice her freedom. Did she give up Harold because her job was more important to her? Social convention, and J.P.'s threats, said that she could not be married and continue in her job. There were probably other factors as well. Ethel was right that Belle's feelings about marriage were ambivalent, to say the least.

It may have been her growing desire to be free from Morgan's control that led her to consider marriage in the first place. But, as she so often equated marriage with a loss of freedom, it was an odd way out. (Perhaps that's why her engagement kept breaking.) Freedom and self-determination were obviously quite important to Belle. Her resolve not to be treated as property, as a mistress, or as a servant, not to mention some of her language evoking enslavement, must be seen in the context of her racial and class background. She had grown up in a family that was distinguished from the majority working class in part because its members were not forced to take menial or servile jobs. Whatever her identity now, she had also grown up hearing adults, including her father, talk about how African Americans were treated, hearing stories about many whites' presumptions of privilege, power, and superiority. Freedom and self-determination were hallmark American values. But they surely meant something slightly different for a family whose ancestors had been slaves. The Fleets' path to freedom had been Henry's ability to buy his wife and children out of slavery. Many of his children had then had to earn their way to full legal emancipation, repaying Henry for their purchase cost. Money and the ability to earn and save it were crucial for maintaining what privileges they had.

Belle had taken this sensibility to heart. Even with her increasingly expensive tastes and her family's continued economic dependence on her, she claimed always to be saving or investing at least one-third of her earnings. By 1912 that meant some $3,300 per year, or around $52,000 in today's currency. At the same time, her need to be stable and safe may have stemmed from a childhood of uneven income and, at least during her teens, the unhappy relationship between her parents. Her job with Morgan was the key to her ability to provide a steady income and very comfortable life for herself and her family. But her job with Morgan also threatened the point of money and security: the freedom to live the life she wanted. Only she and Morgan knew how much was in the will that he threatened to cut out if she married or otherwise left him.

J.P. was not the only man who feared that Belle was slipping out of reach. Mary had returned to I Tatti for the winter and closely watched Bernard as he grappled with these revelations about Belle's men. He had begun to realize, she believed, that Belle was not the person he had thought her to be. He stopped writing to her as often and started to find her letters (no different to Mary's eyes) rather disgusting and confusing. When Belle cabled in mid-October to announce that her plans to come to Europe were completely, finally, utterly off, Bernard seemed to calm down in a strange way. He started to talk about things being over with "B.G." and, much to Mary's exasperated amusement, suddenly found his wife to be much nicer. Nearly a month went by without further word from Belle, and Bernard turned to another dalliance, finding a woman who would respond to his correspondence.[32]

But eventually Bernard began to fall prey to all the possible reasons for her silence. Was she engaged again? Had she come to Europe after all but with another man? Mary's hopes that it was over were premature. Bernard cabled Belle on November 19 to find out what was happening. No answer. Then four days later Belle's reply arrived: "I have been very blue and unhappy and very very tired did not have heart to write but doing so Mauretania be sure of my love always." During the three days it took this cable to reach Bernard, he became nearly suicidal. (In her defense, Belle had sent it on the twentieth.) Bernard was momentarily delighted and vowed to support Belle if Morgan made good on his threat to disinherit her. Mary was appalled. It had begun all over again: the endless letters, the requests that Mary write and

invite Belle to visit. But at least now he was calm and happy again. I
Tatti was rage free.[33]

Then there was more silence: Belle's letter sent via the *Mauretania*
never arrived.[34] More cables, more lost letters. Belle swore that the mis-
placed *Mauretania* letter was the longest one she had ever written; she
had said so much in it that she felt she could never write again. She
cried when she heard it was lost, but she did not try to re-create it.[35]

Belle did address the general scandals he was hearing about her,
though she could not take them seriously. Apparently in Canada they
were now saying she had been engaged to three men simultaneously,
each of whom saw her every day but somehow never met the others!
Perhaps they were also saying she was J.P.'s illegitimate daughter or
the mother of triplets. But Belle was defiant: Why should she care? It
didn't affect her job, her salary, or the friendships that she really cared
about. She didn't want to be "in society" anyway. Yes, she admitted
unrepentantly, she got "hipped" on men constantly, and probably would
continue to do so. But the only time she had ever really been scandalous was with Bernard. So what difference did all the talk make? All
Belle wanted was "a comfortable income, a few good friends and a
chance to travel" and to acquire enough money so that she did not have
to marry after J.P. died.[36]

Still, when Belle realized the effect all of her actions had had on
Bernard she was ashamed, calling herself "pretty damned selfish." She
promised to write every week, reminded him she had given up all her
bad habits except smoking (she had told him over and over again that
she was being good—"behaving like 10000 angels"). But she realized
now that her inconstant correspondence combined with her written
protestations of love were hurting him. She tried to write more regularly after that, although some serious eye trouble made it difficult.
After a week of not being able to read or write at all, which made her
feel "like a manniken," she began wearing glasses.[37]

And she started to send him photos again, as she had in the months
after he first left her in New York over two years ago. She arranged for
sitting after sitting, trying to find the right photographer, the right pose
and look that he would appreciate. She knew he liked thinking of her

as colored, so the first batch, taken at the end of 1911, included a series of poses she called the "Esquimaux-Nigger-Burmese" ones to appeal to his tastes. For Bernard the suspicion or even knowledge that Belle had black ancestry seems to have been part of her allure. After two decades of living in Europe, he may have lost allegiance to the one-drop rule, if he ever had any. For many outsiders, the American insistence that people who looked white were really black was baffling. The other photos were, she said, "mine own self, poor, indifferent and bad." One apparently showed her smoking.[38]

Two series of photos dated 1911 remain in Berenson's archives. One was taken by Clarence White, one of the New York photographers featured in 291 exhibitions and *Camera Work*. In these photos Belle is wearing a close-fitting hat, high-necked lace blouse, and dark jacket with a long skirt and a small spray of flowers on her left collar. In the standing poses she holds her chin high and dangles a purse from her white-gloved hand. In the closer shots her gaze is still far away, her eyes dark and sad. The other set was taken in May 1911 by Theodore Marceau, who had a studio on Fifth Avenue. In these portraits Belle is wearing a dark velvety looking dress with a plunging lace-edged neckline and elbow-length sleeves. She looks much thinner in this set, especially in her one standing pose, where her corseted figure follows the slender curves of fashion in a sleek, elegant line. Even her face appears more angular, accentuating the shape of her nose and deepening her eyes. Perhaps this was the pose that she felt looked more ethnic?

In early 1912 she sat for Baron Adolf de Meyer, whose portrait photographs, including one of Belle, were exhibited at the Ritz Carlton in early 1913. Belle's shared exhibit space with photographs of Anne Morgan, Rita Lydig, Elsie de Wolfe. Several society women posed in Japanese and in Persian costumes, illustrating the popularity of Belle's fondness for dressing up as the exotic other.[39] Belle sent three of the de Meyer photographs to Bernard, asking him to choose one and return the other two unless he really liked them. Apparently she was getting many requests for copies, and they were worth $25 apiece. She worried that Bernard would find them "posey," but everyone else said she looked "deeply, darkly mysterious in it (but not beautiful)." When

Bernard sent no comment on the de Meyer photos for three months (she asked in every letter during that time), she began fishing for compliments, finally admitting that she couldn't help liking them because they made her look "better looking than I am." Finally, in April, he sent a sarcastic and scornful response to the photos, which she tried to laugh off.[40] The de Meyer photographs are stunning; one of them is on the jacket of this book. Belle wears dark gloves, which cover her arms and melt into the short sleeve of her dark dress, a fur shawl thrown over one shoulder, and a long scarf or ribbon wrapped around her upswept hair.

Was it a coincidence that these photos were taken and commissioned just as Belle's notoriety was moving her into the ranks of proto-celebrity? Certainly many of these shots appeared over the next few years in newspaper articles, and not just in New York. The *Washington Post* ran a brief story on her on its society page for no particular reason in early 1912, noting that while many passersby might wish to be allowed inside Morgan's Library, "they would wish even more ardently for admission if they knew about his librarian." Belle da Costa Green of the "slender, girlish figure" had a gentle demeanor but could be "a regular dragon in her guardianship of the treasure."[41] Later that year the *Chicago Daily Tribune* ran a full-page illustrated story calling her the "most clever girl in the country" and noting that she was barely twenty-six, fashionably chic and decidedly pretty with "dark, brilliant eyes." Indeed, she had "the air of a young belle of the 'four hundred' . . . one of the most charming and popular of them all." The bold catch line below the headlines reads like a B movie spy plot: "She wears her hair long and does not use glasses, runs to Europe on secret missions, and is the terror of continental collectors' agents. Her name is Belle Green."[42] One of the Marceau portraits fills over a quarter of the page. Similarly, one of the de Meyer portraits was reprinted in the *New York Times*, which also devoted an entire page to Belle in April 1912. This article emphasized the incredible amounts of money Belle controlled, and the fairy-tale situation with the "extraordinary responsibility which is put on the shoulders of such a small and dainty person."[43] In early 1913 the *Washington Post* listed Belle as one of its featured "Women

Who Are Paid Princely Salaries for Their Rare Ability to Keep Secrets."
The biographical sketch highlighted her $10,000 salary and her
"extraordinary knowledge of early printed books," as well as her love for
them. It was Miss Green's "true feminine scent for a bargain," the *Post*
writer suggested, that allowed her to acquire the one Caxton at the
Hoe sale, and the sixteen in London several years before for twice as
much. Belle's youth and her interest in "fashion and frivolity" were
noted as well. "It is not that she loves the gayeties of this life less which
distinguishes her from the rest of her sex, but that she loves interesting old books more."[44]

What an image to live up to. Belle was both society girl and serious
scholar (all of the articles emphasized her intelligence and incredible
knowledge, and her acceptance as an equal among scholars and dealers). She could be charming and ferocious, controlled hundreds of
thousands of dollars, and had the complete support of J. Pierpont Morgan, one of the most powerful men in the world. What girl, as several
articles asked, would not want to be her? Nowhere in these articles
was there any suggestion that Belle should leave her job to marry and
have children; the tone was entirely celebratory. Nor was there any
question of who Belle was or where she had come from—that would
come later. For now, the media image of Belle was entirely positive,
glamorous, and adoring.

But the reality was somewhat different. Belle was certainly not feeling particularly glamorous that year. Her sister (probably Ethel) was ill,
threatened with the possibility of a hysterectomy. After two months at
the hospital she came home to Belle's apartment, where Belle's maid,
Marie, who had finally returned from Switzerland that fall, took care
of her with a hired nurse. Theodora was going to college (at Belle's
expense), and the eldest, Ethel, had just married, but she and her
"good-for-nothing" husband had also moved in with Belle. Ethel was
confirmed into the Catholic Church that Easter.[45]

Belle's health was also poor. She had been diagnosed with "autointoxication." This medical theory, dominant in the nineteenth and early
twentieth centuries, blamed many diseases on intestinal waste building
up toxins in the body. Belle's treatment included intestinal massages

and what she called stomach pumping—probably colonic irrigation. Meanwhile, problems with her eyes continued to plague her.[46]

Furthermore, Belle was already tired of her apartment on East Fortieth, now too crowded with her sisters and a brother-in-law living with her. She plotted to find another she could afford, wondering whether she could persuade J.P. to buy one that was selling for $35,000 as an investment and rent it to her for $2,500 a year.[47] She also hated the darkness of being on the ground floor and blamed the apartment for her illness the preceding year. By summer she had persuaded her family to spend the hot season in the Pennsylvania Poconos again, at her expense, of course. (They seemed to go somewhere every summer without fail, so why Belle always mentioned an annual debate is a mystery.) Then her brother, Russell, came down with malaria. He had been working as a civil engineer in Florida, so she was looking for work for him near New York. By July things were improving. She had found a lighter, quieter (presumably higher) apartment just a block down the street. Her friend Thomas Ryan had come through with a lead on a job for Russell, and her mother and sisters had enjoyed themselves in their vacation home.[48] When Russell arrived, he, too, moved back in with his sister Belle.

But Belle's worlds were bigger than her own health and family issues. New social issues were coming into focus around her, and her interest and participation accelerated. The new term "feminism" gave a word for an array of movements and changes that were taking place in women's social, economic, and political roles. The suffrage movement, which dated back to the first women's rights convention in 1848 and had been a focus of activists since 1865, was finally making headway, gaining enough popular support to become a serious possibility. Other movements focused more on the social, cultural, and sexual aspects of women's experiences. The campaign for legalizing birth control, reforming the technically illicit but omnipresent practice of prostitution, and teaching sexual "hygiene" especially to counter the spread of syphilis all emerged in the public arena. Over the next few years Belle would become involved with many of these movements, to varying extents and often with some ambiguity.

For example, Belle was a member of the Society of Sanitary and Moral Prophylaxis (SSMP), a reform group that focused on sexual hygiene and education, pushing the media and public to begin talking openly about sexually transmitted diseases. She included in her reading list that spring Eugène Brieux's *Les Avariés,* which she recommended as "a powerful plea against this dreadful syphilis." The play was later rewritten in English by Upton Sinclair as *Damaged Goods* and performed in New York in 1913, with the careful support of ministers, doctors, and politicians intent on addressing a growing public health crisis.[49]

Through this interest Belle began to consider the "White-Slave" question, as prostitution was generally understood to be a primary means of spreading the syphilis infection. She visited night court with a group of her fellow reformers to watch "these poor, diseased, misused women" being sentenced. Belle talked to one of them, promising not to preach, but asking whether she "took good care of herself" by douching. She was shocked that the woman was completely unfamiliar with the practice. After that, Belle said she understood the spread of "that awful disease." She, like many Americans at the time—including those in the medical community—believed that internal washing after intercourse would prevent the transmission of diseases, as well as pregnancy.[50]

Belle said it was the prostitute's health that concerned her more than the moral implications of their trade: the women did not even know how to protect themselves and, according to SSMP statistics, usually became sick and died within seven years. The SSMP advocated prosecuting the male clients as much as, or more than, the female prostitutes. It was the men, they argued, who provided the demand for prostitution in the first place, and who brought diseases like syphilis home to their unsuspecting wives.[51]

It is not clear exactly when Belle's interest in these issues began. Her recent experience with unplanned pregnancy, as well as her London doctor's afternoon of careful explanation and education, may well have given her a personal perspective on a set of social issues that were very much on the public mind in New York.

On those issues Belle was at the forefront of reformist movements, if not radical ones. Suffrage was another matter. In the spring of 1912 New Yorkers were bracing for a large pro-suffrage parade in late April, and it was the talk of the town. Pro and con groups had stepped up their activities, and Belle was very involved. She was a long-standing member of the Anti-Suffrage League and on April 9 made a speech against women's suffrage at their meeting.[52]

But someone must have dragged her to a pro-suffrage meeting— perhaps Katrina Ely Tiffany, whom Belle named as one of her closest friends during that period. Tiffany was an officer of the Woman Suffrage Party of New York and later chaired the War Service Committee of the National American Woman Suffrage Association. Belle came home from that first suffrage event, just a week before the parade, rather unsettled. She had been won over, at least enough to resign her membership in the anti-suffrage group. To her surprise she found them "a pretty competent set of women," noting, "I am more of their type than I am of the Anti's who belong to a past generation." Still, she had doubts. Though she would no longer oppose the suffrage activists, she was not yet ready to join them in marching. When the big day came, Belle and her crowd rented out a room in Delmonico's so that they could watch the display in comfort. Belle's friend Tiffany proudly joined the ten thousand marchers, including a thousand men, parading up Fifth Avenue from Washington Square to Carnegie Hall, flanked by huge crowds of onlookers, cheering and heckling.[53]

In the midst of Belle's spring rounds of reform activities, political debates, work, and friends, disaster struck. After a few dizzying days of rumors and conflicting reports, it was confirmed that the newest ship launched by the White Star Line had hit an iceberg on April 14, 1912 and gone down, killing more than fifteen hundred people. The *Titanic* was the latest in a line of ships (including the *Oceanic* and the *Adriatic*) on which Belle and her friends and acquaintances routinely traveled between New York and Europe. In fact, J.P. Morgan had become part owner of the White Star Line after years as a regular passenger. One of the rumors was that J.P. had planned to be and perhaps was on the *Titanic*'s maiden voyage. It was true that he had booked passage, but it had long since been canceled.[54] He was safe in New York, but others were not.

Newspapers splashed the names of prominent men who went down with the ship, after sending women and children onto lifeboats. John Jacob Astor died; his wife survived. And several members of the Philadelphia Wideners were on board. Belle had known this family for years, from Peter Widener, whose art collection had rivaled that of Morgan's, to his grandson Harry, whose interest in rare books had brought him into the Morgan Library many times. Harry had been Belle's particular favorite. She had even introduced him to her pet New York book dealer, Luther Livingston, with whom the young collector carried on a brisk business. Harry Widener was on the *Titanic* with his parents, Eleanor and George D. Widener, and two of their servants. The three men put Eleanor Widener and her maid on a lifeboat. Belle later heard from the dealer A. S. W. Rosenbach that Mrs. Widener collapsed on the dock when she heard that her husband and son had died. Belle wrote to Bernard that Harry's brother George, who was not onboard, was ill with shock. "My heart almost breaks when I think of dear little Harry Widener. . . . It is the most shocking thing that has happened in my day."[55]

Belle jumped into the quickly formed relief committees, along with many other society women, including Anne Morgan, supporting and raising money for the survivors. But she just as quickly gave it up, after turning over almost $6,000 she had collected. The relief groups were too social, she complained, and she couldn't stand the other women's ideas of helping. She swore never to join a women's committee again.[56] Belle's frustration with women's approaches to such work may have been related to her ambivalence over women's suffrage. Although she now had several female assistants in addition to Ada Thurston, she was used to working in a male-dominated and masculine enviornment. Other women often seemed frivolous and incompetent to Belle.

But the social and emotional impact of the *Titanic* disaster stayed with her. She knew many among the survivors, and others who were lost but did not make the headlines: Edgar Meyer was one such casualty. His wife apparently did not want to leave him behind, as the women were boarded onto lifeboats, but he finally persuaded her to go because they had a child waiting at home for them.[57] Meyer was Florrie Blumenthal's brother and the brother-in-law of Agnes Ernst Meyer, another of Belle's close friends.

Although Bernard was still trying to encourage reconciliation between Belle and Ethel Grant, Belle had turned to new associations.[58] Just as her friendship with Katrina Tiffany reflected her new interest in activism and women's issues, her connection with Agnes followed her growing immersion in modern and Chinese art. Belle described Agnes as both good-looking (blond!) and very intelligent. Born Agnes Ernst, she had been an art student at Barnard and worked as a newspaper reporter at the *New York Sun*. She met Alfred Stieglitz through an interview and became actively involved in the 291 gallery and New York's avant-garde. She first traveled to Europe in 1908, the same year that Belle had made her initial journey. But Agnes was able to live in Paris for over a year, soaking in classical and modern art. In 1910 she married Eugene Meyer, a financier who shared her interest in modern art and had the money to become a collector and patron. Eugene was also Jewish; Agnes probably did not fully appreciate the anti-Semitism she would encounter as the Gentile wife of a Jewish man.[59]

With Eugene's resources Agnes was able to start her own art collection. She was an aficionado of Asian art, influenced in part by her close friendship with Charles Lang Freer, a Detroit-based collector of Chinese art who advised her on her purchases. Agnes also had a strong interest in African art, especially wood carvings and masks, a taste she tried unsuccessfully to transfer to Belle. She once complained that Belle had no respect for "Negro things."[60] But it was her collection of European impressionists and postimpressionists and American modernists, including Picasso, Cézanne, Renoir, and Marin, that most puzzled Belle. Although many of Meyer's acquisitions would soon be recognized as masterpieces, and would later end up in the National Gallery, in the 1910s they were not yet fully recognized as important art. (In fact, many modern artists were significantly influenced by African and other "primitive" artistic traditions. Stieglitz mounted several exhibitions of African sculpture at 291 in the mid-1910s.) Belle loved Agnes for her beauty and her involvement in the New York art scene, but was horrified that she spent so much money and time on the "Impression-Futurist-Cubist-Pointillist School."[61]

By 1913 Belle felt completely surrounded by exhibits of modernist art. Shows at 291 had featured her friend John Marin and Francis Picabia. When the International Exhibition of Modern Art was mounted at the Sixty-ninth Regiment Armory, she bemoaned the upcoming visual array: "[M]ay the dear Lord and angels guard us—I for one, will want to quietly hand in my chips." A seminal moment in American art history, the Armory Show introduced Americans to many European painters and sculptors, and for once 291 was not involved, although Stieglitz played a nominal organizational role. Considering them the "wildest cubism," Belle claimed they were beyond her comprehension and/or below her taste.[62] And although the show included realists, impressionists, and other, more traditional works, it was the "Cubists, Futurists, and out-Futuring Futurists" that received the most attention. Belle was escorted by two of the artists represented, Julian Alden Weir and Francis Picabia, who couldn't remember her name and kept calling her "Miss Da Costa" and "Miss Belgren." Other artists that she knew were there, each one pulling her toward the room or area of his work. John Marin, Pablo Picasso, Marcel Duchamp, Vincent van Gogh, Henri Matisse, Georges Seurat, Claude Monet: it was a whirlwind of styles and periods that led even some of the participants to wonder what the art world was coming to.[63]

Her disdain for modern art, whether real or exaggerated for Bernard's eyes ("What is your friend ART coming to?"), did not prevent her from entering into the social circles and claiming acquaintance of the artists themselves. The same could be said of music. Belle heard the Boston-born pianist George Copeland perform works by Debussy that had never been heard in America. She was surprised at his appearance, describing him as "painted and powdered" but thrilled to hear him play, "like an angel."[64]

In addition to her relationship to art as an aesthetic admirer and a would-be scholar, Belle also became an object of inspiration for several artists, beyond the usual sitting for portraits that elite men and women were expected to do. Belle's interest in collecting artists' portraits of her was more a quest for flattering images of herself than interest in their artistic merit. Belle posed for numerous artists, sometimes nude. By the 1920s she had a small collection of portraits of herself on her bedroom walls and loved to show them off to visitors.[65]

William Rothenstein drew her that year during his visit to New York. Rothenstein was an English portrait artist and a friend of Berenson's. He did several drawings and two pastels of her head, and exhibited one of the pastels in Boston, where it was a great success. Belle did not see why. She felt it looked nothing like her, rather more like a "combination of a Buddha, a suffragette and Jeann d'Arc." Upon meeting her for the first time, Mabel Dodge's husband, Edwin, expressed relief that Belle did not look much like that portrayal. Rothenstein gave her another sketch, which she kept until her death (now held in the Morgan Library), and she sent a photograph of it to Berenson.[66]

The following winter the French portrait artist Paul Helleu did several chalk and pencil drawings of her. Helleu was in New York working on commission to paint the ceiling of the main concourse of the new Grand Central Terminal. His blue-and-gold zodiac was inspired by a medieval manuscript he examined in the Morgan Library. (J. P. Morgan played an instrumental role in the construction of the new terminal.) Helleu also spent some time examining the librarian. Belle was not the only object of Helleu's interest; he had arrived in New York announcing his plans to "capture the charm of American women" and bring it back to France. Belle was only one of dozens of women who sat for a sketch or a portrait during Helleu's three-month stay. One of his sketches remained in Belle's possession until her death and is now owned by the Morgan Library. Another version of the same pose and sitting was published in the *New York Sunday Times* the following spring.[67]

Interviewed as he was departing, Helleu discussed several of the sketches he brought back with him, especially eight that he picked out as types of women that he thought "truly American." One was Belle da Costa Greene. Helleu laughed at the notion of a female librarian—that, too, was a truly American notion, he said. But Helleu was more interested in form and beauty as he described Belle's portrait:

See that line?—and that?—and that? Alive, eh? Truly American! See the cigarette? When I first drew the cigarette,
Miss Green objected: she thought that perhaps it would not
be well that she should be shown with a cigarette.

"Take it away, Monsieur Helleu," she asked, but I said:
"Pardon, mademoiselle! I will not. I cannot. It completes
the picture. I like it. It must stay." And it stayed.

It may have stayed in the sketch that Helleu kept, but there is no cigarette in either the one that remained in her possession or the one published with this *Times* article.[68]

Much as Belle claimed not to care about these representations of
her physical self, she clearly did. Throughout her life she sought out
opportunities to model for photographers, painters, and even sculptors. At some point Henri Matisse sketched her standing nude, with
her back to the viewer. The story has been passed down at the Morgan
Library from a former co-worker of Belle's, Felice Stampfle, that Belle
not only identified herself as the model for this sketch, but explained
that she had to pose with her back to Matisse because "the front
didn't work."[69]

Belle's interest in posing for artists continued at least into the
1920s. In 1919 she planned to sit for American art deco sculptor Paul
Manship, with whom she had been socializing for years. He wanted to
sculpt her head, and she thought it would be a good idea—if she could
get her hair "plastered down sufficiently" for his style.[70] In 1923 a
friend described a tea at the Morgan Library given in honor of the
renowned British portrait artist Augustus John, who was "in a very
grumpy mood and most untidy costume." Belle spent her time "trying
to prevail upon [opera singer Madame] Alda to have 'Mr. Johns' do her
portrait."[71] She was probably successful, for a pencil drawing by John
of a nude female figure was listed among her belongings after her death.

In addition to the Matisse drawing, the Helleu portrait, the John
drawing, and the Hills miniature, Belle's probate records list a pastel
female figure study by A. B. Davies, an unsigned study of three heads,
charcoal drawings by A. Walkowitz, and a nude drawing by E. Shinn,

done in 1904. Only the Hills is identified in the estate list as being a portrait of Belle, but she has been identified as the model for several others and may well have been the model for all of these.[72] She apparently told visitors that she was. One museum director told a Berenson biographer that she had been taken to Belle's bedroom to see some nude drawings that Belle said she had posed for. The visiting director admired the artistry but was quite taken aback by her admission.[73]

Meanwhile, as all of her personal drama, media attention, and social reform interests were going on, Belle had also been very busy at the Library. In addition to her usual tasks of making purchases, working with scholars, and doing general maintenance of the collection, she now was in charge of one of the biggest purchases Morgan had made: a set of about fifty Coptic (Egyptian Christian) manuscripts. Belle loved them before she even saw them because they contained dozens of Byzantine illuminations, and of course they were Egyptian. Scholars of early Christianity were beside themselves because the collection included several unique Coptic scriptures.[74]

Unlike most of the Egyptian treasures Morgan brought to New York during this period, this collection of manuscripts was not found on an archaeological dig he himself had financed. The story of their discovery was a rich one. The ancient books had been unearthed near Hamouli, Egypt, by farmers who were digging for fertilizer in a small mound of ancient ruins. Normally, farmers would not have been allowed to disturb a ruin without the presence of a government antiquities guard, but this particular area had been ruled by a German archaeologist as too insignificant to be excavated. The ruins, however, turned out to be those of the Coptic Monastery of St. Michael, and the farmers soon opened up a room that had a receptacle (*sanduk*) full of books of parchment. Knowing they had a large and valuable find, they divided the books among themselves, their families, and their neighbors. Individuals began bringing them into the city to sell to local merchants for between $100 and $125 per book, or selling them among themselves at $10 per page. This value was confirmed by a German scholar who, after examining the books, thought they were alchemy formulae and of no great value. Nevertheless, because antiquities were now on the market without government approval, the police soon arrived and began forcibly searching the villagers' homes for the manuscripts. About a week later the books began selling for $500 each in Cairo.[75] From there, samples arrived in Paris, and scholars and dealers began to salivate.

Father Thomas Shahan, president of Catholic University of America, first wrote to Belle in the fall of 1911, laying out the case for Morgan's purchase of this "rare and unique treasure." Not only did it contain seventeen complete books of the Coptic Old and New Testament (four times as many as any other European collection), but most of them seemed to predate by 150 to 200 years any of the earliest known Coptic books. The bindings were equally unique, and some were the oldest-known specimens. It must be purchased en bloc, Shahan urged. It would be a "great literary glory" that would make the United States a center for Orientalist studies.[76]

Morgan turned the decision over to Belle, and soon she was swamped with letters and visits from leading scholars and other figures offering advice and wanting a part in the exciting new discovery. Belle negotiated the price down from £60,000 to £40,000 (almost $200,000) pending an examination by her friend Charles Read at the British Museum. Read approved of them, and the manuscripts were sent to the Morgan Library.[77]

Belle took Father Shahan's recommendation and had the French-born scholar-priest Dr. Henri Hyvernat oversee translation and editing of the Testaments and other books. Hyvernat had joined the CUA's faculty in the school's infancy as a scholar of Eastern Christianity. When she hired him for what would be a significant piece of his lifeswork, Belle had met Father Hyvernat only through his scholarly writing. The two soon became oddly kindred spirits. Even in her first introduction to him through writing Belle found his "gentle sarcasm rather delightful." Hyvernat was thrilled with his new responsibilities. He had been involved in the efforts to unite the manuscripts in Cairo and had had a chance to examine and evaluate many of them. He wrote to Miss Greene that he could scarcely believe he was not dreaming. He more than anyone else understood their value.[78]

The Hamouli manuscripts, as they came to be known, arrived at the Morgan Library on December 18, 1911. Father Hyvernat began to track down missing leaves and volumes in Egypt, Germany, and England. Media and scholarly interest was high, but rumors emerged that questioned the worth of the purchase and criticized the price Morgan paid (which was said to be anywhere between $125,000 and $1,000,000).[79] In 1912 the *Journal of Biblical Literature* published a brief piece by Hyvernat announcing the discovery to the academic community. After extolling the literary value and uniqueness of the books, Hyvernat explained why such a large, cohesive collection was so rare. "The Arabs," he explained, "have been wont to tear the manuscripts they discover, so as to give to each member of the tribe his share of the spoils." They would ultimately be able to make more money selling individual sheets as well. "Thanks to Mr. J. P. Morgan, our country is coming to the point where it will have nothing to envy the European countries for."[80] Actually some of the leaves had been lost. For years to come various scholars and dealers presented pages that had to be checked to see whether they belonged to Morgan's Hamouli manuscripts.[81]

Belle decided to have the whole collection photographed immediately, to ensure that the material would be safe, at least for scholarly purposes, if anything happened to the precious originals. Moreover, the ancient manuscripts desperately needed repair work, which Belle eventually determined would be best performed at the Vatican Library. She hated to send them away so soon after procuring them, but there were no comparable facilities in the United States. Morgan would have much preferred to have the work done in America, but Belle emphasized to J.P. that she felt it should be performed by "acknowledged authorities of the world," because it was "too important to be experimented upon by the amateur students now in America." At the Vatican Library, Dr. Franz Erhle, whom Belle had met during her 1910 trip, would supervise the work.[82] In deciding to send the work abroad, Belle angered a number of scholars in the United States, many of whom she would continue to work with in future years. But although she was able to tell many of them that the decision was being made by Morgan or Hyvernat, she did not worry about their response: "My salary, always double theirs, still goes merrily on." By June 1912 Morgan's Coptic manuscripts were on their way to the Vatican.[83]

During the spring of 1912 Morgan also began removing his collections from England to the United States. (He narrowly missed having a sizable portion in the *Titanic*'s cargo bay.) U.S. customs taxes had been reduced, and Morgan was finally bringing home his very expensive art pieces, many of which had been on loan to British museums, especially the Victoria and Albert. Jacques Seligmann was put in charge of the mammoth project of removing, packing, insuring, and shipping Morgan's collections in England.[84] There was much controversy in England over the loss; Charles Read wrote a letter to the *Times* of London defending Morgan's decision. Read raised another probable motive for the move: British estate tax laws would require Morgan's heirs to pay a hefty duty if the collection were still in England when he died.[85] The world was already beginning to speculate that the end might be near for the mighty Pierpont Morgan.

All winter and spring Belle thought about going to Europe again the following fall. She continually daydreamed about how it would be to be with Bernard again, but always cautioned that she could never be sure until J.P. approved it and that they would have to wait until he returned. In the spring of 1912 Morgan was in Egypt; in fact, he had left just two weeks after the manuscripts arrived. It was his first trip to Egypt, a land whose culture and treasures he had helped bring to the United States for years. He had even invited Belle to join him, if she felt the Library could do without them both. She did not.[86]

Belle thought Morgan would finally approve her European plans. She wanted to spend time with Bernard, but she insisted that she would have to bring her mother with her. There was so much gossip already that getting caught traveling unchaperoned with Bernard would be catastrophic: "it would simply mean the finish of me." It was particularly important that J.P. not hear any more talk about his librarian and Mr. Berenson. Still, Belle was aching to travel with B.B. again. She wanted to go to Spain, France, and Italy. And she promised repeatedly that her mother's presence would not "interfere with us in the slightest." Mrs. Greene had not yet met Bernard but had promised to leave him and Belle alone—to provide the appearance of a chaper-one without actually preventing what a chaperone was supposed to pre-vent. "I am the only person she obeys," Belle insisted, "and I can pretty generally make her do as I please."[87] Bernard did not believe that for a minute and was sure Belle was giving him an ultimatum heralding the end of their affair. He persuaded Mary to intervene, and she was able to convince Belle that her mother's presence would not provide much protection and would make it difficult to be alone with Bernard.[88]

With Morgan in Egypt, and much easier to love from afar, Belle began to forget their squabbles and long for his return. "I wish you two were one person," she rather oddly wrote to Bernard, "then I would not have a thought for anyone else in the world."[89] As spring turned to summer (and J.P.'s continued absence allowed Belle to imagine that he had softened and relented in his threats), Belle grew more and more confident that there would be no obstacle to her trip. Even as she con-tinued to remind Bernard that all was contingent on J.P., she began to make plans. She promised to ship her family to Maine where she wouldn't "hear their wails and reproaches" when she departed.[90] Meanwhile, Mary saw Bernard off on a tour with his latest mistress. She could not understand his interest in her but hoped it might at least distract him from "the siren in New York." B.B. claimed to be over Belle, but Mary knew that if the siren turned up in Europe, the affair would be back on again. Belle was well aware that B.B. was still being chased by many beautiful women, and she often assured him that she would not expect him to renounce any of them.[91]

But when Morgan returned in July, she hesitated to bring the sub-ject up. When she did, it turned out he had not softened at all, and in fact had probably heard more gossip in Europe, where he had gone after his Egyptian tour. Morgan now seemed to know that seeing Bernard, not business or vacationing, was Belle's real motive for going to Europe. (Belle was fully aware of the double standard this implied after all of her boss's affairs.) Morgan broke into a rage, accusing her of always planning to desert him. He charged that she cared only about the books, not him, and did not appreciate how much he had given to her. "He doesn't give a damn really," Belle insisted. If one of his "pet ladies" showed up, he would stop his crying and raging and immediately be all smiles, Belle instantly forgotten.[92]

Obviously, Morgan's jealous sense of ownership of Belle had not decreased. When he first saw the 1913 Pierce Arrow roadster she had bought while he was gone, he asked her who gave it to her. Belle was so furious, she said, she could have slapped him: "I just blazed at him speechless." He immediately realized he had gone too far and began to apologize, but she went home and had Marie tell him she was out of town when he called. His implication that she could have gotten such a car only if she were someone's mistress took some time to heal. When she finally accepted his apology the next day, Belle coolly informed him that he was the first person who had ever insulted her in that way to her face. But resentment festered under her apparent calm.[93]

The two were barely speaking to each other when Morgan left for Newport on his yacht to remain away until September. And he had still not settled the question of whether she could go to Europe. She held out hope, but now it would have to be a fall visit, for sure. Bernard begged her not to let him down again, and she complained once more about her inability to leave her job, where she was "commanded to remain" when J.P. was away and "implored" when he was there, an "office boy and amusement agency" all rolled into one. She felt their situation was coming to an impasse. Either she would come to put aside her personal resentment and resign herself to being "a drudge and slave" to him or there would be a final confrontation and she would move to Europe to live. If she wasn't allowed to travel to Europe that year, she would have to decide whether she was ready to give up her job yet. She didn't think she could, because of her family's dependence on her. And even with the difficulties, where else would she find a job so wonderful and so lucrative? Maybe Bernard could come to New York while Morgan was gone, Belle suggested hopefully. There was no danger of arrest anymore; the Duveen case had finally been settled, with the firm paying $1,400,000.[94]

After a week without Morgan, Belle had calmed down considerably. Bernard thought there was some agreement between her and "J.P.M."

that she wasn't telling him. It seemed to him that when Morgan was gone, Belle was free to play, and when he was there he thought he had the right to control her time. Belle would have been much offended and annoyed to hear that she had done nothing but play for the last six months! If nothing else, the Coptic manuscripts had kept her busy. And, of course, there was plenty more—including a Keats bibliography for a London publication. Her name, as usual, would not appear, but she was doing a lot of research for the project. In fact, there was less time for her to do library work with J.P. around, since he kept her so busy with other tasks: "housekeeping, entertaining, politics, art and dogs." While Belle found some of these miscellaneous duties hateful, others proved extremely interesting.[95]

Belle described in great detail the hundreds of visitors who arrived daily. It was her duty, while he was at home, to deal with almost everyone who wanted to see Mr. Morgan "and their name is legion, and they come in every conceivable subject—pictures, books, charities, museums, appeals for help of every variety, everything to see from a baby carriage to Marion Crawford's place in Sorrento." The telephone (a "damnable instrument of torture") also rang every minute. And it was no use hiring someone to answer it, for everyone wanted to speak with Miss Greene. "How I hate that name," she moaned. They were all under the delusion that she controlled him, "a huge joke for he pays, if anything, less attention to what I say outside of the book-line and some of his personal affairs, than to any one else." Her secretary helped, but she still had to write just as many letters that were too personal or sensitive to turn over. And then she was also put in charge of organizing his parties, buying presents, ordering cars, opening mail (unless it looked "blond"), arranging club meetings, even scheduling his "ladies' visits" to make sure they didn't meet each other. And, most important, she was currently "lobbying" for him in the "Untermeyr Case."[96]

Samuel Untermeyr had been appointed lead counsel for the congressional hearings headed by and named for Representative Arsène Pujo, chair of the House Banking and Currency Subcommittee to investigate intercorporate trusts. In part because of the power he had wielded in solving the 1907 panic, Morgan was a prime target of the

Pujo committee.[97] The process was interrupted by the fall 1912 election, and Belle's "lobbying" was probably associated with election campaigning.

Where did all of this leave her librarian skills? Well, at the very least the Coptic manuscripts, now at the Vatican, might be her ticket to Europe, perhaps in November or December. But when Bernard heard that Belle would not be coming in August, he gave up. He told her that Morgan had no right to keep her away, but Belle replied that it was an "unwritten law" between them that allowed it, and her own "very deep and very real feeling for him," which he often used to his advantage. She admitted she was at his beck and call, and he sometimes played with his power over her.[98]

For example, over Labor Day weekend Morgan planned a trip on his yacht, and Belle mentioned she also had plans to go away for the weekend and would return Tuesday, after the holiday. Instead, she ended up driving back to town the morning after she left, because J.P. sent a telegram ordering her to be at the Library at nine-thirty Monday morning. She rushed back, believing something important must have come up to justify coming in on a holiday. But Morgan just laughed: it turned out he only wanted her to sit with him until he left at seven for a dinner. So they spent the entire day sitting together doing nothing, Belle seething silently the entire time. Belle knew it was a display of power—"simply a cussed desire to demand my presence and to show that he has a right to." But she also believed that he really cared for her and would rescue her if she were ever in trouble. It was only her desire to go to Bernard that made her regret the situation she was in. And it was a temporary situation. She reminded Bernard again that she was in J.P.'s will, at a "fairly good figure," and that it was contingent upon her agreeing that she "would never leave him while he was alive." Morgan was seventy-five years old and not in the best of health. It could not be very long, Belle consoled Bernard, adding parenthetically that she hated even writing that.[99]

She still hoped to be able to go over in the fall to Rome, and squeeze in a few weeks at I Tatti. But when Dr. Hyvernat broached the subject with Mr. Morgan, he refused.[100] With this final realization of what should have been obvious all year, Belle accepted that she was not going to get to Europe again that year, and fell into a depression, claiming herself no longer a "free-born" person. She wrote short unhappy letters to Bernard, reminding him that when she was "blue" writing was "a physical impossibility."[101] Perhaps as consolation, Bernard sent her a gift of another painting: *Madonna and Child Enthroned with Four Saints*, by Bernardo Daddi. (Both the Daddi and the Spinello, which Bernard had previously given her, were included in an exhibit at the Fogg Art Museum a few years later.)[102]

Despite her growing resentment of Morgan's control over her, it is hard to imagine that Belle would have considered leaving him that fall. In November 1912 the Pujo committee hearings resumed after the election, and Morgan had already been called to testify before a Senate committee about his previous contributions to Roosevelt's campaigns and his role in the 1907 panic resolution. Belle was J.P.'s constant attendant and fiercest defender while he waited nervously for his turn to be grilled by Untermeyr.[103] After the hearing ended, a much weakened Morgan left New York for another trip to Egypt. There is some evidence that he had suffered a series of small strokes over the past year, which would explain some of his behavior toward Belle. He was certainly in poor health when he left, and his doctor traveled with his party to keep an eye on his health. In Cairo Morgan was nervous, depressed, unable to eat or sleep, and diagnosed with nervous exhaustion brought on by stress and age. By February 1913, reports of his ill health caused a decline in the stock market. In early March the touring party retreated to Rome. Belle was terribly upset but relieved to hear he had arrived safely and seemed to be improving. The art and financial worlds held their breath as John Pierpont Morgan, protected from the public by his family and friends, declined into paranoia and dementia. On March 31, 1913, he slipped from sleep to death.[104] Belle was free.

10

CROSSROADS

I feel as one enveloped in a dense fog, I can neither think nor see into the future. Not even you knew all that he was to me—besides every other relation he was a son and a father confessor. . . . My wonderful life with him is with him now and will be buried with him.

—Belle Greene, 1913[1]

The little village is seething with people who are all either dance-mad, suffrage-mad or like myself politics mad. I don't know where it will all end, for there is not a moment of rest or peace. Also we are all wearing trousers (but indoors). They are grandly comfortable and I love them.

—Belle Greene, 1913[2]

THE DEATH OF J. P. MORGAN brought Belle's emotional and professional life crashing to a halt. The life she had was almost entirely due to him. Through her work and relationship with Morgan, she had gained financial grounding for herself and her family, an introduction to both social elites and the cultural avant-garde, and a respected position in the New York and international art worlds. The eight years since she first walked into his Library had brought her from anonymity to local fame and given her daily access to rare books, artistic treasures, cultural performances, and high society. She had seen some of the great collected and private art of America, England, France, and Italy; she had a solid financial stability and powerful connections with bankers, publishers, scholars, potential patrons or employers, and wealthy would-be husbands. But the man who had made it all possible, and whose work and interests had become her own, was now gone. Her life was, as she said, at a "parting of the ways," and she did not know which direction to follow. The uncertainty of her future would weigh heavily on her in the coming months and years. But first the immediate preparations had to be dealt with.[3]

As she waited for the *France* to reach New York, carrying her patron's body, Belle prepared the Library with red and white roses and wreaths for his "homecoming." Brought straight from the harbor to his office in the Library's West Room, Morgan's body lay in state in the building he had made his final legacy. She felt he had come back to her and to the building he had loved. After a weekend of attending the body, as always feeling herself an intruder among "the family," Belle joined the Morgans and the hundreds of mourners following the casket in horse-drawn carriages to the service at St. George's. At Jack Morgan's invitation, she traveled with him and other family members to the church, and then in their private train and hired cars to the burial spot at the Hartford, Connecticut, Cedar Hill Cemetery. It was, she said, a "terrible ordeal."[4]

As news of the financier's passing spread, the Morgan family received literally thousands of letters and telegrams of condolences as well as public statements of respect, including ones from royalty, Pope Pius X, Kaiser Wilhelm, William Jennings Bryant, and many other national and world figures. Belle personally received, by her own count, over three hundred letters and cards from a somewhat more modest circle. Business acquaintances and friends wrote to her personally. Some sent sympathies for the loss they knew she felt deeply; others focused on the question of her status at the Library and her future now that her employer was gone. Most came from people in her own social and professional circles, but she made particular note of condolences offered by friends of Morgan with whom she had not been well acquainted. She deemed their notice of her a final gift from the man who had opened so many doors for her. Her great consolation was that each assured her she had "done more to lighten and brighten his life than any one person—I marvel that they all should have known how devoted I was to him—and I marvel still more at their kindness in telling me—but it has all helped me and comforted me, for the one thing I could not bear, is to have anyone think I used him—or loved his money or his power."[5]

Professional contacts struggled to balance their desire to send condolences with a fear they were treading into inappropriate intimacy, knowing her relationship with Morgan had been an emotional as well as a professional one. Francis Kelsey, a University of Michigan archaeologist who had helped obtain the Coptic manuscripts, wrote a letter to Belle on the day of Morgan's funeral "expressing the sense of loss which all lovers of art and learning feel." But, he said, he decided not to send that note, for fear "it would seem like the intrusion of a stranger in the hour of affliction."[6]

Scholars and dealers also felt their loss of a patron, and many reflected on their own relationship with Morgan. "I am very proud to have known him and to have had him here many times as my guest and to have worked for him," the miniature expert and book dealer George Williamson wrote from London. "The world does not seem the same without him to day but to you in the Library, the loss must be far more severe and we sympathize with you in your irreparable calamity." F. Wheeler, her old friend from J. Pearson & Co., told her he had hesitated to write, knowing what a "blow" Mr. Morgan's death would be to her.[7] Bernard Quaritch sent his sympathy to all working at the library who would "deeply feel his death." Father Henri Hyvernat sent his condolences and his prayers.[8]

Stock prices had taken a hit upon Morgan's death, and his passing would affect the livelihoods of many dealers. Even the Berensons, who had no direct dealings with Morgan, worried that his death would mean a general decline in the art trade. A few were unable to put financial concerns aside for condolences: Leo Olschki sent Jack Morgan his sympathy and a bill for outstanding purchases, much to Belle's disgust. But the reality was that Morgan's death interrupted many such sales and transactions, often in amounts that forced the unpaid dealers or sellers who had not yet finalized a transaction to hasten to remind Morgan's heirs and employees of his debts.[9] Ongoing scholarly projects had a similar urgency. Sidney Colvin, recently retired from his position as keeper of the Department of Prints and Drawings at the British Museum, wondered whether "the lamented death of Mr. Pierpont Morgan" would affect Belle's "position and authority" at the Library. In this case the inquiry was in large part professional: Colvin wanted transcripts of some of the Keats manuscripts in the Library and was not sure whether Belle could help him anymore. She responded that "Mr. Morgan, Junr" would provide him with the material.[10]

Friends, even estranged friends, tried to support Belle and distract her from her grief. Ethel Grant wrote a "wonderful" letter. Agnes and Eugene Meyers invited Belle to visit Charles Freer with them in Detroit. Eugene hoped that a break from the Library "under the existing sad circumstances" would be helpful and that a period of quiet study of Freer's unequaled collection of Chinese art would bring Belle some relief.[11] A long letter from Junius Morgan, "in which he says the grandest things to me and about me," cheered her greatly. Such praise meant a lot coming from the man who had recommended her for the job with Morgan in the first place. Junius also offered her advice on dealing with the new Mr. Morgan and the Library, telling her to "sit tight" for a year or two before making a decision.[12]

Sydney Cockerell of the Fitzwilliam apparently wrote as well. Belle's response to him mourned "the loss of everything [she] loved and respected and revered."

> I don't dare look ahead very much for it seems so hopelessly dreary and desolate. I had come to rely so much upon telling him everything and talking over everything with

him—both cabbages and kings—and now there seems nowhere to turn or no one to turn to.

And there was her telegram to Berenson, sent in response to his own cable of condolences: "MY HEART AND LIFE ARE BROKEN."[13]

And broken she seemed. It may be an exaggeration to say Belle never recovered from Morgan's death, but she certainly kept him close in her heart. She never forgot the man who had created her career and who had become an emotional center of her world. His memory was a constant touchstone for her, and she felt his absence and his presence throughout her life. Yet she had, as we have seen, suffered the loss of loved ones before. She would rally again, and her life and career were far from over.

Still, in the months that followed J.P.'s death, Belle felt she had "lost everything." Her work brought her back day after day to the place that reminded her most of her loss. The Library no longer radiated "sheer exuberant intoxicating joy" as it once had. Memories of J.P. were everywhere. "Everything I touch and see and do, reminds me so much of him—and I can hardly bear it." For her assistant, Ada Thurston, the fact that Morgan had fallen ill and died so far away made it hard to "think of him as gone. . . . It makes him seem here—and it ever will, a vital presence."[14] For Belle, who had tended to his coffin in the Library, that presence was a ghostly one. She struggled to regain her balance and continue her work. "I feel," she wrote Berenson, "as if the ground itself had been taken from under my feet and it is impossible for me to find any interest in life just at present."[15]

Freedom was the last thing on her mind now that Morgan was gone. Their troubled, vital relationship cut off unexpectedly by his death, she was left alone to deal with her memories of their conversations, fights, and the conflicting emotions she had felt for him. Sometimes she was overwhelmed with grief and regrets for all the times she longed to leave him and begged to go to Europe and for all her "fits of anger and rebellion." She treasured the gifts he had given her—even a small Egyptian statuette she believed to be a fake—and clung to the hope that he, like his friends who wrote her, had known she loved him and not his money.[16]

Her concern that her interest in Morgan would be seen as largely financial could hardly have been allayed by the public attention to the extremely generous bequest Morgan left her. Morgan's death, funeral, and will received detailed attention in the New York papers and, indeed, throughout the United States and Europe. The *New York Times* summarized all of his bequests, including the clause in which Morgan gave "to Miss Belle Da Costa Green [*sic*], who has long been my efficient librarian, the sum of Fifty Thousand Dollars." Morgan had kept his promise. Belle was not the only employee to receive such a gift. His private secretary, Charles King, received $25,000; Belle's assistant, Ada Thurston, $10,000; and all the employees of the Morgan company, a year's salary. But Belle's $50,000 windfall was the largest personal bequest besides family, a dramatic and much publicized detail of Morgan's long and oft-cited final testament. Calculations of comparable worth are complicated, but $50,000 in 1913 is worth the approximate equivalent of $800,000 today, a very grand sum by any calculation.[17]

No doubt Morgan's bequest to Belle caused further speculation about the nature of their relationship. But her friends understood it as a sign of her value to Morgan at the Library. F. Wheeler specifically wrote "how pleased he was to read that Morgan "had placed on record his appreciation of all that [Belle] accomplished for his Library." He added, "Personally, I was perfectly well aware how entirely he relied on your judgment and I recall how he used to like to tease me by inquiring 'what Miss Greene will say to more Bibles and Liturgical books.'"[18]

Her inheritance gave her the financial stability she had been longing for, even holding out for. But Belle's career, once completely defined and controlled by the presence and person of J.P., was now at a crossroads. For the short term she still had her job at the Library, which with its holdings went to Morgan's son, John Pierpont Jr., better known as "Mr. Jack" to Belle. Morgan's will also suggested that Jack should retain Belle as librarian at no less a salary than she was receiving at the time of his death. With a $2,000 raise and a plea that he could not properly assess the contents of the Library without her, Jack committed Belle to at least a year of continued work at the Library. But anyone who knew Belle understood that a raise would not make up for the loss of *her* Mr. Morgan or the plans for the collection toward which they had been striving.[19]

The "new" Mr. Morgan immediately put her to work making a full inventory of his father's artistic holdings, many of which were on loan to the New York Metropolitan Museum of Art, as well as the manuscript and book collection at the Library. The immediate purpose was to deal with the taxes and other financial details required for processing the estate. This was an awesome task, taking the rest of the summer and much of September. Belle went without a vacation at all that year. Each item had to be located and appraised, which meant tracking down the original price, dealer, and sometimes the provenance.[20] It was hot and dirty work, keeping her digging through files and climbing up and down stairs to check references and manuscripts, writing to dealers to confirm original prices and conferring with scholars and curators to determine current value and attributions. For once Belle was glad that New York had emptied of most of her friends and entertainments for the summer. There were still enough men around to take her to lunch every day, but other than these "gents" who were soon "shake[n] . . . from [her] mind and soul," Belle's life revolved around her work. She felt smothered by family at home and was so rude or distant to her friends that they all decided she was suffering a nervous collapse. She did not disabuse them of this notion, because it gave her a reason to stay in.[21]

Her home life suffered in her neglect. In the middle of the inventory, Belle realized that she had been completely ignoring her household duty of overseeing the servants. When she wasn't paying attention, they had stopped "functioning." First she attempted to reform them "with a hell of a yell," but with no results. So she fired everyone except Marie and moved herself and her family to the shore in Rye, New York, about twenty-five miles north of Manhattan. For the rest of the summer she commuted into the heat of the city but slept in comfort under an ocean breeze. Even Marie was soon to leave her—she was finally getting married that fall. Belle complained about the "awful blow" of losing her and despaired of being able to find another maid "so discreet and so devoted" to her.[22] Marie had shown her discretion regarding Belle's romantic life very capably on the European trip with Bernard.

Bernard felt himself again relegated from the fore of Belle's attentions. He wrote repeatedly complaining that she no longer thought about him. Her reply hastened to reassure him he was the only light in her life and that she was counting on him, now more than ever. Belle rejoiced when he announced that he was coming to visit New York later that year. However, she could no longer promise to keep herself completely free for him. If he came during the summer, she would still be working on the price inventory of the 21,000 books, dealing with matters only she understood.[23] So the short term belonged to J.P.'s son and the Library. The inventory must have taken an emotional as well as physical toll on her. Perhaps it kept her too busy to dwell on her grief, but it also brought her through the files of correspondence and sales records that represented not only the years of her hard work but those of Morgan before her arrival. It kept her in the Library that would always be "his," except when it was hers. Working at the Library during the first six months after her Mr. Morgan's death was a mixed blessing for Belle.

Although it was painful to stay and she was often tempted to leave, Belle felt obliged to the memory of J.P. to remain there for a while. She also claimed she needed to continue working, believing that $50,000 could have supported her alone, but was not enough to care for her mother and siblings who were all, she claimed, wholly or partially dependent on her. That summer the weight of her responsibility to her family felt particularly heavy. She complained about their clinging to and swarming her, how much they bored her, how poor her married sisters' husbands were. When Christmas arrived at the end of that fateful year, her family hosted seventeen children, most the offspring of their servants, providing food and gifts for each. Upon seeing how inadequate their clothing was, Belle determined to take care of them all. Although she found them "adorably dirty and common," she was shaken to see the true poverty that existed in her own domestic circle and was grateful to her beloved J.P. that she now had the money to keep them warm.[24]

Still, Belle estimated she would need another $50,000 in savings to set her mother and siblings up well enough that she could leave them without having let them down. Now immersed in the world of investment banking, Belle probably intended to set up trust accounts whose interest would provide an annuity to support her family. All of the Greenes seemed to assume that one person's economic success should be shared by the entire family. This is a value that has been identified as specifically, although not uniquely, African American.[25] It was certainly not understood by most of her friends and colleagues, who rarely had anything good to say about Belle's family. However, in true American fashion, with their upward mobility, the perceived needs of her family and especially of Belle herself had escalated. As soon as she received her bequest, Belle invested the bulk of it. Her one extravagance was to order a Mercedes from Paris that fall to replace her Pierce Arrow. The Mercedes had a ninety-horsepower rating, which meant she could indulge her passion for fast driving; she couldn't wait for it to arrive. It never did. Under Bernard's persuasion Belle canceled the order for the expensive luxury car. But even investing almost all of her money, and even with her connections on Wall Street, she didn't think she could double her investment without some questionable scheme. Still, if she saved and invested well over the next five years, she hoped to quit her job and live in Europe, "if only on $4000 a year— then I will work and study . . . and be happy." Until then, she vowed, she would do nothing but work, without long travels and no vacation over a month long. "I want so much to live my own life—if only after I am 32 or 33—that I am willing to give up these intervening years to it."[26] In fact, she was already thirty-four. For the last two years Belle had put off her relationship with Bernard to keep her bargain with Morgan. The $50,000 was her payoff. Once free, however, she immediately committed herself to put off her own dreams for at least two more years. Although much had changed, Belle still felt bound to the Library in every sense of the word. She could not turn her back on it, yet could not pursue the life of study and travel she desired. If anything, she said, she felt her responsibility to her work even more now that her Mr. Morgan was gone.[27]

Still, she thought a great deal about what her next career move might be. Belle had been tempted by "fabulous salaries" to leave Morgan before his death. Now she supposed some past tempters might make her an offer, unless they had been interested in her only because of her connection to Morgan. Would her knowledge and experience still be valuable without the patronage of the great man? Was her reputation based on her own accomplishments or solely on her association with his name? Some were immediately firm in their estimation of Belle for herself. Charles Read of the British Museum, Sydney Cockerell of the Fitzwilliam, and the private collector Henry Yates Thompson had each offered "to do anything and everything for me when I shall need them." But none were in a position to offer the kind of money she was making for the new Mr. Morgan. Nor did she yet feel free to take them up on their promises.[28]

But just the fact that dealers and scholars were taking her seriously meant a great deal to Belle. They treated her as an equal and seemed to reach out to her just when her usefulness as a conduit to Morgan was gone. Several of her academic idols in London and Paris asked her to collaborate on publications on incunabula or illuminated manuscripts. Belle was flattered but worried that she was misunderstanding the situation and getting conceited. She wrote to Charles Read for advice. His response was prompt and clear: she should get more conceited! It was her lack of conceit, he felt, that had held her back thus far. In fact, Read wanted her to become "the most egotistical, conceited and unreachable person ever." This was difficult for Belle to accept. When she received another flattering letter from another expert in the field, she could not take it to heart:

> It was awfully kind reading but I feel a nigger in the wood-pile—Indeed I do most of the time nowadays. I can't understand why these people seem to have taken such an awful shine to me at this time, when, it seems to me, that any usefulness to them I might have had, is certainly ended.

At the same time, she had to acknowledge that there was a note of "equality" in all of these letters that was encouraging. It was "as if I were now to be recognized for myself and no longer as an adjunct . . .

as myself and on my own—I seem to be more acceptable to them than before."[29]

Eventually, concrete offers did come through. By October she reported an offer with a $25,000 salary, as well as one from an editor at the *New York Times*. Exactly what the jobs were, she didn't say. However, much to her amusement, the same editor immediately added, "If young Morgan allows you to leave that Library, there will be the biggest howl from the Newspapers here that he has ever witnessed." Belle was very gratified to feel now that she was respected for her own abilities, "not because I'm tagged (or was tagged rather) to a big man." Belle did send some feelers out for her future plans, as well. She asked Sydney Cockerell whether he would take her as a pupil if she were to come to London for a few months the next year.[30]

Opportunities of a different kind arose as well. Within a few months Belle reported an epidemic of marriage proposals. She promised Bernard she did nothing to encourage them, always laughed when they "popped," and chalked it up to her suitors' misperception that she was in weak financial and emotional condition. Oddly, she never mentioned that the very public increase of her assets with Morgan's $50,000 bequest may have inspired one or two proposals as well. Nevertheless, Belle said she expected "to go on my lonely maiden (?) way for years and forever," taking the opportunity to tease Bernard about her lost virginity.[31]

Being with Berenson was definitely part of her plans as well, but not in the near future. When he asked her to come to Europe, no doubt pointing out that the one person who had kept her away for the last three years was now gone, she prevaricated:

> I wish I could go to you. . . . I want so much to get away. . . . I want to study a great deal. That is certain—and I want so much to travel and learn in that way—I want to be with the minds (at least or at most!) of the men I know in London and Paris—and—most of all, I want to be with You![32]

But she also sometimes felt that her own dreams and desires were not nearly as important as the work she had done and perhaps still could accomplish at the Library. She had begun something bigger than herself, and she still had aspirations for it that had not yet been reached. If Jack Morgan could just be convinced to put some effort and money into the collection, her plans for it could be realized.

However, in the first months after her Morgan's death, that seemed a dim possibility. "I cannot help but feel that I will not be able to make the Library all that I want it to be. . . . I feel that this darling place is going to degenerate into a 'shell'—a useless and empty reminder of what has been and might be. He [Jack] has the narrow, instead of the broad vision and the bargaining soul." And her greatest fear was that Jack planned to sell off all or most of the collection. Rumors were flying. Dealers were circling like sharks. Although there were certainly a few items Belle would have been happy to get rid of, she now faced the dissolution of the collection she had spent over seven years shaping. All was safe during the inventory: Jack would be unable to sell until the estate was settled, and (much to her relief) he had decided to wait a bit before making any preparations. Bernard reassuringly opined that Jack would "come around."[33]

But a few weeks later it seemed that the Library was already a shell, albeit a beautiful one. And her plans for it were narrowing. If she could not create a growing, vibrant, living collection of artistic and literary treasures, she might at least hope for a "resort for scholars," a place they could come to work on materials. Perhaps that was "all I or anyone else can expect."[34]

She was losing hope that the junior Morgan might be enticed to continue developing the collection, or understood enough about it to add meaningfully to it. Relying on Bernard's discretion, she told him Jack was trying to return all the items J.P. had purchased since November but had not yet paid for—including the Hoentschel collection of early enamels. "I almost fainted when he announced this!" Some of the items, to be sure, merited returning. Belle and several experts, for example, had concluded that a book cover purchased from Maurice de Rothschild, was not a Cellini as attributed, and not nearly as old as represented. But, in fact, Jack wished to return everything that his father had not paid for before his death. Since such payments were often made at regular intervals throughout the year or at year's end rather

than at the time of purchase, this policy took many of his regular dealers unpleasantly by surprise.[35]

Jack's one attempt to add to the collection was hardly encouraging.
Having heard about a recent sale of Browning manuscripts, which
Belle was not very interested in, the new owner of the Morgan Library
decided to buy some of them. The dealer involved offered to presell
them for the starting auction cost and 10 percent, which Belle recognized as an extremely good deal: they would almost certainly go for
much more than that at auction. She was astonished when Jack
"balked" and said he would "wait until they were cheaper!!!! . . . It all
shows how the wind blows—and le Roi est mort [the King is dead]."
Clearly Jack had no understanding of how the art market worked. After
that, waiting to sell also meant waiting to buy, and for some time Jack
refused even to consider purchases of fragments of the Hamouli Coptic manuscripts his father had so famously purchased.[36]

Still unsure of her relationship with her new boss, Belle kept her
reactions to herself—and a few confidants. She reported that she was
very busy and that so far there had been no "difficulties or embarrass-
ments." Her greatest concern was that she could not "put heart and
enthusiasm into my work but I can do it well and they do not know the
difference." Her relationship with J.P. had been so unique she could
not hope to match it (and perhaps did not want to). But she had some
very real concerns about Mr. Jack. He was, she admitted, a "fine,
upright, splendid, even faultless person," but it was that desire for
faultlessness that distressed her. However, she felt better about him
with each meeting they held and by the summer was expressing the
hope that he might turn out just like her Mr. Morgan, although he had
"discouraging and even dismaying" ideas about art. He hated Persian
art ("when I had just gotten my Mr. Morgan awakened to it") and did
not care if a piece was a fake as long as he liked it. There were many
times that year when only the memory of J.P. kept her at her work.[37]

By all accounts Jack was a much more modest man than his father,
even puritanical. He was happily married and did not engage in affairs.
He had no use for (perhaps no knowledge of) the small collection of
erotic literature J.P. kept behind a secret door in his office. Belle qui-

etly removed and disposed of it. So, while Jack had already been filling his father's shoes in the business world, he brought to the Library a very different personality and nature than the one that had shaped it.[38]

By the end of the summer Jack Morgan's waiting period was over. Belle quietly contacted her dealer of choice, Jacques Seligmann, to tell him that Mr. Jack had decided some of the art must be sold because, she noted sardonically, "we seem to 'need the money.'" Belle had suggested that the Library's majolica would be the best collection to dispose of first, as well as obviously unwanted pieces like the Rothschild "Cellini" book cover. Seligmann responded with two letters: one for Jack's eyes and one only for Belle. The latter offered sympathy at this first step in what might be the total dissolution of the Library. He consoled Belle that Mr. Jack could probably be talked out of selling too much and offered to talk to him himself. In the official letter he advised against selling. But Jack was determined. Over the next five months he corresponded with Seligmann, Fairfax Murray, and Charles Read discussing how to liquidate some of what Jack continued to refer to as "Father's things."[39]

Hoping to control the damage, Belle wrote to the new Mr. Morgan suggesting that he sell a list of items she had made up, which she estimated would bring $750,000 but whose loss would not detract from the appearance of the Library. She then proposed that the $750,000 be invested as an endowment, with the annual interest of $30,000 going to the support of the Library. Belle also enclosed a list of paintings and art objects to be sold that amounted to $3.5 million—this profit Jack could use to invest in the more traditional business projects he preferred to art collecting.[40] Jack may have found her suggestions just as impertinent as Belle feared, but he supported the idea of selling only select portions of the Library holdings. None of the precious incunabula or illuminated manuscripts were on Belle's list of disposable items.

By the end of August, Belle was working frantically to finish the inventory before Jack's departure for Europe on September 15. Too busy now to commute to Rye, she was staying in the city, working into the night and through the weekends to complete her task. Her relationship with Morgan Jr. was improving. When she worked late into the night, he left his car and driver for her ride home after work. "Wifey may have to journey to Reno yet," Belle teased Bernard.[41]

Slowly Belle had begun to return to her social life and her friends. One of the first engagements Belle kept after J.P.'s death was with her old friend Charlotte Martins, with whom she had lived and worked in Princeton. Charlotte and some of her family came for lunch and a visit in July. A few months later Belle arranged to visit her "<u>dear</u> Aunt Lottie" in Princeton—a brief escape at the height of the final frenzy of work on the inventory. Belle and her Princeton family had remained close through the years. The preceding year Belle had tried unsuccessfully to raise funds to help her former boss and housemate go to Europe.[42] Now they were among the first people she turned to for support.

Belle gradually returned to some semblance of her former busy life. She was thrilled when Bernard announced he was definitely coming to New York at the end of the year. The gossip mill had been busy talking about his travels and visits with his friend Edith Wharton; Belle teased that the scandal they had created would take the pressure off of her. Buoyed by Bernard's impending arrival in December, she threw herself back into culture, politics, and entertaining, as New York's social, theater, and opera seasons began in the fall. Jack had sold his father's opera theater box (for $200,000), but Belle had enough invitations to get her through the season.[43] She even began traveling again, ready to face friends who knew she had "lost a great deal—in fact everything" since they last saw her. She organized a "Sunday Evening Supper Club" with a group of friends. She gave a talk at a women's club, on libraries, of course. She even made a rare attempt to correct a newspaper article that misquoted her. The *New York Times,* which covered the women's club lecture, had cited her as saying that the British Museum had no catalogue. Someone else then wrote in to correct her. With a small headline "Miss Greene Misquoted," she wrote to the editor that she was very familiar with the "superb printed catalogue" of the British Museum, having begun to study it ten years previously at the Princeton University Library.[44]

In private correspondence Belle revealed that her talk had gone off topic and ended up in a political tirade, which the *Times* had not noted. Her political activities are nearly impossible to trace, and she does not seem to have aligned herself with any one cause for very long. This appearance may be deceptive, however. Socially speaking, Belle was now thoroughly immersed in the Greenwich Village scene, and declared herself part of its "politics mad" circles. Her main focus that year was a local movement against Tammany Hall Democratic city politics, infamous for its broad web of corruption and inside deals. Belle actively supported her friend John Mitchel's Fusion Party candidacy for New York mayor even though it went against the political interests of "all my bosses." While a lawyer, Mitchel had targeted corruption in the police department and had gone on to challenge Tammany Hall's domination of city politics and municipal fiscal waste. His campaign successfully united progressive Republicans and reformists. Belle attended a huge Madison Square Garden rally to support Mitchel and other Fusion candidates, and was further radicalized when she witnessed police intervention there. Her primary role was fund-raising, organizing (she claimed to be attending three to five meetings a night, no doubt an exaggeration), and distributing literature. Her impromptu political speech to the women's club was perfectly timed to be related to this work.[45] Mitchel won his bid and served as mayor from 1914 until 1917, when he was soundly defeated by Tammany Democrats.

Despite her political activism, Belle was worried by some of the radicalism of her fellow activists. She was afraid of being seen as "an haranguer" and repeatedly told Bernard that she had "no use whatever for this damned old suffrage and feminism and all the tommyrot connected with it." She would rather, she affirmed, be called a "masculinist" than a "feminist." Eventually Belle overcame whatever fears or dissembling such comments reflected, for she did become involved actively in suffrage groups.[46]

Her social group that year, however, and particularly the women she admired and disdained, further complicate our understanding of her engagement with not only the campaign to give women the right to vote but the underlying debates over women's proper sphere and role in society. Gaining the vote would mean that women were moving into the public arena that had been restricted to men. Women were expected to have priority within the domestic sphere. But there were increasing numbers of women who chafed at that limitation. Belle was obviously one of them. Yet despite the prominence of her career, perhaps even because of it, Belle resisted openly challenging too many of her culture's restrictions on women's behavior, even while her work and many of her choices broke with tradition. The publicity that occasionally swirled around her touted her as a career woman, evidence of a woman's ability to thrive in traditionally male pursuits. Her response was often to eschew her own example and advocate traditional gender roles for women.

During the mid-1910s she was much sought as a speaker and routinely turned down invitations to speak to women's clubs, graduations at female colleges, and other public events. In 1914 Adelphi College for Women asked her to speak on the subject of "Vocations for Women" at its commencement exercises. Belle agreed because, she said, she could not resist the opportunity to tell all those eager young graduates that marriage and motherhood was the only worthwhile vocation for women. Failing that, they could specialize "in some field—but I'm going to pound in the marriage idea for all I am worth and cite myself and a few others (by name!) as examples of miserable failures in life!" Belle probably thought better of her plan; she ended up not giving the commencement speech at Adelphi. Vassar had also asked her to speak to its graduates, and Belle recruited Thursty (an alumna) to talk on private art collections, using a paper Belle had given to the Bryn Mawr Club.[47]

Belle clearly had some concerns with the obvious disjuncture between her stature as an esteemed independent career woman and the traditional female role of wife and mother she continually rejected. Some of her friends had found ways to compromise between the two. Ethel Grant and Agnes Meyer were both writers and mothers. But neither was dependent on an income for support, their husbands both being wealthy businessmen, and neither was identified as a working woman in the same way Belle was.

Similarly, much as Belle asserted her right to have sexual affairs without any interest in marriage, she was uneasy with some—certainly not all—women who were similarly hewing new paths of sexual expression and feminine behavior. Her distaste for Mabel Dodge, a notorious figure and salon leader in the modernist circles Belle moved in, is a case in point. Dodge was a wealthy heiress, enthusiastically engaged, like Belle, in the social and artistic life of Greenwich Village. Her famous salons attracted writers like Hutchins Hapgood, Carl Van Vechten, and Claude McKay, feminist Margaret Sanger, anarchist Emma Goldman, and socialists like Max Eastman, Bill Heywood, and John Reed. Dodge was also part of the 291 crowd and had been involved in organizing the 1913 Armory Show that so horrified Belle. Dodge had distributed a pamphlet there of Gertrude Stein's "Portrait of Mabel Dodge at the Villa Curonia," providing publicity for both the writer and her subject. Dodge was now estranged from her husband and openly living with John Reed. She publicly discussed her sexual experiences, both heterosexual and homosexual, and loved to talk about orgasms: she even named her dog Climax. She helped organize an Industrial Workers of the World parade in support of striking workers and financed Isadora Duncan's school of modern dance. In short, she was the epitome of a feminist bohemian: shocking, self-supporting, sexually active, energetic.[48]

While Belle admired and even loved other women who fit this general description, Dodge was just too much for her. Belle had met her socially many times—they had many friends in common, including Agnes Meyer, Hapgood, Stieglitz, and Van Vechten. But Belle soon came to consider Dodge a "noodle headed, crazy female" and refused to let her come to the Library, threatening Agnes with exclusion if she tried to bring Dodge and the "whole pig-sty" with her.[49] The difference may have been Dodge's involvement with literary modernists like Gertrude Stein. Immersed in the idea of art as a means of transcendent expression, Belle was able to glimpse the motives and occasionally the meanings of modern art. But Stein's writing was beyond her, although she knew and admired Leo Stein, Gertrude's brother, who was living in New York by then.[50] Belle sent the "Portrait of Mabel Dodge" to Berenson, asking for his opinion on the "post-futurism of words" she described unoriginally as "Matissy and Picassonian." (Leo and Gertrude Stein were early collectors of Matisse and Picasso, embracing the modern artists long before the rest of the world was ready to acknowledge their genius, and the parallels between these artists' work and Gertrude's writing was generally recognized at the time.) With its repetitive lines, wordplay, unorthodox punctuation, and long breathless sentences, Stein's writing baffled Belle even more than the paintings it brought to mind. Stein's interaction with the modernist movement was evident not only in the style of her writing but in her direct engagement with the people and works of the new art. Belle would undoubtedly also have read Stein's word portraits of both Matisse and Picasso in Stieglitz's publication *Camera Work* in 1912. "Matisse" begins, "One was quite certain that for a long part of his being one being living he had been trying to be certain that he was wrong in doing what he was doing and then when he could not come to be certain that he had been wrong in doing what he had been doing. . . ."[51]

Belle also wanted Bernard's opinion on Mabel Dodge, who lived in Florence most of the year, and she referenced Stein's word portrait of her. What Bernard told Belle is not known, but the Berensons had already read the piece on Dodge, sent to them by Gertrude herself. Mary passed a copy on to her family, calling it "horrid" and "horrible," although many were heralding Stein's style as a new departure, the literary equivalent of modern art.[52] Berenson wrote a more careful commentary to Stein herself, first thanking her for the photographs of her Matisse and Picasso paintings that she sent him, which he promised to try to "puzzle out." Of the word portraits he admitted, "It beats me hollow, & makes me dizzy to boot. So do some of the Picasso's [*sic*] by the way."[53]

Belle also owned a copy of Gertrude Stein's *Three Lives*, which included two stories about immigrant women and one, "Melanctha," about a woman of mixed black and white ancestry "pale yellow and mysterious." The book was first published in 1909, but Belle received it in 1910 as a gift from a friend, and again in 1914 from Stein's publisher John Lane, another friend of hers. Although she mentioned the book several times to Bernard and asked whether he had read it, she never recorded her own thoughts on it.[54] She did note, however, that Lane had "gone mad on the subject of futurism in literature" and cited his praise for *Three Lives* as proof.

Belle would hardly have identified with the character, a "subtle, intelligent, attractive, half white girl" who is inexplicably loyal to her full Negro friend, "coarse, decent, sullen, ordinary, black." In Stein's portrayal of Melanctha, it is clear that ancestry, Melanctha's "real white blood," makes the difference, because both have been "brought up quite like their own child by white folks."

> Melanctha Herbert always loved too hard and much too often. She was always full with mystery and subtle movements and denials and vague distrusts and complicated disillusions. Then Melanctha would be sudden and impulsive and unbounded in some faith, and then she would suffer and be strong in her repression.[55]

Despite her superior white ancestry, however, Melanctha is subject to suicidal depression, a result of her "half-black" ancestry. In this depiction Stein drew on common stereotypes that people of mixed ancestry were unstable, prone to physical or mental illness.

Belle did meet Gertrude when she came to New York to join her brother Leo. And Stein included Belle briefly in the first chapter of her *Everybody's Autobiography*. Belle is an onlooker, present at a party Stein and her companion Alice B. Toklas attended in New York. Belle and Gertrude are not yet acquainted: "I had never met Belle Greene before although everybody I knew knew her." But Belle is sitting nearby when someone introduces Mary Pickford to Gertrude:

> Mary Pickford said it would be easy to get the Journal photographer to come over, yes I will telephone said some one rushing off, yes I said it would be wonderful we might be taken shaking hands. You are not going to do it, said Belle Greene excitedly behind me, of course I am going to I said,

nothing would please me better of course we are said I turning to Mary Pickford, Mary Pickford said perhaps I will not
be able to stay and she began to back away, Oh yes you must
I said I will not be long now, no no she said I think I had better not and she melted away. I knew you would not do it,
said Belle Greene behind me.[56]

Stein's concern in the scene is clearly movie star Mary Pickford, who
first suggests having a newspaper take (and presumably publish) their
picture and then changes her mind inexplicably. Belle is literally in
the background in this scene, always "behind me," serving as an echo
of Stein's inner voice of doubt. Still, Belle's presence in this scene
confirms her connection to the avant-garde bohemian circles Stein
describes here.

Furthermore, although Dodge and Stein seemed beyond her, Belle
was very attracted to other independent women, many of them living
a new kind of life in Greenwich Village. She told Bernard she studied
them nightly and thought that they would create a "third sex," at least
in New York. She admitted that this type was "a bit like myself." They
were independent, without fussing about it, and had largely taken on
a "masculine outlook." These were the women who were all, including
Belle, wearing pants instead of skirts, at least at home.[57] Belle extolled
the charms of this type of woman:

Who takes her pleasures as a man does and wearies of them
and throws them aside as a man does—who is economically
independent and so does not have to earn her living through
marriage—Who has no morals, but a sense of decency—no
scruples outside of playing the game square—and who generally has a job, more or less masculine in its nature but who
is even keener than the average girl.[58]

This was more than a bit like Belle, and she was more than an observer
of their social circles. She now openly described herself as a philan-
derer who enjoyed relationships with men, sometimes sexually, and

then moved on to the next when the spark was gone. She was certainly economically independent and had often described marriage as being as much a financial arrangement as anything else. And while she was defying social definitions of morality in her relationships with men, she had a very strong sense of right and wrong and a code of proper behavior to which she tried to adhere.

But these women were not just working in male occupations, throwing off double standards for women's sexual behavior, and developing their own codes of decency and morality. They also, Belle said, cared more for other women than for men. Indeed, they seemed "unaccountably physically attracted toward each other—and have almost a contempt—certainly an amused tolerance for men."[59] Was Belle a bit like this as well? At the very least, she was spending a lot of time with women who were. From Amy Lowell's and Annie Field's Boston marriages, to the overtly pansexual Greenwich Village circles she frequented, there is no doubt that Belle socialized with a crowd that was comfortable with men and women who were bisexual and homosexual. In fact many of the scandals she reported that year involved "ladies . . . living with each other."[60] The rumors about Belle's own possible relationships with women may simply have reflected the company she was keeping.

At the same time, her relationships with women may have meant more to her than any of her existing writing lets on. That year she seemed to be, like the crowd she described above, particularly involved with women, and described two flirtations of her own. One involved Emilie Grigsby, newly returned to New York, but not a stranger to Belle—this was the woman who had offered her a Fortuny wrap in London just as Belle was packing to return to New York. Belle reported that Grigsby was now having an affair with Sidney Colvin, with whom Belle was still working on Keats manuscripts.[61] But she also told Bernard that she and Emilie had had a "very amusing and really interesting 'affair.'" As we have seen with men, Belle's affairs and flirtations were not always physical. But she clearly perceived Emilie's interest in her as sexual.[62]

Belle had met Emilie at Jack Cosgrove's home but she first got to know her personally in 1910 in London. Even then Belle had felt that Emilie's attraction to her was sexual. But she had not been interested at the time, and, even though she saw Emilie again (at more of Jack Cosgrove's dinners), she made no mention of any particular friendship with her until this 1913 reference.[63]

Belle also began flirting with Elisabeth Marbury. Widely believed to be a lesbian, Bessie Marbury had been on the periphery of Belle's social circles for several years. She was older than the new generation of women who lived openly as gay women, but had been living with the young interior decorator Elsie de Wolfe for decades, joined by Anne Morgan in recent years. In early 1913 Belle began to spend time with Bessie, who was then in her early fifties. After her first lunch alone with her, Belle was "more or less ashamed" to confess to Bernard, "I immediately proceeded to fall in love with her." Belle was attracted to the older woman's apparent breeziness and openness. But when she did not hear from Marbury after that lunch, Belle worried that she had been too open herself about her "ideas on the enjoyment of female society." Eventually they got together again, for Belle often mentioned Bessie in her letters over the next few months.[64]

There were obstacles to their friendship, however. For one, Belle disliked both Anne Morgan and Elsie de Wolfe and found it difficult to get to know Marbury "without her Morgan and de Wolfe appendages." Still, she persevered, and Bessie seemed to be cooperating, to the extent that Belle had to remind herself, "I'm a gent's lady!!!" At least, that's what she told Bernard. But she also asked him to talk to Bessie and find out what she thought and felt about her. Belle wondered whether Bessie's interest in her was "purely personal (or impurely physical rather)" or whether she was simply interested in Belle for her career and her position of influence.[65]

There was also the problem that Bessie's relationship with Anne had prompted great resentment from the Morgans. Bessie and Anne had probably had an affair, and the Morgans seemed to know this. Juliet Hamilton in particular, Belle confided, talked about Bessie "as if she were a leper and as if her sister [Anne] had contracted the disease from her."[66] It is not clear whether the Morgans knew about Belle's friendship with Bessie, but if Belle was attracted to or involved with women, it would have been very dangerous for them to find out. A wayward daughter might be excluded from familial bonds; an openly bisexual employee could be quickly fired and thus disassociated from the Morgan name.

So when finally Bernard returned to New York, five years after his last visit, he found Belle once again immersed in a decidedly un-elite, bohemian crowd. Only this time her focus had shifted from singers, musicians, and actors to activists, intellectuals, avant-garde artists, and new women—the modernists who were extending the boundaries of creative expression, political ideology, sexual mores, and gender roles. Marbury would have been acceptable, but the Greenwich Village crowd was not.

On December 10, Bernard and Mary arrived in New York on the *Olympic*, after some frustrating delays. He had already told Belle not to meet him at the dock, but she had expected him to come to her apartment as soon as he could after arriving. She had arranged rooms for the Berensons at the Belmont Hotel, just a few blocks from her home, and offered them the use of her car and her chauffeur's services. (Belle had apparently added a driver to her employment of domestic servants.) The Berensons were in New York for only a few days before leaving for Boston. Nevertheless, Belle and Bernard were together several times in those few days, both publicly, at a dealer's and at the Library, and in private, probably at the Gotham Hotel.[67]

Belle had a new interest in Mary as well, finding that she had "all sorts of new feelings" about her. Mary seemed so generous and big-hearted that she made Belle "feel uncomfortably like a weasel." The attraction may have been partly influenced by Belle's new curiosity about women's relationships. She told Bernard, "[I]f I were with her much and she would let me know her . . . I might be more true to her than I would to you." Belle struggled to explain what she meant: "I suppose it is that a great woman means much more (perhaps impersonally) to another [illegible] woman than any man. But—for Gawd's sake—don't misinterpret."[68]

Bernard had ample time to think that one over on his journeys. It was a short visit. On December 14, Belle and Ada Thurston saw the Berensons off at the station, a rather surreal experience for Belle. Bernard would not be back in New York for nearly a month. But Belle looked forward to joining him on an upcoming trip to Montreal to see a new exhibit of Chinese art and hear John C. Ferguson, a well-known expert on Chinese art and culture, give a lecture on that topic.[69] Still, she was so upset after seeing him off that she skipped a luncheon party at the Colony Club and drove down Fifth Avenue until she reached the hotel they had been at together, where she decided to have a quiet meal alone with her memories. Instead, she found herself pulled into lunch with a "wild bunch of men," including Alfred Stieglitz, John Marin, Marius de Zayas, and Bliss Carman. Marin was an American painter who had returned to New York after several years in Paris and made a public break with representational art in 1912 with an exhibit at the 291 gallery. Always confused by modernism, Belle said of Marin, "[W]hatever he is doing (and God knows I don't know what it is) his whole life is in it—so perhaps something will come of it." And as for Bliss Carman, of his hundreds of poems, he had written "two fine ones and for those two I am grateful." The secessionists pulled her out of her funk with their "outlandish 'futurism'" and unshaven faces, towing her through an afternoon of viewing the latest Picabia, Picasso, and Marin pieces. But after this company she longed for "great sweeps of cold fresh air" and motored for a while, stopped in Greenwich for tea, lingered through dinner, and ended up dancing until two in the morning. "That is what your going away does to me."[70]

So Belle survived. Exhausting days at work could be relieved by a fast drive in her car and a hot bath. If that revived her sufficiently, she could head out again for a dinner party where she might make all the "wimmen folks" furious by monopolizing the men to herself.[71]

Jack also returned to New York a week after the Berensons' brief visit. Belle was terribly pleased when he and his wife, Jessie, both came straight from the boat to the Library, just as J.P. used to do. She was beginning to really like him despite herself. "I steel myself against him, but all the time there are little devils tugging at me and pointing me to see charming traits in him." Jack seemed much nicer to her upon his return, and she eventually figured out it was because all of the "men abroad" in the art and book world had told him how highly they regarded her. Charles Read made a particular point of informing Jack that everyone wanted to bring Belle to England to work there. Mr. Morgan was duly impressed. "It looks as if my job might be interesting and worth while here after all," Belle exulted.[72] Jack was now coming to the Library regularly and listening for hours as she talked him through the collection and tried to make him love it as she did. In his absence Belle had been free to enjoy time alone with her treasures. In fact, a "fit of the blues" led her to cancel all of her plans and spend one Sunday afternoon and evening visiting with some of the manuscripts, especially two early French manuscripts "that I kiss, when I take them up—and kiss when I put them back."[73] If only she could teach Jack to feel even half of that passion for the books that were now his.

After a few months, however, Belle remembered there was a down-side to having an enthusiastic, omnipresent boss. She grumbled that she had "overdone" her plan of getting Jack to appreciate the Library. Now she couldn't get him to leave! When he ordered typewriters ("which frightened me to death"), she determined to make it more uncomfortable for him, as she could not get her work done with his constant interruptions. Whatever her plan was, it did not work.[74]

Finishing the inventory had not ended Belle's tasks. She then embarked on confidential correspondence trying to arrange for the sale of some of the Library's items, while trying to maintain what she believed to be the core of the collection. Jack was still equivocating over whether to liquidate the contents of the Library. Every month that he didn't start to sell, Belle had become more optimistic. But that winter Jack had been in England meeting with Fairfax Murray, the only dealer to whom he would talk directly, much to Belle's dismay. Jack had taken her advice to get assistance assessing the collection, but he now planned to bring Murray in to do it, in addition to Belle's recom-mended adviser, Charles Read. Jack privately explained that his pref-erence for Murray was due to his "not being a Hebrew."[75]

Jack's character and influence has received far less scrutiny than that of his more famous father, but his one biographer dates Jack's strong distrust of Jews to the Pujo hearings, which weakened his father months before his death. Samuel Untermyer and several other anti-trust and anti-Morgan figures were Jewish.[76] Belle's distaste for Fairfax Murray is harder to explain. She had been doing business with him for years; J.P. had acquired an important collection of drawings from Murray as well as several smaller purchases. Belle's attitude appears to have developed after her Italian tryst with Bernard, but it is not entirely clear why she disliked him so vehemently. When dealers fell in and out of her favor, it was usually based on their treatment of her or of people she knew. Jack's anti-Semitism would play a strong role not only in his choice of advisers but in many of his business and personal projects as well. Belle, who could use ethnic slurs of all types very casually, does not seem to have let ethnic or national prejudice enter into business decisions—except when it came to Germans during the war. And even then she made exceptions.

Selling part of the collection was now unavoidable. Jack had decided he needed to reverse his father's recent practice of moving his wealth from capital into art. For a long time Belle did not even confide in Bernard about her project, "as even the most cautious of men are apt to leave papers unburnt."[77] However, she may have let enough slip to make Bernard alert his partners, the Duveens. By the end of 1913 Henry and Joe Duveen approached her to insinuate that she might make some money if she worked with them in selling Morgan's things. Before the conversation got too far, she told them "in a very blank and babyish way" that she worked only for Mr. Jack Morgan. No doubt, she mused, they thought she was a fool or secretly working with Seligmann.[78]

Despite Jack's new interest in the Library and the inevitable movement toward selling, Belle found time to spend with Bernard when he returned to New York in mid-January. Mary had come to terms with the state of their marriage and decided that Belle no longer had the power to torment Bernard as she had so unconsciously for the past three years. Still, the way Bernard kept running to Belle was disconcerting and humiliating. Mary bit her tongue and wrote hopefully to friends and family who were in the know, describing how miserable and tortured her husband was and how "capricious and uncertain and moody and contradictory" Miss Greene was.[79]

In fact, although Belle promised to put herself completely at Bernard's disposal upon his return, she not only made other plans on a few occasions but left town for a weekend in early January for a mysterious visit to Chicago on "important personal business."[80] She was gone the entire first weekend Bernard was back in New York. Capricious indeed. What personal business could Belle have had in Chicago that would be worth missing a weekend with Bernard? There is no record of her ever having gone to Chicago before. Her existing correspondence to Chicago institutes was strictly business and reveals no evidence of personal relationships of the kind she forged with art collectors and scholars in Boston, Philadelphia, Washington, D.C., and London.

Struggling to explain, but clearly trying not to give away any specifics, Belle described the trip that would cost her precious days with Bernard as a visit to meet with someone she had not seen in almost twenty years. "I dread the trip in one way," she explained, "but am overjoyed to take it in another as it is to bring back into my life someone whom I love very much and have not seen since." She assured Bernard she would not have hesitated to tell him everything if she had been the only one involved. But not only was she taking a personal risk in making the trip, "it would bring disaster to several people if it became known that I had seen this person." Despite the danger, however, she was pleased that her trip would help toward "rectifying a very grave wrong and injury" for someone she loved "very dearly." But when Bernard accused her of "pleasuring" in Chicago instead of spending time with him, she retorted that it was a "beastly errand" she was going on.[81]

Whom could Belle have anticipated seeing again with such a powerful complex of emotions? There is absolutely no concrete evidence pertaining to her trip beyond these letters to Bernard. But there was one person living in Chicago who might have inspired this strange reaction. Richard Greener had settled in Chicago in 1906 and was still living there in 1914.

Several pieces of circumstantial evidence point to the strong possibility that in January of 1914 the former Belle Marian Greener went to

Chicago to meet with her estranged father. Her own description holds most of the clues. It had been at least sixteen years since Belle had seen her father; Greener left the United States in 1898 and was estranged from his wife and children for several years before that. Belle had known him as a teenager, not just the "tiny little girl" she described herself as. But Belle's purported age never quite lined up with the true passage of years. In addition, Greener must have been hurt by his family's decision to disassociate from him and live as white. And, of course, it would have been very risky, to Belle herself and to all of her siblings and her mother, had her relationship to Greener become public knowledge.

There is other suggestive evidence that it was her father whom Belle was meeting in Chicago. Greener had a need for a meeting with some of his estranged family at that time. He was in legal limbo over his cousin's will, which left some assets jointly to Richard and his son, Russell Greener. After several years of trying to convince the probate court that Russell could not be found, did not want to be found, and did not need the money anyway, Greener and his lawyer promised to place ads in New York and New Jersey papers looking for his son, who was, of course, now living as Russell de Costa Greene. He had taken a job in New York with the Mexican Petroleum Corporation. And he was married.[82] It was not a good time for his father, whose black ancestry was well known, to reenter Russell's life.

If this was the reason for the trip, why would Belle have gone instead of Russell? She seemed to operate as the head of her family, even though she was neither the oldest nor male. She was certainly the most well traveled, and the only one with a ready excuse for a sudden trip. In fact, she was scheduled to return to Chicago later that summer to give a talk at a weeklong conference on women's achievements organized by the Woman's Association of Commerce. (Other speakers included the Chicago reformer Jane Addams, the Unitarian minister Rowena Morse Mann, and Ella Flagg Young, superintendent of the Chicago Public School system.) Nothing in Belle's description indicated that this was related to her January trip, but it could cover any questions from less intimate sources than Bernard. (Belle pulled out of the meeting at the last minute because the meeting attendees passed a resolution in favor of women's suffrage.)[83]

It is also possible that Richard contacted Belle directly. Despite his claims to the contrary for the court, Richard must have known how to reach the family, especially his most successful child. He would have recognized the images and name of his daughter, which were not only prominent in the New York papers but had appeared several times in the *Chicago Daily Tribune* in the last two years. In these stories she was called Belle Da (or De) Costa Green, a name that would be transparent or at least suspiciously familiar to anyone who knew her as Belle Greener. The August 1912 full-page story had appeared with a photograph of Belle that took up more than a quarter page. And the $50,000 Richard's daughter received from Morgan made the front page in Chicago papers just ten months before her trip.[84]

In 1914 Richard Greener was seventy years old and retired from his legal and political work. He had left the high visibility of his early career and spent his days pursing his own writing and research at nearby libraries. But he was still known in Chicago as a prominent colored man, the first black graduate of Harvard, as a former U.S. consul, and for his work for the Republican Party and civil rights. He continued to give public talks from time to time, and had recently accepted a series of speaking engagements in the city and the surrounding region.

Greener lived in a mostly white neighborhood as a boarder with his cousins, three unmarried sisters: Amelia, Mary, and Ida Platt. Like Greener, the Platts were of mixed black and white ancestry, and the family was alternately listed in federal censuses as white (1860, 1910, 1920), mulatto (1870, 1880), and black (1900).[85] Ida was a lawyer and may have worked with Richard for a time. Mary kept house. Amelia worked as a public librarian; the Chicago libraries had a policy of hiring through color-blind civil service tests. Their listing as white at times was probably due to a combination of their light skin and their residence in a white neighborhood. When, in 1930, Amelia was living in a black neighborhood and still working at the library, she was listed as "Negro." (By 1930 "mulatto" had been dropped as a federal census category.)

It was probably fairly safe for Belle to meet with her father. Despite the previous newspaper coverage, Belle could likely be anonymous in the midwestern city. It would not have been difficult for the father and daughter to find a private place to meet, and strangers noticing them together might have seen only an older white man with a younger white woman.

But while the danger may have been low, the stakes were very high. As Belle da Costa Greene, she had the life her father had never been able to reach. She was surrounded by art, books, masterpieces. She had traveled to Europe twice, immersing herself in art and work, exactly the dream her father had given up as a student. And she was supporting his wife and family in a style that he, with a Harvard degree and a J.D., and the support of leading white politicians, had never been able to provide. With much less formal training, just as much talent, intelligence, and drive, the presumption of whiteness, and the fortunate meeting with J. P. Morgan, Belle was now living a life few Americans not born to privilege could have hoped to achieve. It was a biting indictment of the power of racism over talent and hard work, and the possibilities and privileges available to whites.

If Belle were now to be discovered to be the daughter of Richard T. Greener, Negro consul and lawyer, "her life and future," as she told Bernard, could very well be over. People might be willing to accept speculation about some possible black ancestry, but outright proof and public disclosure might be another matter altogether. Certainly her Library position would be in jeopardy. Even if J.P. had been willing to look beyond ancestry for a talented individual, Jack's refusal to work even with Jewish dealers suggests that he would not have been so inclined.[86] With no job, and her black ancestry made public, what would Belle do? She already yearned to move to Europe, and many with darker skin had found relative acceptance there, often as exotic curiosities. But Belle was aware of the pitfalls of being an ethnically exotic woman in Europe. When a French acquaintance offered to make her the rage of Paris, she laughed bitterly at the vision of herself on the streets wearing nothing but "bells on my toes and breasts."[87] Yet she could have lived her dream, finding a small place to live quietly in Italy or France, pursuing her own studies.

Her family would probably have fared less well. By 1914 all of her siblings but the youngest, Theodora, now called Teddy, were launched in careers or marriages. Belle was still the financial and emotional center of the family, at least from her perspective. The loss of Belle's income would mean a lowering of the entire family's standards. Her mother was no longer working and had become completely dependent on Belle financially. Even as other siblings moved out and established their own households, the elder Genevieve always lived with Belle. The summer rentals at lakes or seashores, the dresses for parties, and the entrée into some of Belle's social circles would all be gone. But it would mean not just the loss of luxuries and comforts; in 1912 one of Belle's sisters had been in and out of the hospital, threatened with a hysterectomy. How would the family deal with such costly medical emergencies in a future in which Belle could no longer be Belle da Costa Greene? By 1914 Ethel became engaged to George Oakley, a wholesale merchant.[88] Would her fiancé change his mind if the family's past emerged?

Belle's job and status had touched every one of her siblings' lives. She helped pay for the college educations of Russell and Louise and was still paying for Teddy's education. When her brother became ill with malaria after working in Florida for several years, Belle was the one who arranged for him to return to the New York area and looked for work for him. Russell moved back in with her for a while, but by 1914 he too was married, to a white woman Belle described as "sassiety." The couple lived in New Jersey, where her brother worked as an engineer and belonged to a golf club.[89] Did his wife know her husband's family history? Would she have cared? The golf club and contracting firm almost certainly would have.

Belle's eldest sister, Louise, had been married for two years. She had met her husband while teaching in the public school system; Frederick Martin was a speech therapist who had overcome his own childhood stuttering and developed a method for treating speech impediments (including the foreign accents of immigrant children). He would write two texts on the subject, and go on to establish a school for training speech therapists that became part of Ithaca College, in western New York.[90] Louise had converted to Roman Catholicism when she married

Fred Martin. Would he accept her black ancestry as a distant, unimportant detail? An impediment to be overcome? An exotic enticement? Or cause for annulment?

And what would Richard Greener feel upon hearing of his children's achievements? He already knew that Russell was doing well; one of his arguments for settling the will without Russell was that his son was well off enough not to need his portion. Of course, Greener would be all too aware that the achievements of the Greene family were possible only because they had distanced themselves from that part of their ancestry that he represented. He was no darker than they, and no less intelligent and gifted. But he was proud of his black ancestry and had devoted much of his career to creating a world where African Americans could achieve exactly what his children had—only without having to deny or hide their African ancestry.

In addition to anger and hurt, Richard must have felt some pride. After all, his children's accomplishments were also a product of their abilities, unencumbered by racism, and a reflection of his own parenting. His daughter Belle especially was living the dreams that he had never been able to pursue. But Belle and her siblings had turned their backs on that most vital of values Greener had hoped to instill in them: that of using their gifts and achievements to advance the opportunities available to the Negro race, and prove that people of African descent were capable of full citizenship. What good did their accomplishments do for those of darker complexion who did not have the option to follow them into whiteness, or those who could but instead chose not to? Knowing how her father had to feel, Belle must have approached this meeting with no small amount of trepidation. It was surely not the first time she had had to face those left behind, still excluded, still demeaned.

Even if Belle and her father had never met in person after her career was launched, she must have thought about him from time to time. Surely all of them wondered what it would be like to see each other again. For those with a sentimental heart, which Belle had for things that mattered to her, every day could have brought memories. At home he was the absence that defined the new Greene family. At work he was the source of countless lessons and memories of books and files and catalogues. Belle was well practiced in pushing out unwanted memories, drowning them in work or drink or opera or parties. Nevertheless, some reminders must have gotten past any defenses she had installed.

For example, how did she react when Asa Bird Gardiner wrote her in 1913, asking whether she was one of the Rhode Island Greenes and claiming her as kin if she was? Mr. Gardiner was actively involved in the sort of genealogical societies that honor descendants of historical figures. He was particularly proud of his ancestor General Nathanael Greene's role in the Revolutionary War.[91] That alone might be enough to remind her of the much more recent and fragile history of her own Greene lineage.

But there was more to fear here if Belle recognized the name. Major Asa Bird Gardiner had served as judge advocate in the 1880 court of inquiry regarding one of Richard Greener's former students, West Point cadet Johnson C. Whittaker. Gardiner had presented the case for the prosecution against Whittaker, with Greener and Daniel H. Chamberlain acting as defense counsel. Gardiner had, moreover, cross-examined Greener, who also served as a witness, having been called to West Point immediately after the attack.[92]

At the time Belle was barely a toddler. She would have known the details of the case only if Greener had continued to talk about it to his family as she grew older. His version would have been a bitter one, about the many outrages of the inquiry, the triumph of racism over justice and common sense. If Gardiner was named, he would have been one of several whites who punished a talented and promising young black cadet for the crime of being a victim of racial violence. Or perhaps some proud family member or friend had told her the story of her father's fighting the good fight in defense of his student, trying to make the argument that white America was not yet able to hear.

Perhaps Belle was unaware of Gardiner's history with her father. But how often did Belle find herself confronting someone who might have known she was Richard Greener's daughter? Greener had lived and worked in New York for over a decade. He was a prominent figure there. It must have happened that she crossed paths with people who knew him and perhaps had known Belle Marian Greener. There is even some evidence that people not only suspected she had some black ancestry but knew who her father was. Early in her research on Morgan, Jean Strouse spoke to a man (now deceased) who told her that Belle's father was the first black man to graduate from Harvard.[93]

Miss Greene's reply to Major Gardiner ignored his question about her name and heritage and made no claim to the kinship he offered.

The risks of having risen to such heights help explain Belle's continued attempts to avoid publicity. Her increasing celebrity in New York would seem to have been a perfect opportunity for one who delighted in being petted and spoiled and the center of attention. But, in the context of her father's identity, Belle's new visibility was a liability. Just a week before her trip to Chicago, *Vanity Fair* had asked her to send Paul Helleu's portrait of her for publication. Belle had already been uncomfortably aware of her celebrity; she had just overheard a man lounging at the Ritz say, "Morgan said she was the cleverest woman he ever met—I don't think she's much on looks." Curious to see whom he was talking about, she found him looking at a picture of herself in a magazine. She pronounced it "disgusting to be discussed in the foyer of an hotel" like an actress.[94] But, of course, Belle loved actresses, and she loved being the center of attention. Perhaps she would have felt differently if the anonymous gentleman had admired her picture. In addition to the worrisome association of this kind of publicity with less respectable women like actresses, such visibility made contact with her father all the more dangerous.

Moreover, Belle believed her visibility was due partly to her dark skin and ambiguous ethnic appearance. Just a week before writing Bernard about her trip to Chicago, she had finally decided not to accompany him and Mary on a trip to Montreal because, she said, "I am so damned black that it is impossible for me to go anywhere, among people whose names are known without being identified."[95] Belle was hardly black in the literal, or even racial, sense but certainly dark enough to stand out among the mostly white circles in which she moved.

Even among her family, Belle was constantly aware of the physical differences between herself and her siblings, and constantly racialized them. Describing a family dinner a few months later, she depicted them as a "queerly assorted bunch": her sister Louise "looking very much like a Japanese lady of exquisite quality . . . extremely pretty in a delicate and fascinatingly aloof way with wonderful masses of mouse coloured hair." "She makes me feel like a hell-hound, like a wild Tassanian [sic] boar and like the gorilla you see in me." We have already seen that Belle especially resented blond women, except perhaps her light-haired sister Ethel, whom she called the "blondish me."[96] And here the pain she attached to her own appearance, which she and others routinely qualified as exotic or unusual, is starkly evident as she identified herself with some of the harshest, most demeaning images of blackness: as evil, savage, animal-like, inhuman. That this self-description is presented in contrast with her sister's Asian-like beauty suggests that it is appearance, not ancestry, that is behind Belle's disatisfaction with herself. Perhaps this was one of the unanticipated costs of shifting from being a very light-skinned woman of color to a not-quite-white-enough white woman. In her mother's community, Belle's pale beige skin and "good" hair would be considered beautiful, as European ideals of facial features and hair type influenced a value system now known as colorism. Belle was still internalizing these ideals, but now was judging herself against women, even her own sisters, who she felt were more beautiful than she could ever be because they were lighter-haired and fairer-skinned.

If, indeed, Belle had just met with her father that winter, that might help explain her heightened awareness of her ethnic ancestry, her darker-than-Anglo appearance, and her need to hide part of her background.

There are no further clues or later references to clarify what happened in Chicago, or whether Belle had any other contact with her father. But, whatever its purpose, Belle's trip to Chicago was not the only impediment to a perfect reunion between her and Bernard. Despite her promises to the contrary, Belle was not willing to put everything aside for her long-separated lover, and could not throw herself back into their romance without ambivalence, especially since Bernard was indeed trying hard to persuade her to give up her bohemian friends and lifestyle.

When she returned from Chicago, Belle met with Mary and told her that although she still cared deeply for Bernard, she was not in love with him anymore and did not think she ever would be again. "She is very straight and frank," Mary observed. Relieved enough to be back-handedly charitable toward her rival yet again, she added, "I really like her, in spite of her social vulgarity." After a few more meetings between the lovers—a lunch at the Gotham Hotel, and an "evening perform-ance" the following Saturday night—Bernard's frustration with Belle was rising. Mary observed, perhaps too optimistically, that "the end must be near," as Bernard was having "an awful time with Miss G. who is not at all the frank & candid person she seemed at first to be." Belle was also strongly resisting Bernard's attempts to disengage her from her unsuitable friends. Bernard explained Belle's unavailability and moodiness by saying she was "overworked and neurasthenic [on the verge of a nervous breakdown]."[97]

Even Mary had to admit that Belle's life was quite hectic. During the few months of their visit, Belle was working every day, and showed no signs of curbing her usual run of lunches, dinners, meetings, and shows. She was still socializing with the same people: Agnes Meyer and the rest of the 291 crowd, her old friends the Truesdales, Charles Freer—who was often in New York because of his illnesses—her good friend and former flame Jack Cosgrove (now Sunday editor of the *World*), and Carl Van Vechten and his crowd.[98]

But neither Belle nor Bernard pretended to monogamy (or bigamy, in B.B.'s case). Agnes Meyer was also flirting with Bernard on that visit, and even Mary referred to her as "B.B.'s lady."[99] There does not seem to have been anything overtly sexual or even romantic in Agnes and Bernard's relationship beyond friendship and flirtation. (This fits Bernard's description of his relationships with women as being prima-rily intellectual and emotional. Whether or not they became physical did not appear to define his interest.) Belle actually seemed to encour-age the dalliance, although she said she was personally tiring of the friend she now referred to as "Agoness" or "Agonies." She persuaded Agnes to plan a trip to Florence to see Italy with Bernard, and wrote to her lover about the trip much as Mary once wrote about her: "I am glad that she is in love with you—I only regret that it probably will not last—but it will certainly last long enough to influence her toward righteousness and certainly being with you in Florence will open her eyes, her mind and I hope her soul."[100]

Nevertheless, when they were in New York, Bernard and Belle saw each other virtually every day—so much so that years later Mary would still recall her humiliation as they conducted their affair almost under her nose.[101] Of course, much of their time together in New York was in the company of Mary or others. The Berensons' schedule was also busy, and their business meetings and trips took away from time between the lovers: most notably, the Berensons' monthlong stay in Boston when they first arrived. Even in New York a typical day for them included trips to see privately owned pictures, meetings with dealers, lunch and dinner with friends and art people, lectures, opera, and even meetings at eleven-fifteen at night.[102] Belle had arranged visits for the Berensons with a number of her friends and accompanied them on some of their meetings. But the best times of the visit for Belle and Bernard came in trips to Detroit and Baltimore.

Outside New York it was perhaps easier for Belle to focus her attention on Bernard. In late February she traveled with the Berensons and the Meyers to Detroit, a trip Agnes and Eugene had been trying to arrange for Belle since Morgan's death. The group stayed with Charles Freer and spent the week studying his collection of Chinese art, paintings, potteries, bronzes, and sculpture under Freer's own tutelage. It was, Belle said, even better than their Italy tour, and many of her subsequent conversations and letters with him and other art experts were about particular pieces she had seen at Freer's and at the various New York dealers' galleries, museums, and private collections.

Belle was captivated by this new arena of Asian art. She wrote to her English friend Sydney Cockerell that the stay with Charles Freer had "revolutionized" her " 'art' life" and freed her from the "weed-choked streams" of European art. She loved "the grandeur, the immensity, the

all-pervading mysticism and selflessness" of Chinese painting, especially the landscapes.[103] Upon her return to New York, Belle immediately arranged to continue her education, putting herself under the
direction of Professor Friedrich Hirth, of Columbia University, who
conducted a series of lessons for her on Chinese history, philosophy,
and culture. That these lessons were usually conducted in German
made it even more challenging for Belle. German was Hirth's native
language, but Belle's German was, as she said, "a thing of the future."[104]

Bernard's interest in Chinese art was both aesthetic and professional. He had been buying pieces of Chinese art in New York, both
before and after their visit to Freer (who accompanied them back east).
By early March, Mary was confident that Bernard could now serve as
an adviser for collectors of this increasingly popular school.

American interest in Asian culture was not new, but the market in
pottery, statues, and paintings had exploded in New York. It was a
potentially lucrative field for the Italian Renaissance experts. Belle's
love for Chinese art was closely connected to her feelings for Bernard
as well. He had first told her about Chinese jade and promised to send
her some. When they saw a jade piece at Freer's that she loved, Bernard purchased it and gave it to her. Belle promised she would treasure it joyously.[105]

Others saw different emotional motives involved in the Detroit trip
and Belle's new interest. Belle's old friend Junius Morgan was sure that
Freer was in love with Belle. (There is little evidence that this was
true.) When she laughed in response, he told her that she "didn't even
have the feelings or sentiment of a fish!" and that she would never love
anyone. Apparently Junius did not know about Bernard, for Belle was
busy rediscovering the depth of her emotional attachment to her
first lover.[106]

Belle also joined the Berensons in Baltimore. She had much less
interest in the collection of Henry Walters there than she had in
Freer's. She loved Walters's private assortment of illuminated manuscripts, which few people ever saw. But the bulk she described as looking like "all the trash of the world had been swept up and <u>dumped</u> into
that poor building." Not unlike her own "Morgan of the Blessed Memory," Walters had a haphazard medley of styles, periods, schools, and

quality. The one good thing was a Greek marble frieze relief that she judged to be sixth century.[107]

Seeing the art with Bernard, however, was what made those trips memorable for Belle. She had finally realized "all that you mean in my life" and regretted that she had not known it when he first arrived. It was the trips to Freer in Detroit and Walters in Baltimore that made the difference in showing her that he was "the 'quality' of life" she wanted. Now she was as much in love with him as she had been four years previously, although she still felt she had to "earn the right to be with you."[108]

Spending time with the Berensons also enhanced Belle's renewed interest in Mary, long frustrated by the older woman's "impersonal attitude" toward her. That made Belle just want to try harder to "climb over the wall" between them. She asked Bernard not to tell his wife but tried to explain her feelings for Mary. "You have no idea how she fascinates my attention—I really force myself to stop staring at her. . . . I sure would make love to her if I were a gent."[109]

Bernard saw Belle off at the train station. She was going back to New York; the Berensons were heading for D.C. and then Pennsylvania. On the train Belle ran into none other than Henry Walters, who insisted on seeing her in his private car and demanded Belle's opinion of his collection. He didn't want to hear about the manuscripts or the Greek frieze: her reactions to those had been clear. When Belle became frustrated by all of his questions and snapped at him, he smiled and said, "Now you are talking like the Miss Belle, Laffan knew and Morgan found invaluable." Walters had known J. P. Morgan and William Laffan well. Then he abruptly asked whether Laffan had been in love with her. She retorted, "perhaps—as much as he could be with anyone but himself." Finally Belle recovered her social balance and started lecturing him. Yes, he was older and a big man and she was a "poor working girl," but she found his questions "damned impertinent." She reminded him that just because he had the power to treat her any way he wanted, it did not mean he should. He apologized, and then they settled down to discuss art, attributions, and Berenson. Belle hoped that Walters would bring her B.B. lots more work.[110]

Back in New York, Belle waited for Bernard to finish his work with the Widener and Johnson pictures in Philadelphia and return to her. Already her newly recovered bliss began to crack under the stretch of their distance. Each complained about the other's unenthusiastic letters.[111] When Bernard began to write romantically, vowing that they were now loving only each other, she immediately objected. Surely Bernard could not really mean that.

> Given our mutual self interests, our mutual desire for the coin and other perquisites of this world, and your great love of people and sassiety, and my one or two tiny ambitions— it is pretty much tommy rot. . . . We can be truly devoted to each other and when together do all that we should, ideally, want to be to each other, but as I, at least, am frank enough to admit that I would not cast aside my material life for you, and as I know you feel the same, why waste time hot airing about it.

Belle did not believe in a "maison à trois [house of three]." Having recognized the impossibility of that, she wanted a real and worthwhile relationship. Both would lead their own lives without interference, and they would meet occasionally "in some relation, outside and above it all."[112] Belle would no longer dedicate her bedroom to Bernard, either in fantasy or in practice. Whether or not Belle ever acted on her new attraction to women, she had certainly turned a corner on her sexuality.

Although she still maintained a professional veneer of respectability, she began to gain a reputation for her ribald comments and her willingness to talk, at least jokingly, about intimate and forbidden topics. Belle was also increasingly willing to be open about her relationships with men and no longer cared quite so much what people said about her. J. P. Morgan's death may actually have freed her from that particular concern. Belle was also maturing, slowly becoming more sure of her position in the world. And, too, times were changing.

Belle, of course, had her usual work and life to distract her. Charles Read was coming soon and seemed to expect Belle to entertain him and weekend with him. Belle told Bernard that she was not looking forward to it. On one of his lessons, Professor Hirth brought a student of his, an unnamed Japanese man who was studying Lao Tzu and Taoism. Belle was enthralled by the handsome, genteel young man at the same time that she repeatedly referred to him as a "Jap" and described him as "uncanny." Still, she was so impressed that she immediately invited him to dinner (alone) at her home.[113]

Bernard returned to New York for a few more days of talks, strategizing about dealers and other art people, and being with Belle. Soon he and Mary returned to Europe again. Their calm parting confirmed Belle's belief that they had reached a higher level of love and trust and were now finally on a smooth course in their relationship. They would not have been capable of it before, she concluded proudly.[114]

Soon after Bernard's departure, Belle observed the first anniversary of Mr. Morgan's death. She and Jack closed the Library and received mourners, flowers, and cards for hours. "It was one of the hardest days I have ever spent and I am still numb and dumb from it."[115] An entire year had somehow passed since his death, and the pain of the loss was still with her, waiting for some unexpected moment to bring it back as fresh and sharp as ever.

11

BATTLEFIELDS

[E]verything in life, with perhaps the exception of one's work is a pis-aller [done for lack of better options]. It's distressing and makes one want to chuck the whole game sometimes.

—Belle Greene, 1916[1]

[T]he world, literary and otherwise, that will emerge from that war will be so vastly differed from the one we have been used to live in, that I wonder whether we shall be able to, or care to continue any of our pre-war undertakings.

—Henri Hyvernat, 1916[2]

WITH BERNARD GONE and the first anniversary of J.P.'s death behind her, Belle's attention turned again to her work and her many outside interests. Having immersed herself in local reformist politics and dabbled with radicalism, Belle was well situated in a front-row seat for New York's response to America's foreign policy and for witnessing Europe's fateful steps toward a war so overwhelmingly large in scope and sheer numbers that it was considered the war to end all wars. The Great War, as it was then known, eclipsed Belle's plans long before the United States entered the military fray in Europe. But it was the Mexican revolution that first drew her attention to the politics of war.

When President Wilson ordered the U.S. Navy to intervene in Mexico's violent upheaval, Belle began attending socialist antiwar meetings. She listened to New York radical Max Eastman, a familiar figure from her Greenwich Village haunts. Although she dismissed most socialist leaders as "dirty and uninteresting maniacs," she "howled with joy" when the handsome California anarchist William "Big Bill" Haywood gave a rousing antiwar and anticapitalist speech at a meeting in Carnegie Hall on April 19, 1914. Haywood was advocating a general strike to protest, and perhaps even prevent, the U.S. entry into the war. Belle reveled in his rhetoric and his invectives against Wilson and capitalists. She remembered his opening sentence as "War is Hell—well then let all the capitalists go to war!"—which the *New York Times* reporter recorded as "Sherman said war was hell. Well, then, let the bankers go to war, and let the interest-takers and the dividend-takers go to war with them. If only those parasites were out of the country it would be a pretty decent place to live."[3] The *Times*'s front-page story labeled the speech treason; and subsequent articles focused on the government's refusal to take Haywood's threats seriously, and labor leaders' lack of interest in following him.

Belle's enthusiastic support of this seditious, or at least anticapitalist, stance is intriguing. She had followed the rise of socialism closely for the last few years and had predicted in 1912 it would soon become a political force in America. But she had denounced the Industrial Workers of the World (IWW) as "purely anarchistic. . . . General riot and disobedience and mutiny is their program." Similarly, she rejected socialism, noting that since younger men tended to be socialists and older men conservative, the latter must be the "result of years of experience and meditation." Furthermore, Belle's own interests were as a rule strongly aligned with New York's elite. Her job depended on the bankers and capitalists Haywood denounced as parasites. Still, she found herself quite sympathetic to the antiwar rhetoric of labor activists and radicals.[4] Unable to find any reason to support or care about the distant conflict in Mexico, Belle declared herself with the activists, because she felt that the rich business owners and politicians who supported the war should be sending themselves and their sons to fight alongside the working-class troops.[5]

But by summer it was Europe that was on the verge of war. This was a place much nearer to Belle's heart and to her professional and social life. Belle watched in horror with the rest of the world as a political assassination in the little-known country of Serbia triggered a widening series of alliances, declarations of war, and mobilizing of troops that soon erupted in violence. America remained politically and militarily neutral until 1917. In the meantime many Americans did not want to enter the war. Socialists and radicals focused on class-based arguments like that of Haywood—that the elite classes would declare war and make money from it while the working classes would be the ones to sacrifice their sons' and husbands' lives. More mainstream isolationists argued that the United States should focus on its own problems and interests rather than involve itself in external conflicts. A popular song in 1916 reflected the nation's feelings: "I Didn't Raise My Boy to Be a Soldier." Hawk politicians like Theodore Roosevelt scoffed at such sentiment. That was like saying, "I Didn't Raise My Girl to Be a Mother," he famously rejoined. But most Americans considered the war in Europe to be strictly a European affair and much preferred that the United States stay out of military involvement.

Like the rest of the country, Belle was ambivalent about what the American political and military response to the European war should be, although she was immediately caught up in the nation's economic response. The first years of the war offered increased opportunities for American business leaders to invest in and market goods to European countries on both sides of the conflict. Some were motivated by profit, some by political loyalties, some by both. Jack Morgan was in the thick of several major deals. Just as J.P. had made money during the Civil War, Jack would later be accused of profiting unduly from the spoils of World War One.[6]

The Bank of France deposited over $10 million in gold with Morgan's London bank. Jack and his peers also began to strategize to protect their interests in the United States and abroad. Eventually they began to actively support England and France by sending money, usually via Canada. Belle's work shifted from running the Library to providing clerical support for Morgan's financial meetings and activities. It was the kind of work she was far overqualified and overpaid for—demeaning tasks for a professional of her status under other circumstances. But, like his father before him, Morgan had come to depend on her, and she thought it was the best way she could assist him and therefore assist the European countries to which she felt most loyal. It was during this period that Belle came to believe that Jack had the potential to be as powerful in the art world as his father had been. She already saw him as greater in the financial world, and now she saw much to admire in his prewar activities. Jack's refusal to bow to Wilson's pressure on him not to finance French munitions while the United States was maintaining neutrality made Belle see the man that Jack was and could become.[7]

Jack and Belle also shared a strong anti-German attitude on the war, one that many of their fellow Americans were quick to adopt as reports came in of German military incursions across Europe. Despite her negative experiences in Munich, Belle had not always disdained Germany as a nation. In fact, the preceding year she had praised Germany's academics, noting that she would rather have one German scholar than a thousand American ones.[8] But as the European war spread, Belle joined many Americans in blaming Germany and extending that anti-German feeling to Americans of German ancestry. To be identifiable as a "hyphenated American" was to be suspect in one's loyalties as a citizen. Belle forbade her mother to continue to shop at their regular butcher and grocer, both of whom were German American.[9]

In Belle's transatlantic world the events in Europe had an immediate impact. Austrian, German, and French men in the United States were ordered to report to their consulates and prepare to be drafted, as were men in Europe. This included some of the scholars, businessmen, and artists in Belle's circles. A few Germans associated with the Metropolitan Museum of Art went to serve in the German military, most notably William Valentiner.[10] Belle later said that she had to respect his actions in the war. "He went over and risked his life for his principles instead of remaining here, pretending neutrality and poisoning the wells." The French army claimed most of George Blumenthal's Paris business partners. He and his wife, Florence, were in France, determined at first to stick the war out in Paris. Jacques Seligmann's son went into the French service as well.[11]

But in England and the United States it was still largely business as usual. Charles Read and Fairfax Murray both arrived from London in early May to appraise the Morgan collection. Throughout May and June, Belle entertained and worked with Read—now Sir Charles Hercules Read—whom she described as an uncle or godfather educating a daughter.[12] She ignored Fairfax Murray socially as much as possible, unwilling to give him any advantage or show of support. On the contrary, Belle was engaged in a silent battle to maneuver him out of the job.[13]

And Belle soon had further reason to hate Fairfax Murray. One evening Agnes and Eugene Meyer hosted Belle and Charles for dinner at their home in Mount Kisco, where their modern art collection was displayed. After dinner Agnes pulled Charles aside to talk about Bernard. Belle ignored them and discussed the Mexican situation with Eugene, until she overheard Agnes mention that Fairfax Murray could tell the best stories about B.B., but that Charles should wait to get him started on it when "Greenie" was not around. Belle was now alerted that Murray was not a friend to Berenson, and her suspicions of Agnes were confirmed as well. Belle also had long believed that Agnes, despite her claims to be Bernard's friend and her plans to tour with him in Italy, was actually critical of Berenson's character and expertise. Finally, she was able to confront Agnes with proof.[14]

Belle was making and breaking a lot of friendships and business acquaintances because of people's hostility to Berenson, to the point that her friends became concerned at the influence he apparently had over Belle. Read pushed her to make up with Agnes, and lectured her that she could better assist Bernard by making those who opposed him change their minds rather than further polarizing them by inserting herself into their disagreements. When Rose Nichols, a good friend of Belle's from Boston, came back from visiting Charles Freer, she told a story that only emphasized the extent to which Belle's name was becoming associated with Bernard's in an unscandalous but equally dangerous way. Freer believed, Rose said, that Belle was "ruled by Mr. B.B." The Detroit collector had observed that Belle and Mary both submerged themselves to Bernard, devoted and deferential in a way that "would have ruined women who were not 'born' as big and vital." The "Queen of Sheba" (Belle) dismissed it all as the work of Agnes, but Freer had had ample opportunity himself to observe the odd three-some when they stayed with him earlier that year.[15] With Berenson's reputation already tarnished by his continued dual role as objective scholar and professional appraiser, Belle's insistence on blindly defending him against all criticisms threatened her own professional reputation.

Read and Murray left, Murray with a charge from Jack Morgan to negotiate sales on his behalf, much to Belle's chagrin.[16]

Belle began to make vague plans for her own trip to Europe the following year. She hoped that Bernard would come again that winter and that she would go over the following summer or fall. She once again planned to bring her mother to Italy to avoid scandal, but promised she would be free to spend the night with Berenson or take occasional side trips alone with him. Besides, she noted, he had so many "devoted ladies on the string" that no one would notice one more.[17]

By July one such lady was already there, perhaps not quite as devoted as B.B. assumed. Agnes Meyer had arrived in Europe, where she saw Bernard and told him her husband was having a "riotous time" with Belle in her absence. Bernard seemed quite willing to believe that an affair was going on, which seemed to be Agnes's purpose.[18] The Meyers' marriage was going through a difficult period. While in Europe, Agnes went unchaperoned to the apartment of a male friend, someone with whom she had been involved before her marriage. Eugene was furious. Perhaps Agnes was willing to tell stories about her own husband and Belle because she wanted to give the impression that he was even more inappropriate than she was. Certainly she was straining under the double standard of behavior permitted for herself and her husband.[19] Or perhaps Belle was having an affair with Eugene Meyer. She flatly denied it. But her sexual life was no longer chaste or monogamous, which left her vulnerable to all sorts of rumors and speculation.

By the time Belle caught wind of this latest gossip, Agnes had moved on to London, where she spent time with Charles Read and told him many of the same stories. Moreover, Agnes and Fairfax Murray were whispering all manner of things about Belle and Bernard in Read's ear, and warning him against Bernard all the while. In fact, Agnes—knowing that Read was devoted to Belle—was trying her best to undermine that attachment by convincing Read that Belle was in love with B.B. Charles did not believe it. In fact, he did not even believe that Agnes believed it. He was sure he was better informed on the subject, and he wrote to Belle to tell her all about it. Belle in turn, for reasons not entirely clear, sent Read's letter on to Bernard, with several lines carefully scissored out. That, of course, renewed Berenson's suspicions that there was something romantic between Belle and Charles. They were still flirting, and Belle certainly was not discouraging Read's continued gifts. He was sending her yet another Chinese statuette.[20] It was a typical tangle of romantic interest, possible affairs, and professional loyalties and reputations on the line.

Belle dealt with the situation by writing Charles plainly that she did like Bernard very much, even though she knew that he did not. Read loved her even more, he said, for having the courage and sense to be open about the situation. Of course, Belle had not been entirely open. She was still using her strategy of telling people how much she liked and respected Bernard to distract them from the deeper truth that he was the love of her life. Read also asked for details when Belle had dinner with Harold Mestre, "your former young man." He wanted, he said, to understand what the younger Belle had been like and, having raised two daughters, thought that he could tell by her description of Harold. Read apparently also did not know that Belle's relationship with Harold had ended only a few years ago, long after Read had met her. Belle ignored his request.[21]

In the meantime Belle's desperation to make enough money to retire to Europe was rising. She was planning a trip in 1915, and in a moment of hatred against New York, America, and perhaps even the Library, she threatened to take an entry-level job at the British Museum and just stay there. She had just heard from an acquaintance whom she disliked that he had seen a ninth-century Chinese carved head and wanted to give it to her. In a fit of frustration she swore she would accept it and sell it to add to her Europe fund. "Of course its rotten of me but I think I'll be rotten from now on until I can come and live with you and then I'll be nice again," she grumbled to Bernard. And she would sell the piece Read was sending her, too, if it was worth anything. To be sure, the next day Belle wrote again taking back the awful letter she had written. "I guess my little tummy must have been out of order," she quipped, referring to Bernard's famous rages and his use of his stomach problems to excuse them.[22]

But Belle's threat to let herself be supported by men's gifts to her was a momentary lapse of one of her most basic rules of decent behavior. She never explicitly laid these rules out, but this one was apparent in her constant horror of women who lived off of men they did not love. One of the earliest examples is seen in her response to the play *The Easiest Way*, which she saw performed in 1909. The main character, Laura, is an actress who supplements her meager income by living as a kept woman of a wealthy stockbroker. When she falls in love with a poor journalist, she agrees to give up her old ways and support herself while waiting for him to make enough money to marry her. But Laura cannot get enough work or make enough money to cover her own bills, and after six months of selling and pawning all of her jewelry and clothes, she returns to her stockbroker. She ultimately loses both her true love and the stockbroker when each discovers she has lied to him.[23]

The Easiest Way shook Belle to her core. She said she was "faint and dizzy and sick at heart" and thought that the horror of it would stay with her forever. The world depicted seemed a devastatingly realistic one "in which honesty and decency is nonexistent—in which love and self-supporting women are jeered at and vice rules triumphant."[24] The odds were stacked against Laura. All around her, men were willing to trade her beauty and charm for their money. And those men also controlled the jobs and their availability, pay, and conditions. No doubt Belle had similar offers to be so supported. At times she seemed to consider marriage just as bad. Still, she did allow some men to buy her things: meals, jewelry, clothing, perfume, and art. But such exchanges of gifts for a woman's time and attention were not considered immoral. Turning those gifts into money, as she threatened to do with the carved head, would have been crossing a moral line for Belle.[25]

Having relationships with other men, on the other hand, was now clearly within Belle's comfort zone. Although she wrote to Bernard frequently during the spring and summer of 1914, it was clear that she was no longer trying to maintain even the façade of fidelity. He had been her first lover, and he was still the love of her life. Their sexual relationship had clearly resumed during his last trip to New York: one of her summer letters to him ended, "I ache with longing for you. I daresay you've forgotten all about those——sweats???" But her letters also reveal a more explicit interest in sex in general. She retold a story Freer regaled her with about "doing his duty" with thirty women one night at an Indian palace, and how eunuchs had "indescribable ways of being most attractive to women"—a point on which Belle very much wanted further information. Bernard was no longer the only man she had been "really scandalous" with. Presumably she was now using birth control, but pregnancy was still a concern. "Thanks be to almighty gawd," she wrote, relieved that her period had arrived.[26]

Belle very likely had many lovers whose identities are lost to history. But one name that began cropping up again and again in her correspondence was that of Mitchell Kennerley, a publisher and book collector who was already quietly dealing and would soon open the Anderson Galleries. As early as 1912 Belle described him as a "frantic admirer of mine," but rarely mentioned his name.[27] In 1913, just before Bernard's visit, Belle had warned him that he might hear she was in love with Kennerley. She did not deny it, but said only that he was a "restful person." Bernard apparently caught on that there was more to it than that. He commanded her to see less of Mitchell, but

Belle soon discovered that wasn't going to work for either Bernard's or her own purposes. "It's a bad plan B.B., 'my angel' because it makes me gladder to see him, when I do." And see him she did. For the next six months she constantly referred to Mitchell coming to her family's house, lending her his car, driving her to the country weekends she continued to attend from time to time, even to the circus.[28] They often lunched together, she picking him up in a cab or he stopping by the Library for her. Kennerley had dinner with her and her mother, and even gave B.B. some competition in poetic romance by reading to Belle from Keats and Shelley and Robert Bridges. Bernard apparently gave up trying to end the liaison from afar. Instead, he and Mitchell began sending each other polite messages through Belle's letters.[29]

Mitchell Kennerley was married, but a renowned womanizer, maybe even one to rival Berenson. His secretary at his publishing firm was a former mistress, and he used an apartment above his business offices as a "love nest." But the secretary could not stand Belle, so she usually waited in the car when they stopped by Kennerley's office. Belle was just one of his many women.[30] Or, it might just as accurately be said, Mitchell was one of her many men.

In addition to being a good friend and probable lover, Kennerley was a source of books for Belle, through both his publications of new pieces and his growing business in manuscripts and rare books. As a publisher, he had gained a reputation for presenting new and often edgy writers. In 1913 Anthony Comstock, who had long been threatening to suppress Kennerley's books, had him arrested for *Hagar Revelly*. Written by the social hygienist Dr. Daniel Carson Goodman, the book offered a morality tale of two sisters, one of whom becomes pregnant by a man who abandons her while the other remains chaste, despite temptation, marries well, and raises her sister's illegitimate child. The moral of the story seems quite traditional, but Comstock's objection was to the detailed seduction and attempted seduction scenes. In 1914 Kennerley's case went to trial, and he was unexpectedly found not guilty by the jury.[31]

Belle often had access to unpublished works that Kennerley was considering. For example, in 1912 she read Frank Harris's *Oscar Wilde:*

His Life and Confessions, which Kennerley had set in type but did not publish under his imprint. Belle, who was already tiring of Harris's lectures (sponsored by Kennerley) and his arrogance, was appalled. She acknowledged "certain things we all know about Oscar and for which, God's knows he paid a heavy penalty," namely his sexual relations with men, for which Wilde had been jailed in England from 1895 to 1897. This was not the basis of her objection; Belle did not disapprove of male homosexuality. When she read about Lord Byron's affairs with men, she told B.B., "it rather tickles my erotic and degenerate self."[32] But Belle thought that, as a purported friend of Wilde's, Harris should have used his book to show the best of Wilde's character, wit, and writing. Instead, Harris had dragged him, and many others, "lower than any court or public opinion ever did." Belle was certain it would never be published in England and might have influenced Kennerley to delay printing. She claimed to have had such influence in previous cases.[33]

That summer Belle also became deeply interested in psychology. Since the highly influential lectures of Sigmund Freud at Clark University in 1909, psychoanalysis had been the rage in New York. Hutchins Hapgood later recalled that the practice had become so popular that "nobody could say anything about a dream, no matter how colorless it was, without his friends' winking at one another and wondering how he could have been so indiscreet." In 1914 Belle met Dr. Paul Federn, a student of Freud's. In New York to treat some cases of neuroses using psychoanalysis, Dr. Federn was taken up by Belle's social circles. She dined with him several times and grilled him on this new school of thought, which fascinated her. With its focus on childhood experiences and sensual desires as keys to understanding adult sexual and social behavior, psychoanalysis was gaining in popularity in the United States. Belle also considered purchasing some of Freud's papers for the Library, especially those related to his 1909 lectures.[34]

But she was most interested in Federn's professional attentions to her. He told her, she bragged to Bernard, that she was the most interesting woman, psychologically speaking, that he had ever met. And he wanted to analyze her. Belle said she was thinking about it, but never said whether she went through with it. It must have been a temptation.

Belle already loved having the concentrated attention of a photographer or artist when she modeled. Imagine being able to confide in a man who wanted nothing more than to understand her inner workings and desires. She had read Freud's *Interpretations of Dreams* earlier that year and had begun trying to remember and understand the meaning of her dreams, which she understood would be a large part of her work with Dr. Federn. These solo experiments had been rather uninteresting, as she realized that her dreams were mostly "little mosaics of details" from her past, even her childhood, albeit reassembled in decidedly bizarre ways.[35]

Nevertheless, two weeks later, Belle experienced something that Federn would probably have been eager to psychoanalyze. She suffered from what she called a hysterical attack and her doctor diagnosed as "nervous prostration." After several weeks of constant work, she had collapsed as soon as she tried to get out of bed. Her mother called a doctor, who brought sedatives. But it was several days before she would walk again. Probably not coincidently, Belle was back on the water wagon for the rest of the summer.[36] (She never mentioned going off it.) If Belle had still been seeing Dr. Federn, he would likely have had a very different diagnosis. But in this case the problem was probably pure exhaustion and stress. Belle was then taking on the job of appraising several huge collections of items that had not been part of the Library inventory. Knowing that she was now doing work, with no bonus or extra pay, that two others had already been paid several times her annual salary to perform could only have worsened her financial frustrations.[37]

She was also quite annoyed with Murray and Read, for different reasons. Read was an ally, but he did not seem willing or able to do the negotiating for the sale of Morgan's art. Murray, who was supposed to be acting as their agent in England, had become incommunicative and untrustworthy, though he might have said the same about her. The Duveens had apparently told him some of the negative things Belle told them in confidence about Murray. Now Belle was furious at the Duveens, resigned to be open enemies with Murray, and disgusted that Read was not stepping up to help her. Having to complete the appraisals that Murray and Read had been paid to do earlier that year was only the final straw.[38]

Meanwhile, the war news grew worse. Friends were stranded in Europe, boats that carried Belle's acquaintances and mail became less dependable and even dangerous. Living and traveling in France was becoming difficult for Americans, and Belle worried that Bernard was still there. Prices on imported goods were rising, like the French perfume (Houbigant Violette Essence) and face powder that Mitchell Kennerley usually provided her—the cost of the perfume alone had risen from $8.50 to $10.50 a bottle. And the price inflation began to affect domestic products as well as imports. By mid-August food costs were escalating alarmingly. This was, Belle felt, unwarranted and due only to store owners' trying to take advantage.[39]

After England entered the war, in August of 1914, such issues as the price of perfume faded in significance. Crowds of people surrounded newspaper boards and electric bulletins posting the latest war news in New York, groaning when news was posted of Germany's advance into Belgium.

> It was the same in two or three vaudeville houses we stopped in for a minute where they showed moving pictures of the various armies etc. I never heard such a wild roar of rage and disgust as broke out when a portrait of the Kaiser was thrown on the screen and they had to take it off pretty quick. Portraits of the King of England and the French army were given prolonged hand-clapping and cheers.[40]

The invasion of Belgium had immediate repercussions. Great Britain, already committed to defend Belgium, declared war on Germany. Other European alliances cascaded into declarations of war. By the end of August, Russia, France, and Great Britain were allied against Austria-Hungary and Germany. Japan had also entered the fray.

The United States continued to remain neutral, but it was clear that most Americans were sympathetic to the British-French alliance. Stories of German atrocities circulated. Belle related two stories to

Berenson that she had heard: one that Germans were chopping off the hands and feet of young Belgian boys, and another of German soldiers raping a Belgian peasant woman in front of her husband. "I am ashamed to say that this tale made me shriek with laughter, but Thursty was really moved to tears. Lillie said that the lady died—from joy, I bet you! I imagine that there is a good deal of that kind of thing going on."[41]

This is a disturbing reaction, but also quite telling, and may provide an important insight into how Belle dealt with things that were painful or frightening to consider. A woman gang-raped to death was arguably a more personal threat to her than young boys maimed so that they were unable to fight. Her laughter, even as her friend Ada Thurston was so upset, and her continued joking as she retold the story and repeated her own "shameful" reaction completely denied the brutality of sexual assault. Belle often glossed over painful subjects or dealt with them with crass, even offensive behavior. Laughing was easier.

Anti-German sentiment was not universal, however. Some pro-German attitudes were beginning to surface in Belle's social circles, not from the German Jews she knew well (Eugene Meyer and the Blumenthals most notably), but from some Americans. Belle noted that Isabella Gardner was reported to be wildly pro-German, something she could not understand and constantly asked Bernard to explain to her. She believed that Edward Robinson of the Metropolitan Museum (a close associate of Valentiner) was also pro-German.[42] Still, she was willing to overlook some of her prejudices—and accept some from others. At a visit with some friends in Mount Kisco, for example, Belle met a German-born man who was strongly connected to German business and political interests. Belle found him surprisingly charming, but felt better when she discovered he had been raised and educated in England and France. She did not buy his "silly, baseless arguments that all of them use" in support of German aggression. However, she did accept that she could not call on Eugene and Agnes Meyer that weekend: her hosts did not recognize their neighbors because Eugene was Jewish. Furthermore, Belle was willing to overcome her prejudices to befriend an individual. That spring and summer one R. Meyer-Riefstahl, a German-born scholar, was often in the Library instructing her on Persian manuscripts. (He also sold her some.) They got along so well that by the summer Belle had to stop seeing him because, she said, he had fallen for her.[43]

By September, Belle's work and world seemed entirely focused on war work and war news—what little they could get that proved reliable. Everything else had, for the time being, been pushed aside. A weekend in New Hampshire brought Belle briefly into company with the very different Winston Churchill and Maxfield Parrish, where she found the conversation so "stimulating and fine" that she accepted every invitation she could where they were to be present. Junius Morgan, who had been living in France, came back from his Paris home with stories of French bravery and poverty.[44]

New Yorkers began to chafe under President Wilson's order to maintain neutrality and started openly to defy his request that they maintain this position in their speech and thoughts. Social gatherings were dominated by talk of German aggression and atrocities, and sympathy for the English and French prompted many to speak of U.S. intervention. Belle began to feel a numbing sense of sadness and helplessness as she followed the escalating events of the war. The Central Powers of Germany and Austria-Hungary (later joined by the Ottoman Empire) stood opposed to the Allies: Russia, France, and Great Britain. By the end of 1914 French casualties had reached over 300,000, with twice as many wounded; Germany's numbers were almost as high. Belle felt, she said, as if the end of the world had come; all "thinking people" she knew had the same response to the war that was both so far away and so near.[45]

The war's economic effects intensified. Belle's stocks stopped paying dividends. She sold her beloved Pierce Arrow to economize. Russell, who had been living in New Jersey, lost his job when his company closed because building was at a near standstill. He and his wife moved in with Belle for a while that summer.[46] By October, Belle told Henri Hyvernat that she was finally on her knees praying—for peace. "Surely God seems very far away," she added. Her desire for peace was near-universal, but apparently her turn to prayer was a new development. Father Hyvernat was glad she was praying—he may have been long encouraging it—but the French-born priest asked Belle to pray for "peace without humiliation for France" (his native country). Anything else, he said, would only be "the peace of death."[47]

But some things continued as usual. Harold Mestre—the man Belle had been engaged to in the summer of 1911—had returned to New York. "The child," as Belle referred to him, had developed into a fine person and had made a good deal of money in Central America. Unfortunately he found her even more attractive than before and swore he would marry her yet. She wasn't interested: she thought he would make "a most magnificent lover, but never a husband."[48]

Underneath the usual busy rhythm of her life, Belle was becoming quite depressed. With apparently very little encouragement from Bernard, she had begun to count on his return, with or without Mary, to the United States for the winter of 1914–15, or perhaps even for the duration of the war. When she finally realized he was not coming, her emotional state sank to a new low. She stopped writing to him, and anyone else except for business, and turned inward in contemplation. For the first time she realized how emotionally dependent she was on him, how entirely her inner life had centered on him, in a way that was utterly unsustainable, given his marriage and his distance. "I'm really cross with you that you made me love you so finally this last time you were here, it makes everything else so useless and uninteresting and uncompelling."[49] It didn't matter that she now had other lovers, and that she sometimes hated or, worse, felt entirely indifferent to Bernard. Still, she kept coming back to realizing how deeply he was embedded in her emotional life. Devastated that he wasn't coming, she recognized that she was now paying for all the times she had disappointed him. Even her mother, who she seldom felt understood or sympathized with her, saw how distraught her daughter was that Bernard was not returning.

To make matters worse, Belle turned thirty-five in November of 1914 and said she felt "horribly old ever since." (She never mentioned to B.B. exactly how "horribly old" she really was.) When her thoughts turned to suicide, she cast around for some activity to distract and revitalize her. Ironically, she found it in resuming her Italian lessons.

When Bernard finally cabled her frantically in early December, she had recovered enough to resume writing regularly. And she soon began to socialize and work outside of the Library again. She traveled to Detroit, staying again with Charles Freer and continuing her education on Chinese art under his guidance.[50]

Back in New York, Belle faced a far less welcome diversion. Jack now proposed to sell the Duveens his father's collection of Chinese porcelains. At least, to Belle's great satisfaction and glee, Fairfax Murray was no longer in Jack's confidence. Murray had returned on his own in the fall to assess more of the Morgan collection for sale. This time Belle made good on her vow to get him off the job and went to work showing him up in front of Jack. By the time Murray left, she had persuaded her new boss not to work with him, having made a "laughing stock and fool of him over here."[51] But with Murray out of the picture, and Seligmann unwilling or unable to take on such big sales, Belle herself now had to take over the project of disposing of "these damned art objects." At least she wasn't selling off her beloved books. First she sold the Chinese porcelains, held at the Metropolitan Museum, to the Duveens—who were fronting for Joseph Widener—for three million dollars. The Duveens had offered two million; Jack was ready to settle on two and half. Belle locked Jack in his office to keep him from interfering in her negotiations with the Duveens. They thought that she was giving them a good deal because of Bernard's relationship with them, but Belle walked away with three million dollars. At auction she figured they would have brought at least four million, but she consoled herself that she had saved them the trouble of an auction and that Jack could make up the difference with investments.[52] By early February 1915 she was focusing on Henry Clay Frick as her target purchaser for the Fragonards, a collection of large eighteenth-century French paintings. Belle was also eying Frick for some of the antique furniture and paved the way by suggesting he get rid of all the eighteenth-century furniture he already had.[53]

Apparently Belle was now fully aware of the agreement between Berenson and the Duveens. It had occurred to her that all of their dealings with the Duveens now might be damaging Bernard's business with them. If they were investing millions of dollars on Morgan's collections, they would not have the time or the money to invest in the Italian art Bernard was still specializing in. (The Berensons' plans to expand their dealing and appraising into Chinese art had not proved fruitful.) The Duveens themselves kept telling Belle that their business was great "except for paintings" and began talking about getting out of paintings altogether. She suspected they were hoping she would pass this on to Bernard, so she did so, with a promise to keep track of them and make sure they weren't doing business in paintings behind his back.[54]

Berenson was also worried that his lucrative partnership with the Duveens was effectively over. Belatedly, he tried to enter into a large transaction with Jack Morgan, asking Belle whether she would consider selling to Arthur Joseph Sulley (often referred to simply as Sully), a London dealer with whom Bernard was beginning to work. With the Duveens' attentions elsewhere, Bernard and Mary were casting about for new avenues of business themselves. But Belle was too far into negotiations and did not believe Sully had the capital for the amount she was seeking. By February, Belle had sold the Fragonards to the Duveens for $1,250,000. She expected them (correctly) to immediately sell them en bloc to Frick; he had offered her the same amount that morning, but she preferred, she said, to work through dealers.[55]

Meanwhile publicity caught up with the sales. Throughout the year Belle had been telling all inquirers that Jack was not selling yet. But newspapers caught wind of the porcelain deal, probably alerted by the Duveens themselves. They announced the purchase price as $3,900,000, which Belle had told Duveen he could say, even though the price was actually $3,000,000.[56] Jack was furious, and Belle (neglecting to mention her foreknowledge and approval) commiserated. Matters became worse when the Metropolitan Museum director Edward Robinson issued a carefully worded statement that expressed the museum's shock and "disappointment" at hearing about the impending departure of over fourteen hundred pieces in the Morgan collection of Chinese porcelain, the bulk of their entire holdings in that area. Robinson emphasized the enormity of the loss for the museum, for scholarship, and for New York City (the New York papers had already been highlighting these concerns). Furthermore, he reminded the public that while Morgan's will had left it up to Jack to decide the future of the collections, J.P. had specified his hope that the bulk of it would remain available to the public.[57]

Belle was very offended. She thought the statement was "rather nasty," especially its charge that Morgan senior had intended the collection to stay at the museum. In response she wrote an article for the *New York Times* to emphasize everything her Mr. Morgan had done for the museum. He was the only collector who had placed so many of his "things" on public display, and she was furious that his generosity was being lost in the criticism of his son's dispositions. Belle did not sign the article, which appeared uncredited under the title "Morgan Gifts to the Metropolitan" with two pages of text and illustrations of donated paintings. Despite the recent sale of the pottery and the Fragonards, Belle estimated that more that $10,000,000 of Morgan's art had been lent to the museum for the short and the long term. "Such loans in their importance and the length of their continuance constitute a gift in themselves," Belle argued, because they gave the public access to art and objects that would otherwise be completely unavailable. One case in point was the museum's Egyptian department, of which Morgan was a primary donor.[58]

Despite the negative publicity, Belle was quite pleased with the state of affairs at the Library as Jack prepared to leave for Europe again. She declared her mission in "tying Jack M. up to the Library" to be nearly complete. Even more, she had apparently tied him to her as well. He was coming in daily and confiding in her about his financial and personal affairs. Their relationship was now much like the one she had had with his father, without the flirtations and sexual undertones. She told her loyal friend Junius that Jack was immune to her beauty and charm, but "as a confidant I'm his soul mate." This was particularly ironic because she had always thought Jack disapproved of her and her close friendship with his father.[59]

After Jack left for Europe, Belle finalized one more sale with the Duveens, for an allotment of eighteenth-century furniture, clocks, and some decorative items. This sale disgusted her, she said, for it went for less than she had wanted, but again Jack was willing to settle for a lesser amount and this time she couldn't stop him.[60] According to George Blumenthal, members of the Wall Street crowd were all outraged that Jack was giving her nothing of the $3,000,000 profit she had bargained for him over the three bloc sales. They thought she deserved a 10 percent commission at least. Knowing she had done work worth $300,000 but wasn't seeing any of it put her $50,000 inheritance and her $12,000 a year salary into a very different perspective.[61]

Belle still had an eye on her retirement. This determination to be independent and free of work no doubt explains Belle's obsession with the stock market that year. Although she had always put part of her earnings into stocks, she now had her inheritance to invest. Her friend Eugene Meyer was handling much of it, and throughout the year she passed on several stock tips to Bernard, advising him to invest in particular companies. However, Belle was already wavering in her determination to leave the Library by 1915. Mr. Jack had decided he wanted her to stay and was already talking about raising her salary at the end of her two years with him to keep her. But, Belle sighed to Bernard, she felt she had been working her entire life and wanted to get away from it "to the glories of the great big world and to you." She continued to plan for her life after leaving the Library, plotting years of travel and study in Italy, France, Greece, Russia, China, Japan, India, and Egypt. She considered ways she could make money, joking that she could always hire herself out as a travel companion or cicerone to "nice, kind, rich and handsome gents."[62]

Having taken on the role of an agent that Fairfax Murray or Charles Read might have played (without making the commissions or fees that a third party would have), Belle now began seriously to contemplate becoming a dealer herself, and probably began dabbling in the market and putting out feelers. In early 1915 she mentioned that she was "becoming a first rate little dealer." And by the end of the year she was clearly brokering sales—instructing Florrie Blumenthal, for example, in Chinese art and helping her buy some things from Belle's favorite New York dealer for Chinese items, C. T. Loo.[63] In the early years of the war, American businessmen were making so much money that the art market was picking up. It was, Belle said, a "disgustingly easy" game, and she now knew she was as good at the selling side of it as at the buying side. She was not the only one to consider this career shift for her. The Duveens were after her to "go into business with them." Bernard Berenson, Belle da Costa Greene, and Joe and Henry Duveen would have been a powerful combination, indeed.[64]

Meanwhile, Belle was continuing to pursue her own interests. She attended the opera, including rehearsals. The usual opera crowd was around: Enrico Caruso, Geraldine Farrar, Lillie Lawlor, conductor Arturo Toscanini, and Polish coloratura Marcella Sembrich, and celebrated operatic actor Antonio Scotti. She visited the newly opened Frick home, where the Morgan Fragonard panels had been installed, and disparaged the rooms that Elsie de Wolfe decorated. She tried unsuccessfully to understand and appreciate Japanese art, and continued her independent study of Chinese culture and art. She studied a new collection of Chinese paintings at the Metropolitan Museum with Lodge and spent more time with John Ferguson, who had lectured on Chinese art in Montreal during the trip the Berensons had taken without her the preceding year.[65]

She also resumed her liaisons with other men. When spring 1915 bloomed, her pagan nature revived and she wanted to "make love to someone, but you [B.B.] insist you are Nobody." In addition to her continuing relationship with Mitchell Kennerley, Belle mentioned several other men with whom she was flirting that spring. Maurice Sterne was one. Sterne was a painter and photographer who had exhibited at 291. Belle admired his pictures of Balinese women for their "highly patinated bronze" bodies and graceful carriage. Sterne wanted to do a portrait of her, and Belle was tempted as she suspected he could do one that would appeal to both Bernard and herself, but she did not want to give him a commission. Sterne later married Mabel Dodge. Belle also reported a "mad flirtation" with Herbert Satterlee, one of J.P.'s sons-in-law, who later wrote a biography of his famous father-in-law. However, whenever Bernard suspected she was having a serious affair with someone, Belle usually reverted to her old habit of total denial.[66]

In fact, Belle became so immersed in her own life that she temporarily lost interest in war news. She told Bernard she could not "grasp your ravings" about either the Germans or "your absorbtion to your own ill health." Italy had not yet become involved in the fighting, but Bernard was dealing with the effects of war on a daily basis. His German name made local Americans and Italians suspect him of being a spy, and the Berensons were hosting four convalescing Australian officers in 1915. But for Belle the war had become "so remote and meaningless" that she was wrapped up in her own affairs. Ghastly but true, she admitted.[67] The war relief efforts around her seemed pointless, especially those launched by her peers. She was tired of "damn fool" benefits where people paid for a theater performance, ball, dinner, or some other entertainment. Everyone bought new dresses and jewels because it was a society event, paying more for these luxuries than they donated to the cause. Furthermore, after all the food, workers, and actors were paid for, the net earnings were insignificant. Instead, Belle gave everything she could directly to relief funds for Allied countries. She turned down a request to chair a fund-raising committee for the Red Cross because she didn't want money going to Germans. The Red Cross's policy was "mercy knew no caste, creed, color etc."; Belle's policy regarding the German wounded was "Leave 'em rot."[68] America might still be neutral, but Belle was not.

Even worse than the society fund-raisers that Belle now avoided, women everywhere were knitting socks for the troops. They knit at the theater, in restaurants, at the Metropolitan Museum of Art. Bessie Marbury picked Belle up one day and spent the entire car ride knitting "the most hideous pair of brown socks I have ever laid my eyes on." (Bessie was also responsible for one of the theater benefits Belle disdained.) Another friend who went with her to the theater worked on a pair between acts that she said she had been knitting for four days. Belle was aghast, "Why," she exclaimed, if her friend just "sold the smallest diamond she had in her necklace" or took champagne off her dinner menu she could have purchased a thousand socks "and sent them by the *Lusitania* tomorrow."[69]

Belle's criticism of the inefficiency of knitting socks instead of buying them mirrored similar critiques offered by feminist-pacifists who refused to participate in war support. If Belle was still hanging out in Greenwich Village, she would likely have come into contact with such sentiments. In fact, earlier that year Belle reported that she had been asked to join the Women's International Peace "union" but had, as she said sarcastically, "refused the honor."[70] She shared their disdain for women's traditional war relief work, but not their impassioned opposition to the war.

In May, however, the loss of the *Lusitania* started to turn the tide of Belle's, and America's, lack of interest in the war. The sinking of the British-owned transatlantic ship off the coast of Ireland by German U-boats outraged Americans; over a hundred of their countrymen lost their lives. The tragedy shook the nation and heightened anti-German feelings. But even this attack on civilians did not shift America's isolationist tendencies enough to change the policies of President Woodrow Wilson, who won reelection on the slogan "He kept us out of war."

When Belle finally had the heart to write to Bernard (also explaining that a long letter and a color picture of her in an orange tea gown had been lost with the ship), she tried to convey how deeply this "murderous trick" had affected her and everyone around her. The anti-German feeling was so strong that Belle feared it would take "only a tiny spark to set afire a huge anti-German blaze in this country," which would mean disaster for the huge German American population. Belle nonetheless maintained that she and most Americans wanted to remain neutral.[71]

Now unable to ignore war, Belle fell into a lethargy that lasted through the summer of 1915. She moved her family into a smaller house, as her stocks were down and she expected them to remain low throughout the war. She was wrong about that. By the end of the war, her stocks had recovered, thanks in large part to increased production for the war effort. In July her sister Ethel ("the quasi-blond") married George Oakley. Belle thought she would be happy. Their youngest sister, Teddy, also wanted to marry, but Belle was determined to prevent it. The man in question had no money and nothing to recommend him.[72] Teddy was now Belle's only unmarried sibling, still living at home with Belle and Mrs. Greene.

But as she went through the motions of her job and her life, "for the most part hating existence and in my happiest moments ignoring it," Belle once again withdrew from her friends and her social life. In May, Italy declared war on Austria-Hungary and from June to December launched a series of attacks. Belle began seriously to fear for Bernard in Italy and begged him and Mary to come to the United States until the war was over. "Somehow even you seem incredibly far away and out of my life."[73] Also she was worried about Morgan's Coptic manuscripts, still at the Vatican. Henri Hyvernat wanted to go over and retrieve some of his notes and the photographs of the manuscripts and arrange for their security should the battles come to Rome.[74] Work soon came to a standstill as the Vatican, like many museums and libraries throughout Europe, packed up and stored its treasures safely away from possible attacks. The Morgan Library stopped paying Hyvernat's salary for the duration of the war.[75]

Ironically, however, it was Jack Morgan who suffered a physical attack in the summer of 1915. The German sympathizer who shot Jack twice in the stomach and later killed himself had a history of instability and violence. Belle nevertheless believed him to be "a perfectly sane, true and loyal son of Germany," and considered the assassination attempt an act of war in the same realm as the invasion of Belgium and the attack on the *Lusitania*. In its aftermath the Library was secured to be "crank- fire- and bomb- proof," and Jack Morgan had armed bodyguards for the rest of his life.[76]

Worried as Belle was about Bernard, the passion between them was fading. Since he failed to come back to the States in 1914, she realized she was "not much more than a side issue in your life." She didn't object to that (she said), but she thought it relieved her of the responsibility of writing daily. Why should he expect her to focus her time and thought on him when he no longer did the same? She claimed her love for him was still "the one deep and abiding feeling of my life," but she was done trying to accommodate his need for hours of daily or even weekly writing.[77] Still, Bernard could not understand it. He was equally baffled by her periods of not writing and by her "glowing devoted" dispatches. Upon receiving one such ardent letter, Bernard could only comment, "It is a mystery why she lapses into such silences." Mary considered Belle—and anyone who refused to write letters—rude and selfish, even "inhuman" compared with the "civilized class of humanity which does write letters."[78]

By fall Belle was able to tell Bernard about her melancholy. It was the war, she said, when she finally wrote to Bernard after months of silence. It was in her nerves and in her dreams. She was sorry he took her "silences" so seriously, but added, "[I]f you don't know by this time how I feel about you I don't see how I'm ever going to make you know." At first it seemed he did know, for he offered to come over to New York if she wanted. Of course she did. She promised that her mother and Teddy would "do anything for us—so that we need not fear being disturbed."[79]

But Bernard did not come, and Belle stopped writing altogether for another four months, except for a cable in January saying she had been ill. This time the silence was due not to another man but to her own internal need to be alone to work out her emotional confusion. She had even stopped seeing Mitchell Kennerley, because he "would not leave me free (mentally or spiritually) to live out this unknown problem which confronted me." Belle never said what the problem was exactly. There were certainly many issues she had avoided dealing with in her fast-paced life, many pains she had numbed by staying busy and never letting herself think about them. She may have finally found a way to work through all of them, a process that would have been difficult, to be sure.[80]

Belle later blamed her "curious period" of melancholy on the "glimpse of Chinese living and art which has taken such an extraordinarily unrelenting grip" on her after her trips to Charles Freer in Detroit.[81] It was her immersion in Chinese philosophy and art, as much as the psychological effect of the war, that she now believed triggered her period of spiritual and emotional reflection. She repeatedly described the contemplative effect of Chinese painting, and believed that the emphasis on meditation in the Tao philosophy and practice may have reinforced her state as well. Even the jade statuette that Bernard had given her could transfix her for hours "in absolutely joyous contemplation." Just when that contemplation lost its joy is not clear. However, she continued to see a lot of Charles Freer, enjoying his companionship and his new acquisitions. But by 1916 she was growing disillusioned with the Chinese art market, with Freer (who she felt was taking advantage of Eugene Meyer in art-buying deals), and with the nature of Asian art itself. Her "Western blood and training," she believed, made it impossible "to approach the inner significance of the art—I feel this very strongly in trying to live daily with the few things in my house—They simply do not belong to me—or rather I do not belong to them." She had come to see in her once beloved pieces a "frightful monotony, sameness and repetition."[82]

Belle was now trying to educate herself about modern art. Despite all her previous predictions, it no longer seemed to be a passing fad or a hopeless mess. She was spending lots of time with Leo Stein, discussing Cézanne, Renoir, Matisse, and other "futurists." (There are distinctions between postimpressionists, cubists, futurists, and so on, but Belle pretended not to know them and routinely used any or all schools to describe any or all artists.) Stein was likely tutoring her in these very distinctions and in how to look at the new styles and approaches to painting.[83] In January 1915 Belle contributed a brief response to the question "What does 291 mean to me?" which Alfred Stieglitz had posed to many artists, patrons, and regulars of his gallery.

Belle's response has been read as a simple paean to Stieglitz. It was that, in part, "'291' is Stieglitz. . . . Yes, Stieglitz, in spite of your 'art stuff' you are *It*. In spite of your endless drool you are the magnet of Life." However, Belle's entry also reveals a more nuanced appreciation of the art she had seen at 291. She mentioned the "thrills received" from seeing Picasso and Matisse, the "glorious topsy-turvydom" of John Marin. But, most important, she explained her own uneasy relationship to 291 and the kind of art it represented. Belle distinguished herself from the other regulars at the gallery:

> they, at least have seen the Light—they *know* that Rembrandt, Leonardo, Raphael, Velasquez and the other old fogies are weak, flabby and hopelessly defunct, *they know* that the Metropolitan Museum is but a morgue and as such

should be relegated to its proper place under ground—but I, oh Stieglitz, am still groping in darkness—my eyes are still unopened—and when you are not looking, I creep back to that same Morgue, and find there, as I have at "291," the glory you radiate.[84]

With her usual ironic wit, Belle declared her ability to find life and inspiration in the classical art that she loved, as easily as she found it in the exhibitions at 291. She, of course, would never really believe that the old masters had nothing more to say to the world, nothing to contribute to humanity. But she was now willing to look for and sometimes find the same beauty at 291 as she did in her Renaissance paintings and medieval illuminations.[85]

In February 1916 her melancholy broke, and she awoke feeling energized and joyful once more. She wrote to Bernard to catch him up on her life. She felt like a different person, she said, recalling a theory she had once read that intellectually curious people remake themselves every seven years. As for romantic affairs, she felt far away from the time when she "indulged in such empty amusements." Fully aware that Bernard would likely be unable to reconcile this to her not writing, she told him, "[O]ne of the greatest things I got out of my 'retreat' [was the] fact that you belong in my every existence."[86]

Newly invigorated and sure again of her love for him, Belle wanted to see Bernard that year. She could not arrange to travel to Europe but once more began begging him to come over.[87] Bernard was eager to oblige this time, especially since art dealing had almost come to a standstill in Europe and the only hope for business was the neutral and wealthy United States. (Jack Morgan was not the only American businessman profiting on the European War.) Bernard and Mary went into negotiations. She had no interest in a trip to New York, confiding to Senda that she feared reliving the humiliation of their 1914 visit, but Bernard insisted on her presence if he went. They considered summer, considered November, and settled on October. Bernard would go alone first to spend time with Belle before Mary joined him so that she would not have to witness the resumption of the affair that had nearly ended her marriage. She refused to go at all unless he "behaved discreetly and correctly" while she was there.[88]

By summer Belle was planning for the Berensons' visit, promising to give him four weeks in the fall to travel somewhere together. In September, however, Bernard suddenly cabled that the trip was canceled. No explanation followed. It was a complete reversal of her doomed attempts to come to him in 1911 and 1912. For weeks Belle waited for clarification. This time the silence was on Bernard's end. When he finally attempted to justify his change of mind, she was completely unsatisfied.[89]

The explanation Belle never received was that Mary and Bernard had struck an unhappy deal. Throughout the summer they had debated back and forth and around and around all the advantages and disadvantages of going to America. In addition to their business needs, their U.S. passports needed to be renewed again. But would they be allowed back in Italy if they left? Would they even be allowed to leave the United States? Here, Bernard's Lithuanian birth became a problem. Lithuania was now occupied by Germany, and the name Bernard Berenson (still often spelled Bernhard Berenson) sounded very German. It was during this period that Bernard dropped the *h* in his name. Privately, Mary confided to her sister Alys that a big factor for her was knowing that if they did not go, it would mean her husband would effectively be giving up "Miss G." Finally Bernard proposed to forgo the New York trip altogether and stay in Italy until the war was over, if Mary agreed to do the same. This was a bitter deal for Mary, as she had planned to see her family before joining Bernard in New York. Karin had just had her first child, Ray's daughter Barbara needed an operation, and Ray was expecting again.[90]

Completely unaware of this marital drama, Belle was stunned and devastated by the sudden change in plans. For the first time, she revealed to Bernard that Jack had wanted her to go to Europe that fall to buy books for the Library. She had refused in order to be in New York when Bernard came. Now Jack was in Europe himself, and she was stuck in New York having made weeks' worth of arrangements for Bernard. However, she recovered soon enough to contact Jack and arrange a trip to London and quickly began making arrangements to meet Bernard there or travel with him somewhere else in Europe. She assured him that she no longer worried about "scandal" and that it was perfectly safe for them to travel together, even in the United States. They were too old and both "so obviously interested in such multitudes of people" that no one would think twice now or care what they were doing together. Belle thought she had found a sort of safety in her "philandering." She had done so much flirting with nothing ever coming of it that everyone now saw her as more focused on her work than anything else and so left her alone. It was a bit boring to no longer be of interest, she said, but useful.[91]

Now Bernard was in a tough situation. He had promised Mary he would stay at I Tatti for the duration of the war and had forced her to do the same. But it was becoming more and more difficult to stay. Their large villa was feeling smaller by the day. Bernard proposed leaving Europe altogether to spend a year traveling in the East but complained that he could not do so with Mary's inexplicable devotion to her daughters and grandchildren. He derided her as "a squaw who needs to run back to her papooses every four months." The two finally agreed to leave Italy but remain in Europe. He went to Paris, where Mary worried he would meet with Belle. But she had other things to focus on. She arrived in time to assist Ray's delivery of a son.[92]

Belle had spoken too soon about her own disappearance from the gossips' interest. Just as she was arranging for her trip, rumors began to circulate that she was once again engaged, or about to become engaged. This time the papers were running the story. *Town Topics,* a gossip sheet that routinely covered the doings of society, reported in September that Belle had resigned, giving her upcoming wedding as the reason. Other papers picked up the story, and at least one dispatched a reporter to the Rye house, where Belle's mother told them, "In my daughter's absence I would not care to say anything definite about her engagement just yet." Belle's noncommittal response: "It sounds silly."[93]

This time Belle addressed the rumors publicly. She called a reporter into her Library office and gave an interview emphatically denying the whole story. She was still "heart whole and fancy free," Miss Greene announced, surrounded by the books and manuscripts that were her life. Belle promised that if she ever did become engaged, she would announce it herself. "As far as interest goes I have found nothing thus far to equal my position as librarian of the Morgan library." One Mickey McKee sent her a clipping of the denial and teasingly wrote, "I wondered how you could disown me thusly Oh Belle Deerie! is it all off—and yet—may I hope???"[94]

Belle may have had to agree to give another rare interview to get her denial out exactly as she wanted. A few weeks later the same paper, the *Evening Sun,* ran a feature article on her. The headline read, "Opportunity Will Come to the Prepared and Success Is a Matter of Undivided Loyalty So Says Belle da Costa Greene, Whose Ten Years of Hard Work Had Made Her Ready to Become Curator of the Morgan Library." Belle was touted as one of the most powerful career women in the world. The article gave many details (but few concrete facts) about Belle's preparation for her job at the Library, emphasizing that she had worked long and hard to be as experienced and prepared as she could be when the opportunity arose. It was a paean to the possibility of hard work, traditional values, and the fruition of the American dream.[95] It was exactly the sort of publicity Belle hated and generally sought to avoid. She must have taken the engagement rumors very seriously indeed to submit to the questioning for this story.

No sooner did the *Sun* article appear than Belle was on her way to England, despite the risk of wartime travel and the fears of her friends. Once in London she quickly discovered that the situation in Europe was much worse than she had realized. Rooms were almost nonexistent, prices had nearly doubled since her last visit, and everyone was in a state of tense watchfulness. It would be more difficult to get from London to Paris than it had been to come to London from New York. There were new regulations and tracking of movements in and out of every major European city. Belle had to register with the local police whenever she traveled from London to the countryside or elsewhere in England. Crossing an international border meant submitting paperwork ten days in advance and delays on both sides. Once again Belle was stuck in London unable to reach Bernard in Paris.[96]

Belle immediately prevailed upon Bernard to come to her, since she did not have time to go through such lengthy channels and he would surely know people who could speed up the process. Mail was almost as slow, and the couple tried to communicate about their plans by telegram. At least the staff of Claridges remembered her. They asked after Bernard and gave her the same suite of rooms she had had before. Unfortunately, she could not stay there long, since they had a confirmed guest in her rooms starting in a week. Approaching hotels by herself to ask about rooms seemed oddly beyond her sense of propriety. She was finally in Europe again, after six years of longing, and it was turning out to be a disaster. To top it all off, Jack Morgan, who was supposed to meet her in London, failed to make an appearance for almost a week. When he did, he absolutely forbade her to travel to France.[97]

By then she had Bernard's answer: it was too late for him to make arrangements to join her, given the time it would take to get papers. But there was more to it than that for Bernard. Although he was tempted to come to her and thought he could manage it if he really wanted, he had many reasons not to try. He told Mary, "I honestly no longer feel that I want that sort of thing, altho' I dare say I could still be made to soon enough." Nor did he encourage Belle to come to him. The irrepressible B.B. had also fallen for yet another new woman: the openly lesbian Natalie Barney, who hosted a literary salon. The two immediately became fast friends, and it took Bernard a while to realize that his physical interest in Barney was not mutual. Bernard referred to Barney's lesbianism as her "No. 2 illness wh[ich] she holds to with fierce zeal and pride," but the two remained good friends for years.[98]

The severity of the travel situation was apparent in Mary's last letter to Bernard before preparing to sail from France to England herself. She asked him, in the event that they were torpedoed, to take care of Ray and her children "as if they were thine" and particularly to see to granddaughter Barbara's education.[99] Mary arrived safely in England, where she pointedly did not visit Belle.

Another reason Bernard did not want to go to London was that Belle was now associated in his mind with the Duveens and the whole business of art dealing. Bernard was aching to leave that world behind. He confessed to Mary,

> I feel about it as I did once as a small boy when I had to return to a school that I hated. Of course everybody else has such repulsions and in my case the material reward is great. And yet even you would be surprised if you clearly realized how much of my life is scarred and fouled by their connection.[100]

Here Bernard came perhaps as close as he ever did to casting off the dubious, but lucrative, role of art dealer for the higher, if significantly less profitable, life of a scholar. And at the same time Belle was considering entering the shady business world of dealing.

Mary was not as ready as Bernard to give up on the business, and she saw opportunities and dangers in Belle's imminent movement into the field. She suggested to Bernard that he could probably indebt the Duveens to him again if he could "detach" Belle from Jacques Seligmann. Dealer gossip told her that the Duveens feared Belle's "joining forces against them" with Seligmann and that they wanted Belle to work with or for them. (This much, Belle had already told Bernard.) Mary connected the dots even further. "If she is a faithful ally to thee, she c[oul]d help thee a lot, I fancy." Perhaps Bernard should change his mind, pull a few strings, and make the trip to London, if only to ensure that Belle did not turn against him. If Belle went into business with the Duveens or just signed a contract like the one Bernard had, she and Bernard could work together and make a lot of money.[101]

But Bernard did not have the time or the stomach for a personal visit or further negotiations with the Duveens. Besides, Bernard knew that Joe Duveen had already "mortally offended her—as he does everybody," and there was no chance of Belle's working with them beyond her duties for Jack Morgan. Furthermore, Duveen told Bernard that he believed Belle was in London as an agent for a New York dealer named French. Bernard hesitated to let Belle know about these newest rumors, which he judged "contemptible." But eventually Belle figured it out and ordered Bernard to tell her everything he had heard. Duveen was being friendly to her, she said, but he was watching her like a cat. She denied that she had any connection with P. W. French & Co. other than through her work for Morgan.[102]

Although she did not express it immediately, Belle was furious at Bernard's attempt to interfere, or perhaps just his willingness to believe that she would work on the side with a dealer, as he did. She certainly could not in good conscience both keep the job with Morgan and have a secret deal with a dealer. She later explained to Bernard that Duveen probably started the story out of resentment that she had sold some of Morgan's collection to the rival dealers instead of to the Duveens.[103]

As it turned out, Belle was considering a business offer, but not from the Frenches. Jacques Seligmann had proposed that she take over the New York end of his business. He had wanted her to come to Paris to discuss it, and Eugene Glaenzer had gone to New York to talk to her earlier that year. Belle had not yet given them an answer when she went to London. She was tempted. If she left the Library and went into dealing, she was sure she could make the money she needed to retire in five years. Seligmann wasn't her only option. Other dealers in New York besides the Duveens had asked her to go into business with them, but not French. She turned all of them down, hoping to find some cleaner way to make money.[104] Dealing would compromise her reputation as an authority in the field, and Belle had long disparaged the crooked dealings and price fixing that made it such a lucrative trade. This was a tacit indictment of Bernard's own decision to do just what she refused to do.

So instead of a romantic liaison with Bernard, Belle got a further long-distance cooling off of their romance. However, she also enjoyed a few weeks of heady socializing in London among a much more aristocratic crowd than she had known before. Jack Morgan's financial support to England and France was well known, and Belle was reaping the social benefits. She became good friends with the Robert Bensons. She had met the English financier and art collector before but was now utterly charmed by his wife. "I have never fallen victim to a female as

I have to Mrs. Benson." Given her avowed crush on Emilie Grisby and
her internal debates over Bessie Marbury, that may not have been an
empty phrase. Rumors that Belle was a lesbian had been circulating for
at least a year by now, and she knew it. She promised B.B. she would
have a "public scandal with some gent" to counter this particular tale
and vowed to prove more privately to Bernard that it was not true. It
was only her new indifference to men that prompted such talk anyway,
she assured Bernard.[105]

Still, she was hardly indifferent to the high life she experienced in
London, especially after such a disconcerting beginning. The Morgans
were quite impressed when she dined with a countess. People she had
never heard of sent their cards and asked whether they could call. The
wife of the American ambassador gave her a dinner, and all in all Belle
felt treated like an actress or a celebrity. None of them, Belle discovered, seemed to know anything about her and Bernard, not even Benson, who was friends with the Berensons. But they did know who Jack
Morgan was, and that she was his trusted librarian, and they seemed
to think, she laughed, that made her a very important person. She was
having the time of her life.[106]

Bernard was unimpressed—he knew the Benson circle and patron-
izingly opined that Belle did not understand London class structures if
she thought her new friends so highly placed. He was probably correct,
but Belle claimed it was not their status that she was enjoying but the
thrill of a new experience. Charles Read also believed she was carried
away by the names and titles of her new acquaintances, and was visibly hurt that she preferred their company to that of his own family.
Belle was sorry for that; she recalled that Read had befriended her
when she was completely unknown. She did make time for her old
friend, and Read apparently forgave her. Before she left England, he
gave her two wooden African statuettes. Belle loved them, "so simply
and so brazenly sculpted." It was one of the few times she expressed
an admiration for African art.[107]

Her friend Henry Yates Thompson called her "an American snob"
for her new social interests, but she saw him as well. And she met with
her "dear" Alfred Pollard, head of the British Museum Library. She also

spent several days with Sydney Cockerell, who seemed to have finally "awakened to the 'sex' side" of her, or was at least making "a sort of antiquarian wavering in that direction." When he took her to vespers at King's College Chapel, she was emotionally overcome by the singing and the setting. Cockerell held her hand all the way back. This seems to have been the extent of any physical flirtation between them, although Cockerell is sometimes listed as one of Belle's reputed lovers.[108] Belle no longer seemed to be hiding her other liaisons from Bernard.

She was also doing business with George Durlacher, a London art dealer who, along with his brother Henry, owned Durlacher Brothers. Durlacher had had a business correspondence with Belle since 1908 and made near-annual trips to New York. The two had quickly formed a fond friendship, and Belle often did business with him. In 1912 she had quipped that "a kind and loving family" such as his was exactly what she needed, and suggested he raise the possibility of adopting her with J. P. Morgan. Durlacher often wrote about his wife, their daughter, and her son, who, the doting grandfather claimed, was "worth more than all your [Belle's] library and the whole of the collection on loan at the Metropolitan."[109]

Ironically, while Belle played in London, contemplated a career change to dealing, and continued to hope that Bernard would join her, the Berensons were once again considering going to New York. Fundamentally it was a decision about whether to try to stay in the art business during the war. Little trade was happening in Europe, and with the increasing difficulties with travel, America was the only place to be doing business in the art world. Also, a personal visit might refocus Joe Duveen's interest on Italian art and the Berensons. Mary wanted to go, but Bernard was still afraid that once out of Europe it would be too difficult to get back.[110] Furthermore, he was afraid that returning to New York "would inevitably lead to [his] becoming totally a dealer," if it worked out at all. B.B. shuddered at such a fate. He decided he preferred "severe retrenchment" to going deeper into dealing. Sully, the London dealer who hoped to go into business with Bernard, was out of luck—for a while. Eventually Bernard relented and made an arrangement to share 50 percent of the profits with Sully on items Berenson helped him broker.[111]

At the last minute before Belle left, Jacques Seligmann arrived in London from Paris. He made it clear, in both word and action, that Bernard could have made the same journey to visit Belle if he had really wanted to. But if Belle was Seligmann's reason for coming, it was a lost cause. She turned down his offer and did not see Jacques again on that trip. In fact, the dealer who had helped J.P. make some of his earliest and most important purchases would soon find himself unwelcome at the Morgan Library. His inability or unwillingness to help Jack Morgan dispose of the unwanted portion of his father's collection would carry a heavy price.[112]

Belle returned to New York on the *Liverpool* (which she denounced as the most rotten boat in the history of the world), flirting with British military officers all the way, and arriving back in New York on December 3, 1916.[113] The next time she saw Europe, it would be a different place. In April 1917, just four months after Belle's return, the United States officially abandoned its three-year stance of neutrality and entered the Great War on the side of the Allies: Great Britain, France, and Russia.

Soon Belle was back in her usual rush. Family celebrations quickly followed. While in London, Belle had bought some lingerie for Teddy's trousseau. The baby of the family was getting married, leaving Belle and her mother "able to roam about the world as we please." But the wedding plans were marred by the preparations for war. Teddy's fiancé, Robert MacKenzie Leveridge, the son of a New York physician, was probably a member of the New York National Guard. They were called into service in July to become the Twenty-seventh Division of the U.S. Army, informally known as the Empire Division. (The division later expanded by recruiting.) On September 1, 1917, the young couple married. Soon the groom was in South Carolina with the Twenty-seventh for training, which lasted nearly a year. The New York papers followed their local troops' training closely, reporting several times a week throughout the winter as the men faced tough training, high illness rates, and a meager Christmas celebration. By spring the coverage focused on the need to recruit more volunteers to fill out the Twenty-seventh and some of the entertainments the men developed to keep themselves amused.[114]

In early summer 1918 the Twenty-seventh returned to New York before shipping overseas. The new husband and wife were together again briefly. But by July the division was overseas, and rumor had it that they were at or near the front. Teddy moved back into Belle's house.[115] She had been married for almost a year, but had barely seen her husband. When Private Leveridge left for Europe, he probably did not yet know that his wife was pregnant.

Belle was proud that all of the men in her family were "in it" and bragged that no tears had been shed in her household when Robert left for France that summer. Exactly how all of her male relatives were involved is unclear. Leveridge seems to have been the only one with a military record. At thirty-five her brother Russell was at the upper end of the draft range. He registered for the draft, but did not serve. Yet his new work as a civil engineer was almost certainly focused on war-related production. Later that year Belle wrote to the London dealer George Durlacher, "I thank whatever Gods there be that we are now in it with you to crush the scourge of civilization."[116]

Those left behind on the homefront found their lives significantly changed. Belle entered the very war work she had come to disdain in previous years. In the one existing letter she wrote to Bernard in 1917, she reported that she had been given some "rather important work," which she could not write about. When that was finished, she went to work for the Red Cross, which had been reorganized by Henry Davison, a partner in Morgan's firm. She also helped raised money for a series of Liberty Loans and Red Cross drives. One such event, an exhibition of Italian primitives, sounds suspiciously like the kind of society events she was scoffing at a few years earlier. Belle contributed one of her own paintings (probably one of Bernard's gifts) for the event, as well as arranging for Jack Morgan to lend one of the main attractions: *Madonna and Child with Angels* by Fra Angelico. Belle even overcame her aversion (probably more bluster than substance) to women's groups and became an officer of the Women's City Club, which was involved with both local politics and social work, and actively engaged in war work. By 1918 the WCC had a women's ambulance and a surgical unit in France.[117]

With her usual overstatement, Belle pronounced her family "terrifically poor." She had to give up her house and was looking for something smaller and cheaper. Prices had sky-rocketed, including rents. Sugar, wheat, and beef were in short supply. In the winter they couldn't heat the house adequately. But she spent Christmas helping a large number of poor families who had much less food and heat than did the Greenes. And she was constantly worried about the friends and family who were fighting overseas.[118]

Belle's antiwar sympathies of 1914 had reversed themselves completely. She wholeheartedly supported the movement to criminalize the antiwar activities and speech she had once participated in, applauding the government's "rounding up the pacifists, Germans and other vermin." Some of the very men she had cheered on in early 1914 as they denounced American military involvement in Mexico now found themselves indicted under the Espionage Act of 1917 and the Sedition Act of 1918. William Haywood was arrested, like many other IWW leaders, and received a twenty-year prison sentence. Max Eastman faced two prosecutions, each of which resulted in a hung jury.[119]

Far more of Belle's political and social acquaintances supported and served in the war in various functions. Her friend John Mitchel, the former New York mayor, enlisted in 1918 and died in a plane crash during his training. Edward Forbes of Harvard University's Fogg Museum went to Italy to do Red Cross work in late 1918. Paul Sachs, also of the Fogg Museum, was now Captain Paul J. Sachs. He was stationed in Paris when the armistice was declared on November 11, 1918.[120] Bernard spent the later war years in Paris, where he was offered a commission by the U.S. Intelligence Department, but ultimately ended up doing "secret and unofficial" work advising on Italian and German matters. He was staying with Edith Wharton, whose cousin Tom Rhinelander came over after the fighting to search for his son, still missing in action. Bernard had gone to Harvard with Tom Rhinelander, and he felt deeply for this acquaintance who had lost his child in the war.[121] Henri Hyvernat was still at Catholic University of America, which he described as completely militarized and turned over to war work. His job was reading and translating Turkish publications. Hyvernat's housekeeper, Amalia, was a German immigrant who had not yet filed for naturalization. She, like all enemy aliens, had to leave D.C. for six months until her citizenship paperwork went through.[122]

Nearly everyone's life was interrupted by the war and the sacrifices it entailed, but some sacrifices were more permanent. George Durlacher's nephew died "from the effects of shell shock," after surviving several years of fighting for the British. Belle empathized as she worried daily that bad news would arrive about her brother-in-law or one of her dearest "beaus," both fighting overseas. And she had no sympathy for healthy able men who did not enlist. When Harold Mestre came back again in 1918, she refused to even see him, sending word that she "had time for soldiers only." Although Harold, like her brother, was too old to be drafted, Belle was disgusted he had not signed up to fight anyway. "Thank Gawd I'm not tied up to anything like that." She promised "Sir Hercules," her old friend Charles Read, "If the men get all killed off, we women will go over."[123]

For once, Belle had no love life to scandalize friends. She told Charles she had not even "flirted with my eyes" since the war began. "Sad indeed. Hope old age does not overtake me before I get another opportunity." Belle also told Charles about her sister's pregnancy, perhaps complaining about Teddy's lack of contraceptive care. Read apparently chided her for neglecting to educate her younger sister on these matters. Noting wryly that it must be the "married portion of her family" that would offer such advice, Belle maintained that she personally found "prevention wiser than cure in most instances in life." Belle could have helped Teddy procure contraception, had it been wanting or wanted.[124]

But when Teddy gave birth on January 24, 1919, to an "A.1. peach of a boy," with blond hair and blue eyes, Belle fell in love. Blond women may have been her ideal of feminine beauty, but apparently she preferred men to be darker, for the one hope the devoted aunt had for her nephew was that his hair might darken as he grew older. It did.

Belle said that the child showed signs of high intelligence, which she predicted would make him either a prodigy or a "bad un." Most striking for her was that the baby's head was shaped "almost bone for bone" like her Mr. Morgan's. Belle showed Morgan's death mask to Bobbie's doctor, who thought the likeness so striking that he joked, "[N]ow, if he had been your baby!"—referring to the old rumor about Belle and Morgan senior.

But Teddy, newly married and now a mother, was also a widow. Private Robert M. Leveridge Sr. was killed in action, probably late in 1918 and was honored posthumously for rescuing two men in his company under heavy fire. Fatally wounded soon afterward, he also refused medical attention until others had been treated.[125] He never saw the son who bore his name.

12

LADY DIRECTRESS

*Of course—you are right—the lady is a most peculiarly tantaliz-
ing one—does it on purpose too, I believe—goes about the world
making people hate her and love her all at once and in the same
breath and heart beat—but, and it's a great big but, she has the
most peculiar quality of making people think about themselves,
of making them haul out their weights and measures and touch-
stones and go over their standards and tables of thought and conduct and life.*

—William Ivins, 1925[1]

*Miss Greene's personality filled the building, the electric tension
in the air as she approached, noisily, energetically alive and alert,
displaying what was once so delicately described as "a certain
imperious pungency of temperament." . . . [She] animated the
Morgan Library.*

—Aline B. Louchheim, 1949[2]

AS SOON AS the fighting stopped, Belle began to make plans to return to Europe. She had several business reasons for the trip. She was anxious to visit the Vatican to deal with the Coptic manuscripts and get them back on task. Also, her good friend Henry Yates Thompson was selling some of his renowned book collection at auction in January in London through Sotheby's; Belle wanted to make purchases for the Library. January was too early for her to travel, so she used her connections to postpone the sale until May, a telling example of her buying power in the book world.[3] Business was returning to normal, and the art world would see a brisk trade in the decade to come. But the death, disease, and destruction that this first world war had brought would not soon be forgotten.

Belle's interest in the Thompson sale also indicated her return to Library business. The war had brought Belle's work there to an almost complete stop for two years. Whatever progress she had made in supplementing her income by brokering private sales, whatever plans she had for her career, whatever hopes for retiring by 1921, all had crumbled. Even her correspondence had all but ceased. Very little in 1919 was as it had been in 1916.

Perhaps it is not too surprising, then, that when Belle first contacted Bernard to tell him she was heading to Europe his response was not very warm. She quickly assured him that he need not see her at all. She had heard that he was "quite surrounded by ladies and perhaps you thought I, in some way, would try to interfere with your 'indoor sports.' Far be it from me, dearest B.B.—Live and let live, is my motto."[4] Bernard was indeed in Paris with a new woman. And he was dealing with Mary's greatest emotional breakdown. She was in England with her daughters and sister, recovering from an attempted suicide. Geoffrey Scott was engaged to marry Lady Sybil Cutting, destroying Mary's hopes to somehow keep him permanently connected to I Tatti and making it impossible for her to remain close to him. Lady Sybil was one · of Bernard's first mistresses, and Mary could not stand her. With Bernard doing his intelligence work in Paris, Mary had been alone at I Tatti during the war, battling illness and spending hours meditating on her grievances and depression. Bernard reluctantly agreed that she could join him, but he was now involved in a passionate affair with Baroness Gabrielle La Caze, a socialite who rejoined his sexual interest with enthusiasm. Never one for tact, Bernard wrote from one of his trysts to Mary that the memories of Mary's "young eyes, of Miss Greene's and of Madame La Caze's . . . at a sexual crisis" were all he cared to "take from this world to the next." Mary was undone. Haunted by the phrase, feeling abandoned by both B.B. and Geoffrey, she spiraled downward for months and finally tried to jump from a window. Ray arrived to bring her, sedated, to a London hospital, where she grappled with her physical and emotional problems. The couple exchanged long, emotional letters, trying to work out their problems—his women and rages, her depression and frustration—on paper. Arguing that his presence would only make her mental instability worse, Bernard refused her pleas to join her and sent her to a sanatorium.[5]

By March, Belle had decided to postpone her trip anyway. Although the fighting had ended, she had received too many reports about scarcity not just of comforts but even of food in postwar Europe. Instead, she used Edmund Dring, a manager for Bernard Quaritch's rare-book dealers, as her agent to make some purchases. Still, even from New York, she was connected enough to be able to provide Yates Thompson with information after his sale about who was behind bids and what pre- and postsale dealers' gossip was. She told her friend "in all due modesty" that if she had been there, she could have "made things 'hum' a bit more, of course not where I was interested!"[6] Her own purchases brought her great pleasure, and she exulted, "[Jack is] a continual joy to me as a collector. In his sense of appreciation, discrimination, of rapidly increasing knowledge and sure recognition of the best, he will (I fear!!) soon surpass even his great Father." She also counseled Dring, who would soon be meeting with Morgan face to face, how to deal with the wealthy collector. In advice reminiscent of her earlier guidance to Berenson regarding the senior Morgan, she warned Dring not to talk down to Morgan, to admire Morgan's sense of art.[7]

Belle had become used to working with Jack on his financial deals during the war. When Charles King, Morgan's business secretary, died, Belle asked Jack to let her take over King's tasks and perform them at the Library, promising to explain when she saw him that the idea was not as crazy as it sounded.[8] But it was; Jack hired a new secretary for his Wall Street office, John Axten, and Belle found herself more than busy enough with the Library as business started back up again after the interruption of the war. Still, her offer indicates how much she considered herself Jack Morgan's assistant and support. They emerged from the war closer than ever, writing fondly to each other during his annual European stays and making loving references about family members. When his son Henry S. Morgan became engaged, the young couple made the rounds of the Library and the bride-to-be was introduced to the famous Miss Greene. Belle wrote Jack that she felt "a bit like a 'maiden aunt' about Harry—and quite grudge him to any one except his mother." Jack replied with more niceties about the engagement and sent "My love to the librarians and Library, which Mrs. Morgan joins."[9] Belle felt similarly proprietary about Junius S. Morgan Jr., Jack's other son.

Now unable to reach Rome herself that year, Belle began putting long-distance pressure on the Vatican, primarily through Henri Hyvernat, to resume and complete the repairs on the Coptic manuscripts interrupted by the war. She urged Father Hyvernat to finish his work on a checklist of the collection and asked him to go to Italy to speak with the Vatican directly. By August she was sending him lists of other places that might finish the work if the Vatican Library could not do it.[10] Belle feared that the officials in the Holy See might have gotten so used to having the manuscripts in their hands—it had been nearly a decade—that they considered them their property. This had happened with other manuscripts that Morgan lent out. Finally, by the end of the year, with Belle doing much of the cataloguing, they got the checklist out, which not only detailed the contents of the collection but publicly reminded the world that it belonged to Jack Morgan.[11]

After Morgan's polite threats to remove the manuscripts to another location to complete repairs, the project became a Vatican priority. Even the pope embraced the manuscripts—"to his Holy Bosom," she told Berenson—and was bending over backwards to accommodate them. Belle was still suspicious. She, like many Americans, already considered Pope Benedict XV to be pro-German. On the other hand, she was now "utterly devoted" to Father Hyvernat. She called him, alternately, "Mon Cher Pére" (my dear father) and "Most Reverend Sir," and assured him, "You are one of the all too few people in the world for whom I have a constant respect and deep affection and humility." Henri Hyvernat left for Rome in the fall of 1919. He met directly with Benedict XV and arranged to add extra hands to the job. By the following spring Hyvernat could confidently report that repair efforts had more than doubled and would continue as fast as was safe.[12]

The checklist was published in September of 1919, and Belle immediately began planning a full catalogue of the Coptic manuscripts. She asked Bernard to work on the illustrations, promising him access to the books at the Vatican. Her plan was for Bernard to write not only descriptions of the pictures in the manuscripts but also an essay in his unique style on Coptic art. This was a new departure in their professional relationship. Belle and Bernard had always conferred on professional issues—mostly involving specific pieces one or the other was studying or considering for purchase. This was the first time she had directly approached him about a job for the Morgan Library. Jack would not have been happy about it: he tolerated Berenson in the Library only because Belle insisted. She had already apologized to Jack for sending Berenson a copy of the Coptic checklist. She knew her boss might " 'writhe' at the sight" of his name, but justified her intent to include Berenson in the catalogue raisonné. Involving Bernard with the manuscripts meant bringing one of the world's experts on art to her biggest ongoing project. But it would also bring the very devoted, paternalistic Hyvernat into Belle's relationship with Bernard.[13] Hyvernat could be just as protective and patronizing as J. P. Morgan, albeit in a much gentler manner and with no secular authority behind him. He did, however, have a spiritual authority as a priest, which Belle definitely respected and took very seriously. Mostly.

Meanwhile, Belle's correspondence with Bernard had picked up again. They never seemed to address the conflict over dealers that had driven them apart in 1916. By September, Belle told him, "I can no more help loving you always than I can help flirting." Even if they separated and didn't communicate for years, she said, she now had much deeper feelings for him that she now knew only came with age and maturity. She added, "[A]ll my philandering (to put it mildly to myself) has not changed the real me at all. Even if perhaps it has scratched and muddied the surface." At least, she said, she had not pretended to be faithful "at least physically."[14]

When they did meet again, Belle warned him, he would find her greatly changed. After all, it had been a very difficult five years since they last saw each other. She was now "a rather mature and different person" and had even been told that she was dull and no longer had a sense of humor.

> I feel thousands of years old and am quite sure I look it. In fact, one of my friends told me the other day that I looked "dowdy." That was a blow. But all these chickens of 40–50 dressing as children has rather put me off the idea of preserving such youth as I might have.[15]

Belle would turn forty in a few weeks, but was still confident in her ability to attract men. She promised B.B. that "a well settled down, middle-aged 'loveréss'" would be good for him and assured him that while he may have spent the war years "scattering [his] 'wild oats' very recklessly," she had been most respectable. When she vacationed with a group of veterans in their new-fashioned, very revealing bathing suits, Belle enjoyed the sight, but "sighed a sigh for the bygone days" when she would have certainly taken "a fall" with one of them.[16]

Her newfound maturity did not mesh well with a nation caught up in the euphoria of victory and homecoming celebrations. Belle could not resist all of the invitations and bragged about meeting the Prince of Wales twice, once at a very exclusive ball. She also attended a few all-night parties in honor of returning war heroes, but confessed that she was "pretty well fed up with heroes and uniforms."[17] Her own family's war hero was not coming home. Robert M. Leveridge was buried overseas. His young widow and infant child still lived with Belle. Teddy had no job and could not support herself and Bobbie on the small pension the army provided. Belle was, once again, supporting her youngest sister and now her nephew, whom she absolutely adored.[18]

Having an infant in her home led Belle to consider, for the first time apparently, why she had never had a child herself. She was not the only one considering motherhood as her next step. Several men in her life, including two doctors with whom she said she had had "harmless" affairs, were also talking about Belle's having a child. One, an obstetrician, had examined her and declared her able to do her "bit in the baby line" for another five years. But there were only two men Belle would have considered to father her children. One was Bernard. And here, in a parenthetical query, Belle showed the first and only recorded regret for her abortion: "Why did we ship me off to London?"[19]

Belle remained fascinated by the idea of having children. In 1921 she made a passing reference to the "immaculate" frogs that Jacques Loeb had produced by means of artificial conception. Loeb pioneered the in vitro procedures that have now become a mainstay of human fertility treatments. But Belle's idle wish that Loeb could "produce a baby for me" with his method was several decades ahead of scientific technique. Despite her occasional expressions of regret for the road not taken, however, Belle almost certainly avoided motherhood by choice, although she might have wished for a world in which she could have a child and remain unmarried and working, as several of the actresses and dancers who populated her social circles in the early 1910s had done. Belle would not name the other man whom she had considered as a father for her speculative child. All she said was that he, like Bernard, was miles away from her, although more faithful than Bernard would ever be—not a difficult accomplishment.[20]

The years immediately following the war were turbulent ones. The United States had proved itself a major world power, a position it would continue to hold into the twenty-first century. But internally the nation seemed far from stable. As the speeches and parades and all-night parties gave way to the decade remembered as the Jazz Age or the

Funeral procession for J. Pierpont Morgan, 1913.

The *Lusitania* docking in New York, 1907.

John Pierpont "Jack" Morgan Jr., circa 1919.

Mary Garden.

Emilie Grigsby.

Agnes Meyer.

Anne Morgan.

Joseph Duveen.

Mitchell Kennerley.

Belle da Costa Greene, portrait by Laura Coombs Hill, 1910.

Portrait by Rene Piot, probably of Belle da Costa Greene, 1910.

Belle da Costa Greene,
portrait by Paul Helleu,
1912.

Female Nude Before a Figured Curtain, by Henri Matisse,
probably of Belle da Costa Greene.

Miss Green. Librarian to Pierpont Morgan

Sketch of Belle da Costa Greene by William Rothenstein.

Belle DeAcosta (*sic*) Greene, date unknown, probably 1920s.

Belle da Costa Greene, date unknown.

Page from
Thomas Mallory's
Le Morte D'Arthur.

Page from one of the
Morgan Library's
Coptic manuscripts.

UPTIAE
FACTAE
sunt inchana
galilee · & erat mater ihu ibi ·
uocatus ē autem & ihe · & disci

Detail from Gospel lectionary, Salzburg, Austria, late eleventh century.

School of Tintoretto, *Portrait of a Moor*.

Father Henri Hyvernat, 1939.

Belle's nephew,
Robert M. Leveridge Jr., circa 1939.

Belle da Costa Greene, early 1950. Note the *Portrait of a Moor*
hanging behind the desk.

Roaring Twenties, not everyone was celebrating. Class divisions were stronger than ever, as even Belle noticed. Everyone around her, she said, was "dreadfully poor except the millions of newly rich,"[21] Labor unrest broke out in violence throughout the year, and resentment of the rich, whether new or old, grew. The Red Scare marked escalated fears that immigration was bringing socialist and anarchist revolutions into the country, and governments began to scrutinize and crack down on ethnic and foreign-language unions, newspapers, and social organizations. Racial tensions were also mounting. Black veterans in uniform were attacked in the streets by whites who did not want to recognize either the contribution blacks had made in the war or the rights of citizenship it implied. Race riots broke out in urban areas throughout the country.[22]

The passage of the Nineteenth Amendment, giving women the right to vote in 1919 (ratified in 1920), did not end debates over women's proper social roles. New opportunities opened in professional careers, and women like Belle came to be celebrated as pioneers for this new wave of professional working women. A small but highly visible and controversial group began to push social and cultural boundaries even farther. The young flapper emerged with her short straight dresses, bobbed hair, and long cigarettes to gyrate to the new jazz dance crazes and completely reject Victorian definitions of proper behavior. Conservative social mores and Christian fundamentalism were also on the rise. The Eighteenth Amendment prohibited the manufacture, transportation, and sale of alcoholic beverages after January 1920. The Volstead Act, which provided for enforcement of the prohibition amendment, allowed exemptions for sacramental and medicinal purposes, as well as homemade vinegar, cider, and wine.[23]

Belle was too old to join the flapper generation, too well-off to suffer greatly in the economic upsets of the postwar era, consciously removed from the continuing struggles of African Americans, and well connected enough to obtain alcohol. But she was still affected by many of these changes swirling around her. She was not rich enough to merit the attention of radical socialists, but her boss certainly was. In September of 1920 a horse-drawn wagon loaded with dynamite was detonated outside of the Morgan building on the corner of Wall Street and Broadway. Although the culprits were never identified, the attacks were widely assumed to be the work of anarchists. Belle was shaken by the "inconceivably heartless outrage" of the attack, which cost over thirty lives, wounded hundreds, and left a spray of mortar scars still visible in the building's limestone wall. Jack Morgan was on a hunting holiday in Scotland, but two of his employees were killed and his elder son, Junius, was injured.[24]

Nor did the passage of suffrage resolve Belle's uneasy relationship with women's rights. She continued to attend meetings of feminist organizations, like the Lucy Stone League, which was founded in 1921 for the initial purpose of encouraging women to keep their birth names after marriage. Named for a nineteenth-century abolitionist and women's rights activist who made the then radical decision to keep her name when she married Henry Blackwell, the group soon expanded its focus. But in 1922 Belle participated in a debate on the subject of women's names. All of the pro and con speakers were men, as were all of the respondents mentioned in the paper coverage, except for Belle. She considered it an "indisputable right and privilege" for a woman to keep "the personality of her own name" if she wanted.[25] After all, Belle had exercised her right to change her own name to match a new public identity twenty years before.

Belle did find herself caught up in the new interest in and recognition of women who were pioneering educational and professional spheres formerly occupied by men. Her friend Gertrude Atherton published an homage to women's war work and celebration of feminism. Belle appeared as an example of women performing men's work with outstanding success. Atherton claimed that Belle had purchased every book and item in the Library since her arrival and that Morgan made no purchases without consulting her. (This was a bit of an exaggeration.) Writing in 1917, Atherton predicted that suffrage would pass after the war, but was more interested in transforming society into a gender system that trained women in professions, arranged for men to support them during their childbearing and early child-rearing years, and then allowed them to venture back into the workplace unencumbered by prejudice.[26] This was a radical view even by feminist standards. Atherton's vision would have resolved the problem that Belle had tacitly faced in choosing between children and her profession.

Belle was probably unimpressed. Her rising professional status made her a visible example of this movement, but she did everything she could to avoid notice. When the editor of the *Ladies Home Journal* offered her $500 for a one-page article on the topic "Woman's Supremacy in Man's Field," Belle retorted that she "did not know what he was talking about and never heard of any such phenomenon." She did, however, accept the Palmes d'Officier de l'Instruction Publique awarded her by the French government in 1921, and several similar honors.[27]

Belle's attention in the years following the Great War was primarily on her own life: her work, her family, her friends. By the end of 1919 she was making plans again to sail for Europe later in the winter. Bernard had not come to New York after all, and she wanted to see him. But this time her priority was Rome and the Coptic manuscripts, which Father Hyvernat was still busily overseeing.

Belle's departure was delayed by the illnesses of her mother and her sister Louise. Mrs. Greene was feared to have typhoid fever; Louise required an operation. With New York still dealing with the tail end of a influenza epidemic, Belle could not find a private nurse and stayed up nights with her mother for a week before getting her to a hospital. The influenza (also called flu or grippe) was a continual health inconvenience, but a highly virulent form killed over 600,000 Americans in 1918–19 and an estimated 50 million worldwide. More American soldiers died from the disease during the war than in battle. By 1920 the deadly "Spanish flu" virus was dwindling, but the memory and the fear remained. Belle could not leave until she knew her mother and sister were safe.[28]

Finally sailing in late February 1920, Belle landed in France and found a train strike prevented her from traveling to Rome for several weeks. The luxury trains were not running, and she could not bear to take the regular trains, having arrived ill herself and in need of a doctor's care. Her first stop was supposed to be Rome and the Coptic manuscripts, but Belle decided to go to London first and sent notice to both Bernard and Hyvernat of the delay.[29]

Although Belle had decided to avoid I Tatti, her plans to visit Tuscany, and Bernard's desire to see her in Rome, had already disrupted the Berensons' ever bumpy household. Mary had since returned to the villa after recovering from her suicide attempt. She was still physically and emotionally weak, but she and Bernard had managed to find a new equilibrium for their friendship, marriage, and partnership. This was helped in part by I Tatti's new permanent resident, Nicky Mariano. Hired by Bernard to be his personal secretary and librarian, Mariano held a position that had some parallels to Belle's in her first years at the Morgan Library. Although she was far from the first employee to try to fill this role, Nicky would be the last. Unlike other assistants, she brought balance to the villa and to the relationship between its owners. Mariano eventually became involved with Bernard, and this time bringing a third party into the rocky Berenson marriage seemed to make things better, not worse.

But in early 1920 Nicky was not yet caught up on the intricacies and details of the Berensons' past relationship. One evening she left the two alone after dinner, and Bernard used the private moment to talk to Mary about Belle's proposed visit. When Nicky returned, she found Bernard alone and angry and had to search the house twice before discovering Mary in another room curled up on the couch in the dark. Nicky was mystified.[30]

Bernard was no doubt upset that Belle was delayed and not planning to visit Florence at all. She had also had lots of bad things to say about the Duveens' and Carl Hamilton's doings in the New York art world.[31] Carl Hamilton was a new presence in New York. Although he appeared to be a wealthy collector entering the market, Belle was suspicious and was letting Bernard know how skeptical everyone was about Hamilton and his relationship with the Duveens. Any bad news about the Duveens' business prospects was unwelcome to B.B., but Belle had no inkling of the significance of this bit of gossip to him.

Mary eventually let some bitter comments slip about the woman who would soon be arriving. She told Nicky that Belle had played a "dangerous part in B.B.'s life." Still, Mary calmed herself enough to write Belle a "delightfully cordial letter" assuring her she was welcome at I Tatti. Belle wrote to Bernard to confirm that Mary's health really was good enough for her to come.[32]

It was. But the visit would have to wait until the trains began running to Italy again. In the meantime Belle went to London. Before leaving Paris, however, she took a few days to be fitted for new clothes and found that fashions were moving faster than she could assimilate them. The French dressmakers all thought her crazy for insisting that her skirts cover her knees. In fact, when she did wear one of her new dresses that barely reached her calves, she caught a cold. Furthermore, in the postwar economy even these modern designs that used so much less fabric seemed to be no less expensive in Paris than in New York.[33] The two reasons for buying clothes in Paris—getting the latest fashions and the lower prices—were now gone.

Belle had reached the age where she had stopped trying to keep up with the latest trends, and could only look askance at the appalling new styles the younger women were wearing, which became even shorter and scantier as the years went on. Belle was comfortable with some of the inevitable effects of reaching middle age (not that she yet admitted she had reached forty). When she returned to New York, her seamstress grumbled at having to let all her belts and waists out a whole inch, mourning the slight addition to her formerly "svelte" figure. Belle thought it was "grand."[34] And when confronted a few years later with the "queer" spectacle of a young flapper in the Library, Belle was both mystified and mildly approving. The girl was apparently wearing a jingle dress: Her clothes made so much noise that Belle could barely hear her words. But Belle rather envied the "exclusive finality of her" and her general attitude of "I'm all the Hell there is—there isn't any more."[35]

And that first experience wearing a shorter skirt (still below the knee) could not have helped. By the time Belle arrived in London, her cold was worsening, and she worried it was actually the flu. The Bensons and their crowd of lords and ladies embraced her again, and Mrs. Benson, once she realized Belle was ill, insisted that she come stay with them until she had recovered. So when Bernard hinted again that this crowd might only be using her for her position, Belle went into a written rant about their good qualities, her long relationship with many of them, and their social ties to the Jack Morgans. If Bernard felt negatively about them, she said, it was probably owing to the Duveens or other trouble-making dealers planting stories to feed B.B.'s infamous grudges.[36] She was, she told an unconvinced Bernard, perfectly aware that those in her new crowd were not the true "sassiety" aristocrats he socialized with. "Your Lady Cunard's-Astor's etc. etc. would sniff the air at me—I don't know them and never expect to—My only point was that I was meeting real England, in that they were all so desperately, solidly British—awful clothes—wonderful houses—awful food—and wonderful hearts." Still, she admitted to Dring, she hated to leave "these adorable people, who have almost succeeded in turning my head."[37]

After four days in bed Belle ventured out to attend the Catholic Mass at Westminster Cathedral. This would have surprised a number of people for a number of reasons. For one, Belle did not have the reputation of being a particularly religious person, although she and her mother were members of the Episcopalian St. Thomas Church in New York. (St. Thomas's French Gothic architecture would have pleased her aesthetic sensibilites as well as her spirit.) Furthermore, Catholicism was still very much a minority and often disparaged denomination in the predominantly Protestant world of New York's social elite. Although a number Catholics were among the upper circles of Belle's world (among them Bessie Marbury—who converted as a young adult, much to her family's consternation—John Ryan, and Bernard Berenson, the latter at least nominally), the majority of Catholics in the United States were immigrants or descendants of recent immigrants from Ireland, Poland, and Italy. Anti-Catholicism was rising, along with anti-immigration sentiments. When the Ku Klux Klan reconstituted in the postwar era, it appealed to native-born whites' anti-Semitism and anti-Catholicism as much as to anti-Negro prejudices.

Many non-Catholic tourists sat in on Mass at Westminster Cathedral for the experience. But Belle's interest in Catholicism was deeper. She complained to Father Hyvernat that she did not understand much of the Catholic Mass, since the priests seemed to be talking mostly to themselves in Latin and the congregation was silent the whole time. "You must instruct me in the service so that I can, at least, follow it."[39] Her interest was serious, and she probably did receive some instruction, at least informally, from her devoted scholar-priest. Even her interest in illuminated manuscripts took on new meaning. She later concluded, "I'm surely intended for the Catholic Church, for its what all these pictures and places are 'remembering' that impresses me most."[38]

But now that Belle had recovered enough to go out, she had work to do at the British Museum and collections and dealers to see. Her favorite Englishmen were waiting for her as well: Charles Hercules Read, Henry Yates Thompson, and Sydney Cockerell. When Belle dined alone in her rooms with Cockerell, she discovered, to her great amusement, that he still had "an awful crush" on her. On her last visit, in 1916, she had also realized this, but it seemed to catch her by surprise again. No doubt this was in part for Bernard's benefit, and she assured him, "I have little time for a rather thick set, beginning-to-be-elderly chap, with a wife and 3 children and all the typical British instincts and barriers—but out of consideration for our friendship I did let him kiss me on the cheek and neck."[40] This sort of "consideration" could have been enough to spark those rumors that they had an affair. An early Morgan biographer, with access to letters no longer available, confirmed that Greene and Cockerell were "intimate friends." Belle apparently signed letters with "yours eternally" and teased Sydney from time to time: "Are you nice and chubby, or are you just dull?" One of the letters recounted a flirtation Belle had with a rich westerner in New York for a few weeks. The lumberman put "himself and his checkbook" in Belle's hands, so she made the rounds of New York society and art dealers with him, instructing him to buy several paintings, a private train car, and numerous meals and entertainments. Perhaps a bit dazed, the man returned to the slower pace of life west of the Mississippi. But the experience apparently stayed with him, for a few weeks later he cabled her, "When will you marry me?" She replied that "all such proposals would be considered alphabetically after my 50th birthday," and told Cockerell that she found the proposal "screamingly funny."[41]

In any case, there is no doubt that their friendship was based largely on a shared love and understanding of books and manuscripts. The two spent hours looking at the rare books at various college libraries. "I almost wept over the Milton manuscript at Trinity— What would I not give to own the leaves containing Lycidas!" Belle never found the six months she had wanted to study with Cockerell, but she managed to sneak a few days in every time she was in England.[42]

Men like Sydney Cockerell and William Ivins also shared Belle's more modest background. Ivins was head of the prints and drawings department at the Metropolitan Museum of Art and one of Belle's new beaus. Belle pronounced him really worthwhile, loving both his intelligence and knowledge and his sharp wit, which could (and often did) challenge her own in not quite deadly duel. Cockerell and Ivins were both working professionals who found themselves in a field of wealthy men. When Ivins was elected vice president of the Grolier Club, he confided to Cockerell that it was a position for the "well to do," not for a "poor museum official" like himself.[43] This experience and the skills necessary to socialize as equals may have been a bond between Belle, Sydney, and "Billy"—as Belle called her favorite Met man.

But by 1920 Belle was more than capable of holding her own with aristocrats and economic powers. Henry Yates Thompson, whose own background was decidedly not modest, threw a party for her, inviting many other bibliophiles who had gathered for another auctioning of his collection. However, word was that Thompson had lost the respect of his peers by putting too much of his collection on the block. Belle worried that he would never again be the center of London's group of collectors, curators, and critics, as he had been. But she loved him anyway.[44] He too had been a friend long before she was anything but Morgan's unknown assistant.

And Edmund Dring, now Belle's "Cher Nunkie" and "oncle Confesseur," was there as well. Dring was older and married—two qualities Belle apparently still found very attractive in a man. They may have sailed together, passing the time in some unusual, or perhaps not so unusual, ways, developing a much more playful and intimate relationship than their previous correspondence suggested. For example, Belle sent Dring a handwritten invitation, apparently while they were onboard, for a whimsical series of lectures given by herself. Topics included "Sons-in-law & Why I have em" and "The Rise, Progress,

History (Economic, Political & Intimate) and Bibliography of Mothers-in-law."

Whether this was a cover for a physical relationship or not, Edmund and Belle certainly enjoyed a flirtation that spring. She saw him several times in London, but only briefly. He gave her a cigarette holder and some prints, which she returned, perhaps trying to discourage his attentions or to signal that their tryst was over.[45] Dring also sent her a letter he'd received from a mutual friend that began, "So our beloved Bella is with you all, over there. The Witch!! . . . The Witch will soon be here. . . ."[46] There is little doubt that the bulk of Belle's rumored affairs were simply friendships in which affectionate repartee, clever innuendo, and very real ties of feeling and interest sometimes evoked the appearance of sexual intimacy. Belle and Edmund Dring clearly had that kind of bantering friendship.

It was mid-April before Belle arrived in Rome. She had begged Father Hyvernat to find her rooms at the Excelsior ("you don't want a thin yaller ghost corpse on your hands, do you?") and her "Le Petit saint Père" came through, although he couldn't get her an en suite room.[47] Bernard arrived a few days later, although Belle had hardly encouraged him. She warned him to try not to arrive at the same time she did, and certainly not to stay at the same hotel. "I don't see any point," she said, "in starting the old scandal afresh— If you were not coming to America so soon it would be quite different."[48] Since this was the same concern she had dismissed a year before, saying they were too old to be suspected of scandal, something else must have been going on. Belle also urged Bernard to keep all of his own engagements as she would not have much time for "visiting" with him in Rome.

Their long-awaited reunion got off to a rather rocky start. It had been such a long time since they had seen each other. Belle also later blamed her own state of mind at the time. She was tired of seeing people after her romp in London and wanted to just be in Rome alone.[49] But Belle felt some ambivalence about resuming their relationship. Her love for Bernard had been her emotional center for years. She still loved him, but she now had a great deal more maturity through which to view him. Few men could have lived up to the idealized image that distance and youthful passion could create. Belle was no longer young, and her passion was now tempered by her experiences.

Still, there was a lasting bond there. Despite their troubles in Rome, Belle accompanied Bernard to Settignano, where she met Nicky in person and saw Mary, but also managed several long walks alone with Bernard in the surrounding hills overlooking Florence. Already falling in love with Bernard herself, Nicky scrutinized Belle, trying to see what the attraction was.

> The first impression was not agreeable. Great vitality and plenty of intelligence, a provocatively exotic physical type and something unharmonious, almost crude, in speech and manner. In later years I got to know her better and was able to enjoy her wit and her zestful approach to her work. But I never got a sense of real harmony with her.[50]

Belle found Nicky more to her liking. She left her two pairs of the "New York" stockings the younger woman had admired, and told Bernard that the new assistant was a godsend for him "if she be not spoiled."[51]

Back in Rome, Belle fell in with three young Americans attached to the U.S. embassy in Rome. After dinner they went to the Colosseum, where, as she had been on that first visit to Rome ten years earlier, Belle was enchanted by the sight of the ancient structure in the moonlight. Again she was reminded of how different some of her social circles were from those of Bernard and Mary. But when the young men began singing popular songs—"Over There" and "Another Little Drink"—even Belle got a bit disgusted. (We might imagine that a few drinks had been consumed with dinner.) But still, she "loved them for their clean youth, their freshness. . . . I felt—and still feel, as if I were 16 and if for nothing else, I would love them for that." This was one of Belle's secrets to maintaining the vitality, if not the appearance, of youth. Even as she aged and became undeniably older, she was able to—even loved to—connect with young people.[52]

Most of her time in Rome was spent with Hyvernat. Belle may have felt that his age and status as a priest (not to mention her maturity and professional standing) eliminated the need for an escort. Of course, they were often in the Vatican Library, and in the company of other scholar-priests working at the Vatican and on the Coptic texts. But they traveled alone together daily between the Vatican and their lodgings in Rome—she at the Excelsior Hotel, he on Via S. Luigi, where they often had tea in his room, which she called his "most austere and yet most lovable 'cell.'" And they also made a tour of the Via Appia, an ancient Roman road that winds away from the city, and made their own moonlit visit to the Colosseum.[53] This was enough to cause some scandal about her behavior at the Vatican. Belle scoffed that the "dear centenarian friends" she had been with were too old to require an escort or to merit such speculation.[54] Hyvernat was only twenty-one years her senior, in his early sixties, hardly a centenarian. Still, there is no evidence that anything untoward took place between the priest and his "chela." There was, however, a close bond between Belle and Father Hyvernat. She was his spiritual daughter, she said, his ever devoted "child-in-sanctity."[55]

What Belle remembered most of that visit was the "physical Rome." She described "warm, scented, sunlit days" and "intoxicating moonlit nights." In late spring, she concluded, Rome was "almost as dangerous a place as Venice," suggesting that romance was in the air.[56] She often wished to be there entirely alone, except perhaps for the Catholic Church (and Father Hyvernat?), which seemed to her to be an intrinsic part of the natural beauty of the ancient modern city. Bernard, who no longer practiced Catholicism, would not have been impressed with Belle's new interest.

Train strikes threatened again in early May, and Belle had to cut short her stay in Italy, returning quickly to France so that she would not miss her boat. Hyvernat left her at the station and went to church to pray for her. Then he went about making arrangements to meet with Pope Benedict XV on her behalf.[57] He brought a gold medal scapular for Benedict to bless for Belle, asking her to accept it as a token of their personal attachment and to always wear it inside her dress. He promised to explain its full meaning and symbolism when she was ready, but

told her that in the meantime it placed her under the protection of the
Virgin Mary and Jesus Christ. Such scapulars have varied traditions
and manifestations in Roman Catholicism, but generally are intended
to be worn daily and to bind or signify the relationship between the
wearer and Mary and Jesus. In some traditions persons who died wearing one were assured they would not go to hell. In others it was
intended as a reminder of the need for prayer, not a guarantee of sal-
vation. Hyvernat hoped it would remind Belle that "someone is ever
praying—and encourage you to pray yourself—that God may enlighten
you to see and straighten you to do His will." Whether Belle actually
wore the medal is unknown, but years later, when Hyvernat was very
ill, she sent him a medal, perhaps this very one.[58]

On May 21 the *Adriatic* docked in New York, and Belle was home
again. She was now taking nearly a decade off of her age; she was
almost forty-one but told customs she was thirty-two. A trail of letters
from both Hyvernat and Berenson followed her across the Atlantic.
Hyvernat confessed that he missed her and was trying to feel lucky for
the time they had had together. He called her "most precious daughter," "dear daughter," and, most daringly, "o desired one!" Belle was not
quick to respond, and the priest had to wait some time before hearing
back from her.[59]

This time she really had a good excuse. A swollen jaw that hampered
her enjoyment of the return trip turned out to be an impacted wisdom
tooth that had worked its way up toward her eye. A friend of Hyvernat's, Dr. Dunn, met Belle at the boat and took her under her care.
(Belle seemed unsurprised to be cared for by a female physician.) She
was in the hospital for ten days and took a few more weeks to recuperate. Later she blamed the ether she received during and after the wisdom tooth removal for a depression that followed, lasting several
months.[60]

But within a month she had recovered enough to arrange the annual
family move to the shore and begin a hopeless search for hotel lodging
for Bernard and Mary. Rooms were in short supply, and she was
relieved when the Berensons announced that they would be staying in
Carl Hamilton's apartment on Park Avenue. The Duveens arranged

this setup to advertise the collection. The idea was that the Berensons would bring people in for entertaining and talk up the pieces to help sell them. Bernard had already written an article on one of the many pieces Hamilton had supposedly purchased from Duveen. Most of his purchases were "on credit," and most ended up back in the Duveens' stockrooms to be sold to more solvent collectors. Belle's information had been correct.[61]

Both Belle and Bernard were eager to resume their affair in New York. He told her that it was pointless to worry about gossip. Belle agreed this time, in part because everyone around her seemed to be assuming that she was already hiding something big. Even her mother believed there was some "large secret sorrow" her one unmarried daughter kept to herself. Belle said it was probably because she was not flirting anymore. Edmund Dring might have been surprised to hear that.[62]

There was a change in her. She continued to show a deepening interest in religion, and in the Roman Catholic faith in particular. She began to take vacations at Catholic retreats, one at a convent in New Jersey where most of the nuns were converts from prominent Protestant families. She loved the quiet and the rest but was not always able to succumb to the spirit of such places. Once, after feeling "very pure and holy" the first few days, she was appalled to suddenly find herself "filled with wicked, scandalous thoughts." And when she interviewed the "wayward girls" who were on the grounds for training, she found that most were "pure as lilies compared to myself," guilty only of disobedience or staying out after curfew.[63] Belle may have been drawn to the rituals, the ancient traditions, and the grandeur of Roman Catholicism, but she had a hard time fitting her sensual nature into its proscriptions and rules and its expectations for women.

The Berensons arrived on November 24 on the *Olympic*, with Henri Hyvernat close behind the following week. Mary and Bernard settled uncomfortably into Hamilton's apartment. Mary complained to her daughter that they soon found out that Joe Duveen had placed them there as "decoy-ducks" to strengthen Hamilton's credit, although it had been her idea to begin with. Again, Mary did not want to be in New

York. This time it was her sister Alys's poor health that pulled her heart to England. But there was greater need for them to be in New York with new buyers entering the market and other dealers and scholars trying to push the Berensons out of the business. Mary dutifully prepared a series of lectures on the paintings in Hamilton's collection.[64]

The Berensons were back in their usual New York whirl of parties and dinners and entertainments with the wealthy elite. Prohibition did not stop the champagne and wine from flowing at their tables, and the deprivations of war made the jewels and delicacies and ostentatious spending they represented even more repellent. Unfortunately, their visit coincided with a financial panic, so business was not as good as they had hoped. "I do not think we shall ever come again. It isn't our life," Mary wrote prophetically to Alys.[65]

Mary also reported that Belle was "very much to the fore" in New York and tried hard to use her prominence to help them. But Bernard felt put out because Belle was friends with some people he considered his enemies. Bernard was convinced, probably correctly, that there were dealers and even collectors in the art world who were out to destroy his reputation and living. He expected those who would be his friends to choose a side and make his presumed enemies their enemies.[66] Jacques Seligmann was one such suspect. Belle gave Bernard a letter that the Duveens' rival had sent her. Belle probably meant for Bernard to realize that Seligmann was not working against him, but Jacques also wrote about his belief that Bernard and the Duveens were plotting against Seligmann's own company. The Blumenthals were another. Bernard was having a conflict with them about the attribution of a painting they had purchased from the Duveens with Berenson's assurance that it was as a Titian. Belle did not understand why he thought it was impossible for her to be friends with them (she and Florrie were very close now) and with Bernard. She pointed out that he must be close to people who did not like her. This was certainly true, Mary being only the most obvious case in point.[67]

Bernard was also having difficulties that went beyond his role in dealing and attribution. Despite his multiple conversions, he was still known as a Jew, and there is some evidence that the prejudices he had faced in Italy had now transformed to official inquiries into his loyalty to the United States. In fact, during this trip an investigation began of the Berensons' activities, looking into his possible connection with Zionism or communism. The inquiry found nothing and was quickly dropped, but the taint of suspicion, combined with rising anti-Semitism in the 1920s, remained.[68]

The Berensons went north for their usual family and business visits in Boston, where Isabella Gardner, half paralyzed and bedridden, received them for the last time. They traveled south, making their usual stops in D.C. and Philadelphia. Bernard wrote to Belle, "[H]ow simple it would all be if I did not care so much for you." Belle jumped on the phrase and began analyzing their relationship. How would not caring simplify his life? Wasn't she just an "ineradicable memory" that rarely intruded on his daily life. She understood that she had to give him space when he was in New York, as he wanted the "Rush and Wear and Tear" more than he wanted her. She was the same way in Europe. And she admitted that she still had some "hostility toward him." The roots, she mused, lay in that first trip together in Italy, in the "world-excluding worship" she once felt for him. "Certainly I can never give anything approaching it to anyone else—for the simple reason that it is no longer existent." She lost it, she now realized, when she went to London.[69] Rethinking that episode may also have been affecting Belle's feelings for Bernard. Or maybe she was just coming to recognize the effect it had had on her when her first great love affair ended in an aborted pregnancy.

Belle even suggested it might be time she and Bernard "released" each other. Their constant disagreements about people and loyalties were only the tip of the iceberg. It had, after all, been thirteen years. Thirteen years, five visits, untold numbers of other affairs for each of them, and one world war. They were truly, as Belle said, not the people they had been when they met at the end of 1908 and had their Italian idyll in 1910. And he had younger, more beautiful, and equally intelligent women to occupy his time. Belle referred to them as "the kindergarten." When she met one, Evangeline Johnson, she said she felt like Rip Van Winkle, or as if she were seeing a moving picture of herself when she was first in love with Bernard. She could no longer pretend to be the naïve and all-accepting protégée she once was. And there were other indications that her faith in him was no longer absolute. When he wrote enthusiastically about some people (unnamed) she thought poorly of, she simply hoped he would never be disillusioned. But, she added, it gave her "further pause . . . in blindly accepting your verdicts."[70] Belle was becoming disillusioned with Bernard. And Bernard was starting to believe that Belle might be more loyal to his suspected enemies than to him.

Among the people about whom they disagreed were some of the scholar-priests at the Vatican. Belle wrote a confidential letter to Father Hyvernat about the matter, a letter that he seems to have destroyed at her request.[71] In his reply Hyvernat said only that he was not surprised by her warning but that he was taken aback by Bernard's apparent comments on some of his Holy See colleagues. They were, he said, "so silly that he must either be a fool or think you are one." The priest promised to be on his guard in further communication with Bernard, especially if Belle's name came up. He told Belle he was too busy writing a university report to worry about the matter, but on the same day he spent some time itemizing what he knew about Berenson. His "Facts about B.B." list included the observation that Bernard's partnership with Duveen interfered with the integrity of his scholarship, and that he tended to set people against each other and attack persons or projects he felt did not serve his benefit. But Hyvernat also wrote that Berenson "[p]retends vehemently to be utterly devoted to B.G. (personally) but in fact is trying to use her," adding that Jack Morgan hated Bernard. Furthermore, Hyvernat now had evidence that Berenson resented Belle's ties with the Vatican and the people there and was trying to convince Belle that they were using her to get at Morgan's money and name. Underlying all this was Belle's decision not to have B.B. write part of the Coptic manuscripts catalogue. Exactly how and why she changed her mind is not clear, but it was another sign that Belle and B.B.'s friendship was growing distant.[72]

In mid-March, Belle retreated to the Yama Farms Inn, in Napanoch, New York, a select resort for "invited" guests (including Nelson Rockefeller, Thomas Edison, and Henry Ford). Increasingly, Belle used her vacations to retreat from both the "reeking, hydrahead, infested" city and the company of society to retreats like Yama and, when she had more time, Wyoming and Montana. There, on long walks in the wooded trails, Belle had ample time to reflect on her situation with Bernard. She told him that "the time had come when we ought to be constructively friends or mere acquaintances." After several weeks of thinking about him and working through the "mixture of feelings" she had for him, she had arrived at "a most heavenly peace" about him. Her clarity did not last long: a week later, with Bernard's departure just a few days away, Belle was overcome with a grief that "successively benumbs me, freezes me, burns me and causes me to ache with a bitter, intolerable pain." She had, she said, often "idly speculated upon the particular Hell-on-Earth which undoubtedly awaited me—Is this It?"[73]

With Bernard gone again, and their relationship at an uncertain crossroads, Belle turned to socializing and busyness, trying to "banish the insistent thought" of him. Within a few weeks, however, she had calmed down enough to sigh philosophically that there wasn't much point in saying anything about their relationship. "Ô douceur—ô poison [o softness, o poison]," she sighed.[74]

Bernard apparently suggested that he held "others in my arms to symbolize you," but Belle claimed that didn't work for her. It was not because Bernard was still the only lover in her life (although she would still hold him apart from her other men, at least in the letters she wrote to him). Still, she mourned, "I am but a poor disciplinarian after the arm-holding state has been reached, and so find it wiser to prevent any such happening." She still did not feel herself a "free person, in any sense, and a constant awareness of my bondage prevents the enjoyment of casual or even something more than casual encounters." Besides, her "wild past" was just that, in the past. Of course, for Belle the past was never really behind her, and the reputation for wildness now preceded her. When she invited psychologist Morton Prince back to her house for a drink after a night out on the town, she laughed, "I may as well have the game . . . as the name!" She was no longer even trying to protect her reputation. Well aware that she was known to have taken many lovers (the name), Belle figured she might as well enjoy herself and have more affairs (the game). Times were changing. Sexual purity, or the appearance thereof, was no longer an absolute requirement for social status. Although there were many who would still judge women like Belle who were sexually active outside of marrige, there were now also those who would celebrate her or at least smile knowingly.[75]

April was always a difficult month for Belle. She once again went to J.P.'s grave in Hartford on the anniversary of his death, on March 31. "By the time I reached his tomb I wanted nothing but to creep in and stay there with him forever." Even after she left his grave, he haunted her. She felt him with her constantly over the next weeks, she said, urging her to "come away." When Bernard told her he had heard (again) the rumor that Belle was J.P.'s illegitimate daughter, she retorted she would consider it a blessing to be so, and would never hide such news. Earlier that year she had heard a rumor that her own house was a gift from Henry Davison, one of Morgan's partners with whom she had worked on Red Cross projects during the war. "My only comment was that he had better taste both in architecture and females." It was useless to worry about such rumors.[76]

Meanwhile, Father Hyvernat, unaware that Belle's loyalty to Bernard was not so easily shaken, arrived in New York from Washington and started to talk about the Bernard situation with her. Belle shook him off and refused to discuss the subject anymore. Or at least that's what she told Bernard—and it may have been true. Belle did not love blindly, but she did have a different measuring stick for Bernard than for anyone else. On the other hand, she may just have been trying to assure her jealous and grudge-bearing lover that he had nothing to fear or resent from her beloved Henri Hyvernat, who was now her confidant.[77]

Belle's musings about her one unplanned pregnancy and her childlessness may have been weighing heavily on her that year for other reasons. In 1921 Belle became her nephew's legal guardian when Teddy got married again to another man, Robert M. Harvey. Harvey was probably a disappointment to Belle, who believed that marriage should bring financial stability, by which she meant wealth. Harvey was the grandson of Irish immigrants who grew up on an unnamed road in Allegheny County, Pennsylvania, where his father worked as a mechanical laborer. By 1920 he had moved to Paxtang, where he worked as a carpet factory manager before his marriage and as a salesman in a print shop by 1930. Belle denounced Harvey as a "penniless nobody, but one of those 'God-fearing' Methodists."[78] Of course, Belle had had something negative to say about every one of her siblings' spouses.

Teddy moved out, but Bobbie now lived with Belle and Mrs. Greene, although he continued to see his mother on family visits for at least the next four or five years. During this period Belle occasionally mentioned Teddy's presence and referred to her as the "mother of my dear Boy." In late 1922 Teddy returned to Belle's home to give birth to a daughter. It was traditional for a woman's female relatives to be present at her labor and delivery; Teddy had been living with Belle and given birth to her son at home. Teddy named the infant Belle Greene Harvey, perhaps hoping that her namesake would assume some responsibility for the girl's education as well. Whether she did is not known, but Belle seems to have had little interest in her niece, never mentioning her in correspondence, and her relationship with Teddy deteriorated over the next twenty years.[79]

As a parent, Belle behaved as most women in her economic class did. She largely continued her own activities, secure in the knowledge that other women were caring for her child during the day. In Belle's case this included her mother as well as hired servants. Belle had found another discreet lady's maid, Elisabeth Hogan, an Irish-born woman who also helped with Bobbie. When Elisabeth married in 1926, her cousin Marie Mullins took over her position. Mullins's grandson recalls that her duties included taking care of Belle's wardrobe, performing personal tasks, and helping her entertain guests. She also sometimes cared for Bobbie.[80]

Belle now sent Bobbie and her mother to the country for the summer. When she could, she spent her nights with them, making her usual summer train commute every day; Belle loved sleeping with the

ocean breeze and watching Bobbie tan in the sun.[81] Other summers
her mother and Bobbie traveled without Belle. In the summer of 1921
Belle reveled in finally, finally living alone. (Her mother and nephew
were visiting her sister Ethel in the country.) She reported gleefully
that she now understood the delights of the bachelor life, or perhaps
that of the married man whose wife and children were gone for the
summer. The most interesting men appeared for her to flirt with. Inviting some home to dinner, she made herself vampy but aloof. And, she
told Bernard, she usually headed upstairs to bed by herself, but not
always.[82] She knew what her reputation was, but did not care. And she
was still able to maintain a façade of respectability among those who
knew her only professionally. When a new acquaintance who struck
her as "being very 'correct' socially" asked her to dine with him, she
shyly told him that her mother was out of town and she would therefore be unable to do so. "What a scream! May he never meet any of my
friends or enemies who will put him wise!" Her summer was full of
dinners, dances, and weekends at Newport. A series of English friends
were in town. She brought Sydney Cockerell to see Billy Ivins at the
Met, and entertained Charles Read again.[83]

Although young Robert was now a constant presence in Belle's life,
very little is known about his childhood, schooling, or upbringing.
Belle, like most of her correspondents, mentioned children only in
passing in her letters to her friends and colleagues. Few stories about
his escapades appear in her correspondence to friends. This should not
be taken to indicate a lack of interest in him on Belle's part. It is clear
from the references that do survive that Belle's friends and even
acquaintances were well aware of her new role and were interested in
Bobbie's development. But the wealth of information about him was
no doubt destroyed with her personal papers, and children rarely enter
historical documents, publications like newspapers, or other available
sources.[84]

Belle's new family structure may seem very modern, but it was far
from unusual. In 1921 the New York Times reported that over 100,000
women in lower Manhattan were listed as "heads of families" for
income tax purposes. Most of them, like Belle, were unmarried women

who were supporting parents or siblings. The *Times* article was careful to distinguish these women from the "new women" who were getting so much negative attention. The difference was that these heads of household, although not biological mothers, were "engaged in mothering an army of dependents."[85] Belle had solved the problem of single motherhood by adopting her nephew, although she never called herself his mother.

In 1922 Mrs. Greene, still living with her one unmarried and most successful child and now a grandmother, truly became a widow. Richard Greener was still living in Chicago with the Platt sisters on Ellis Avenue when he died of a cerebral hemorrhage. The *Chicago Tribune* published a death notice, but none of the major East Coast papers reprinted it. Greener had faded from prominence in mainstream politics and society long before his death. The *Washington Post*'s last mention of Greener during his lifetime was in 1913, and even then it noted that not many people in D.C. would remember him. The *New York Times* had not mentioned him since soon after his consular position in Vladivostok ended. The black press still remembered him, however. The *Cincinnati Union* called him the "Last of the old Guard" and the *Chicago Broad Ax* praised him as one of the "most prominent colored men" in the country.[86] In fact, the *Broad Ax* marked Richard's passing with a front-page story that outlined his career in a few brief paragraphs. Richard continued to list himself as "married" until his death, although none of his obituaries mentioned his wife and children. He was buried in the Platt family plot in Graceland Cemetery in Chicago.[87]

Whether the Greenes knew of his death and how they responded is unknown. The rest of the Greener/Greene family remained close. Belle's siblings were now all married and on their own. Only Teddy and Robert Harvey had left New York, although Louise and Frederick Martin were soon to move to Ithaca. Russell and Josephine Greene, and Ethel and George Oakley all lived in the city near Belle, Genevieve, and Bobbie. Before she left, Louise seems to have briefly worked for Belle at the Library. Louise shared Belle's interested in manuscripts. She studied Latin and, no doubt with Belle's aid, became an expert in

Latin manuscripts. Records of her work at the library indicate only that she performed secretarial and stenographic work, typing and copying catalogue cards at the rate of one dollar per hour.[88] But no doubt her education was greatly enhanced by her exposure to the Morgan Library treasures and by working with Belle in her element.

The catalogue was not the only project under way. Now that work on the Coptic manuscripts had resumed, Jack Morgan had allowed the release of several press stories about them.[89] By 1921 Belle was also making arrangements to have the manuscripts returned to the Morgan Library. The Vatican Library prefect confirmed that the bulk of the collection was ready to go back. All the codexes were restored and bound, and the original bindings had been repaired. Only the fragments were still in progress. Belle hoped to go to Europe again in 1922 or, if she could put it off, the spring of 1923 to oversee the process herself. She was particularly excited when her friend Cardinal Ratti was elected pope in 1922, becoming Pope Pius XI. Ratti had been in charge of the Vatican Library when the Coptic manuscripts first arrived, and Belle considered him a "good and learned" man who would "lead us all to the light in these troubled times."[90]

But some feathers had been ruffled a bit lower in the Roman Catholic hierarchy. Apparently Monsignor Mercati, the head of the Vatican Library, had sent a letter to Archbishop Bonzano, an apostolic delegate in Washington, D.C., complaining about the situation. Hyvernat managed to smooth things over and thought the problem was that the 1919 negotiations to resume work at the Vatican had been done directly with the Holy See. In other words, they had gone over Monsignor Mercati's head. In any case, Belle's push to finish and clear out had been misinterpreted. The Vatican thought Mr. Morgan was annoyed that the work had taken so long, and now an offended Mercati wanted the manuscripts out as soon as possible. Belle immediately wrote a complacent letter to the archbishop assuring him that the Library had nothing but gratitude for the work the Vatican had done. The only reason for pressing for completion, she claimed, was to relieve the Vatican of the burden of the project.[91]

Belle also suspected that Father Hyvernat may have played a role in fueling the fire. Was he upset that his "devoted hand-maiden" had not gone to Rome that year? In any case, there was nothing to be done. Belle outlined a plan for removing the books, complaining all the way about how much she had wanted to go there herself, to see everyone who had contributed to the work, and especially to help make the presentation of the reproductions to "my librarian friend, His Holiness!"[92]

All was forgiven when His Holiness signed a photograph for Belle and one for Jack, something Hyvernat assured Belle was almost never done for non-Catholics. And Belle's old librarian friend sent on the hope that she would have his photo framed and placed on her desk. "I should give much to have the Pope do so much for me," Hyvernat told her. "You lucky daughter of mine!" Belle copied the letter out for Jack and wrote underneath, "Of course this reconciles me to everything! B.G."[93] Jack was not impressed with a papal autograph, but he later personally presented the pope with the full-size photographic reproductions of the manuscripts that the Morgan Library commissioned and distributed to a select and very limited number of libraries.[94]

The bulk of the Hamouli Coptic manuscripts finally came back to the Morgan Library. But Belle would not return to Italy until 1925. Her job was to blame, although not in the same way that it had been over a decade ago when J.P. extracted her promise not to travel to Europe while he was still alive. Now that Jack was almost as devoted to the Library as his father had been, and the war was over, the work was piling up. Projects and trips that had been postponed during the war were now on again. Belle complained that there were so many visitors that she was forced to spend her evenings and nights doing the library work that she couldn't get to during the day. She told Jack's business secretary to warn him that she was "considering a Union—any old Union that promises to protect ageing librarians."[95]

Under Jack's patronage the Library was open not only to scholars and social visitors but to clubs, lectures, and visiting classes. One young Harvard student later recalled his first visit to the Library with the Harvard professor Paul Sachs. The group of twenty students had come into the vestibule and were looking up at the lapis columns and trying to heed Professor Sachs's cautions not to bump into the furniture or artwork. His wife, Meta Sachs, sat down in one of the chairs, only to have it collapse, dropping her to the floor. Miss Greene, the student recalled, was very gracious, sweeping up the pieces and lightly assuring her friend: "This happens all the time, we just glue them together." The student, Henry Sayles Francis, later became a curator at the Cleveland Museum of Art and got to know Miss Greene as a prominent figure in the manuscript field. For young students coming of age in the 1920s, Belle was a commanding personage and a recognized authority in her field.[96]

Established authors and scholars also came to give lectures. For example, in 1921 Amy Lowell, a longtime acquaintance of Belle and J.P., came—with her partner Ada Dwyer Russell—to speak to a private club on Keats. In return Belle allowed Amy to examine some of their Keats collection in the comfort of her hotel, a complete deviation from their usual rules. Such lectures were not open to the public, but academics, students, and interested parties could hope for invitations from Belle or Jack.[97]

Sometimes even Belle could be persuaded to give a talk to students or a visiting group, as long as she was approached correctly. Margaret Jackson of the New York Public Library first appealed to Belle in 1919 to give a lecture on manuscripts to a group of students. Jackson organized an annual class on "the artistic side of bookmaking" intended for NYPL staff and some outside librarians. Her course seemed to be somewhat similar to the Amherst summer program Belle had attended so long ago, with a more specialized focus. Belle, however, refused to give anything called a lecture or address. She said the idea terrified her. And she refused to have her name listed in the syllabus. Still, she invited the class to visit the Library and offered to "show them the manuscripts and explain the technique and the position they occupy in the history of art—but quite informally!"[98] This was actually much more than Jackson had been hoping for, and it was a great success. Nonetheless, she had not understood the distinction Belle made between giving a lecture and just talking about the books that she loved, about which she knew almost everything there was to know. The next year Jackson wrote again, asking Belle to repeat "the talk" that she gave, which made "sleeping things live." Belle repeated her offer to host the students, but again refused to give "a formal talk." By 1921 Jackson had learned how to word her requests to Belle. This time she asked for "the same informal (but informing) talk" Belle had given the preceding year, and Belle agreed without objection.[99]

Belle continued to try to avoid publicity. French Strother of *World's Work* repeated his request that she write an article on American collectors and rare books so many times that she finally gave in. "My brain," she admitted, "simply refuses to conjure up a new excuse." Belle promised to write the article just as soon as she found time. Mr. Strother is still waiting. When a reporter from the *Sunday World Magazine* asked for an interview to add to a series on career women, Belle sent word through her secretary, "Miss Greene has adhered very closely to a rule which she made several years ago, refraining from all interviews, and everything savoring of publicity."[100]

Belle was also involved in some independent projects outside of the Morgan Library. In 1922 she began working with several scholars organizing a new art journal that she referred to as the "Harvard-Princeton" journal, because all of the editors (Frank Jewett Mather Jr. and Paul Sachs), associate editors (Charles Rufus Morey and A. Kingsley Porter), and advisory councils were either at Harvard or Princeton University. Belle had been involved in the organizing board and had wanted to bow out once the journal was launched, but as the men "very flatteringly insisted upon my inclusion," she stayed on. One of the first things she did was enlist Bernard to write for them. He also donated $250. Belle then recruited Roger Howson (of Columbia University) to write an article. *Art Studies: Medieval, Renaissance and Modern* was launched in 1923 and published until 1931.[101]

Belle may not have been dealing, but she was planning an active role in assisting some deals. George Widener, whose father and brother had died on the *Titanic,* was one of the few big collectors who was making major purchases in the immediate postwar era. Belle helped weed out his collection and taught him how to set up purchases as exchanges, where he sold back or sold some of his less important pieces as part of his purchase agreements, usually amounting to half of the cost of his new items. Few dealers escaped this setup: Widener was buying from Sulley, Duveen, and Durlacher.[102]

Belle rarely spoke about leaving the Library now. The economy was very unstable, and adopting her nephew entailed an unexpected financial responsibility. Belle sold her car and began investing in foreign loans (through the Morgan company) on Bobbie's behalf.[103]

Moreover, her relationship with Jack had strengthened during the war. Although she said her feelings for him did not approach those for his father, he was now, she said, the only person whose feelings about her were "of vital importance to my life." The feeling, she thought, was mutual. She described him as "lashed to the mast," and she spent vacation time with his family in the Adirondacks. In the years that followed, Jack even began loosening up enough to flirt a bit and to tease Belle. When she considered an invitation from two scholars, including her old friend Albert Clay, to join them for a trip down the Euphrates, Jack retorted, "In what capacity do you go? As the official concubine of the party?" Gleeful at Jack's attempt at off-color humor, Belle sighed that unfortunately his newly wayward manner was only talk. It would take a more fundamental change to bring him to the point where she would really fall for him.[104] At any rate, he was party to some of her family life now. In a 1923 letter to Jack, Belle related a story about taking Bobbie shopping for warm clothes for a visit to the country. Belle had told him there would be woods, even a forest there. So the four-year-old boy wanted to buy a gun for bears that might be in the woods and an ax and saw to help the men chop down the trees and cut them up![105]

By 1923 Belle was also referring to herself as director of the Library, and confided in Bernard that they would soon be incorporating. By 1924 it was official: Jack established the Library as a permanent public institution and turned it over to a board of trustees. Belle told Bernard she had been working on Jack to make this happen since his father's death, to make it a memorial to J.P. The Pierpont Morgan Library, now generally known as the Morgan Library, was no longer a private institution, with access only at the approval of the owner or librarian. This was what she had envisioned: a collection that would serve both scholars and the public and give everyone access to the incredible collection of human artistry and thought housed there.[106]

Belle officially became the director and promised to stay on for at least five years, one of which was to be a sabbatical year. After that, she hoped she would have the courage and the freedom to finally leave it. She still held the dream of traveling and studying in Europe. "Pray that I don't weaken!!! in 1929," she exhorted B.B.[107] Jack stayed on as a trustee, along with his wife and their sons Junius Spencer Morgan and Henry Sturgis Morgan.

Old friends came out of the woodwork to send congratulations to Belle on her new position and the Library's transformation. F. Wheeler wrote with mixed feelings. He was proud that J. Pearson & Co. had participated in the formation of Morgan's original collection, but it was a bittersweet pride. His company had never had the publicity that larger firms did, and it was soon closing.[108] Ruth Granniss, librarian of the Grolier Club, sent her congratulations and her acknowledgment of the great role Belle had played in the transformation.[109] Henri Hyvernat teasingly called her "My Dear Director Greene." He had quickly discovered that Belle was becoming busier than ever. In fact, that spring he asked her to come to Washington for a meeting precisely because it was now impossible to discuss things with her at the Library "on account of your being so constantly interrupted."[110]

Public accolades followed as well. Henry Todd of Columbia University wrote to the *Times* pointing out the encouragement and aid Belle had always given to scholars publishing studies of the Library's holdings. He described Belle as "the wise and ever gracious presiding genius of the place."[111]

Almost immediately after the Library was incorporated as a public institution, Belle mounted an exhibition of rare manuscripts at the New York Public Library. Because of its small size and the need to protect its treasures, the Morgan Library would still have to restrict public access to its holdings. The exhibit opened at the end of March, attracting hundreds of visitors daily to view letters and manuscripts by American founding fathers, colonial figures, and writers like Edgar Allan Poe and Ralph Waldo Emerson, and Henry Wadsworth Longfellow.[112] The letters of George Washington received particular attention in the *Times,* which published several of them in full, noting that Washington and the time he lived in survived in these letters. In February 1925, an article in *The Bookman* revealed that Belle had blithely claimed to have destroyed several of George Washington's letters. Edward Larocque Tinker reported that he had visited the Library when it was still private. His impressions were immediately negative: he described a "mausoleum-like interior" and a "gorgeous but depressing" reading room. But his ideals of artistic and historical preservation were stunned when the "lady dictator" and "czarina of the library" cheerfully admitted she had eliminated the papers in question because "they were smutty . . . so I did not want them ever to become public and destroy the ideal of Washington that has flourished for so long." Tinker was appalled and launched a long tirade on the relativism of such judgments and the loss to history and humanity if all writings deemed inappropriate at one time or another were so obliterated by the "lethal whitewash brush." He was not alone in his censure of Belle's reputed act.[113]

Going public was quite an adjustment for Miss Greene. There were exhibits to mount, more lectures to arrange, and an ever-growing stream of visitors wishing to see the "'Oh My!' stuff," Library lingo for the pieces that most impressed nonexperts.[114] Policy changes could be difficult to impose. New rules were required for providing access to the unique and often fragile books and manuscripts, new policies for lending pieces. Although she was still under the auspices of a board of trustees, Belle had far more independence and control over the day-to-day operations of the Library than she had ever had before. Staffing relationships were affected as well. Belle later mentioned that Ada Thurston, who had been with her since the beginning, "increasingly feels her subordinance to me in the Library. That, I can do nothing about, because she does not go ahead and I have to increasingly supervise."[115] And she was under a great deal of stress as they tried to resolve the theory and practice of going public. The transition was sometimes bumpy.

When Belle lost her temper with Sydney Cockerell over a lent-out manuscript that he was not finished with, Jack Morgan had to intervene and smooth things over. In a letter to Cockerell he apologized for "Miss Greene who, I think, wrote you more vigorously than, perhaps, she really meant too." Jack also appealed to his director to "have extreme patience, which I know is difficult for you as for me."[116] How many millionaires have had to write a soothing letter covering for their librarian's tantrum? William Ivins, keeper of books and prints at the Metropolitan, mentioned to Cockerell that he had heard about Belle doing "her best impersonation of Damnyou Beatit, the Tartar Queen." When Billy stopped by, somewhat nervously, he found her quite cheerful. He concluded that she must like him after all.[117]

Belle began to develop a reputation for her temper. Although always there below the surface, she was now, perhaps, more free to wield it. One story told and retold involved a manuscript of Saint Augustine's *City of God*. A dealer had brought the book in for Belle to inspect, and she had it out on her desk waiting for a scholar to come consult with her on the possible purchase and left it there when she went to lunch. It was a social luncheon, the story goes, and a few drinks may have been consumed. Upon returning to her office she panicked: the expensive book had disappeared. Out of her office she strode, roaring, "Where the hell is the *City of God*?!" It was safe: the scholar had arrived in her absence, and the book had been removed to the reading room for him to examine.

Belle's new responsibilities made a vacation impossible that year. Instead, Belle rented a summer cottage "for Bobbie." Presumably her mother went too. When Belle was not weekending with "the Rich," she spent lazy days sleeping on the beach, even though tanning made her "blacker than ever—or than seems possible," and watching her now six-year-old nephew play.[118] Tanning was the new fad among middle- and upper-class white Americans, who had once zealously protected their skin from the effects of the sun. The ability, or willingness, of whites to darken their skin further blurred the boundaries between white and brown that imperfectly defined some racial and ethnic boundaries. Why a woman supposedly trying to hide her black ancestry would sit unprotected in the sun for the purpose of darkening her skin is a little hard to explain. But many other white women were doing it, so perhaps it became an odd form of fitting in. Also, Belle could use tanning to both further highlight ("blacker . . . than seems possible") and undermine her own darkness (she was "black" only because she allowed herself to tan).

Tanning also represented yet another of the many forms of racial

crossing and boundary blurring taking place in 1920s American culture, music, and social life, especially in Manhattan. Belle was playing
with many of them. She often dragged Billy Ivins or visiting Europeans
up to Harlem.[119] Harlem's nightlife was only the most visible example
of the crucial role African American culture played in the deveopment
of modern American culture. Many whites thronged to the bars and
clubs and even parties in Harlem. Belle's presence, however, may have
brought her to the attention of African Americans who might have
known or guessed her own black ancestry. Perhaps it no longer mattered if people knew or guessed. Belle was now a director of a major
public institution, no longer working at the whim of an individual rich
man. She undoubtedly had received a substantial pay hike as well.

Public demand for entry into the new Library in its old building continued. At the end of 1924 the Morgan Library mounted another
exhibit at the New York Public Library, this time of manuscripts by
English authors. Belle oversaw the selection, transport, and setup of
the exhibit. She and the trustees also arranged for Friday afternoons to
be reserved for junior and high school students to see the original manuscripts of such classic authors as Sir Walter Scott, Charles Dickens,
Thomas Paine, and Rudyard Kipling. Intended to last three months,
the exhibit was so popular it was extended into April 1925. A record
170,000 people attended the exhibit during its five months, including
6,000 high school students. But, despite its popularity, the exhibit had
to close so that the books and letters would once again be available to
scholars.[120]

Back at the Library, Belle reported that they had recorded an average of thirty people a day, all with questions and needs to be attended
to. Some days saw only a handful (which would have been a normal
day before going public); others saw dozens every hour, mostly students or visitors who had some particular item or area of interest.
Clearly the Library would have to grow to meet the new demands.

Belle somehow found time to socialize heavily that year, her usual
response to increased stress. In January she bragged that one day she
held a luncheon for "Famous Ruined Ladies" and a dinner for "Famous
'Ruiners.'"[121] In the summer she returned to her old habits, attending

multiple events every evening, and constantly entertaining, despite the fact that her resulting lack of sleep accentuated a new problem: wrinkles.[122] And she had an intense affair, a "harrowing 6 months emotional debauch" that ended at the end of 1924. She never identified the man in question, and her description of it doesn't match any of the men who were demonstrably in her life that year.

> I pray the dear god of such things that he will "call it a day"
> and leave me in peace for the rest of my life on this earth.
> I've had all of it I want and can stand—and feel exactly as if
> I had been skinned—and am so raw that I must be wrapped
> up in soothing oil and cotton for a long time before I can
> again be touched without its causing agony. I'm sure that
> sounds theatrical. I wish it were not so damned true! . . .
> But now Thank God, I'm FREE—and intend to stay so.

Her one saving grace was that she knew she would recover when most women—"yes dear especially at my age!"—would not. Bernard was almost as curious about Belle's real age now as he had been about her ethnicity when they first became involved. Her letters often teased him about her age: "I wonder just really why my age bothers you so much—It appears to be a real 'complex' with you—a never ceasing source of aggravation."[123]

And now Belle wanted to see her B.B. again. It was beginning to look as if the two ex-lovers still had enough affection for each other and the emotional distance necessary to be real friends. Belle had already sent William Ivins to visit the Berensons at I Tatti. Mary was offended by his "virulent picturesque slang," but Bernard was enchanted. This was predictable given their respective responses to Belle's ribald humor and love of "bowery" slang. The two men became fast friends and lifelong correspondents. Nicky Mariano speculated that their bond was created in part because they had both been in love with Belle. Certainly their subsequent correspondence was liberally sprinkled with gossip and discussion of their shared frustration and adoration of one Belle da Costa Greene.[124]

Billy provided Bernard with the details about Belle's life that she
would or could not give him herself. He described a day spent with
Belle, art collector George Northrop, and art critic and historian
Richard Offner and concluded that "to say nothing of her other qualities, B.G. is twice the man that they would be if rolled in one." And a
lunch with Belle at a restaurant that was subsequently closed for Prohibition violations was followed by a "barbaric temptation" in a shop
selling Native American silver jewelry "where she fell, splash, for a
necklace of silver squash blossoms—ten of them—signs of fertility!
But she's a dear, and no two ways about it. I'm rapidly coming to think
of her as my Mother Confessor, if there is such a thing?"[125] Billy confessed that he loved Belle dearly but seemed quite happy to share her
with Bernard and probably others as well. He envied her vitality, her
sauciness, and her common sense, and fondly called her "such a nice
mutt!" and Arabella, or the Queen of Sheba—when she wasn't being
Damnyou Beatit the Tartar Queen, that is. Belle's wit and even her
temper were such a welcome change from Ivins' staid colleagues at the
Metropolitan Museum of Art that he declared, "[E]ven to quarrel with
her like mad is so much better than what I put up with here."[126]

Billy may have been one of the four new beaus Belle bragged about
to Bernard that spring. Another was a titled Englishman—Belle said
she might marry him if it weren't for the title. But the "grand English
beau" did not last long. She preferred having several to the intensity of
one, but was baffled when they all wanted to marry her. "I'm sure I do
not know how all this purity came so suddenly to pass," she mourned.
Now she swore not to marry before turning sixty, by which time she
hoped she would be sterile. And she mentioned that her doctor said
she was still fertile and would be for some time, suggesting that she
was keeping close tabs on her contraceptive needs. Adopting her
nephew seemed to have satisfied her desire for a child; Belle never
again in the written record mourned for the lost pregnancy in London
or that lack of access to in vitro techniques in humans. And she teased
Bernard that Billy appeared to have a crush on both of them. "I did not
know that you were either of you that kind of gent," Belle poked, but
added that she was confident enough in B.B.'s attraction for her that
she was willing to accept his "bi-detexerity."[127]

In the summer of 1925 Belle made good on her promise to see Bernard and Italy again. She was losing weight and reaching complete exhaustion from her work, and hoped that the trip would help her recuperate from "the most trying year" she had ever known. She now had to pay for her own travel, but decided it was worth the financial cost. Billy saw Belle off on the *Majestic*, waving from the shore as she made faces and rude gestures at him. He wrote to Bernard that she was on her way and warned him the "mutt" was very worn out and would need to get lots of rest. When he didn't hear from her for a month, Billy sighed to Bernard that Belle had apparently dropped them both and was probably off dining with aristocracy or having a wild affair.[128]

Belle arrived in Europe at the end of June, staying first in London and Paris, where she had hectic days of business and visiting with old friends. In Paris she haunted the Bibliothèque Nationale, feasting on its manuscripts with Henri Auguste Omont, the library's paleographer. When she found out that Omont had been gathering material for an edition of their Greek manuscripts but could not find a publisher willing to bear the costs of printing it, she offered to underwrite it with funds she now controlled at the Morgan Library. Belle was astonished when Omont was moved to tears. With America moving into a period of prosperity and seemingly endless economic growth, she had not realized how the war continued to affect Europe's economy. Publishing, especially of books so expensive and limited in appeal, was at a standstill.[129]

By the time Belle arrived in Rome, she was cranky and tired and on the verge of illness. She hated her hotel, but was forced to spend increasing amounts of time there. By the end of the visit, she was dragging herself out of bed to meet with the pope ("friend Ratti"), who blessed crucifixes for Bobbie and Elisabeth Hogan, her maid. Her main task, however, was making arrangements with Father Hyvernat, also in Rome that summer, and the Vatican Library to bring the last few manuscripts and bindings back to the United States.[130]

Finally Belle retreated to the Dolomites for a rest cure, as always never specifying the nature or extent of her illness. She postponed her plans to visit Florence, where Bernard and some color photos of the Coptic manuscripts awaited her. Hyvernat swore to keep her poor health a secret. Jack's wife was seriously ill, and Belle did not want to add further worry to him or anyone else in New York. Belle wrote to Hyvernat that she hated to leave Rome, which always seemed wonderful since she been there with him. "You are so much mon Père et mon frère et mon oncle et mon neveu—that I feel as if I had lost an entire sainte Famille when I have left you."[131]

Once recovered, Belle moved on to Florence, where she stayed at the Grand Hotel with her friend Marie Louise Emmet. Bernard had left I Tatti by then, and in late July Belle and Marie Louise joined him and Nicky Mariano in Perugia. Nicky reported to Mary that Belle looked about the same as she had in 1920, and described Mary Louise as young, shy, and good-looking but prone to awkward pronouncements and slang. Nicky thought Belle was "rather wild and shrieky," but the party got along well and traveled around Tuscany. For the first time since her ill-fated first visit to northern Italy, in 1910, Belle returned to the small towns of Tuscany, including Orvieto and Siena.[132]

Mary stayed away from them. She still put up with Bernard's other affairs, which Nicky was learning to deal with as well. But Mary no longer pretended to tolerate Belle, whom she now called an "out & out vulgarian." Besides, her presence as chaperone was no longer needed. It is not clear whether Belle and Bernard revisited their affair that trip. Bernard and Nicky were involved at this point, and Belle seemed quite aware that she had younger competition. She told Bernard that she did not envy Nicky her job, but did envy her charm, and Bernard's love for her. Belle also felt that she had "grown so 'witchily' old and wrinkled and everything—that I could not now put up any fight against her at all." So Belle was mentally prepared to face, for the first time, one of Bernard's other women besides Mary.[133]

While Belle was with Bernard, she consulted with him directly about an issue she had broached already in writing. Bernard was considering willing his library and collection to a museum or university. Already in a close working relationship with Paul Sachs and Edward Forbes at Harvard University, Bernard's alma mater, Belle intervened on their behalf to encourage Bernard to move in that direction. Arguing against another option Bernard was considering (donating his things to the new National Gallery planned for Washington, D.C.), Belle wrote carefully about the financial details of such a bequest. Reporting back to her Harvard friends at every turn, Belle suggested that Bernard either transfer his collection to the Fogg Museum or allow Harvard to operate I Tatti as a library and center of scholarship. In the latter case, she pointed out, Bernard would need to either leave enough money for an endowment to support the institution or work with Harvard to try to raise such a fund.[134] Mary, who had long since realized that Bernard considered all the money they earned to be his, wanted her share of the profits they both worked for to go to her daughters and grandchildren. She supported the idea of a foundation or institution for Harvard, but could not convince Bernard that she had the right to control her portion of their money.[135]

Belle's conversations with Bernard about the future of I Tatti went smoothly, but there were other bumps in their reunion. Most disturbingly to Bernard, Belle was enchanted by Mussolini's Fascist government, which had come into power in 1922. Bernard could not dissuade her. He was disgusted with the new Fascist regime; its local leaders were the same people who had caused him so much trouble during the war. Nicky dismissed Belle's opinion as typically American: "she had no discrimination about where information on European affairs came from. One source was as good as another and the first one more likely to be preferred."[136]

Marie Louise Emmet's presence as Belle's traveling companion was a bit of a mystery. Bernard suspected that Marie Louise, whom they referred to as "M.L.," was a lesbian and dubbed her "the papoose," for reasons unknown. But a series of postcards the party sent to Billy Ivins during their tour suggests an open acceptance of the situation: Bernard had multiple women, and some of them got along just fine. The cards refer to "B.B. . . . and his harem," and the women call themselves "Cherubim No 2," 3, and 4. If M.L. was a lesbian and Belle's traveling companion, the implication was that the two women were lovers. There is no direct evidence of this, and precious little information exists about Emmet at all. Still, when she left Bernard to return to Paris, Belle responded to B.B.'s speculation by telling him that M.L.

had thought it was Nicky who was "the Lesbian plus" and concluded that they all must be very sexually frustrated to be so suspicious of the sexual activities of everyone around them.[137]

Interestingly, Belle immediately followed this episode by creating more scandal, of a decidedly heterosexual nature, about herself.

> A rather famous female in Paris asked me if I was not fright-fully annoyed by the type of very fascinating man who was deep-rootedly highly moral also. I said no—that, in fact I thanked God for him, and played with him as much as I could, as it gave one a chance to breathe and "cross one's legs!"

Even before Belle left Paris, she noted with unconvincing pique that "the damned bitch" had repeated this story at every social gathering she could. "I'm sorry to say its true," Belle repented half-heartedly.[138] Belle had just fanned the flames of her own reputation as sexually promiscuous—with men.

Billy was intrigued by the whole Marie Louise situation. He wanted more details from Bernard and demanded M.L.'s "name age and previous condition of servitude." Not only had Billy never met "the papoose," even though she lived in New York, he confessed he knew almost nothing about Belle's private life. She was always vague about whom she was seeing and where she was going. When Billy later met Marie Louise himself at a luncheon well lubricated with scotch, he reported to B.B., "I don't wonder at many things I've heard of last summer. However it's none of my business or game and so I shan't worry or think of it."[139]

Billy seemed to think Bernard's suspicions were correct. In any case, Marie Louise and Belle were often together over the next five or six years. If they were lovers, then Belle's ribald jokes about her sexual relations with men may have been a smoke screen or another way to hide in full view. Better, perhaps, to have a bad reputation as a promiscuous heterosexual woman than to be known as a lesbian. If they were not, Belle seemed unaffected by the rumors. It was not until 1932 that

Billy reported that "the papoose" was no longer Belle's "shadow and constant attendant."[140]

Belle's trip was cut short when Jack's wife suddenly took a turn for the worse. Ill with a sleeping sickness, she had lapsed into a coma. Belle wrote the Jack Morgans fearfully from Siena, pouring all of her anxiety and sympathy into the words that always seem so powerless at times like that. When Jessie Morgan passed away, Belle took the next available boat home, knowing that Jack would be heartbroken. She could not make it in time for the funeral but wanted to be in New York to comfort her friend.[141]

On the voyage home Belle went on the water wagon again and challenged another beau, Basil Howard, to join her.[142] She also used the time to contemplate her reunion with Bernard and the state of their relationship.

> Now then, I've only this to tell you—with the exception of your very vitriolic tongue about everyone-in-the-world (I'm sure including me!) dear B.B.—I do love you. And had I been big enough to surmount, or swallow in silence, that only-one thing this time, I could have made you feel my love rather deeply.[143]

But whatever that only-one thing was, it had apparently prevented them from resuming an affair, or from truly reconnecting.

Bernard complained to Billy about Belle's "husks and burrs," her inapproachability. Billy commiserated:

> I'm quite sure that even so you were able to talk more real stuff with her than with anyone else these several years past. You see, dear B.B., she plays hob with you because she puts her warm hand right about your heart—and thus suddenly makes you aware of that organ's existence—very upsetting it is, too, for the middle-aged scholar and "intellectual," to have his heart beats accelerated, to have his "spark advanced," for it makes his poor chassis hop about

> the bumps on the road in the most unpredictable manner—
> interferes with contemplation and disinterestedness. But
> just think! how damned lucky you have been to have got all
> stirred up that way. There's mighty few can do it![144]

This probably says more about Billy's feelings than about Belle and
Bernard. However, by that fall Belle had decided that she and Billy
were no longer in love, but that she still liked and admired him. The
following year Belle suggested that it was Billy's own sense of virtue
that made her keep her emotional distance, and she implored B.B. not
to discuss her lack of respectability with Billy. "His morals are his all
. . . don't try to impeach or shatter them."[145]

One thing Bernard had guessed correctly was that there was an
important man in Belle's life—one she was never to joke about or even
name in her correspondence to him. Once safely away, Belle confessed
that she was now trying to get rid of all of her men to be monogamous
with this mystery man. Her strategy of dating multiple men at once
had not worked, and in at least one case Belle was quite ashamed of
how much her rejection hurt a man.

> I'm cleaning up the messy battleground of my life for the
> past 8 or 9 years & trying to bury the dead neatly and in
> order. . . . I have a sudden virtuous-old-age urge to come
> clean and monogamous from now on. Personally I'd be
> grateful if God would exercise his omniscience and charity
> and completely paralyze me—No amount of resolutions are
> half as effective.[146]

At the age of forty-six, Belle was clearly still attracted and attractive to
men. The few surviving photographs of her from this period show
the effects of stress and time on her face. But her beauty still shone in
her energy and her spirit, the camera only capturing her face in
midexpression.

Since Belle never named or otherwise identified the man who
inspired this new resolution, we can only speculate who it was. One
possibility (and one whose identity she would surely want to keep from

Bernard) was an Italian prince, Amadeo Umberto Isabella Luigi Filippo Maria Giuseppe Giovanni, who would become Duke d'Aosta upon his father's death in 1931. Amadeo served in Mussolini's government. Belle's relationship with him would explain her defense of fascism and her reputation (already well deserved) for socializing with royalty. He was the grandson of the former king of Spain, also a Duke d'Aosta, and a cousin of King Victor Emmanuel III, of Italy.

Belle left no record of her romance with Amadeo, and it is impossible to know exactly when it would have taken place. Meta Harrsen, who worked with Belle at the Morgan Library in the 1930s and 1940s, recalled that when the duke died during the Second World War, Queen Elena sent the Italian ambassador to the Library with several pieces of jewelry he had left Belle. These included a dagger-shaped insignia with emeralds, rubies, and diamonds, which Harrsen often saw her wear on her winter turbans. According to Harrsen, d'Aosta also left Belle the contents of his London apartment, which included a pet tiger. (Belle apparently donated the tiger to the London Zoo.) Belle's rendition of this story to Meta never mentioned any engagement or wedding plans. But she had a Venetian lace wedding dress made in Paris, and Harrsen speculated that it may have been intended for marriage to her duke.[147] This romance might also explain Belle's positive image of fascism, which was supported by many of Italy's aristocrats, including Amadeo.

Whatever the reason, Belle was no longer falling all over herself to keep B.B. happy. Three weeks after she left, Bernard bitterly complained that she had not written a word since her departure. Her silence, however predictable and familiar, still had the power to pull him into depression.[148]

Belle returned to New York and immediately wanted to leave again. New York was blooming in the ever-increasing financial boom. New buildings, new businesses, new neighborhoods, everything was moving and growing and expanding. But for Belle it just meant dirt and noise and chaos. "It's just a huge noisy, grating and grinding machine." And she could not get used to it after her blissful (in hindsight) months in Europe.[149]

It may have been particularly uncomfortable that fall, as New York newspapers renewed their fixation on the Rhinelander case. The media scandal started in late 1924 when Leonard Kip Rhinelander, son of the wealthy real estate magnate Philip Rhinelander, was discovered to have married the middle-class, probably mixed-race woman he had been involved with for several years. All New Yorkers recognized the Rhinelander name; Belle knew several members and had done real estate business with Charles Rhinelander.[150]

But it was Leonard's bride who made the story a national scandal. Alice Beatrice Rhinelander, née Jones, probably had some black ancestry, just as Belle did. But her parents were both English immigrants; her mother was white and her father had been raised only by his white mother. Alice lived in a white neighborhood in the small town of New Rochelle, where her friends and neighbors knew or assumed that she was mixed race but did not object when she said she was white. She had lived largely outside of or in between racial categories, until her marriage threatened the name and reputation of one of New York's most prominent families.[151]

Within a few months of Belle's return, the long-awaited juried annulment trial commenced just to the north in the city of White Plains, Westchester County. Belle was mercifully (or perhaps conveniently) out of town as the tabloids and even mainstream newspapers splashed daily headlines and photographs of the trial across their front pages. Alice Rhinelander suddenly found herself labeled Negro, Negress, black, mulatto, quadroon, dusky, dark, colored. Her own lawyers decided to concede that she had some "colored blood in her veins" and focused instead on arguing that she had not hidden that fact from her husband. Interracial marriage was not illegal in New York, so Leonard's case rested on a charge of misrepresentation, claiming that Alice had represented herself as white. In the Harlem Renaissance writer Nella Larsen's *Passing*, the fictional characters who were confronted with a woman passing as white reflect on the legal and social implications of the Rhinelander case. What Belle might have thought about it can only be surmised. Even if she managed to escape the nearly six weeks of deliberation, she could not have been unaware of the case.

In trying to defend and save her marriage against the annulment suit

she believed her husband's family was forcing him to bring, Alice
Rhinelander found her love life a matter of public record as private letters were read before the court. She also partially disrobed before the
jury to prove that her husband, having had sex before their marriage,
should have seen that she was not white. Belle might have taken comfort in the jury's decision, however, especially if she paid attention to
the much overlooked argument it made about the definition of whiteness. Not only did the twelve white men deny Leonard Rhinelander
his annulment, but they reasoned—entirely against the judge's instructions and the legal point of the case—that Alice was not really black
any more than a gallon of water with a cup of whiskey in it was really
whiskey. Under that logic, Alice and Belle could both claim whiteness.
But Belle never mentioned the Rhinelander case, or the topic of racial
identity and the definition of blackness that it engendered.

Nor did Belle have significant connections with African Americans
in New York. Had Belle lived as an African American in New York, she
would surely have gravitated to the vibrant community of writers,
artists, musicians, and singers who launched the Harlem Renaissance
in the 1920s. Instead, she seems to have patronized the clubs and theaters of Harlem as a spectator, along with hundreds of other middle-
and upper-class white New Yorkers looking for entertainment. Her
only known link to the community was through Carl Van Vechten, a
white patron of several Harlem writers and artists.

In 1921 when Belle saw Charles Gilpin in one of his most celebrated roles as Eugene O'Neill's Emperor Jones, she deemed it "tremendously interesting from the psychological point of view—and the
chief part, the Emperor Jones, taken by a real (New York) darky—and
amazingly well done—really magnificent acting."[152] When she was a
child, had a black man won such acclaim for his acting skills in mainstream theater, she would certainly have been brought to the play, if
possible, or at least had him pointed out as an example of Negro
accomplishment and a success for "the race." After over two decades
of living as white, she removed herself from identification with blackness by calling the actor a "darky" at the same time that she praised his
acting skills.

By spring of 1926 Belle declared herself "on the ragged edge of prostration." She was drinking again; Prohibition seemed to have little effect on her access to alcohol. One afternoon after a "rousing and sousing" lunch seeing some friends off on the *Mauretania,* she impulsively spent $300 on several leaves from an illustrated Koran, and $100 on a gold-lettered seventeenth-century book of Muslim prayers. "I was sorter drunk at the time," she admitted, but she still loved her purchases and happily added them to her growing collection at home. Belle stumbled through the next few months alternately sick with colds and flus and partying with friends, as she made plans to return to Italy for "a last absolutely final fling at life." She invited Hyvernat to join her (he did not) and Bernard to come "play," but not for the whole time, because she had other dates.[153] She warned him,

> I look like Hell—
> wrinkles
> crows feet
> pimples
> old-fashioned hair
> no new clothes.

She also considered bringing Bobbie, by then almost seven years old. Would he be safe from fever in Venice at the height of summer? she asked Bernard. "[B]ut I forgot, you're not interested in children," she added pointedly.[154] Young Robert stayed behind that year.

On August 1 Belle landed in Naples and slowly made her way north to Venice, "purpling Italy with passion" all the way, or so Bernard heard. He stayed away, but had plans to see her toward the end of her trip in early September. He confided to Billy that he wished he had the guts to run away from Belle and their impending reunion. He wished it was Ivins coming to visit him instead of Belle: "dear Billee I love even the thought of you." But, as it was, B.B. and Belle would soon "meet in the flesh if not in the spirit."[155]

This trip was as close as Belle had come yet to living her dream. She did not seem to have business to do for the Library and spent the entire two months in Italy, most of it in Venice. And what she did most was study and see "things." Father Hyvernat gave her letters of introduction to the libraries in Venice, Naples, Ravenna, and Milan. Belle wrote teasing endearments, sending "My Passionate LOVE to all the Holy Fathers! And to you—a most reverent kiss on the hand." Later she promised, "[M]y head and both knees are bowed in filial submission."[156]

Once in Venice, Belle stayed at the Grand Hotel in Venice, on the main canal. She first tried to take in all of the city at once—it had been sixteen years since she had been there with Bernard, Mary, and Geoffrey Scott. But she made herself ill again. She hated San Marco's dazzling, treasure-filled interior: gold everywhere, thankfully muted by age, mosaic floors, beautiful, wild, and almost Escher-esque, and chamber after chamber filled with statues, paintings, frescoes. "Is it old age?" she asked B.B. "I loathed it"—except for the glittering Pala d'Oro, a large medieval gold enamel, and the stones. "Gawd damn the rest." Maybe it would be different if she could ever see it without "1000 German & American" tourists. But somehow the crowds seemed part of the whole experience of a church crowded with examples of art and other plunder from multiple periods and cultures.[157]

Then she discovered the Lido, a long strip of land between Venice and the open sea, where she found quiet and sanity. After a few days of rest there, she was able to settle into a routine. Every day Belle visited the Santa Maria dei Miracoli, a small simple church tucked into one of Venice's many hidden corners. The Santa Maria is about as unlike San Marco as an Italian church gets. Its quiet beauty and soft, soothing pale marble walls invite tourists to put away their guidebook and itinerary and just sit in silent meditation. But she also loved the Frari, a large medieval stone-and-brick building with plain, unfrescoed pillars and walls, then huge ornate multistory baroque marble façades and an array of tombs and paintings by masters like Titian, Bellini, and Donatello.

And every day she spent two hours at San Lazzaro, an Armenian monastery and former leper colony on its own small island. The "fathers" there clustered about her as she worked, and she finally learned their schedule and came in between their hours of duties and prayers so that she would not disturb their devotions. She was less respectful of the assistant librarian who, she said, "spends all his time looking at my drooping breasts . . . his eyes glued to my nipples every moment. I loathe him." Still, the collection included several thousand Armenian manuscripts, some from the eighth and ninth centuries, as well as many other rare books. Belle was rapt. She had always loved Middle Eastern illuminated manuscripts, and the Morgan Library had only a handful. In the next few years Belle added several more Armenian gospels to the Morgan collection.[158]

Belle had hoped to travel with Bernard alone, but acquiesced gracefully when he insisted that Nicky accompany them. She realized that he was nervous about the visit, and it was now well established that Bernard's stomach problems were made worse by stress. In fact, their travel plans were almost canceled when his stomach acted up. Bernard thought it was because he and Belle had been exchanging "insulting and vilifying caresses" in their letters. One of hers was so bad he tore it up.[159]

Belle was also still tracking the I Tatti–Harvard deal behind the scenes, and was thrilled when an agreement was reached. She sent Bernard a long letter of congratulations and immediately moved on to her next suggestion:

> In my deeply-considered opinion your name must be connected with it—It simply must be known as your foundation. . . . The thing I Tatti stands for—no class room stuff etc. etc. but culture in the real sense of the word—a soaking in of an atmosphere, which means to me more than anything all the consolidated Universities of the world can give.[160]

Her only complaint was that Berenson had not made her "one of the high muckie mucks" and that she would thus not have an excuse to go to Italy every year. But Belle may have been oblivious of Bernard's interpretation of her actions and words. She did not seem to realize, for example, how much she was the cause of his discomfort. She offered to come cuddle him at I Tatti and then make her rounds of Tuscany by herself.[161] Belle particularly wanted to revisit Ravenna with him, which she had last seen with him in 1910.

Bernard recovered enough to resume their plans, and he and Nicky toured Ravenna with her. Belle was energized and ready to see anything Bernard wanted. She was also full of dealers' gossip and confided to Nicky that Bernard had been shamefully manipulated by the Duveens on his last trip. Duveen knew that Hamilton would have to return much of his collection, Belle insisted, and used the Berensons' stay to be sure the pictures would sell well. Bernard feigned skepticism when Nicky passed on this bit of information, but he knew perfectly well that that's what had happened.[162]

The gossipers all wanted to know who slept with whom on that trip. Nicky Mariano reported that she roomed with Belle at least three times. Belle carefully explained to a very curious Billy Ivins that Nicky had stayed with Bernard. Whether or not Belle and Bernard were still physically intimate on this trip seems almost beside the point.[163] She had long since decided that sex was "a crust very near the surface." "I only realized about a year ago, why your damned old sex gets all het-up, and I'm sure its because I throw it all off, sorter sweat it out—in seeing things I like, in interest in the job and all sorts of things and people connected with it."[164]

Bernard and Nicky then accompanied Belle to Genoa. Her own ship had been delayed, and she had taken passage on a new Italian ship, the *Roma*, which was making its maiden voyage. Again Bernard and Belle argued over fascism. Belle could not help being impressed by the "fascisti" boat, which was feted by a large party before it left, with endless champagne and countless Italian officials on board. Her rooms were large and full of red silk and velvet. Nonetheless, she complained, so much work was still being done on it that there were more workmen than passengers on the ship. The *Roma* survived a storm and arrived safely in port in New York, although it did not make the record time Mussolini had hoped for. The American papers were full of stories about this newest and best Italian liner, and Belle sent clippings to Bernard.[165]

Leo Olschki once again complained that she did not come to

see him while she was in Florence. Someone told him that "Miss Greene will never come neither to my Library nor to my Bookstore" and his honor was deeply offended. Miss Greene declined to send an answer.[166]

Now, with a budget and funds at her command, Belle's purchasing power increased. But when the Earl of Leicester indicated that he might be willing to part with four extraordinary manuscripts in his collection, for the right price, Belle sent Jack to handle the negotiations. After obtaining photographs and preparing a report on their value and provenance, she sent him off with the charge to buy. Jack balked at the high price, and negotiations were not forthcoming; the seller didn't really need the money and would keep the books if he did not feel their value was met. Morgan went home to consider but returned the next day, confessing, "My librarian told me she wouldn't dare spend so much of my money, but just the same I wouldn't be able to face her if I went home without the manuscripts."[167]

The year 1927 was one of work. Belle rarely went out, working at the Library until midnight four nights a week. She had become "rude and cross" to her friends, but Billy reported that the "Morganian Sibyl of Murray Hill" still smiled on him.[168] So quiet was the year that she was shocked to hear that Billy Ivins was reporting scandal about her again: "I've done nothing—seen no one—neither loved (or even 'affected') anything nor any one for so long—that I'm sure I've lost all technique for being even a quasi-human person again." She told Bernard, "[Y]ou will doubtless be my Omega as you are my Alpha."[169]

But the big project at the Library was the building of the new annex, which expanded its space considerably. Belle played a significant role in planning the general layout for the interior, especially the exhibit space. She visited other institutions for lighting ideas and had the final say on wall coverings and curtains. By the spring of 1928 she was moaning that the "damned thing" was killing her. When the building was done, she professed to hate the exterior; she delightedly quoted art historian Charles Loeser, who said it looked as if it was intended as her tomb, similar to the Grant Monument. Belle swore she would rot on the sidewalk before allowing her body to be entombed there.[170]

Father Hyvernat fell ill in France, where he was living at Jack Morgan's expense, editing and publishing the oldest-known version of the Gospels. Belle was so busy that she had her secretaries send her usual profusions of love to Hyvernat instead of writing herself. But she sent him a token that had been blessed for his recovery.[171]

In 1928 Eric Millar, of the Department of Manuscripts at the British Museum, spent two months at the Morgan Library reassembling an illuminated book that had been cut apart and rebound incorrectly in the early nineteenth century. (Millar later thanked Belle for her kindness, which made his visit "one of the most pleasantest and most inspiring two months" that he had ever spent.) This book was purchased in 1927 from the Holdford estate, along with the Reims Gospel. The latter is still considered one of the finest Carolingian manuscripts at the Morgan Library and was one of Belle's favorites. Its gold-ink text and brilliant, deep-hued illuminations also rank it among the "Oh My!" books that delight lay visitors as well as scholars and experts.[172]

But as soon as she could get away, Belle retreated to Switzerland with Bobbie, mostly trying to regain her health at a series of resorts and cures, followed by a few weeks of travel throughout southern France. She returned with a renewed sense of self and health (although, she assured Berenson, "just as UGLY" as ever), having (mostly) kept her promise to Morgan and other friends to avoid people and excitement. She did, of course, see some manuscripts and art, but mainly she relaxed, walked, and sought that escape from work and urban life that modern Americans have come to seek regularly in their vacations. She took long walks through postcard vistas of mountains and glaciers in Switzerland, and she found Avignon, France, divine and enchanting, especially under a moonlit sky.[173]

But she did not find time on this trip to visit with Berenson, who might easily have arranged to meet her in Paris in early September. He sent his response to her snub in a letter that awaited her upon her return. She pretended not to understand its meaning, "save that it bites, snarls and scratches and icily terminates with 'Cordially B. Berenson' or something like that."[174]

The new sense of health Belle had found in Europe did not last many months. Within two months she had developed what would be another series of bad colds. Her increased responsibilities at the Library started to wear on her previously unflagging energies. Around her, Manhattan was still riding high as the buildings and the stock market climbed ever closer to the clouds. Belle hated the construction and even the skyscrapers. She was sick of New York and all such cities, complaining that she had not even seen the sky since leaving Europe. More than ever she longed to escape and live in the country, across the Atlantic, anywhere quiet where she could be surrounded by both nature and art. Still, she was profiting on the stock market—her path to that dream of retirement. Had she picked up on some of the fears that it could not continue to rise endlessly?

13

A WOMAN OF A CERTAIN AGE

I don't believe that any female ought to be allowed to linger in any official position after 50.

—Belle Greene, 1914 (age 34)[1]

I distinctly like being old—honestly. There are heaps of benefits and not half as many losses as I had expected. Howsumever I admit that I should love to stay at the present age and in the present physical condition, feeble as it may be compared to yesteryears—for about 40 years more! There is so much doing— and going-to-be-done throughout this world.

—Belle Greene, 1936 (age 55)[2]

THE YEAR 1929 BEGAN like many others. Early in the year Belle was sick with a series of colds and flus, and under continual stress from her work at the Library. She wrote to the object of one of her newer flirtations, Eric Millar, that her life was "even more hectic than

that of a cork in Niagara Falls," a favorite expression of hers.[3] Millar
was a slightly younger man, who worked in the manuscripts department of the British Museum and had published a two-volume study of
early English manuscripts in the 1920s.[4] He was not the only man with
whom she conducted a "scandalous" correspondence—when she
could find the time to write—but he was typical of her taste in men in
the 1930s. Belle seems to have discarded artists, aristocrats, and stockbrokers (what good was a stockbroker after 1929?) in favor of her ever-
increasing fondness for scholars and other learned men. Eric Millar,
Arthur Hind, of the prints department at the British Museum, and
Adolph Goldschmidt, a German art historian who taught for several
years at Harvard and New York University in the 1930s, were all among
her "pets" that decade. Each shared with her, when he visited New
York, "innocently amusing times" in Harlem or downtown Manhattan.[5]

Continuing her habit of using travel as a curative, Belle actually went
to Europe twice in 1929, first returning to Avignon, France, in February and then to Sweden in August. The first trip was unusual:
February was not her usual travel time. But Avignon's medieval history
and gothic churches provided ample opportunity for sightseeing and
perhaps purchasing as well as recuperating. The Sweden trip, although
it may also have involved vacation time, was primarily for business.
When she returned in early October, she brought with her an early
tenth-century illuminated manuscript of the Four Gospels that she
had purchased for $50,000, and an Italian Venetian Bible from 1471
priced at $18,000.[6]

That fall Jack Morgan was also making purchases. He brought A
Portrait of a Moor now attributed to the school of Tintoretto but then
listed as a work of the master himself. The near-Tintoretto hangs today
in the West Room of the original Morgan Library, the former office of
J. P. Morgan and Jack. The identity of the subject is not known, but he
is a beige-skinned man with short, curling hair, dark almond-shaped
eyes, and a thin mustache. Presumed to be an ambassador to the
Venetian court for which Tintoretto painted portraits, the subject looks
remarkably like a former American commercial agent to Siberia,
Richard Greener.[7]

On Thursday, October 24, the stock market crashed, rallied (in part because a consortium of bankers, led by the house of Morgan pumped hundreds of millions of dollars into the market), and then crashed again the following week, not to recover for over a decade. Rumors flew of stockbrokers jumping to their deaths. Some did do so, although none of the Morgans and their ilk. It was generally not the financiers who lost everything overnight; it was the more modest stockbrokers and the smaller investors.[8] Like Belle.

Belle had witnessed terrible panics, runs, and recessions before. And it was not immediately clear that the impact of this crash would extend for and define the next decade. Heavily invested in the market since at least 1913, Belle must have suffered terrible financial losses. For the first year or two she probably waited the market out, as she had before. She had never lived off of her stock earnings, holding them as savings toward her retirement, only drawing on them occasionally for a trip or an unexpected expense. In the wake of losing her savings, however, she was fortunate to have a secure job with a sizable income. Jack Morgan, his partners, and many of their peers had suffered enormous financial losses. But their personal wealth was so great that it cushioned them from feeling the devastation of the economic crash that would soon ripple out and affect a nation of workers and their dependents.

To add insult to injury, Belle da Costa Greene turned fifty years old in November 1929, a landmark that only her mother and siblings would have noticed, had she allowed them to speak of it. She continued to deduct a solid decade or more from her age, telling friends and census officials alike that she was nearing her fortieth birthday. Older men were no longer quite so appealing.[9]

But first and foremost in Belle's mind that year was her work. In 1929 and 1930 she was compiling a five-year report on the status and progress of the library in its first half decade as a public institution. It was the culmination of her struggles since 1924 to adjust to working for a board of trustees, having the added responsibilities of being open to the public, and the increased use of the reading room. Throughout the year, Belle and her staff worked at a breakneck pace gathering information, compiling statistics, checking facts, writing, and editing.

There is some evidence that before October 1929 Belle was beginning to plan for her replacement. In 1927 she told Bernard that she
would be ready to leave by 1932. She wanted to find two men to
replace her—she preferred an English director with an American assistant. Belle believed that by then she would have enough money to set
up trusts for her mother and Bobbie for the rest of their lives. If there
was nothing left for herself, she would marry "some damn old rich
slob" and live in Europe. On a more practical level, she solicited advice
from her friend George Parker Winship on what kind of person she
should look for to head the Library in her place, telling him her "two
man" plan. Winship, who had left the John Carter Brown Library in
1915 to head the Widener Library at Harvard University at Belle's recommendation, now returned the favor. He made a list of qualities the
director must have (be pleasing to Jack Morgan and trusted by other
board members) and what they ought to be (good judge of people and
things, careful buyer, natural conservator, supportive of scholarship),
as well as other roles that Belle's replacement would play ("tactful
bouncer," good manager, and neat housekeeper). Impossible to find in
one person, of course, but the director could have two or three of the
"ought" list if the assistant director had the others. The only absolute
necessity, Winship professed, was a "personality that inspires confidence." Belle was impressed.[10]

Professionally speaking, it would have been an appropriate time to
retire. The Morgan Library had become what she had always wanted
it to be: a leading and permanent collection of illuminated manuscripts
that had nurtured the development of American scholarship on the
field and allowed public access to its treasures. In her report Belle
detailed some of the 46 illuminated or textual manuscripts, 19 leaves,
over 500 letters, documents, or draft manuscripts, almost 5,000
printed books, plus drawings, etchings, and mezzotints that the Morgan Library had purchased in its first five years as a public institution.
The Reims Gospels, the facsimile publication of the illuminated Coptic manuscripts, and the purchase of the Rembrandt etchings all
received special mention. But most important were the testaments to
the significance of the Morgan collection, and its activity in making its
treasures accessible to the public.

Belle confirmed with several leading scholars that there had not been any colleges or universities in the country that offered study in early books, or any leading American scholars in the subject prior to the opening of Mr. Morgan's Library.[11] The Pierpont Morgan Library was now, she proclaimed, one of the most significant collections in the country and perhaps the world, thanks in large part to the younger Mr. Morgan. She must have been particularly proud of the scholar who called it the "Bibliothèque Nationale of America" for students of manuscripts. This was exactly what she had envisioned for it in 1909, and what she hoped its transformation into a public institution would encourage.[12]

Belle's report also highlighted the New York Public Library exhibits. In addition, William Ivins testified that the Morgan's loans to the 1924 exhibit called "The Arts of the Book" at the Metropolitan Museum of Art had single-handedly provided "an unrivalled and complete historic series of books and manuscripts," representing the artistic development of the book over eight centuries. New Yorkers were now able to see for themselves "the fact that their city contained one of the great collections of beautiful books in the world."[13]

Once published, the report was distributed to libraries and museums throughout the world. It rated notice in the local press and interest throughout the art and book world. The *New York Herald Tribune* praised the report, "written with learning and grace by Miss Belle da Costa Greene, the director," and summarized its listing of acquisitions, scholarly publications, and the history of the Library itself.[14] Praise came also from the colleagues and peers who best understood the amount of work that went into such a publication, not to mention the actual work of the Library that the report summarized. Ruth Granniss of the Grolier Club told Belle that everyone had good things to say about the new Library. Did Belle realize, Miss Granniss enthused, what the new accessibility of the Library's resources meant for the whole country?[15] She did.

But by the time the report was published, in 1930, Belle's financial situation had become too precarious for her to consider immediate retirement. She could not afford to retire, given her stock market losses. She put Winship's letter away. With her latest major project behind her, Belle tried to catch up on her correspondence and other work at the Library. She was too tired to make another trip to Europe in 1930. Instead, she caught up on news of Bernard when their mutual friend Rose Nichols spent a night talking with her about him. Nichols was a landscape designer who had been part of Belle's Boston circles since 1910. Rose left for Europe the next day with a gift for Bernard from Belle: a Japanese bottle for smelling salts. Belle went to Wyoming for a rural vacation.[16]

By 1930 Belle was starting to have serious health problems. Exactly what they were, she never specified. But her illnesses were no longer merely colds and flus. She confided to her "Most Holy & Reverend 'Petit-Saint-Pére'" Hyvernat that she was "exhausted, disheartened . . . and skinny." She began seeing more doctors, including a nerve special- ist and a surgeon. Each warned that she was heading for a "crash" of her own, so Belle was determined to get fat and healthy. She wasn't afraid of dying, she said, at least that would bring peace and quiet. But she did fear becoming an "under-sexed nervous wreck," one of those neurotic "wimmin" she always complained about.[17]

No one else seemed to see these unwanted characteristics in her. Bryson Burroughs of the Metropolitan Museum visited Belle at the Library in 1931. He reported back to William Ivins that he had seen the "Lady Directress" and described her as a "grand old sport! No sob- stuff about her." Belle did not seem to be going anywhere, but talked about her planned travel and activities. "[S]he's full of pep and only shows slightly, in her face and manner, the excitements and worries she's been through."[18] Burroughs may have been referring to any num- ber of worries. It should be noted that he never identified Belle by name, but there were no other female directors of such institutions in New York.

Despite her physical and psychological concerns, Belle was doing relatively well financially. Even without her investments to fall back on, she was able to send Bobbie to private boarding schools and keep her servants employed. Around her, unemployment rates were sky- rocketing, families were losing their homes, and the public presence of poverty was invading even the tony Murray Hill District in which she lived and worked. By 1932, however, she had to move out of that neighborhood to a less expensive flat, which she described as an "enlarged railroad car." Her new home was almost two miles north of the Library, a block east of Central Park. Belle complained to Bernard that if the present financial situation continued she would have to "sit on the front steps of the Library with a patch and a tin cup."[19] Homeless families slept in public parks and unemployed men begged for money on the city's sidewalks, but Belle was in no danger of joining their ranks, and she knew it. While she was forced to cut back and downsize her budget, and no doubt felt the loss of accustomed luxuries, she had the resources to weather the Depression.

The impact of the economic downturn on her immediate and extended family is more difficult to assess. In 1930 or 1931 Ethel moved back in with Belle. Her husband, George Oakley, does not appear to have joined her; he may have had relocate to find work. Ethel continued to teach high school. Louise was still living in Ithaca with her husband, Frederick Martin, whose Institute for Speech Therapy had become part of Ithaca College. They probably also had to cut back but were financially secure. Teddy and her second husband, Robert M. Harvey, were still living in Paxtang, Pennsylvania. He was a salesman at a printing firm, and she was raising their seven-year-old daughter.[20]

Members of Belle's extended family who were not living as white did not fare as well. Belle's cousin Henry Grant, for example, was still living in D.C. in 1930, following the family trade of teaching music. His wife was a singer. Their son Henry L. Grant was in Brooklyn with his wife, Sarah, and a son. Although the Brooklyn Henry worked as a candy store clerk in 1920, he was unemployed in 1930, probably one of the tens of thousands who found their jobs disappearing overnight. Sarah supported the family working in a toy factory.[21]

The Depression hit the Library, as well. Jack had provided a sizable endowment to fund the Library, but acquisitions had to be approved by the entire board of trustees. In practice, Belle appears to have had a budget she was free to use at her own discretion, but large purchases needed to go through the trustees. During the years following the crash, the board was understandably reluctant to authorize sizable acquisitions.[22] Belle was often frustrated not to be able to dominate sales anymore as she had in the 1910s and 1920s. In 1932 she had to advise a friend who was hoping to sell her collection that an auction would be disastrous, since no one was buying and prices had plummeted. In 1934 the situation was made worse by the levying of income taxes on the Library, which Belle bitterly complained were eating up their already dwindling earnings.[23]

Belle compensated by shifting her focus to developing programs that increased the academic standing of the Library. She began to organize more lecture series and graduate courses, including a lecture course given by Charles Rufus Morey, chair of the Department of Art and Archaeology, and Erwin Panofsky, a former student of Adolph Goldschmidt's, who had just begun teaching at Princeton University. Arthur Hind, now keeper of prints and drawings at the British Museum, gave two talks in 1931 on the Rembrandt etchings acquired in the late 1920s. Laurence Binyon, former keeper of prints and drawings at the British Museum, lectured on William Blake in 1935. Such events, often coordinated with exhibitions, were highly successful. With the new addition completed, the Library was able to mount twenty-six exhibitions between 1930 and 1935. Scholarly use of the collections in the reading room increased from just over 150 visits in 1930 to almost 1,000 in 1935; public attendance at exhibitions jumped from 2,500 in 1930 to over 15,000 in 1935.[24]

The Morgan Library also continued to lend its unique books and manuscripts to other institutions. Never comfortable when her treasures were out of her control, Belle saw her worst fears realized when the manuscript of Sir Walter Scott's *Guy Mannering,* one of J. P. Morgan's earliest acquisitions, was stolen from the Columbia University exhibit in 1932. When Belle found out about the theft, she leaped into action. In quick order she contacted trustees Junius and Henry Morgan (Jack was out of town), called the insurance company, stepped up security at the Library just in case, and canceled Visitors Day that week. She did not immediately tell any of her employees what happened, and it was several months before the story went to the newspapers. The manuscript was quietly returned six months after it disappeared.[25]

By the time of the next published report, in 1935, the impact of spending cuts was clear. Belle had been able to acquire only half the number of preprint manuscripts and leaves that she had in the preceding five-year period, and only a fraction of the rare books, manuscripts, and original documents. On the other hand, she had acquired over ten thousand photographs and one thousand slides of manuscripts, artwork, illustrations, and other visual reproductions of use to scholars.[26] These were amassed through a combination of purchases and gifts as Belle appealed to friends and colleagues at private and public collections to provide her with photos or slides of their items.

One enthusiastic respondent to her pleas was Bernard, who had long been building his own photograph library. Belle and Bernard were still corresponding, a few times a year now, rather than a few times a month. Belle's letters always included regards to Mary and affection to Nicky and some indication of "purple love" or other form of devotion to Bernard.[27] The last embers of their passion had long since cooled, but the memory of what she had once felt for him kept a very real fondness alive.

But her few, long letters were concerned primarily with business. When his 1932 *Italian Pictures of the Renaissance* came out, Belle was startled to find that Bernard had revamped his attribution system and had changed his opinion on some of the Morgan Library's and Belle's own pieces.[28] Belle demanded details. Why was the Castagno-Botticelli now Pollaiuolo? Why did he think that another panel was not by Bellini? And above all, she chided, his new attribution of a Fra Filippo Lippi as now "in the school of" would have saved the Library a lot of money if he hadn't attested that it was "unsurpassed" as a Fra Filippo Lippi in his letter to the Duveens, from whom the Library had purchased it. With deceptive nonchalance, Belle wondered whether there were pictures of the painting taken before the Duveens acquired it. Such photos would document any changes that had been made in the name of restoration to make a would-be masterpiece more salable. Belle knew that the Duveens and other dealers had made similar "restorations" in other cases. But she did not pursue the matter, satisfying herself with calling Berenson a "wretched Great Man."[29]

Despite the economic difficulties, Belle was able to make several trips to Italy in the 1930s. In the summer of 1932 she even took a vacation. Belle decided to ignore her financial situation and bring thirteen-year-old Bobbie to Italy. Her health and exhaustion demanded a break. Her main purpose was the restorative sea voyage, but she wanted to take Bobbie to Venice to show him around, and then go to the beach for a few weeks to relax. As she planned her itinerary, she fretted that the Grand Hotel was now beyond her means—in fact, the whole plan was beyond her means, but she needed to get away, and Bobbie had never seen her beloved Italy.[30]

The boat trip was as relaxing as she had hoped, and once they reached Italy, it became a "local," stopping at almost every port for several hours. Belle and Bobbie did end up staying at the Grand Hotel for almost a week, giving the youth a taste of Venice at the height of luxury on the Grand Canal. Then they traveled south to meet the boat in Genoa, stopping several times along the way. I Tatti was not one of the stops, and Bernard was not on Belle's itinerary. She explained that she needed to recuperate her "frayed body, mind and nerves" on the voyage, and the journey through Italy was for her nephew's sake.[31]

Bobbie was boarding at the equivalent of high school at Malcolm Gordon School in Garrison-on-the-Hudson, near Poughkeepsie, New York.[32] It was a small and very exclusive school: in 1933 the graduating class consisted of six students, and Eleanor Roosevelt spoke at the ceremony. Belle's co-worker Meta Harrsen archly noted that the school administrators there would not play favorites, which Harrsen thought the young boy sorely needed. There are precious few clues to Robert's childhood, but this one seems to indicate that he had become too accustomed to privilege and entitlement—a common enough problem with the first generation of a newly well-to-do family. Bobbie's adolescence was apparently a bumpy one, but there are only vague references to trouble, with no specific information about why or what kind.[33]

In 1932 Bobbie performed in the one-act play *The Marriage Proposal*, which Malcolm Gordon students presented, along with some other entertainment, at the Amateur Comedy Club. As a parent and patron of the school, Belle supported the students' annual theatrical productions. The social status of the parents and other patrons led to annual notices in the *New York Times*.[34] After a few years at Malcolm Gordon, Robert had developed high academic aspirations. By 1934 he was planning to apply to Harvard, which even his doting aunt worried was a bit too lofty a goal.

As the Morgan Library director, Miss Greene continued to be a powerful figure in the New York art world. When the Metropolitan Museum hired a new director (Herbert E. Winlock) and elected a new president (William Sloane Coffin), Belle took on the task of "teaching" them "the way they should go." Belle's new assistant Meta Harrsen noted that both gentlemen were frequently at the Library for that service. Belle had also informally advised the trustees of the Frick Library as they set up their institution on the basis of the collections of Henry Clay and Helen Frick.[35] In 1933 Belle was working hard with a number of assistants on an exhibit of illuminated manuscripts from the Morgan Library at the New York Public Library, and a catalogue of that exhibit. While purchases may have slowed during the Depression, the activities of the Morgan Library certainly did not.[36]

Time magazine reviewed the exhibit, paying close attention to the "dark vivacious woman" who had guarded the "Morgan Treasures" for over twenty years. The writer noted that Librarian Greene had "managed to keep her early history to herself" but suggested that she was of "Portuguese-Virginia ancestry." Others suggested New Orleans, Spain, Latin America, or the Caribbean, though Portuguese-Virginia (Belle's own story) was the most common theory repeated in media coverage of Belle Greene. But many also noted that she was secretive about her origins—one report called her private life "almost as cloistered as that of a nun." A 1932 feature article described her as "of slight medium height, with fluffy brown hair, gray eyes and vivacious, smiling expression," and mentioned that "she shrinks from personal publicity." A 1949 *Time* article suggested that she had been born abroad, perhaps in Portugal. Rumors about her ancestry thus entered the public record in a manner that was fairly obtuse and indirect.[37]

Belle literally collapsed after the illuminated manuscript exhibit was mounted. This physical crash came after a year of not only hard work but personal loss. In 1933 Belle's sister Louise unexpectedly died of complications from influenza at the age of fifty-three. In Ithaca, Louise was remembered as the wife of the director of the Martin Institute for Speech Correction. Her own accomplishments included competitive golfing and Latin scholarship, some of which she may have gained at the Morgan and under Belle's tutelage. She was particularly known for her expertise on Latin manuscripts. She and her husband, Frederick, her obituary reported, had traveled widely and amassed a valuable collection of antiques and medieval and Asian art.[38] There is no record of the nature of Belle's relationship with Louise after the Martins moved to Ithaca, but their shared interests and familial connection kept them close. Louise's body was brought back to Belle's home for burial. The family held a small funeral at the St. Thomas Church chapel with only a few friends present. One was Meta Harrsen, who notified Bernard of Belle's unexpected loss. Meta called Louise "an extraordinarily fine and gifted woman," a rare compliment from one of Belle's friends to one of her family.[39]

Belle's collapse may have been a delayed reaction to this combination of stress at work and personal grief. Or her health may have been a continuing problem as well. For any or all of those reasons, Belle seems to have been preparing for retirement by the mid-1930s. When the trustees began searching for an assistant director in 1932, they appear to have had the idea in mind that the new hire would serve in that position for a few years before taking over the directorship. Several men—only men—were considered, and in 1934 the Library hired Philip Hofer as its first assistant director. Hofer was a graduate of Harvard and curator of the New York Public Library's Spencer Collection. He was also a well-known book collector, focusing on German, Iberian, and Italian early print books. Hofer donated one of his own items, a thirteenth-century Latin Bible, to the Morgan Library in 1935.[40] Curt Bühler was also hired in 1934, in part to replace Ada Thurston, who was retiring after twenty-eight years at the Morgan Library. Thurston continued to work at the Library for a while, producing a checklist of its incunabula. Eventually, she retired to Poughkeepsie, near her alma mater, Vassar College. Belle publicly noted that Ada's value to the Morgan Library was demonstrated by the need to distribute her duties among three different departments.[41]

Hofer probably believed that he was in line for Belle's position. As early as 1932 Bernard heard a report that Hofer was succeeding Belle. By then Bernard had heard so little from Belle that he appealed to William Ivins for an explanation. Belle would not answer him, Bernard said. (And it was true that she rarely wrote him now unless she was planning a trip or was in Europe.) Ivins assured him that "the Morgantuan Arabella" was "still in command" at the Library. When Hofer was hired, Bernard sent him a congratulatory note: "I could envy you for many reasons, not least of all that you are brought in continual [contact] with the most vitalizing person I have ever known."[42]

In the summer of 1934 Belle went alone to France to rest her "tired old bones" at a beach resort in La Baule and to do some business in Paris and London. To her dismay, she found Paris dismal and bitter, full of radicalism and communism, rude servants and high prices, and practically empty of tourists. But London was bustling with business and energy. Idly hoping to meet up with Bernard, she wrote to him from La Baule and London but neglected to mail either letter until she was back in New York. Perhaps he would come to New York, she suggested, "before I pass out of old age."[43]

He would not. Mary was ill with a number of ailments: rheumatism, infections, bladder problems. The diagnoses varied: Bernard thought she was a hypochondriac, Nicky described a mild case of manic depression, and Mary offered physical descriptions like "glandular blood poisoning in the groin." In fact, she had come very close to dying in 1932 but had recovered.[44] She was never herself again, however, and although Bernard still traveled a bit, he spent most of his time at I Tatti, working slowly, being near Mary. And Belle, while still a beloved memory, was no longer reason enough for him to go to New York, if she ever had been. Bernard was now relying on mutual friends—Meta Harrsen, William Ivins, and a new young friend, Daniel V. Thompson—to keep him updated on Belle's doings.

But Ivins, still at the Metropolitan Museum, seemed to be distancing himself from Belle. Now widowed and living with his daughter,

Ivins remained good friends with Bernard, however, and the two men sprinkled their continued correspondence with references to her. For example, Billy reported that Miss Greene had returned from a boat trip to San Francisco with manicured finger nails, which she kept long for several years in what he considered a Chinese fashion. Ivins was now finding Belle "most polite and horribly insulting," and he expected that she was critical of his own scholarship. Ivins and Berenson were also both skeptical of Belle's fixed loyalty to Englishmen.[45]

For Ivins a mix of both personal and professional jealousies were apparent. He scoffed when Belle entertained Arthur Hind, of the British Museum's Department of Prints and Drawings, for three weeks, "providing dinners and dames and parties for his delectation." This was the kind of attention Belle had once paid to Billy, but she also was now caught in an academic dispute over approaches to the subject of prints, which was the field of both Hind and Ivins.[46] Billy assured Bernard there had not been an actual split between them. However, he resented "the "Sachses and Greenes of the World . . . the Fogg and Morgan Library crowds" for what he viewed as their partiality to European scholars over American ones, and their emulation of traditional approaches to art and scholarship at the cost of innovation. Berenson was "inevitably and unavoidably American" in Billy's mind and thus exempt from his contempt of the Euro-centrism of the American art world. Yet a few years later Belle invited Billy to give a series of lectures at the Morgan Library on Renaissance illustration, which were later published.[47]

Although Belle no longer occupied his daily thoughts, Bernard still wanted to be kept informed. In 1933 he wrote to Belle thanking her for a letter and telling her that a mutual friend had given him good news about Belle's continued health, happiness, and ribald talk. "Temps da jades. How far away and long ago—if only it were so! The damn fact is it's all so near. Yours, B.B." But two years later Bernard sighed that he had "no recent news of her at all, at all."[48]

He soon heard from her when Belle returned to Europe in 1935. She wrote to Bernard several times, and this time even remembered to mail the letters in a timely manner. However, she did not reach Italy to see B.B., promising to try again the next summer, if the political situation allowed. Bernard still traveled a bit with Nicky, but his old practices of spending more time in Paris hotels than at I Tatti were over.

Bernard was not the only one feeling cut off by Belle's propensity to ignore personal correspondence. Adolph Goldschmidt, the German art historian who had taught at Harvard and become friends with Belle, was now coming to teach for a year at New York University. She had fallen in love with him in 1928 while he was at Harvard—a harmless crush, she told B.B, because of his age. Belle was attracted to Goldschmidt's intellect "unhampered by any 'isms,'" his memory, and his "kris kringle" humor. But Goldschmidt wrote to Meta Harrsen when planning his 1936 trip to New York since Belle was "too high" to write to directly. Belle got the hint and replied to her friend herself.[49]

Before Goldschmidt's arrival in New York, Belle visited him in Berlin in the summer of 1936, where he introduced the seventeen-year-old Robert to sauerkraut, wurst, and beer.[50] Goldschmidt departed for New York, leaving Belle and Bobbie to stay in his apartment in Berlin with his housekeeper, a servant, and a library full of art books. They were lucky to have such a place to stay that year. Berlin was filling with tourists in anticipation of the Olympic Games. Before Belle left, the African American runner Jessie Owens had won three of his four gold medals, dashing Adolf Hitler's hopes to use the games to prove German Aryan superiority and Nazi claims of nonwhite inferiority. Belle mentioned the Olympics only to complain about the crowds.[51]

Belle did not make good on her promise to Berenson to visit Italy on that trip.[52] But she wrote to him from Berlin and invited him to meet her in Salzburg. She, too, still retained a sentimental fondness for her first love, even if she no longer tried to maintain close contact. After several weeks in Berlin, Belle continued her tour of Germany and Austria, seeing the museums and libraries and doing some business. Bernard was waiting in Salzburg when she arrived, probably with Nicky in tow. Neither left a record of their reunion, except for Bernard's injured memory that Belle had not allowed him to meet her nephew. Belle later wrote that she hoped to see him and even travel with him again [53]

After Bernard departed, Belle got down to business, entering into deep negotiations with a very business-minded representative of Salzburg's St. Peter's Church, one Jacobus Reimer, O.S.B. (Belle had, she said, her own way of interpreting those initials). Belle described the encounter:

> [T]hen ensued a game of verbal "tag"! He assured me, by all the signs of the Cross, that noone since the time of the Swarzenski publication had seen it, by command of the Order—it being their most precious possession. That it was kept in a strong chest in the Schatzkammer, to which noone but himself had the key. That it had never been offered to anyone (all the dealers were LIARS) nor seen by anyone, etc. etc. ad inf. etc. Both of us most smilingly—even playfully polite with each other—he however with twinkling eyes throughout. Finally the proceeding struck as being so typically a "dealer's" one that I giggled and said "Well—as the Church never falsifies (I didn't dare say lies) the various dealers who wrote me of their negotiations with you, must be inaccurate—shall we put it that way?" He threw back his head and laughed and said "You are very kind"— Of course I knew that he knew—that we both were playing a game.[54]

Finally Belle was allowed to see the precious multivolume illuminated book, and eventually she procured it. Such negotiations often required Belle's presence in order to be finalized, even when dealers had begun the process, as they certainly had in this case.

The manuscript Belle brought home that year from Salzburg is absolutely gorgeous. An eleventh-century illuminated lectionary of liturgical readings, the brightly colored illustrations (Mary on her way to Jerusalem, Thomas doubtfully touching the risen Christ) bring the narratives of humanity and divinity to life. Decorative pieces are sensuously inked, particularly the gold-script C on a background of deep reddish-purple, interlaced with indigo, teal, and orange. Initial letters of a page or book were often highly decorated.[55]

After her triumph at St. Peter's, Belle became ill again with her "so-called bronchitis." Her years of smoking seem to have been catching up with her. She ignored the "less than middle class" Germans and Americans on the boat home, although she happily allowed Bobbie to run around with a group of Harvard students he met on board.[56] It was a good transition for him. A few weeks after he returned from Germany, he enrolled as a freshman at Harvard College, where he was part of the same graduating class as John F. Kennedy.

There is no way to know whether Robert Leveridge Jr. knew that his grandfather had also gone to Harvard, or who his grandfather was. Although his blond hair had darkened considerably by the time he reached adulthood, Robert would have had no reason to question his whiteness if no one else did. It is unlikely that rumors of his aunt's ancestry had reached him. Such things would have been discussed in hushed tones, in confidential whispers, and not outside of certain circles. Besides her father and Bernard, whom Belle apparently did not wish her nephew to know, Belle had many friends on the faculty and staff at Harvard, especially her good friends Paul Sachs and Edward Forbes at the Fogg Museum, with whom she had ventured on the *Art Studies* experiment. Belle had talked to them about her nephew, but Robert's acceptance was dependent on his academic performance. Obviously, he had done well.[57]

Henri Hyvernat, on the other hand, may have wished to have a bit less of her attention that decade. Belle was very frustrated that his catalogue of the Coptic manuscripts had not yet been finished, and in 1931 she threatened to cancel the whole project. The elderly Hyvernat was in and out of the hospital in 1933. Still, now working with the help of an assistant, Theodore Christian Petersen, Hyvernat reported progress year after year, while Belle pressed for completion. In 1933 he seemed ready to send it but wanted it retyped first. Belle urged him to deliver it to her for duplication. In 1935 she planned to visit him, but took a sudden fall and injured both of her legs, or her "nether limbs," as she told Hyvernat. He chuckled at what he called her "Anglo-Saxon modesty."[58] Two years later Belle still had not received Hyvernat's text. Indeed, she seemed to have forgotten about it, although it is much more likely that she simply did not have the time or heart to coax the papers away from him. Finally, in the summer of 1937, Belle returned her attention to her elderly friend Hyvernat and the Coptic manuscripts. She traveled to Washington, D.C., where she enjoyed a reunion with her dear petit-Saint-Père, whose health seemed renewed. She returned with the catalogue manuscript in hand.[59] It was never published, but it remains in the reference collection of the Morgan Library reading room, and it would be almost sixty years before another scholar would complete a catalogue of the Morgan Coptic manuscripts.[60]

The Coptic manuscripts were only one of many purchasing triumphs and scholarly projects for which Belle was responsible. She oversaw numerous scholarly editions of manuscripts owned by Morgan. And she made at least one significant discovery for which she actually did receive credit—the identification of an individual painter working in the late nineteenth century to forge Renaissance art. She dubbed him "The Spanish Forger" and, using the methods she had learned from Berenson and her decades of experience, set about identifying several dozen pieces attributable to the same artist.[61]

The "Lady Directress" was now an iconic figure in her world. Her approval could give a young scholar a break or a would-be bibliophile a windfall; a dealer or seller could live for months, even years, off of the profit of a sale. Scholars, agents, and new workers arrived on her doorstep with no small amount of trepidation. Roger Howson, librarian of Columbia University, teased her that her walls were "hung with scalps of defeated book agents." Perhaps that was why all the dealers he saw were bald.[62] Stories began to circulate, and her reputation often preceded her. As one London visitor told her, the Morgan Library had been a "romantic dream" before he came and was now a "romantic reality." Belle herself, an "often imagined figure," was part of that allure.[63]

Still, she was not the glamorous figure she had once been. Decidedly middle-aged now, she was no longer described by contemporaries as graceful, exotic, or charming. Noting the contrast between the gorgeous photographic images of her younger self with her usual work attire, Margaret Stillwell noted,

[S]he was masculine. She would stride about in a tweed
suit, throwing colorful remarks offhand over her shoulder.
Or, with her jacket removed, she would stand belligerently
while she talked with you, forever poking her blouse into
her skirt, which always seemed to be a bit too large at the
waistline.[64]

No longer a "girl librarian" whose feminine charm belied her authority
and temper, Belle was now a nationally known figure widely respected
as a professional woman at the top of her game. And she was well-
known enough to make a cameo appearance in national print. In 1939
Time magazine described her at work at an auction, bidding on an original manuscript of *Look Homeward Angel*, by Thomas Wolfe. The bidding began:

> "I'll start with $50," volunteers Belle Green, [*sic*] represent-
> ing the J. P. Morgan Library . . ."$750" another bids . . .
> "Gosh," protests the Morgan agent, "we're not Rockefellers."[65]

Belle's sphere of professional influence continued to extend beyond
the Morgan Library. She was one of the first women to become a fellow of the Mediaeval Academy of America, and was nominated as a
fellow of the Academy for the Advancement of American Scholarship
in the Middle Ages. She was a fellow in perpetuity of the Metropolitan
Museum of Art and served on the advisory council for Princeton University's Department of Art and Archaeology. She was elected to the
board of the College Art Association and the editorial boards for the
Gazette des Beaux Arts and *ARTnews*. And she served on committees
for the Museum of Costume Art, which became the Costume Institute
at the Metropolitan Museum of Art in 1937. On several occasions
Belle was offered honorary degrees from American universities, which
she always turned down. Colleagues and friends explained that it was
her modesty or her "complete submergence of the self" in her work at
the Library that motivated these refusals.[66]

As more private collectors began turning their treasures over to the public either through gifts or bequests, the Morgan Library served as a model for transforming a personal collection into a public institution. Belle was one of four experts appointed to an advisory board for the newly formed Walters Art Gallery, based on the collection of Henry Walters, who died in 1931. She recommended one of her own employees, Dorothy Miner, to take over the work that she and Meta Harrsen had begun in organizing and cataloguing the collection. Miner was one of a group of younger women who worked under Belle at the Library in the 1930s. This was the generation who had entered universities and professions on the wave of feminist expansions in the 1920s. While Belle had grumbled at the time, uncomfortable in her role as unwilling pathbreaker, she supported many of the women who came to her for guidance, instruction, and experience. Dorothy had a Ph.D. from Columbia University and had received a Carnegie Foreign Fellowship to study abroad. From Baltimore she kept Belle updated on her progress, addressing her as "Dearest BG" and signing herself "Your Keed [Kid]."[67] Belle herself received a quarterly honorarium of $250 for her service to the board, which she regularly endorsed back to the gallery, suggesting that her finances were improving.[68]

In the late 1930s the American economy did seem to be recovering. Franklin Roosevelt's New Deal programs provided jobs and support for millions of unemployed Americans. But it was the business opportunities offered by the renewed European military buildup that sparked the systemic recovery of the American economy. Americans watched the fascist Adolf Hitler rise to power in Germany. Soon after Mussolini invaded Ethiopia in 1935, German troops occupied the Rhineland. Belle's old flame was appointed viceroy of Abyssinia (Ethiopia). Prince Amadeo, now the Duke d'Aosta, implemented Mussolini's policies of racial segregation, maintaining African inferiority and racial purity. He did, however, give a greater role to the Ethiopian ruling class than Mussolini had directed.[69] By the end of 1936 Italy and Germany had formed an alliance, much to the consternation of England, France, and the United States.

Most Americans still hoped to stay out of the European conflicts, and few protested as the National Socialists began to escalate their physical and verbal attacks on Jews in Germany. Many believed the anti-Semitic stereotypes that formed the Nazi party line: that the Jews were both wealthy and powerful, and corrupt and inferior. American racialism was not very far away from the theories that led Hitler's regime to exterminate millions of Jews, along with Polish, homosexual, and other supposedly inferior groups.

What Belle thought of all this is impossible to know. She had many Jewish friends, and certainly knew of Berenson's background, and she had already rejected the anti-Semitism of Henry Ford and her own beloved Jack Morgan. At the same time she was interested in heredity, a curiosity Meta Harrsen explained as being "due to her nephew." Her interest may well have been related to her own situation. Many women of mixed ancestry who wished to live as white avoided having children because of the common belief that they might give birth to a "coal-black" baby. There is no way to know whether this was what was behind Belle's curiosity, but the fact that only one of her four married siblings ever had children is highly suggestive.[70]

Rumors about her racial ancestry were circulating widely by now. Publications often referred obliquely to the mystery of Belle's lineage and past, like the 1933 *Time* magazine reference to her hiding her early history and having Portuguese ancestry. But more explicit conjectures and explanations were circulating in private correspondence, diaries not meant for immediate publication, and undoubtedly in conversation and gossip as well.

In 1921 the French art dealer René Gimpel described her in his diary as "Miss Greene, with her tanned complexion." He had heard she had been born in Cuba and that she was "even said to be a mulatto; her hair is frizzy, her cheeks are thick, her lips big." Gimpel saw evidence of her black ancestry in her behavior as well: "She's a figure sculpted by a savage of genius. And she's a 'savage' herself: she is savage in her furies, in her preconceived notions, even in her marvelous intelligence." Like Isabella Gardner so many years before, Gimpel was sure Belle was of mixed ancestry. For Gardner, that allowed her to dismiss the then young upstart as a half-breed who couldn't help lying. But Gimpel saw no contradiction between her "savage" nature and her obvious intelligence and judgment. He credited her as the "architect" of Morgan's "famous, precious" book collection and said she had universal knowledge of ancient books and manuscripts.[71]

That these rumors had reached far beyond her social circles and accompanied her growing professional reputation is evident in a 1934 report by Emmett Maun, an agent sent to do some bookselling business with Miss Greene by M. L. Parrish of the Princeton Library. Neither man had yet met Belle, but Parrish had apparently heard the rumors and was curious about her appearance. He surely must have requested the detailed physical report his agent provided along with an account of their meeting about the copies of Dickens's *A Christmas Carol* that she was considering for purchase. Maun's portrayal of Belle compels the conclusion that he was told to check for himself whether the rumors of Belle's having black ancestry were true. She would have loved that he thought her "fortyish" (she was firmly in her midfifties) and could not have objected to his description of her black velvet outfit in a classic cut with bits of chartreuse lace or his notice of her horn-rimmed glasses. But the rest of his rendering was decidedly unflattering. He described her nose as "bulbous" and suggested she had "caught" it from the numerous photographs of J. P. Morgan that hung in Belle's office. (As early as 1921 Belle's own brother had called it "one hell of a blob.") And Maun's first impression was that Belle seemed not fat but bloated, "as if she had a touch of dropsy or perhaps drank too much." She did have a series of dental problems around that time. Finally, however, he noted that her skin "must be very swarthy," under the white face powder that she used. The result was a "speckled gray" that he compared to "the Negro you see pouring dusty cement into mixers on building construction jobs."[72]

Maun also detailed her graciousness and her comments on the *Christmas Carol* editions, and every aspect of their conversation and transaction. But the incredible detail given to her physical appearance can be explained only by a specific curiosity about her appearance and ancestry. Parrish must have told Maun he had heard she might be part black. He sent his agent not merely to try to sell their Dickens books but also to scrutinize Miss Greene in person and report back on the results. Did she look as if she had black ancestry? Apparently Maun thought she did, as did many others who were aware of the rumors. But hundreds of people met her or saw her every year and did not suspect. Few photos survive from her later life. But in the United States the racial identity of a person of ambiguous appearance lay very much in the eye and expectations of the beholder.

At the same time that knowledge of Belle's ancestry was spreading, her reputation and status were only growing. Undoubtedly at least some of the people who recommended and voted for her for the many positions and awards she received in the 1930s and 1940s had heard the rumors about her ancestry. Some of them probably believed it. Belle was so powerful at that point that the rumors never seem to have been turned against her in any direct way. She had always been the kind of person people either loved or hated. There were probably people who would have been eager to tarnish her reputation, and found her ancestry one way to do so. But accusations of racial passing never came out—at least not in any public or documented manner. Even those who had clear problems with Miss Greene had to be circumspect in how they handled them.

For example, in 1937 Assistant Director Philip Hofer left the Morgan Library on bad terms. As Meta Harrsen later put it, "he and Belle clashed and off he went." Hofer himself left no written account of his departure. He did confront Belle in person with his reasons for doing so, but wrote to Junius Morgan only that he was sorry that "the connection which we all entered with hope, has not worked out as anticipated."[73] There are a number of possible reasons for Hofer's departure. If he was expecting the Lady Directress to retire, three years of waiting without a sign of movement in that direction may have been enough. Some evidence suggests that there were also tensions between Hofer and Greene during those years. He later called her a "formidable opponent" and told a writer interviewing him about Bernard Berenson that "B.B. was not half as ruthless as Belle Greene. . . . I'd take on B.B. anytime in battle. She was a real tartar. You'd have to work under her to know it." Hofer also suggested that some advice he received from William Ivins was "not without bearing" on his decision.[74]

After he left, Philip Hofer tried to get his donated Latin Bible returned. By 1938 he had been hired by the Harvard University librarian William Jackson to head its new Department of Printing and Graphic Arts. The exchanges—increasingly bitter on his part and unmovingly polite on the Library's—dragged on for almost ten years. Belle's personal response was far from polite, but the correspondence was limited to Junius Morgan Jr., representing the board of trustees. The board voted unanimously not to return the Bible, in part because the Library's status as a public institution prohibited it from giving gifts without reciprocation.[75]

As the 1930s came to a close, Belle's life was becoming more work centered, and much less social and family oriented. Her immediate family had scattered, except for her mother, who still lived with her. Louise had died; Ethel had long since rejoined her husband and was living in Goshen, New York; at some point in the 1930s she became a widow. The Harveys were still in Pennsylvania, but Belle never mentioned Teddy and her new family. Russell and Josephine still lived in New York. Belle and her brother remained close, but she had little use for his wife. By 1941 Belle and Genevieve had moved back down to the neighborhood of the Morgan Library, into a spacious Park Avenue apartment across from the Colony Club (a move that merited mention in local papers.)[76]

In the spring of 1939 Bobbie went out to California, where he worked in a series of jobs, including those of airplane engine mechanic, reporter, public relations person, and film editor and writer. This would have been quite a blow for Belle; Robert left college a year before he would have graduated. A Harvard alumni publication noted that he had studied medicine, and he may have planned to continue elsewhere. Still instead of entering medical school immediately, Robert seems to have followed a much more modern career path and one that may have seemed frivolous to his aunt and perhaps disappointing to his mother and her memory of his father.[77]

But as Germany and Italy began military incursions outside of their borders, the European world began to mobilize for war. The preparations brought familiar worries and fears stemming from the memories of the Great War, which now seemed not to have ended all war. Long before the United States entered the war in 1941, Belle, whose daily correspondence included reports from friends and associates throughout Europe, became deeply involved.

Painfully aware of Jack Morgan's anti-Semitism, Belle turned to a network of international art figures to try to persuade and aid German Jews to leave, first Germany and then Europe altogether. Adolph Goldschmidt, for example, was back home in Berlin despite Belle's and other friends' pleas that he stay in New York. Paul Sachs, who had known him from his Harvard days, even went to Berlin in 1938 to appeal directly to the aging art historian to leave. Belle and others offered to fund his trip and help support him in the United States. However, Goldschmidt refused to leave his home country, although he allowed his friends to help his nephew Martin and Martin's wife and child leave Germany for the United States. Adolph believed that his age, accomplishments, and loyalty to his native country would protect him despite the increasing restrictions and violence against Jews. In 1939, when he was barred from entering the library of the university where he was professor emeritus, Adolph Goldschmidt finally left for Switzerland.[78]

Fascist Italy was also becoming a dangerous place for Belle's friends. The Italian-born Dr. Joseph Martini, who had lived in New York for several years, returned to Italy in the 1920s to set up his own business, much to his regret. By 1940 he described Italy and Europe to Belle as "a cage of . . . insane people, which are slaughtering each other at any chance and at any occasion."[79]

When Mussolini declared war on France and England in June of 1940, the Berensons were still holed up in I Tatti. Two servants, English citizens, immediately fled: both were captured, one escaped. Mary, who had never fully recovered from her near-death experience, was unable to travel, and the American ambassador assured Bernard that his age would protect him. Florence police honored this promise, even when radical Fascists demanded Berenson's arrest and threatened him with violence. The Berensons were effectively confined to their home and immediate environs. The American embassy staff left

Italy in June 1942, but Bernard refused to join them if Mary's nurse and Nicky could not come with them. As the property of enemy aliens, I Tatti was now subject to seizure, but a sympathetic Italian official completed a seventy-page inventory of its possessions and quietly set it aside. When Mussolini was overthrown a year later, the Berensons were still there, sequestered up on their hill above Florence, both working on their own writing projects.[80]

Like Bernard, Belle continued to work through the first years of the war, keeping an uneasy eye on news reports. In 1940 and 1941 she was still fielding the usual array of requests and projects. When the American Historical Association met in New York, Dwight C. Miner, of Columbia University, set up a visit to the Morgan Library. Belle arranged instead to have one of her colleagues, Lawrence Wroth, speak to the historians and agreed, against her usual policy, to say "about ten words" of welcome and introduction. It may have helped the usually recalcitrant nonspeaker that Dwight was the brother of Dorothy Miner, Belle's friend and protégée.[81]

When Alain Locke wrote that fall asking to include a photograph or print of Tintoretto's *Portrait of a Moor* in his book *The Negro in Art*, Belle sent the permission, commenting only that Locke should be sure to note that Jack owned it. Did Alain Locke, or other Harlem figures, know that Belle da Costa Greene was Belle Marian Greener, daughter of Richard T. Greener? Most of them were too young to have known Greener when he was a public figure in Gilded Age New York. But African American communities often kept track of (and kept quiet about) people with black ancestry who were living as white. Surely someone knew.[82] Even more unknowable is Belle's personal response, if any, to this request. Did she consider the implications of the *Portrait of a Moor* being included in a volume on artistic portrayals of Negroes? Did she think of her father when she looked at that painting hanging in the West Room, which was once Mr. Morgan's office?

But by the end of 1940 Belle had more pressing personal problems to focus on. After returning from her usual summer vacation at a Wyoming mountain resort, which usually revived her enough to face another year of work, she had another bad fall, this time breaking her arm. It took several months to heal, and Belle was demoralized as well. She could not even visit her beloved Father Hyvernat in D.C. that following January when he became critically ill. She wrote to his assistant Dr. Peterson that if it were not for "a broken arm, a broken head and a broken heart," she would be there immediately, but that she was able to travel only from her home to the Library and back again.[83] In April, Dr. Peterson wrote to Belle to inform her that Hyvernat was dying; he had cancer and was beyond medical intervention.

Belle was unable to visit Henri Hyvernat before his death in May. She had an even closer death to mourn. On March 22, 1941, her mother died. Genevieve Ida Van Vliet Greene was in her early nineties. Her surviving children buried her in a private funeral; Belle made all of the arrangements. Belle's friends, many of whom had met the mysterious Mrs. Greene, sent their condolences. Eric Millar wrote of his devotion to the elderly woman and how impressed he had been and how often he had thought with "real joy of the close bond between you two." He knew what a heartbreaking shock her sudden death must have been.[84]

Genevieve had been a powerful force in her children's lives, long into their adulthood. It was her aspirations for them and her understanding of race that had prompted their decision to change their name from Greener to Greene and stop identifying themselves as colored. While Richard had believed his children capable of supporting themselves at the age of eighteen, as he himself had been a wage earner at a much younger age, Genevieve had worked to support her children's higher education and careers. Moreover, she had trained Belle to play the same role. At the age of sixty-two, Belle was now truly living alone for the first time in her life.

14

SHINING THROUGH
THE DARKNESS

Here are [medieval Europe's] religion, art, history, and literature;
here are the doing and thinking of humble scribe, of illuminator,
bookbinder, metal worker, and wood carver, of tellers of tales and
chroniclers as well as of great princes and mitred lords. . . . The
manuscripts . . . shine through the darkness of those years,
through their confusion and seeming hopelessness, through the
barriers set up by later ideologies. Looking upon them we see the
qualities of aspiration, gaiety, love of beauty, gentleness, and
humor devoid of cynicism. If so much beauty needs excuse, this
is it.

—Lawrence C. Wroth, 1949[1]

In these terrible days I . . . remind myself that after all we knew
a grand time and lived a grand life. What have the kids—and
others—got to look forward to?

—Belle Greene, 1945[2]

THE WAR CAME HOME to Belle Greene and her family four
months before the infamous attack on Pearl Harbor. On August 18,
1941, Robert Leveridge enlisted. War had not been declared; there
was no draft yet. But Robert, twenty-two years old with three years of
college and some work as a plane mechanic under his belt, entered the
Air Corps as an aviation cadet. Congress had just created this new category as part of government and military preparation for what seemed
the inevitable involvement in the European war. Certainly Belle
expected America to enter the war and supported "a union of English-
speaking people," even though there was still popular opposition to
U.S. involvement. But danger did not wait for combat. Ten days after
he enlisted, the landing gear broke on Leveridge's PT-13A during a
training flight at Hemet Airdrome in California. Both Robert and the
civilian flight instructor, who was at the controls during the landing,
were uninjured. The instructor was found to be at fault and placed on
probation.[3]

Whatever disappointment Belle may have felt when Robert dropped
out of Harvard before graduating would have been more than compensated for when he enlisted and entered pilot training. During World
War One, Belle had been determined that her male relatives and
friends fight or work in support of the war. She was older now, and her
pride would have come with great fear. If her enthusiasm for patriotic
duty had not faded, it was certainly now accompanied by a real understanding of the suffering war would bring. Those who have lived
through one catastrophic war rarely welcome another.

The day after the Japanese attack on Pearl Harbor, the United
States officially entered the war. The Ninety-second Bombardment
Group (Heavy) was constituted on January 28, 1942; Robert joined its
327th Squadron and relocated to MacDill Field in Florida.[4] Two days
later Belle wrote to Adolph Goldschmidt that Bobbie had been training for a year and a half and expected to be sent into the war very soon.
(Belle may have been exaggerating, but it is possible that he had left
school to work as a plane mechanic in order to prepare for pilot training.) Aware that she was writing to someone who had already fled Ger-

many but was still in Europe, Belle commented only that, having been free of war for so long, Americans found it "rather hard" to have "our boys go off."[5]

In Florida the four bombardment squadrons of the Ninety-second trained at a furious rate with new B-17F's. But Robert's hopes for a combat mission were not soon realized. In August 1942 the squadrons flew to Dow Field in Maine and began to practice long-range flying in preparation for the transatlantic trip. Exactly one year after he enlisted, Robert flew with the 327th to Newfoundland, moving on the next day to Scotland, and finally on to England.

Stationed outside of the small town of Bovington in Dorset County, the Ninety-second was one of the first groups of the American Air Corps to arrive in England. Although the facilities were starker than their training bases had been, the men found themselves a welcome curiosity and struck up a good relationship with the English citizens whose armed forces the Americans were there to support. Military success was not immediate. An aerial demonstration for several generals, including Dwight D. Eisenhower, did not go well. Within a few weeks the group lost its new B-17F's to another bomb group slated to be deployed to Africa. The Ninety-second was left with older B-17E models for its first combat mission in early September. As new troops came into Europe, various sections of the Ninety-second were put in charge of training them. Nevertheless, Leveridge participated in occasional bombing raids, including (Belle believed) the raid on Dieppe. Robert survived his first combat flight, but Belle wrote to a scholar who was coming to lecture at the Library, "I dare not think how often that may happen."[6]

Exactly what Bobbie's role was is unclear from Belle's letters. She described him both as a bombardier and as a pilot, two different positions in the air crews that flew each mission. Belle was not alone in her confusion. The bomber pilot became so glorified in the American imagination that the Air Force turned to the media to help recruit and support the other air crewmen who were essential to the bombing missions that defined much of World War Two combat. By 1943 the dominant image was of the teamwork and cooperation between the pilot, navigator, bombardiers, gunners, engineers, and radio operators who manned each flight mission.[7]

Meanwhile, there was new work to be done at the Library. Following the example of libraries and museums throughout Europe, the trustees of the Morgan Library decided to put their irreplaceable treasures into underground storage. In hindsight the danger of an aerial German attack on New York was remote, but domestic security was a real concern at the time, especially on the coasts. Blacked-out harbors and air raid drills became familiar experiences to New Yorkers. Jack was particularly determined not to wait to make plans to secure the Library's art and manuscripts, pointing out the foresight the British Museum had shown in removing its holdings long before bombs started dropping in London. By June 1942 Belle was able to report that the materials had been "evacuated . . . to divergent places for safekeeping" until the war was over. This meant that almost all of the business of the Library was now shut down for the duration. Helen Franc, newly hired as curator of drawings and paintings, found she had nothing to curate with the collection in storage. She resigned to do war work. Curt Bühler also left for military service, as did several other employees; Junius S. Morgan had a commission as a lieutenant commissioner.[8]

Although the war effort on the homefront was even more organized and urgent than it had been thirty years ago, Belle did not return to the same the level of relief work. She was involved in some fund-raising activities. The Red Cross War Fund had a "Museums and Private Libraries Division," which had raised over $23,000 by the spring of 1942. However, Belle's lowered participation was to be expected: She was now in her sixties and in poor health. The woman who had managed to continually subtract five to fifteen years from her age was slowing down. Throughout 1942–43 she seemed to be confined to her bed every few months, and in 1945 began going to Saratoga Springs regularly for "cures." The "Queen of Spas" of the Victorian period had developed into a medical center, and Belle took advantage of both the luxury hotels, which offered her an old-fashioned rest cure, and the presence of doctors with state-of-the-art technologies. In 1943 she wrote to her friend and dealer "Rosey" Rosenbach, sympathizing when he, too, had been confined to bed. She confided ruefully that she was still under orders to turn in by six o'clock. "Noone—not even a blond Adonis—can ever mention bed to me again!"[9]

Nor did she repeat her work assisting Jack Morgan with business as she had in the First World War. In part this was because the Morgan company decided not to return to its World War One strategy of funding the European Allies while the United States was neutral.[10] Even if they had, Belle would likely not have become involved again. The Library's independence had not separated it from the Morgan family, but it had removed her from the Morgan business. Similarly, J. P. Morgan & Co. was transforming itself from a private partnership into a corporation, which further removed it from Jack Morgan's control and, therefore, from the relatively informal processes followed by Jack and his father in the Library in the 1910s.[11]

When Jack Morgan died at the age of seventy-six, on March 13, 1943, two weeks after a stroke and a series of heart attacks, Belle felt the loss deeply. He had been one of her "staunchest friends," she mourned.[12] She must also have been reminded of his father's death, almost exactly thirty years before. Jack's funeral was at St. George's as well, and even the same baritone sang; respects poured in from around the world, and newspaper memorials noted his financial and philanthropic accomplishments. Belle pronounced the funeral "like himself, very simple and dignified."[13] Even his will raised inevitable comparisons: like his father, Jack bequeathed $50,000 to Belle da Costa Greene. It was not worth as much as the same amount had been thirty years ago, but it reflected his esteem for her. And once again, no amount would be enough to offset his death and the losses that were to come.

Belle received many personal condolences from old employees, dealers, and friends. Ada Thurston congratulated her not on the amount but on the "real meaning behind your legacy," which she understood as "a real tribute to your assistance in his development from his closed personality to one of a greater appreciation of all sorts of people and interests. Perhaps he never fully realized this and very likely his family did not but you can 'lay it to your soul.'"[14] Belle missed

Jack's presence at the Library "to an almost unbelievable extent." It was both a personal and a professional loss. Belle felt that no one else on the board had the same passion for the Library as Jack had. She confided to a friend a few years later that she had had some "struggles" with the trustees as a result after Jack's death. And she could not get used to his being gone. She never expected to suffer such a loss twice, she wrote to Ada, just as she had never expected to live through another war. Moreover, she had once again to deal with the estate, which included some pieces housed at the Library (like the *Portrait of a Moor*) but not the Library's collection itself. Still, the executors of his will were all bankers and needed Belle's help in going through Jack's many art pieces and books. By summer Belle was recovering from her grief, still not back to work full-time but her "dear old self again," as one friend declared.[15]

But in August the worst news possible left Belle completely devastated. Six months after Jack's death, the War Department sent notification that Robert MacKenzie Leveridge had been killed in action in Europe. Bobbie survived one year of active duty in England; he was twenty-four years old. It was Belle's nightmare.

The circumstances of Robert's death are rather mysterious, and what few details the Air Force had were almost certainly not communicated to the family. He was not actually killed in action; he died during a period when his battalion was not engaged in battle. At some point at the end of July or the beginning of August, he was declared missing in action. But according to his military files, First Lieutenant Robert MacKenzie Leverage died on August 3, 1943, of brain injuries caused by "Gunshot Wounds Self Inflicted While Mentally Unsound." The names of two other men in his unit, whose deaths were also listed as not battle related, appear in his file. But there is no evidence of an inquiry, and Leveridge's file contains no explanation of the circumstances of his death and how or whether these other men were involved.[16]

Robert was buried temporarily in Brookwood American Military Cemetery in England with a Protestant military funeral. His belongings were fastidiously itemized and included one package of medals and insignias, two pairs of sunglasses, one box of shaving and toilet articles, twenty-four boxes of soap, clothes, $18.76, and an outstanding tailor bill. Robert Leveridge smoked a pipe (he had seven), played chess, cards, and cribbage, and carried calling cards—the last no doubt reflected his aunt's influence. He had blue eyes and a scar over his right eyebrow, perhaps from a childhood injury.[17]

It took four years for Leveridge's body and personal items to reach their final destination. The delay was due partly to the sheer bureaucracy required to keep track of so many bodies, grieving families, and trunks of clothing. But there was also some confusion about where to send the effects. When he enlisted, Robert named Belle as his emergency contact and executor of his will and gave her power of attorney; he listed his mother and half sister as his beneficiaries. The resulting confusion offers a rare glimpse into the relationship between Belle and her sister Teddy. Army paperwork began to send the items to Belle, but Teddy successfully appealed to the Army Effects Bureau (AEB) in May 1944 to have them sent to her instead. She explained the situation that led to her sister's taking custody of her son. The shock of her husband's death in the First World War had "broken my health down completely so my sister adopted my son and clothed and educated him until he was 21." Belle already had some of Robert's belongings that he left behind. "For sentimental reasons" Teddy wanted the things associated with her son's military service.[18] Teddy clearly had not given up her identity and claim as Robert's biological mother. If this was her understanding of her arrangement with Belle, she may have regretted her decision after she recovered.

Belle's lawyer, Nathan G. Goldberger, who had known Robert since he was an infant, confirmed for the quartermaster that Belle had adopted her nephew but that she had not been his guardian since he turned twenty-one. Robert had, however, granted her power of attorney and appointed her executor of a will that was not being probated, because there was no significant estate to disburse. However, Belle did not challenge her sister's request for Robert's belongings, and Goldberger promised that if she received them she would allow "the boy's

Mother" to distribute them. The AEB determined that since the will had not been probated and the mother was a closer relative than the aunt, Teddy would receive the items. A footlocker and cardboard box containing 109 pounds of clothing and personal items was sent to the Harvey residence in Reading, Pennsylvania, in the late spring of 1944. Her health failing at this point, Teddy delayed confirming receipt, but finally wrote, thanking the AEB for its help and comfort. It made her feel, she said, that Robert had died for a cause.[19]

In 1947 Leveridge's remains were removed from the temporary Brookwood Cemetery and permanently interred at the American Cemetery in Cambridge, England, at his mother's request. Like the families of many officers, she believed he would rather be buried with his comrades. Four years after his death Robert had reached his final resting place.[20]

Already very ill, Belle was devastated by Bobbie's death.[21] Looking for a cause and giving meaning to his loss, along with hundreds of thousands more, was very much on her mind as well. She found solace in her friend Archibald MacLeish's memorial poem "The Young Dead Soldiers," which she called "one of the finest and most important things" she had read in a long time. MacLeish, a poet and magazine writer who served as Librarian of Congress under Franklin D. Roosevelt, wrote the poem in 1943. At first it was distributed anonymously, immediately picked up by newspapers and printed on envelopes and cards. But Belle knew MacLeish and knew that the poem was his; he donated the original manuscript to the Morgan Library. MacLeish dedicated the poem to Lieutenant Richard Myers, a combat flier who had also died in 1943. In 1946 Lieutenant Myers's mother contacted Belle Greene, wanting to see the original manuscript. MacLeish had told her that Belle had also lost a child she had raised.[22] If Mrs. Myers did visit the Library, the two women may have met and found comfort in their shared sorrow. But even in their correspondence it is clear that their losses connected them.

MacLeish's poem is a haunting one, written at a low point in the war, when the end was nowhere in sight and victory uncertain:

THE YOUNG DEAD SOLDIERS

The young dead soldiers do not speak,
Nevertheless they are heard in the still houses, who has
　　not heard them?
They have a silence that speaks for them at night and
　　when the clock counts.
They say, We were young. We have died. Remember us.
They say, We have done what we could but until it is
　　finished it is not done.
They say, We have given our lives but until it is finished no
　　one can know what our lives gave.
They say, Our deaths are not ours. They are yours: they
　　will mean what you make them.
They say, Whether our lives and our deaths were for peace
　　and a new hope or for nothing we cannot say; it is you
　　who must say this.
They say, We leave you our deaths: give them their mean-
　　ing; give them an end to the war and a true peace; give
　　them a victory that ends the war and a peace after-
　　wards; give them their meaning.
We were young, they say. We have died. Remember us.[23]

For Belle, so early in a decade that already seemed defined more by death than by life, her nephew's passing was the greatest personal blow. She tried to keep her head up by focusing on "how many countless others have suffered similarly."[24] But this was a bereavement from which she would truly never recover. By the end of 1943 Belle suffered an episode that she described as a fall and a friend later said was a stroke. She now had difficulty walking and started making references to her "game legs."[25] What role Bobbie's death played in this physical collapse can only be speculated.

　　Bernard heard about Robert's death almost two years later. He wrote to Belle, trying to rebuild the bridge of letters that was once the only direct connection between the long-distance lovers. He had not heard from her (or had not saved any letters) since 1939. In the spring of 1941, when Belle was reeling from the death of her mother, Bernard was complaining to yet another mutual acquaintance that the "fair lady" had "Freudishly if not deliberately forgotten my existence."[26]

Since then Bernard had had more vital concerns. When German troops occupied northern Italy in 1943 and began moving southward, Bernard—born a Jew and therefore always a Jew in the eyes of Nazis—finally had to leave I Tatti, where he had spent the early years of the war. The same sympathetic official who protected the villa from being occupied during the early years of the war now secreted Bernard and Nicky away under diplomatic flags to a safe house. Mary, confined to her bed and in much less danger, stayed behind with her nurses. Friends arrived to pack away the most valuable paintings and manuscripts for safekeeping, and hide much of Berenson's library. Belle was much relieved when she heard Bernard had made his way to France. But he and Nicky were actually still in Italy. Their hiding place was only three miles away from I Tatti, and they remained in touch with Mary through letters delivered by friends. A year later, in September 1944, the Allied forces drove the German troops out of southern and central Italy. Florence was safe again, and Bernard and Nicky returned to I Tatti and to Mary.[27] Six months later Mary Berenson died quietly after over a decade of intermittent illness and several years of confinement to her bed. Although he knew her death had brought an end to her pain, Bernard could feel only grief at losing her.[28] He never married Nicky Mariano, but he was devoted to her. (Mary had given them her blessing, but neither felt the need to legalize their decades-long relationship.)

Bernard's interest in Belle is hard to assess at this point. The years had worn away the edges of their disagreements and muted the pain of decades-old betrayals and disappointments. By 1945 Belle was mostly the "eradicable memory" she had long believed herself to be, but B.B. clearly wanted this living memory to show more loyalty and interest in him. Belle was probably more willing to acknowledge that it was easier to remain affectionate toward a former lover when actual contact was kept infrequent.

Bobbie's death softened Bernard to Belle and perhaps made it easier for her to reach out to him as well. He told a mutual friend, Daniel Thompson, that he was particularly sorry to hear that Robert had "turned out so well before the end. It makes his loss so much harder to bear." Thompson sent him a pen portrait of Robert as well. And when Belle received Bernard's letter, she apparently showed it or sent it to Thompson, for it survived the destruction of her papers and was archived with his own. It had been nine years since Bernard and Belle had last seen each other, and neither would be able to make the journey again. Bernard was, he proudly wrote, an octogenarian. He told her he now really regretted not meeting Bobbie those many years past in Salzburg, and he begged her to visit him: "Dear Belle," he concluded his note, "I want to see you to enjoy your presence again. You must come over as soon as you can and stay here for as long as you can stand my company." He signed the letter, "Ever yrs. B.B."[29]

Bernard considered Belle's response to be the "first real letter" she had written him in years. She could not tell him, she wrote, what it meant to hear from him. This last war had sapped her of her energy and any optimism she had left for the world. At least their generation had "lived a grand life." She found it hard to believe that the ones to come would ever know such a life. And her own world was growing smaller and smaller. In two years she had lost her mother, Jack, her nephew, and many others. At least Bernard was now safe at I Tatti again. Belle signed her letter, "Devotedly, as always, Your Belle." The loss of her nephew, Bernard mused, had humanized her.[30]

The other losses Belle had suffered during the war years included Ada Thurston, who had been living in Poughkeepsie, New York, since her retirement. Ada died in 1944. Adolph Goldschmidt also passed away in 1944, while living in Switzerland.[31] And, of course, she had already lost her mother and Father Hyvernat just before the start of war. And Belle's family losses were not finished. Just a month after she wrote to Bernard, her favorite sister, Ethel, died. Already widowed, Ethel was still living in upstate New York. She had probably long since retired from her career as a public school teacher. Ethel had been the sister nearest in age and temperament to Belle, and her death in 1945 hit hard. Now Belle's only family were her estranged sister, Teddy, with whom she was still negotiating the estate of her nephew, and her brother, with whom she continued to spend time.[32] As Belle wrote to a friend, informing her of this new loss, "The last three years have been really just about too much for me, and I don't believe I can take much more."[33]

Amazingly, Belle—now sixty-five but very much weakened by her emotional losses and her health—was still able to muster some of the spark and bawdy humor of her old self. She continued to exchange biting insults with William Ivins, who was equally known for his sometimes deadly repartee, responding to one of his digs with her "usual and well-known ladylike restraint" and concluding her subsequent outburst by sending "love and affection and all the amenities of the season"—including smallpox.[34] And she continued to work, although her health began to take her away from the Library more often and for longer periods.

Belle was sick again and was having further trouble with her legs. She told Bernard that she was so "weak in the legs" as to be "partly crippled there," which meant that she would never travel to Italy and him again. But she continued to write to him two or three times a year, usually during the holidays or her summer vacations. She had probably by this time developed the cancer that would eventually take her life. Rarely specific about her illnesses, Belle left no written record of this or any other serious diseases. Cancer, in particular, was a disease that often went unnamed. Writing during her treatment in 1946, she told Berenson only that she was trying to get "revitalized after a bad two or three years" and that she would be back at work in a few weeks. (By this point Belle had heard rumors that Bernard and Nicky had married. Their commitment was that of a married couple, but Belle was no longer concerned with the details of B.B.'s love life.)[35] The war was over and business was returning to normal, but Belle's health kept her from resuming her full-time work. Still, she kept coming in to the Library as often as she was able.

When she heard in 1947 that Eric Millar was retiring from the British Museum and planning a trip to New York in 1948, she was thrilled and wrote him immediately. She wanted him to lecture at the Library, but mostly she wanted to see him. However, she did warn him that her health was not good, although her tongue was still going strong. And when she fell again, further adding to her "physical debility," she joked that she "did not believe in doing things by halves!"[36]

Belle's "falls" were probably small strokes. At least that's how Billy Ivins described this latest one, which rendered her unable to walk without a cane or other support. He described "poor old BG" in brutal detail for Bernard:

> Two years or so ago, I forgot exactly, she had what I imagine might be called a stroke—her legs went completely out from under her—and she now teeters painfully with a cane if she has to move only a few steps, if more she hangs heavily and clumsily on the nearest and stoutest arm. The deaths of her mother and sister shocked her and then the loss of her nephew Bobbie in the war hurt her cruelly. In spite of the brave face she wears, the zip and élan are fading. In public she puts up a gallant fight but off stage I imagine she does as little as possible. It's pitiful—but it's likely that many people have developed a new respect for her.[37]

In between treatments and periods of recuperation, Belle was still a strong presence at the Morgan Library, the "reigning queen at 36th St." with her deep gruff voice and her impatient ways. She had begun work on a memoir about "the two J.P.M.'s"—J.P. and Jack—and asked old friends and colleagues to share their reminiscences of the elder one. When she asked Bernard, she recalled, "[Y]ou two did not get along so awfully well," because of Seligmann's machinations (something she never mentioned at the time—she may have meant Joseph or Henry Duveen) and because of her "known friendship" with Bernard.[38] Once so dramatically important, that triangle was now a fuzzy memory.

In 1947 Billy Ivins visited "Lady Arabella" and concluded that she would probably give up altogether if she could not go to work; her life now revolved so entirely around the Library. By the end of the year he was shocked to find her "very badly crippled." He suspected she was very lonely and depressed, but still thought she might "achieve a sort of handsomeness."[39] Bernard was glad to have the news, even if it wasn't good. Belle was now sixty-five, he reflected (he was pretty close—she was actually sixty-nine), and should take her age into consideration.

Belle would have retorted that she was already making many, many concessions to her age and condition. And she did have a group of friends who watched over her in her declining health, as much as she would let them. Meta Harrsen, a longtime work colleague, had now become a close friend. And one of Belle's few social activities had brought her into a new circle of friends. During the war years she had become a founding member of the Hroswitha Club, an exclusive group for women interested in books and book collecting. Belle was one of the few professional women in the original group. The others were Ruth Granniss, librarian of the Grolier Club, and Shakespeare scholar Henrietta Bartlett.[40] A later member, Margaret Stillwell, described the wistfulness and reverence the other women—all wealthy, cultured, well traveled, and intelligent—had for the few who worked among rare books and manuscripts.[41] Several members of this group would become close friends of Belle's in her later years, especially Anne Sherman Haight, a book collector who had published a listing of books that had been banned at one time.[42]

Belle was not able to attend Hroswitha Club meetings regularly, but she did when she could, and in 1948 she hosted the group and gave them full access to the vault of rare manuscripts.[43] She wrote a brief letter to Bernard herself in early 1948 to wish him a good new year, and reported that she could only "hobble along on canes." Since she could afford taxis, however, she was still making it in to the Library regularly. But her renewed, scattered correspondence was not enough for Bernard; he seems to have asked about her every time he wrote a mutual friend. He heard reports that she was in "very bad shape" but complained that she was not returning his letters. "I cannot understand people who so utterly forgo the past!" he vented at Billy Ivins.[44]

In late 1947 or early 1948, Belle told the Morgan Library trustees that it was finally time to find a successor. It was a difficult decision, but a necessary one, given her very poor health. The trustees, who had probably been generously waiting for Belle to accept that the time had come, immediately began making lists of possible candidates. All were men, all had at least a B.A. and significant work experience, and most had M.A.'s or Ph.D.'s. The requirements for the position had increased substantially since Junius Morgan brought Belle to meet J. P. Morgan Sr. for the first time over forty years earlier. The Library itself had expanded almost exponentially, and the position now required specialized knowledge, judgment, and administrative abilities.[45]

Nor is it too surprising that no one considered replacing Belle with another woman. In 1950 a study in *Library Journal* found that in the ten largest library systems in the nation, 84 percent of head librarians were men, in a field in which 90 percent of librarians and librarian's assistants were women. Since most of these institutions were controlled by boards of trustees or directors who were themselves primarily men, the study concluded that their cultural biases toward men were keeping women out of economic competition and advancement.[46] But there was one thing everyone involved in the search agreed on: it would be no easy task to replace Belle Greene, and, as one consultant gravely observed, "[a]n equal is out of the question."[47]

In May 1948 Belle underwent an operation at St. Luke's Hospital. She recovered well, but, under orders to take the entire summer off from work, she went again to Saratoga. The trustees considered closing the Library for the season, but decided to remain open even in her absence. Miss Green's loyal staff members were well able to manage day-to-day matters on their own.[48]

After getting Belle's approval, Junius Morgan offered the directorship to William A. Jackson, of the Houghton Library at Harvard. Jackson turned the position down, saying that he wanted to finish what he had started at Houghton. Junius then asked his advice on whom else to consider. Jackson mentioned Stanley Pargellis, of the Newberry Library, who had all of the qualifications except buying experience. However, Jackson suggested, if Pargellis followed Belle's own strategy when she first began of "obtaining the best advice from the most learned people in each field," he would do just fine.[49]

The search continued. In October, just one month before Belle's official departure, the trustees hired Frederick B. Adams Jr. Adams was a Yale graduate who had some postgraduate education but no further degrees. He was an avid book collector and independent scholar, but had never had an academic, library, or museum posting. At the time of his hire, he was working for his father's manufacturing firm, Air Reduction Company. But he was wellborn, well-connected, and respected in his field. He was a great-nephew of Henry Walters and a cousin of Franklin D. Roosevelt, far more a part of the Morgans' world and experience than Belle had been. Adams was no doubt a comfortable hire for the trustees, and they breathed a sigh of relief that they had found someone suitable in time.

If Belle was contacted in the process, there is no record of it. She still had a vested interest the Library. In fact, she had already surreptitiously returned to work in July, just an hour or two a day, against her frustrated doctor's orders. She said she felt it was much more beneficial to heal her mind with the work.[50] When she heard Adams had accepted the position, she wrote him a welcoming letter and arranged to meet with him to start the handover. What Belle thought of Adams is not recorded, but if her staff is any reflection, she did not like him. Meta Harrsen complained obliquely about the new director for years, even threatening to resign in 1953.[51] And the transition period may have lasted somewhat longer than Adams had anticipated. After she retired, Belle was no longer responsible for the Library business, but she continued to come in a few days a week, working on her memoir of the Morgans. It could not have been easy to be a new director there, with such a strong and dominating former leader still on the premises. Belle's staff would likely have been more attuned to her than to him, and some were quietly hostile to the newcomer.

In April 1949 the Library opened an exhibit in honor of Belle da Costa Greene, marking the twenty-fifth anniversary of the Library's public incarnation. The exhibit featured over 250 of the best items Belle had purchased. The Reims Gospels were there, and a French psalter—perhaps the very one that she used to kiss every time she put it away. So were the Armenian Gospels she had purchased after her studies in the Armenian monastery in Venice, and several Caxton books she had acquired since becoming director. (The sixteen Caxtons she had obtained from Lord Ashbury in 1908 the night before his auction and the *Morte d'Arthur* she had bid $42,800 for at the Hoe sale in New York in 1911 were not there, having been purchased before the Library's celebrated transformation in 1924.) Lawrence Wroth gave a speech honoring her accomplishments, but—playing to an experienced and adoring audience—highlighting her personal characteristics with vignettes that humorously illustrated her "imperious temperament" and "characteristic enthusiasms." He likened her ability to recognize quality to the gift of perfect pitch in a musician, and noted that her "inherent taste" had been molded "through years of association with great men, great books, and great productions of artist and craftsman." He read letters of tribute sent on the announcement of her retirement, and shared Frederick Adams's discovery that every book, manuscript, and original drawing was accompanied by lists of notes, attributions, scholars' comments, and references, some dating back over thirty years, some written in the last year: "a continuous, living record of the growth of knowledge." Such an effort, Wroth suspected, could have been possible only if Belle stayed after hours, when the correspondence, visitors, and employees had all gone home. He imagined "round-the-clock industry" and "a complete submergence of self in the interests of the Library."[52]

Newspaper coverage of Belle's retirement and the exhibit in her honor showed the mythology that was already beginning to form around her life story. Articles noted that her private life was a "mystery" and that she had lived a life "of European tours, of chats with kings and diplomats," even including the incongrous image of her "bustling in brocade" through the narrow backroom corridors of the Library. The "Where the hell is the *City of God*" story was now in public circulation, as was the Spanish Forger identification. Journalists noted that it was not until after her arrival that Morgan started purchasing "really great paintings." Her very last purchase was noted (fifteenth-century Ethiopian Gospels). *Time* magazine dubbed her "Belle of the Books."[53]

None of the articles mentioned that Belle attended the reception in her honor in a wheelchair. Billy Ivins was there, and he later reported to Bernard that Belle was practically paralyzed, "completely burned out," and unable to recognize people. He thought it was the result of "all her many wicks having flared at all their ends for too long a time." Conversation, he said, had long been impossible.[54] However, his bleak description contradicts those of Belle's co-workers and replacement.

It was true that Belle was in a wheelchair, and she may have had some of the other common symptoms of a stroke—difficulty speaking and selective memory loss. But she could not have been nearly as incoherent or impaired as Billy's description implied. She continued to work at the Library until the spring of 1950. With a new director in her former office, she now had a desk in the Print Room, where she sat three mornings a week dealing with her correspondence, receiving very select visitors, and, Meta Harrsen told Bernard Berenson, still inspiring her former staff. Said staff was also willing to lie for her to unwanted visitors, telling them she was rarely there.[55]

During this period Belle was still corresponding with friends, usually typewritten (possibly dictated), though sometimes in her now very shaky hand.[56] Her last letter to Bernard, written just a few weeks before her party, sounded very much like herself. She thanked him for a book on behalf of the "wolves of learning, that come daily to the library to feed." And she still could manage a flirt: "I can think of nothing that I would not willingly exchange for your visit to Istanbul this summer. Do propose yourself." She signed off, "Ever thine."[57]

Similarly, Frederick Adams reported to Junius Morgan that Belle was still doing a lot of work. She wanted to write a history of the Library collections, which Adams supported. He feared the Library's records would never tell its whole history and that only Belle, whose memory was still "remarkably good," could fill in the gaps. Adams also knew that Belle could not write such a history herself and thought she was starting to realize it as well. Adams proposed hiring a ghost writer to help her with the task of writing and organizing her thoughts, but Belle refused to let the Library hire anyone, preferring, she said, to sell some of her jewels if necessary.[58]

Meanwhile Meta Harrsen, Dorothy Miner, Anne Sherman Haight,

and some of Belle's other friends began planning a festschrift, a collection of articles to be published as a book in her honor. They solicited contributions, both academic and financial, from scholars with whom she had worked. Proceeding in secrecy, they planned to surprise Belle with the volume upon its completion. Meta Harrsen contacted Bernard Berenson for an article, knowing that Belle's "'Italian period' was one of the happiest, as well as one of the most profound experiences of her life." Bernard immediately agreed and contributed to the costs as well. This contact began a correspondence that kept Bernard apprised of Belle's status through her last days.[59]

Even after some difficult dental work that winter drained still more of Belle's dwindling energy, she continued to come in to the Library. Her co-workers hoped that the warmth of spring would give her its usual boost. Sometime during that season, someone took a photograph of Belle seated in the West Room, at Mr. Morgan's desk. According to Frederick Adams she was looking at one of her favorite manuscripts— the ninth-century Reims Gospels. When Bernard saw the picture, he said he did not recognize the woman he knew at first but "discovered all of her as I looked further—not so far gone as I had feared."[60]

Soon after this photo was taken, Belle fell again, this time injuring her back. She could no longer leave her home, and she was no longer taking life in her stride. In fact, she was preparing to die. Belle was still religious. There were rumors she had converted to Catholicism, and some had certainly tried to convert her. But Belle was probably less interested in denominational differences than in the transcendent truths and experiences of the divine. She had always been equally comfortable confronting herself and the sublime in nature and in church. If she shared the Christian belief in an afterlife, its promise surely would have comforted her as she faced her own death. So many of those she had loved most had gone before her: her mother, her sisters, her nephew. Did she still think about her father? Surely in heaven she could be with him if she wanted without worrying about such human fabrications as race.

Her preparation was practical as well as spiritual. Belle destroyed her personal papers, including the hundreds, possibly thousands of letters from Bernard.

Harrsen, one of her closest companions in those final months, visited Belle faithfully at home. In early April, Meta contacted Rose Nichols, an old friend of Belle's, to explain Belle's situation and arrange a visit. When Rose arrived, she found Belle bedridden, but talkative, even cheerful at times, especially when they discussed Bernard. Belle had become, Rose reported to B.B., very gentle and affectionate, begging her not to leave and to come again soon.[61]

Rose did return and brought a letter from Bernard. B.B.'s letter, and Rose's conversation with Belle, focused on her family and her origins. Her friends apparently all now believed that Belle and her family had "crossed the color line." At the end of her life, they encouraged her to talk to them about it. B.B. mentioned how beautiful Belle's mother had been and talked about the sacrifices Mrs. Greene had made to give her daughters an education. But, Rose reported, Belle did not respond and refused to answer any questions about her father. Nor did Belle explain to Rose why she destroyed Bernard's letters, which had "contributed so largely to her education." At some point, perhaps through a third party like Rose, Belle asked Bernard to destroy her letters to him as well. Bernard hesitated; Frederick Adams, and probably many others as well, urged him to preserve them. She had destroyed his autobiography, he mourned, but he could not bring himself to destroy hers.[62]

Soon after this lunch with Rose Nichols, Belle had a final stroke that left her completely unable to speak or to move her right side. She returned to St. Luke's Hospital, in the same neighborhood she had lived in when she first came to work for J. P. Morgan. Her room was filled with huge bouquets of flowers, mostly roses, sent by her many friends and colleagues, including Junius Morgan.[63] Belle was still alert and very aware of her surroundings, but she was not expected to live more than a few days. Meta Harrsen described her first visit to Belle at St. Luke's after this last debilitating stroke:

> Her wonderful eyes alone showed that she was fully conscious of everything that was said to her. So, although we had wanted to surprise her with the accomplished Festschrift, in the brief moments I was with her, I told her what a magnificent tribute her friends had been working on for a

year. Her eyes lighted up and with her one good left hand she pulled me down to her and kissed me. So, at least, she knows and it gave her a moment of joy. That is something for which we can all be thankful.[64]

Dorothy Miner arrived from Baltimore. She, Meta, and Anne Haight took turns visiting the hospital when they were allowed and when Belle was awake. Bernard began writing a final letter for them to read to her, but it was too late.

On May 10, Meta wrote Berenson that Belle was "peacefully breathing her last" and was not expected to survive the day. She was sleeping more and more and responding to her friends' visits less and less. Only her eyes, Meta said, had shown any life the last time she had seen her conscious. Everyone who was with Belle during her final week, however, felt that she looked "far off and safe," as if she were, as a friend's telegram put it, "in the hollow of God's hand." Despite her condition, Belle had completely charmed the nurses who cared for her. And her illness had brought her friends closer together as well. Meta explained to Bernard that they were now calling each other by their given names and invited Mr. Berenson to do the same, signing herself "Meta." Soon she was using the familiar "B.B."[65]

If Belle's friends are to be believed, her brother and sister did not come to see her during her final days. This is perhaps understandable, given the bitterness and loss that had come between Belle and Teddy. Sharing a child proved too difficult for the sisters, and when he died their last connection was severed. More surprising is the apparent absence of Russell. Belle had mentioned being close to her brother as recently as 1943 and 1944, but in her final visit with Rose she apparently let it be known that Russell "no longer counts in her life."[66] It may also have been a dangerous time for her remaining siblings to be present. In illness and death Belle was losing control over—among many other things—her ability to contain the rumors about her ancestry. Even on her deathbed her friends were questioning the identity of her father and her mother's background. Belle still had the mental faculties to maintain her protective silence on the matter, but her siblings may not have been sure that she would, or could. Whatever the reasons for their absence, Belle's final days were spent in the company of hospital staff and a few loving friends. Anne Haight took care of the many personal details involved in arranging for Belle's care.

Belle died at five minutes to eleven on the night of May 10. According to the nurse on duty, she simply stopped breathing in her sleep. Meta noted bitterly that "the brother" called the next day and mistakenly told the papers she had died on the eleventh.[67] Junius Morgan sent telegrams to all the Library trustees who were abroad, as well as to Fred Adams, who had left the day before for his vacation and was on the *Queen Mary*. All simply said, "Miss Greene died yesterday."[68]

Epilogue

THE PASSING OF BELLE GREENE

She was one of the great women of our time and of the world.

—W. G. Constable, 1950[1]

Institutions are funny places and their true histories are never written,—even the surviving documents for them are carefully eradicated from their records,—and so we shall never know about what she really accomplished and the reverberations of the rattle and bang will soon fade.

—William Ivins, 1950[2]

FUNERAL SERVICES FOR BELLE da Costa Greene were held at St. Thomas Church on May 15 with a regular Episcopal service. Meta Harrsen chose hymns and readings she knew Belle would like: "Ein' festre Burg ist unser Gott" (A Mighty Fortress Is Our God), Psalm 23 ("The Lord Is My Shepherd"), and "Onward Christian Soldiers." The coffin was covered with crimson roses from the Library. Two hundred friends gathered from all over the eastern seaboard. Meta believed that "there was great rejoicing in Heaven, when she met Bobby and both Mr. Morgans and old Prof. Hyvernat and all the others." Her body was later cremated and the ashes buried in Kensico Cemetery, Valhalla, New York. If her three remaining family members were there, Belle's friends did not record their presence.[3]

Friends were left behind to memorialize, mourn, blame, and otherwise try to make meaning of Belle's life and death. If it was true that her family had abandoned her (or that she had cut them off), then it seems apparent that the same had happened with some of her friendships. Meta recommended Anne Haight to Bernard Berenson as "one of the small select company that remained watchful and true through the dark times, overlooking insults, and remembering all the fine things and happy times she owed Belle." Rose Nichols later reminisced that Belle had loved a "lively quarrel." Rose believed she had escaped scot-free "probably because of my insignificance," but that was only because she hadn't read Belle's letters. Even her faithful and beloved Miss Harrsen had "felt the lash of her tongue."[4]

Some blamed her death on her own bad behavior. Billy Ivins believed her death was caused by "dipso[mania]" or alcoholism. Bernard might have agreed. He thought her "suicidal faults" had brought her to a premature end. She had surely lived her life at full throttle, stealing hours out of the night to fit more into the day, pushing her body past its limits many times to work harder, play longer, and love more joyfully than most of her peers ever could. Still, her life was hardly tragically short. Belle was just over seventy when she died, certainly premature to someone still going strong into his eighties as Bernard was, but well within, perhaps even beyond, the life expectancy of a woman of her generation.[5]

Neither man seemed to be aware that Belle had battled cancer in the last years of her life. Without knowing Belle's exact diagnosis, we cannot judge whether her life choices had anything to do with her final illness. Smoking could have caused certain kinds of cancer (and the one reference to Belle's "so-called bronchitis" suggests she may have had lung problems), but many others have no relationship to behavior.

And it is impossible to say whether the hearty drinking she enjoyed, when she was not on the wagon, translated into health problems. The mere fact that Belle was able to give up alcohol so easily when her doctor or her own whims decreed it suggests that Billy's diagnosis of alcoholism may have been as exaggerated as his claim that she could not speak or recognize anyone at her retirement celebration.[6]

Regardless of how they viewed her final years, all of her friends worried that Belle and her accomplishments would be forgotten. For the next decade several of them worked hard to make sure that would not happen. The main theme in their correspondence with each other was remembering Belle, both publicly and privately. Anne Haight was the most determined. She began collecting letters and materials related to Belle almost immediately, planning to write a biography. Many of Belle's friends supported this project. Meta Harrsen promised to visit the Princeton Library records and look for some of Belle's "nebulous vital facts." (She would have been unsuccessful: no such records exist in its archives.) Harrsen also arranged for Haight to interview several people in Princeton about Belle's early training and associates there. So much "conjecture and fantastic rumor" surrounded Belle's background and early experiences that they were determined to get an accurate chronology and facts. Haight planned a trip to Italy to interview Berenson, and she may have made it, for she reportedly had copies of many of Belle's letters to Bernard.[7] Bernard must have had second thoughts, however, because he told Rose Nichols that he had decided not to let Haight include any of his letters in her biography. Rose also decided not to turn over any of hers. "If I should have any of them published," she said, "I would rather interpret them in my own way."[8] She never did.

Belle's letters truly do need interpretation, particularly as she specialized in the ironic tone and did not mind leaving impulsive rants in ink. Haight, who had been reading Belle's letters to Berenson, grappled with the question of whether to publish portions in which Belle vented anger at J.P.'s demands and games and jealousies. Harrsen agreed that it was too soon to air such "devastating criticism" of J.P. and Anne Morgan, Herbert Satterlee, and Juliet Hamilton. Too many family members were still alive. Meta attributed it all to the pressure Belle was under, and both women understood that "much of what is objectionable was just her feeling at the moment—and her reaction and sorrow for Mr. Morgan at his death fully shows that."[9]

Scholars could memorialize Miss Greene in other ways. Bernard dedicated the English version of *Seeing and Knowing* "To the Memory of Belle Greene, Soul of the Morgan Library." But he did not find his emotional life much affected by her passing. True, she had been part of his very self for twenty years, he wrote a friend, but it had been a long time since she had haunted his daily life. A few years later Rose Nichols told him, "You did more for Belle than any of her friends or lovers. She was devoted to you and could not bear to differ with you about people or things."[10]

The work of the festschrift continued, and in 1954 *Studies in Art and Literature for Belle da Costa Greene* was published. A small group of friends gathered to celebrate the occasion at a restaurant near the Morgan Library: Meta Harrsen invited Dorothy Miner, Rose Nichols, and Anne Haight to join several of the faithful Morgan staff: Violet White, Felice Stampfle, and Curt Bühler. They sent a card, signed by all, to Bernard Berenson telling him, "The only person we miss at this occasion more than B.G. is yourself!" Meta also wrote to describe their celebration, at which Belle's "loving spirit and cheer" showed up and infected them. And Meta made a not so loving and cheerful point of telling Bernard that she did not invite Frederick Adams to the luncheon. Belle's friends had wanted the Morgan Library to host an event commemorating the festscrift but received no encouragement from its new director.[11]

Studies in Art and Literature was indeed something to celebrate. At least four times the size and weight of a standard hardcover book, it was, as Bernard had predicted, massive. Not exactly conducive to reading in bed, Hroswithian Rachel Hunt suggested, but beautiful.[12] With five hundred pages of text and almost four hundred illustrative plates, it includes both direct tributes to Belle and scholarly articles written in her honor. Contributors included Bernard Berenson, William Ivins, Arthur Hind, Eric Millar, Theodore Petersen, Charles Morey, the

Duke of Alba, Cardinal Eugene Tisserant, Cardinal Giovanni Mercati, and the Earl of Ilchester. Several Morgan Library employees were also represented: Curt Bühler, Lawrence C. Wroth, and Felice Stampfle. There were, as one reviewer put it, "curators, keepers, and professors of most of the major museums, libraries, and universities of the western world."[13]

And the community of friends and colleagues who contributed was larger still. Donors included Frederick Adams; fellow Hroswitha members Henrietta Bartlett, Anne Haight, Rachel Hunt, and Rose Nichols; Paul and Meta Sachs; John D. Rockefeller Jr.; the Rosenbach brothers; Meta Harrsen; Dorothy Miner; the trustees and fellows of the Pierpont Morgan Library; Belle's brother, Russell da Costa Greene; and her lawyer, Nathan Goldberger. Russell was also surprisingly supportive of Anne Haight's biography plans.

Belle would have loved her festschrift, would have spent hours devouring every detail of every page that considered a hundred different books or works of arts, as well as general issues in the field: punctuation marks in Copic manuscripts, the state of pre-Christian Asia, the illustrations in one of her Armenian lectionaries, the meaning of the ostrich egg in a Piero della Francesca alterpiece, or the first published study of the last illuminated manuscript she purchased. About half of the essays were on medieval subjects, many on medieval manuscripts Belle had acquired herself. The volume served to honor her in the way that she would have appreciated deeply, by contributing scholarship in the areas she most supported and highlighting the development and worth of the Morgan Library. Many of the articles focused either on specific manuscripts or items held in the Library, and others on general fields represented by its collections. The volume was, one enthusiastic reviewer rejoiced, "as wide as her interests and as miscellaneous as her enthusiasms."[14]

Lawrence Wroth's article (drawn from the talk he gave to the American Historical Association in 1941 at Belle's request) highlighted the worth of the Morgan collection to historians. E. A. Lowe's article on the Golden Gospels (M 23), an illuminated manuscript written in gold letters on purple parchment, discussed various theories on its date, concluding that it was probably tenth century. Bernard Berenson offered a sketch of a book he did not think he would complete on the decline and recovery of figure arts, offering analytic criteria for future students to follow. And Patrick Skehan's study of M 828, an Ethiopian Four Gospels, compared Belle to the princess who commissioned the manuscript, speculating that her pleasure upon receiving it could not have equaled the "sparkling joy . . . with which Miss Greene saw to its inclusion in the Pierpont Morgan Library."[15]

In her foreword, Dorothy Miner mourned the biography that would never be written and remembered "Belle's loyalty and her sense of fun, her crushing forthrightness of speech and her surpassing generosity," and her "astonishing capacity for people." These had been her lasting contributions to scholarship, in lieu of a list of publications to be read by future generations. Belle had befriended and supported scholars thoughout her career, the sages and the students alike, encouraging, challenging, questioning. Although Miner had a distinguished formal education, she clearly considered herself a student of "B.G." as much as of any professor.[16]

Dorothy Miner received many accolades for her work in compiling and editing the volume. The Walters Art Gallery trustees (still her employers) cited her work on this "fitting memorial to . . . Miss Greene's great contributions to the appreciation of works of art and literature." The Hroswithians, many of whom had become acquainted with Dorothy during Belle's final illness and the work on the festschrift, made her a member soon after *Studies in Art and Literature* appeared. Three years later Meta was elected as well.[17]

The Hroswitha Club also hoped to commemorate Belle's life. As late as 1961 they were still collecting funds and discussing plans with Adams on where in the Library they might place a memorial to her. Adams suggested that the club donate decorative plaques showing the development of printing machines in her name, with a plaque noting the donation. The Hroswithians agreed. They presented sixteen carved printers' marks to the Library in Belle's memory.[18]

While these various memorials to Belle's scholarship and friendship were in progress, her material possessions were being disseminated through her social circles as well. Her will took a while to untangle. Oddly, although she had known she was seriously ill for years, she had not updated it in over a decade. Three of her heirs had proceeded her in death: her mother, her nephew, and Ethel. Russell, along with her lawyer of many decades, Nathan Goldberger, were the executors; only Teddy and her daughter remained to inherit Belle's sizable estate. The Morgan Library would receive some of the share allotted to Bobbie. At the time of her death Belle's net worth was almost $200,000. Some of the money was given as outright bequests to family members, executors, and servants. Her family, her lawyer, and presumably some representative of the Morgan Library agreed to place the rest of her assets (about $175,000) in a trust fund. Teddy would receive an annuity of $3,600, and the Library would receive any additional earnings the fund might have made that year. The trust was held by Morgan & Co.[19]

As for her collected works of art, books, jewelry, and other valuables, Belle had dispersed many of the choice items to her family or the Library. She left her antique jewelry to the Library, and her modern pieces to her family—her sister and niece got those. But her colleagues and friends had the opportunity to purchase, at appraisal prices, some of her other personal items: glassware, pottery, and especially books. Meta helped Adams divide up Belle's private library. Some stayed at the Morgan, some went to the Hroswitha Club, some to the New York Public Library. Bobbie's medical books went to the American Academy of Medicine, and staff members were allowed to select from the remainder. Meta chose one—Heinrich Heine's *Buch der Lieder*, a collection of nineteenth-century German poems—to send to Bernard.[20]

Stories about Belle went into circulation as well. Whenever people met who had known her, Meta said, they instantly began to exchange reminiscences that brought her vital presence back. This turned out to be another way to memorialize her, as many of these stories have been passed down to current generations of curators, librarians, and biographers. By this time the friends of Belle who had rallied around her in her final days had become fast friends of one another as well. It was always satisfying, Meta remarked, "when B.G. enthusiasts meet."[21]

Meta herself loved to recall, when writing to mutual friends, Belle's beauty, her ribald comments, and "the procession of *beaux*" who were in and out of favor during their association. She listed a few for Bernard: Mitchell Kennerly was the first she had known, but he was "on the verge of being dismissed" by then. There was a Count Sala, a young Norwegian man (a "flash-in-the-pan with Belle while it lasted"), Lord Ilchester, Billy Ivins, Joe Breck, the Duke of Alba (whom Belle called "my cousin"), Adolph Goldschmidt, and Eric Millar. Belle's beaus might find themselves "in a Harlem night club or perhaps at the Beaux Arts Ball," Meta recalled. Unfortunately, she added, that side of Belle would not be recorded for posterity.[22] Little did she know: Belle's affair with Berenson would make its way into almost every biography of the art scholar.

Unfortunately, Anne Haight was not able to complete her biography of Belle. She and Dorothy Miner did coauthor an entry in the 1971 biographical reference work *Notable American Women*. They said Belle was born in Alexandria, Virginia, on December 13, 1883. This was four years late, but it still revealed her to be significantly older than her friends had realized. Mrs. Greene was described as a native of Richmond, Virginia, "a proud and cultivated lady of old-fashioned dignity" who moved to Princeton with her children to teach music after separating from her husband. Since Anne Haight also had possession of Belle's letters to Sydney Cockerell, her claims that he played a central role in tutoring her in manuscript illuminations are probably valid. But the new details (almost entirely wrong) of Belle's early life suggest that someone, perhaps Russell or B.B., may have fed misinformation to Belle's friends. And even stranger, Haight and Miner also wrote that Belle did not meet Bernard until after J. P. Morgan's death in 1913 when Berenson came to appraise the Morgan art collection. Anyone with full access to Belle's letters to Bernard would have known this to be untrue. Belle's first letter to Bernard was dated early 1909, and Berenson played no role in appraising the estate. Most likely Belle's friends sought to protect her reputation, even after her death, just as they did not put into writing their suspicions or knowledge about her racial ancestry.

Still, despite its many errors and missed guesses, Dorothy and Anne were able to place Belle and her career into the public record for later generations to read and consider. By the time Anne Haight wrote this article, she was already so ill that she had to abandon the biography project. Dorothy may have been enlisted to help for this reason. But Haight spoke with at least two biographers probably in the 1960s as well. She shared letters with Cass Canfield, for his *Incredible Pierpont Morgan*, and spoke with Meryle Secrest, who wrote so vividly about Belle in her Berenson biography.[23]

In fact, so widespread were these suspicions, that they made it into at least one newspaper notice of Belle da Costa Greene's death. Most obituaries lauded her work, recounted the glamor of her early career, the highlights of her purchases: the $42,800 *Morte d'Arthur*, the sixteen Caxtons bargained away from the auction table in London. But several publications also mentioned that Belle's friends were of the opinion that she and her family had crossed the color line.

For many, Belle's significance will continue to lie in her identity, especially her racial identity. She was a glamorous librarian, whose image lends panache to an often undervalued profession, an astute collector who shaped an internationally renowned library of rare written and artistic treasures from around the world. Her complicated performance of her gender in both her social and her professional worlds drew on often contradictory messages about women's proper behavior, appearance, and access to authority. She was a flamboyant and creative woman who, despite herself, helped pave the way for a new generation of working women even as she wavered on her public stance on women's roles. Her complicated performance of race and ethnicity also illuminates much on America's racial landscape in the early twentieth century. As Belle da Costa Greene, of mysterious, exotic origins, rumored to be from Cuba, Portugal, New Orleans, suspected to have some black ancestry, Belle gained far greater privilege and freedom than that which Belle Marion Greener, daughter of the first black man to graduate from Harvard College, could ever have inherited in this period of history. Still, Belle did so not by simply becoming white or passing as white. She implicitly claimed whiteness while letting speculation about her ancestry continue and feeding but never confirming rumors about her own background.

Belle would have wanted her story to end, of course, at the Library. Many institutions manifest her influences, but none more clearly than her own beloved collection on East Thirty-sixth Street. In April 2006, ninety years and a few months after she first began her work for Mr. Morgan, the Library opened its doors on yet another incarnation. The Pierpont Morgan Library and Museum is now a four-story modern building boasting brightly lit exhibit rooms, new offices and reading room, and even an auditorium. The newest renovations nestle around the original marble building Belle first entered in 1905. Given her resistance to modern aesthetics, Belle would probably have been dubious about the architecture. (Then again, she did grow to love Matisse.) But she would have loved the multiple exhibits on display in the summer of 2006: medieval and Renaissance manuscripts, printed books and bindings, and ancient Near Eastern seals and tablets, to name a few. It is not an American Bibliothèque Nationale, but the landscape of American libraries and museums has changed radically since Belle had that vision. The Morgan Library is highly prestigious and almost unique, precisely for its vast holdings of rare books and manuscripts, as well as bindings, papers, and art. The institution she shaped and promoted tirelessly is clearly growing in both its mission to serve scholars and its role as a public institution.

Nor is Belle forgotten by those who now keep the collection growing and living. There are plans to reinstall the printers' marks donated in her honor in the new bindery area.[24] Her name will be remembered within the Library that stands as a continued testament to her life and accomplishments. It is Belle da Costa Greene's most concrete legacy.

Acknowledgments

IT IS A PLEASURE to reach the point of publicly recognizing the many people and institutions that helped support this project. First, Jeff Kleinman introduced me to Belle da Costa Greene and has been an enthusiastic supporter and advocate ever since. Our fabulous editor for *Love on Trial*, Amy Cherry, introduced me to Jeff and wanted to work with me again on the project that became this book. Amy was unfailingly positive in the broad issues, and scrupulously attentive to details of writing and of history.

Before the official funding found me, Benedict Giamo, then chair of the American Studies Department at the University of Notre Dame, and Greg Sterling, associate dean in the College of Arts and Letters, helped make ad hoc funding happen for my first trip to Italy and a laptop to take with me. Jason and Jeni Ardizzone-West hosted me while I worked at the Morgan Library, allowing me to complete preliminary research before it closed for renovations. If it had not been for this early assistance, I might not have been able to earn the grants and fellowships that funded the following years of research travel: a Francis M. Kobayashi Research Travel Grant, a Faculty Research Program Grant from the Graduate School's Office of Research, and an Interim Grant from the Institute for Scholarship in the Liberal Arts, all at the University of Notre Dame, as well as an Everett Helms Visiting Fellowship from the Lilly Library at the University of Indiana, Bloomington. I am completing this manuscript in 2006 instead of 2008 because of all this assistance and because of a yearlong leave from teaching in 2005–2006.

Like all researchers, I am indebted to the expertise and generosity of numerous librarians, archivists, and curators. Because much of my research was done in art museums or archives related to art and art history, I also benefited from the interests and stories Belle da Costa Greene continues to generate in that world. Almost everyone had a story to tell, and although not all aprocryphal tales of the notorious B.G. made it into the book, all helped inform my image of her and her impact. I am particularly grateful to Christine Nelson, curator of Literary and Historical Manuscripts of the Morgan Library, who shared discoveries, allowed me access in cramped quarters to uncatalogued collections while the Library was closed for renovations, and helped me double-check citations as the Library was reopening. William Voelkle, curator of Medieval and Renaissance Manuscripts of the Morgan Library, enthusiastically shared collected stories about Belle da Costa Greene, and some of his sources as well. Three guardians of the Morgan Library Reading Room, Sylvia Merien, Inge Dupont, and Vanessa Pintado, protect, preserve, and make accessible the manuscripts and books to which Belle devoted her life.

In the Biblioteca Berenson at Villa I Tatti's Harvard University Center for Italian Renaissance Studies, Fiorella Superbi and Giovanni Pagliarulo welcomed me warmly day after day for three months. Eve Borsook, Susan Arcamone, and Patrizia Carella also helped make my time at I Tatti memorable, as did Hectore. Anne and Lorenzo Martini oriented me to Italy's culture, food, and language and provided a sense of home and familiarity for my first, eye-opening experience of the country of half my ancestors. Conrad Rader and Anne Millen Martini helped me explore Rome, Florence, and Venice and trace Belle's path through several Tuscan towns.

My research, particularly the compilation of a database of Belle's correspondence, was assisted by a series of brilliant young Notre Dame students, including Maura Malloy, Joyce De Leon, and Katherine Cardinalli. My thanks to the Dean's Office in the College of Arts and Letters for funding their work. John Clark assisted with last-minute footnote checks. Professional World War Two researcher William Beigel located Robert M. Leveridge Jr.'s military records for me and helped me interpret them.

I am also indebted to several circles of scholars whose work and support made this project possible. Biographers of Bernard Berenson kept the mythology of Belle Greene in print through the 1960s and 1980s. I have relied most heavily on Ernest Samuel's two-volume biography for background on the Berensons' family and professional life. Jean Strouse identified Belle's parents in her biography of J. Pierpont Morgan. Her discovery brought Belle da Costa Greene's story back into circulation, setting the wheels in motion for this book. Michael Mounter wrote an encyclopedic intellectual biography of Richard T. Greener as a dissertation and was exceedingly generous with his time and additional information as we swapped information and resources via e-mail.

Numerous people responded to early presentations or drafts of my writing, talked to me about the project, or offered suggestions, stories, or advice. The Gender History Group and the Africana Studies Erskine Peters Fellows' Writing Workshops have provided just the kind of intellectual community all scholars hope to find. Special thanks to Gail Bederman, Emily Osborn, Susam Ohmer, Ben Giamo, Brandi Brimmer, Kathleen Pyne, Sophie White, Quincy Mills, Richard Pierce, Margaret Meserve, Margaret Abruzzo, Hilary Jones, and Valerie Sayers. My undergraduate students in "American Men, American Women," "Race, Gender, and Women of Color," and "Homefronts during War" have all helped me stay focused on the big picture while keeping me aware of how much an individual's life can both complicate and illuminate our meta-narratives of history. Alexis Stokes and Diane Sampson did heroic work, reading a near-final draft of my entire manuscript and offering just the right balance of encouragement and criticism. My thanks also to Otto Sonntag, for his most careful and extremely helpful copyediting, and to other, unknown readers and editors at Norton. Also to Lydia Fitzpatrick, my fabulous editor's assistant

Friends and decidedly nonintellectual activites helped keep me sane and balanced. My thanks to the folks at the South Bend Regional Art Museum, the Niles Readers Theater workshop, the Niles District Community Library, the Four Flags Players, Juliana Bergsma Jiminez, Gina Shropshire, Sara McKibben, Jessica Chalmers, Nancy Studebaker, and the Oblates of Blues, who forever changed my image of theologians. My thanks also to everyone who left me alone and forgave my neglect when balance became temporarily impossible.

My parents, Wendy and Richard Ardizzone, are at the core of everything I do. My birth family still sustains me even when the visits are all too few. My new family has proven to be an ideal environment for writing, among other things. Conrad Rader wisely refused all offers to become my full-time unpaid personal assistant, but he kept the cats out of the office and the dishes washed, dragged me out to Warren Dunes Beach at least once a week, and provided a calm center in my life. For that and so much more, I dedicate this book to him.

Notes

CITATION FORMS AND ABBREVIATIONS

I have made every attempt to cite archived documents in a manner that both fits the individual preferences of the archives and allows for consistency between archives in my notes. Generally notes give citation information in the following pattern: document identification, date of document, archive, collection, and file or box name, if relevant or necessary for finding the document.

Primary sources were often in the form of handwritten documents. Belle's handwriting varied from her own self-described "scrawl" to her professionally taught, evenly rounded printing. The former was usually used in personal correspondence, however. Belle punctuated primarily with dashes, underlines, capital letters and unorthodox spellings ("daaarling"), as did some of her correspondents. In longer quotations, I occasionally replaced dashes with commas or periods for clarity, wrote out "and" for "+" and, in all sources, quietly corrected spelling errors when they were small and obvious and did not affect the meaning of the phrase. Ambiguous, illegible, or missing words are noted with brackets. Underlines, capitalizations, and other written inflections are reproduced faithfully.

The following abbreviations are used for archives and collections (the names of collections are listed here under the archive in which they are currently found):

VIT   Bernard Berenson Archive, Harvard Center for Italian Renaissance Studies, Villa I Tatti, Florence

PML   The Pierpont Morgan Library, New York
              Literary and historical manuscripts owned by the Morgan Library are identified by accession number in footnotes.

AML   Archives of the Pierpont Morgan Library, New York
              Correspondence and records pertaining to the business of the Morgan Library itself are identified by collection.
              MCC   Morgan Collections Correspondence ARC 1310

Most letters in MCC are individually catalogued in Cosair, the PML online database. Those that are not are identified by file. MCC records begin before Belle's arrival in 1906 and generally run through the 1920s, although some files run well into the 1940s.

DOG   Records of the Director's Office (Greene)

Chronology between MCC, RDOG, and RDOGA is inconsistent. Generally representing the later years of Belle Greene's directorship (1920s–1940s), these records are not catalogued and are here identified by file.

RDOG-A   Records of the Director's Office (Greene-Adams)

This record set generally contains files from the 1940s and later, and seems to have been organized by Frederick Adams, when he assumed the directorship. Only papers up to 1950 are available to researchers at this time.

JPMJ   John Pierpont Morgan Jr. Papers

Overlapping in chronology with MCC and RDOG, these papers represent Jack Morgan's files. Because of the moving involved with the reopening of the Morgan Library in 2006, I was unable to double-check some of my citations from this collection. Every effort has been made to ensure accuracy.

EC   Edward S. Curtis Papers, ARC 1307

ICOR   Institute of Christian Oriental Religion, Catholic University of America

    HH   Henri Hyvernat Papers

       PPM   Professional Papers, Morgan Collection

This collection contains many duplicates of letters (both in drafts and in typed copies) contained in Hyvernat's correspondence at the Morgan Library. Wherever possible, I have cited the location of the original letter.

    TCP   Theodore C. Peterson Papers

Hired as an assistant to Henri Hyvernat, Father Peterson took over correspondence and much of the work on the Morgan Hamouli Coptic manuscripts.

LLIU   Lily Library, Indiana University

    HWS   Hannah Whitall Smith MSS

    HYT   Henry Yates Thompson MSS

FGA   Freer Gallery of Art and Arthur M. Sackler Gallery Archives, Smithsonian Institute

    CF   Charles Lang Freer Papers

HLHU   Houghton Library, Harvard University

HUAMA	Harvard University Art Museums Archive
PS	Paul Sachs Papers, Fogg Art Museum

MSRC:HU	Moorhead-Springherd Research Collection, Howard University
FJG	Frances J. Grimke Papers

CAH	The Center for American History, University of Texas, Austin
NYJAM	*New York Journal,* American [Clippings] Morgue

GC	Grolier Club Library
HC	Hroswitha Club

PUA   Princeton University Archives

PHS   Princeton Historical Society

ACASC   Amherst College Archives and Special Collections

BLM	British Library Manuscripts
SC	Sydney Cockerell Papers
WC	Walter Crum Papers

AAAS	American Art Archives, Smithsonian
WI	William Ivins Papers
MF	Mary Fanton Papers
DVT	Daniel V. Thompson Papers

SC   Smith College

AHRC   Army Human Resources Command, Alexandria, Va.

Personal names that appear often in the footnotes are abbreviated as follows:

AC	Albert T. Clay		BQ	Bernard Quaritch
AF	Annie Adams Fields		CM	Charlotte Martins
AG	Adolph Goldschmidt		CR	Sir Charles Hercules Read
AH	Anne Sherman Haight		DVT	Daniel Varney Thompson
AM	Agnes Meyer		EG	Ethel Grant
AP	Alfred Pollard		EHD	Edmund Hunt Dring
AR	Alys (Smith) Russell		EM	Eric Millar
AT	Ada Thurston		ER	Emile Rey
BB	Bernard Berenson		FA	Frederick Adams
BG	Belle da Costa Greene		FJG	Francis J. Grimké

FW	F. Wheeler	LL	Luther Livingston
FK	Francis W. Kelsey	LO	Leo Olschki
GD	George Durlacher	LW	Lawrence Wroth
GS	Geoffrey Scott	MB	Mary Berenson
GW	George Williamson	MF	Mary Fanton
HF	Helen Franc	MH	Meta Harrsen
HH	Henri Hyvernat	MJ	Margaret Jackson
HSM	Henry S. Morgan	PH	Philip Hofer
HWS	Hannah Whitall Smith	PS	Paul Sachs
HYT	Henry Yates Thompson	RC	Rachel Costelloe
ISG	Isabella Stewart Gardner	RG	Ruth Granniss
IW	Isaiah Wears	RH	Roger Howson
JCW	Jacob C. White	RN	Rose Nichols
JEB	John E. Bruce	RTG	Richard Theodore Greener
JM	Joseph Martini	SB	Senda Berenson
JPM	John Pierpont (J. P.) Morgan	SC	Sir Sydney Cockerell
JPMJ	John Pierpont (Jack) Morgan Jr.	TP	Theodore Petersen
JS	Jacques Seligmann	TS	Thomas Shahan
JSM	Junius Spencer Morgan (son of JPMJ)	WI	William (Billy) Ivins
		VS	Vladimir Simkhovitch

INTRODUCTION

1. "Belle of the Books," *Time*, 11 April 1949, 76–77.
2. BG to BB, 19 Jan. 1912, VIT.
3. This quotation is attributed to the British portrait photographer Ernest Walter Histed. William M. Voelkle, "Livre la Chasse," *Princeton*, 2005, 22.
4. Jean Strouse does not believe the two were lovers, given Morgan's preference for women somewhat closer to his age and station, and given that her voice in addressing him in letters was very different from that used for lovers. I would add that she was perfectly capable of writing formally to lovers, but I, too, have found no evidence that Belle and Morgan had an affair. Strouse does note, "As flirts, they were in the same league." Strouse, *Morgan: American Financier* (New York: Harper Perennial, 2000), 516.
5. Inge Dupont and Hope Mayo, eds., *Morgan Library Ghost Stories* (New York: Fordham University Press, 1990).
6. Aline B. Louchheim, "The Morgan Library and Miss Greene," *New York Times*, 17 May 1949.
7. Gertrude Atherton, *The Living Present* (New York: Frederick A. Stokes, 1917), 296.
8. John H. Burma, "The Measurement of Negro 'Passing,'" *American Journal of*

Sociology 52, (July 1946): 18–22; James E. Conyers and T. H. Kennedy, 1964, "Reported Knowledge Negro and White College Students Have of Negroes Who Have Passed as Whites," *Journal of Negro Education* 33 (Autumn 1964): 454–59. 1932. Caroline Bond Day, *A Study of Some Negro-White Families in the United States*, foreword by Earnest A. Hooton (Cambridge: Peabody Museum of Harvard University, 1932; reprint, New York: Negro Universities Press, 1970).

9. Meryle Secrest, *Being Bernard Berenson: A Biography* (New York: Holt, Rinehart and Winston, 1979), 291.

10. Nicholas Basbanes, *A Gentle Madness: Bibliophiles, Bibliomanes, and the Eternal Passion for Books* (New York: Henry Holt, 1995).

11. Dorothy Miner, ed., *Studies in Art and Literature for Belle da Costa Greene* (Princeton: Princeton University Press, 1954), x–xi.

12. Secrest, *Being Bernard Berenson*, 294; Ernest Samuels, *Bernard Berenson: The Making of a Legend* (Cambridge: Harvard University Press, Belknap Press, 1987), 541.

13. I spent two weeks in the summer of 2002 and nearly three months in the spring of 2003 transcribing these letters. According to archivists there, I was the first scholar to look at all of her letters and the first to transcribe them in their entirety, although others certainly have looked at them and made full use of her irresistibly quotable writing style.

14. BG to BB, 19 April 1909, VIT.

CHAPTER 1: RAISED EXPECTATIONS

1. Dorothy Miner, "Foreword," in Dorothy Miner, ed., *Studies in Art and Literature for Belle da Costa Greene* (Princeton: Princeton University Press, 1954), xi.

2. Jacqueline M. Moore, *Leading the Race: The Transformation of the Black Elite in the Nation's Capital, 1980–1920* (Charlottesville: University Press of Virginia, 1999).

3. Various versions of their meeting and Greene's usual biography include Louis Auchincloss, *J. P. Morgan: The Financier as Collector* (New York: Harry N. Abrams, 1990), and Aline B. Louchheim, "The Morgan Library and Miss Greene," *New York Times,* 17 April 1949.

4. BG to BB, 10 July 1909, 22 Nov. 1910, VIT.

5. During Belle's lifetime the terms "Negro" and "colored" were most often used to refer to all people of African ancestry. Both terms sometimes had other meanings as well, but generally were intended to include people of mixed black and white ancestry. The terms "black" and "Afro-American" were also in use at the time, although not as common. "Black" sometimes was used to distinguish people of mixed ancestry from those whose ancestry was predominantly African, but it could be used inclusively as well. I tend to use all of these terms when I am paraphrasing or otherwise trying to invoke the language and sensibility of the time. I also use the contemporary term "African American" to refer to all Americans with recognized African ancestry. People of mixed black and white ancestry were often called "mixed-bloods," "mulattoes," "quadroons," or "octoroons" in the nineteenth- and early twentieth-century public discourse, and sometimes referred to by other, more descriptive terms as well: "brown," "yellow," "tan," "near-white." During slavery free African Americans were often called "people of color." Although all of these terms, as well as the term "white," could appropriately be

placed in quotes to emphasize their socially constructed nature, I do so only when discussing a particular term or quoting.

6. Although many previous publications had reported or repeated rumors and speculation about Belle's black ancestry, Jean Strouse was the first scholar to confirm Belle's background and identify her parents. Strouse, *Morgan: American Financier* (New York: Harper Perennial, 2000), 509–16; W. E. B. Du Bois, "Talented Tenth," in *The Negro Problem* (New York: J. Pott, 1903), 34–35.

7. BB to DVT, 17 May 1934, AAAS:DVT, "Correspondence: Berenson."

8. Michael Robert Mounter, "Richard Theodore Greener: The Idealist, Statesman, Scholar and South Carolinian" (Ph.D. diss., University of South Carolina, 2002), 6–7. My discussion of Richard Greener and his background draws heavily on Mounter's thorough dissertation. U.S. census, 1880, Ohio; ancestry.com, *U.K. and U.S. Directories, 1680–1830* [database online] (Provo, Utah: MyFamily.com, 2003). All federal census records cited are also from ancestry.com, unless otherwise noted. The younger Jacob moved to Ohio and had a family there. By 1880 he was living with his married daughter in Toledo. He was a barber; his son-in-law, a hotel waiter. His grandson, Jacob C. White, later corresponded with Richard T. Greener.

9. For histories of interracial mixing, see Martha Hodes, *White Women, Black Men: Illicit Sex in the Nineteenth-Century South* (New Haven: Yale University Press, 1997); Joel Williamson, *New People: Miscegenation and Mulattoes in the United States* (Baton Rouge: Louisiana University Press, 1995); and Stephan Talty, *Mulatto America: At the Crossroads of Black and White Culture: A Social History* (New York: HarperCollins, 2003).

10. Mounter, "Greener," 5–9.

11. Mounter, "Greener," 10–11.

12. "Extract from the 1851 report of the Cambridge School Committee," in William Cooper Nell, *The Colored Patriots of the American Revolution, with Sketches of Several Distinguished Colored Persons* (Boston: Robert F. Wallcut, 1855), 360–61, in Mounter, "Greener," 12–14.

13. "Richard T. Greener: The First Black Harvard College Graduate," in Werner Sollors, Caldwell Titcomb, and Thomas A. Underwood, eds., *Blacks at Harvard: A Documentary History of African-American Experience at Harvard and Radcliffe* (New York: New York University Press, 1993), 37–41; Mounter, "Greener," 28–48.

14. Harvard's Medical School had admitted a very few African Americans prior to Greener's entrance in Harvard College, including Martin R. Delany. See Caldwell Titcomb, "The Black Presence at Harvard: An Overview," in Sollors et al., eds., *Blacks at Harvard*, 2; Mounter, "Greener," 49–55.

15. U.S. census, 1870.

16. Frances Anne Rollin Diary in Dorothy Sterling, ed., *We Are Your Sisters: Black Women in the Nineteenth Century* (New York: Norton, 1984), 454–59.

17. Mounter, "Greener," 49–55. Greener's senior thesis was on Irish land reform; he remained interested in Irish rights for years.

18. Frederick Douglass, *My Bondage and Freedom* (rev. ed., 1892), reprinted in *Life and Times of Frederick Douglass: His Early Life as a Slave, His Escape from Bondage, and His Complete History, Written by Himself* (New York: Collier Books, 1962).

19. David Herbert Donald, *Charles Sumner and the Coming of the Civil War* (New York: Knopf, 1960).

20. On debates over the Fifteenth Amendment among suffrage activists, see Angela Davis, *Women, Race, and Class* (New York. Vintage, 1983), and Paula Giddings, *When and Where I Enter: The Impact of Black Women on Sex and Race in America*, 2d ed. (New York: Amistad, 1996). There are numerous studies of the patterns of African American participation in Reconstruction politics. A founding work is Eric Foner, *Reconstruction: America's Unfinished Revolution, 1865–1877* (New York: Harper Perennial, 1989). An example of a detailed local study is James Lowell Underwood and W. Lewis Burke Jr., eds., *At Freedom's Door: African American Founding Fathers and Lawyers in Reconstruction South Carolina* (Columbia: University of South Carolina Press, 2000). See also Elsa Barkley Brown, "To Catch a Vision of Freedom: Reconstructing Southern Black Women's Political History, 1865–1880," in Vicki L. Ruiz and Ellen C. DuBois, eds., *Unequal Sisters: A Multicultural Reader in U.S. Womens History*, 2d ed. (New York: Routledge, 1994), 124–46. For the role of free people of color, see Thomas Holt, *Black over White: Negro Political Leadership in South Carolina during Reconstruction* (Urbana: University of Illinois Press, 1977).

21. Mounter, "Greener," 72–76.

22. U.S. census, 1870; Moore, *Leading the Race*, 22; Mounter, "Greener," 83–85.

23. Dorothy S. Provine, ed., *District of Columbia Free Negro Registers, 1821–1861* (Bowie, Md.: Heritage Books, 1996), Registration, no. 192, Manumission, 2 Nov. 1822 (this entry actually records Henry's freeing of his wife and one daughter, Airy, but refers back to the earlier purchase); Paul E. Sluby Sr. and Stanton L. Wormley Jr., *History of the Columbian Harmony Society* (Washington, D.C.: Columbian Harmony Society, 2001), 8; Letitia Woods Brown, *Free Negroes in the District of Columbia, 1790–1846* (New York: Oxford University Press, 1972), 89, 117. I have not been able to identify George Beall with certainty. There were at least two George Bealls or Bells in the D.C. area who were white slaveholders, one of whom was a cofounder of Georgetown. There was also a former slave named George Beall who was a member of the free black community in Georgetown.

24. *Free Negro Registers, Liber A. Q. 41: 7*, 2 Feb. 1818.

25. Wesley Pippenger, comp., *District of Columbia Probate Records, 1818–1831* (Westminster, Md.: Family Line Publications, 1996). "Turner, Patience of Washington D.C. 2 Jun 1807, 1 Jul 1807."

26. Mounter, "Greener," 222. For background on the Grimké brothers, see Willard B. Gatewood, *Aristocrats of Color: The Black Elite, 1880–1920* (Bloomington: Indiana University Press, 1990).

27. Brown, *Free Negroes*, 14, 97, 111–17; Constance McLaughlin Green, *The Secret City: A History of Race Relations in the Nation's Capital* (Princeton: Princeton University Press, 1967), 16–19. See also Barbara Fields, *Slavery and Freedom on the Middle Ground: Maryland during the Nineteenth Century* (New Haven: Yale University Press, 1987), Ira Berlin, *Slaves without Masters: The Free Negro in the Antebellum South* (New York: Vintage, 1976), and Carter G. Woodson, ed. and comp., *Free Negro Owners of Slaves in the United States in 1830, Together with Absentee Ownership of Slaves in the United States in 1830* (New York: Negro Universities Press, 1968).

28. Nevertheless, the dangers of delaying manumissions are apparent in the brief records of one Charles Gusta, who wrote a will a few months before his death in May 1807. Gusta left "friend George [Beall] . . . my wife and four children whom I purchased but neglected to manumit." Gusta's four daughters were five, four, three, and two weeks old. This George Beall was a free man of color, a carpenter who owned several lots of land and helped start one of the first schools for Negroes in D.C. He did sometimes purchase slaves for other free blacks in Georgetown, and he promised Gusta to free his young children immediately and "bind" them out as laborers and apprentices until adulthood. Such apprenticing was a common practice in both the free white and black community—a way to train and educate children for a job and remove the financial burden of feeding and clothing them from parents. D.C. Probate Records, 1818–1831, "Gusta, Charles of Washington, D.C., 30 Jan 1807, 25 May 1807, 32"; Brown, Free Negroes, 89, 105, 135–36; Free Negro Registers, 45. See also Woodson, ed., Free Negro Owners, v.

29. D.C. Probate Records, 1818–1831, "Swan, Jane, 7 Aug. 1822, 27 Nov. 1822"; Paul E. Sluby Sr. and Stanton L. Wormley Jr., Blacks in the Marriage Records of the District of Columbia, Dec. 23, 1811–Jun. 16, 1870, vol. 1 (Washington, D.C.: Columbian Harmony Society, 1988); Free Negro Registers, 41.

30. Brown, Free Negroes, 133–34, 141; Gatewood, Aristocrats, 74. Both Jameses were listed as musicians or music teachers in all censuses and city directories. These two James Fleets have been confused by other scholars, and the records are confusing. But given the chronology, I am certain that Henry Fleet was Genevieve's great-great-grandfather, not her great-grandfather. The elder James, Henry's son, was born in the late 1790s and purchased by his father in 1804. He would have been almost fifty when Hermione and James H. Fleet married in 1845. Furthermore, the 1850 census finds a J. Fleet and a J. H. Fleet, both living in the same household. J. Fleet is fifty-five, a few years older than P. Grant, who must be Patience Grant (James's sister, living there with her husband). J. H. F eet is thirty-five, only ten years older than H. Fleet—his wife, Hermione.

31. John Peters stipulated in his will that a slave he referred to only as "my Negro man" should be freed four years after Peters's death. It is possible the man was a relative, but his language suggests otherwise. D.C. Probate Records, 1818–1831, "Peter, John, of D.C. 18 Sep. 1832; 13 Oct. 1837." Two of Genevieve's daughters may have been named after her mother's side of the family: Hermione's brother, John Theodore Augustin, and her mother, Louisa (one of Hermione's sisters was also named Louisa).

32. Sluby and Wormley, Blacks in the Marriage Records, Louisa Peters (black) to Edward Garey in 1848.

33. Brown, Free Negroes, 213, n. 27.

34. Not surprisingly, these names were shortened and often misspelled in official records. Bellini appears variously as Belem, B.D., B.C.; and Mendelsohn is usually listed as Mendi or Mendel. Mendelsohn seems to be spelled with one s, a common variant of Mendelssohn. But, as no two documents spell his name exactly the same way, it is unclear with the Fleets intended. Wesley E. Pippenger, ed., District of Columbia Death Records, August 1, 1874 to July 31, 1879 (Westminster, Md.: Family Line Publications, 1997), "Fleet, Mendleshon B., 21y C[olored], D.C. 09 May 1878. Harmony"; MSRC:HU, Fifteenth St. Presbyterian Church Records, box 34–1, folder 3.

35. Mounter, "Greener," 300; Wesley E. Pippenger, comp., *District of Columbia Marriage License: June 28, 1877 to October 19, 1885* (Lovettsville, Va.: Willow Bend Books, 1997), 155, 261; U.S. census, 1880.

36. Moore, *Leading*, 32, 35.

37. Seven children are listed in 1860, but the two youngest children are not in the 1870 census, most likely having died.

38. Mounter, "Greener," 98–99.

39. James Lowell Underwood, "African American Founding Fathers: The Making of the South Carolina Constitution of 1868," in Underwood and Burke, eds., *At Freedom's Door*, 1–2.

40. Franklin J. Moses, trustee, and *Journal of the House of Representatives of the State of South Carolina, 1873–1874* (Columbia, 1874), 91, quoted in Mounter, "Greener," 116; Mounter, "Greener," 114–32.

41. Mounter, "Greener," 140–50.

42. Green, *Secret City*, 23.

43. Mounter, "Greener," 145, 157.

44. Mounter, "Greener," 164–67, 176–77.

45. Mounter, "Greener," 181–96.

46. MSRC:HU, Fifteenth St. Presbyterian Church Records, box 34–1, folder 3. Russell was probably also baptized at the church, but is not listed in its records.

47. Mounter, "Greener," 191–202, 215.

48. Green, *Secret City*, 93–94.

49. U.S. census, 1880.

50. Ibid. Two years later Mozart and Adie buried their second son, Mozart Reginal, at the age of nine months.

51. U.S. Department of Commerce, Bureau of the Census, *Twenty Census Population and Housing Questions, 1790–1980* (Washington, D.C.: GPO, Oct. 1979), 16, 22; Heidi Ardizzone, "Red-Blooded Americans: Mulattoes and the Melting Pot in United States Racialist and Nationalist Discourse, 1890–1930" (Ph.D. diss., University of Michigan, 1997), 192–94.

52. Ardizzone, "Red-Blooded Americans," 194–95.

53. Gatewood, *Aristocrats*, 48; Mounter, "Greener," 222, 269–70.

54. Mounter, "Greener," 269–70. See also Kevin K. Gaines, *Uplifting the Race: Black Leadership, Politics, and Culture in the Twentieth Century* (Chapel Hill: University of North Carolina Press, 1996); Gatewood, *Aristocrats*, 39–68; and Moore, *Leading*. I discuss the politics of respectability and mixed-race identity in my "'Such Fine Families': Photography and Race in the Work of Caroline Bond Day," *Visual Studies* 21, no. 2 (Oct. 2006): 106–32.

55. Archibald Grimké quoted in Gatewood, *Aristocrats*, 44. Archibald married a white woman, named their daughter after her famous aunt, and raised her on his own after his wife left him.

56. The dark-skinned Nanny Burroughs had difficulty finding acceptance in D.C.'s elite community of color. Moore, *Leading*, 30–31.

57. Moore, *Leading*, 29, 30.

58. Moore, *Leading*, 33, 49.

59. For histories and studies of such communities, see Adele Logan Alexander, *Ambiguous Lives: Free Women of Color in Rural Georgia, 1789–1879* (Little Rock: University of Arkansas Press, 1991); Virginia R. Dominguez, *White by Definition: Social Classification in Creole Louisiana* (New Brunswick: Rutgers Uni-

versity Press, 1986); Willard B. Gatewood, *Aristocrats of Color: The Black Elite, 1880–1920* (Bloomington: Indiana University Press 1990); and Joel Williamson, *New People: Miscegenation and Mulattoes in the United States* (Baton Rouge: Louisiana State University Press 1995).

60. BG to BB, 25 Dec. 1910, 19 June 1914, VIT.
61. Stephanie Shaw, *What a Woman Ought to Be and Do: Black Professional Women Workers during the Jim Crow Era* (Chicago: University of Chicago Press, 1996), 15.
62. Moore, *Leading*, 33, 49.
63. Mounter, "Greener," 222, 228–34, 255–64, 273–76.
64. The episode was made into a movie in 1994: *Assault at West Point: The Court-Martial of Johnson Whittaker,* a made-for-TV movie, starred Samuel L. Jackson as Richard Greener and Sam Waterston as Whitaker's counsel Daniel Chamberlain. It was written and directed by Henry Moses.
65. Mounter, "Greener," 304–9, 331–36; *New York Evening Post,* 16 Oct. 1883. Twenty years later, Greener had not reconciled himself to Jim Crow. He returned to South Carolina in 1907, traveling in the white train cars when he was unknown and in the "Jim Crow" cars when he was identified. He wrote to Grimké, "Every where the signs of caste appear, 'colored lunch' 'white lunch' 'waiting room for colored.' Inside the cars, 'white' stares at you from the one; 'colored' grins at you in the other. At times you can imagine my feelings. Always I am ruminating on the problem." RTG to FJG, 18 Nov. 1907, MSRC:HU, Francis J. Grimké Papers, box 40, folder 3, 109.
66. *Washington Bee*, Feb. 7, 1885, quoted in Mounter, "Greener," 336.
67. William Henry Crogman, "Negro Education—Its Helps and Hindrances," in Philip S. Foner and Robert James Branham, eds., *Lift Every Voice: African American Oratory, 1787–1900* (Tuscaloosa: University of Alabama Press, 1998), 623–24, 632; Mounter, "Greener," 331.
68. Richard T. Greener, in *Southwestern Christian Advocate,* 17 June 1886, in Mounter, "Greener," 352–54.

CHAPTER 2: GILDED DREAMS IN NEW YORK

1. *New York Times*, 8 Jan. 1881.
2. BG to BB, 3 Aug. 1909, VIT.
3. For discussions of Greener's involvement in the Grant Monument Association, see David Quigley, *Second Founding: New York City, Reconstruction, and the Making of American Democracy* (New York: Hill and Wang, 2004), 176–83; Michael Robert Mounter, "Richard Theodore Greener: The Idealist, Statesman, Scholar and South Carolinian" (Ph.D. diss., University of South Carolina, 2002), 341–81.
4. Mounter, "Greener," 341–45.
5. There are many possible reasons why Genevieve did not join Richard immediately. The older children were in school, for one thing. Despite the erosion of black civil rights in D.C., the schools were still strong; other African American families moved to D.C. so that their children could go to school there. She may also not have been ready to try to raise four young children without the support of her mother and sister-in-law.
6. Quigley, *Second Founding*, 179–80.
7. Mounter, "Greener," 370–71.

8. RTG to J. E. Bruce, 16 Sept. 1885, NYPL:SC, Bruce Papers.

9. For background on art and culture in New York at the turn of the century, see M. H. Dunlop, *Gilded City: Scandal and Sensation in Turn-of-the Century New York* (New York: Morrow, 2000); W. G. Constable, *Art Collecting in the United States of America: An Outline of a History* (London: Thomas Nelson, 1964); Germain Bazin, *The Museum Age,* trans. Jane van Nuis Cahill (New York: Universe Books, 1967); and Eric Homberger, *Mrs. Astor's New York: Money and Social Power in a Gilded Age* (New Haven: Yale University Press, 2002).

10. Mounter, "Greener," 347–48, 50; *New York Times,* 21 Feb. 1886, 2.

11. Quigley, *Second Founding,* 180.

12. Charlotte Forten Grimké reported in her diary that their "dear friends the G's, whom we are soon about to lose," had their baby baptized on Christmas Day. MSRC:HU, FJG Papers, box 40–46, folder 1824.

13. W. E. B. Du Bois, *The Black North in 1901: A Social Study* (New York: Arno Press, 1969), 5–11.

14. U.S. census, 1880, 1900.

15. Winifred Howe, *History of the Metropolitan Museum of Art* (New York: Gillis Press, 1913).

16. Bernard Berenson, *The Venetian Painters of the Renaissance, with an Index to Their Work* (New York: G. P. Putnam's Sons, 1894); John W. Osborne, "A Liaison to Remember: The Friendship of Belle da Costa Greene and Bernard Berenson," *Biblio,* Nov. 1997, pp. 38–41.

17. Mounter, "Greener," 361–63, 365. Greener never explained why his mother had never met his wife and children. The class differences between the Fleets and Richard's mother may have been part of the problem.

18. FJG Sermon, 14 July 1895, MSRC:HU, FJG Papers, box 15, folder 667.

19. *New York Age,* 22 Feb. 1892.

20. Mounter, "Greener," 373, 381–83.

21. Mounter, "Greener," 391, 402. Teachers' College does not have records of a Belle or Marian Green, Greene, or Greener. This is most likely because its records do not seem to go back before 1899, the year after Teachers' College united with Columbia University. Personal conversation with Registrar's Office, April 2006.

22. Ellen Collins to Booker T. Washington, 23 Aug. 1892; Thomas Junius Calloway to Booker T. Washington, 2 May 1894, in Louis R. Harlan, ed., *The Booker T. Washington Papers,* vol. 3, *1889–1895* (Urbana: University of Illinois Press, 1974), 258, 416.

23. Mounter, "Greener," 401, 421–29.

24. RTG to JEB, NYPL:SC, John E. Bruce Papers.

25. *New York Times,* 18 March 1886, p. 3.

26. RTG to IW, 24 April 1898, MSRC:HU, JCW Papers, box 115–3, folder 166; Mounter, "Greener," 436.

27. This story of Richard Greener's meeting with his Japanese common-law wife, Mishiyo Kawashima, was recounted to me by Michael Mounter, who spoke with one of the woman's grandchildren. Greener and Kawashima never married, but lived together in Siberia and had three children. After Greener returned to the United States in 1905, Kawashima moved with her children to China. Her children later emigrated to the United States. (Personal correspondence, Michael Mounter to the author.) Several tantalizing unidentified pages of a letter in the

Jacob C. White Papers possibly support this. One page describes a visit to Vladi-vostok. Another mentions a "lively old gentleman" who had a "Japanese wife" and was the "only genuine negro here." But there is no way to determine whether these fragments describe Greener. Unidentified letter fragments, n.d., MSRC: HU, JCW Papers, box 115–3, folder 174.

28. RTG to IW, 7 Jan. 1899, MSRC:HU, JCW Papers, box 115–3, folder 166.
29. Rose Nichols to BB, 5 May [1950], VIT. The date written on the letter is 1949, but internal evidence fixes the year as 1950. Nichols often omitted dates altogether.
30. Paul E. Sluby Sr. and L. Wormley Stanton Jr., *History of the Columbian Harmony Society* (Washington, D.C.: Columbian Harmony Society, 2001), 1, 8; Wesley E. Pippenger, *District of Columbia Death Records, August 1, 1874 to July 31 1879* (Westminster, Md.: Family Line Publications, 1997), 113. Mendelsohn Fleet, Genevieve's brother, was also buried in Harmony. In the 1970s the graves in the Columbia Harmony Cemetery were moved to National Harmony Memorial Park in Landover, Md. When I contacted the park on a trip to Maryland, officials were unable to locate any of the Fleets in their database.
31. U.S. census, 1900.
32. Greener, "Suffrage for Women," *New National Era*, 1873.
33. Stephanie Shaw, *What a Woman Ought to Be and Do: Black Professional Women Workers during the Jim Crow Era* (Chicago: University of Chicago Press, 1996).
34. Mounter, "Greener," 289, 321.
35. Mounter, "Greener," 158, 272; MSRC:HU, FJG Papers, box 40–44.
36. Marriage Certificate No. 26074, State of New York, Manhattan, Department of Health.
37. Willard B. Gatewood, *Aristocrats of Color: The Black Elite, 1880–1920* (Bloom-ington: Indiana University Press, 1990); Constance McLaughlin Green, *The Secret City: A History of Race Relations in the Nation's Capital* (Princeton: Prince-ton University Press, 1967), 207–9.
38. BG to BB, 6 April 1909, VIT.
39. BG to BB, 24 May 1909, VIT.
40. Andrew Sinclair, *Corsair: The Life of J. Pierpont Morgan* (Boston: Little, Brown, 1981), 182.
41. Ernest Samuels, *Bernard Berenson: The Making of a Legend* (Cambridge: Har-vard University Press, Belknap Press, 1987), 72–73; Cass Canfield, *The Incred-ible Pierpont Morgan: Financier and Art Collector* (New York: Harper & Row, 1974), 146; Meryle Secrest, *Being Bernard Berenson* (New York: Holt, Rinehart and Winston, 1979), 290.
42. On transitions of racial classification systems in the early twentieth century, see Virginia R. Dominguez, *White by Definition: Social Classification in Creole Louisiana* (New Brunswick: Rutgers University Press, 1986); Joel Williamson, *New People: Miscegenation and Mulattoes in the United States* (Baton Rouge: Louisiana State University Press, 1995); David Fowler, *Northern Attitudes towards Interracial Marriage: Legislation and Public Opinion in the Middle Atlantic States and the States of the Old Northwest, 1780–1930* (New York: Gar-land, 1987); and Heidi Ardizzone, "Red-Blooded Americans: Mulattoes and the Melting Pot in American Racialist and Nationalist Discourse, 1890–1930" (Ph.D. diss., University of Michigan, 1997).

43. Jessie Fauset, "Fabiola," *World Tomorrow*, 5 March 1922, pp. 77–78.

44. Gertrude Atherton, *The Living Present* (New York: Frederick A. Stokes, 1917), 296. Atherton also asserts that Belle traveled to Europe and studied for ten years after Princeton, which is patently untrue. "Class of 1900 Employment 1901," ACASC: Amherst Summer School Records, 1878–1906, 1:4. The New York Public Library system was not yet fully developed. Belle may have worked at one of the two privately funded libraries mentioned above, but records are unavailable.

CHAPTER 3: PRINCETON: EARLY INFLUENCES

1. Woodrow Wilson, 1904, cited in Editors, "Woodrow Wilson and the Negro Question at Princeton University," *Journal of Blacks in Higher Education* (Autumn 1997): 120.

2. BG (from Princeton University) to BB, 7 July 1910, VIT.

3. Room, board, and books cost an additional thirty to fifty-five dollars. Belle would not have needed the additional instruction in French, but the extra class offered in "Vertical Round" handwriting gives a specimen that looks somewhat similar to Belle's formal hand, although nothing like her informal scrawl. Wm. I. Fletcher, A.M., "Summer School of Library Economy" (Amherst College Library: July 15 to Aug. 16, 1901). ACASC: Amherst Summer School Records, 1878–1906, 1:2.

4. Princeton University Library records are incomplete in these early years, and some have speculated that Belle Greene began work there before her first appearance in the archives in 1903. Years later Belle recalled that she had worked at Princeton for "nearly 3 years." BG to BB, 25 Aug. 1910, VIT.

5. Allowing an employer to assume that one was white was the best-known form of passing in the black community. In these situations, individuals often led dual lives, living in a black neighborhood with family and friends, working in a white or segregated office as a white colleague. Belle could have practiced this form of extreme division between her public identity at work and at home. But with the whole Greene family now living as white, her entire life was conforming to a public white identity.

6. *Princeton Press*, 27 Dec. 1902, 28 Jan., 17 June 1905.

7. Some writers have suggested that Belle's entire family moved to Princeton, but I have found no evidence of any Greene family members other than Belle in Princeton, and ample evidence that they remained in New York.

8. Princeton University Library, Report of the Librarian, June 1902, PUA.

9. BG to Moses Taylor Pyne, 25 April 1911, AML:MCC, "II Misc: Ho-Hoskier."

10. Federal census, 1910.

11. Charlotte Martins to BG, 6 Feb. 1912, AML:MCC.

12. U.S. census, 1860, 1870. In 1870 the family had moved to Baltimore, and Anna's husband, Warren Hyde (an engineer), and their infant lived with them.

13. N.J. state census, 1905.

14. Donald Robert Come, "The Influence of Princeton on Higher Education in the South before 1825," *William and Mary Quarterly* 2 (Oct. 1945): 359–96. The Divinity School did admit a few African Americans.

15. Editors, "Woodrow Wilson," 120.

16. Marcia G. Synnott, "The Admission and Assimilation of Minority Students at Harvard, Yale, and Princeton, 1900–1970," *History of Education Quarterly* 19

(Autumn 1979): 285–304; Dan Klein, "The Young Man Who Pushed Princeton toward Racial Integration," *Journal of Blacks in Higher Education* (Spring 1996): 85.

17. N.J. state census, 1905, Princeton Township and Borough of Princeton.
18. Lloyd Brown, *The Young Paul Robeson: On My Journey Now* (Boulder, Colo.: Westview Press, 1997), 22–23.
19. *Princeton Press,* 23 Jan. 1904; Wilda D. Logan, JCW Papers Finding Aid, "Scope Note," June 1980, MSRC:HU.
20. Sheila Tully Boyle and Andrew Bunie, *Paul Robeson: The Years of Promise and Achievement* (Amherst: University of Massachusetts Press, 2001), 12–14.
21. Brown, *Robeson,* 63–64; BG to BB, 20 March, 7 July 1909.
22. Roger C. Slaughter '28 to President John G. Hibben, 9 Feb. 1931, PHS.
23. Secretary, Princeton University, to Editor, *Kansas City Times,* 18 Feb. 1931, unsigned copy, PHS.
24. Lawrence C. Wroth, *The First Quarter Century of the Pierpont Morgan Library: A Retrospective Exhibition in Honor of Belle da Costa Greene* (New York: Pierpont Morgan Library, 1949).
25. JPMJ to Perry Laming, 29 Sept. 1925, AML:JMPJ, box 173.
26. Graduation weekends were the highlight of the season for those on campus. Townspeople often left town for the duration, renting out their homes to visiting alumni and graduates' families. For those who stayed and participated, the frolic and extravagance of the celebration was memorable. The *Princeton Press* noted the shift from somber graduation exercises to "[s]pectacular processions and imposing ceremonies" with some concern, but concluded that "it was natural for the students, with their overflowing animal spirits and their freedom from the restraints of the year, to go to opposite extremes and seek the jovial, grotesque and boisterous." *Princeton Press,* 27 Feb. 1904.
27. BG to BB, 14 April 1909, VIT.
28. Belle actually recalled in 1909 finding herself at a dinner party with an unidentified man to whom she had once "in a weak moment allowed [her]self to become engaged." She described him as a Princeton graduate and a financier. BG to BB, 3 Aug. 1909, VIT.
29. *Princeton Press,* 25 Nov. 1905.
30. Boyle and Bunie, *Robeson,* 13–15.
31. See, e.g., *Princeton Press,* 20 Feb., 28 May 1904, 22 July, 18 Aug., 2 Sept. 1905.
32. *Princeton Press,* 7 May 1904.
33. *New York Evening Sun,* 19 Oct. 1916. Greene routinely denied the accuracy of interviews—even accusing newspapers of inventing entire conversations. But on this point Belle told a similar story in private. BB to MB, 25 Aug. 1910, VIT.
34. Belle Greene, *The Pierpont Morgan Library: A Review of the Growth, Development and Activities of the Library during the Period between Its Establishment as an Educational Institution in Feb. 1924 and the Close of the Year 1929* (New York: Pierpont Morgan Library, 1930), 14.
35. Frederick B. Adams Jr., *An Introduction to the Pierpont Morgan Library* (New York: Pierpont Morgan Library, 1964), 9–10; Louis Auchincloss, *J. P. Morgan: The Financier as Collector* (New York: Harry N. Abrams, 1990), 12–13.
36. Lewis C. Branscomb, *Ernest Cushing Richardson: Research Librarian, Scholar, Theologian 1860–1939* (Metuchen, N.J.: Scarecrow Press, 1993), 22–24. All

biographical information on Richardson is taken from this one published biography on him.

37. BG to BB, 25 Aug. 1910, VIT; Princeton University Library, Librarian's Reports, PUA.

38. *Evening Sun*, 10 Oct. 1916.

39. She had been quoted as saying the British Museum had no catalog, when she meant it had no card catalog. "Miss Greene Misquoted," Letter to the Editor, *New York Times*, 7 Dec. 1913.

40. His wife, Grace Duncan Ely, had family money, allowing them some independence from his job. He negotiated with then Princeton University president Woodrow Wilson to be out of residence one semester of each year, and used many of those months to travel.

41. Unlike her first mentor, who had financial resources beyond his salary, Belle would have to wait until Morgan sent her to Europe on official business. In an article advocating regular travel for librarians, Richardson himself estimated that a four-month trip would cost "only" $500, just over Belle's total annual wages as his employee. Branscomb, *Richardson*, 15, 22–24, 85–89.

42. Princeton University Library, Librarian's Report, June 1902, PUA.

43. Jean Strouse, *Morgan: American Financier* (New York: Harper Perennial, 2000), 380; R. W. G. Vail, "10. Grolierii et Amicorum," in Alexander Davidson Jr. et al., eds., *Grolier 75: A Biographical Retrospective to Celebrate the Seventy-fifth Anniversary of the Grolier Club in New York* (New York: Grolier Club, 1959), n.p.

44. Arthur Rau, "Junius Spenser Morgan," in Davidson et al., eds., *Grolier 75*, 156–57; "Acquisitions to the University Library," 4 March 1905; "Library News," 20 May 1905, *Princeton Press*. Quaritch was one of the many dealers Belle would become very familiar with in her work for J. P. Morgan.

45. BG to BB, 18 April 1921, 10 July 1914, VIT.

46. BG to BB, 13 Sept. 1922, VIT.

47. BG to BB, 1 June 1909, 26 Dec. 1913, 31 Aug. 1909, VIT. See also BG to BB, 17 Aug. 1909, VIT.

48. BG to BB, 6 Jan., 9, 10 June 1914, VIT.

49. BG to BB, 14 March 1914, VIT.

50. Lauder Greenway, "Harry Watson Kent," in Davidson et al., eds., *Grolier 75*, 146–48.

51. Rau, "Morgan," 156–59.

52. Adams, *Introduction*, 9–10; Auchincloss, *Morgan*, 12–13.

53. Princeton University Library, Librarian's Report, 1906, PUA.

CHAPTER 4: BELLE GREENE, GIRL LIBRARIAN

1. Gertrude Atherton, *The Living Present* (New York: Frederick A. Stokes, 1917), 295.

2. *Chicago Daily Tribune*, 11 Aug. 1912, G2.

3. N.Y. state census, 1905.

4. BG to Henry Guppy, 6 Aug. 1908, AML:MCC.

5. *New York Herald Tribune*, 2 Oct. 1930.

6. BG to JPM, 23 April 1909, VIT; Jean Strouse, *Morgan: American Financier* (New York: Harper Perennial, 2000), 510.

7. BG to Walter Cook, 30 Oct. 1929, AML:MCC.

8. The meaning of using first names has changed markedly over the last century. Instead of continually referring to individuals as "Mr.," "Miss," and "Mrs.," as people in formal or professional situations referred to each other, I often use first names. This indicates that the individuals had the close relationships we associate with first-name use. I also use first names to distinguish between different people with the same last name, for clarity.

9. All family information taken from Strouse, *Morgan*.

10. Strouse, *Morgan*, 290–91, 486–87; Frederick B. Adams Jr., *An Introduction to the Pierpont Morgan Library* (New York: Pierpont Morgan Library, 1964), 5, 9–10.

11. *New York Times*, 4, 5, 26 July 1902.

12. Ron Chernow, *The House of Morgan: An American Banking Dynasty and the Rise of Modern Finance* (New York: Atlantic Monthly Press, 1990), 114.

13. St. George's did have an African American singer, Harry Burleigh, who sang at J. P. Morgan's funeral and at that of his son.

14. *New York Times*, 2 Feb. 1904, p. 9; Chernow, *House*, 555–56. Chernow describes the later impact this relationship had on Morgan company business in postwar Japan. George died in 1916, leaving an inheritance to Yuki Morgan, who returned to Japan. The Morgan family oversaw the annuity payments, except during World War II, when they could not reach her. After the war Yuki was located, and the missed payments, with compounded interest, were delivered. Yuki, by this point, was a legendary figure in Japan. A former geisha, she was the subject of a romantic musical that depicted her as forced to abandon a Japanese lover when her contract was sold to George Morgan.

15. Susie Jin Lee, "The Content of Character: The Role of Social Capital in the Expansion of Economic Capital," vol. 1 (Ph.D. diss., Cornell University, 2004), 181–82, 184–87. Lee argues that the Morgans' anti-Semitism cannot be dismissed as normal for their time. Her focus, however, is on the 1920s and later.

16. *New York Times*, 5 July 1907, 3.

17. *New York Times*, 6 June 1944, 17; Student Records, Pratt Institute Archives, Brooklyn, N.Y. Ada's listing notes that she was in the class of 1902 but did not take a full course. She received A's in both classification and cataloguing. Herbert Satterlee's biography describes Belle as being hired as the librarian with several assistants under her; since he showed Belle a draft of the manuscript, in which she made copious corrections, it is likely that this was Belle's version of events as well. Satterlee, *J. Pierpont Morgan: An Intimate Portrait* (New York: Macmillan, 1939), 435.

18. BG to BB, 22 Feb., 2 May 1911, 14 Dec. 1913, 6, 22 May 1914, VIT.

19. Satterlee, *Morgan*, 435. Satterlee (Morgan's son-in-law) consulted with Belle when writing his biography and turned over a draft to her to comment on. This passage, then, probably reflects her memory of this first year at the Library.

20. BB to MB, 25 Aug. 1910, VIT; Aline B. Louchheim, "The Morgan Library and Miss Greene," *New York Times*, 17 April 1949.

21. There are relatively few records from the first years of Belle's work at the Morgan Library. Most of the files from this period are filled with receipts, lists of items, and brief business correspondence. I have selected those records which reflect Belle's early work and show her professional development. The sources I chose are atypical, then, of the records during these years in that they demonstrate the relationships with dealers and other curators and librarians which came to characterize Belle's business dealings.

22. Sales could be negotiated individually or "en bloc," and she could request information on specific titles if she needed. They would sometimes distribute catalogues of their holdings, sometimes send photographs of an item, sometimes send the book itself for inspection. J. Pearson to BG, 9 Nov. 1906, AML:MCC; Strouse, *Morgan*, 291, 381.

23. FW to BG, 9 Nov. 1906, AML:MCC.

24. BG to FW, 10 Sept. 1907, AML:MCC; BG to BB, 15 July 1909, VIT.

25. AML: Curtis, ARC 1307.

26. Auchincloss, *Morgan*, 16; Frederick Lewis Allen, *The Great Pierpont Morgan* (New York: Harper, 1949), 269.

27. Allen, *Morgan*, 269.

28. BG to LO, 26 Oct., 1907; LO to BG, 7 Dec. 1907, AML:MCC. Leo and Aldo Olschki were publishers and booksellers based in Florence.

29. LO to BG, 8 Jan. 1908, AML:MCC.

30. BG to LO, 8 April 1908, AML:MCC.

31. LO to BG, 10 April 1908, AML:MCC.

32. Jon Moen and Ellis Tallman, "Lessons from the Panic of 1907," *Federal Reserve Bank of Atlanta Economic Review* 75 (May–June 1990): 2–13.

33. Chernow, *House*, 121–25.

34. Chernow, *House*, 126–27; Andrew Sinclair, *Corsair: The Life of J. Pierpont Morgan* (Boston: Little, Brown, 1981), 182; undated Associated Press release, CAH:NYJAM.

35. Chernow, *House*, 127–28. In fact, of all the secrets Belle took with her to her grave, some of the biggest in her mind were those pertaining to Morgan and her knowledge of many equally significant but much less known behind-the-scenes deals. She was always working on a study of his life and work, even before his death.

36. "Bibliophiles and Bibliophiles," *Nation*, 17 Dec. 1908, 596.

37. *New York Times*, 4 Dec. 1908, 1.

38. George Charles Williamson, *Catalogue of the Collection of Miniatures, the Property of J. Pierpont Morgan*, 4 vols. (London: Chiswick Press, 1906–08). Williamson also compiled volumes on Morgan's jewels in 1910 and on his watch collection in 1912.

39. George Williamson to BG, 16 June 1908; Claude L. Hagen to BG, 21 Feb. 1910; John Gilliland to BG, 23 Jan., 28 Feb. 1912, AML:MCC.

40. BB to WI, 11 June 1950, AAAS:WI, "Correspondence: Berenson"; Lawrence C. Wroth, *The First Quarter Century of the Pierpont Morgan Library: A Retrospective Exhibition in Honor of Belle da Costa Greene* (New York: Pierpont Morgan Library, 1949), 17–18.

41. James Osborne Wright, *Catalogue of the American Library of the Late Samuel Latham Mitchill Barlow* (New York: D. Taylor, 1889). Wright also helped prepare catalogues of Henry Ward Beecher's valuables, art, and furnishings for auction after the Reverend Beecher's death (New York: Press of J. J. Little, 1887), compiled a price list of the Daly Library (New York: James O. Wright, 1900) and a catalogue of Robert Hoe's collection of pre-eighteenth-century English books (New York: Gillis Press, 1903), and edited the collected poems of John Ruskin (New York: J. Wiley, 1884).

42. J. O. Wright to BG, 3, 7, 10 Aug. 1908, AML:MCC; Charles Dickens, *The Adventures of Oliver Twist; or, The Parish Boy's Progess,* with twenty-four illustra-

tions on steel, by George Cruikshank (London: Bradbury & Evans, 1846.), PML:6661.

43. BG to BB, 8 March 1910, VIT.
44. *New York Times*, 24 March 1906, 5; 8 Nov. 1908, 3:15; 24 April 1909, BR261.
45. BG to BB, 29 April 1909, VIT.
46. BG to BB, 9 May 1909, VIT; *New York Times*, 11 Feb. 1923, 3.
47. EG to BB, 4 Dec. 1911, VIT.
48. There is only one business letter from Laffan in the Morgan Library archives. W. T. Walters, Stephen Bushell, and William M. Laffan, *Oriental Ceramic Art* (New York: Crown, 1896); J. P. Morgan, Stephen Bushell, and William M. Laffan, *Catalogue of the Morgan Collection of Chinese Porcelains* (New York: Metropolitan Museum of Art, 1907).
49. BG to BB, 8 March 1914, VIT.
50. BG to BB, 11 April 1910, VIT.
51. Except for the few letters cited here, Belle left no record of her experiences or impressions of her first European trip; Passport Record, 1908, NYPL.
52. *New York Times*, 7 April 1912, SM8.
53. *New York Times*, 7 April 1912, SM8.
54. *New York Times*, 3, 4, 7 Dec. 1908.
55. GW to BG, 11 Dec. 1908, AML:MCC.
56. GD to BG, 19 Jan., 14 July 1909, 17 June 1910, AML:MCC.
57. BG to BB, 29 June 1909, VIT; J. H. Fitzhenry to BG, 2, 20 Nov. 1909, AML: MCC. Fitzhenry routinely signed his letters "Fitz."
58. Strouse, "Introduction," in Pierpont Morgan Library, *The Morgan Library: An American Masterpiece* (New York: Pierpont Morgan Library, 2000), 21–22.
59. Strouse, *Morgan*, 257–56; BG to GD, n.d. (reply to his letter of 14 July 1909), AML:MCC.
60. AP to BG, 13 Sept. 1909, AML:MCC.
61. Ormonde Maddock Dalton, *Sir Hercules Read, 1857–1929* (London: Humphrey Milford, [1930]), 7.
62. CR to BG, 3 Jan. 1909, AML:MCC.
63. VS to BG, 25 Jan. 1909, AML:MCC.
64. LO to BG, 6 March 1909; BG to Charles King, n.d., AML:MCC.

CHAPTER 5: A TURN IN THE ROAD

1. Ernest Samuels, *Bernard Berenson: The Making of a Legend* (Cambridge: Harvard University Press, Belknap Press, 1987), 73.
2. BG to BB, 9, 23 April 1909, VIT.
3. Israel Zangwill, *The Melting Pot: Drama in Four Acts* (New York: Macmillan, 1909).
4. Ernest Samuels, *Bernard Berenson: The Making of a Connoisseur* (Cambridge: Harvard University Press, Belknap Press, 1979), 2–6. Although Bernard did not change the spelling of his name until the World War One era, I use "Bernard" throughout this book, as is standard in scholarship on Berenson.
5. Samuels, *Connoisseur*, 12–13.
6. Rollin Van N. Hadley, ed., *The Letters of Bernard Berenson and Isabella Stewart Gardner, 1887–1924, with Correspondence by Mary Berenson* (Boston: Northeastern University Press, 1987), xviii–xix; Samuels, *Connoisseur*, 35.

7. Samuels, *Connoisseur*, 46–49.
8. Samuels, *Connoisseur*, 50, 54, 65–66, 86.
9. Sylvia Sprigge, *Berenson: A Biography* (Boston: Houghton Mifflin, 1960), 103.
10. Much less has been written about Mary Smith Costelloe Berenson than about her more famous husband, Bernard. Unless otherwise noted, biographical information about Mary Berenson is from Samuels, *Connoisseur*. See also Barbara Strachey, *Remarkable Relations: The Story of the Pearsall Smith Women* (New York: Universe Books, 1980), and Robert Allerton Parker, *The Transatlantic Smiths* (New York: Random House, 1959).
11. MB to HWS, 12 Sept. 1891, quoted in Barbara Strachey and Jayne Samuels, eds., *Mary Berenson: A Self-Portrait from Her Letters & Diaries* (New York: Norton, 1983), 22–23.
12. Sprigge, *Berenson*, 103.
13. MB to HWS, 1 Dec. 1908, LLIU:HWS, "Correspondence: Berenson." Many of the letters sent by Hannah Whitall Smith's clan, including her daughter Mary, seem to have been "round robined." Sometimes they are simply addressed to "Family." More often they are addressed to an individual, but penciled initials in the upper right-hand corner of the letter seem to note who has read it. I identified the initials of Mary's sister A[lys], brother L[ogin], and daughters K[arin] and R[ay]. Some letters do seem to be private, although rarely marked as such. Here I list letters by the person to whom they are addressed, and only note private mail when it is explicitly labeled as such.
14. MB to HWS, 10 Jan. 1909, LLIU:HWS, "Correspondence: Berenson."
15. Marbury generally spelled her name "Elisabeth" and her nickname "Bessy," although scholars sometimes use her given spelling "Elizabeth." Many contemporaries, including Belle, spelled her nickname "Bessie," which I have used here.
16. Anne Morgan to MB, 1 Dec. 1908, LLIU:HWS, "Correspondence: Berenson."
17. Strouse, *Morgan*, 521; Jane S. Smith, *Elsie de Wolfe: A Life in the High Style* (New York: Atheneum, 1982), 109–10; MB to HWS, 10 Jan. 1909; LLIU:HWS, "Correspondence: Berenson."
18. Louis Auchincloss, *J. P. Morgan: The Financier as Collector* (New York: Harry N. Abrams, 1990), 16.
19. BB to MB, 10 July 1910, VIT; MB to HWS, 1 Dec. 1908, LLIU:HWS, "Correspondence: Berenson."
20. MB Diary, 1 Jan. 1908, in Strachey and Samuels, eds., *Mary Berenson*, 144.
21. Letters from both Bernard and Mary fix the date of their visit to Morgan as Thursday, which would have been 3 Dec. in 1908. BB to ISG, 5 Dec. 1908, in Hadley, ed., *Letters*, 426: "We saw the famous Morgan Library on Thursday. . . ." MB to HWS, 1 Dec. 1908, LLIU:HWS, "Correspondence: Berenson." "Her father has asked us to come see his famous Library on Thursday." Neither mentions Belle in the extant correspondence in Dec. 1908. Bernard's letter mentioning that he "met her [Miss Greene] at Morgan's library last winter and saw her several times afterwards" was written a year later. By that time Bernard was deeply in love with Belle and (as always) desperately trying to hide that fact from his nosy and mischievous patroness. He often fudged details or outright lied to Gardner about personal matters; in this case Gardner was upset about something Belle had said, and Bernard's main purpose was to smooth things over. BB to ISG, 1 Jan. 1910, in Hadley, ed., *Letters*, 463. The dates of the Caxton purchase

in London are incontrovertible (see chapter 4). It was a public sale, and Morgan's coup was announced almost immediately. It is possible that Belle was not present there, as she claimed, but I find it highly unlikely. Although details of her story may be exaggerated, the fact that she was in London that week for the auction would have been a difficult thing to lie about, given that so many important figures in the book world were in attendance. The story about her making the deal circulated during her lifetime, based on newspaper interviews in legitimate papers, and she never tried to deny it. Correspondence cited in chapter 4 also supports the timing of her trip.

22. S. N. Behrman, *Duveen* (London: Hamish Hamilton, 1972), 34. Behrman's book is an example of one in which Belle plays virtually no role in the narrative, but a picture of her appears nonetheless.

23. According to Colin Simpson, Morgan had been duped out of a substantial deposit on nonexistent bronze doors from an Italian cathedral. Earlier biographers, who did not have access to the evidence in the Duveens' papers that Simpson evidently gained, blame the source of Morgan's dislike of Berenson on dealers like Fairfax Murray who made their own living on the commissions of Morgan and other collectors and resented Berenson's entrance into the field. Colin Simpson, *Artful Partners: Bernard Berenson and Joseph Duveen* (New York: Macmillan, 1986), 96; Samuels, *Connoisseur*, 422.

24. BB to ISG, 5 May 1901; Samuels, *Connoisseur*, 356.

25. Auchincloss, *Morgan*, 108; Strouse, *Morgan*, 413–15. The seven altarpiece panels were recently reunited for an exhibition at the Metropolitan Museum of Art. *New York Times*, 23 June 2006.

26. BB to ISG, [1906], in Hadley, ed., *Letters*, 388 (this letter is placed in Nov. by Hadley).

27. The Morgan Library owns a limited edition of *The Drawings of the Florentine Painters* (New York: Dutton, 1903) and two editions of *Central Italian Painters* (New York: Putnam, 1908; 2d ed., 1908).

28. MB to HWS, 31 Dec. 1908, LLIU:HWS, "Correspondence: Berenson."

29. BB to ISG, 5 Dec. 1908, in Hadley, ed., *Letters*, 426–27.

30. BG to BB, 23 April 1909, VIT.

31. Samuels, *Legend*, 69, 73–74; MB to HWS, 15 Dec. 1908, LLIU:HWS, "Correspondence: Berenson."

32. BG to BB, 23 April 1909, VIT.

33. MB to HWS, 15 Jan. 1909, LLIU:HWS, "Correspondence: Berenson."

34. MB to HWS, 2 Dec. 1908, LLIU:HWS, "Correspondence: Berenson"; Samuels, *Legend*, 74.

35. MB to HWS, 9 Feb., 8 March 1909, LLIU:HWS, "Correspondence: Berenson."

36. MB to HWS, 15 Jan. 1909, LLIU:HWS, "Correspondence: Berenson."

37. Simpson, *Artful Partners*, 124–25.

38. Nicky Mariano, *Forty Years with Berenson* (New York: Knopf, 1966), 36.

39. BG to BB, 23 April 1909, VIT.

40. MB to RC, 18 Feb. 1909, LLIU:HWS, "Correspondence: Berenson."

41. MB to HWS, 23 Feb. 1909, LLIU:HWS, "Correspondence: Berenson." A few days later she described Belle as Morgan's "extraordinary young secretary." MB to HWS, 28 Feb. 1909, LLIU:HWS, "Correspondence: Berenson."

42. MB to RC, 28 Feb. 1909, LLIU:HWS, "Correspondence: Berenson."

43. MB to RC, 17 Feb. 1909, LLIU:HWS, "Correspondence: Berenson."

44. BG to BB, 1 March 1910, VIT. Karin did not have as nice a time in the States that year. Mary was also preoccupied throughout the winter with doctor's appointments, trying to find a hearing aid for her younger daughter, who was nearly deaf.

45. RC to Smith Family, 5 March 1909, LLIU:HWS, "Correspondence: Strachey."

46. MB to HWS, 9 March 1909, LLIU:HWS, "Correspondence: Berenson."

47. BG to BB, 23 Feb. 1909, VIT.

48. This letter was destroyed, but Belle referred to it in a later letter to BB after she had gone back and reread all of his letters to her. BG to BB, 8 Dec. 1914, VIT.

49. BG to BB, 1, 5 March 1909, VIT. Alice Ditson is probably best remembered now for having made to Columbia University a large bequest that funds a number of awards, fellowships, and music programs.

50. BG to BB, 1, 5, n.d. March 1909, VIT.

51. BG to MB, 8 March 1909, VIT.

52. BG to BB, 7 March 1909, VIT. The poem is by Alice Rollitt Coe and was clipped from *Scribner's Magazine*, n.d.

53. BG to BB, 8, 9 March 1909, VIT.

54. BG to BB, 15 Oct. 1909, 12 Aug. 1912, VIT.

55. BG to BB, 12 Aug. 1912, VIT.

56. BG to BB, 3 Aug. 1909, 11 April 1910, VIT.

57. BG to BB, 17 March 1909, VIT.

58. Samuels, *Legend*, 79.

CHAPTER 6: "THE WHIRL IN WHICH I LIVE"

1. BG to BB, 2 Feb. 1910, VIT.

2. Hutchins Hapgood, *A Victorian in the Modern World* (New York: Harcourt, Brace, 1939), 152. Belle was friends with Hapgood.

3. BG to BB, 21 Ju[ne] 1909, VIT.

4. Nicky Mariano, *Forty Years with Berenson* (New York: Knopf, 1966), 96.

5. BG to BB, 30 April, 9 May, 21 Ju[ne] 1909, VIT.

6. BG to BB, 17 March 1909, VIT.

7. Several scholars have argued that the issue of respectability and controlling one's public image was particularly crucial to African American middle-class women's self-expression and community organizing during the first decades of the twentieth century. Darlene Clark Hine, "Rape and the Inner Lives of Black Women in the Middle West," *Signs* 14 (Summer 1989): 912–20. Others have noted that some African American women were among those who were pushing the boundaries of women's sexual freedom and self-expression. Hazel Carby, "It Jus Be's Dat Way Sometime: The Sexual Politics of Women's Blues," in Vicki L. Ruiz and Ellen C. DuBois, eds., *Unequal Sisters: A Multicultural Reader in U.S. Women's History*, 2d ed. (New York: Routledge, 1994), 238–49. The blues women whom Carby highlights were performing and in many cases living in New York during Belle's lifetime. There is no evidence that Belle interacted with these women or even was aware of their music, although her common reference to having "the blues" suggests she may have been. We can only speculate on what influence her upbringing in an elite community of color had on Belle's understanding of the dangers and joys that might result from expressing her sexuality.

8. BG to BB, 19–20 April 1909, VIT.

9. Printed out, double-sided and single-spaced, my transcripts of her letters to Bernard fill a two-inch binder.

10. BG to BB, 29 April 1909, VIT.

11. BG to BB, 30 April 1909, VIT.

12. BG to BB, 6 April 1909, VIT.

13. BG to BB, 29 Oct. 1909, VIT.

14. BG to BB, 22 March 1910, 19 Nov. 1909, VIT.

15. BG to BB, 22, 24 May 1909, 29 June 1909, VIT. Cass Canfield's account of Belle suggested that she owned her own horse, but I have found no evidence of this. She loved to ride, but only did so at various weekend parties or country clubs. Canfield, *The Incredible Pierpont Morgan: Financier and Art Collector* (New York: Harper & Row, 1974), 152–53.

16. BG to BB, 24 May 1909, VIT. For a history of images and products of feminine beauty, see Kathy Peiss, *Hope in a Jar: The Making of America's Beauty Culture* (New York: Metropolitan Books, 1998).

17. BG to BB, 4 May 1909, VIT.

18. BG to BB, 17, 24 Aug. 1909, VIT. BB to IG, 10 April 1909, in Roland Hadley, *The Letters of Bernard Berenson and Isabella Stewart Gardner, 1887–1924* (Boston: Northeastern University Press, 1987), 441.

19. BG to BB, Easter Sunday [11 April] 1909, VIT.

20. BG to BB, 23 April 1909, 10 July 1909, VIT.

21. BG to BB, 3 Aug., 30 April 1909, VIT.

22. BG to BB, 29 March 1910, VIT.

23. BG to BB, 24 May, 6 July, 20 Aug. 1909, VIT.

24. BG to BB, 17 Aug. 1909, VIT.

25. BG to BB, 23 April 1909, VIT.

26. BG to BB, 20 Aug. 1909, VIT.

27. BG to BB, 20 Aug. 1909, VIT. Mrs. Reggie Vanderbilt was Cathleen Gebhard Neilson, first wife of Reginald Claypoole Vanderbilt. After their marriage ended in divorce, Reginald Vanderbilt married Gloria Laura Mercedes Morgan. Their daughter, Gloria Vanderbilt, became a leading fashion designer.

28. BG to BB, 30 April 1909, VIT.

29. BG to BB, 12 Nov. 1909, VIT.

30. BG to BB, 12 Nov. 1909; "New Theatre Boxes," AML:MCC, "N Misc. Na–Ne." Belle was not alone in this complaint, and the theater was never a success. In 1929 it was demolished.

31. In one of her letters to BB, Belle enclosed a notepaper signed "J.D.R." with a whimsical poem about a silent owl. "The less he spoke the more he heard—/ Why can't I be like that wise old bird?" JDR to BG, n.d. enclosed in BG to BB, 19 April 1909, VIT.

32. BG to BB, 29 March 1910, VIT.

33. BG to BB, 19 April, 9 May 1909, VIT.

34. BG to BB, 19 April 1909, VIT.

35. BG to BB, 12 Nov., 13 Dec. 1909, VIT.

36. BG to BB, 30 July 1909, VIT.

37. BG to BB, 19 Oct. 1909, 17 Dec. 1913, VIT.

38. ISG to BB, 18 Dec. 1909, in Hadley, ed., *Letters*, 462–63.

39. BG to BB, 27 Dec. 1909, VIT.

40. BB to ISG, 1 Jan. 1910, in Hadley, ed., *Letters*, 463.

41. BG to BB, 10 March 1914, VIT; Judith Roman, *Annie Adams Fields: The Spirit of Charles Street* (Bloomington: Indiana University Press, 1990), 109–44.

42. BG to BB, 13 Dec. 1909, 6 Jan. 1914, VIT.

43. BG to BB, 3 Feb. 1915, VIT; Amy Lowell to BG, 3, 5 Feb. 1921, HLHU, bMS Lowell 19 (560). After her death, Dwyer burned most of Lowell's personal correspondence.

44. JPM to Amy Lowell, 4 March 1925, HLHU, bMS Lowell 19 (865). Edwin Wolfe II, with John F. Fleming, *Rosenbach: A Biography* (Cleveland: World Publishing, 1960).

45. Gardner M. Lane to JPM, 15 Jan. 1909; Sarah Orne Jewett to Gardner M. Lane, 14 Jan. 1910, AML:MCC.

46. AF to BG, 16 Dec. 1909, AML:MCC.

47. BG to AF, 11 Jan., 18 Feb. 1910; receipt signed 28 March 1910; AF to BG 3 April 1910, AML:MCC.

48. ER to BG, 21 July 1912, AML:MCC.

49. BG to BB, 24 Aug. 1909, 27 Dec. 1909, VIT.

50. BG to BB, 14 July 1909, VIT.

51. BG to BB, 15 July 1909, VIT; A. K. McComb, ed., *The Selected Letters of Bernard Berenson* (Boston: Houghton Mifflin, 1964), 296.

52. BG to BB, 12 Nov. 1909; MB to BB, 18 Sept. 1909, VIT.

53. BG to BB, 15 Oct. 1909, VIT.

54. BG to BB, 10 July, 15 Oct. 1909, VIT.

55. BG to BB, 26 Nov. 1909, 24 Feb. 1910, VIT.

56. Both were published by G. P. Putnam's Sons in 1909; *Central Italian Painters* was first published in 1897. BG to BB, 27 Dec. 1909, VIT.

57. BG to BB, 29 Oct. 1909, VIT.

58. BG to BB, 13 Dec. 1909, 6, 18 Jan. 1910, VIT.

59. BG to BB, 23 April 1909, VIT.

60. Morgan's final will was dated in Jan. 1913. No earlier versions with which to compare it have survived, so there is no way of knowing whether his bequest to her changed from the 1910 draft to the final one.

61. BG to BB, 23 Jan. 1910; Senda Berenson to BB, 28 Jan. 1910, VIT. She took her to the opera one night, where Senda immediately noticed Rita Lydig, who also had a box at the New Theatre, and asked who she was. Belle called Rita her "hated rival" and then was afraid that Senda took her seriously.

62. *New York Times*, 20 April 1910, pp. 1–2; BG to BB, 19 April 1910, VIT.

63. BG to BB, 21 March 1910, 20 March 1914, VIT.

64. BG to BB, 29 Oct. 1909, 11 April 1910, VIT.

65. *New Yorker*, Feb. 14, 1948, 72; BG to BB, 21 June 1910, VIT.

66. *New York Times*, 20 April 1910, 1–2; BG to BB, 19 April 1910, VIT.

67. M. H. Dunlop, *Gilded City: Scandal and Sensation in Turn-of-the-Century New York* (New York: Morrow, 2000).

68. Penelope Niven, *Steichen: A Biography* (New York: Clarkson Potter, 1997); Jay Bochner, *An American Lens: Scenes from Alfred Stieglitz's New York Secession* (Cambridge: MIT Press, 2005).

69. Edward Steichen to BG, n.d., AML:MCC.

70. BG to BB, 1 March 1910, VIT.

71. Ernest Samuels, *Bernard Berenson: The Making of a Legend* (Cambridge: Har-

vard University Press, Belknap Press, 1987), 66.

72. BG to BB, 1 March 1910, VIT.

73. BG to BB, 1 March 1910, 23 April 1914, VIT; Gertrude Atherton, *Sleeping Fires: A Novel* (New York: Frederick A. Stokes, 1922), inscription "To the one and only Belle Greene," PML, ARC 648.

74. BG to BB, 1 March 1910, VIT.

75. BG to BB, 24 Feb. 1910, VIT; *New York Times*, 10 Oct. 1909, SM13; 12 Jan. 1910, p. 9; 20 March 1910, p. 11.

76. BG to BB, 24 Feb., 21 March 1910, VIT.

77. BG to BB, 17 Aug., 23 April 1909, VIT.

78. BG to BB, 1 June 1909, VIT.

79. BG to BB, 3 Aug. 1909, VIT.

80. BG to BB, 26 Nov. 1909, VIT.

81. BG to BB, 15 April, 2 Feb. 1910, VIT.

82. BG to BB, 6 May, 21 June 1910, VIT.

83. BG to BB, 19 Nov. 1909, VIT.

84. BG to BB, 19 Jan., 8 March 1910, VIT.

85. BG to BB, 17 March 1911, VIT; BG to MF, n.d. 1910, AAAS:MF, "Belle Greene."

86. Meryle Secrest, *Being Bernard Berenson* (New York: Holt, Rinehart and Winston, 1979), 291.

87. BB to Margot Barr, 23 June 1926, HLHU, bMS Am 1801.

88. BG to BB, 23 April 1910, 17 May 1912, VIT.

89. BG to BB, 29 March 1910, VIT.

90. *New York Times*, 16 Jan. 1909, 5; 27 Nov. 1909, 1.

91. BG to BB, 22 March, 8 Feb. 1910, VIT.

92. BG to BB, 24 Aug., 21 March 1910, VIT.

93. Christine Stansell, *American Moderns: Bohemian New York and the Creation of a New Century* (New York: Henry Holt, 2000); Andrea Barnet, *All-Night Party: The Women of Bohemian Greenwich Village and Harlem, 1913–1930* (Chapel Hill: Algonquin Books of Chapel Hill, 2004); Gerald W. McFarland, *Inside Greenwich Village: A New York City Neighborhood, 1898–1918* (Amherst: University of Massachusetts Press, 2001).

94. BG to BB, 29 June 1909, VIT.

95. BG to BB, 6 May 1910, VIT.

96. BG to BB, 6 May 1910, VIT.

97. Secrest, *Being Bernard Berenson*, 291. Secrest does not identify the origin of this story, or her source for it.

98. BG to BB, 9, 18 April 1921; BB to MB, 6 Sept. 1920, VIT.

99. Henry Louis Gates discusses this phenomenon in "The Passing of Anatole Broyard," in *Thirteen Ways of Looking at a Black Man* (New York: Random House, 1997), 180–214. Broyard, like Greene, grew up as a light-skinned African American and, according to Gates, lived as white as an adult, becoming a well-known figure in the New York literary world in the 1960s. Interestingly, other acquaintances have claimed that Broyard's black ancestry was not a secret.

100. Secrest, *Being Bernard Berenson*, 290.

101. BG to BB, 22 Nov. 1910, VIT.

102. BG to BB, 22 March [1910], VIT.

103. Strouse, *Morgan*, 558.
104. BG to BB, 6 July 1909, VIT
105. BG to BB, 22 March, 9 April 1909, VIT.
106. BG to BB, 23 April 1910, 19 Nov., 27 Dec. 1909, VIT.
107. BG to VS, 5 Jan. 1910, AML:MCC.
108. BG to Ernest North, 16 Feb. 1910, AML:MCC.
109. AC to BG, 23 April 1910, AML:MCC. See also AC to BG, 1 Jan. 1910, and AC to JPM, 12 Jan. 1910, AML:MCC.
110. George C. Keidel to BG, 28 June 1910, AML:MCC.
111. BQ to BG, 27 Jan. 1910, AML:MCC.
112. BG to BB, 30 March, 23 April, 10 July 1909, VIT.
113. BG to BB, 7 June 1910, VIT; Samuels, *Legend*, 105.
114. BG to BB, 7 June 1910, VIT.
115. BG to BB, 7 June 1910, VIT.
116. No record of this portrait survives.
117. BG to BB, 7 June 1910, VIT. The black-and-white photo is still at the Berenson Archives.
118. BG to Laura Hills, 5 Jan. 1912, AML:MCC.
119. BG to BB, [July 1910], VIT.
120. BG to BB, 21 June 1910, VIT.
121. BG to BB, 6 July 1910, VIT.
122. BG to BB, 21 June 1910, VIT.
123. BG to BB, 24 Feb. 1910, VIT.
124. BG to BB, 24 Feb. 1910, VIT.
125. BG to BB, 21 July 1910, VIT.
126. BB to MB, 22 July [1910]; MB to BB, 23 July 1910, VIT.

CHAPTER 7: BELLA ITALIA

1. BG to BB, 18 Jan. 1911, VIT.
2. BG to BB, 4 Jan. 1921, VIT.
3. BB to MB, 18 Aug. 1910, VIT.
4. BG to BB, 19 Oct. 1910; MB to BB, 18 Aug. 1910, VIT.
5. MB to BB, 27 Aug. 1910, VIT.
6. MB to BB, 21 Aug. 1910, VIT.
7. BG to BB, 17 Aug. 1909, VIT.
8. BG to BB, 30 July 1909, VIT.
9. BG to BB, 14 Dec. 1913, VIT.
10. BB to MB, 25 Aug. 1910, VIT.
11. BB to MB, 21 Aug. 1910, VIT.
12. BB to MB, 21 Aug. 1910, VIT.
13. BB to MB, 25 Aug. 1910, VIT.
14. BB to MB, 27, 29 Aug. 1910, VIT.
15. BB to MB, 25, 28 Aug. 1910, VIT.
16. BB to MB, 29 Aug. 1910; BG to BB, 22 Sept. 1911, VIT.
17. BB to MB, 22 Aug. 1910, VIT.
18. MB to BB, 23 Aug. 1910, VIT.
19. BB to MB, 25, 26 Aug. 1910, VIT.
20. BB to MB, 21 Aug. 1910, VIT.

21. BB to MB, 26 Aug. 1910, VIT.
22. MB to BB, 25 Aug. 1910, VIT.
23. MB to BB, 21 Aug. 1910, VIT.
24. BG to BB, 16 Sept. 1912, VIT.
25. Carl Hovey, *The Life Story of J. Pierpont Morgan* (London: Heinemann, 1912), 338–39; A. K. McComb, ed., *The Selected Letters of Bernard Berenson* (Boston: Houghton Mifflin, 1964), 295.
26. BB to MB, 3 Aug., 7 Sept. 1910; MB to BB, 3 Sept. 1910, VIT.
27. BB to MB, 25, 30 Aug. 1910, VIT.
28. BB to MB, 22 Aug., 21 Sept. 1910, VIT.
29. MB to BB, 1 Sept. 1910, VIT.
30. BB to MB, 4 Sept., 31 Aug. 1910, VIT.
31. BB to MB, 31 Aug. 1910; BG to BB, 15, 18 Oct. 1910, VIT.
32. BG to BB, 29 Oct. 1910, VIT.
33. BG to BB, 16 May 1911, 19 March 1912; BB to MB, 8 Sept. 1910, VIT.
34. BG to BB, 31 May 1911, 19 March 1912, VIT.
35. BG to MB, 7 Sept. 1912, VIT.
36. MB to BB, 3, 4 Sept. 1910, VIT.
37. BG to BB, 6 Jan. 1911, VIT.
38. BG to BB, 19 March 1912, VIT.
39. MB to BB, 9 Sept. 1910, VIT.
40. BB to MB, 12 Sept. 1910, VIT.
41. BB to MB, 12 Sept. 1910, VIT. The Vatican Museum today employs several people during peak tourist season to stand in the Sistine Chapel and constantly quiet the crowds.
42. BG to BB, 17 Sept. 1910, VIT.
43. BG to BB, 14 Oct. 1913, VIT.
44. BG to BB, 17 Sept. 1910, VIT.
45. BB to MB, 13 Sept. 1910, VIT.
46. BG to BB, 17 Sept. 1910, VIT.
47. MB to HWS, 18 Sept. 1910, LLIU:HWS, "Correspondence: Berenson."
48. BG to BB, 9 May 1915, VIT.
49. Barbara Strachey and Jayne Samuels, eds., *Mary Berenson: A Self-Portrait from Her Letters & Diaries* (New York: Norton, 1983), 151. For more on Geoffrey Scott and his relationship with the Berensons, see Richard M. Dunn, *Geoffrey Scott and the Berenson Circle: Literary and Aesthetic Life in the Early 20th Century* (Lewiston, N.Y.: Edwin Mellen Press, 1998).
50. MB to HWS, 23 Sept. 1910, LLIU:HWS, "Correspondence: Berenson."
51. LO to AT, 11 Nov. 1910, AML:MCC.
52. BG to BB, 17 Sept. 1910, VIT.
53. BG to HWS, 19 Sept. 1910, LLIU:HWS, "Correspondence: Berenson."
54. MB to BB, 20 Sept. 1910, VIT.
55. HWS to MB, 22 Sept. 1910; MB to HWS, 23 Sept. 1910, LLIU:HWS, "Correspondence: Berenson."
56. HWS to MB, 12, 23, Sept. 1910, LLIU:HWS, "Correspondence: Berenson"; RC to MB, 29 Sept. 1910, LLIU:HWS, "Correspondence: Stephens."
57. HWS to MB, 4 Oct. 1910, LLIU:HWS, "Correspondence: Berenson."
58. MB to HWS, 25 Sept. 1910, LLIU:HWS, "Correspondence: Berenson."
59. BG to BB, 14 Oct. 1913, VIT.

60. MB to HWS, 1 Oct. 1910, LLIU:HWS, "Correspondence: Berenson."

61. Scott did follow up, with a real estate prospectus for a villa neighboring I Tatti that he was selling on behalf of the owner. Belle obliged him by distributing the description but no further correspondence on the matter exists. GS to BG, 23 Jan. 1912; BG to GS, 27 Feb. 1912, AML:MCC.

62. MB to HWS, 26 Sept. 1910, LLIU:HWS, "Correspondence: Berenson."

63. BG to BB, 15 Jan. 1911, VIT.

64. MB to HWS, 26 Sept. 1910, LLIU:HWS, "Correspondence: Berenson"; FW to BG, 30 Sept. 1910, AML:MCC; BG to BB, 12 Aug. 1912, 29 Oct. 1909, VIT.

65. BG to MB, 21 Oct. 1910, VIT.

66. BB to MB, 3, 4, 6 Oct. 1910, VIT.

67. MB to BB, 6, 7 Oct. 1910, VIT.

68. MB to BB, 10, 13, 14, 17 Dec. 1912, VIT. See also Strachey and Samuels, *Mary Berenson*, 98.

69. Andrea Tone, *Devices and Desires: A History of Contraceptives in America* (New York: Hill and Wang, 2001); Carole R. McCann, *Birth Control Politics in the United States, 1916–1945* (Ithaca: Cornell University Press, 1994); Virginia Nicholson, *Among the Bohemians: Experiments in Living, 1900–1939* (New York: Morrow, 2002), 31–66.

71. BG to BB, 26 Sept. 1919, 4 Jan. 1921, VIT. Although Belle and Bernard met again, there was no other time that she left him to go to London, except for Oct. 1910.

72. BG to BB, 9 Oct. 1910, VIT.

73. BG to BB, 22 Oct. 1910, VIT.

74. BG to BB, 12 Oct. 1910, VIT.

75. BG to BB, 12 Oct. 1910, VIT.

76. EG to BB, 13 Oct. 1910, VIT.

77. MB to BB, 9, 14, Oct. 1919; BG to BB, 10 Oct. 1910, VIT.

78. BG to BB, 11 Oct. 1910; BB to MB, 12 Oct. 1910, VIT; Ernest Samuels, *Bernard Berenson: The Making of a Legend* (Cambridge: Harvard University Press, Belknap Press, 1987), 115.

79. BG to BB, 12 Oct. 1910; BB to MB, 13 Oct. 1910, VIT.

80. BG to BB, 14 Oct. 1910, VIT.

81. BG to BB, 15 Oct. 1910, VIT.

82. BB to MB, 16, 17 Oct. 1910, VIT.

83. BG to BB, 17 Oct. 1910, VIT.

84. BG to BB, 17 Oct. 1910, VIT.

85. BG to BB, 18 Oct. 1910, VIT; MB to Judith Berenson, 15 Nov. 1912, HLHU, bMS Am 2013 (43). Judith was Bernard's mother.

86. MB to BB, 16 Oct. 1910; BB to MB, 19 Oct. 1910, VIT.

CHAPTER 8: HIDING IN THE LIGHT

1. BG to BB, 29 Oct. 1910, VIT.

2. BG to BB, 6 Jan. 1911, VIT.

3. BG to BB, 19 Oct. 1910, VIT.

4. Ernest Samuels, *Bernard Berenson: The Making of a Legend* (Cambridge: Harvard University Press, Belknap Press, 1987), 78.

5. BG to BB, 19 Oct. 1910, VIT.

6. EG to BB, 19 Oct. 1910, VIT.

7. BG to BB, 19 Oct. 1910, VIT; Nina Auerbach, *Ellen Terry: Player in Her Time* (New York: Norton, 1987).

8. BG to BB, 19 Oct. 1910, VIT.

9. BG to BB, 19 Oct. 1910, VIT.

10. BG to BB, 19 Oct. 1910, VIT.

11. BG to BB, 19 Oct. 1910, VIT.

12. EG to BB, 25 Oct. 1910, VIT; Oliver Herford and Ethel Watts Mumford Grant, *The Cynic's Calendar of Revised Wisdom for 1904* (San Francisco: P. Elder, 1903).

13. BG to BB, 28 Oct. 1910, VIT.

14. *New York Times*, 27 Oct. 1910, p. 11; BG to BB, 29 Oct. 1910, VIT. The papers also noted the return of Anne Morgan and the arrival of Ellen Terry on the same boat, and mentioned only that Belle had been visiting England. This same article was reprinted in Belle's hometown paper, the *Washington Post*, 28 Oct. 1910, p. 6.

15. On the Duveen case, see Samuels, *Legend*, 114, 122, 133–34, and Colin Simpson, *Artful Partners: Bernard Berenson and Joseph Duveen* (New York: Macmillan, 1986), 127–29.

16. BG to BB, 8, 22 Nov. 1910, VIT.

17. MB to BB, 1 Oct. 1909, VIT.

18. BG to BB, 29 Oct. 1910, VIT.

19. BG to BB, 28 Oct. 1910, VIT.

20. BG to BB, 31 May 1911; EG to BB, 15 Nov. 1910, VIT.

21. BG to BB, 29 Oct., 11 Nov. 1910, VIT.

22. BG to BB, 31 May 1911, VIT; CR to BG, 14 June 1911, AML:MCC.

23. BG to BB, 3 Nov. 1910; EG to BB, 21 Oct. 1911, VIT.

24. BG to BB, 3 Nov. 1910, VIT.

25. BB to MB, 1 Nov. 1910; BG to BB, 29 Oct., 25 Dec. 1910, VIT.

26. BG to BB, 3 Nov. 1910, VIT.

27. BG to BB, 19 Sept. 1916, VIT.

28. BG to BB, 3 Nov. 1910, VIT. This is an example of Belle's forgetting what she previously wrote to Bernard. Three months later, she wrote about having dinner with Eugene Glaenzer and repeated a similar conversation about her trip to Italy and an unspoken agreement between them that he would protect her and "B.B." BG to BB, 7 Feb. 1911, VIT.

29. BG to BB, 21 May 1911, VIT.

30. BG to BB, 17 Nov. 1910, VIT.

31. BG to BB, 3 Jan. 1911, VIT.

32. BG to BB, 29 Oct. 1910, VIT.

33. Rey was Seligmann's partner, and a good friend of Belle's. George Blumenthal, in addition to having many business and social ties to Belle, was a good friend of Jacques Seligmann's. And Thomas Ryan, also a businessman and art collector, wanted to warn Seligmann through Belle not to hire a particular lawyer who had blackmailed Ryan in the past.

34. BG to BB, 24 Jan. 1911, VIT.

35. BG to BB, 19 Jan. 1911, VIT.

36. BG to BB, 9 May 1911, VIT.

37. BG to BB, 15 Jan. 1911, VIT; BG to Otto Kahn, 27 Jan. 1911, PU, CO 269, 34: 9. A series of letters from BG to Kahn about New Theater is in this file. *New York Times*, 10 May 1913, 11.

38. G to BB, 19 Dec. 1910, VIT.

39. Arthur Gold and Robert Fizdale, *The Divine Sarah: A Life of Sarah Bernhardt* (New York: Knopf, 1991).

40. BG to BB, 25 Dec. 1910, VIT.

41. BG to BB, 28 Dec. 1910, 24 Jan., 22 Feb. 1911, VIT.

42. BG to BB, 27 Feb., 15 Jan. 1911, VIT.

43. Michael T. R. B. Turnbull, *Mary Garden* (Portland, Ore.: Amadeus Press, 1997).

44. Turnbull, *Mary Garden*, 79–95.

45. BG to BB, 7, 28 Feb., 21 March 1911, 13 Feb. 1912, VIT.

46. BG to BB, 25 Dec. 1910, VIT.

47. Jean Strouse identifies Lady Johnstone as the former Antoinette Pinchot. Jean Strouse, *Morgan: American Financier* (New York: Harper Perennial, 2000), 633.

48. BG to BB, 11 Nov. 1910, VIT.

49. MB to BB, 1, 3 Nov. 1910, VIT.

50. Samuels, *Legend*, 112–17; MB to Family, 28 Oct. 1910, LLIU:HWS, "Correspondence: Berenson."

51. MB to Family, 13, 21 Nov. 1910, LLIU:HWS, "Correspondence: Berenson."

52. MB to BB, 17 Nov. 1910; BG to BB, 19 Dec. 1910, VIT.

53. BG to BB, 17 Nov., 13, 25, 28 Dec. 1910, VIT.

54. BG to BB, 25, 28 Dec. 1910, VIT. See also BG to BB, 10 March 1914, VIT: "but as my old nurse used to say 'she sure is powerful mistook.'"

55. U.S. census, 1880.

56. U.S. census, 1910.

57. BG to BB, 4 May 1909, 19 Oct. 1910, VIT.

58. It is also possible that Annie wasn't a nursemaid at all. Explaining an undeniably dark-skinned family member as a maid or servant had helped many a fictional and historical individual "pass" as white and maintain some ties to darker-skinned family members. But which of Belle's family members could this have been? Both her grandmothers had died long before 1910. She did have numerous aunts, great aunts, and assorted cousins who might have lived with the family. But none are ever listed as living with the Greenes, and these names don't match family records.

59. NYC directories list Van Vliet Green or Greene "wid DeAcosta" at 142 East 40th Street from 1912 to 1916; Bella Greene, librarian, is listed at 104 East 40th Street. Today those addresses are a full block away from each other, on opposite sides of Lexington Avenue, which does not fit Belle's description. This may be a typographical error—140 East 40th Street would abut 142.

60. BG to BB, 19, 28 Dec. 1910, 6, 24 Jan. 1911, VIT.

61. BG to BB, 13 Dec. 1910, VIT.

62. BG to BB, 25, 27 Dec. 1910, 6 Jan. 1911, VIT.

63. MB to AR, 24 May 1911, LLIU:HWS, "Correspondence: Berenson"; Samuels, *Legend*, 125, 140.

64. BG to BB, 19 Jan. 1911, VIT.

65. The lengths of Belle's silences have been exaggerated by many of Berenson's biographers, in part, no doubt, because of Mary's propensity to greatly exaggerate how long it had been since she was last heard from. A few times Mary claimed it had been several, even four months, yet there is no time during these years when Belle waited more than a month after her last letter to write again. Bernard usually made a note when letters arrived late, especially when he had been anxiously awaiting them.

66. EG to BB, 15 Nov. 1910; BG to BB, 29 Oct., 11 Nov. 1910, VIT.

67. BG to BB, 6 Jan. 1911, 31 Dec. 1910, VIT.

68. BG to BB, 24 Jan. 1911, VIT.

69. BG to BB, 27 Dec. 1910, VIT.

70. BG to BB, 12 Nov. 1909, 22 Nov. 1910, VIT.

71. BG to BB, 6 Jan. 1911, VIT.

72. BG to BB, 3 Jan. 1911, VIT.

73. BG to BB, 18 April 1911, 11 Feb. 1913, VIT.

74. BG to BB, 19 Jan. 1911, VIT.

75. BG to BB, 3 Jan. 1911, VIT.

76. BG to BB, 15 Jan. 1911; MB to BB, 9 July 1911, VIT.

77. BG to BB, 25 Dec. 1910, VIT.

78. BG to BB, 19 Dec. 1910, VIT. The story actually continued. Apparently the man then went to California, where he immediately found a female friend reading one of Bernard's books—more proof that his competition was out of his league.

79. BG to BB, 18, 19 Jan. 1911, VIT.

80. BG to BB, 24 Jan. 1911, VIT.

81. BG to BB, 10 March 1911, VIT.

82. BG to BB, 3 Nov. 1910, VIT.

83. BG to BB, 29 July 1910, VIT.

84. BG to BB, 29 July 1910, VIT.

85. BG to BB, 15, 19 Jan. 1911, VIT.

86. BG to BB, 1 Feb. 1911, VIT.

87. BG to BB, 15 Jan. 1911, VIT.

88. BG to BB, 1 Feb. 1911, VIT.

89. BG to BB, 1 Feb. 1911, VIT

90. BG to BB, 31 May 1911, VIT.

91. BG to BB, 3 Aug. 1909, VIT.

92. SB to BB, 2 Feb. 1911, VIT.

93. SB to BB, 2 Feb. 1911, VIT.

94. BG to BB, 1 Feb. 1911; SB to BB, 2 Feb. 1911, VIT.

95. BG to BB, 7, 17 Feb. 1911, VIT.

96. BG to BB, 14, 22 Feb. 1911, VIT.

97. MB to BB, 22, 23 Feb. 1911, VIT.

98. BB to MB, 25 Feb., 12 March 1911; MB to BB, 1 March 1911, VIT.

99. Stephen M. Vallillo, "Broadway Revues in the Teens and Twenties: Smut and Slime?" *Drama Review: TDR* 25, no. 1 (March 1981): 25–34. See also Linda Mizejewski, *Ziegfeld Girl: Image and Icon in Culture and Cinema* (Durham: Duke University Press, 1999).

100. BG to BB, 22 Feb. 1911, VIT.

101. BG to BB, 28 Feb., 14, 16 March 1911, VIT.

102. There is no direct evidence linking this Baird to Belle prior to 1913 when they were both founders of the Century Opera Company (formerly the City Club opera organization). But it is hard to imagine that Belle did not know another passionate opera supporter. *New York Times,* 17 Nov. 1910, 4; 10 May 1913, 11; 16 May 1913, 11.

103. EG to BB, 15 Nov. 1910, 15 March 1911, VIT.

104. BG to BB, 21 March 1911, VIT.

105. BG to MB, 2 May 1911, VIT.

106. BG to BB, 3, 14, 24 April 1911, VIT. Most of the four other letters she wrote were much shorter. Berenson called them "curt indifferent notes," worse than nothing at all. BB to MB, 2 May 1911, VIT.

107. CR to BG, 9 Nov. 1909, AML:MCC. Belle continued to help national museums, especially the British Museum, acquire and keep national treasures in their country when possible. Frederick G. Kenyon, "A Tribute from the British Museum," in Dorothy Miner, ed., *Studies in Art and Literature for Belle da Costa Greene* (Princeton: Princeton University Press, 1954), 4–5.

108. *New York Times*, 25 April 1911, 1.

109. *New York Times*, 30 April 1911, SM13.

110. *World Magazine*, 21 May 1911, 1.

111. Undated Associated Press release, CAH:NYJAM.

112. *New York Daily Tribune,* 28 May 1911; BG to ER, 1 June 1911, AML:MCC, "Seligmann."

113. BG to BB, 25 April 1911, VIT.

114. She called the Huntington purchases a result of "absolute ignorance backed by seemingly limitless means" and was appalled that anyone who knew Morgan would suggest he fell in the same category. Wheeler's response was defensive, but he did not challenge Belle's right to speak for Morgan. He only denied his intentions to raise values and assured her that, even if he did, he would not do so for her: "I am neither foolish enough nor ungrateful enough to thus repay 23 years of Mr. Morgan's patronage and confidence." BG to FW, 26 May 1911; FW to BG, 6 June 1911, AML:MCC.

115. Among other things, Belle had apparently introduced Harry Widener to Livingston in 1909, resulting in lucrative business for Livingston & Dodd. LL to BG, n.d. [1911], AML:MCC. See correspondence in folder "Dodd, Mead & Co."

116. BG to LL, 19 April 1911, AML:MCC.

117. BG to MF, 1 Jan. 1912, AAAS:MF, "Belle Greene."

118. AC to JPM, 6 April 1911, AML:MCC.

119. Guy Lesser, "Browsing for Gold," *Harper's Magazine,* Jan. 2002, 39–52.

120. Margaret Bingham Stillwell, *Librarians Are Human: Memories in and out of the Rare-Book World, 1907–1970* (Boston: University Press of New England, 1973), 288.

121. *New York Times*, 7 April 1912, SM8.

CHAPTER 9: A MODERN WOMAN

1. BG to BB, 3 Nov. 1913, VIT.

2. BG to BB, 14 March 1914, VIT.

3. BG to BB, 31 May 1911, VIT.

4. Caroline Gerrit Smith to BG, 20 March 1912, AML:MCC; BG to BB, 9 May 1911, VIT.

5. BG to BB, 27 June 1911; MB to BB, 5 July 1911, VIT.

6. BG to BB, 4 July 1911, VIT.

7. MB to AR, 24 May 1911, LLIU:HWS, "Correspondence: Berenson." Alys was Mary's sister, who was married to philosopher Bertrand Russell.

8. MB to BB, 12 July 1911, VIT.

9. BB to MB, 8 July 1911, VIT.

10. BG to BB, 18 July 1911, VIT.

11. BG to BB, 11, 22 Aug., 11 Oct. 1911, VIT.

12. BG to BB, 9 May 1911, VIT. Reports of Marbury's affairs with women had been circulating for years. When Mary heard the gossip about Bessie, she wrote Bernard, "I don't really disapprove either of Lesbianism (I think I approve of it) nor using one's charms in a mercenary way." MB to BB, 1 June 1909, VIT.

13. BG to BB, 17 May 1911, VIT.

14. BG to BB, 16 May 1911, VIT.

15. BB to MB, 8 July 1911, VIT.

16. BG to BB, 18 July 1911, VIT.

17. BG to BB, 9 May, 11 Aug. 1911, VIT.

18. BG to BB, 2 Sept. 1911, VIT.

19. BB to MB, 24, 28 Aug. 1911; MB to BB, 26 Aug. 1911, VIT.

20. GS to EB, 30 Aug. 1911, HLHU; BG to BB, 22 Sept. 1911, VIT.

21. BG to BB, 2, 14 Sept., 11 Oct. 1911, VIT.

22. BG to BB, 11 Oct. 1911, VIT.

23. MB to BB, 22 Sept. 1911, VIT. Bessie actually wrote to Mary's daughter Karin Costelloe, who read the letter to her mother, who was still staying with them. Mary immediately wrote to Bernard.

24. "Mestre, Harold de Villa Urrutia," in *The National Cyclopaedia of American Biography*, vol. 29 (New York: James T. White, 1941), 485–86.

25. EG to BB, 4 Dec. 1911, VIT.

26. Hubert B. Ross, Amelia Marie Adams, and Lynne Mallory Williams, "Caroline Bond Day: Pioneer Black Physical Anthropologist," in *African-American Pioneers in Anthropology*, ed. Faye V. Harrison and Ira E. Harrison (Chicago: University of Illinois Press, 1999); Heidi Ardizzone, "Red-Blooded Americans: Mulattoes and the Melting Pot in United States Racialist and Nationalist Discourse, 1890–1930" (Ph.D. diss., University of Michigan, 1997).

27. EG to BB, 21 Oct., 4 Dec. 1911, VIT.

28. BG to EG, 1 Feb. 1912, VIT.

29. EG to BG, 2 Feb. 1912, VIT.

30. Mary Berenson thought that Belle was writing twice about the same incident mentioned in BG to BB, 21 Aug. 1911. But since Ethel describes the engagement as being off and on again several times and since there are some significant differences in the stories, it is more likely that Belle and J.P. had two confrontations, one with each wave of gossip as she became engaged, broke it off, and became engaged again.

31. BG to BB, 11 Oct. 1911, VIT.

32. MB to EB, 22, 24, 28, 30 Oct., 5, 12 Nov. 1911, HLHU:BP, bMS Am 2013 (42).

33. MB to EB, 19, 23, 27 Nov. 1911, HLHU, bMS Am 2013 (42); BG to BB, 20 Nov. 1911, VIT

34. BG to BB, 2 Dec. 1911, VIT; MB to EB, 2 Dec. 1911, HLHU: BP, bMS Am 2013 (42).

35. BG to BB, 5, 12 Dec. 1911, VIT.

36. BG to BB, 9 Jan. 1912, VIT.

37. BG to BB, 18 July 1911, 1, 13 Feb. 1912, VIT.

38. BG to BB, 15 Dec. 1911, 9 Jan. 1912, VIT.

39. *Washington Post*, 12 Jan. 1913, ES10.

40. BG to BB, 9 Jan., 17, 20 Feb. 1912, VIT.
41. *Washington Post,* 8 Jan. 1912, p. 7.
42. *Chicago Daily Tribune,* 11 Aug. 1912, G2.
43. *New York Times,* 7 April 1912, SM8.
44. *Washington Post,* 16 Feb. 1913, MT4.
45. BG to BB, 9, 26 April 1912, VIT; *New York Times,* 7 Jan. 1912.
46. BG to BB, 1, 17 Feb., 19 March 1912, VIT; E. Ernst, "Colonic Irrigation and the Theory of Autointoxication: A Triumph of Ignorance over Science," *Journal of Clinical Gastroenterology* 24 (June 1997): 196–98.
47. BG to BB, 26 March, 7 June 1912, VIT.
48. BG to AC, 2 July 1912; AC to BG, 19 March 1912, AML:MCC; BG to BB, 1 July, n.d. April 1912, VIT; Albert Clay provided Belle's mother and sisters with motorboat rides.
49. BG to BB, 2 April 1912, VIT.
50. BG to BB, 1 Feb. 1912, VIT.
51. *New York Times,* 23 May 1913, 8; 10 April 1914, 10; 16 Dec. 1914, 22.
52. BG to BB, 9 April 1912, VIT.
53. BG to BB, 26 April, 3 May 1912, VIT; *New York Times,* 5 May 1912, p. 1.
54. BG to BB, 9 April 1912, VIT; FW to BG, 29 July, 23 April 1912, AML:MCC; Jean Strouse, *Morgan: American Financier* (New York: Harper Perennial, 2000), 643.
55. ASWR to BG, 20 April 1912, AML:MCC; BG to BB, 24 April 1912, VIT.
56. BG to BB, 26 April 1912, VIT.
57. BG to BB, 23 April [1912]. A number of letters had also gone down with the ship, and the practical as well as emotional fallout of the *Titanic* is evident in her professional correspondence. HH to BG, 19 April 1912; FW to BG, 23 April 1912, AML:MCC; Strouse, *Morgan,* 643.
58. BG to BB, 7 June 1912, VIT.
59. Douglas Hyland, "Agnes Ernst Meyer and Modern Art in America, 1907–1918" (M.A. thesis, University of Delaware, 1976), 1–14; Katharine Graham, *Personal History* (New York: Knopf, 1997).
60. AM to BG, n.d. [1914], VIT; Hyland, "Meyer," 43.
61. BG to BB, 9 April 1912, VIT.
62. Penelope Niven, *Steichen: A Biography* (New York: Clarkson Potter, 1997), 364, 370–74; BG to BB, 20 Jan. 1913, VIT.
63. BG to BB, 11 Feb. 1913, VIT.
64. BG to BB, 3 Feb. 1915, 26 April 1912, VIT.
65. Meryle Secrest, *Being Bernard Berenson: A Biography* (New York: Holt, Rinehart and Winston, 1979), 291.
66. BG to BB, 12 Dec. 1911, VIT; William Rothenstein to BG, 13 Feb. 1912, AML:MCC.
67. BG to BB, 31 Dec. 1912, VIT. The manuscript in question depicted the heavens from above, not below, explaining the backwards orientation of the zodiac.
68. *New York Times,* 16 March 1913, SM8.
69. Probate Record, "Belle daCosta [sic] Greene," New York County Clerk's Office, Manhattan, New York County Surrogate's Court, File No. P. 1771-1950.
70. BG to BB, 31 March 1919, VIT.
71. WI to SC, 28 April 1923, BLM, 52726 ff., 160–293.

72. Probate Record, "Belle daCosta [*sic*] Greene," New York County Clerk's Office, Manhattan, New York County Surrogate's Court, File No. P. 1771-1950.
73. Secrest, *Berenson*, 291. This story is apparently from Adelyn Breeskin, who was one of the first female museum directors, beginning her career at the Metropolitan Museum of Art's print department.
74. BG to BB, 2 Sept. 1911, VIT.
75. David Askins to FWK, 11 Feb. 1915, AML:MCC. Later Askins heard from local dealers that the Cairo merchant had sold 150 of the books to Mr. Morgan for a million dollars. Askins doubted that 200 books had actually been found, dismissing that estimate as "only a grossly exaggerated native story."
76. TS to BG, 11 Sept. 1911, AML:RODG, "CUA." Father Shahan initially hoped that Morgan would purchase the collection and give it to CUA, but quickly gave up on that option and supported Morgan's purchasing and housing the manuscripts.
77. BG to BB, 22 Sept. 1911, VIT; BG to TS, 23 Sept. 1911, AML:RODG, "CUA"; Leo Depuydt, *Catalogue of Coptic Manuscripts in the Pierpont Morgan Library* (Leuven: Uitgeverij Peeters, 1993), lx.
78. BG to TS, 23 Sept. 1911, AML:RODG, "CUA"; HH to BG, 19 April 1912, ICOR: HH/PPM, 4:1; HH, Report on Progress of Work, 29 Jan. 1915, AML:MCC.
79. Depuydt, *Catalogue*, lxi; *New York Times*, 10 March 1912, 12; David Askren to FWK, 11 Feb. 1915, BG to FWK, 14 June 1912, AML:MCC.
80. Henri Hyvernat, "The J. P. Morgan Collection of Coptic Manuscripts," *Journal of Biblical Literature* 31, pt. 1 (1912).
81. BG to HH, 18 Jan., 12 April 1912, ICOR:HH/PPM, 4:1.
82. BG to JPM, 31 May 1912; Richard Gottlieb to BG, 3 June 1912 AML:RODG, "Coptic Manuscripts—General"; BG to BB, 1 July 1912, VIT. Belle mentions that Charles Rufus Morey of Princeton came to talk about his own qualifications.
83. FK to BG, 29 July 1912, AML:MCC; BG to BB, 1 July 1912, VIT.
84. BG to BB, 13 Feb. 1912, VIT.
85. *Times* (London), 27 Jan. 1912. Jacques Seligmann sent a set of clippings from London papers.
86. BG to BB, 31 Dec. 1912, VIT.
87. BG to BB, MB to EB, 2 April 1912, HLHU, bMS Am 2013 (42); BG to BB, 17 Feb. 1912, VIT.
88. BG to BB, 26 March [1912], VIT.
89. BG to BB, 19 March 1912, VIT.
90. BG to BB, 26 April, 7 June, 9 July 1912, VIT.
91. MB to EB, 6 April, 7 May 1912, HLHU, bMS Am 2013 (42); BG to BB, 19 Jan. 1912, VIT. Mary was not the only one to refer to Belle as a siren. In 1914 Belle received a copy of *Sirenica* published by her friend John Lane. The author inscribed her copy, "To B.G. the Siren of Today." Belle loved the book, telling B.B., "I feel almost as if I had written it myself." W. Compton Leith, *Sirenica* (New York: John Lane, 1913). PML:ARC 0654; BG to BB, 22 June 1914, VIT.
92. BG to BB, 12 Aug. 1912, VIT.
93. BG to BB, 12 Aug. 1912, VIT.
94. BG to BB, 12 Aug. 1912, VIT. The lawyer Louis Levy (who had also defended Gardner in her customs case) had successfully bargained the $10 million penalty down to $1.4 million. He pointed out that the Duveens' private clients included

not only financiers but also powerful politicians, among them President Taft. With the Duveens threatening to challenge the penalty assessment in court, calling their clients as codefendants, the collector of customs, a political appointee, reduced the fee and the Duveens paid. This story is told in the most detail in Colin Simpson, *Artful Partners: Bernard Berenson and Joseph Duveen* (New York: Macmillan, 1986).

95. BG to BB, 8 Oct. 1912, VIT.
96. BG to BB, 6 Nov. [1912], VIT.
97. Strouse, *Morgan*, 4–5, 659–60.
98. BG to BB, 20 Aug. 1912, VIT.
99. BG to BB, 6 Sept. 1912, VIT.
100. BG to BB, 27 Aug., 6 Sept., 8 Oct. 1912, VIT.
101. BG to BB, 22 Oct. 1912, VIT; [BG] *unsigned* to JPM, 9 Jan. 1912, AML:MCC, enclosed in George Williamson folder.
102. BG to BB, 6 Dec. 1912, 5 March 1915, VIT; Edward Forbes to BG, 13 Feb. 1915, AML:MCC; Ernest Samuels, *Bernard Berenson: The Making of a Legend* (Cambridge: Harvard University Press, Belknap Press, 1987), 140.
103. BG to BB, 30 Oct. 1912, VIT.
104. Strouse, *Morgan*, 674–80; BG to CR, 14 March 1913; FK to BG, 8 March 1913, AML:MCC.

CHAPTER 10: CROSSROADS

1. BG to BB, 12 April 1913, VIT.
2. BG to BB, 3 Nov. 1913, VIT.
3. BG to BB, 12 April 1913, VIT.
4. BG to BB, 12, 21 April 1913, VIT.
5. BG to BB, 21 April 1913, VIT.
6. FK to BG, 8 March, 3 May 1913, AML:MCC; BG to BB, 21 April 1913, VIT. Mary reported that Annie Morgan was receiving letters from Belle saying that her "heart was broken and life was ended." MB to BB, 22 Aug. 1913, VIT.
7. GW to BG, 1 April 1913; FW to BG, 22 April 1913, AML:MCC.
8. BQ to BG, 10 April 1913, AML:MCC; AT to HH, n.d. [April 1913], ICOR: HH/PPM, 4:1.
9. MB to GS, 25 Oct. 1913, VIT; LO to JPMJ, 24 April 1913, AML:MCC. See also BG to BQ, 25 April 1913, AML:MCC.
10. Sidney Colvin to BG, 16 April 1913; BG to SC, 25 April 1913, AML:MCC.
11. Eugene Meyers to Charles Freer, 21, 24 April 1913, AAAS:CF, "Eugene Meyers."
12. BG to BB, 19 May 1913, VIT.
13. BG to SC, 29 April 1913, BLM, 52717, 778A f 5. Cockerell's letter may not have been saved. The file containing his correspondence to the Morgan Library is missing from its archives. BG to BB, 2 April 1913, VIT.
14. BG to BB, 9 May 1913, VIT; AT to HH, n.d. [April 1913]; BG to HH, 25 April 1913, ICOR:HH/PPM, 4:1.
15. BG to BB, 21 April 1913, VIT.
16. BG to BB, 21 April 1913, VIT.
17. *New York Times*, 20 April 1913, 2.
18. Belle had gathered many of these letters, presumably those that paid respects to

Morgan and his collection, into a file to show Jack Morgan—a file that was not returned to or saved in her records at the Morgan Library. Some examples that did survive in individuals' correspondence files include GW to BG, 1 April 1913; BQ to BG 10 April, 1913; Sir Sidney Colvin to BG, 16 April 1913; FW to BG, 22 April 1913, AML:MCC, "Pearson"; FK to BG, 3 May 1913, AML:MCC. See also BG to BB, 9 May 1913, VIT.

19. MB to BB, 22 Aug. 1913, VIT.
20. For an example of Belle's notes from the summer of 1913 taken during the inventory, see AML:MCC, "Duveen Bros. corresp. 1906–1923." In cases where she did not have original sale lists or appraisals, she had to contact dealers for details from their records. See BG to EHD, 24 Aug. 1913, AML:MCC.
21. BG to BB, 9 July 1913, VIT.
22. BG to BB, 17 July 1913, VIT.
23. BG to BB, 21 April 1913, VIT.
24. BG to BB, 26 Dec. 1913, VIT.
25. Carol B. Stack, *All Our Kin: Strategies for Survival in a Black Community* (New York: Harper & Row, 1974); Elsa Barkley Brown, "Constructing a Life and a Community: A Partial Story of Maggie Lena Walker," *Magazine of History* 7, no. 4 (Summer 1993); Jacqueline Jones, *Labor of Love, Labor of Sorrow: Black Women, Work, and the Family from Slavery to the Present* (New York: Basic, 1985).
26. BG to BB, 4 Sept., 21 April, 9 May 1913, VIT.
27. BG to BB, 19 May 1913, VIT.
28. BG to BB, 21, 29 April 1913, VIT.
29. BG to BB, 20 Sept. 1913, VIT.
30. BG to BB, 14 Oct., 29 April 1913, BLM, 52717, 778A f 5.
31. BG to BB, 24 June 1913, VIT (parentheses and question mark in original).
32. BG to BB, 29 April 1913, VIT.
33. BG to BB, 17 June 1913, VIT.
34. BG to BB, 9 May 1913, VIT.
35. BG to JS, 9 May 1913; JS to BG, 21 May 1913, AML:MCC.
36. BG to BB, 9 May 1913, VIT; HH to BG, 18 June 1913, ICOR:HH/PPM, 4:1.
37. BG to BB, 9, 17 July 1913, VIT; BG to HH, 22 Sept. 1913, ICOR:HH/PPM, 4:11; BG to FW, 18 Sept. 1913, AML:MCC, "Pearson."
38. Ron Chernow, *The House of Morgan: An American Banking Dynasty and the Rise of Modern Finance* (New York: Atlantic Monthly Press, 1990), 168–71; Jean Strouse, *Morgan: American Financier* (New York: Harper Perennial, 2000).
39. BG to JS, 29 July 1913; JS to BG, 11 Aug., 17 Sept. 1913, AML:MCC.
40. BG to JPMJ, 7 Oct. 1913, AML:JPMJ (364).
41. BG to BB, 22 Aug. 1913, VIT.
42. Charlotte Martins to BG, 29 July 1913, AML:MCC, "M Misc." Charlotte had appealed to Belle to ask the Princeton Library trustees to fund a trip to Europe ($500) as a merit award after thirty years of work. Belle tried and promised to contribute $100 herself, but was not able to raise the additional funds.
43. BG to BB, 3 Nov. 1913, VIT. In the preceding season, papers had noted that she was the guest of Mrs. Giulio Gatti-Casazza, who was also entertaining Viscount and Viscountess Selby. *New York Times*, 24 March 1912, XA1. Belle was often listed in society pages beginning in 1912, through the 1920s.

44. BG to Lilian (Woodman) Aldrich, 24 Nov. 1913, HLHU, bMS Am 1429; BG to MF, 4 Nov. 1913, AAAS:MF, "Belle Greene." Unfortunately the list of members that Belle enclosed was not saved. *New York Times*, 22 Nov., 7 Dec. 1913. During Belle's lifetime the British Library was physically part of the British Museum. It is now housed separately in a new building.

45. BG to BB, 3 Nov. 1913, VIT.

46. BG to BB, 3 Nov. 1913, 18 June 1914, 15 Feb. 1915, VIT; BG to Agnes Morgenthau, 21 March 1918, SC:SSC.

47. BG to BB, 18 April 1914, VIT. Dr. Charles Albertson gave the commencement speech at Adelphi in 1914. There is no record of his message. Eugene T. Neely, University Archivist and Special Collections Librarian, Adelphi University, personal communication, 24 May 2006.

48. Christine Stansell, *American Moderns: Bohemian New York and the Creation of a New Century* (New York: Metropolitan Books, 2000), 231–34.

49. BG to BB, 11 Feb., 4 March, 4 Sept. 1913, 17 March 1914, VIT.

50. BG to BB, 4 Sept. 1913, VIT.

51. Gertrude Stein, "Matisse," *Writings, 1903–1932* (New York: Library of America, 1998), 278.

52. MB to Family, 21 Nov. 1914, quoted in Patricia R. Everett, ed., *A History of Having a Great Many Times Not Continued to Be Friends: The Correspondence between Mabel Dodge and Gertrude Stein, 1911–1934* (Albuquerque: University of New Mexico Press, 1996), 77.

53. BB to Gertrude Stein, 23 Nov. 1912, in Donald Gallup, ed., *The Flowers of Friendship: Letters Written to Gertrude Stein* (New York: Knopf, 1953), 66.

54. BG to BB, 11 Oct. 1914, VIT.

55. Gertrude Stein, *Three Lives: Stories of the Good Anna, Melanctha and the Gentle Lena* (New York: John Rodker, 1927), 86–90.

56. Gertrude Stein, *Everybody's Autobiography* (New York: Cooper Square Publishers, 1971), 7–8.

57. BG to BB, 3 Nov. 1913, VIT.

58. BG to BB, 20 Sept. 1913, VIT.

59. BG to BB, 20 Sept. 1913, VIT.

60. Stansell, *American Moderns*, 250–51; George Chauncey, *Gay New York: Gender, Urban Culture and the Makings of the Gay Male World, 1890–1940* (New York: Basic Books, 1994).

61. Sir Sidney Colvin was working on the biography *John Keats: His Life and Poetry, His Friends, Critics and After-Fame* (New York: Scribner, 1917).

62. It is worth noting that "No. 2," the term that Belle (and Bernard) used for same-sex desire, may have suggested that same-sex relationships were a secondary option if the first or even preferred cross sex was not available. If Belle herself did feel the same kind of romantic and sexual attraction to women as she did to men, she used a term to describe them that suggested that her same-sex flirtations were of merely secondary importance. I have not found other examples of this slang term and therefore have not been able to determine its origins or, indeed, whether it was even used beyond Belle's and Bernard's circle of friends. BG to BB, 20 Sept. 1913, VIT.

63. BG to BB, 17 Oct. 1910, 21 March 1911, VIT.

64. BG to BB, 17 March 1911, VIT.

65. BG to BB, 17 March, 21, 29 April 1913, VIT (parentheses in original).

66. BG to BB, 9 July 1913, VIT. Jean Strouse suggests that this was Anne Morgan's first love affair but that Frances Morgan (Anne's mother) welcomed Elsie and Bessie as friends of her daughter. Jane Smith notes that Juliet Hamilton "reportedly stiffened at the mere mention of the name Elsie de Wolfe." Strouse, *Morgan*, 524; Jane S. Smith, *Elsie de Wolfe: A Life in the High Style* (New York: Atheneum, 1982), 120.

67. BG to BB, 13 Aug. 1913, 3 Nov. [1913], 9 Dec. 1913, VIT.

68. BG to BB, 14 Dec. 1913, VIT.

69. Most of our knowledge of the conversations and activities of Belle and Bernard in Italy come from his letters to Mary. Because Mary was with Bernard for most of his travels in the United States in 1913–14, much less information is available about this visit. John C. Ferguson to BB, 14 March 1915, AML:MCC.

70. BG to BB, 14 Dec. 1913, VIT.

71. BG to BB, 17 Dec. 1913, VIT.

72. BG to BB, 22 Dec. 1913, VIT.

73. BG to BB, 4 Jan. 1914, VIT. The two manuscripts were a twelfth-century psalter and a thirteenth-century Bible.

74. BG to BB, 13 March 1914, VIT.

75. JPMJ to Lewis [Walters?]; AML:JPMJ, (364). Jack's full description of Murray reads, "He is rather deformed, but with a fine straightforward countenance, and, not being a Hebrew, I have hope that we can get along all right together."

76. John Douglas Forbes, *J. P. Morgan, Jr., 1867–1943* (Charlottesville: University Press of Virginia, 1981), 74, 115–17.

77. BG to BB, 14 Oct. 1913, VIT; Forbes, *Morgan, Jr.*, 80–81.

78. BG to BB, 16 Dec. 1913, VIT.

79. MB to Senda Abbott, 5 March 1916, typed copy; MB to GS, 2 Jan. 1914, typed copy, LLIU:HWS, "Misc. Halpern"; MB to Alys Russell, 6, 8 Sept. 1916, LLIU: HWS, "Correspondence: Berenson."

80. BG to BB 4 Jan. [1914], VIT.

81. BG to BB, [5, 7 Jan. 1914], VIT.

82. It is not clear whether these ads were actually placed. Michael Robert Mounter, "Richard Theodore Greener: The Idealist, Statesman, Scholar and South Carolinian" (Ph.D. diss., University of South Carolina, 2002), 514, and personal correspondence.

83. BG to BB, 18 June 1914; *Chicago Tribune,* 7 June 1914, F7.

84. *Chicago Daily Tribune,* 11 Aug. 1912, G2; 20 April 1913, 1–2.

85. The Platts were born in Chicago. Their father, Jacob, was a lumber merchant from New York, and their mother, Amelia, was born in Pennsylvania and may have been related to Richard's mother.

86. Belle was well aware of Jack's "very strong aversion to Jews." BG to BB, 26 Dec. 1913, VIT.

87. BG to BB, 2 Jan. 1914, VIT.

88. BG to BB, 1 Feb., 19 March 1912, VIT.

89. BG to BB, 7 June, 9 July 1912, 22 June, 21 Oct. 1914, VIT.

90. *New York Times,* 30 March 1919, p. 57; 14 March 1920, xx1.

91. Asa Bird Gardiner to BG, 7 Feb. 1913, AML:MCC, "G Misc., Ga–Gev."

92. Mounter, "Greener," 254–58.

93. Jean Strouse, "The Unknown J. P. Morgan," *New Yorker*, 29 March 1999, 75.

94. BG to BB, 5 Jan. 1914, VIT.

95. BG to BB, 29 Dec. 1913, VIT.

96. BG to BB, 26 Sept. 1919, VIT.

97. MB to GS, 2 Jan. 1914; Mary Berenson to Senda (Berenson) Abbott, 19 Jan. 1914, typed copies, LLIU:HWS, "Misc. Halpern"; BG to BB, 21, 22 Jan. 1914, VIT. See also Ernest Samuels, *Bernard Berenson: The Making of a Connoisseur* (Cambridge: Harvard University Press, Belknap Press, 1979), 171–74.

98. BG to BB, 3, 4 March 1914, VIT.

99. MB to Family, 1 March 1914, VIT.

100. BG to BB, 5 March 1914, VIT.

101. MB to SB, 5 March 1916, typed copy, LLIU:HWS, "Misc. Halpern."

102. MB to Judith Berenson, 5 Feb. 1914, HLHU, Berenson Papers, bMS Am 2013 (43).

103. BG to BB, 1, 10 March 1914, VIT.

104. BG to BB, 1, 14 March 1914, VIT.

105. MB to Family, 1 March 1914; BG to BB, 20 March 1914, VIT.

106. BG to BB, 5 March 1914, 9 June 1914, VIT. Freer's biographers make little or no mention of Belle, and nothing in the correspondence I have seen indicates anything more than a professional friendship. Thomas Lawton, *Freer: A Legacy of Art* (Washington, D.C.: Freer Gallery of Art, Smithsonian Institution, 1993).

107. BG to SC, 10 March 1914, BLM, Add 52717 f 6–8.

108. BG to BB, 8 March 1914, VIT.

109. BG to BB, 8 March 1914, VIT.

110. BG to BB, 8 March 1914, VIT.

111. BG to BB, 12, 13 March 1914, VIT.

112. BG to BB, 13 March 1914, VIT.

113. BG to BB, 1, 16 March 1914, VIT. This man disappears from the record almost immediately. He sends a "delicious" golden lacquer box filled with violets, and she has him to dinner again, with her German professor who also spoke Japanese. BG to BB, 4 March 1914, VIT.

114. BG to BB, 20, 29 March 1914, VIT.

115. BG to BB, [1 April 1914], VIT.

CHAPTER 11: BATTLEFIELDS

1. BG to BB, 13 Nov. 1916, VIT.

2. HH to Walter Crum, 23 June 1916, BLM. Add 45685 ff 131–210.

3. *New York Times*, 20 April 1914, 1.

4. BG to BB, 21 April 1914, VIT.

5. BG to BB, 17 May 1912, 26 April 1914, VIT.

6. John Douglas Forbes, *J. P. Morgan, Jr., 1867–1943* (Charlottesville: University Press of Virginia, 1981), 87–103.

7. BG to BB, 12 Aug., 17 Sept. 1914, VIT; René Gimpel, *Diary of an Art Dealer*, trans. John Rosenberg (New York: Farrar, Straus and Giroux, 1966), 163.

8. BG to BB, 28 July 1913, VIT.

9. BG to BB, 4 Aug. 1914, VIT.

10. BG to BB, 10 Sept. 1914, VIT.

11. JS to BG, 8 Aug. 1914, AML; BG to BB, 13 June 1921, VIT.

12. BG to BB, 13 May 1914, VIT.

13. BG to BB, 1 July 1914, VIT.

14. BG to BB, 5 May 1914, VIT.

15. BG to BB, 13 May 1914, VIT.

16. BG to BB, 28 May 1914, VIT.

17. BG to BB, 3 Aug. 1914, VIT.

18. AM to BG, n.d., VIT (enclosed in a letter marked by Berenson as received 10 July 1914).

19. Katharine Graham, *Personal History* (New York: Vintage, 1998), 21.

20. CR to BG, 3 July 1914, VIT, in Greene Correspondence.

21. CR to BG, 21, 22 July 1914, VIT, in Greene Correspondence.

22. BG to BB, 6, 7 July 1914, VIT.

23. Eugene Walter, "The Easiest Way" (1908), in Thomas H. Dickinson, ed., *Chief Contemporary Dramatists, Second Series* (Boston: Houghton Mifflin, 1921).

24. BG to BB, 29 May 1909, VIT.

25. Kathy Peiss, *Cheap Amusements: Working Women and Leisure in Turn-of-the-Century New York* (Philadelphia: Temple University Press, 1986). Of course, her desire to save money did not get in the way of the extravagances she had come to regard as necessities. When her mother celebrated her birthday, Belle's sister Louise hosted a party, and they all provided luxurious gifts: Ethel and Teddy gave her an opera wrap; Louise and Belle gave her a diamond brooch and matching hairpiece. The main entertainment seemed to be making their mother miserable by trying to figure out her actual age. (She would have been in her fifties.) BG to BB, 18 May 1914, VIT.

26. BG to BB, 1 May, 4 July, 16 Dec. 1914, VIT.

27. BG to BB, 21 Sept. 1914, VIT. In this early reference, Belle did not name Kennerley, referring to him only as the publisher considering Frank Harris's book on Oscar Wilde. See also BG to MF, n.d. [1912], AAAS:MF, "Belle Greene."

28. BG to BB, 16 Dec. 1913, 16 March 1914, VIT. See also BG to BB, 29 March, 9, 18 April, 9, 15 May, 11, 22 June, 26 Oct. 1914, VIT.

29. BG to BB, 5 May 1914, 19 Oct. 1915, VIT. Belle even claimed in this last letter that Mitchell had chastised her for not writing to B.B. for a while.

30. Matthew J. Bruccoli, *The Fortunes of Mitchell Kennerley, Bookman* (New York: Harcourt Brace Jovanovich, 1986), 75.

31. Bruccoli, *Fortunes,*, 68–73; BG to BB, 6 Jan. 1914, VIT.

32. BG to BB, 13 July 1914, VIT. This phrase is followed by "Since then I have xxxxxxxxxx" with a line crossed out illegibly.

33. BG to BB, 6 Sept., 31 Dec. 1912, VIT; Bruccoli, *Fortunes*, 40–41.

34. Hutchins Hapgood, *A Victorian in the Modern World* (New York: Harcourt, Brace, 1939), 20, n. 75; Sigmund Freud to Edward Bernays, 27 Nov. 1924, PML, MA 5043,

35. BG to BB, 18 July 1914, VIT.

36. BG to BB, 29 July, 10, 12 Aug. 1914, VIT.

37. BG to BB, 18 July 1914, VIT.

38. BG to BB, 2, 10, 13 July 1914, VIT.

39. BG to BB, 12 Aug. 1914, VIT.

40. BG to BB, 7 Aug. 1914, VIT.

41. BG to BB, 22 Sept. 1914, VIT.

42. BG to BB, 3, 19 Feb. 1915, 21 Sept. 1914, VIT.

43. Receipt, 2 June 1915, AML:MCC; BG to BB, 3 March, 20 April, 12 July 1915, VIT.
44. BG to BB, 8, 10 Sept. 1914, VIT.
45. BG to HH, 8 Sept. 1914, AML:RODG, "Hyvernat, Henri, 1911–15"; BG to BB, 8 Sept. 1914, VIT.
46. BG to BB, 4, 21 Oct. 1914, 12 July 1915, VIT.
47. BG to HH, 6 Oct. 1914, ICOR:PPM, 4:1 "Miss Greene, 1912–1914"; HH to BG, 17 Oct. 1914, AML:RDOG, "Hyvernat, Henri, 1911–15."
48. BG to BB, 15, 27 Aug. 1914, VIT.
49. BG to BB, 1 Nov. 1914, VIT.
50. BG to BB, 1 Nov., 5 Dec. 1914, VIT.
51. BG to BB, 1 Nov., 7 Dec. 1914, 2 Jan., 15 Feb. 1915, VIT.
52. BG to BB, 10, 15 Jan. 1915, VIT; Ernest Samuels, *Bernard Berenson: The Making of a Connoisseur* (Cambridge: Harvard University Press, Belknap Press, 1979), 195.
53. BG to BB, 3 Feb. 1915, VIT; AML:JPMJ.
54. BG to BB, 15 Feb., 20, 29 Jan. 1915, VIT.
55. BG to BB, 19 Feb. 1915, VIT.
56. *New York Times*, 9 Feb. 1915, 1, 2; 10 Feb. 1915, 10.
57. *New York Times*, 11 Feb. 1915, 8; BG to BB, 3 March 1915, VIT.
58. BG to BB, 3 March 1915, VIT; *New York Times*, 7 March 1915.
59. BG to BB, 15 Feb. 1915, VIT.
60. BG to BB, 3, 25 March 1915, VIT.
61. BG to BB, 19 Sept. 1916, VIT.
62. BG to BB, 14 March 1914, 22 July 1915, 29 Dec. 1914, VIT.
63. BG to BB, 29 Jan. 1915; BG to BB, 28 Sept. 1915, VIT.
64. BG to BB, 25 March 1915, 19 Sept. 1916, VIT.
65. BG to BB, 29 Jan., 3 Feb. 1915, VIT; John C. Ferguson to BB, 14 March 1915, AML:RDOG, "F Misc."
66. BG to BB, 20 April, 28 May 1915, VIT.
67. BG to BB, 3 March 1915, VIT; Samuels, *Connoisseur*, 196–98.
68. BG to BB, 1 Nov., 8 Aug. 1914, VIT.
69. BG to BB, 1 Nov. 1914, VIT.
70. BG to BB, 27 Oct. 1914, VIT; Erika Kuhlman, *Petticoats and White Feathers: Gender Conformity, Race, the Progressive Peace Movement, and the Debate over War, 1895–1919* (Westport, Conn.: Greenwood, 1997), 116. The New York City Women's Peace Party also criticized the practice of knitting socks as unnecessary, but further complained that middle- and upper-class women were depriving working-class women of jobs.
71. BG to BB, 14 May 1915, VIT.
72. BG to BB, 12 July 1919, VIT.
73. BG to BB, 19 Oct., 14 May 1915, VIT.
74. HH to BG, 3 June 1915, AML:RODG, "Hyvernat, Henri, 1911–15"; HH to BG, 6 July 1915; BG to HH, 8 July [1915] ICOR:HH/PPM 4:2.
75. HH to BG, 10 Aug. 1917; BG to HH, 17 Sept. 1917; HH to TS, 29 Sept. 1917; BG to TS, 11 Oct. 1917; ICOR:HH/PPM 4:2. Morgan had been paying $2,300 annually. Belle did continue to send Hyvernat money quietly to help him keep his work going, and he was still a faculty member at Catholic University of America, which took over his salary.

76. BG to BB, 12, 22 July 1915, VIT. See also FK to BG, 3 July 1915, AML:MCC; BG to HH, 6 July 1915, ICOR:HH/PPM 4:2; Forbes, *Morgan, Jr.*, 93–94.
77. BG to BB, 30 July 1915, VIT.
78. Ibid.; MB to BB, 8 Aug. 1915, VIT.
79. BG to BB, 19, 27 Oct. 1915, VIT.
80. BG to BB, 10 Feb. 1916, VIT.
81. BG to BB, 17 Jan., 10 Feb. 1916, VIT.
82. BG to BB, 3 March 1915, 19 Sept. 1916, VIT.
83. BG to BB, 29 Jan. 1915, VIT.
84. Belle Greene, "291," *Camera Work,* Jan. 1915, 64.
85. It is worth noting that Belle's first response to Stieglitz's request was to worry that she was in "bad grace" at 291. He brushed her concern away, chiding that he was worried she might have "given us a black cross or two. But we knew they could not be very heavy ones." Alfred Stieglitz to BG, 10, 14 July 1914, AML:MCC.
86. BG to BB, 10 Feb. 1916, VIT.
87. BG to BB, 29 Feb. 1916, VIT.
88. MB to SB, 5 March 1916, VIT; MB to AR, 8 Sept. 1916, LLIU:HWS, "Correspondence: Berenson."
89. BG to BB, 8, 15, 19 Sept., 4 Oct. 1916, VIT.
90. MB to AR, 6, 8 Sept. 1916, LLIU:HWS, "Correspondence: Berenson."
91. BG to BB, 13, 19 Sept. 1916, VIT.
92. Bernard Berenson, unidentified source, quoted in Samuels, *Connoisseur,* 206.
93. *Town Topics: The Journal of Society,* 21 Sept. 1916, unidentified clipping, 22 [Sept.] 1916, CAH:NYJAM. See also *Boston Globe,* 23 Sept. 1916, 22.
94. Mickey McKee? to BG, 23 Sept. 1916, AML:RODG, "M." Unidentified clipping enclosed, subsequently identified as *New York Evening Sun,* 22 Sept. 1916, 9.
95. *New York Evening Sun,* 10 Oct. 1916.
96. FK to AT, 21 Oct. 1916, AML; BG to BB, 20 Oct. 1916, VIT.
97. BG to BB, 21 Oct., 4 Nov. 1916, VIT.
98. BB to MB, 29 Oct. 1916, 11 Nov. 1917, VIT.
99. MB to BB, 3 Nov. 1916, VIT.
100. BB to MB, 7 Nov. 1916, VIT.
101. MB to BB, 9 Nov. 1916, VIT.
102. BB to MB, 12 Nov. 1916; BG to BB, 27 Sept., 6, 15, 17 Nov. 1916, VIT.
103. BG to BB, 29 June 1920, VIT.
104. BG to BB, 27 Sept., 9 Nov. 1916, VIT.
105. BG to BB, 12 July 1915, VIT.
106. BG to BB, 6, 17 Nov. 1916; VIT.
107. BG to BB, 10, 13, 19 Nov. 1916; AM to BG, n.d. [1914],VIT.
108. BG to BB, 17 Nov. 1916, VIT.
109. BG to GD, 2 July 1912; GD to BG, 18 Dec. 1913, AML:MCC.
110. BB to MB, 19, 20 Nov. 1916, VIT.
111. BB to MB, 7, 21 Nov. 1916, VIT; Colin Simpson, *Artful Partners: Bernard Berenson and Joseph Duveen* (New York: Macmillan, 1986), 196.
112. BG to BB, 3 Dec. 1916, VIT; JS to BG, 28 Oct. 1921; BG to JS, 2 Nov. 1921, AML:RODG, "Seligmann and Co. Inc. II."
113. BG to BB, 30 Nov.–3 Dec. 1916, VIT.

114. *New York Times*, 31 July 1917; 14 Dec. 1917, 8; 20 Dec. 1917, 3; 12 April 1918, 11; 15 April 1918, 6.
115. *New York Times*, 8 July 1918, 7; BG to BB, 18 July 1918, VIT.
116. BG to GD, 19 Sept. 1917, AML:MCC. Belle did refer to having a brother-in-law who was a cavalry officer; Leveridge was a private in the army. George Oakley is the likeliest possibility, and several George Oakleys are listed in the records, but I cannot confirm any of them as Ethel's husband.
117. BG to BB, 14 Sept. 1914, VIT; *New York Times*, 9 June 1918, 7; 11 Nov. 1917, 70.
118. BG to BB, 14 Sept. 1917, VIT; BG to CR, 23 July 1918, AML:MCC, "Read . . . 1913–1924"; BG to HH, 3 Jan. 1918, ICOR:HH/PPM 4:2.
119. BG to GD, 8 April 1919, AML:MCC.
120. Edward Forbes to BG, 30 Sept. 1918, AML:MCC, "Fogg Museum of Art"; PS to WI, 11 Nov. 1918, AAAS:WI, box 4, "Correspondence: Sachs."
121. BB to MB, 6, 9 Dec. 1917, 20 Dec. 1918, VIT.
122. HH to Walter Crum, 22 Oct. 1918, BLM: Add 45685 ff 131–210; HH to BG, 7 May 1918, ICOR:HH/PPM 4:3.
123. GD to BG, 6 June 1918; BG to GD, 18 July 1918, AML:MCC; BG to CR, 23 July 1918, AML:MCC, "Read . . . 1913–1924."
124. BG to CR, 23 July 1918, AML:MCC, "Read . . . 1913–1924." What conversations Belle may or may not have had with her sisters about such matters, we can only guess. Certainly she was aware of her sisters' sex lives. She once explained to Bernard that a letter went out late because she had given it to "one of sister's lovers" to post and discovered the next day that he had spent the night. "I told [Fatty?] that as it was my furniture he was wearing out, the least he could have done, would be to run out and post my letter in between courses." BG to BB, 17 March, 1914, VIT.
125. *New York Times*, 16 March 1919, 18–19.

CHAPTER 12: LADY DIRECTRESS

1. WI to BB, 26 Aug. 1925, VIT.
2. Aline B. Louchheim, "The Morgan Library and Miss Greene," *New York Times*, 17 April 1949.
3. BG to EHD, 14 Feb. 1919, AML; BG to BB, 21 Feb. 1919, VIT.
4. BG to BB, 21 Feb. 1919, VIT.
5. BB to MB, 12, 16, 21 Jan. 1919, VIT; Ernest Samuels, *Bernard Berenson: The Making of a Connoisseur* (Cambridge: Harvard University Press, Belknap Press, 1979), 229–36.
6. BG to HYT, 10 June 1919, LLIU:HYT.
7. BG to EHD, 24 June, 21 Aug. 1919, AML:MCC, "Quaritch."
8. BG to JPMJ, 3 Sept. 1920, AML:JPMJ, box 169.
9. BG to JPMJ, 30 June 1922; JPMJ to BG, 17 July 1922, AML:JPMJ, box 174.
10. JPMJ to HH, 15 Aug. 1919, ICOR:HH/MPP, 4:3.
11. BG to BB, 31 March, 26 Sept. 1919, VIT.
12. BG to BB, 11 Feb. 1920, VIT; BG to HH, 18 March 1920; HH to BG, 24 March 1920, ICOR:HH/MPP, 4:4.
13. BG to JPMJ, 17 Sept. 1919, AML.RODG, "Hyvernat 1919–1920."
14. BG to BB, 5 Sept. 1919, VIT.
15. BG to BB, 21 Oct. 1919, VIT.

16. BG to BB, 26, 29 Sept., 23 Dec. 1919, VIT.
17. BG to BB, 5 Sept., 26 Nov. 1919, VIT.
18. U.S. census, 1920; Genevieve Harvey to Army Service Forces, Kansas City Quartermasters Depot, 24 Jan. 1944, Air Force Historical Research Agency, Maxwell AFB, Ala.
19. BG to BB, 26 Sept. 1919, VIT.
20. BG to BB, 10 May 1921, VIT.
21. BG to BB, 27 Dec. 1919, VIT.
22. For background on race riots and labor-related violence, see William M. Tuttle, *Race Riot: Chicago in the Red Summer of 1919* (New York: Atheneum, 1970); Nell Painter, *Standing at Armageddon: The United States, 1877–1919* (New York: Norton, 1987); and Cliff Brown, *Racial Conflict and Violence in the Labor Market: Roots in the 1919 Steel Strike* (New York: Garland, 1998).
23. For background on changes in gender images and women's activism, see Betty DeBerg, *UnGodly Women: Gender and the First Wave of American Fundamentalism* (Minneapolis: Fortress Press, 1990); Alison Parker, *Purifying America: Women, Cultural Reform, and Pro-Censorship Activism, 1873–1933* (Urbana: University of Illinois Press, 1997); and Brian Donovan, *White Slave Crusades: Race, Gender, and Anti-Vice Activism, 1887–1917* (Urbana: University of Illinois Press, 2006).
24. BG to BB, 29 Oct. 1920, VIT.
25. *New York Times*, 13 March 1922, VIT.
26. Gertrude Atherton, *The Living Present* (New York: Frederick A. Stokes, 1917), 206, 261.
27. BG to BB, 24 April 1924, VIT; *Chicago Tribune*, 12 June 1921, D10.
28. BG to BB, 11 Feb. 1920, VIT; BG to HH, 11 Feb. 1920, ICOR:PPM, 4:4.
29. BG to HH, 5 March 1920, ICOR:PPM, 4:4; BG to BB, 6, 7 March 1920, VIT.
30. Nicky Mariano, *Forty Years with Berenson* (New York: Knopf, 1966), 32.
31. BG to BB, 13, 6 March 1920, VIT.
32. BG to BB, 19 March 1920, VIT; Mariano, *Forty Years*, 32.
33. BG to BB, 6, 19 March 1920, VIT.
34. BG to BB, 14 April 1921, VIT.
35. BG to WI, 13 Sept. 1922, AAAS:WI, box 2, "Greene."
36. BG to BB, 19 March 1920, VIT.
37. BG to BB, 1 April 1920, VIT; BG to EHD, 6 April 1920, AML:MCC, "G Misc, Gre–Gu."
38. BG to BB, 28 Aug. 1925, VIT.
39. BG to HH, 12 April 1920, ICOR:HH/MPP, 4:4.
40. BG to BB, 19 March 1920, VIT.
41. BG to SC, unidentified letters, quoted in Cass Canfield, *The Incredible Pierpont Morgan: Financier and Art Collector* (New York: Harper & Row, 1974), 153. Canfield notes only that Anne Sherman Haight shared copies of Belle's letters to Cockerell with him. As discussed in chapter 14 and the epilogue, Haight was working on a biography of Greene.
42. BG to BB, 1 April 1920, VIT.
43. WI to SC, 13 Feb. 1924, BLM:CP, 52726 ff. 160–293; BG to BB, 2 Jan. 1925, VIT.
44. BG to BB, 1 April 1920, VIT.
45. BG to EHD, 6, 15 March 1920, AML:MCC, "G Misc, Gre–Gu."

46. Lily Sawyer to EHD, 6 April 1920, AML:MCC, "G Misc, Gre–Gu."
47. BG to HH, 12, 15 April 1920, ICOR:HH/PPM, 4:4.
48. BG to BB, 19 March 1920, VIT.
49. BG to BB, 30 July 1920, VIT.
50. Mariano, *Forty Years*, 32–33.
51. BG to BB, 12 May 1920, VIT.
52. BG to BB, 2 May 1920, VIT; Dorothy Miner, ed., *Studies in Art and Literature for Belle da Costa Greene* (Princeton: Princeton University Press, 1954), xi.
53. BG to HH, 16 June 1920, ICOR: HH/MPP, 4:4. Most likely there were two such visits. Certainly, when one compares letters she sent to Berenson and Hyvernat about the same time, her propensity to create details and sprinkle her truths with decorative fabrications becomes a little more obvious.
54. Helen Frick, the daughter of Henry Clay Frick and an up-and-coming art collector herself, seemed to be behind much of this round of gossip, reported as saying that she was sorry to see herself "'in such bad company' in Italy." Belle retaliated in her usual style, telling jokes about her and Perkins (he as wet nurse). BG to BB, 28 Oct. 1925,14 Jan., 23 April 1926, VIT.
55. BG to HH, 21 Feb. 1923, ICOR:HH/MPP, 4:6.
56. BG to EHD, 24 May 1920, AML:MCC, "G Misc, Gre–Gu."
57. The *Washington Post* reported that Belle had accompanied Father Hyvernat on his visit, which was the initial plan. But Belle's letter makes it clear that her hurried departure caused her to miss the meeting. 7 May 1920, 8.
58. HH to BG, 5 May 1920, AML:RODG, "Hyvernat 1919–1920"; BG to TP, 21 June 1929, ICOR:HH/MMP, 4:4. This letter reached Belle just before she left Europe, but she did not have time to collect the medal from the post office before her ship sailed. It was sent after her.
59. HH to BG, 20 May 1920, [23 May] Day of the Pentecost 1920, 10 June 1920, n.d. AML:RODG, "Hyvernat 1919–1930."
60. BG to HH, 29 July 1920, ICOR:HH/MPP, 4:4.
61. BG to BB, 10 June 1920, VIT; BG to HH, 16 June 1920, ICOR:HH/MPP, 4:4. Although Belle wrote to Hyvernat almost a week after she wrote to Berenson, she assured the priest that his was the first letter she had written since returning.
62. BG to BB, 29 June 1920, VIT.
63. BG to BB, 13 June 1921, VIT.
64. MB to AR, 2 Dec. 1920; MB to RC, 30 Dec. 1920, LLIU:HWS, "Correspondence: Berenson." According to Colin Simpson, Mary had full knowledge of the situation before leaving Europe and had devised the plan of using their visit to publicize the collection, which Hamilton could then sell to pay his many debts (including those to Duveen, of which the Berensons would be owed a substantial amount). The ruse failed, and the Duveens repossessed most of Hamilton's purchases in 1922. Colin Simpson, *Artful Partners: Bernard Berenson and Joseph Duveen* (New York: Macmillan, 1986), 196–202.
65. MB to AR, 7, 21 Dec. 1920, LLIU:HWS. Mary pointed out that this was the third time their arrival had coincided with a panic.
66. BG to BB, 31 Dec. 1920, VIT.
67. BG to BB, 29, 31 Dec. 1920, VIT.
68. Samuels, *Connoiseur*, 285–86.
69. BG to BB, 4 Jan. 1921, VIT.
70. BG to BB, 4 Jan., 11 March, 28 Feb. 1921, VIT.

71. In Hyvernat's reply he reports that he destroyed this letter, as she requested. But his notes make it clear that the subject was Berenson.
72. HH to BG, 28 Jan. 1921; HH notes, n.d., ICOR:HH/MPP, 4:4.
73. BG to BB, 4, 11, 18 March 1921, VIT.
74. BG to BB, 21 March, 10 April 1921, VIT.
75. BG to BB, 15, 10 April, 10 May 1921, VIT.
76. BG to BB, 18 Jan. 1921, VIT.
77. BG to BB, 18 April 1921, VIT.
78. U.S. census, 1910, 1920, 1930; BG to Earl of Ilchester, 21 Feb. 1944, AML:RODG, "Ilchester, Earl of."
79. BG to HH, 6 Oct. 1922, ICOR:HH/MPP, 4:5. "Bobbie" is sometimes spelled "Bobby" in Belle's and others' letters, but I use the former (which occurs somewhat more often) for clarity.
80. When Marie married, Belle gave her a bridal veil and $100. Raymond Vogel Jr. to Christine Nelson, 28 Jan. 2002, PML, ARC 2639.
81. BG to HH, 29 July 1920, ICOR:HH/MPP, 4:4
82. BG to BB, 13 June 1921, VIT.
83. BG to BB, 25 April, 12, 14 July 1921, VIT.
84. Belle rarely mentioned Bobbie to Bernard, probably quite consciously, because Bernard (she often reminded him) had no interest in children. Records involving legal guardianship and adoption are sealed except to involved parties or their descendants.
85. *New York Times*, 17 Feb. 1924.
86. *Chicago Broad Ax*, 13 May 1922, 1; *Chicago Tribune*, 4 May 1922; *Washington Post*, 3 Dec. 1913, 6; Mounter, "Richard Theodore Greener: The Idealist, Statesman, Scholar and South Carolinian" (Ph.D. diss., University of South Carolina, 2002), 524–25.
87. U.S. census, 1910, 1920; Mounter, "Greener," 524–25. Ironically, Greener was identified as white on his death certificate. Michael Mounter attributes this to his light skin and gray hair and the fact that he lived in a white neighborhood.
88. The evidence is largely circumstantial. A woman named Louise Martin definitely worked at the Morgan Library for a short period in 1921. Receipts, signed Louise Martin, 20 Jan., 1 June 1921, n.d., AML:MCC. She is never identified in Library records as Belle's sister, and she refers to her in professional correspondence as Miss Greene. Her handwriting is very similar to Belle's, and she is on close terms with friends of Belle's like Henri Hyvernat, sending him her "love" and calling him "my dear Father." Louise Martin to HH, 7 April 1921, ICOR:HH/MPP, 4:5. Furthermore, when she died over a decade later, Meta Harrsen, who did not socialize outside of the Library, notified Bernard Berenson and wrote about Mrs. Martin in very familiar terms. MH to BB, 8 Feb. 1933, VIT. It is also suggestive that this Louise Martin does not appear in the Morgan Library records after 1922. In late 1921 Frederick Martin resigned from his position in the New York school system. By 1923 Belle's sister and brother-in-law were in Ithaca, N.Y. *New York Times*, 1 Dec. 1921, 16; "Mrs. Mary L. Martin Dies in Hospital after Flu Attack," *Ithaca Journal*, 7 Feb. 1933; various receipts in AML:MCC, "Misc, Ho–Hoskier," "Misc M."
89. "Coptic Collection of J. P. Morgan Is to Be Translated," *Catholic News Sheet*, 24 May 1920, ICOR:HH/MPP, 6:51.
90. Mons. Mercati to HH, 14 June 1922, AML:RODG, "Coptic Manuscripts—General"; BG to HH, 20 April 1922, AML:RODG, "CUA."

91. HH to BC, 16 Aug. 1922, ICOR:PPMC, 4:5; BG to Archbishop Bonzano, 18 July 1922, ICOR:PPMC, 4:5. Bonzano was archbishop of Melitene.
92. BG to HH, 20 July 1922, ICOR:PPMC, 4:5.
93. HH to BG, 25 July 1923, AML:RODG, "Hyvernat, 1923–1925"; BG to HH, 21 Feb. 1923, ICOR:HH/MPP, 4:6.
94. BG to HH, 6 Oct. 1922, ICOR:HH/MPP, 4:5. In addition to the scholarly interest, there was a great deal of enthusiasm among American Catholics that Morgan's manuscripts were bringing attention to the Vatican and Catholic University. John B. Kennedy (Knights of Columbus) to BG, 6 Jan. 1923, AML:MCC. *Times Literary Supplement*, 15 Nov. 1923; *Catholic University Bulletin*, Oct.–Dec. 1922, no. 7, ICOR:HH/MPP, 6:53.
95. BG to John Axten, 18 Oct. 1921, AML:JPMJ, 170.
96. Paul Sachs brought students every term to visit the Library and examine its treasures. Francis did not specify what year he visited, but he was at Harvard between 1921 and 1924. Oral history interview with Henry Sayles Francis, conducted by Robert Brown, Walpole, N.H., 28 March 1974, AAAS, www.aaa.si.edu/collections/oralhistories/transcripts/franci74.htm.
97. Amy Lowell to BG, 3 Feb. 1921, HLHU, bMS Lowell 19 (560); BG to Amy Lowell, 4, 7 Feb., 23 Nov. 1921, HLHU, bMS Lowell 19 (519).
98. MJ to BG, 16 Oct., 4 Dec. 1919, 16 Jan. 1920; BG to MJ, 10 Dec. 1910, AML:MCC, "New York Public Library."
99. MJ to BG, 23, 29 Oct. 1920,12 Dec. 1921; BG to MJ, 29 Oct. 1920, AML: MCC, "New York Public Library." Interestingly, the list of lecturers and course registrants reveals that this was a class essentially for and by women. All of the lecturers were women, including Ruth Granniss, the librarian of the Grolier Club, Alice Lerch, who worked at the New York Public Library, Henrietta Bartlett, a well-published librarian and scholar, and Grace Cornell, assistant professor of fine arts at Teachers' College, Belle's former school. All but one of the students were women; all of the women were unmarried. Belle continued to give these lectures for several more years. Alice G. Higgins to BG, 24 Nov. 1922, AML:MCC, "New York Public Library."
100. French Strother to BG, 26 Sept. 1922; BG to French Strother, 12 Oct. 1922, AML:MCC; Sarah MacDougall to BG, 1 June 1923; Secretary to Sarah Mac-Dougall, 4 June 1923 (unsigned copy), AML:MCC, "W Misc, Wh–Wy."
101. BG to BB, 6 Feb. 1922, VIT. BG to RH, 15 May 1922, AML:MCC. Belle was not impressed with the first issue of their "poor frail child," and she was not the only one. Billy Ivins apparently communicated his comments with his characteristic lack of tact. Belle retorted, "The soul of me is shedding bluddy tears. Believe you me, it's the time a feller needs a friend—not a vitriolic bath." She called it an appalling horror and was ashamed every time she met one of the men who had contributed money to it. BG to WI, 26 Feb. 1923, AAAS:WI, box 2, "Greene." BG to BB, 16 May, 26 Dec. 1923, VIT.
102. BG to BB, 6 Feb. 1922, VIT.
103. BG to BB, 25 April 1921, VIT. Although Jack had been called down to the White House to discuss these loans, Belle reported that they were very popular, largely because the interest rates (8 percent) were much higher than those on domestic investments and loans.
104. BG to BB, 29 June 1920, 25 April, 13 June 1921, VIT.
105. BG to JPMJ, n.d. 1923, AML:JPMJ, box 170.

106. BG to BB, 13 June 1921, 12 Feb. 1924, VIT. The *New York Times* celebrated the transition with the headline "J. P. Morgan Gives Library to the Public," noting in a subheading "Belle da Costa Greene to Remain in Charge." The story was a description of the Library, the collection itself, especially a display case of medieval books "bound in gold with their covers studded with precious gems." *New York Times*, 17 Feb. 1924.

107. BG to BB, 2 Feb. 1924, VIT.

108. FW to BG, 18 Feb. 1924, AML:MCC, "Pearson."

109. RG to BG, 14 March 1924, GC, "Corres. 1924–1930."

110. HH to BG, 17 March, 3 April 1924, ICOR:HH/MPP, 4:7.

111. *New York Times*, 2 March 1924, E6.

112. *New York Times*, 12 March 1924, p. 14; 29 March 1924, p. 17.

113. Edward Larocque Tinker, "Whitewashing," *The Bookman*, February 1925, 719–22.

114. *New York Times*, 17 Feb. 1924.

115. BG to BB, 4 March 1926, VIT.

116. JPMJ to SC, 15 Nov. 1924; JPMJ to BG, 24 Nov. 1924, AML:JMPJ, box 173.

117. WI to SC, 18 March [192?], BLM:SC, 52726 ff 160–293.

118. BG to BB, 9 April 1924, VIT.

119. Ann Douglas, *Terrible Honesty: Mongrel Manhattan in the 1920s* (New York: Noonday Press, 1996). The African American press had pointed out the irony of the new aesthetic of tanning and the continued discrimination against people with naturally brown skin. Kathy Peiss, *Hope in a Jar: The Making of America's Beauty Culture* (New York: Metropolitan Books, 1998), 150–51, 224.

120. *New York Times*, 2 Jan. 1925, p. 8; 8 April 1925, 25.

121. BG to WI, 28 Jan. 1924, AAAS:WI, box 2, "Greene."

122. BG to BB, 6 Aug. 1924, VIT.

123. BG to BB, 14 May 1921, VIT.

124. Mariano, *Forty Years*, 117.

125. WI to BB, n.d. March 1925, VIT.

126. WI to BB, 1 July, 14 June 1925, 17 Aug. 1924 [1925], VIT.

127. BG to BB, 6 April, 3 May 1925, VIT.

128. BG to HH, 25 April 1925, ICOR:HH/MPP, 4:7; WI to BB, 14 June, 11 July 1925, VIT.

129. BG to BB, 17 Aug. 1925, VIT; Henri Auguste Omont, *Miniatures des plus anciens manuscrits grecs de la Bibliothèque nationale du VIe au XIVe siècle* (Paris: H. Champion, 1929).

130. BG to HH, 6 July 1925, ICOR:HH/MPP, 4:7.

131. BG to HH, 13 July 1925, ICOR:HH/MPP, 4:7.

132. Mariano, *Forty Years*, 125.

133. MB to SB, 7 Jan. 1923, typed copy, LLIU:HWS, "Misc. Halpern," 10; BG to BB, 6 March 1925, VIT.

134. BG to BB, 9 April, 6 Aug. 1924, VIT; BG to PS and Edward Forbes, 29 July 1924; BG to PS, 16 July 1926, HUAMA:PS, "Greene, Belle de [*sic*] Costa, 1916–1927"; Edward Forbes to BG, 1 Aug. 1924, AML:MCC. Despite the continuing problems with *Art Studies*, Belle had great respect for Paul Sachs. She told him he gave her "new faith in the 'art world'" and considered him honest, simple, and having character. BG to PS, 30 July, 7 Oct. 1926, HUAMA:PS, "Greene."

135. Samuels, *Connoisseur*, 225.

136. Mariano, *Forty Years*, 125; Samuels, *Connoisseur*, 326–27.

137. BG to BB, 28 Aug. 1925, VIT; undated postcards in BG's and BB's handwriting to WI, [mid-July 1925], AAAS:WI, box 1, "Correspondence: Berenson."

138. BG to BB, 28 Aug. 1925, VIT.

139. WI to BB, 22 Dec. 1925, VIT.

140. Walter Cook to BG, AML:RODG, "Cook, W.S.S."; WI to BB, 24 Jan. 1932, VIT.

141. John Douglas Forbes, *J. P. Morgan, Jr., 1867–1943* (Charlottesville: University Press of Virginia, 1981), 148.

142. BG to BB, 28 Aug. 1925, VIT.

143. BG to BB, 28 Aug. 1925, VIT.

144. WI to BB, 26 Aug. 1925, VIT.

145. BG to BB, 4, 18 March 1926, VIT.

146. BG to BB, 8 Sept. 1925, VIT.

147. MH to BB, 14 July 1954, VIT. There is one problem with Meta's story. Amadeo was born in 1898, making him twenty years younger than Belle—or almost ten years according to her count. His father, the Duke d'Aosta before him, was of a more suitable age for Belle, but Meta's memory of the timing and circumstances of Belle's duke identify him as Amadeo. Amadeo married his cousin Princess Anne in 1927.

148. BB to WI, 21 Aug. 1925, AAAS:WI, box 1, "Correspondence: Berenson."

149. BG to BB, 8 Sept. 1925, VIT.

150. Belle was probably closest to Olive Frances Rhinelander, who practiced the art of illuminating manuscripts using natural inks and colors. The Morgan Library owned some of her works, and Belle was so well acquainted with her that one of Olive Rhinelander's sisters asked Belle to write her obituary in 1942. H. Bennett to BG, n.d. [1942], AML:DCI, "B Misc, Ba–Be"; *New York Times*, 13 June 1942, 15.

151. Earl Lewis and Heidi Ardizzone, *Love on Trial: An American Scandal in Black and White* (New York: Norton, 2001).

152. BG to BB, 10 May 1921, VIT (parentheses in original).

153. BG to BB, 23, 26 May, 4, 18 March 1926, VIT; BG to HH, 28 June 1926, ICOR:HH, PPMC, 4:8.

154. BG to BB, 18 March, 6 April 1926, VIT.

155. BB to WI, 31, 11 Aug. 1926, AAAS:WI, box 1, "Correspondence: Berenson."

156. BG to HH, 4 June 1925, 22 July 1926, ICOR:HH/PPMC, 4:7.

157. BG to BB, 18, 21 Aug. 1926, VIT.

158. BG to BB, 18 Aug. 1926, VIT. In 1928 she purchased a thirteenth-century Armenian Four Gospels from Mrs. John D. Rockefeller (PML, MS: M 740), and another in 1929 in Paris (PML, MS: M 749).

159. BB to WI, 16 Aug. 1926, VIT. The remaining letters (and there were several dozen that year) don't seem particularly insulting, although Belle called one of his "'snooty' as an early Chinese martyr" and blamed it on "overdoses of female hand nursing." She called another one a "hissy, spitty the-God-of-Moses letter." But in all she told him she loved him, "not the famed critic, or the sardonic wit, or the scalding arbiter—just the Human Being, I love." BG to BB, 4, 30 March 1926, 6, 28 April 1926, VIT.

160. BG to BB, 8 July 1926, VIT.

161. BG to BB, 8 July, 21 Aug. 1926, VIT.

162. Mariano, *Forty Years*, 153.

163. Mariano, *Forty Years*, 153; BG to BB, 5, 7 Oct. 1926, VIT.

164. BG to BB, 26 May 1926, VIT.

165. BG to BB, 24 Sept. [1926], 5 Oct. 1926, VIT.

166. LO to BG, 29 Sept. 1926, AML:MCC. BG wrote "No answer" on top. This is the last letter from Olschki.

167. Lawrence C. Wroth, *The First Quarter Century of the Pierpont Morgan Library: A Retrospective Exhibition in Honor of Belle da Costa Greene* (New York: Pierpont Morgan Library, 1949), 19; PML, MSS M 708–11.

168. BG to BB, 18 April 1928; WI to BB, 18 Jan. 1927, VIT.

169. BG to BB, 22 Jan. 1928, VIT.

170. BG to BB, 22 Jan. 1928, VIT; Records of the Morgan Library, Box 1381, Buildings-Annex 1926; J. Axten to Mr. Morris, 6 July 1928, AML:JPMJ, Letterpress Book 41, p. 313.

171. BG to BB, 18 April 1928, VIT; *Washington Star*, 31 July 1927, n.p. [clipping], ICOR:HH/PPMC, 6:51; BG to HH, 6 Jan. 1928; Violet White to HH, 28 Dec. 1928, ICOR:HH/PPMC, 4:8.

172. Belle purchased both manuscripts from the Holdford estate in 1927. Belle Greene, *The Pierpont Morgan Library: A Review of the Growth, Development and Activities of the Library during the Period between Its Establishment as an Educational Institution in Feb. 1924 and the Close of the Year 1929* (New York: Pierpont Morgan Library, 1930), 27–29; PML, MS M.728, MS M.729; EM, quoted in Wroth, *First Quarter Century*, 26.

173. BG to BB, 23 Sept. 1928, VIT; AT to HH, 6 July 1928, AML:RODGA, "Goldschmidt, Dr. Adolph"; BG to WI, 28, 30 Aug. 1928; AAAS:WI, box 2, "Greene."

174. BG to BB, 23 Sept. 1928, VIT.

CHAPTER 13: A WOMAN OF A CERTAIN AGE

1. BG to BB, 13 March 1914, VIT.

2. BG to BB, n.d. Aug. 1936, VIT.

3. BG to EM, 30 Jan. 1929, AML:RODG, "British Museum."

4. Eric Millar, *English Illuminated Manuscripts from the Xth to the XIIIth Century* (Paris: G. van Oest, 1926), and *English Illuminated Manuscripts from the XIVth to the VIth Century* (Paris: G. van Oest, 1928).

5. EM to BG, 15 March 1929; BG to EM, 22 Nov. 1929, AML:RODG, "British Museum"; BG to BB, 4 Nov. 1930, VIT.

6. BG to WI, 25 Feb. 1929, AAAS/WI, box 2, "Greene"; BG to HSM, 30 Sept. 1929, JPMJ, box 174.

7. According to the Morgan Library records the portrait was purchased in Dec. 1929, but it was most likely agreed to earlier in the year. Andrew Sinclair, *Corsair: The Life of J. Pierpont Morgan* (Boston: Little, Brown, 1981).

8. In fact, the total number of suicides was not markedly higher in 1929, and those who did commit suicide usually found more private methods. If Belle knew any of these people, she never mentioned it. John Kenneth Galbraith, *The Great Crash:1929* (Boston: Houghton Mifflin, 1955), 148–49.

9. U.S. census, 1930; BG to BB, n.d. Aug. 1936, VIT.

10. George Parker Winship to BG, 25 March 1929, AML:JPMJ; BG to BB, 29 Jan. 1915, 22 April 1927, VIT.

11. BG to Walter Cook, 30 Oct. 1929; Walter Cook to BG, 31 Oct. 1929, AML: RODG, "Cook."

12. Belle Greene, *The Pierpont Morgan Library: A Review of the Growth, Development and Activities of the Library during the Period between Its Establishment as an Educational Institution in Feb. 1924 and the Close of the Year 1929* (New York: Pierpont Morgan Library, 1930), 1, 15.

13. Greene, *Review of the Growth,* 4–5.

14. *New York Herald Tribune,* 2 Oct. 1930, p. 16.

15. RG to BG, 23 Jan., 30 Oct. 1930, GC, "Corres. 1924–1930."

16. BG to BB, 28 May, 31 July 1930, VIT.

17. BG to HH, 17 May 1930, ICOR:HH/MPP 4:10; BG to BB, 28 May 1930, VIT.

18. Bryson Burroughs to WI, 3 May 1931, AAAS/WI, box 1, "Correspondence: Burroughs."

19. BG to BB, 1 June 1932, VIT.

20. U.S. census, 1930.

21. Another James Fleet, possibly her uncle, worked as a laborer in D.C. U.S. census, 1910, Washington D.C. I could not determine whether this James Fleet was indeed Genevieve's brother James, but the age and birth city match. The biggest discrepancy is his occupation and that of his daughter Rose, who worked as a cook. Of course, it is entirely possible that a branch of the family, identified as black, whose members remained in the increasingly segregated District of Columbia fell on hard times or were able to find work only in menial and service jobs.

22. BG to Germaine Seligmann, 9 Jan. 1930, AML:RODGA, "Seligmann, Arnold Rey & Co"; BG to FW, 9 May 1933, AML:MCC, "Pearson"; BG to BB, 21 Aug. 1932, VIT.

23. BG to Lena Adams, 16 Oct. 1932, AML:MCC, "Misc, A"; BG to HH, 14 Oct. 1934, ICOR:HH/PPM, 5:1. BG to BB, 30 Aug. 1935, VIT; John Douglas Forbes, *J. P. Morgan, Jr., 1867–1943* (Charlottesville: University Press of Virginia, 1981), 141.

24. Belle Greene, *The Pierpont Morgan Library: Review of the Activities and Acquisitions of the Library from 1930 through 1935: A Summary of the Annual Reports of the Director to the Board of Trustees* (New York: Pierpont Morgan Library, 1937), 3–9.

25. BG to JSM and HSM, 25 Oct. 1932; RH to JPMJ, 17 April 1933, AML:RODG, "Columbia University."

26. Greene, *Review, 1930 through 1935,* 14.

27. BG to BB, 31 July 1930, 26 Feb. 1932, 20 Feb. 1934, VIT.

28. Bernard Berenson, *Italian Pictures of the Renaissance: A List of the Principal Artists and Their Works, with an Index of Places* (Oxford: Clarendon Press, 1932).

29. BG to BB, 26 Feb. 1932, VIT.

30. BG to BB, 14 July 1932, VIT.

31. BG to BB, 15 Aug. 1932, VIT.

32. Belle had initially wanted him to attend Phillips Academy, but Phillips has no record of a Robert Leveridge in attendance.

33. *New York Times*, 28 May 1933, N2; MH to BB, 2 Feb. 1932, VIT.
34. *New York Times*, 9 April 1930, 32; 17 March 1932, 18; 20 March 1933, 27.
35. MH to BB, 2 Feb. 1932, VIT. Henry Clay Frick had asked her to serve as a trustee for his gallery after his death, but Belle refused. She later regretted it, when she saw the list of trustees and realized she had as much experience as, or more than, any of them. In 1921 a trustee, anticipating a vacancy in the next few years, asked whether she would accept the position. BG to BB, 13 June 1921, VIT.
36. Belle da Costa Greene, Meta Harrsen, and Charles Rufus Morey, *The Pierpont Morgan Library Exhibition of Illuminated Manuscripts Held at the New York Public Library* (New York: Pierpont Morgan Library, 1934).
37. *Time*, 11 Dec. 1933; undated Associated Press release, CAH:NYJAM; *New York Evening Sun*, 2 May 1932; *Time*, 11 April 1949.
38. *Ithaca Journal*, 7 Feb. 1933.
39. *Ithaca Journal*, 7 Feb. 1933; MH to BB, 8 Feb. 1933, VIT.
40. Owen Morshead to JPMJ, 12 Oct. 1932; BG to JPMJ, 9 Dec. 1932, AML:JPMJ, box 174, MS 791.
41. Greene, *Review, 1930 through 1935*, 11–14; Ada Thurston and Curt F. Bühler, comps., *Check List of Fifteenth Century Printing in the Pierpont Morgan Library* (New York: Pierpont Morgan Library, 1939).
42. BB to WI, 9 Jan. 1932, AAAS:WI, box 1, "Correspondence: Berenson"; BB to PH, 26 Nov. 1934, AML:MCC.
43. BG to BB, 21 Aug., 3, 24 Sept. 1934, VIT; BG to HH, 14 Oct. 1934, ICOR: HH/PPM, 5:1.
44. Ernest Samuels, *Bernard Berenson: The Making of a Connoisseur* (Cambridge: Harvard University Press, Belknap Press, 1979), 413, 419.
45. WI to BB, 3 Oct. 1930; 24 Jan. 1932, VIT; BB to WI, 9 Jan.1932, AAAS:WI, box. 1, "Correspondence: Berenson."
46. WI to BB, 3, 31 Oct. 1930, 2 Feb., 1 March 1931, VIT.
47. WI to BB, 24 Feb., 14 June 1933, 14 July 1933, 28 March 1937, VIT.
48. BB to BG, 3 Jan. 1937, AML:MCC; BB to WI, 19 March 1935, AAAS:WI, box 1, "Correspondence: Berenson."
49. BG to BB, 18 April 1928, VIT; AG to MH, 10 Feb. 1936; AG to BG, 2 March 1936, AML:RODGA, "Goldschmidt, Dr. Adolph."
50. BG to BB, 27 July 1936, VIT; AG to BG, 10 Nov. 1937, AML:RODGA, "Goldschmidt, Dr. Adolph."
51. BG to BB, [Aug. 1936], VIT.
52. Earlier in 1936 she sent her friend Helen Franc, who had been working at the Library for a few years. Franc visited the Berensons for lunch, where Mary made an unusual appearance, and wrote a glowing report back to Belle. BG to Hamilton Coltier, 6 May 1936, AML:RODG, "Princeton, 1936–1940"; HF to BG, 16 May 1936, AML:RODGA, "Franc, Helen."
53. The next year Belle also hoped to "go East—near and far" and invited Bernard and Nicky to join her. "Otherwise," she snorted, "I'll slam my first love-affaire down on your head and go off with a rich beau (another benefit of age—there's practically nothing new in a damning way they can say about one)." But that trip never materialized either, leaving Bernard to continue to quiz his American contacts: "Do you ever see the puissanta princess Belle Greene? How is she aging?" BG to BB, 1 Aug. 1936, VIT; BB to WI, 19 Feb. 1938, AAAS:WI, box 1, "Correspondence: Berenson."

54. BG to BB, 31 Aug. 1936, VIT.

55. Images of this and other manuscripts can be viewed at the Morgan Library Web site: www.morganlibrary.org.

56. BG to BB, 31 Aug. 1936, VIT.

57. BG to PS, 17 June, 8 July 1936, HUAMA:PS, "Greene"; *Harvard Class of 1940, Twenty-fifth Anniversary Report* (Cambridge, 1965), v.

58. HH to MH, 1 Aug. 1935; MH to HH, 5 Sept. 1935, ICOR:HH/MPP 5:4.

59. TP to BG, 2 Sept.1931; BG to TP, 20 Dec. 1933; HH to BG, 22 Dec. 1933; BG to HH 4 Jan. 1934; MH to HH, 1 July 1937; BG to HH, 7 July 1937, ICOR: HH/PPM, 5:4.

60. Henri Hyvernat, "Catalogue of Coptic Manuscripts in the Pierpont Morgan Library," Reference Collection, PML c. 1935; Leo Depuydt, *Catalogue of Coptic Manuscripts in the Pierpont Morgan Library*, 2 vols. (Leuven: Uitgeverij Peeters, 1993).

61. Albrecht Rosenthal to BG, 2 June 1939, AML:RODG, "Rosenthal, Albrecht"; BG to EM, 4 May, 24 July 1939, AML:RODG, "British Museum"; BG to Charles Cunningham, 27 Sept. 1939, AML:MCC, "Boston Museum of Art." After her death, the Morgan Library mounted an exhibition of works by the Spanish Forger. *New York Times*, 26 May 1978. In the accompanying catalogue, William Voelkle, then associate curator of medieval and Renaissance manuscripts, notes that while Belle was not the first to identify that this artist was modern, she was the first to collect and catalogue his work, and she gave him the name he is still known by. Voelkle, "Preface," in *The Spanish Forger* (New York: Pierpont Morgan Library, 1978).

62. RH to BG, 1 April 1932, AML:RODG, "Columbia University."

63. Cosmo Gordon to BG, 28 April 1934, AML:RODG, "Misc, G."

64. Margaret Bingham Stillwell, *Librarians Are Human: Memories in and out of the Rare-Book World, 1907–1970* (Boston: University Press of New England, 1973), 228.

65. Leonard Lyons, "The New Yorker," *Washington Post,* 23 Feb. 1939, p. 8.

66. Irene Lewishon to BG, 22 Sept. 1937, AML:RODG, "Museum of Costume Art"; AML:RODG, "Princeton"; BG to George Sarton, 24 Nov. 1930, HLHU, bMS Am 1803 (666); Wroth, *The First Quarter Century of the Pierpont Morgan Library: A Retrospective Exhibition in Honor of Belle da Costa Greene* (New York: Pierpont Morgan Library, 1949), 17, 28.

67. Belle suggested that the permanent position of librarian carry a salary of at least $2,500 to start. Dorothy Miner was eventually hired at $3,000. Dorothy Miner to BG, 1 Feb. 1938, n.d. [1938]; Minutes of Advisory Committee, 17 March 1934; BG to Francis Henry Taylor, 19 June 1934; BG to FHT, 8 Nov. 1935, AML: RODG, "Walters Art Gallery, 1938–1939."

68. Walters Art Gallery to BG, 25 Nov. 1939, AML:RODG, "Walters Art Gallery 1938–1939."

69. Alberto Sbacchi, "Italy and the Treatment of the Ethiopian Aristocracy, 1937–1940," *International Journal of African Historical Studies* 10, no. 2 (1977): 209–31. D'Aosta died in 1941 of illness in an Allied prisoner camp.

70. BG to BB, 29 Dec. 1920, VIT; HH to BG, n.d. [1933], AML:RODG, "Hyvernat, Henry, 1930—"; MH to HH, 11 Oct. 1934, BG to HH, 25 Nov. 1934, ICOR:HH/PPM, 5:1.

71. René Gimpel, *Diary of an Art Dealer,* trans. John Rosenberg (New York: Farrar, Straus and Giroux, 1966), 162.

72. Emmett Maun to M. L. Parrish, 27 March 1934, CO 171, 22:10, "Greene Corres.," PUA.

73. MH to BB, n.d. [probably late 1953 or early 1954], VIT; PH to JPMJ, 27 May 1937, AML:JPMJ, 174.

74. Hofer, Ivins, and Greene all had strong personalities, which sometimes led to resentments and grudges. Hofer and Ivins themselves had a falling out several years later. PH to WI, 12 July 1937, 19 June 1946, AAAS:WI, box 3, "Correspondence: Hofer, Philip"; Meryle Secrest, *Being Bernard Berenson: A Biography* (New York: Holt, Rinehart and Winston, 1979), 291.

75. PH to JPMJ, 24 July 1947, AML:JMPJ, box 171, "1941–1947."

76. Unidentified clipping, 17 Aug. 1941, CAH:NYJAM.

77. "Robert M. Leveridge," Record Group 64: Records of the National Archives and Records Administration; Series: World War II Army Enlistment Records, 6/1/2002–9/30/2002; *Harvard Class of 1940*, 783.

78. BG to PS, 22 Nov. 1938, HUAMA:PS; PS to BG, 22 Nov. 1938; PS to C. R. Morey, 19 Dec. 1938, AML:RODGA, "Fogg Art Museum"; Martin Goldschmidt to BG, 30 Dec. 1938; BG to Martin Goldschmidt, 28 Dec. 1944, AML:RODG, "G Misc."

79. JM to BG, 16 Aug. 1940, AML:RODG, "Martini, Dr. Joseph 1930."

80. Ernest Samuels, *Bernard Berenson: The Making of a Legend* (Cambridge: Harvard University Press, Belknap Press, 1987).

81. Dwight C. Miner to BG, 10 Nov. 1940; BG to Dwight C. Miner, 13 Nov. 1940, AML:MCC, "Misc, Amb–And."

82. BG to John Axten, AML:JPMJ, box 172, "1930–1941"; J. A. Rogers wrote about interracial mixing and people of mixed ancestry who lived as white in his *Sex and Race*, vol. 2, *A History of White, Negro, and Indian Miscegenation in the Two Americas* (St. Petersburg, Fla.: Helga M. Rogers, 1942). Rogers revealed no identifying details to betray those individuals. Although his scholarship was dismissed by white publishers as "gossip," Rogers refused to name names except for historical figures.

83. MH to HH, 26 Aug. 1940; BG to TP, 13 Jan. 1941, ICOR:HH/PPM, 5:4; Helen Woodruff to BG, 25 Sept. 1940; BG to E. Baldwin Smith, 1 Nov. 1940, AML:MCC, "Princeton University, 1936–1940."

84. *New York Times*, 24 March 1941. No probate file exists for Genevieve. Her death certificate lists her birthplace as Richmond, Va., and her parents as Robert Van Vliet and Genevieve DaCosta. (Belle signed the form.) Certificate of Death 6902, Bureau of Records, Department of Health, Borough of Manhattan; EM to BG, 2 July 1942, AML:RODG, "British Museum."

CHAPTER 14: SHINING THROUGH THE DARKNESS

1. Lawrence C. Wroth, *The First Quarter Century of the Pierpont Morgan Library: A Retrospective Exhibition in Honor of Belle da Costa Greene* (New York: Pierpont Morgan Library, 1949), 21. Wroth is describing the illuminated and textual manuscripts exhibited in 1949, selected from the hundreds that Belle had purchased during her tenure as director.

2. BG to BB, 28 April 1945, VIT.

3. War Department, "Report of Death"; War Department, "Technical Report of Aircraft Accident Classification Committee," Air Corps Training Detachment,

Air Force Historical Research Agency, Maxwell AFB, Ala., file 293, "Leveridge, Robert M."

4. Information about the training and movements of the Ninety-second comes from Robert D. Elliot, *92nd Bomb Group (H): Fame's Favored Few* (Paducah, Kyu Turner Publishing, 1996).

5. BG to AG, 30 Jan. 1942, AML:RODGA, "Goldschmidt, Dr. Adolph."

6. BG to Edgar Wind, 21 Sept. 1942, AML:RODGA, "Dr. Edgar Wind"; BG to unknown, 21 Sept. 1942, AML:RODGA, "Boston Museum of Fine Arts."

7. Philip A. St. John, *Bombardier: A History* (Paducah, Ky.: Turner Publishing, 1993), 19–20.

8. JPMJ to BG, 28 July 1941; BG to JSM, 4 June 1942, AML:JPMJ, box 171; HF to BG, 23 July 1942, AML:RODGA, "Franc"; Francis Henry Taylor to BG, 3 April 1942, AML:RODGA, "Metropolitan Museum 1940–43."

9. BG to ASWR, 28 July 1943, AML:RODG, "Rosenbach"; Ann Mosher to LW, 23 Nov. 1942; BG to Samuel Chew, 4 Aug. 1945, AML:RODG, "Professor Samuel C. Chew"; BG to Dr. Henry Sigerist, 7 Sept. 1945, AML:RODG, "Misc S"; Ann Mosher to TP 19 April 1943, ICOR:TCP/RP "1932–1946."

10. Ron Chernow, *The House of Morgan: An American Banking Dynasty and the Rise of Modern Finance* (New York: Atlantic Monthly Press, 1990), 440–41.

11. The Morgan company's various international branches and relationships still played important financial roles during the war. See Chernow, *House,* 430–81.

12. BG to PS, 26 March 1943, HUAMA:PS, "Greene."

13. TP to BG, 19 March 1943, ICOR:TCP, "Research Papers, 1932–1946."

14. AT to BG, AML:RODG, "T Misc." See also Edward K. Rand to BG 12 April 1943, "Rand, E.K."; Germain Séligmann to BG, 30 April 1943, AML:RODGA, "Seligmann, Arnold Rey & Co."; LW to BG, 12 May 1943, AML:RODG, "Lawrence C. Wroth."

15. BG to EM, 29 June 1945, AML:RODG, "British Museum"; BG to AT, 19 March 1943, AML:RODG, "T Misc."; BG to LW, 13 Jan. 1944, AML:RODG, "Lawrence C. Wroth"; BG to Lorraine Sherwood, 9 March 1944, AML:RODG, "Misc S"; ASWR to BG, 25 June 1943, AML:RODG, "Rosenbach."

16. War Department, "Report of Death," File 293, "Leveridge, Robert M.," AHRC.

17. War Department, "Report of Death."

18. Genevieve Harvey to Army Service Forces, Kansas City Quartermasters Depot (ASF, KSQD), 24 Jan. 1944, Department of the Army, AHRC.

19. Nathan G. Goldberger to ASF, KCQD, Depot, 28 Jan. 1944; W. F. Hehman to Nathan G. Goldberger, 16 Feb. 1944; Genevieve Harvey to ASF, KCQD, AHRC.

20. Genevieve Harvey to ASF, KCQD, n.d. [1947], AHRC.

21. BG to Edgar Wind, 22 Sept. 1943, AML:RODG, "W Misc."

22. Alice Lee Meyers to BG, 2 April 1946, AML:MCC, "American Library in Paris"; Cary Nelson, "Martial Lyrics: the Vexed History of the Wartime Poem Card," *American Literary History* 16, no. 2 (2004): 270–71.

23. This poem was first published under MacLeish's name in *Actfive and Other Poems* (New York: Random House, 1948), 60. Copyright permission is now credited to *Collected Poems* (New York: Houghton Mifflin, 1962).

24. BG to EM, 29 June 1945, AML:RODG, "British Museum."

25. BG to ASWR, 8 Nov. 1943, AML:RODG, "Rosenbach."

26. BB to Margot Barr, 22 April 1941, quoted in A. K. McComb, ed., *The Selected Letters of Bernard Berenson* (Boston: Houghton Mifflin, 1964), 182.

27. BG to Aurelia Henry Reinhardt, 7 June 1940, AML:RODG, "R Misc."; Ernest Samuels, *Bernard Berenson: The Making of a Connoisseur* (Cambridge: Harvard University Press, Belknap Press, 1979), 469–89.

28. BG to DVT, 23 March 1945, AAAS:DVT, "Berenson."

29. BB to BG, 11 July 1945, AAAS:DVT, "Berenson." Unfortunately, the pen sketch was not filed among Thompson's letters in the Berenson archive.

30. BG to BB, 28 April 1945; BB to DVT, 10 July 1945, AAAS:DVT, "Berenson."

31. *New York Times*, 6 June 1944, 17; BG to Martin Goldschmidt, 28 Dec. 1944, AML, "G Misc."

32. BG to ASWR, 31 May 1944, AML:RODG, "Rosenbach."

33. BG to HF, 8 June 1945, AML:RODGA, "Franc, Helen."

34. BG to WI, 17 April 1947, AAAS:WI, box 2, "Greene."

35. BG to BB, 10 April, 29 July 1946, VIT.

36. BG to BB, 18 June 1947, VIT; BG to EM, 2 June 1947, AML:RODG, "British Museum."

37. WI to BB, 7 March 1946, VIT.

38. BG to BB, 2 June 1947, VIT.

39. WI to BB, 23 June, 23 Dec. 1947, VIT.

40. At the first meeting they considered the name Hroswitha Club after a ninth- or tenth-century German scholar and book collector. Belle noted that there was some question of the historical Hroswitha's authenticity, but the name was eventually adopted and the members became the Hroswithians, which challenged many a tongue.

41. Minutes, Hroswitha Club, 16 Dec. 1944, 14 Nov. 1946, GC:HC, "Assorted Minutes in Binders"; Sarah Fife to Mrs. Dickey, GC:HC, Unlabeled Blue Folder; Margaret Bingham Stillwell, *Librarians Are Human: Memories in and out of the Rare-Book World, 1907–1970* (Boston: University Press of New England, 1973), 292–93.

42. Anne Lyon Haight, *Banned Books: Informal Notes on Some Books Banned for Various Reasons at Various Times and in Various Places* (New York: R. R. Bowker, 1935).

43. BG to Sarah Fife, 13 Dec. 1946, AML:RODG, "F Misc"; Minutes, Hroswitha Club, 15 Jan. 1948, GC:HC, "Assorted Minutes in Binders."

44. BB to WI, 29 Jan. 1946, AAAS:WI, box 2, "Greene."

45. Keyes Metcalf to JSM, 12 Dec. 1947, AML:JPMJ, box 171.

46. Unidentified clipping [*Library Journal*, 1950] in GC:HC, "Material about Hroswitha"; BG to Albert Boeckler, 13 Jan. 1949, AML:RODG, "B Misc."

47. JSM to H. M. Lyndenberg, 16 Jan. 1948, AML:JPMJ, box 171.

48. AM to LW, 1 May 1948; Elisabeth Dodd to LW, 6 May 1948, AML:RODGA, "Lawrence C. Wroth"; Lucille Miller to BG, 18 May 1948, AML:RODG, "D Misc"; MH to Millard Meiss, 11 June 1948, AML:RODGA, "Columbia University, 1937–"; Morgan Library Trustee's Meeting Minutes, 5 May 1948, AML: JPMJ, 208, "1948–1950."

49. JSM to William A. Jackson, 30 Aug. 1948; WAJ to JSM, 17 Aug., 1 Sept. 1948, AML:JPMJ, 171, "1941–1947."

50. BG to Juliet Hamilton, 8 Sept. 1948, AML:RODGA, "Hamilton, Mrs. W. P."

51. FA to JSM, 11, 13 Oct. 1948, AML:JPMJ, box 208; MH to BB, 7 April 1953, VIT.

52. Wroth, *First Quarter Century*, 9–17.

53. *Time,* 11 April 1949, pp. 76–77; *New York Times*, 17 April 1949.

54. WI to BB, 5 July 1950, VIT.

55. MH to Maurice Brockwell, 15 Sept. 1949, AML:RODG, "B Misc"; MH to BB, 7, 11 Nov. 1949, VIT.

56. BG to PS, 1 Jan. 1950, HUAMA:PS, "Greene."

57. BG to BB, 31 March 1949, VIT. This was the last letter Belle wrote Bernard; on the back of the letter, Bernard penned a cross and the date of her death.

58. FA to JSM, 25 Feb. 1949, AML:JPMJ, box 208.

59. MH to BB, 7 Nov. 1949, VIT.

60. MH to BB, 9 Jan. 1950; HF to BB, 4 Aug. 1950, VIT; BB to AF, 31 Aug. 1950, AML:RODGA, "Berenson."

61. RN to BB, 8, 18 April [1950]; MH to BB, 2 May 1950, VIT.

62. RN to BB, 5 May 1950; FA to BB, 24 Jan. 1952, VIT; Samuels, *Legend*, 541.

63. MH to JSM, 16 May 1950; BG to Juliet Hamilton, 8 Sept. 1948, AML:RODGA, "Hamilton, Mrs. W. P."

64. MH to BB, 2 May 1950, VIT.

65. MH to BB, 10 May 1950, VIT.

66. BG to ASWR, 31 May 1944, "Rosenbach," AML:RODG, "Rosenbach"; RN to BB, 5 May 1949, VIT.

67. MH to BB, 18 May 1950, VIT.

68. JSM to RR, JSM to RN, JSM to FA, 11 May 1950; RR to JSM, 12 May 1950; FA to JSM, 14 May 1950; MH to JSM, 16 May 1950, AML:JPMJ, box 208. Adams was not surprised, given how feeble she had been in the last few weeks. He worried about the "emotional gap" her death would leave at the Library and hoped that his absence would make it easier for the old staff to deal with it. Meta collected a "sheaf" of letters and telegrams sent to the Library in condolences for Belle's death and sent them to Junius Morgan.

EPILOGUE: THE PASSING OF BELLE GREENE

1. Minutes, Hroswitha Club, 2 May 1950, GC:HC, "Assorted Minutes in Binders."

2. WI to BB, 5 July 1950, VIT.

3. MII to BB, 18 July 1950, VIT; Dorothy Miner and Anne Lyon Haight, "Belle da Costa Greene," in Edward T. James and Janet Wilson James, eds., *Notable American Women: A Biographical Dictionary* (Cambridge: Harvard University Press, Belknap Press, 1971), 83–85.

4. MH to BB, 18 Sept. 1950; RN to BB, 26 Oct. 1954, VIT.

5. WI to BB, 5 July 1950, VIT; BB to WI, 11 June 1950, AAAS:WI, "Correspondence: Berenson." Life expectancy is difficult to determine. A woman born in 1900 had a life expectancy of just over 48, if she was white, and 33.5 if she was black. Belle clearly outlived either statistic, although she was born in 1879. However, a woman who was 65 in 1950 (when Belle was 71) had a life expectancy of 15 more years. U.S. Department of Health and Human Services, Centers for Disease Control, National Center for Health Statistics, *Health, United States, 2005* (Hyattsville, Md.: GPO, 2005), 83, 184.

6. My request for Belle's death certificate was denied because she died after 1948, their cutoff date for public access; there is no copy in her probate file.

7. MH to BB, 21 May 1951, VIT; MH to AH, n.d., GC:HC, Women Printers Materials, "Wightman/Waysblum." Anne Haight's daughter donated these letters and other notes to the Morgan Library in the 1980s, but they have apparently disappeared.

8. RN to BB, 26 Oct. 1954, VIT.

9. MH to AH, 27 Nov. 1968, GC:HC, Correspondence, "Letters 1950s."

10. Ernest Samuels, *Bernard Berenson: The Making of a Connoisseur* (Cambridge: Harvard University Press, Belknap Press, 1979), 541; RN to BB, 26 Oct. 1954, VIT; Bernard Berenson, *Seeing and Knowing* (New York: Macmillan, 1953).

11. MH to BB, 27 June 1954, VIT.

12. Rachel Hunt to AH, 22 June 1954, GC:HC, "Correspondence, 1950s"; Dorothy Miner, ed., *Studies in Art and Literature for Belle da Costa Greene* (Princeton: Princeton University Press, 1954).

13. John R. Spencer, review in *Renaissance News* 8 (Autumn 1955): 142–45.

14. Francis Wormald, "Review: In Honor of Belle da Costa Greene," *Burlington Magazine* 97 (June 1955): 185. For other reviews, see Robert Scranton, in *Classical Philology* 50 (July 1955): 225–26, and Kenneth John Conant, in *Speculum* 30 (April 1955): 289–91.

15. Miner, ed., *Studies*.

16. Miner, ed., *Studies*, x–xiii.

17. "Resolution," Walters Art Gallery Board of Trustees, 5 Oct. 1954, GC:HC, Correspondence, "Letters 1950s."

18. Minutes, Hroswitha Club, 16 Nov. 1961, GC:HC, "Assorted Minutes in Binders."

19. There are no records at the Morgan Library to trace these negotiations. Probate Record, "Belle daCosta [sic] Greene," New York County Clerk's Office, Manhattan, New York County Surrogate's Court, File No. P. 1771-1950.

20. MH to BB, 22 Dec. 1950, 6 June 1954, VIT.

21. MH to BB, 7 Aug. 1950, VIT.

22. MH to BB, 5 April 1954, VIT.

23. Miner and Haight, "Greene," 85–85. See also Mary Tolford Wilson, "Belle da Costa Greene," in Edward T. James and John A. Garraty, eds., *Dictionary of American Biography, Supplement Four, 1946–1950* (New York: Scribner, 1974), 344–46, and Constance Koppelman, "Belle da Costa Greene," in John A. Garraty and Mark C. Carnes, eds., *American National Biography*, vol. 9 (New York: Oxford University Press, 1999), 518–19.

24. Frederick B. Adams Jr., *Printers' Marks in the Pierpont Morgan Library* (New York: Spiral Press, 1968). My thanks to William Voelke for this information.

Select Bibliography

Adams, Frederick B., Jr. *An Introduction to the Pierpont Morgan Library*. New York: Pierpont Morgan Library, 1964.

Ardizzone, Heidi. "Red-Blooded Americans: Mulattoes and the Melting Pot in American Racialist and Nationalist Discourse, 1890–1930." Ph.D. diss., University of Michigan, 1997.

Atherton, Gertrude. *The Living Present*. New York: Frederick A. Stokes, 1917.

Auchincloss, Louis. *J. P. Morgan: The Financier as Collector*. New York: Harry N. Abrams, 1990.

Balken, Debra Bricker. *Debating American Modernism: Stieglitz, Duchamp, and the New York Avant-Garde*. Singapore: American Federation of Arts in association with Distributed Art Publishers, 2003.

Barnet, Andrea. *All-Night Party: The Women of Bohemian Greenwich Village and Harlem, 1913–1930*. Chapel Hill: Algonquin Books of Chapel Hill, 2004.

Behrman, S. N. *Duveen*. London: Hamish Hamilton, 1972.

Berlin, Ira. *Slaves without Masters: The Free Negro in the Antebellum South*. New York: Vintage, 1976.

Bochner, Jay. *An American Lens: Scenes from Alfred Stieglitz's New York Seccession*. Cambridge: MIT Press, 2005.

Branscomb, Lewis C. *Ernest Cushing Richardson: Research Librarian, Scholar, Theologian, 1860–1939*. Metuchen, N.J.: Scarecrow, 1993.

Brown, Elsa Barkley. "To Catch a Vision of Freedom: Reconstructing Southern Black Women's Political History, 1865–1880." In *Unequal Sisters: A Multicultural Reader in U.S. Women's History*, edited by Vicki L. Ruiz and Ellen C. DuBois, 268–83. 2d ed. New York: Routledge, 1994.

Bruccoli, Matthew J. *The Fortunes of Mitchell Kennerley, Bookman*. New York: Harcourt Brace Jovanovich, 1986.

Calo, Mary Ann. *Bernard Berenson and the Twentieth Century*. Philadelphia: Temple University Press, 1994.

Canfield, Cass. *The Incredible Pierpont Morgan: Financier and Art Collector*. New York: Harper & Row, 1974.

Carby, Hazel. "It Jus Be's Dat Way Sometime: The Sexual Politics of Women's Blues." In *Unequal Sisters: A Multicultural Reader in U.S. Women's History*, edited by Vicki L. Ruiz and Ellen C. DuBois. 2d ed. New York: Routledge, 1994, 330–41.

Chauncey, George. *Gay New York: Gender, Urban Culture, and the Makings of the Gay Male World, 1890–1940*. New York: Basic, 1994, 330–41.

Chernow, Ron. *The House of Morgan: An American Banking Dynasty and the Rise of Modern Finance*. New York: Atlantic Monthly Press, 1990.

Come, Donald Robert. "The Influence of Princeton on Higher Education in the South before 1825." *William and Mary Quarterly* 2 (October 1945): 359–96.

Constable, W. G. *Art Collecting in the United States of America: An Outline of a History*. London: Thomas Nelson, 1964.

Davidson, Alexander, Jr., et al., eds. *Grolier 75: A Biographical Retrospective to Celebrate the Seventy-fifth Anniversary of the Grolier Club in New York*. New York: Grolier Club, 1959.

Davis, Angela. *Women, Race, and Class*. New York: Vintage, 1983.

Depuydt, Leo. *Catalogue of Coptic Manuscripts in the Pierpont Morgan Library*. Leuven: Uitgeverij Peeters, 1993.

Dominguez, Virginia R. *White by Definition: Social Classification in Creole Louisiana*. New Brunsick: Rutgers University Press, 1986.

Douglas, Ann. *Terrible Honesty: Mongrel Manhattan in the 1920s*. New York: Noonday Press, 1996.

Dunlop, M. H. *Gilded City: Scandal and Sensation in Turn-of-the-Century New York*. New York: Morrow, 2000.

Dunn, Richard M. *Geoffrey Scott and Berenson Circle: Literary and Aesthetic Life in the Early 20th Century*. Lewiston, N.Y.: Mellen Press, 1998.

Dupont, Inge, and Hope Mayo, eds. *Morgan Library Ghost Stories*. New York: Fordham University Press, 1990.

Fields, Barbara. *Slavery and Freedom on the Middle Ground: Maryland during the Nineteenth Century*. New Haven: Yale University Press, 1987.

Fleming, Edwin Wolfe II, with John F. Fleming. *Rosenbach: A Biography*. Cleveland: World Publishing, 1960.

Foner, Eric. *Reconstruction: America's Unfinished Revolution, 1865–1877*. New York: Harper Perennial, 1989.

Forbes, John Douglas. *J. P. Morgan, Jr., 1867–1943*. Charlottesville: University Press of Virginia, 1981.

Gaines, Kevin K. *Uplifting the Race: Black Leadership, Politics, and Culture in the Twentieth Century*. Chapel Hill: University of North Carolina Press, 1996.

Gatewood, Willard B. *Aristocrats of Color: The Black Elite, 1880–1920*. Bloomington: Indiana University Press, 1990.

Gimpel, René. *Diary of an Art Dealer*. Translated by John Rosenberg. New York: Farrar, Straus and Giroux, 1966.

Ginsberg, Elaine K. "Introduction: The Politics of Passing." In *Passing and the Fictions of Identity*, edited by Elaine K. Ginsberg. Durham: Duke University Press, 1996.

Graham, Katharine. *Personal History*. New York: Knopf, 1997.

Green, Constance McLaughlin. *The Secret City: A History of Race Relations in the Nation's Capital*. Princeton: Princeton University Press, 1967.

Greene, Belle. *The Pierpont Morgan Library: A Review of the Growth, Development and Activities of the Library during the Period between Its Establishment as an Educa-*

tional Instutiton in February 1924 and the Close of the Year 1929. New York: Pierpont Morgan Library, 1930.

———. *The Pierpont Morgan Library: Review of the Activities and Acquisitions of the Library from 1930 through 1935: A Summary of the Annual Reports of the Director to the Board of Trustees*. New York: Pierpont Morgan Library, 1937.

Hine, Darlene Clark. "Rape and the Inner Lives of Black Women in the Middle West." *Signs* 14 (1989): 912–20.

Holt, Thomas. *Black over White: Negro Political Leadership in South Carolina during Reconstruction*. Urbana: University of Illinois Press, 1977.

Homberger, Eric. *Mrs. Astor's New York: Money and Social Power in a Gilded Age*. New Haven: Yale University Press, 2002.

Hovey, Carl. *The Life Story of J. Pierpont Morgan*. London: Heinemann, 1912.

Hyland, Douglas. "Agnes Ernst Meyer and Modern Art in America, 1907–1918." M.A. thesis, University of Delaware, 1976.

Jones, Jacqueline. *Labor of Love, Labor of Sorrow: Black Women, Work, and the Family from Slavery to the Present*. New York: Basic, 1985.

Koppelman, Constance. "Belle Da Costa Greene." In *American National Biography*, edited by John A. Garraty and Mark C. Carnes, 518–19. New York: Oxford University Press, 1999.

Kroeger, Brooke. *Passing: When People Can't Be Who They Are*. New York: Public Affairs, 2003.

Kuhlman, Erika. *Petticoats and White Feathers: Gender Conformity, Race, the Progressive Peace Movement, and the Debate over War, 1895–1919*. Westport, Conn.: Greenwood, 1997.

Lawton, Thomas. *Freer: A Legacy of Art*. Washington, D.C.: Freer Gallery of Art, Smithsonian Institution, 1993.

Lee, Susie Jin. "The Content of Character: The Role of Social Capital in the Expansion of Economic Capital." Ph.D. diss., Cornell University, 2004.

Louchheim, Aline B. "The Morgan Library and Miss Greene." *New York Times*, 17 April 1949, x8.

Mariano, Nicky. *Forty Years with Berenson*. New York: Knopf, 1966.

McFarland, Gerald W. *Inside Greenwich Village: A New York City Neighborhood, 1898–1918*. Amherst: University of Massachusetts Press, 2001.

Mellow, James R. *Charmed Circle: Gertrude Stein & Company*. New York: Praeger, 1974.

Miner, Dorothy. *Studies in Art and Literature for Belle Da Costa Greene*. Princeton: Princeton University Press, 1954.

Miner, Dorothy, and Anne Lyon Haight. "Belle da Costa Greene." In *Notable American Women, 1607–1950: A Biographical Dictionary*, edited by Edward T. James and Janet Wilson James, 83–85. Cambridge: Harvard University Press, Belknap Press, 1971.

Mizejewski, Linda. *Ziegfeld Girl: Image and Icon in Culture and Cinema*. Durham: Duke University Press, 1999.

Moore, Jacqueline M. *Leading the Race: The Transformation of the Black Elite in the Nation's Capital, 1880–1920*. Charlottesville: University Press of Virginia, 1999.

Mounter, Michael Robert. "Richard Theodore Greener: The Idealist, Statesman, Scholar, and South Carolinian." Ph.D. diss, University of South Carolina, 2002.

Nicholson, Virginia. *Among the Bohemians: Experiments in Living, 1900–1939*. New York: Morrow, 2002.

Niven, Penelope. *Steichen: A Biography*. New York: Clarkson Potter, 1997.

Parker, Robert Allerton. *The Transatlantic Smiths*. New York: Random House, 1959.

Patterson, Jerry E. *The First Four Hundred: Mrs. Astor's New York in the Gilded Age*. New York: Rizzoli, 2000.

Peiss, Kathy. *Cheap Amusements: Working Women and Leisure in Turn-of-the-Century New York*. Philadelphia: Temple University Press, 1986.

———. *Hope in a Jar: The Making of America's Beauty Culture*. New York: Metropolitan Books, 1998.

Quigley, David. *Second Founding: New York City, Reconstruction, and the Making of American Democracy*. New York: Hill and Wang, 2004.

Roman, Judith. *Annie Adams Fields: The Spirit of Charles Street*. Bloomington: Indiana University Press, 1990.

Saarinen, Aline B. *The Proud Possessors: The Lives, Times, and Tastes of Some Adventurous American Art Collectors*. New York: Random House, 1958.

Samuels, Ernest. *Bernard Berenson: The Making of a Connoisseur*. Cambridge: Harvard University Press, Belknap Press, 1979.

———. *Bernard Berenson: The Making of a Legend*. Cambridge: Harvard University Press, Belknap Press, 1987.

Secrest, Meryle. *Being Bernard Berenson: A Biography*. New York: Holy, Rinehart and Winston, 1979.

———. *Duveen: A Life in Art*. New York: Knopf, 2004.

Seligman, Germain. *Merchants of Art: 1880–1960: Eighty Years of Professional Collecting*. New York: Appleton-Century-Crofts, 1961.

Shaw, Stephanie. *What a Woman Ought to Be and Do: Black Professional Women Workers during the Jim Crow Era*. Chicago: University of Chicago Press, 1996.

Simpson, Colin. *Artful Partners: Bernard Berenson and Joseph Duveen*. New York: Macmillan, 1986.

Sinclair, Andrew. *Corsair: The Life of J. Pierpont Morgan*. Boston: Little, Brown, 1981.

Smith, Jane S. *Elsie De Wolfe: A Life in the High Style*. New York: Atheneum, 1982.

Sollors, Werner, Caldwell Titcomb, and Thomas A. Underwood, eds. *Blacks at Harvard: A Documentary History of African-American Experience at Harvard and Radcliffe*. New York: New York University Press, 1993.

Sprigge, Sylvia. *Berenson: A Biography*. Boston: Houghton Mifflin, 1960.

Stansell, Christine. *American Moderns: Bohemian New York and Creation of a New Century*. New York: Metropolitan Books, 2000.

Stillwell, Margaret Bingham. *Librarians Are Human: Memories in and out of the Rare-Book World, 1907–1970*. Boston: University Press of New England, 1973.

Strachey, Barbara. *Remarkable Relations: The Story of the Pearsall Smith Women*. New York: Universe Books, 1980.

Strachey, Barbara, and Jayne Samuels, eds. *Mary Berenson: A Self-Portrait from Her Letters & Diaries*. New York: Norton, 1983.

Strouse, Jean. *Morgan: American Financier*. New York: Harper Perennial, 2000.

Synnott, Marcia Graham. *The Half-Opened Door: Discrimination and Admissions at Harvard, Yale, and Princeton, 1900–1970*. Westport, Conn.: Greenwood, 1979.

Talty, Stephen. *Mulatto America: At the Crossroads of Black and White Culture: A Social History*. New York: HarperCollins, 2003.

Tone, Andrea. *Devices and Desires: A History of Contraceptives in America.* New York: Hill and Wang, 2001.

Turnbull, Michael T. R. B. *Mary Garden.* Portland, Ore.: Amadeus Press, 1997.

Tuttle, William M. *Race Riot: Chicago in the Red Summer of 1919.* New York: Atheneum, 1970.

Underwood, James Lowell, and W. Lewis Burke Jr., eds. *At Freedom's Door: African American Founding Fathers and Lawyers in Reconstruction South Carolina.* Columbia: University of South Carolina Press, 2000.

Voelkle, William M., and Susan L'Engle. *Illuminated Manuscripts: Treasures of the Pierpont Morgan Library, New York.* New York: Abbeville Press, 1998.

Wetzsteon, Ross. *Republic of Dreams: Greenwich Village: The American Bohemia, 1910–1960.* New York: Simon & Schuster, 2002.

Williamson, George C. *Behind My Library Door: Some Chapters on Authors, Books and Miniatures.* London: Selwyn & Blount, 1921.

Williamson, Joel. *New People: Miscegenation and Mulattoes in the United States.* Baton Rouge: Louisiana University Press, 1995.

Wilson, Mary Tolford. "Belle Da Costa Greene." In *Dictionary of American Biography, Supplement Four, 1946–1950,* edited by Edward T. James and John A. Garraty, 344–46. New York: Scribner, 1974.

Woodson, Carter G. *Free Negro Owners of Slaves in the United States in 1830, Together with Absentee Ownership of Slaves in the United States in 1830.* New York: Negro Universities Press, 1968.

Wroth, Lawrence C. *The First Quarter Century of the Pierpont Morgan Library: A Retrospective Exhibition in Honor of Belle Da Costa Green.* New York: Pierpont Morgan Library, 1949.

Photograph Credits

Every effort has been made to identify and credit the artists, photographers, and copyright holders on these photographs.

Insert between pp. 212 and 213: 1a: Harvard University Archives, call # HUP Greener, R.T. (2); 1b: Harvard University Archives, call # HUP Greener, R.T. (3); 2a: LC:PPD, # LC-USZ62-68287; 2b: LC:PPD, # LC-USZ62-40466; 3a: photograph by Heidi Ardizzone; 3b: LC:PPD, # LC-D4-16648, Detroit Publishing Company Collection; 4a: LC:PPD, #LC-USZ62-94188; 4b: LC:PPD, # LC-USZC4-6403, illustration in *Puck*, 21 June 1911, centerfold; 5: LC, PDD, #LC-D4-70688, Detroit Publishing Company Collection; 6: AML, photography by Tebbs & Knell, North Room of the Morgan Library; 7a: Archives of the Pierpont Morgan Library, New York (AML) ARC 1904, West Room of the Morgan Library; 7b: AML ARC 1635, East Room of Morgan Library, before 1928; 8, 9: Berenson Archives, Harvard University Center for Italian Renaissance Studies, Villa I Tatti (VIT), Clarence White, photographer; 10, 11: Berenson Archives, VIT, Theodore Marceau, photographer; 12: AML ARC 2702, Ernest Walter Histed, photographer, photograph of Belle da Costa Greene; 13, 14, 15: Berenson Archives, VIT; 16: *Chicago Tribune*, 11 August 1912, G2.

Insert between pp. 362 and 363: 1a: LC:PPD, # LC-USZ62-86692; 1b: LC:PPD, # LC-USZ62-64956, N. W. Penfield; 2: LC:PPD, # LC-USZ62-105820; 3a: LC:PPD, # LC-USZ62-55586; 3b: LC:PPD, # LC-USZ62-105441; 4a: © CORBIS; 4b: LC:PPD, # LC-B2- 3622-1, George Grantham Bain Collection; 5a: LC:PPD, # LC-USZ62-103851, detail, George Grantham Bain Collection.; 5b: LC:PPD, # LC-G432-1101, Arnold Genthe Collection; 6: Berenson Archives, VIT, portrait by Laura Coombs Hill; 7a: Berenson Archives, VIT, sketch by Rene Piot; 7b: The Pierpont Morgan Library, New York, (PML) 1950.12, Paul Helleu, *Portrait of Belle da Costa Greene*; 8: PML 1950.14, Henri Matisse, *Female Nude Before a Figured Curtain*; 9: PML 1956.6, William Rothenstein, *Head of Belle da Costa Greene*; 10: LC:PPD, # LC-DIG-ggbain-50224, cropped, George Grantham Bain Collection; 11; LC:PPD, # LC USZ62-93225, George Grantham Bain Collection; 12a: PML 17560, Sir Thomas Malory, *Le Morte D'Arthur*, Westminster: Wm. Caxton, 31 July 1485; 12b: PML

Index